# The Constitution of the Presbyterian Church (U.S.A.)

## Part I
## Book of Confessions

# THE CONSTITUTION
# OF THE
# PRESBYTERIAN CHURCH (U.S.A.)

## PART I

## BOOK OF CONFESSIONS

PUBLISHED BY
THE OFFICE OF THE GENERAL ASSEMBLY

100 Witherspoon Street
Louisville, KY 40202-1396

Copyright © 2016
by the Office of the General Assembly
Presbyterian Church (U.S.A.)

No part of this publication may be reproduced, stored in a retrieval system, or transmitted in any form or by any means, electronically, mechanically, photocopying, recording, or otherwise (brief quotations used in magazine or newspaper reviews excepted), without the prior permission of the publisher.

The sessions, presbyteries, and synods of the Presbyterian Church (U.S.A.) may use sections of this publication without receiving prior written permission of the publisher.

**Library of Congress Cataloging-in-Publication Data**
978-0-9837536-8-1

Printed in the United States of America

Additional copies available at $10.00 each
from Presbyterian Distribution Services (PDS),
100 Witherspoon Street, Louisville, KY 40202-1396,
or by calling 1-800-524-2612 (PDS).

Please specify PDS order #OGA-16-017

# CONTENTS

|  | Reference Numbers | Page Numbers |
|---|---|---|

Notes on the Paging and the Indexing ................................................................. i

Preface ................................................................................................................ iii

Confessional Nature of the Church Report ........................................................ v

The Assessment of Proposed Amendments to the *Book of Confessions* ......... xxvi

Confessions

| | | Reference Numbers | Page Numbers |
|---|---|---|---|
| 1. | The Nicene Creed | 1.1–1.3 | 1–3 |
| 2. | The Apostles' Creed | 2.1–2.3 | 5–7 |
| 3. | The Scots Confession | 3.01–3.25 | 9–26 |
| 4. | The Heidelberg Catechism | 4.001–4.129 | 27–73 |
| 5. | The Second Helvetic Confession | 5.001–5.260 | 75–143 |
| 6. | The Westminster Confession of Faith | 6.001–6.178 | 145–202 |
| 7. | The Shorter Catechism | 7.001–7.110 | 203–221 |
| 8. | The Larger Catechism | 7.111–7.306 | 223–278 |
| 9. | The Theological Declaration of Barmen | 8.01–8.28 | 279–284 |
| 10. | The Confession of 1967 | 9.01–9.56 | 285–297 |
| 11. | The Belhar Confession | 10.1–10.9 | 299–306 |
| 12. | A Brief Statement of Faith– Presbyterian Church (U.S.A.) | 11.1–11.6 | 307–318 |

Index ........................................................................................................ 319–435

# NOTES ON THE PAGING
# AND THE INDEXING

The *Book of Confessions* contains eleven confessional statements commencing with the Nicene Creed on page numbered 1.1–3. The boldface marginal references indicate the confession number to the left of the decimal and the paragraph numbers to the right of the decimal.

The Apostles' Creed is on page numbered 2.1–.3.

The Scots Confession begins on page numbered 3.01–.03. On this numbered page are found Chapters I through III. The boldface marginal references indicate the confession number to the left of the decimal and the chapter numbers to the right of the decimal.

The Heidelberg Catechism begins on page numbered 4.001–.002. The boldface marginal references indicate the confession number to the left of the decimal and the question numbers to the right of the decimal.

The Second Helvetic Confession begins on page numbered 5.001–.004. The boldface marginal references indicate the confession number to the left of the decimal and the paragraph numbers to the right of the decimal.

The Westminster Confession of Faith begins on page numbered 6.001–.002. The boldface marginal references indicate the confession number to the left of the decimal and the paragraph numbers to the right of the decimal.

The Shorter Catechism begins on page numbered 7.001–.012. The boldface marginal references indicate the confession number to the left of the decimal and the question numbers to the right of the decimal.

The Larger Catechism begins on page numbered 7.111–.119. The boldface marginal references indicate the confession number to the left of the decimal and the question numbers to the right of the decimal.

The Theological Declaration of Barmen begins on page numbered 8.01–.04. The boldface marginal references indicate the confession number to the left of the decimal and the paragraph numbers to the right of the decimal.

The Confession of 1967 begins on page numbered 9.01–.07. The boldface marginal references indicate the confession number to the left of the decimal and the paragraph numbers to the right of the decimal.

The Belhar Confession begins on page number 10.1–3. The boldface marginal references indicate the confession number to the left of the decimal and the paragraph numbers to the right of the decimal.

BOOK OF CONFESSIONS

The Brief Statement of Faith begins on page numbered 11.1–.3. The boldface marginal references indicate the confession number to the left of the decimal and the paragraph numbers to the right of the decimal.

The index references refer to the marginal numbers and page numbers. For example, the references to Image of God are 3.03, 4.006, 4.115, 5.034, 6.023, 7.010, 7.035, 7.127, 7.185, 11.3 (pages 11, 32, 68, 86, 154, 205, 208, 226, 235, 311). The references are to Chapter III of the Scots Confession, Questions 6 and 115 of the Heidelberg Catechism, paragraph 34 of the Second Helvetic Confession of Faith, Questions 10 and 35 of the Shorter Catechism, Questions 17 and 75 of the Larger Catechism, and Line 30 of A Brief Statement of Faith.

# PREFACE

The Constitution of the Presbyterian Church (U.S.A.) consists of two volumes. Part I of the Constitution is the *Book of Confessions*, which contains the official texts of the confessional documents. Part II of the Constitution, the *Book of Order*, is published separately and consists of four sections: The Foundations of Presbyterian Polity, the Form of Government, the Directory for Worship, and the Rules of Discipline.

Chapter Two of The Foundations of Presbyterian Polity—"The Church and Its Confessions"—sets forth the church's understanding of the role and function of the confessions in the life of the church.

**F-2.01      The Purpose of Confessional Statements**

The Presbyterian Church (U.S.A.) states its faith and bears witness to God's grace in Jesus Christ in the creeds and confessions in the *Book of Confessions*. In these statements the church declares to its members and to the world who and what it is, what it believes, and what it resolves to do. These statements identify the church as a community of people known by its convictions as well as by its actions. They guide the church in its study and interpretation of the Scriptures; they summarize the essence of Reformed Christian tradition; they direct the church in maintaining sound doctrines; they equip the church for its work of proclamation. They serve to strengthen personal commitment and the life and witness of the community of believers.

The creeds, confessions and catechisms of the *Book of Confessions* are both historical and contemporary. Each emerged in a particular time and place in response to a particular situation. Thus, each confessional document should be respected in its historical particularity; none should be altered to conform to current theological, ethical, or linguistic norms. The confessions are not confined to the past, however; they do not simply express what the church was, what it used to believe, and what it once resolved to do. The confessions address the church's current faith and life, declaring contemporary convictions and actions.

The 197th General Assembly (1985) adopted "Definitions and Guidelines on Inclusive Language." This document, reaffirmed by the 212th General Assembly (2000), states that "Effort should be made at every level of the church to use inclusive language with respect to the people of God." Some of the church's confessional documents, written before the church committed itself to inclusive language for the people of God, use male language to refer to men and women. Although the original language is retained in the *Book of Confessions*, readers are reminded of the church's policy and the commitment the policy expresses.

Specific statements in 16th and 17th century confessions and catechisms in the *Book of Confessions* contain condemnations or derogatory characterizations of the Roman Catholic Church: Chapters XVIII and XXII of the Scots Confession; Questions and Answer 80 of the Heidelberg Catechism; and Chapters II, III, XVII, and XX, of the Second Helvetic Confession. (Chapters XXII, XXV, and XXIX of the Westminster Confession of Faith have been amended to remove anachronous and offensive language. Chapter XXVIII of the French Confession does not have constitutional standing.) While these statements emerged from substantial doctrinal disputes, they reflect 16th and 17th century polemics. Their condemnations and characterizations of the Catholic Church are not the position of the Presbyterian Church (U.S.A.) and are not applicable to current relationships between the Presbyterian Church (U.S.A.) and the Catholic Church. [Note: These sections have been marked with an asterisk.]

The tension between the confessions' historical and contemporary nature is a fruitful tension within the church. The confessions are not honored if they are robbed of historical particularity by imagining that they are timeless expressions of truth. They are best able to instruct, lead, and guide the church when they are given freedom to speak in their own voices. The confessions are not respected if they are robbed of contemporary authority by imagining that they are historical artifacts. They are best able to instruct, lead, and guide the church when they are given freedom to speak now to the church and the world.

> The creeds and confessions of this church arose in response to particular circumstances within the history of God's people. They claim the truth of the Gospel at those points where their authors perceived that truth to be at risk. They are the result of prayer, thought, and experience within a living tradition. They appeal to the universal truth of the Gospel while expressing that truth within the social and cultural assumptions of their time. They affirm a common faith tradition, while also from time to time standing in tension with each other. (*Book of Order*, F-2.01)

# CONFESSIONAL NATURE OF THE CHURCH REPORT*

The Advisory Council on Discipleship and Worship appointed a task force in 1982 to prepare a report on the confessional nature of the church. Soon thereafter the Council on Theology and Culture was invited to participate in the study and appointed two persons to join the membership of the task force. The urgency of the study was heightened when the 195th General Assembly (1983) recognized it as a basic resource for the work of the Special Committee on a Brief Statement of Faith and instructed that committee to be in consultation with the task force as it pursues its work.

The task force sought first to discover how the confessions are actually used by questioning the presbyteries and seminaries of the church, persons attending the 195th General Assembly (1983), and readers of *Monday Morning*. These surveys substantiated the need for a careful study that would clarify and encourage proper use of the church's confessions.

In light of the results of these surveys the task force concentrated its study on ten questions: (1) Are creeds different from confessions? (2) Why are confessions written? (3) How do confessions relate to Scripture? (4) How do confessions relate to their historic context? (5) Why do we have more than one confession? (6) How do the confessions in the *Book of Confessions* relate to each other? (7) How do Reformed confessions relate to other confessions? (8) How can confessions be used in the teaching ministry? (9) How can confessions be used in other parts of congregational life and mission? (10) How do confessions relate to ordination?

This paper is an attempt to deal with these questions as they arise in the following discussion of (1) the nature and purpose of church confessions in general, (2) the unique role of confessions in the Presbyterian-Reformed tradition, (3) the *Book of Confessions*.

## I. The Nature and Purpose of Confessions

Many people are confused by talk of "confessing," "confessions," and "confessional" churches. Both inside and outside the church confession is ordinarily associated with admission of wrongdoing and guilt: criminals "confess" that they have committed a crime; famous people write "true confessions" about their scandalous lives; persons visit a "confessional" to tell of their sin. In Christian tradition, however, confession has an earlier, positive sense. To confess means openly to affirm, declare, acknowledge or take a stand for what one believes to be true. The truth that is confessed may include the admission of sin and guilt but is more than that. When Christians make a confession, they say, "This is what we most assuredly believe, regardless of what others may believe and regardless of the opposition, rejection, or persecution that may come to us for taking this stand."

---

*This text was added by action of the 209th General Assembly (1997). See *Minutes*, 1997, Part I, p. 162, paragraph 19.0013. The text for this report can be found in the *Minutes*, 1986, Part I, pp. 516–27.

A distinction must be made between confession as an act of Christian faith and a confession as a document of Christian faith.

On the one hand, all Christians are by definition people who confess their faith—people who make their own the earliest Christian confession: "Jesus Christ is Lord." The Christian church, called and held together by Jesus Christ himself, lives only through the continual renewal of this fundamental confession of faith that all Christians and Christian bodies make together.

On the other hand, a confession of faith is an officially adopted statement that spells out a church's understanding of the meaning and implications of the one basic confession of the lordship of Christ. Such statements have not always been called confessions. They have also been called creeds, symbols, formulas, definitions, declarations of faith, statements of belief, articles of faith, and other similar names. All these are different ways of talking about the same thing, though "creed" has ordinarily been used for short affirmations of faith, while other names have been used for longer ones.

While the first and primary meaning of confession as an act of faith must always be kept in mind, this paper will concentrate on the second meaning, confession as an officially adopted church document.

Presbyterian and Reformed churches are not the only churches with confessional standards. The Roman Catholic, Eastern Orthodox, Lutheran and to a lesser extent the Anglican, Episcopal, and Methodist churches are also confessional bodies. Even so-called "free" churches that acknowledge only the Bible as their creed have often made semi-authoritative confessions of faith. Most Christian churches officially or informally share the faith of the Apostles' and Nicene Creeds. Therefore what is said in this section about the role of creeds and confessions is applicable not only to Presbyterian and Reformed churches but to the Christian church as a whole. Most of the examples cited come from the Reformed tradition but similar examples could also be drawn from other traditions.

A. *The Three Directions of Confessions of Faith*

A confession of faith may be defined more precisely as a public declaration before God and the world of what a church believes.

A confession is a public declaration of what a church believes. Individual Christians may and should confess their own personal faith, but a confession of faith is more than a personal affirmation of faith. It is an officially adopted statement of what a community of Christians believe. This communal character of confessions of faith is made explicitly clear in confessions such as the Scots and Second Helvetic Confessions and the Barmen Declaration, which speak of what "we" believe. But it is also implicit in such confessions as the Apostles' Creed and Heidelberg Catechism, which speak of what "I" believe, and in other confessions such as Westminster and the Confession of 1967, which speak more objectively. Whatever their form, confessions of faith express what a body of Christians believe in common.

These affirmations of the church's faith always have three reference points: God, the church itself, and the world. Confessions of faith are first of all the church's solemn and thankful response to God's self-revelation, expressed with a sense of responsibility to be faithful and obedient to God. Secondly, in a confession of faith members of a Christian community seek to make clear to themselves who they are, what they believe, and what they resolve to do. Finally, Christians confess their common faith not only to praise and serve God and not only to establish their self-identity but to speak to the world a unified word that declares who they are and what they stand for and against. Confessions thus have a social and political as well as theological and ecclesiological significance.

B.  *The Time for Confession*

Throughout the history of the Christian movement churches have written confessions of faith because they feel that they must do so, not just because they think it would be a good idea. Confessions of faith may result from a sense of urgent need to correct some distortion of the truth and claim of the gospel that threatens the integrity of the church's faith and life from within the church. They may result from some political or cultural movement outside the church that openly attacks or subtly seeks to compromise its commitment to the gospel. Sometimes the urgency to confess comes from the church's conviction that it has a great new insight into the promises and demands of the gospel that is desperately needed by both church and world. Frequently, all three occasions—internal danger, external threat, and great opportunity—are behind the great confessions of the church at the same time. In any case, the church writes confessions of faith when it faces a situation of life or a situation of death so urgent that it cannot remain silent but must speak, even at the cost of its own security, popularity, and success. Or to put it negatively, when all the church has to say is the restatement of what everyone already knows and believes, or when it has no word to speak other than safe generalities that ignore or cover over the concrete, specific issues of a crisis situation—then it is not the time for confession even though what is confessed might be true in itself.

C.  *The Content of Confessions of Faith*

At the heart of all confessions is the earliest confession of the New Testament church, "Jesus is Lord." (Strictly speaking, therefore, Christians confess not what but in whom they believe.) But the church discovered very early that in order to protect this simple confession from misunderstanding and misuse, it had to talk about the relation between Jesus and the God of Israel, and between Jesus and the Holy Spirit. The earliest Christological confession became a Trinitarian confession. That led to further reflection on biblical witness to the reality and work of God the Father, Son, and Holy Spirit in the past, present, and future history of the world in general, in the particular history of the people of God, and in the life of every individual Christian. Moreover, the church could not talk about the "lordship" of Jesus without also talking about the claim the triune God has on the lives of people in their personal and social relationships in the church and in the world. The confession "Jesus is Lord" necessarily led to the development of a full theology and ethic.

The length and focus of the church's confessions have varied according to which elements of this developing and expanding faith it has believed should be emphasized to meet the needs and challenges of particular situations.

Sometimes the situation has called not for a summary of everything Christians believe but for a short pointed confession dealing with one or more specific issues. The Nicene and Chalcedon Creeds, for instance, were the church's response to fundamental heresies in the ancient church concerning the identity of Jesus Christ. The Barmen Declaration was the response of some Reformed and Lutheran churches in Germany to what they believed was the one most critical issue in their situation in 1933, the relation between loyalty to Jesus Christ and loyalty to the state. The Confession of 1967 reformulated important themes of Christian doctrine in confessional literature and showed their social ethical implications.

Other confessions such as the Apostles' Creed are short summaries of elements of the whole of Christian faith.

The Lutheran and Reformed confessions of the sixteenth and seventeenth centuries tended to be longer and more comprehensive summaries of faith. In reforming the church they dealt with the most critical theological and political issues that divided Roman Catholics and Protestants—and Lutheran, Reformed, and Anabaptist Protestants—in the Reformation and post-Reformation period.

In every time and place the church is called to make the implications of its fundamental confession of the Lordship of Jesus Christ unmistakably clear and relevant. But in order to do that it has had in every new situation to decide afresh what to say and what to leave unsaid, how much and how little to say, what to emphasize and what for the time being to pass over, which internal and external dangers are critical and which are less critical.

D. *The Functions of Confessions*

The shape of confessions has been determined not only by the historical situation in which they were written but also by the uses for which they have been intended.

1. *Worship.* Like the Apostles' and Nicene Creeds, some creeds and confessions have been used as acts of worship in the church's liturgy. This use is a reminder of the fact that the church's confessions are first of all acts of praise, thanksgiving, and commitment in the presence of God.

2. *Defense of orthodoxy.* Most confessions have been intended as polemical defense of true Christian faith and life against perversion from within as well as from attacks from outside the church. They are the church's means of preserving the authenticity and purity of its faith.

3. *Instruction.* The confessions have been used for the education of leaders and members of the church in the right interpretation of Scripture and church tradition and to guard against the danger of individuals or groups selecting from the Bible or church tradition only that which confirms their personal opinions and desires.

Confessions written in question-and-answer form (like the Heidelberg and Westminster Catechisms) were written to prepare children and adult converts for baptism and participation in the fellowship of believers.

4. *Rallying-point in times of danger and persecution.* Confessions have often prepared and strengthened Christians to stand together in faithfulness to the gospel when they have been tempted to surrender to powerful forces of political, racial, social, or economic injustice.

5. *Church order and discipline.* Some churches, like the Presbyterian Church (U.S.A.), have sought to preserve the purity and unity of the church by requiring its ministers and church officers to accept the teachings of its confessions in order to be ordained. The government of these churches is also determined by their confessions of faith.

Some confessions were originally intended to serve more than one of these purposes. Others have in fact served multiple purposes though their writers may not have foreseen how they would be used.

E. *The Historical Limitations of Confessions*

Confessions address the issues, problems, dangers, and opportunities of a given historical situation. But confessions are related to their historical situation also in another way. Even when their writers have believed they were formulating Christian truth valid for all time and places, their work has been directed not only to but limited by their particular time and place. Throughout the history of the church—and also in our time—confessions have been deliberately or unconsciously expressed in the language and thought forms that were commonly accepted when they were written. God's self-revelation in Jesus Christ has sometimes been clarified but also distorted by the language and presuppositions of this or that ancient or current philosophy. The great classical confessions were written before the discoveries of modern science and reflect an outdated understanding of the structure of the world and its natural processes (just as our "modern" confessions will one day seem outdated and "primitive" to a later world). The theology and ethics of confessions of every age are shaped by what seem to be the normative or preferable sexual, familial, social, economic, cultural, and political patterns of a particular period of history. Even those confessions that have sought to be grounded exclusively in biblical revelation have often confused the revelation itself with various historically conditioned thought forms and cultural patterns in which it was received and preserved by people who lived in the ancient Near East. Modern scholarship has shown how extensively earlier confessions of faith saw in Scripture only the confirmation of what they thought they already knew about God, the world and human life in it (just as future scholarship will reveal how we have done the same thing in our time).

The confessions of the church, in other words, have indeed interpreted, defended, and preserved biblical-Christian truth. They have united the Christian community in its one task of bearing witness to the one Christian confession that Jesus is Lord. But at the same time, despite all good intentions, they have also distorted the truth revealed in Jesus Christ, been unable to grasp parts of the biblical witness to God's presence and work in Christ, and divided the church into churches with conflicting views of what Christian faith and life are all about. Is there any way to distinguish between the truth to which confessions of faith seek to bear witness and their inadequate witness to the truth? Christians in the Presbyterian-Reformed tradition believe they know at least how to go about this task. Their solution will be discussed in the proper place in the following section of this paper.

## II. Confessions of Faith in the Reformed Tradition

Everything we have said about confessions in general apply also to Reformed confessions. But now we turn to some of the most important characteristics of the Reformed understanding of the nature and purpose of confessions that distinguish it from other confessional traditions and theological movements.

A. *The Ecumenical Character of Reformed Churches*

From the very beginning and throughout their history the Reformed churches have sought to represent the church catholic. Their confessions do not speak only of what Reformed churches or Presbyterians believe but seek to confess what Christians believe. They have not claimed to be the only true church, with a monopoly on Christian faith and life, but have always been open to learn from other churches and traditions and eager to participate in conversations with them that could lead to mutual correction and reconciliation.

We must not exaggerate this ecumenical openness, of course. Individuals, groups, and whole denominations who claim to be Reformed have sometimes assumed or openly declared that only this or that particular Reformed church is the true church, that all other churches (including other Reformed denominations) are false or at least fatally corrupted, and that conversation with them can only compromise the true understanding of Christian faith and life which is completely, infallibly, and unchangeably contained in this or that particular Reformed confession. But such an attitude is itself un-Reformed and contrary to the very confessional documents used to support it.

Characteristic of the ecumenicity of the genuine Reformed tradition and its confessions is this statement in the confession of the Synod of Berne in 1528:

> But where something is brought before us by our pastors or by others, which brings us closer to Christ, and in accordance with God's word is more conducive to mutual friendship and Christian love than the interpretation now presented, we will gladly accept it and will not limit the course of the Holy Spirit, which does not go backwards towards the flesh but always forward towards the image of Jesus Christ our Lord.

B. *Faith and Practice*

It is typical of confessions in the Reformed tradition, that they emphasize not only what Christians believe but also how Christians live, not only orthodox Christian faith but also thankful and obedient Christian "practice," not only justification by grace through faith but also sanctification by grace evidenced in "good works." All Christian traditions acknowledge the fact that faith without works is dead. But in Reformed confessions the active Christian life is given special and unique emphasis.

1. *The Claim of God on all of Life.* Reformed confessional tradition follows Calvin in emphasizing the authority of God over every area of human life: over personal and familial relationships, over the organization and government of the Christian community, and over social, economic, and political "secular" communities as well. Reformed confessions therefore contain both personal and social ethics, a gospel of salvation and a social gospel. (See, for instance, the comprehensive and detailed exposition of the Ten Commandments in the Westminster Larger Catechism.)

Reformed confessions of different periods differ in their understanding of precisely what God requires. Sometimes they have been too certain that the will of God was identical with the historically and socially conditioned presuppositions of Reformed Christians in a particular time and place. Sometimes they have confused the rule of God in the world with the rule of the church. But however they differ and whatever mistakes they may have made, a consistent theme in Reformed confessions of all periods and places is the responsibility of individual Christians and the Christian church to seek to order all of human life according to the sovereign will of the God who is known in Jesus Christ through Scripture. No room is left for the belief of Christians in some other traditions that there are some areas of individual and social life that are not claimed by God and in which they are excused or prohibited from serving God.

2. *Grace and Law.* Reformed confessional tradition follows Calvin in believing that because the meaning and purpose of God's sovereign will is made known in Jesus Christ, and because sin separates humanity from God and each other, God's rule over and in the world must be understood as gracious rule exercised for our good. God gives us commands and requirements in order to guide and help us to the achievement of wholeness and happiness in our individual lives and justice, freedom, and peace in human society. The Heidelberg Catechism therefore expresses the theology of all Reformed confessions when it puts its exposition of the law of God under the heading "Thankfulness." The demands of God are understood in Reformed tradition as the good gift of God to be received with gratitude, exercised for the welfare of all human beings, and obeyed in confidence that God's grace gives us the ability to do what God's law requires. Law, in other words, is a part of the gospel of saving grace, not something opposed to it or some alternative to it.

This theology of grace and law is one of the most important things that distinguishes the Reformed tradition from other traditions and theologies. (a) It distinguishes Reformed Christians from other Christians who understand obedience to God's commandments as a means of earning or cooperating with the saving grace of God rather than as a thankful response to saving grace already freely given and powerfully at work. (b) It distinguishes Reformed Christians from other Christians who believe that the law of God serves primarily the negative purpose of exposing sin, leading to repentance, and leading to the gospel of God's saving grace rather than the positive purpose of guidance offered by the gospel. (c) It distinguishes Reformed Christians from the belief of some other Christians that Christian freedom is freedom from rather than freedom for obedience to the commands of God. (d) It distinguishes Reformed Christians from other Christians for whom obedience to the law is an end in itself rather than a means of loving and serving God and other people. (e) Finally, it distinguishes Reformed Christians from those who use the law of God to justify oppressive "order" in society for the benefit of a few rather than to achieve a free and just society for all.

One can of course find in the present as well as in the past individuals, groups, and whole denominations of Christians who call themselves Reformed yet understand and use the law of God in all of the un-Reformed ways we have mentioned. But insofar as they do so, they have misunderstood and misused the very theology of grace and law based on God's gracious sovereignty that is one of the most distinctive elements of their own Reformed confessions.

C. *The Authority of Confessions in the Reformed Tradition*

The Reformed tradition is unique in its understanding of the authority of its confessions. The most revealing clue to this unique understanding is the great number of confessions it has produced. Other Protestant confessional traditions have been content with only a few confessional statements written by a few people within narrow geographical or historical limits. All the Lutheran confessions, for instance, were written by a few Germans in Germany between 1529 and 1580. Authoritative Roman Catholic teaching comes from church councils or from the Pope. But from beginning of the Reformation wherever the Reformed church spread, Reformed Christians made new confessions of their faith, first city by city then country by country. The confessions of Bern, Basel, Zurich, Geneva, and other Swiss cities were followed by one or more confessions written for Germany, Switzerland, Belgium, Holland, Hungary, and Scotland. The great period of confession writing came to an end for two centuries after the seventeenth century (because under the influence of Protestant orthodoxy the Reformed churches lost sight of the reason for multiple confessions and because of the liberal theology that dominated the eighteenth and nineteenth centuries was suspicious of confessional restraint.) But the twentieth century has seen a revival of Reformed confessional writing. Reformed churches have participated in the preparation of well over thirty new confessions that have been completed or are in process.

This multiplicity of confessions, written by many people in many places over such a great span of time, obviously means that the Reformed tradition has never been content to recognize any one confession or collection of confessions as an absolute, infallible statement of the faith of Reformed Christians for all time. In the Reformed tradition confessional statements do have authority as statements of the faith of Reformed Christians at particular times and places, and there is a remarkable consistency in their fundamental content. Some have had convincing power for a long time. Nevertheless, for Reformed Christians all confessional statements have only a provisional, temporary, relative authority.

Reformed confessions themselves provide three interrelated reasons for this unique attitude toward confessional authority:

1. Confessions have a *provisional authority* (and are therefore subject to revision and correction) because all confessions are the work of limited, fallible, sinful human beings and churches. In our time we have perhaps become more aware than most of those who wrote and adopted Reformed confessions in the past that even when confessions intend to serve only the revealed truth and will of God, they are also influenced by the sexual, racial, and economic biases and by the scientific and cultural limitations of a particular situation. But from the very beginning and throughout its history Reformed Christians and their confessions have acknowledged with the Westminster Confession of 1646 that: "All synods or councils since the apostles' times, whether general or particular, may err, and many have erred; therefore they are not to be made the rule of faith and practice, but to be used as a help in both" (XXIV–XXXII).

2. Confessions have a *temporary authority* (and are therefore subject to revision and correction) because faith in the living God present and at work in the risen Christ through the Holy Spirit means always to be open to hear a new and fresh word from the Lord. As the multiplicity of Reformed confessions indicates, Reformed Christians have never been content to learn only how Christians before them discerned and responded to the word and work of God; they have continually asked in every new time, place, and situation, "What is the living Lord of Scripture saying and doing here and now, and what do we have to say and do to be faithful and obedient in our time?" The Barmen Declaration speaks for the best intentions of the whole Reformed tradition when it says, "Jesus Christ, as he is attested for us in Holy Scripture, is the one Word of God which we have to hear and which we have to trust and obey in life and in death."

3. Confessions have a *relative authority* (and are therefore subject to revision and correction) because they are subordinate to the higher authority of Scripture, which is the norm for discerning the will and work of God in every time and place. A frequently repeated theme in Reformed confessions is their subjection of their own theological and ethical thought—including their interpretation of scripture itself—to this higher authority, or to the authority of the Holy Spirit who speaks through it:

> We protest that if any man will note in this confession of ours any article or sentence repugnant to God's holy word, that it would please him of his gentleness and for Christian charity's sake to admonish us of the same in writing; and we upon our honor and fidelity, by God's grace do promise unto him satisfaction from the mouth of God, that is, from his holy scriptures, or else reformation of that which he shall prove to be amiss. (Preface to the Scots Confession.)

> The Supreme Judge, by which all controversies of religion are to be determined, and all decrees of councils, opinions of ancient writers, doctrines of men, and private spirits, are to be examined, and in whose sentence we are to rest, can be no other but the Holy Spirit speaking in the Scriptures. (Westminster Confession, 6.010.)

> Confessions and declarations are subordinate standards in the church, subject to the authority of Jesus Christ, the Word of God, as the Scriptures bear witness to him. No one type of confession is exclusively valid, no one statement is irreformable. Obedience to Jesus Christ alone identifies the one universal church and supplies the continuity of its tradition. ... (Preface to the Confession of 1967, 9.03.)

Reformed Christians are put in a difficult position with their self-limiting, self-relativising confessions. On the one hand they are bound: so long as they are faithful members of a Reformed church they are not free to interpret Christian faith and life (or even Scripture itself) however seems best to them personally, but are committed to submit themselves to the authority and guidance of the confessional standards of their church. On the other hand they are free: the very confessions to which they are bound allow—require—them to remember the human limitations and fallibility of their church's confessional standards, to be open to hear a new and perhaps different word from the living Lord the standards confess, and to examine critically the church's teachings in the light of further study of Scripture. It is not surprising, then, that Reformed Christians and whole Reformed denominations have sometimes been unable to maintain this balance between authority and freedom. Some have contradicted the very Reformed tradition they confess by claiming for this or that confession the absolute, infallible, unchangeable truth and authority that the Roman Catholic church has traditionally claimed for its official teaching. Others, while calling themselves Reformed, have acted as if they were members of a nonconfessional "free" church, insisting on their freedom to interpret Scripture for themselves without regard for the guidance and restraint of their church's confessional consensus. Those who choose confessional authority over personal freedom make impossible the continual reformation of the church called for by Reformed confessions themselves. They run the risk of idolatrously giving to the church the ultimate authority that belongs alone to the living God we come to know in Jesus Christ through the Bible. On the other hand, those who choose personal freedom over the confessional consensus of the church destroy the church's unity, cut themselves off from the guidance of the church as they interpret Scripture, and run the risk of serving not biblical truth but the personal biases they read into Scripture.

Difficult as it is to find the way between church authority without personal freedom or personal freedom without church authority, a distinctive mark of the Reformed tradition is the belief that it is only by seeking this difficult way that the church can be a united community of Christians who are both "reformed and always being reformed."

## III. The Presbyterian Book of Confessions

This section will deal with some questions concerning the particular confessional documents included in the Constitution of the Presbyterian Church (U.S.A.).

A. *Why a Book of Confessions*

For most of their history Presbyterians in the United States were guided by essentially a single confessional standard: the Westminster Confession with the Larger and Shorter Catechisms that translated it into question and answer form for educational purposes. It is not surprising then that many Presbyterians have been disturbed by the idea of a book of confessions: Is it not contrary to Reformed tradition? Does not the adoption of a plurality of confessions water down or compromise the confessional nature of the Presbyterian Church? Will not Presbyterians be confused by so many documents, especially since they do not always say the same thing? Will they not tend to pay little attention to any of them because they are overwhelmed by so much confessional material? Two answers can be given to these questions, the first historical and the second theological.

In the first place there is a historical answer. Although the idea of a collection of confessions is relatively new for North American Presbyterians, it is not at all new in the history of the Reformed tradition. In 1581 (still in the period of the Reformation itself) the Reformed churches of Europe issued a *Harmonia Confessionum Fidei* (*A Harmony of Confessions of Faith*) which set out in parallel form the main doctrines of the confessions of eight Reformed and three Lutheran churches. This harmony listed the agreement between the various confessions but pointed out the disagreements as well. Moreover, in the eighteenth century, the Church of Scotland officially authorized eight different confessional documents besides the Westminster Confession as teaching instruments of the church. Both the Heidelberg Catechism and the Second Helvetic Confession have long been standards for most Reformed bodies around the world. Reformed churches in America have been the exception rather than the rule with their single standard. Most Reformed churches have believed that a plurality of confessions enriches rather than compromises Reformed faith and practice.

Secondly, there is a theological reason for a book of confessions. We have just discussed the reasons why Reformed Christians cannot recognize any one confession as a final, infallible encapsulation of true Christian faith and life for all Christians, everywhere, now and forever. A book of confessions that includes some classical Reformed confessions and leaves room for new confessions makes unmistakably clear one of the most distinctive marks of the Reformed tradition.

B.  *Why This* Book of Confessions

The most immediate explanation for the content of the *Book of Confessions* is that it is the result of the combination of doctrinal standards that came with Presbyterian reunion in 1983. This amounted to adding the Larger Catechism from the three Westminster documents that were standards in the former Presbyterian Church in the United States to the *Book of Confessions* already adopted by the former United Presbyterian Church in the United States of America.

But the question remains, why this selection from the great number of authentic Reformed confessions that could have been chosen? The answer is that the *Book of Confessions* contains a cross-section of ecumenical and Reformed confessions with wide geographical and historical representation.

The Nicene and Apostles' Creeds from the ancient church come as close as any other confessional statements to expressing the faith of all Christians, of all traditions, throughout church history. Their inclusion points to the ecumenical character of our church.

The Scots Confession (1560) was written mostly by John Knox, student of Calvin and father of English-speaking Reformed Christianity.

The German Heidelberg Catechism (1563) and the Swiss Second Helvetic Confession (1566) are, as we have noted, probably the two most widely accepted confessional statements among Reformed Christians throughout the world.

The originally British Westminster Confession and Catechisms (1647) have been the primary standard for the Presbyterian branch of the Reformed family not only in our country but wherever Presbyterian Churches have sent missionaries.

The Barmen Declaration (1933), written by Lutheran and Reformed Christians working together (and thus another ecumenical document), confesses the lordship of Christ especially in relation to political issues that are critical for all Christians in the modern world.

The Confession of 1967, the only specifically American confession in the book, addresses critical issues of Christian faithfulness in our time and place.

The *Book of Confessions* as a whole enriches our understanding of what it means to be Reformed Christians, helps us escape the provincialism to which we have been prone, and expresses our intention to join the worldwide family of Reformed churches that is far bigger and more inclusive than our particular denomination.

C.  *The Relation of the Confessions in the Book to Each Other*

There is both unity and diversity in the theological and ethical teachings of the various confessions in the book.

1.  *Unity*

Comparison of the individual confessions in the book with each other reveals an easily recognizable fundamental agreement among them:

   a. All the confessions in the book share the same convictions about Jesus Christ as the one truly human and truly divine Mediator, Lord, and Savior.

   b. All explicitly or implicitly confess the doctrine of the Trinity.

   c. All the specifically Reformed confessions acknowledge the unique authority of Scripture and agree on principles for the right interpretation of Scripture.

   d. All the Reformed confessions assume or articulate the conviction that the Holy Spirit is the source of all right interpretation of Scripture and true Christian faith and life.

   e. All the Reformed confessions have the same theology concerning the true preaching of the Word and right administration of the Sacraments.

f. All the Reformed confessions emphasize God's sovereign claim on both personal and corporate life, and thankful human obedience to it. (All the catechisms contain expositions of the Ten Commandments and the Lord's Prayer.)

g. With the exception of the Nicene and Apostles' Creeds, comparison of any of these confessions with the confessional literature of other Christian traditions clearly reveals the same distinctively Reformed understanding of Christian faith and life.

2. *Differences*

There are of course differences in style, purpose, and sometimes content among confessions written by different people directed to the problems and issues of different situations and shaped by the patterns of thought of different periods of history.

The most obvious differences are differences in form. The Apostles' Creed is a very brief summary of Christian faith in general. The Scots, Second Helvetic, and Westminster Confessions are extended theological discussions that cover all or most of the main elements of Reformed faith in particular. The Nicene Creed, Barmen Declaration, and Confession of 1967 concentrate on a few major critical issues without intending to be comprehensive. The Heidelberg and the two Westminster Catechisms are written in question and answer form for the sake of the Christian education of children and adults. The Westminster documents and the Confession of 1967 differ from all the other confessions in the book in confessing our faith mostly in objective language rather than in terms of what "I" or "we" believe. So long as there is no expectation for any confession to serve purposes for which it was not written, these differences are not confusing or disturbing but can only help the church as it uses different confessions in the book to meet different needs.

But there are also differences, even apparent contradictions, in theological and ethical content that are more difficult to deal with. Without attempting to be exhaustive, the following point to some of the more important of them:

a. The sixteenth and seventeenth century confessions, most notably the Scots, contain an anti-Roman Catholic polemic that would be unfair and inappropriate in contemporary confessions.

b. The classical confessions show little interest in the mission of the church in the world, seeming to imply that the church's task is exhausted in worship, preaching, and Sacraments. Barmen and the Confession of 1967 reflect the awareness of the church in our time that the church does not exist for itself but for the sake of mission.

c. The doctrine of "double predestination" in Chapter III of the Westminster Confession is not taught in the doctrine of election in Chapter VIII of the Scots Confession, or in Chapter X of the Second Helvetic Confession. The Heidelberg Catechism has no explicit doctrine of predestination at all.

d. With the exception of Chapter II of the Second Helvetic Confession, the classical confessions were not concerned with the historical interpretation of

Scripture, whereas the contemporary Confession of 1967 of necessity deals with this issue.

  e. Chapter XXV of the Scots Confession and Chapter XX of the Second Helvetic Confession reflect the sixteenth century view that women should not be allowed to preach or administer the Sacraments. Contemporary confessions do not express this view, and the present Form of Government precludes it.

  f. Chapter XVIII of the Scots Confession, 8.11 of the Declaration of Barmen and 9.27 of the Confession of 1967 have a Christocentric understanding of the authority of Scripture, holding that Scripture is to be understood as witness to Jesus Christ. This Christocentric emphasis is missing in Chapters I and II of the Second Helvetic Confession and in Chapter I of the Westminster Confession.

  g. Speaking or praying in "tongues" is forbidden in Chapter XXII of the Second Helvetic Confession and in Chapter XXIII (XXI) of the Westminster Confession, but not in the other confessions of the book.

  h. Some issues that in the confessions of the sixteenth and seventeenth centuries were important enough to be issues of fundamental Christian faithfulness seem relatively unimportant in our time—for instance the observance of canonical hours or the choice of food in fasting (Second Helvetic Confession) or the taking of oaths and vows (Westminster Confession).

 3. *Dealing with the Differences*

Presbyterians who expect one right answer to every theological and ethical question are especially confused and deeply disturbed by these differences. ("What then does our church believe?") But the differences also puzzle others who understand that there is room for variety within the fundamental unity of the church. It is therefore important that agreement be reached on some guidelines for dealing with divergences among the confessions. Following are some suggestions based on the theology of the confessions themselves:

  a. Differences should not be exaggerated but should be understood and evaluated in light of the Christological and Trinitarian faith shared in common by all the confessions.

  b. Differences should be judged central or peripheral, critical or relatively unimportant, in light of the confessions' common Christological and Trinitarian faith, and in consideration of the most pressing problems and needs that confront the church in our time.

  c. Where there are conflicts, decision in favor of one or another alternative—or in favor of a totally new alternative—should be sought by subjection of all confessional statements to possible correction in light of fresh reading of Scripture.

  d. In light of the confessions' acknowledgment of their own fallibility, differences between them should be understood and evaluated with consideration of the scientific limitations, cultural influences, and theological language and style of the particular time in which they were written.

e. Both Scripture and the confessions teach us to have confidence in the Holy Spirit's continuing guidance of the church through the centuries as the Spirit enables the church to hear the Word of God through Scripture in every new time and situation. Therefore when there are differences between the confessions, initial priority should be given to contemporary confessions. This is only initial preference because further reflection may reveal that at some points the church in earlier times was more able and willing to be guided by the Spirit than the contemporary church.

f. The confessions are the church's confessions. Therefore when a governing body of the church has ruled in favor of one over another alternative in the confessions, the consensus of the whole church should take precedence over the opinions of individual church members or groups of church members. Because individual members or groups who disagree with the consensus of the church sometimes may have a better understanding of Scripture and be more open to the guidance of the Spirit than the church as a whole, the church should listen to them respectfully, with openness to be reformed by them. But until such time as the church as a whole is convinced that it should change its position, its interpretation of the confessions should be considered authoritative.

g. So long as the church as a whole has not taken a stand on differences among the confessions, its ministers and officers should have the freedom to choose the confessional interpretation that they believe best reflects the witness of Scripture.

h. When there is no real consensus in the church, differences among the confessions should ordinarily be allowed to stand until such time as a genuine consensus is possible and necessary. Even if a bare majority were able to defeat a very large minority in voting for one option in preference to another, it would ordinarily be premature and dishonest for the church to claim, "This is what we Presbyterians believe."

D. *The* Book of Confessions *and Ordination*

The church does not require acceptance of the church's confessions for church membership. All who acknowledge Jesus Christ as Lord and Savior are welcome to join and participate in fellowship. But to ensure that those who lead the church do so in faithfulness to its doctrine and form of government, the church does require ordained ministers, elders, and deacons to declare their adherence to the confessions of the church. In order to understand what they commit themselves to when they do this, it is important to note the sequence of questions asked at ordination and the precise wording of the third question. The first five questions are:

a. Do you trust in Jesus Christ your Savior, acknowledge him Lord of all and Head of the church, and through him believe in one God, Father, Son, and Holy Spirit?

b. Do you accept the Scriptures of the Old and New Testaments to be, by the Holy Spirit, the unique and authoritative witness to Jesus Christ in the church universal, and God's word to you?

c. Do you sincerely receive and adopt the essential tenets of the Reformed faith as expressed in the confessions of our church as authentic and reliable expositions of what Scripture leads us to believe and do, and will you be instructed and led by those confessions as you lead the people of God?

d. Will you fulfill your office in obedience to Jesus Christ, under the authority of Scripture, and be continually guided by our confessions?

e. Will you be governed by our church's polity, and will you abide by its discipline? Will you be a friend among your colleagues in ministry, working with them, subject to the ordering of God's Word and Spirit?

These questions are very carefully worded to preserve in the church the same understanding of the authority of confessions characteristic of the Reformed tradition in general. That is, they seek to protect both freedom and variety in the church and the authority and unity of the church. The following two sections of this paper must therefore be held closely together.

1. *Freedom and Variety in the Church*

The same freedom and variety that is characteristic of the Reformed tradition in general is expressed in the questions asked of candidates for ordination in the Presbyterian Church (U.S.A.):

a. Ordained persons are asked to acknowledge the *Book of Confessions* as "authentic and reliable expositions of what Scripture leads us to believe and do." These words limit the authority of the book by making its authority subordinate to the higher authority of Scripture—which in turn (according to the first two questions) derives its authority from its witness to the triune God revealed in Jesus Christ who alone has the right to claim absolute and unqualified loyalty and obedience.

b. Ordained persons are required to be "instructed and led" and "continually guided" by the church's confessions. These words demand study of the confessions. They also provide freedom from a demand for unqualified assent to everything the confessions ask us to think, say, and do and freedom from a legalistic interpretation of the confessions.

c. Since 1983 ordained persons are asked to receive and adopt the "essential tenets" of the Reformed faith as expressed in the confessions. Although some other wording may better express the intent, the phrase "essential tenets" is intended to protect freedom with the limits of general commitment to the confessions. That this is indeed the purpose of the phrase is made clear by the fact that both the former United Presbyterian Church in the U.S.A. and Presbyterian Church in the U.S. repeatedly answered in the negative overtures requesting that the church make a precise list of a few fundamental doctrines (once called "essential and necessary articles of faith") that must be accepted by ordained officers. Moreover, while Chapter II of the Form of Government lists a number of general theological affirmations to summarize the broad general character of Presbyterian faith and life, it too prescribes no specific understanding of any of these affirmations to test the acceptability of people for ordained office in the church.

The ordination question that asks for commitment to the "essential tenets" of the confessions brings freedom in the church at several levels. Ordained persons are free to be "instructed," "led," and "continually guided" by the confessions without being forced to subscribe to any precisely worded articles of faith drawn up either by the General Assembly or by a presbytery. (Presbyteries, too, are bound to the constitutional language that excludes demand for adherence to any specifically worded interpretations of a few selected doctrines. In a presbytery the decision for ordination is always determined by the concrete encounter between the presbytery and the candidate.) Presbyteries (in the case of ministers) and church sessions (in the case of elders and deacons) are free to decide for themselves what acceptable loyalty to the confessions means in their particular situation without being bound to any "check list" prescribed by higher governing bodies of the church.

2. *The Authority and Unity of the Church*

The ordination questions make room for freedom in the church but not for unlimited freedom. They also protect the authority and unity of the church:

a. To be an ordained Presbyterian is not only to acknowledge the superior authority of God in Christ as proclaimed by Scripture but also to recognize the church's confessions as "authentic and reliable expositions of what Scripture leads us to believe and do."

While confessional standards are subordinate to the Scriptures, they are, nevertheless, standards. They are not lightly drawn up or subscribed to, nor may they be ignored or dismissed. The church is prepared to counsel with or even discipline one ordained who seriously rejects the faith expressed in the confessions (*Book of Order*, G-2.0200 [F-2.02 in the current *Book of Order*]).

b. To be an ordained Presbyterian is to promise to be "instructed," "led," and "continually guided" by the confessions of the church—not just by one's personal theological and ethical preferences or even by one's own personal understanding of God or Jesus Christ or Scripture. The church should not "bind the conscience" of those who disagree with its confessions and interpretation of their meaning. When an individual or group of individuals disagree with the consensus of the church, the church must first examine itself to see whether it needs to reform its confessional stance. Nevertheless, in the Presbyterian Church the consensus of the church concerning the meaning of faith and life takes precedence over the opinions and preferences of individuals and groups in the church, and may lead to the refusal of ordination to those who disagree with the church.

c. To be an ordained Presbyterian is to acknowledge the authority of each individual confession in the *Book of Confessions* and the book as a whole, not just the authority of selected sections from the confessions or the authority of one or another preferred confession in the book. While reception and adoption of the *Book of Confessions* means freedom from the imposition of a list of specific doctrinal formulations, it does not mean freedom to select from the book whatever an individual or group in the church chooses. An appropriate governing body as a whole may decide that some statements in the confessions are central and others peripheral, some no longer authoritative and others still authoritative for the church in our place and time. It may decide that there is or is not room for difference in the church regarding the authority of this or that statement. But in the Presbyterian Church the decision about what is "essential and necessary" belongs not to individuals or groups in the church but to the appropriate governing body of the church as it makes decisions in particular cases.

It is important to emphasize that it is not only individual ordained persons but also general assemblies, presbyteries, and synods that are to be instructed, led, and continually guided by the church's confessions.

3. *Guidelines*

In light of the foregoing discussion of the freedom and variety and authority and unity of the church, the following guidelines may be seen as conclusions drawn from these discussions and as guidance for individuals and groups concerned with the ordination of pastors, elders, and deacons.

a. General Assemblies, synods, presbyteries, and sessions, as well as individual church officers, should be led, instructed, and continually guided by the whole *Book of Confessions*.

b. The confessions of the *Book of Confessions* are standards, in response to the historical context of the time, which are subordinate to Scripture; they are subject to criticism in light of the word of God in Jesus Christ as witnessed in the Scriptures of the Old and New Testaments and may be revised by the Church following duly prescribed procedures.

c. The confessions are serious statements and are "not to be taken lightly." While neither the General Assembly nor any presbytery or session should demand adherence to any specific list of beliefs or doctrinal formulations as if the content of the faith could be reduced to a few selected and precisely worded statements of doctrine, General Assemblies, synods, presbyteries, and sessions have the responsibility of determining on a case by case basis whether candidates for ordination adhere to the standards of doctrine as set out in the confessions.

d. When individuals or groups in the church call into question some aspect of the confessions or of the church's interpretation of them, those who hear that objection should consider the possibility that the dispute may point to a deficiency in present confessional standards, remembering that, indeed, synods or councils may err and that the church is always to be reformed (sempter reformanda). However, after due consideration, the court of jurisdiction must decide whether such objection is to be allowed to stand or is to be ruled as being out of conformity with the confessional standards of the church.

e. Thus, when individuals or groups in the church persist in disagreeing with the confessions or the church's interpretation of them, the appropriate church body has the responsibility of determining whether the disagreement is sufficient to prevent the approval of a candidate for ordination to the office of pastor, elder, or deacon.

f. So long as presbyteries do not contradict specific interpretations of the confessions made by the General Assembly, and so long as sessions do not contradict those made by the Assembly or by their presbytery, presbyteries and sessions have the right and responsibility to interpret for themselves whether candidates for ordination and ordained persons, for whom they are responsible, hold to the "essentials" of the faith as articulated by the confessions of the church (the constitutional right of appeal being understood).

E. *Other Important Uses of the* Book of Confessions *in the Church*

If our church is to be a truly confessional church in the Reformed tradition, every aspect of its life must be informed and shaped by the understanding of Christian faith and life expressed in the *Book of Confessions*. Without attempting to be exhaustive in discussing them, we suggest the following areas in which the book should have the normative function the church acknowledges it to have:

1. *The church's ministry in general.* Prerequisite to faithful and responsible use of the book in every particular aspect of the church's life is its being carefully taught in the seminaries, seriously and properly used in the ordination process, and continually studied and utilized by the leaders and governing bodies of the church at all levels.

2. *Worship.* Remembering that one of the main functions of confession in the New Testament and in the ancient church was liturgical, we should seek ways to use the language of the confessions in the church's worship so that people in our congregations may make them their own confessions of faith before God and the world. Even when explicit language of the confessions would be inappropriate, their theological and ethical teachings should determine decisions about the order, forms, content, and purpose of worship.

3. *Preaching.* The task of preaching is to proclaim the God we meet in Jesus Christ through the biblical witness, not to proclaim the theology of the confessions. Nevertheless, preachers may, and should also be "instructed," "led," and "continually guided" by the confessions as they choose and interpret their biblical texts and prepare their sermons.

4. *Christian education.* After the Bible itself, the *Book of Confessions* should be a primary resource and standard of the church's responsibility to enable children, youth, new and long-time Presbyterians to understand what it means to be a Christian in the Reformed tradition, claim that tradition for themselves, and be guided by it in every area of their daily lives. If this is to happen: (a) Unordained as well as ordained teachers in the church should understand, be able to interpret, and be

themselves committed to the Reformed faith as contained in the confessions of our church. (b) Ministers must be teachers and especially the teachers of teachers. (c) The best education theories and methods must be chosen and used in a way consistent with the Reformed tradition so that true learning and claiming of the tradition can take place and authoritarian indoctrination or brainwashing avoided. (d) The *Book of Confessions* itself should be part of the church's educational curriculum—especially in officer and teacher education, in confirmation instruction, and in adult church school classes. (e) All curriculum material need not be informed by the Reformed tradition, but all curriculum material should be continually evaluated and taught in light of that tradition as expressed in the *Book of Confessions*.

5. *Pastoral care*. Faithful and effective pastoral care in our time requires ministers gratefully and diligently to use the wisdom, tools, and skills of such "secular" disciplines as psychology and sociology, and (increasingly) to be able to deal with issues raised by modern medical science and technology. If pastors are to be faithful to their ordination vows and if they are to offer people in need the distinctive resources of Christian and Reformed faith, they must continually evaluate the presuppositions, claims, methods, and goals of these disciplines in light of the theological and ethical teaching of the church's confessions. Pastors should also find guidance in the theology and language of the confessions for what they should say and do in ministering to people both in crisis situations and in situations of everyday life.

6. *Evangelism*. The theology of the confessions should shape the motives, content, methods, and goals of the church's evangelistic programs. Special care must be taken lest concern for "results" or "success" lead to evangelistic preaching and techniques that compromise either the fundamental commitment of our confessions to the gospel of salvation by God's grace alone or their emphasis on costly Christian discipleship in every area of life.

7. *Mission*. The church must continually evaluate its mission programs, strategies and goals to be sure that they are determined by the theology and ethics of its confessions and not by this or that liberal, conservative, or revolutionary ideology or by the cultural or racial preferences of the leaders and members of the church.

8. *Administration*. Governing bodies of the church and church leaders properly seek the most efficient styles of leadership, management, decision-making, and priority and goal-setting. But all administrative and operational processes and goals should be measured by the confessional standards of the church and choices determined by the "essential tenets of the Reformed faith" expressed in them.

Our church will have become a truly confessional church when we no longer have to remind ourselves to test what we think and say and do by reference to the *Book of Confessions*, but when we do so automatically, and when it becomes so much a part of us that we are always unconsciously guided by our commitment to the Reformed tradition it expresses and serves.

CONFESSIONAL NATURE OF THE CHURCH REPORT

## Selected Reading

Calvin John. *Institutes of the Christian Religion.* Edited by John T. McNeill. 2 vols. The Library of Christian Classics. Philadelphia: Westminster, 1960. The greatest theological classic of the tradition.

Cullman, Oscar. *The Earliest Christian Confession.* London: Lutterworth, n.d. (Not in print.) A review of confessional materials found primarily in the New Testament.

Dowey, Edward A. *A Commentary of the Confessions of 1967, An Introduction to the Book of Confessions.* Philadelphia; Westminster, 1968. (Not in print.) A book useful to ministers and theological students, it has a helpful synopsis of the creeds in a two-page chart.

Fuller, Reginald H. *The Foundations of New Testament Christology.* New York: Scribner's, 1969. (Not in print.) A helpful background book for students and ministers.

Guthrie, Shirley C. *Christian Doctrine.* Atlanta: John Knox, 1968. A very readable volume.

Keesecker, William F. *A Layperson's Study Guide to the Book of Confessions.* General Assembly of the United Presbyterian Church in the U.S.A., 1976. A practical study guide.

Leith, John H. *Creeds of the Churches.* Richmond; John Knox, 1982 paper. A comprehensive collection not limited to the Reformed tradition and ranging from the Old Testament to C'67.

Leith, John H. *Introduction to the Reformed Tradition.* Atlanta: John Knox, 1977, 1981 paper. A standard for Presbyterians.

Rogers, Jack. *Presbyterian Creeds, A Guide to the Book of Confessions.* Philadelphia: Westminster, 1985. A readable introduction to some of the main themes put into a case study format.

Schaff, Philip. *The Creeds of Christendom*, Vol. III. Grand Rapids; Baker, 1983. A scholar's tool for work on Protestant confessions. Vol. II is on the Greek and Latin creeds.

# THE ASSESSMENT OF PROPOSED AMENDMENTS TO THE *BOOK OF CONFESSIONS*†

## I. Preamble

The Constitution of the Presbyterian Church (U.S.A.) consists of the *Book of Confessions* and the *Book of Order*. The *Book of Confessions* includes the following: "The Nicene Creed, The Apostles' Creed, The Scots Confession, The Heidelberg Catechism, The Second Helvetic Confession, The Westminster Confession of Faith, The [Westminster] Larger Catechism, The [Westminster] Shorter Catechism, The Theological Declaration of Barmen, The Confession of 1967, and A Brief Statement of Faith—Presbyterian Church (U.S.A.)."[1]

The Presbyterian Church (U.S.A.) does not recognize any one confession or collection of confessions as an absolute, infallible statement of the faith for Christians of all times and places. In the Reformed tradition, the authority of all confessional statements is "subject to the authority of Jesus Christ, the Word of God, as the Scriptures bear witness to him,"[2] and therefore provisional, temporary, and relative. Thus, any confession or collection of confessions is subject to revision and correction. Nevertheless, as a constitutional matter, change in the *Book of Confessions* is a momentous decision, affecting the church's understanding of its faith and life.

When the Presbyterian Church (U.S.A.) considers amending the *Book of Confessions* by the inclusion or deletion of a confessional document, it has enduring resources for assessing the wisdom of the proposal. In its *Book of Order* and the General Assembly study, *The Confessional Nature of the Church*, Presbyterians have articulated an understanding of the place of confessions in the church's life. This understanding embodies considerations that guide the church in its determination of the scope and shape of the *Book of Confessions*.

Chapter Two of The Foundations of Presbyterian Polity, *Book of Order*, "The Church and Its Confessions," clarifies the significance of confessions for the faith and life of the church. Any proposed change in the *Book of Confessions*—whether by inclusion of an additional confessional document, by deletion of a current confessional document, or by clarification of a current confessional document—should be considered in light of these constitutional understandings, grounded in the church's theological tradition and expressed in the *Book of Order*.

Possible changes in the *Book of Confessions* cannot be governed by a formula or a brief checklist of criteria. As the church weighs any proposal for altering its confessional standards, it must consider carefully a broad range of issues. The following considerations are drawn from the church's articulated position in the

---

† [This text was added by action of the 209th General Assembly (1997). See *Minutes*, 1997, Part I, p. 162, paragraph 19.0013. The text for this report can be found in the *Minutes*, 1997, Part I, pp. 162–64.]

## ASSESSMENT OF PROPOSED AMENDMENTS

*Book of Order* and *The Confessional Nature of the Church*. They do not exhaust the issues related to the place and function of confessions in the church. They do provide a necessary framework for actions affecting the scope and shape of the *Book of Confessions*.

### II. Confessional Standards

The *Book of Order* is clear that "confessional statements are subordinate standards in the church, subject to the authority of Jesus Christ, the Word of God, as the Scriptures bear witness to him."[3] This order of authority—Christ, Scriptures, Confessions—is nicely expressed in the fourth ordination question:

> d. Will you fulfill your office in obedience to Jesus Christ, under the authority of Scripture, and be continually guided by our confessions?[4]

While all creeds and confessions, including those in the *Book of Confessions*, are subordinate standards, they are *standards* for the church and its ordered ministries. "[The confessions] are not lightly drawn up or subscribed to," states the *Book of Order*, "nor may they be ignored or dismissed."[5] Thus, the church requires that ministers of the Word and Sacrament, elders, and deacons give affirmative answer to an ordination question that specifies the source and the function of confessional authority:

> Do you sincerely receive and adopt the essential tenets of the Reformed faith as expressed in the confessions of our church as authentic and reliable expositions of what Scripture [teaches] us to believe and do, and will you be instructed ... by those confessions as you lead the people of God?[6]

Because the church's confessions are central to its identity and integral to its ordered ministries, changes in the *Book of Confessions* require an exacting amendment process. Nevertheless, the church is clear that obedience to Jesus Christ opens it to the reform of its standards of doctrine. Change in the *Book of Confessions* is an ever-present possibility that must always be approached with discernment of the truth of the gospel and the leading of the Holy Spirit.

### III. The Church and Its Confessions

The church's commitment to its confessions is an expression of its determination to shape its life in faithful response to the grace of the Lord Jesus Christ, the love of God, and the "koinonia" of the Holy Spirit. The church's confessions are far more than ecclesial artifacts or intellectual abstractions, for

> The Presbyterian Church (U.S.A.) states its faith and bears witness to God's grace in Jesus Christ in the creeds and confessions in the *Book of Confessions*. In these confessional statements the church declares to its members and to the world
> who and what it is,
> what it believes,
> what it resolves to do.[7]

Thus, any proposed change to the *Book of Confessions* should enhance the church's understanding and declaration of who and what it is, what it believes, and what it resolves to do. There are numerous reasons to know, respect, and use creeds and confessions that may not be sufficient to warrant their inclusion in the *Book of Confessions*. The central functions of identifying and proclaiming the church's faithful identity, beliefs, and actions are necessary elements in determining the content of the *Book of Confessions*.

A. *The Church Declares to Its Members and to the World Who and What It Is*

   1. *The Faith of the Church Catholic*

"In its confessions, the Presbyterian Church (U.S.A.) gives witness to the faith of the one, holy, catholic, and apostolic Church. ..."[8]

Thus, any confession within the *Book of Confessions* should articulate the breadth and depth of what Christians believe, not only the distinctive features of what Reformed churches or Presbyterians believe. The Presbyterian Church (U.S.A.) affirms that there is one church and that "the unity of the Church is a gift of its Lord. ..."[9] Thus the confessional standards of the Presbyterian Church (U.S.A.) should acknowledge gratefully the gift of unity as they seek faithfully the visible oneness of the Church catholic.

   2. *The Affirmations of the Protestant Reformation*

"In its confessions, the Presbyterian Church (U.S.A.) identifies with the affirmations of the Protestant Reformation."[10] The Presbyterian Church (U.S.A.) understands itself to be part of the tradition emerging from the sixteenth century Reformation in Europe. Thus, any confession within the *Book of Confessions* should be compatible with the "Protestant watchwords"—Christ alone, grace alone, faith alone, Scripture alone—that remain guides to Christian faith and life.

   3. *The Faith of the Reformed Tradition*

"In its confessions, the Presbyterian Church (U.S.A.) expresses the faith of the Reformed tradition."[11] The Presbyterian Church (U.S.A.) understands itself to be one ecclesial expression of the Reformed tradition. Thus, any confession within the *Book of Confessions* should be compatible with central elements of Reformed faith and life. As one church within the Reformed family of churches, the Presbyterian Church (U.S.A.) should ensure that its confessions enrich understanding of what it means to be Reformed Christians. Historical and geographic representation help the church overcome a tendency toward provincialism and reflect the church's intention to be a member of the worldwide family of Reformed churches.

B. *The Church Declares to Its Members and to the World What It Believes*

   1. *Affirmations*

Ecclesial confessions "identify the church as a community of people known by its convictions. ..."[12] As an expression of what a body of Christians believe in common, any confession within the *Book of Confessions* should help members of the community define and give witness to what they believe.

## ASSESSMENT OF PROPOSED AMENDMENTS

2. *Renunciations*

Ecclesial confessions of faith speak a unified word that declares what the church opposes as well as what it affirms. Confessions within the *Book of Confessions* should help members of the community resist the seductions of ideologies, institutions, and images that are inimical to the gospel, and should embolden the church to announce its opposition to all that denies the good news.[13]

3. *Scripture Tradition, Doctrine, Proclamation*

As expressions of the "yes" and the "no" of the gospel, the confessions within the *Book of Confessions* should

—guide the church in its study and interpretation of the Scriptures;

—summarize the essence of Christian tradition;

—direct the church in maintaining sound doctrine;

—equip the church for its work of proclamation.[14]

4. *Unity*

The *Book of Confessions* evidences a fundamental theological unity. While confessional unity does not mean uniformity, confessions within the *Book of Confessions* should display consistent convictions concerning central affirmations of Christian faith.

C. *The Church Declares to Its Members and to the World What It Resolves to Do*

1. *Mission*

Confessions of faith are not timeless abstractions, but expressions of the actual life of communities of faith. They identify the church as a community of people known by its actions as well as by its convictions.[15] Thus, confessions within the *Book of Confessions* should shape the church's faithfulness and courage in its mission:

> The Church is called to undertake this mission even at the risk of losing its life, trusting in God alone as the author and giver of life, sharing the gospel, and doing those deeds in the world that point beyond themselves to the new reality in Christ.[16]

2. *Actions*

The *Book of Confessions* is meant to be used in the church. Thus, the church should ask how a proposed confessional statement might function in the life of the church. Among the possibilities are the following:

—In the church's ministry and mission: the church's confessions should be used to shape faithful witness and service in the world.

—In worship: the church's confessions are acts of praise, thanksgiving and commitment in the presence of God: confessions should help to shape the liturgy in addition to their use as elements within the liturgy.

—In teaching: the church's confessions should be used for the education of leaders and members of the church in the right interpretation of Scripture, Tradition, theology and ethics.

—In preaching: preachers should be instructed, led, and guided by the confessions of the church as they proclaim the gospel.

—In church order and discipline: the confessions of the church should be used to preserve the peace, unity, and purity of the church by serving as standards for ordered ministry and governance.

—In defense of the gospel: the confessions of the church may be elements in resisting perversions of the faith from within and temptations or attacks from without.[17]

## IV. The Confessional Collection

The *Book of Confessions* includes creeds, catechisms, and confessions from the early church, the Reformation and post-Reformation eras, and the twentieth century. Each document was a genuine expression of Christian faith in its own time and place. Each has been received by the Presbyterian Church (U.S.A.) as a significant expression of Christian faith for our time and place.

Confessional statements emerge from a variety of circumstances in the church's life. Among the realities that lead to the formulation and reception of creeds, catechisms, and confessions are the following:

1. A sense of urgent need to clarify the faith over and against some distortion of the gospel that threatens the integrity of the church's faith and life.

2. A political or cultural movement outside the church that openly attacks or subtly seeks to compromise the church's commitment to the gospel.

3. The church's conviction that it has a new insight into the promise and demand of the gospel that is needed by both church and world.

When the church considers a proposal to add a confessional document to the *Book of Confessions*, all considerations are sharply focused by the issue of the church's reception of the proposed confession.

1. When a *new confession* is proposed for inclusion in the *Book of Confessions*, the church must understand the occasion for its formulation. However, the *intention* of the new document should be tested by a period of reception in the church. A confessional statement should prove itself foundational to the church's faith and life before it is proposed for inclusion in the church's confessional standards.

2. When the proposed confession is a *historic document*, the church should understand the original circumstances of formulation and reception. Additionally, the contemporary need for the confession and the possibilities for reception should be demonstrated. Then, the value of the historical confession should be tested by a period of reception in the church. A confessional statement should prove itself foundational to the church's faith and life before it is proposed for inclusion in the church's confessional standards.

Thus, the creeds and confessions of this church reflect a particular stance within the history of God's people. They are the result of prayer, thought, and experience within a living tradition. They serve to strengthen personal commitment and the life and witness of the community of believers.[18]

ASSESSMENT OF PROPOSED AMENDMENTS

## Endnotes

1. *Book of Order*, G-1.0501 (F-3.04 in the current *Book of Order*).
2. *Book of Order*, G-2.0200 (F-2.02 in the current *Book of Order*).
3. *Book of Order*, G-2.0200 (F-2.02 in the current *Book of Order*).
4. *Book of Order*, G-14.0207d, passim (W-4.4003d in the current *Book of Order*).
5. *Book of Order*, G-2.0200 (F-2.02 in the current *Book of Order*).
6. *Book of Order*, G-14.0207c, passim (W-4.4003c in the current *Book of Order*).
7. *Book of Order*, G-2.0100a (F-2.01 in the current *Book of Order*).
8. *Book of Order*, G-2.0300 (F-2.03 in the current *Book of Order*).
9. *Book of Order*, G-4.0201 (F-1.0302a in the current *Book of Order*).
10. *Book of Order*, G-2.0400 (F-2.04 in the current *Book of Order*).
11. *Book of Order*, G-2.0500 (F-2.05 in the current *Book of Order*).
12. *Book of Order*, G-2.0100b (F-2.01 in the current *Book of Order*).
13. *The Confessional Nature of the Church*, 29.120.
14. Taken from the *Book of Order*, G-2.0100b (F-2.01 in the current *Book of Order*).
15. *Book of Order*, G-2.0100b (F-2.01 in the current *Book of Order*).
16. *Book of Order*, G-3.0400 (F-1.0301 in the current *Book of Order*).
17. *The Confessional Nature of the Church*, 29.129–.135; 29.211–.219.
18. *Book of Order*, G-2.0500b (F-2.01 in the current *Book of Order*).

# THE NICENE CREED

[TEXT]

## The Nicene Creed

In the first three centuries, the church found itself in a hostile environment. On the one hand, it grappled with the challenge of relating the language of the gospel, developed in a Hebraic and Jewish-Christian context, to a Graeco-Roman world. On the other hand, it was threatened not only by persecution, but also by ideas that were in conflict with the biblical witness.

In A.D. 312, Constantine won control of the Roman Empire in the battle of Milvian Bridge. Attributing his victory to the intervention of Jesus Christ, he elevated Christianity to favored status in the empire. "One God, one Lord, one faith, one church, one empire, one emperor" became his motto.

The new emperor soon discovered that "one faith and one church" were fractured by theological disputes, especially conflicting understandings of the nature of Christ, long a point of controversy. Arius, a priest of the church in Alexandria, asserted that the divine Christ, the Word through whom all things have their existence, was *created* by God before the beginning of time. Therefore, the divinity of Christ was similar to the divinity of God, but not of the same essence. Arius was opposed by the bishop, Alexander, together with his associate and successor Athanasius. They affirmed that the divinity of Christ, the Son, is of the same substance as the divinity of God, the Father. To hold otherwise, they said, was to open the possibility of polytheism, and to imply that knowledge of God in Christ was not final knowledge of God.

To counter a widening rift within the church, Constantine convened a council in Nicaea in A.D. 325. A creed reflecting the position of Alexander and Athanasius was written and signed by a majority of the bishops. Nevertheless, the two parties continued to battle each other. In 381, a second council met in Constantinople. It adopted a revised and expanded form of the A.D. 325 creed, now known as the Nicene Creed.

The Nicene Creed is the most ecumenical of creeds. The Presbyterian Church (U.S.A.) joins with Eastern Orthodox, Roman Catholic, and most Protestant churches in affirming it. Nevertheless, in contrast to Eastern Orthodox churches, the western churches state that the Holy Spirit proceeds not only from the Father, but from the Father *and the Son* (Latin, *filioque*). To the eastern churches, saying that the Holy Spirit proceeds from both Father and Son threatens the distinctiveness of the person of the Holy Spirit; to the western churches, the *filioque* guards the unity of the triune God. This issue remains unresolved in the ecumenical dialogue.

## THE NICENE CREED

**1.1**  We believe in one God,
  the Father, the Almighty,
  maker of heaven and earth,
  of all that is,
    seen and unseen.

**1.2**  We believe in one Lord, Jesus Christ,
  the only Son of God,
  eternally begotten of the Father,
  God from God, Light from Light,
  true God from true God,
  begotten, not made,
  of one Being with the Father;
  through him all things were made.
  For us and for our salvation
    he came down from heaven,
    was incarnate of the Holy Spirit and the Virgin Mary
    and became truly human.
    For our sake he was crucified under Pontius Pilate;
    he suffered death and was buried.
    On the third day he rose again
    in accordance with the Scriptures;
    he ascended into heaven
    and is seated at the right hand of the Father.
    He will come again in glory to judge the living and the dead,
    and his kingdom will have no end.

**1.3**  We believe in the Holy Spirit, the Lord, the giver of life,
  who proceeds from the Father and the Son,
  who with the Father and the Son is worshiped and glorified,
  who has spoken through the prophets.
  We believe in one holy catholic and apostolic Church.
  We acknowledge one baptism for the forgiveness of sins.
  We look for the resurrection of the dead,
  and the life of the world to come. Amen.

# THE APOSTLES' CREED

[TEXT]

# The Apostles' Creed

Although not written by apostles, the Apostles' Creed reflects the theological formulations of the first century church. The creed's structure may be based on Jesus' command to make disciples of all nations, baptizing them in the name of the Father, the Son, and the Holy Spirit. In a time when most Christians were illiterate, oral repetition of the Apostles' Creed, along with the Lord's Prayer and the Ten Commandments, helped preserve and transmit the faith of the western churches. The Apostles' Creed played no role in Eastern Orthodoxy.

In the early church, Christians confessed that "Jesus is Lord" but did not always understand the biblical context of lordship. The views of Marcion, a Christian living in Rome in the second century, further threatened the church's understanding of Jesus as Lord. Marcion read the Old Testament as referring to a tyrannical God who had created a flawed world. Marcion believed that Jesus revealed, in contrast, a good God of love and mercy. For Marcion, then, Jesus was not the Messiah proclaimed by the prophets, and the Old Testament was not Scripture. Marcion proposed limiting Christian "Scripture" to Luke's gospel (less the birth narrative and other parts that he felt expressed Jewish thinking) and to those letters of Paul that Marcion regarded as anti-Jewish. Marcion's views developed into a movement that lasted several centuries.

Around A.D. 180, Roman Christians developed an early form of the Apostles' Creed to refute Marcion. They affirmed that the God of creation is the Father of Jesus Christ, who was born of the Virgin Mary, was crucified under Pontius Pilate, was buried and raised from the dead, and ascended into heaven, where he rules with the Father. They also affirmed belief in the Holy Spirit, the church, and the resurrection of the body.

Candidates for membership in the church, having undergone a lengthy period of moral and doctrinal instruction, were asked at baptism to state what they believed. They responded in the words of this creed.

The Apostles' Creed underwent further development. In response to the question of readmitting those who had denied the faith during the persecutions of the second and third centuries, the church added, "I believe in the forgiveness of sins." In the fourth and fifth centuries, North African Christians debated the question of whether the church was an exclusive sect composed of the heroic few or an inclusive church of all who confessed Jesus Christ, leading to the addition of "holy" (belonging to God) and "catholic" (universal). In Gaul, in the fifth century, the phrase "he descended into hell" came into the creed. By the eighth century, the creed had attained its present form.

## THE APOSTLES' CREED

**2.1**   I Believe in God the Father Almighty, Maker of heaven and earth,

**2.2**   And in Jesus Christ his only Son our Lord; who was conceived by the Holy Ghost, born of the Virgin Mary, suffered under Pontius Pilate, was crucified, dead, and buried; he descended into hell; the third day he rose again from the dead; he ascended into heaven, and sitteth on the right hand of God the Father Almighty; from thence he shall come to judge the quick and the dead.

**2.3**   I believe in the Holy Ghost; the holy catholic Church; the communion of saints; the forgiveness of sins; the resurrection of the body; and the life everlasting. Amen.

# THE SCOTS CONFESSION
[TEXT]

## The Scots Confession

Three documents from the period of the Reformation are included in the *Book of Confessions*, each originating in a different country: Scotland, Germany, and Switzerland. These three centers of the Reformation remain significant in Reformed and Presbyterian thought to this day.

The Scots Confession was written at a turning point in the history of the Scottish nation. When the Queen Regent Mary of Guise died in her sleep in 1560, the Protestant nobility of Scotland was able to secure English recognition of Scottish sovereignty in the Treaty of Edinburgh. To the Scots, this favorable conclusion to the civil war with Mary's French-supported forces represented a providential deliverance.

The Scottish Parliament, having declared Scotland a Protestant nation, asked the clergy to frame a confession of faith. Six ministers, including John Knox, completed their work in four days. In 1560, the document was ratified by Parliament as "doctrine grounded upon the infallible Word of God."

Beginning with a pledge of unconditional commitment to the triune God who creates, sustains, rules, and guides all things, the first eleven chapters of the Scots Confession narrate God's providential acts in the events of biblical history. The kirk (church) of the present and future is continuous with the kirk of God's people going back to Adam. While affirming that the Bible is the norm by which the kirk judges itself, the Scots Confession also sees the Scriptures as a sacred history in which the present day church, through the Holy Spirit, participates until the end of time. God's providential deliverance is a continuing, not merely a past, reality.

The Scots Confession sets forth three marks of the true and faithful church: "the true preaching of the Word of God," "the right administration of the sacraments of Christ Jesus," and "ecclesiastical discipline … whereby vice is repressed and virtue nourished."

"Cleave, serve, worship, trust" are key words in this document. As a call to action in a turbulent time, the Scots Confession reflects a spirit of trust and a commitment to the God whose miraculous deliverance the Scots had experienced firsthand.

# THE SCOTS CONFESSION[1]

## CHAPTER 1

### God

3.01   We confess and acknowledge one God alone, to whom alone we must cleave, whom alone we must serve, whom only we must worship, and in whom alone we put our trust. Who is eternal, infinite, immeasurable, incomprehensible, omnipotent, invisible; one in substance and yet distinct in three persons, the Father, the Son, and the Holy Ghost. By whom we confess and believe all things in heaven and earth, visible and invisible, to have been created, to be retained in their being, and to be ruled and guided by his inscrutable providence for such end as his eternal wisdom, goodness, and justice have appointed, and to the manifestation of his own glory.

## CHAPTER II

### The Creation of Man

3.02   We confess and acknowledge that our God has created man, i.e., our first father, Adam, after his own image and likeness, to whom he gave wisdom, lordship, justice, free will, and self-consciousness, so that in the whole nature of man no imperfection could be found. From this dignity and perfection man and woman both fell; the woman being deceived by the serpent and man obeying the voice of the woman, both conspiring against the sovereign majesty of God, who in clear words had previously threatened death if they presumed to eat of the forbidden tree.

## CHAPTER III

### Original Sin

3.03   By this transgression, generally known as original sin, the image of God was utterly defaced in man, and he and his children became by nature hostile to God, slaves to Satan, and servants to sin. And thus everlasting death has had, and shall have, power and dominion over all who have not been, are not, or shall not be reborn from above. This rebirth is wrought by the power of the Holy Ghost creating in the hearts of God's chosen ones an assured faith in the promise of God revealed to

---

[1] Reprinted from *The Scots Confession*: 1560. Edited with an Introduction by G. D. Henderson. Rendered into modern English by James Bulloch. The Saint Andrew Press, Edinburgh, 1960, pp. 58–80. Used by permission.

us in his Word; by this faith we grasp Christ Jesus with the graces and blessings promised in him.

## CHAPTER IV

### The Revelation of the Promise

**3.04** We constantly believe that God, after the fearful and horrible departure of man from his obedience, did seek Adam again, call upon him, rebuke and convict him of his sin, and in the end made unto him a most joyful promise, that "the seed of the woman should bruise the head of the serpent," that is, that he should destroy the works of the devil. This promise was repeated and made clearer from time to time; it was embraced with joy, and most constantly received by all the faithful from Adam to Noah, from Noah to Abraham, from Abraham to David, and so onwards to the incarnation of Christ Jesus; all (we mean the believing fathers under the law) did see the joyful day of Christ Jesus, and did rejoice.

## CHAPTER V

### The Continuance, Increase, and Preservation of the Kirk

**3.05** We most surely believe that God preserved, instructed, multiplied, honored, adorned, and called from death to life his Kirk in all ages since Adam until the coming of Christ Jesus in the flesh. For he called Abraham from his father's country, instructed him, and multiplied his seed; he marvelously preserved him, and more marvelously delivered his seed from the bondage and tyranny of Pharaoh; to them he gave his laws, constitutions, and ceremonies; to them he gave the land of Canaan; after he had given them judges, and afterwards Saul, he gave David to be king, to whom he gave promise that of the fruit of his loins should one sit forever upon his royal throne. To this same people from time to time he sent prophets, to recall them to the right way of their God, from which sometimes they strayed by idolatry. And although, because of their stubborn contempt for righteousness he was compelled to give them into the hands of their enemies, as had previously been threatened by the mouth of Moses, so that the holy city was destroyed, the temple burned with fire, and the whole land desolate for seventy years, yet in mercy he restored them again to Jerusalem, where the city and temple were rebuilt, and they endured against all temptations and assaults of Satan till the Messiah came according to the promise.

## CHAPTER VI

### The Incarnation of Christ Jesus

**3.06**  When the fullness of time came God sent his Son, his eternal wisdom, the substance of his own glory, into this world, who took the nature of humanity from the substance of a woman, a virgin, by means of the Holy Ghost. And so was born the "just seed of David," the "Angel of the great counsel of God," the very Messiah promised, whom we confess and acknowledge to be Emmanuel, true God and true man, two perfect natures united and joined in one person. So by our Confession we condemn the damnable and pestilent heresies of Arius, Marcion, Eutyches, Nestorius, and such others as did either deny the eternity of his Godhead, or the truth of his humanity, or confounded them, or else divided them.

## CHAPTER VII

### Why the Mediator Had to Be True God and True Man

**3.07**  We acknowledge and confess that this wonderful union between the Godhead and the humanity in Christ Jesus did arise from the eternal and immutable decree of God from which all our salvation springs and depends.

## CHAPTER VIII

### Election

**3.08**  That same eternal God and Father, who by grace alone chose us in his Son Christ Jesus before the foundation of the world was laid, appointed him to be our head, our brother, our pastor, and the great bishop of our souls. But since the opposition between the justice of God and our sins was such that no flesh by itself could or might have attained unto God, it behooved the Son of God to descend unto us and take himself a body of our body, flesh of our flesh, and bone of our bone, and so become the Mediator between God and man, giving power to as many as believe in him to be the sons of God; as he himself says, "I ascend to my Father and to your Father, to my God and to your God." By this most holy brotherhood whatever we have lost in Adam is restored to us again. Therefore we are not afraid to call God our Father, not so much because he has created us, which we have in common with the reprobate, as because he has given unto us his only Son to be our brother, and given us grace to acknowledge and embrace him as our only Mediator. Further, it behooved the Messiah and Redeemer to be true God and true man, because he was able to undergo the punishment of our transgressions and to present himself in the presence of his Father's judgment, as in our stead, to suffer for our transgression and disobedience, and by death to overcome him that was the author of death. But because the Godhead alone could not suffer death, and neither could manhood overcome death, he joined both together in one person, that the weakness of one should suffer and be subject to death—which we had deserved—and the infinite and invincible power of the other, that is, of the Godhead, should triumph, and purchase for us life, liberty, and perpetual victory. So we confess, and most undoubtedly believe.

## CHAPTER IX

### Christ's Death, Passion, and Burial

3.09  That our Lord Jesus offered himself a voluntary sacrifice unto his Father for us, that he suffered contradiction of sinners, that he was wounded and plagued for our transgressions, that he, the clean innocent Lamb of God, was condemned in the presence of an earthly judge, that we should be absolved before the judgment seat of our God; that he suffered not only the cruel death of the cross, which was accursed by the sentence of God; but also that he suffered for a season the wrath of his Father which sinners had deserved. But yet we avow that he remained the only, well beloved, and blessed Son of his Father even in the midst of his anguish and torment which he suffered in body and soul to make full atonement for the sins of his people. From this we confess and avow that there remains no other sacrifice for sin; if any affirm so, we do not hesitate to say that they are blasphemers against Christ's death and the everlasting atonement thereby purchased for us.

## CHAPTER X

### The Resurrection

3.10  We undoubtedly believe, since it was impossible that the sorrows of death should retain in bondage the Author of life, that our Lord Jesus crucified, dead, and buried, who descended into hell, did rise again for our justification, and the destruction of him who was the author of death, and brought life again to us who were subject to death and its bondage. We know that his resurrection was confirmed by the testimony of his enemies, and by the resurrection of the dead, whose sepulchres did open, and they did rise and appear to many within the city of Jerusalem. It was also confirmed by the testimony of his angels, and by the senses and judgment of his apostles and of others, who had conversation, and did eat and drink with him after his resurrection.

## CHAPTER XI

### The Ascension

3.11    We do not doubt but that the selfsame body which was born of the virgin, was crucified, dead, and buried, and which did rise again, did ascend into the heavens, for the accomplishment of all things, where in our name and for our comfort he has received all power in heaven and earth, where he sits at the right hand of the Father, having received his kingdom, the only advocate and mediator for us. Which glory, honor, and prerogative, he alone amongst the brethren shall possess till all his enemies are made his footstool, as we undoubtedly believe they shall be in the Last Judgment. We believe that the same Lord Jesus shall visibly return for this Last Judgment as he was seen to ascend. And then, we firmly believe, the time of refreshing and restitution of all things shall come, so that those who from the beginning have suffered violence, injury, and wrong, for righteousness' sake, shall inherit that blessed immortality promised them from the beginning. But, on the other hand, the stubborn, disobedient, cruel persecutors, filthy persons, idolators, and all sorts of the unbelieving, shall be cast into the dungeon of utter darkness, where their worm shall not die, nor their fire be quenched. The remembrance of that day, and of the Judgment to be executed in it, is not only a bridle by which our carnal lusts are restrained but also such inestimable comfort that neither the threatening of worldly princes, nor the fear of present danger or of temporal death, may move us to renounce and forsake that blessed society which we, the members, have with our Head and only Mediator, Christ Jesus: whom we confess and avow to be the promised Messiah, the only Head of his Kirk, our just Lawgiver, our only High Priest, Advocate, and Mediator. To which honors and offices, if man or angel presume to intrude themselves, we utterly detest and abhor them, as blasphemous to our sovereign and supreme Governor, Christ Jesus.

## CHAPTER XII

### Faith in the Holy Ghost

3.12    Our faith and its assurance do not proceed from flesh and blood, that is to say, from natural powers within us, but are the inspiration of the Holy Ghost; whom we confess to be God, equal with the Father and with his Son, who sanctifies us, and brings us into all truth by his own working, without whom we should remain forever enemies to God and ignorant of his Son, Christ Jesus. For by nature we are so dead, blind, and perverse, that neither can we feel when we are pricked, see the light when it shines, nor assent to the will of God when it is revealed, unless the Spirit of the Lord Jesus quicken that which is dead, remove the darkness from our minds, and bow our stubborn hearts to the obedience of his blessed will. And so, as we confess that God the Father created us when we were not, as his Son our Lord Jesus redeemed us when we were enemies to him, so also do we confess that the Holy Ghost does sanctify and regenerate us, without respect to any merit proceeding from us, be it before or be it after our regeneration. To put this even more plainly; as we willingly disclaim any honor and glory for our own creation and redemption, so do we willingly also for our regeneration and sanctification; for by ourselves we are not capable of thinking one good thought, but he who has begun the work in us alone continues us in it, to the praise and glory of his undeserved grace.

## CHAPTER XIII

### The Cause of Good Works

3.13   The cause of good works, we confess, is not our free will, but the Spirit of the Lord Jesus, who dwells in our hearts by true faith, brings forth such works as God has prepared for us to walk in. For we most boldly affirm that it is blasphemy to say that Christ abides in the hearts of those in whom is no spirit of sanctification. Therefore we do not hesitate to affirm that murderers, oppressors, cruel persecutors, adulterers, filthy persons, idolators, drunkards, thieves, and all workers of iniquity, have neither true faith nor anything of the Spirit of the Lord Jesus, so long as they obstinately continue in wickedness. For as soon as the Spirit of the Lord Jesus, whom God's chosen children receive by true faith, takes possession of the heart of any man, so soon does he regenerate and renew him, so that he begins to hate what before he loved, and to love what he hated before. Thence comes that continual battle which is between the flesh and the Spirit in God's children, while the flesh and the natural man, being corrupt, lust for things pleasant and delightful to themselves, are envious in adversity and proud in prosperity, and every moment prone and ready to offend the majesty of God. But the Spirit of God, who bears witness to our spirit that we are the sons of God, makes us resist filthy pleasures and groan in God's presence for deliverance from this bondage of corruption, and finally to triumph over sin so that it does not reign in our mortal bodies. Other men do not share this conflict since they do not have God's Spirit, but they readily follow and obey sin and feel no regrets, since they act as the devil and their corrupt nature urge. But the sons of God fight against sin; sob and mourn when they find themselves tempted to do evil; and, if they fall, rise again with earnest and unfeigned repentance. They do these things, not by their own power, but by the power of the Lord Jesus, apart from whom they can do nothing.

## CHAPTER XIV

## The Works Which Are Counted Good Before God

3.14　　We confess and acknowledge that God has given to man his holy law, in which not only all such works as displease and offend his godly majesty are forbidden, but also those which please him and which he has promised to reward are commanded. These works are of two kinds. The one is done to the honor of God, the other to the profit of our neighbor, and both have the revealed will of God as their assurance. To have one God, to worship and honor him, to call upon him in all our troubles, to reverence his holy Name, to hear his Word and to believe it, and to share in his holy sacraments, belong to the first kind. To honor father, mother, princes, rulers, and superior powers; to love them, to support them, to obey their orders if they are not contrary to the commands of God, to save the lives of the innocent, to repress tyranny, to defend the oppressed, to keep our bodies clean and holy, to live in soberness and temperance, to deal justly with all men in word and deed, and, finally, to repress any desire to harm our neighbor, are the good works of the second kind, and these are most pleasing and acceptable to God as he has commanded them himself. Acts to the contrary are sins, which always displease him and provoke him to anger, such as, not to call upon him alone when we have need, not to hear his Word with reverence, but to condemn and despise it, to have or worship idols, to maintain and defend idolatry, lightly to esteem the reverend name of God, to profane, abuse, or condemn the sacraments of Christ Jesus, to disobey or resist any whom God has placed in authority, so long as they do not exceed the bounds of their office, to murder, or to consent thereto, to bear hatred, or to let innocent blood be shed if we can prevent it. In conclusion, we confess and affirm that the breach of any other commandment of the first or second kind is sin, by which God's anger and displeasure are kindled against the proud, unthankful world. So that we affirm good works to be those alone which are done in faith and at the command of God who, in his law, has set forth the things that please him. We affirm that evil works are not only those expressly done against God's command, but also, in religious matters and the worship of God, those things which have no other warrant than the invention and opinion of man. From the beginning God has rejected such, as we learn from the words of the prophet Isaiah and of our master, Christ Jesus, "In vain do they worship Me, teaching the doctrines and commandments of men."

## CHAPTER XV

## The Perfection of the Law and the Imperfection of Man

3.15　　We confess and acknowledge that the law of God is most just, equal, holy, and perfect, commanding those things which, when perfectly done, can give life and bring man to eternal felicity; but our nature is so corrupt, weak, and imperfect, that we are never able perfectly to fulfill the works of the law. Even after we are reborn, if we say that we have no sin, we deceive ourselves and the truth of God is not in us. It is therefore essential for us to lay hold on Christ Jesus, in his righteousness and his atonement, since he is the end and consummation of the Law and since it is by him that we are set at liberty so that the curse of God may not fall upon us, even though we do not fulfill the Law in all points. For as God the Father beholds us in the body of his Son Christ Jesus, he accepts our imperfect obedience as if it were perfect, and covers our works, which are defiled with many stains, with the righteousness of his Son. We do not mean that we are so set at liberty that we owe no obedience to the Law—for we have already acknowledged its place—but we affirm that no man on earth, with the sole exception of Christ Jesus, has given, gives, or shall give in action that obedience to the Law which the Law requires. When we have done all things we must fall down and unfeignedly confess that we are unprofitable servants. Therefore, whoever boasts of the merits of his own works or puts his trust in works of supererogation, boasts of what does not exist, and puts his trust in damnable idolatry.

## CHAPTER XVI
### The Kirk

3.16 As we believe in one God, Father, Son, and Holy Ghost, so we firmly believe that from the beginning there has been, now is, and to the end of the world shall be, one Kirk, that is to say, one company and multitude of men chosen by God, who rightly worship and embrace him by true faith in Christ Jesus, who is the only Head of the Kirk, even as it is the body and spouse of Christ Jesus. This Kirk is catholic, that is, universal, because it contains the chosen of all ages, of all realms, nations, and tongues, be they of the Jews or be they of the Gentiles, who have communion and society with God the Father, and with his Son, Christ Jesus, through the sanctification of his Holy Spirit. It is therefore called the communion, not of profane persons, but of saints, who, as citizens of the heavenly Jerusalem, have the fruit of inestimable benefits, one God, one Lord Jesus, one faith, and one baptism. Out of this Kirk there is neither life nor eternal felicity. Therefore we utterly abhor the blasphemy of those who hold that men who live according to equity and justice shall be saved, no matter what religion they profess. For since there is neither life nor salvation without Christ Jesus; so shall none have part therein but those whom the Father has given unto his Son Christ Jesus, and those who in time come to him, avow his doctrine, and believe in him. (We include the children with the believing parents.) This Kirk is invisible, known only to God, who alone knows whom he has chosen, and includes both the chosen who are departed, the Kirk triumphant, those who yet live and fight against sin and Satan, and those who shall live hereafter.

## CHAPTER XVII

### The Immortality of Souls

**3.17** The chosen departed are in peace, and rest from their labors; not that they sleep and are lost in oblivion as some fanatics hold, for they are delivered from all fear and torment, and all the temptations to which we and all God's chosen are subject in this life, and because of which we are called the Kirk Militant. On the other hand, the reprobate and unfaithful departed have anguish, torment, and pain which cannot be expressed. Neither the one nor the other is in such sleep that they feel no joy or torment, as is testified by Christ's parable in St. Luke XVI, his words to the thief, and the words of the souls crying under the altar, "O Lord, thou that art righteous and just, how long shalt thou not revenge our blood upon those that dwell in the earth?"

## CHAPTER XVIII*

### The Notes by Which the True Kirk Shall Be Determined from the False, and Who Shall Be Judge of Doctrine

**3.18** Since Satan has labored from the beginning to adorn his pestilent synagogue with the title of the Kirk of God, and has incited cruel murderers to persecute, trouble, and molest the true Kirk and its members, as Cain did to Abel, Ishmael to Isaac, Esau to Jacob, and the whole priesthood of the Jews to Christ Jesus himself and his apostles after him. So it is essential that the true Kirk be distinguished from the filthy synagogues by clear and perfect notes lest we, being deceived, receive and embrace, to our own condemnation, the one for the other. The notes, signs, and assured tokens whereby the spotless bride of Christ is known from the horrible harlot, the false Kirk, we state, are neither antiquity, usurped title, lineal succession, appointed place, nor the numbers of men approving an error. For Cain was before Abel and Seth in age and title; Jerusalem had precedence above all other parts of the earth, for in it were priests lineally descended from Aaron, and greater numbers followed the scribes, pharisees, and priests, than unfeignedly believed and followed Christ Jesus and his doctrine ... and yet no man of judgment, we suppose, will hold that any of the forenamed were the Kirk of God. The notes of the true Kirk, therefore, we believe, confess, and avow to be: first, the true preaching of the Word of God, in which God has revealed himself to us, as the writings of the prophets and apostles declare; secondly, the right administration of the sacraments of Christ Jesus, with which must be associated the Word and promise of God to seal and confirm them in our hearts; and lastly, ecclesiastical discipline uprightly ministered, as God's Word prescribes, whereby vice is repressed and virtue nourished. Then wherever these

---

* See Preface for discussion of our current understanding of such condemnations.

notes are seen and continue for any time, be the number complete or not, there, beyond any doubt, is the true Kirk of Christ, who, according to his promise, is in its midst. This is not that universal Kirk of which we have spoken before, but particular Kirks, such as were in Corinth, Galatia, Ephesus, and other places where the ministry was planted by Paul and which he himself called Kirks of God. Such Kirks, we the inhabitants of the realm of Scotland confessing Christ Jesus, do claim to have in our cities, towns, and reformed districts because of the doctrine taught in our Kirks, contained in the written Word of God, that is, the Old and New Testaments, in those books which were originally reckoned canonical. We affirm that in these all things necessary to be believed for the salvation of man are sufficiently expressed. The interpretation of Scripture, we confess, does not belong to any private or public person, not yet to any Kirk for pre-eminence or precedence, personal or local, which it has above others, but pertains to the Spirit of God by whom the Scriptures were written. When controversy arises about the right understanding of any passage or sentence of Scripture, or for the reformation of any abuse within the Kirk of God, we ought not so much to ask what men have said or done before us, as what the Holy Ghost uniformly speaks within the body of the Scriptures and what Christ Jesus himself did and commanded. For it is agreed by all that the Spirit of God, who is the Spirit of unity, cannot contradict himself. So if the interpretation or opinion of any theologian, Kirk, or council, is contrary to the plain Word of God written in any other passage of the Scripture, it is most certain that this is not the true understanding and meaning of the Holy Ghost, although councils, realms, and nations have approved and received it. We dare not receive or admit any interpretation which is contrary to any principal point of our faith, or to any other plain text of Scripture, or to the rule of love.

## CHAPTER XIX
### The Authority of the Scriptures

**3.19** As we believe and confess the Scriptures of God sufficient to instruct and make perfect the man of God, so do we affirm and avow their authority to be from God, and not to depend on men or angels. We affirm, therefore, that those who say the Scriptures have no other authority save that which they have received from the Kirk are blasphemous against God and injurious to the true Kirk, which always hears and obeys the voice of her own Spouse and Pastor, but takes not upon her to be mistress over the same.

## CHAPTER XX
### General Councils, Their Power, Authority, and the Cause of Their Summoning

**3.20** As we do not rashly condemn what good men, assembled together in general councils lawfully gathered, have set before us; so we do not receive uncritically whatever has been declared to men under the name of the general councils, for it is plain that, being human, some of them have manifestly erred, and that in matters of great weight and importance. So far then as the council confirms its decrees by the plain Word of God, so far do we reverence and embrace them. But if men, under the name of a council, pretend to forge for us new articles of faith, or to make decisions contrary to the Word of God, then we must utterly deny them as the doctrine of devils, drawing our souls from the voice of the one God to follow the doctrines and teachings of men. The reason why the general councils met was not to make any permanent law which God had not made before, nor yet to form new articles for our belief, nor to give the Word of God authority; much less to make that to be his Word, or even the true interpretation of it, which was not expressed previously by his holy will in his Word; but the reason for councils, at least of those that deserve that name, was partly to refute heresies, and to give public confession of their faith to the generations following, which they did by the authority of God's written Word, and not by any opinion or prerogative that they could not err by reason of their numbers. This, we judge, was the primary reason for general councils. The second was that good policy and order should be constituted and observed in the Kirk where, as in the house of God, it becomes all things to be done decently and in order. Not that we think any policy or order of ceremonies can be appointed for all ages, times, and places; for as ceremonies which men have devised are but temporal, so they may, and ought to be, changed, when they foster superstition rather than edify the Kirk.

## CHAPTER XXI

### The Sacraments

3.21 As the fathers under the Law, besides the reality of the sacrifices, had two chief sacraments, that is, circumcision and the passover, and those who rejected these were not reckoned among God's people; so do we acknowledge and confess that now in the time of the gospel we have two chief sacraments, which alone were instituted by the Lord Jesus and commanded to be used by all who will be counted members of his body, that is, Baptism and the Supper or Table of the Lord Jesus, also called the Communion of His Body and Blood. These sacraments, both of the Old Testament and of the New, were instituted by God not only to make a visible distinction between his people and those who were without the Covenant, but also to exercise the faith of his children and, by participation of these sacraments, to seal in their hearts the assurance of his promise, and of that most blessed conjunction, union, and society, which the chosen have with their Head, Christ Jesus. And so we utterly condemn the vanity of those who affirm the sacraments to be nothing else than naked and bare signs. No, we assuredly believe that by Baptism we are engrafted into Christ Jesus, to be made partakers of his righteousness, by which our sins are covered and remitted, and also that in the Supper rightly used, Christ Jesus is so joined with us that he becomes the very nourishment and food of our souls. Not that we imagine any transubstantiation of bread into Christ's body, and of wine into his natural blood, as the Romanists have perniciously taught and wrongly believed; but this union and conjunction which we have with the body and blood of Christ Jesus in the right use of the sacraments is wrought by means of the Holy Ghost, who by true faith carries us above all things that are visible, carnal, and earthly, and makes us feed upon the body and blood of Christ Jesus, once broken and shed for us but now in heaven, and appearing for us in the presence of his Father. Notwithstanding the distance between his glorified body in heaven and mortal men on earth, yet we must assuredly believe that the bread which we break is the communion of Christ's body and the cup which we bless the communion of his blood. Thus we confess and believe without doubt that the faithful, in the right use of the Lord's Table, do so eat the body and drink the blood of the Lord Jesus that he remains in them and they in him; they are so made flesh of his flesh and bone of his bone that as the eternal Godhood has given to the flesh of Christ Jesus, which by nature was corruptible and mortal, life and immortality, so the eating and drinking of the flesh and blood of Christ Jesus does the like for us. We grant that this is neither given to us merely at the time nor by the power and virtue of the sacrament alone, but we affirm that the faithful, in the right use of the Lord's Table, have such union with Christ Jesus as the natural man cannot apprehend. Further we affirm that although the faithful, hindered by negligence and human weakness, do not profit as much as they ought in the actual moment of the Supper, yet afterwards it shall bring forth fruit, being living seed sown in good ground; for the Holy Spirit, who can never be separated from the right institution of the Lord Jesus, will not deprive the faithful of the fruit of that mystical action. Yet all this, we say again, comes of that true faith which apprehends Christ Jesus, who alone makes the sacrament effective in us. Therefore, if anyone slanders us by saying that we affirm or believe the sacraments to be symbols and nothing more, they are libelous and speak against the plain facts. On the other hand we readily admit that we make a distinction between Christ Jesus in his eternal substance and the elements of the sacramental signs. So we neither worship the elements, in place of that which they signify, nor yet do we despise them or undervalue them, but we use them with great reverence, examining ourselves diligently before we participate, since we are assured by the mouth of the apostle that "whosoever shall eat this bread, and drink this cup of the Lord, unworthily, shall be guilty of the body and blood of the Lord."

## CHAPTER XXII*

### The Right Administration of the Sacraments

Two things are necessary for the right administration of the sacraments. The first is that they should be ministered by lawful ministers, and we declare that these are men appointed to preach the Word, unto whom God has given the power to preach the gospel, and who are lawfully called by some Kirk. The second is that they should be ministered in the elements and manner which God has appointed. Otherwise they cease to be the sacraments of Christ Jesus. This is why we abandon the teaching of the Roman Church and withdraw from its sacraments; firstly, because their ministers are not true ministers of Christ Jesus (indeed they even allow women, whom the Holy Ghost will not permit to preach in the congregation to baptize) and, secondly, because they have so adulterated both the sacraments with their own additions that no part of Christ's original act remains in its original simplicity. The addition of oil, salt, spittle, and such like in baptism, are merely human additions. To adore or venerate the sacrament, to carry it through streets and towns in procession, or to reserve it in a special case, is not the proper use of Christ's sacrament but an abuse of it. Christ Jesus said, "Take ye, eat ye," and "Do this in remembrance of Me." By these words and commands he sanctified bread and wine to be the sacrament of his holy body and blood, so that the one should be eaten and that all should drink of the other, and not that they should be reserved for worship or honored as God, as the Romanists do. Further, in withdrawing one part of the sacrament—the blessed cup—from the people, they have committed sacrilege. Moreover, if the sacraments are to be rightly used it is essential that the end and purpose of their institution should be understood, not only by the minister but by the recipients. For if the recipient does not understand what is being done, the sacrament is not being rightly used, as is seen in the case of the Old Testament sacrifices. Similarly, if the teacher teaches false doctrine which is hateful to God, even though the sacraments are his own ordinance, they are not rightly used, since wicked men have used them for another end than what God commanded. We affirm this has been done to the sacraments in the Roman Church, for there the whole action of the Lord Jesus is adulterated in form, purpose, and meaning. What Christ Jesus did, and commanded to be done, is evident from the Gospels and from St. Paul; what the priest does at the altar we do not need to tell. The end and purpose of Christ's institution, for which it should be used, is set forth in the words, "Do this in remembrance of Me," and "For as often as ye eat this bread and drink this cup ye do show"—that is, extol, preach, magnify, and

---

* See Preface for discussion of our current understanding of such condemnations.

praise—"the Lord's death, till He come." But let the words of the mass, and their own doctors and teachings witness, what is the purpose and meaning of the mass; it is that, as mediators between Christ and his Kirk, they should offer to God the Father, a sacrifice in propitiation for the sins of the living and of the dead. This doctrine is blasphemous to Christ Jesus and would deprive his unique sacrifice, once offered on the cross for the cleansing of all who are to be sanctified, of its sufficiency; so we detest and renounce it.

## CHAPTER XXIII
### To Whom Sacraments Appertain

3.23   We hold that baptism applies as much to the children of the faithful as to those who are of age and discretion, and so we condemn the error of the Anabaptists, who deny that children should be baptized before they have faith and understanding. But we hold that the Supper of the Lord is only for those who are of the household of faith and can try and examine themselves both in their faith and their duty to their neighbors. Those who eat and drink at that holy table without faith, or without peace and goodwill to their brethren, eat unworthily. This is the reason why ministers in our Kirk make public and individual examination of those who are to be admitted to the table of the Lord Jesus.

## CHAPTER XXIV
### The Civil Magistrate

3.24   We confess and acknowledge that empires, kingdoms, dominions, and cities are appointed and ordained by God; the powers and authorities in them, emperors in empires, kings in their realms, dukes and princes in their dominions, and magistrates in cities, are ordained by God's holy ordinance for the manifestation of his own glory and for the good and well being of all men. We hold that any men who conspire to rebel or to overturn the civil powers, as duly established, are not merely enemies to humanity but rebels against God's will. Further, we confess and acknowledge that such persons as are set in authority are to be loved, honored, feared, and held in the highest respect, because they are the lieutenants of God, and in their councils God himself doth sit and judge. They are the judges and princes to whom God has given the sword for the praise and defense of good men and the punishment of all open evil doers. Moreover, we state that the preservation and purification of religion is particularly the duty of kings, princes, rulers, and magistrates. They are not only appointed for civil government but also to maintain true religion and to suppress all idolatry and superstition. This may be seen in David, Jehosaphat, Hezekiah, Josiah, and others highly commended for their zeal in that cause.

Therefore we confess and avow that those who resist the supreme powers, so long as they are acting in their own spheres, are resisting God's ordinance and cannot be held guiltless. We further state that so long as princes and rulers vigilantly fulfill their office, anyone who denies them aid, counsel, or service, denies it to God, who by his lieutenant craves it of them.

## CHAPTER XXV

### The Gifts Freely Given to the Kirk

Although the Word of God truly preached, the sacraments rightly ministered, and discipline executed according to the Word of God, are certain and infallible signs of the true Kirk, we do not mean that every individual person in that company is a chosen member of Christ Jesus. We acknowledge and confess that many weeds and tares are sown among the corn and grow in great abundance in its midst, and that the reprobate may be found in the fellowship of the chosen and may take an outward part with them in the benefits of the Word and sacraments. But since they only confess God for a time with their mouths and not with their hearts, they lapse, and do not continue to the end. Therefore they do not share the fruits of Christ's death, resurrection, and ascension. But such as unfeignedly believe with the heart and boldly confess the Lord Jesus with their mouths shall certainly receive his gifts. Firstly, in this life, they shall receive remission of sins and that by faith in Christ's blood alone; for though sin shall remain and continually abide in our mortal bodies, yet it shall not be counted against us, but be pardoned, and covered with Christ's righteousness. Secondly, in the general judgment, there shall be given to every man and woman resurrection of the flesh. The seas shall give up her dead, and the earth those who are buried within her. Yea, the Eternal, our God, shall stretch out his hand on the dust, and the dead shall arise incorruptible, and in the very substance of the selfsame flesh which every man now bears, to receive according to their works, glory or punishment. Such as now delight in vanity, cruelty, filthiness, superstition, or idolatry, shall be condemned to the fire unquenchable, in which those who now serve the devil in all abominations shall be tormented forever, both in body and in spirit. But such as continue in well doing to the end, boldly confessing the Lord Jesus, shall receive glory, honor, and immortality, we constantly believe, to reign forever in life everlasting with Christ Jesus, to whose glorified body all his chosen shall be made like, when he shall appear again in judgment and shall render up the Kingdom to God his Father, who then shall be and ever shall remain, all in all things, God blessed forever. To whom, with the Son and the Holy Ghost, be all honor and glory, now and ever. Amen.

Arise, O Lord, and let thine enemies be confounded; let them flee from thy presence that hate the godly Name. Give thy servants strength to speak thy Word with boldness, and let all nations cleave to the true knowledge of thee. Amen.

# THE HEIDELBERG CATECHISM
[TEXT]

# The Heidelberg Catechism

The Reformation was not a singular movement. Soon after Luther posted his ninety-five theses, reform movements sprang up throughout Europe. As Lutheran thought moved down the Neckar River, Reformed thought traveled up the Rhine from Switzerland. They met at Heidelberg, seat of the oldest university in Germany and capital of the province known as the Palatinate. Tension between Lutherans and Reformed Christians was intense. Because the Reformed did not believe in the real, bodily presence of Christ in the bread and wine, Lutherans believed that they were desecrating the Lord's Supper.

Acting to end the controversy, Frederick the Elector, ruler of the Palatinate, asked two young men of Heidelberg—Zacharias Ursinus, professor of theology, and Kaspar Olevianus, preacher to the city—to prepare a catechism acceptable to both sides. They revised an earlier catechism that Ursinus had written, using its outline and some ninety of its questions and answers. Completed in 1562, the Heidelberg Catechism was published in January of the following year.

The Heidelberg Catechism opens with two questions concerning our comfort in life and death. The knowledge that our only comfort is Jesus Christ frames the remainder of the catechism. Each of its three parts corresponds to a line of Romans 7:24–25 (NRSV), where Paul cries: "Wretched man that I am; Who will rescue me from this body of death? Thanks be to God through Jesus Christ our Lord;" Thus, questions 3–11 deal with our sin and misery, questions 12–85 with the way in which God in Jesus Christ frees us, and questions 86–129 with the manner in which we express gratitude to God for our deliverance.

Each question of the catechism is personal, addressed to "you." Each answer draws as much as possible on biblical language. The catechism's tone is irenic, showing nothing of the controversy that called it forth. Its theology is both catholic, universal in appeal, and evangelical, setting forth the gospel of Jesus Christ. Providing a basis for peaceful coexistence between Lutheran and Reformed Christians, the catechism denied that the bread and wine become the very body and blood of Christ but affirmed that "by this visible sign and pledge ... we come to share in his true body and blood through the working of the Holy Spirit ..." (paragraph 4.079).

The influence of the Heidelberg Catechism in the church's preaching and teaching continues to be felt in Germany, Austria, Holland, Hungary, parts of Eastern Europe, Scotland, Canada, and the United States.

The biblical citations in this text are those found in the German 3rd edition of 1563 and the Latin translation of 1563. The citations in the German 3rd edition include book and chapter without verse numbers, inviting the reader to use the Catechism as an aid to the study of larger passages of Scripture. The citations in the Latin edition are often a place to begin reading on a topic, or the conclusion of a relevant passage, rather than simple proof-texts. Placement of the notes varies slightly in the German, the Latin, and here in English according to the nature of the language.

Here, citations in ordinary type reflect the citations of the Latin where the Latin simply adds verse numbers.

Citations in *italics* indicate texts present in the German original but omitted from the Latin edition.

Citations in **bold** indicate texts not found in the German original but added in the Latin edition.

Square brackets [ ] indicate the present editors' corrections of apparent typographical errors in the 1563 texts as well as necessary clarifications.

# THE HEIDELBERG CATECHISM[1]

**LORD'S DAY 1**

**4.001** 1 Q. **What is your only comfort in life and in death?**

A. That I am not my own,[1]
but belong—
body and soul,
in life and in death—[2]
to my faithful Savior, Jesus Christ.[3]

He has fully paid for all my sins with his precious blood,[4]
and has set me free from the tyranny of the devil.[5]
He also watches over me in such a way[6]
that not a hair can fall from my head
without the will of my Father in heaven;[7]
in fact, all things must work together for my salvation.[8]

Because I belong to him,
Christ, by his Holy Spirit,
assures me of eternal life[9]
and makes me wholeheartedly willing and ready
from now on to live for him.[10]

1. 1 Cor. 6:19
2. Rom. 14:8
3. 1 Cor. 3:23
4. 1 Pet. 1:18; 1 John 1:7; 2:2
5. 1 John 3:8
6. John 6:39
7. Matt. 10:30; Luke 21:18
8. Rom. 8:28
9. 2 Cor. 1:22; 5:5; Eph. 1:14; Rom. 8:16
10. Rom. 8:14

**4.002** 2 Q. **What must you know to live and die in the joy of this comfort?**

A. Three things:[1]
first, how great my sin and misery are;[2]
second, how I am set free from all my sins and misery;[3]
third, how I am to thank God for such deliverance.4

1. Luke 24:47; 1 Cor. 6:11; Tit. 3:3
2. **John 9:41**; John 15:[6–]7
3. John 17:3
4. Eph. 5:10

---

[1] Reprinted from *The Heidelberg Catechism, 400th Anniversary Edition, 1563–1963*, Copyright © 1962 United Church Press. All rights reserved. Used by permission.

## Part I: Misery

### LORD'S DAY 2

**4.003** 3 Q. **How do you come to know your misery?**
A. The law of God tells me.[1]
1. Rom. 3:20

**4.004** 4 Q. **What does God's law require of us?**
A. Christ teaches us this in summary in Matthew 22:37–40:

"'You shall love the Lord your God
with all your heart,
and with all your soul,
and with all your mind.'
This is the greatest and first commandment.

"And a second is like it:
'You shall love your neighbor as yourself.'

"On these two commandments hang
all the law and the prophets."

**4.005** 5 Q. **Can you live up to all this perfectly?**
A. No.[1]
I have a natural tendency
to hate God and my neighbor.[2]
1. Rom. 3:10; 3:23; 1 John 1:8
2. Rom. 8:7; Eph. 2:3

### LORD'S DAY 3

**4.006** 6 Q. **Did God create people
so wicked and perverse?**
A. No.[1]
God created them good and in his own image,[2]
that is, in true righteousness and holiness,
so that they might
truly know God their creator,
love him with all their heart,
and live with God in eternal happiness,
to praise and glorify him.[3]
1. Gen. 1:31
2. Gen. 1:26–27
3. 2 Cor. 3:18; Col. 3:10; Eph. 4:24

4.007  7  Q. **Then where does this corrupt human nature
           come from?**
        A. The fall and disobedience of our first parents,
               Adam and Eve, in Paradise.[1]
           This fall has so poisoned our nature
               that we are all conceived and born
               in a sinful condition.[2]
        1. Gen. 3; Rom. 5:12, 18–19
        2. Ps. 51:5; **Gen. 5:3**

4.008  8  Q. **But are we so corrupt
           that we are totally unable to do any good
           and inclined toward all evil?**
        A. Yes,[1] unless we are born again
           by the Spirit of God.[2]
        1. John 3:6; **Gen. 6:5**; Job 14:4;15:16, [35]; Isa. 53:6
        2. John 3:5

## LORD'S DAY 4

4.009  9  Q. **But doesn't God do us an injustice
           by requiring in his law
           what we are unable to do?**
        A. No,[1] God created human beings with the ability to keep the law.
           They, however, provoked by the devil,[2]
               in willful disobedience,
               robbed themselves and all their descendants of these gifts.
        1. Eph. 4:[22–23], 24–25
        2. **Luke 10:30[–37]**

4.010 10  Q. **Does God permit
           such disobedience and rebellion
           to go unpunished?**
        A. Certainly not.[1]
               God is terribly angry
               with the sin we are born with
               as well as the sins we personally commit.

           As a just judge,
           God will punish them both now and in eternity,
           having declared:
               "Cursed is everyone who does not observe and obey
               all the things written in the book of the law."[2]
        1. Rom. 5:12; Heb. 9:27
        2. Deut. 27:26; Gal. 3:10

4.011 11 Q. **But isn't God also merciful?**
A. God is certainly merciful,[1]
but also just.[2]
God's justice demands
that sin, committed against his supreme majesty,
be punished with the supreme penalty—
eternal punishment of body and soul.

1. Exod. 34:6
2. Exod. 20:5; Ps. 5:5; 2 Cor. 6:14

*Part II: Deliverance*

**LORD'S DAY 5**

4.012 12 Q. **According to God's righteous judgment
we deserve punishment
both now and in eternity:
how then can we escape this punishment
and return to God's favor?**
A. God requires that his justice be satisfied.[1]
Therefore the claims of this justice
must be paid in full,
either by ourselves or by another.[2]

1. Exod. 20:5; 23:7
2. Rom. 8:3–4

4.013 13 Q. **Can we make this payment ourselves?**
A. Certainly not.
Actually, we increase our debt every day.[1]

1. Job 9:3; 15:15; Matt. 6:12

4.014 14 Q. **Can another creature—any at all—
pay this debt for us?**
A. No.
To begin with,
God will not punish any other creature
for what a human is guilty of.[1]
Furthermore,
no mere creature can bear the weight
of God's eternal wrath against sin
and deliver others from it.[2]

1. Heb. 2:14
2. Ps. 130:3

**4.015** 15 Q. **What kind of mediator and deliverer should we look for then?**

A. One who is a true[1] and righteous human,[2]
  yet more powerful than all creatures,
  that is, one who is also true God.[3]

  1. 1 Cor. 15:21
  2. Jer. 33:15; **Isa. 53:9**; *Ps. 53*; 2 Cor. 5:21
  3. Heb. 7:[15–]16; Isa. 7:14; Rom. 8:3; Jer. 23:6

## LORD'S DAY 6

**4.016** 16 Q. **Why must the mediator be a true and righteous human?**
A. God's justice demands
  that human nature, which has sinned,
  must pay for sin;[1]
  but a sinful human could never pay for others.[2]

  1. Rom. 5:12, 15
  2. 1 Pet. 3:18; Isa. 53:3–5, 10–11

**4.017** 17 Q. **Why must the mediator also be true God?**
A. So that the mediator,
  by the power of his divinity,
  might bear the weight of God's wrath in his humanity[1]
  and earn for us
  and restore to us
  righteousness and life.[2]

  1. Isa. 53:8; Acts 2:24; 1 Pet. 3:18
  2. John 3:16; **1 John 1:2, 4:12**; Acts 20:18 [28]; *John 1[:4,12]*

**4.018** 18 Q. **Then who is this mediator— true God and at the same time a true and righteous human?**
A. Our Lord Jesus Christ,[1]
  who was given to us
  to completely deliver us
  and make us right with God.[2]

  1. Matt. 1:23; 1 Tim. 3:16; Luke 2:11
  2. 1 Cor. 1:30

**4.019** 19 Q. **How do you come to know this?**
A. The holy gospel tells me.
  God began to reveal the gospel already in Paradise;[1]
  later God proclaimed it
    by the holy patriarchs and prophets[2]
  and foreshadowed it

> by the sacrifices and other ceremonies of the law;[3]
> and finally God fulfilled it
> > through his own beloved Son.[4]

1. Gen. 3:15
2. Gen. 22:18; 49:10–11; Rom. 1:2; Heb. 1:1; Acts 3:22–24; 10:43
3. John 5:46; Heb. 10:7 [1–10]
4. Rom. 10:4; Gal. 4:4

## LORD'S DAY 7

**4.020** 20 Q. **Are all people then saved through Christ just as they were lost through Adam?**

A. No.
Only those are saved
who through true faith
> are grafted into Christ
> and accept all his benefits.[1]

1. John 1:12; **3:36**; Isa. 53:11, Ps. 2:11[–12]; Rom. 11:17, 19; Heb. 4:2; 10:39

**4.021** 21 Q. **What is true faith?**

A. True faith is
not only a sure knowledge by which I hold as true
> all that God has revealed to us in Scripture;[1]
it is also a wholehearted trust,[2]
> which the Holy Spirit[3] creates in me by the gospel,[4]
> that God has freely granted,
> > not only to others but to me also,
> > > forgiveness of sins,
> > > eternal righteousness,
> > > and salvation.[5]
These are gifts of sheer grace,
granted solely by Christ's merit.[6]

1. Heb. 11:1, 3; James 2:19
2. **Rom. 4:16[–25]; James 1:6;** Rom. 5:1; *Rom. 10[:9–10]*
3. *2 Cor. 4[:6, 13]; Eph. 2[:8, 18];* **Matt. 16:17; John 3:[5–]13; Gal. 5:22; Phil. 1:29**
4. Rom. 1:16; **10:17**
5. *Heb. 2[:9–11]; Rom. 1[:16];* **Heb. 10:38;** Hab. 2:4; Matt. 9:2; **Eph. 2:7–9; Rom. 5:1**
6. *Eph. 2[:8];* Rom. 3:24–25; **Gal. 2:16**

**4.022** 22 Q. **What then must a Christian believe?**

A. All that is promised us in the gospel,[1]
> a summary of which is taught us
> in the articles of our universal
> and undisputed Christian faith.

1. John 20:31; Matt. 28:20

4.023  23  Q. **What are these articles?**
  A. I believe in God, the Father almighty,
     creator of heaven and earth.

  I believe in Jesus Christ, his only begotten Son, our Lord,
     who was conceived by the Holy Spirit
     and born of the virgin Mary.
     He suffered under Pontius Pilate,
     was crucified, died, and was buried;
     he descended to hell.
     The third day he rose again from the dead.
     He ascended to heaven
     and is seated at the right hand of God the Father almighty.
     From there he will come to judge the living and the dead.

  I believe in the Holy Spirit,
     the holy catholic church,
     the communion of saints,
     the forgiveness of sins,
     the resurrection of the body,
     and the life everlasting. Amen.

## LORD'S DAY 8

4.024  24  Q. **How are these articles divided?**
  A. Into three parts:
     God the Father and our creation;
     God the Son and our deliverance;
     and God the Holy Spirit and our sanctification.

4.025  25  Q. **Since there is only one divine being,[1]
     why do you speak of three:
     Father, Son, and Holy Spirit?**

  A. Because that is how
     God has revealed himself in his Word:[2]
     these three distinct persons
     are one, true, eternal God.

  1. Deut. 6:4
  2. Isa. 61:1; Ps. 110:1; Matt. 3:16–17; Matt. 28:19; 1 John 5:7[–8]

*God the Father*

## LORD'S DAY 9

4.026  26  Q. **What do you believe when you say,
     "I believe in God, the Father almighty,
     creator of heaven and earth"?**

A. That the eternal Father of our Lord Jesus Christ,
   who out of nothing created heaven and earth
      and everything in them,[1]
   who still upholds and rules them
      by his eternal counsel and providence,[2]
is my God and Father
   because of Christ the Son.[3]

I trust God so much that I do not doubt
   he will provide
      whatever I need
         for body and soul,[4]
   and will turn to my good
      whatever adversity he sends upon me
      in this sad world.[5]

God is able to do this because he is almighty God[6]
and desires to do this because he is a faithful Father.[7]

1. Gen. 1; Ps. 33:6
2. Ps. 104; Ps. 115:3; Matt. 10:29; Heb. 1:3,
3. John 1:12; Rom. 8:15; Gal. 4:5-7; Eph. 1:5
4. Ps. 55:22; Matt. 6:25-26; Luke 12:22
5. Rom. 8:28
6. Rom. 10:12
7. Matt. 6:32; 7:9

## LORD'S DAY 10

4.027  27 Q. **What do you understand
         by the providence of God?**
   A. The almighty and ever present power of God[1]
         by which God upholds, as with his hand,
            heaven
            and earth
            and all creatures,
         and so rules them[2] that
            leaf and blade,
            rain and drought,
            fruitful and lean years,
            food and drink,[3]
            health and sickness,[4]
            prosperity and poverty—[5]
            all things, in fact,
            come to us
               not by chance
               but by his fatherly hand.

1. Acts 17:25[–28]
2. Heb. 1:3

3. Jer. 5:24; Acts 14:17
4. John 9:3
5. Prov. 22:2

**4.028** 28 Q. **How does the knowledge of God's creation and providence help us?**

A. We can be patient when things go against us,[1]
thankful when things go well,[2]
and for the future we can have
good confidence in our faithful God and Father[3]
that nothing in creation will separate us from his love.[4]
For all creatures are so completely in God's hand
that without his will
they can neither move nor be moved.[5]

1. Rom. 5:3; James 1:3; Job 1:21
2. Deut. 8:10; 1 Thess. 5:18
3. **Rom. 5:5–6**
4. Rom. 8:38–39
5. Job 1:12; **2:6**; Acts 17:28; Prov. 21:1

*God the Son*

## LORD'S DAY 11

**4.029** 29 Q. **Why is the Son of God called "Jesus," meaning "savior"?**

A. Because he saves us from our sins,[1]
and because salvation should not be sought
and cannot be found in anyone else.[2]

1. Matt. 1:21; **Heb. 7:25**
2. Acts 4:12

**4.030** 30 Q. **Do those who look for their salvation in saints, in themselves, or elsewhere really believe in the only savior Jesus?**

A. No.
Although they boast of being his,
by their actions they deny
the only savior, Jesus.[1]

Either Jesus is not a perfect savior,
or those who in true faith accept this savior
have in him all they need for their salvation.[2]

1. 1 Cor. 1:13, 31; *Gal. 3[:1–4]*; **Gal. 5:4**
2. **Heb. 12:2**; Isa. 9:6; Col. 1:19–20; 2:10; John 1:16

### LORD'S DAY 12

**4.031** 31 Q. **Why is he called "Christ," meaning "anointed"?**

A. Because he has been ordained by God the Father and has been anointed with the Holy Spirit[1]
to be
our chief prophet and teacher[2]
who fully reveals to us
the secret counsel and will of God concerning our deliverance;[3]
our only high priest[4]
who has delivered us by the one sacrifice of his body, and who continually pleads our cause with the Father;[5]
and our eternal king
who governs us by his Word and Spirit,
and who guards us and keeps us
in the freedom he has won for us.[6]

1. **Ps. 45:[7]**; Heb. 1:9
2. **Deut. 18:15; Acts 3:22**
3. **John 1:18; 15:15**
4. Ps. 110; Heb. 7:21; **10:12**
5. Rom. 8:34; 5:9–10
6. Ps. 2:6; Luke 1:33; Matt. 28:18; **John 10:28**

**4.032** 32 Q. **But why are you called a Christian?**

A. Because by faith I am a member of Christ[1]
and so I share in his anointing.[2]
I am anointed
to confess his name,[3]
to present myself to him as a living sacrifice of thanks,[4]
to strive with a free conscience against sin and the devil
in this life,[5]
and afterward to reign with Christ
over all creation
for eternity.[6]

1. Acts 11:26, **1 Cor. 6:15**
2. 1John 2:27; **Isa. 59:21;** Acts 2:17; Joel 2:28; Mark 8:[34–38]
3. Rom. 12:1; Rev. 5:8[–14]; **1 Pet. 2:9**
4. Rom. 6:12; Rev. 1:6
5. **1 Tim. 1:19**
6. **2 Tim. 2:12**

### LORD'S DAY 13

**4.033** 33 Q. **Why is he called God's "only begotten Son" when we also are God's children?**

A. Because Christ alone is the eternal, natural Son of God.[1]
   We, however, are adopted children of God—
      adopted by grace through Christ.[2]
1. John 1:29; Heb. 1:2
2. Rom. 8:15; Eph. 1:[5–]6

4.034  34 Q. Why do you call him "our Lord"?
A. Because—
   not with gold or silver,
   but with his precious blood—
   he has set us free
      from sin and from the tyranny of the devil,
   and has bought us,
      body and soul,
   to be his very own.[1]
1. 1 Pet. 1:18–19; 2:9; 1 Cor. 6:20; **7:23**

**LORD'S DAY 14**

4.035  35 Q. What does it mean that he
   "was conceived by the Holy Spirit
   and born of the virgin Mary"?
A. That the eternal Son of God,
   who is[1] and remains
   true and eternal God,[2]
took to himself,
   through the working of the Holy Spirit,[3]
   from the flesh and blood of the virgin Mary,
a truly human nature[4]
   so that he might also become David's true descendant,[5]
   like his brothers and sisters in every way[6]
      except for sin.[7]
1. John 1:1; **17:5**; Rom. 1:4
2. Rom. 9:5; *Gal. 4[:4]*
3. Matt. 1:18, 20; Luke 1:27, 35; *Eph. 1*
4. John 1:14; **Gal. 4:4**
5. Ps. 132:11; Rom. 1:3
6. Phil. 2:7
7. Heb. 4:15; **7:26**

4.036  36 Q. How does the holy conception and birth of Christ benefit you?
A. He is our mediator[1]
   and, in God's sight,
   he covers with his innocence and perfect holiness
   my sinfulness in which I was conceived.[2]
1. **Heb. 2:16–17**
2. Ps. 32:1; 1 Cor. 1:30

### LORD'S DAY 15

**4.037** 37 Q. What do you understand
by the word "suffered"?

A. That during his whole life on earth,
but especially at the end,
Christ sustained
in body and soul
the wrath of God against the sin of the whole human race.[1]
This he did in order that,
by his suffering as the only atoning sacrifice,[2]
he might deliver us, body and soul,
from eternal condemnation,
and gain for us
God's grace,
righteousness,
and eternal life.

1. 1 Pet. 2:24; **3:18**; Isa. 53:12
2. 1 John 2:2; 4:10; Rom. 3:25

**4.038** 38 Q. Why did he suffer
"under Pontius Pilate" as judge?

A. So that he,
though innocent,
might be condemned by an earthly judge,[1]
and so free us from the severe judgment of God
that was to fall on us.[2]

1. Luke 23:14; John 19:4
2. Ps. 69:5; Isa. 53; 2 Cor. 5:21; Gal. 3:13

**4.039** 39 Q. Is it significant that he was "crucified"
instead of dying some other way?

A. Yes.
By this I am convinced
that he shouldered the curse
which lay on me,[1]
since death by crucifixion was cursed by God.[2]

1. *Gal. 3[:10]*
2. Deut. 21:[23]; Gal. 3:13

### LORD'S DAY 16

**4.040** 40 Q. Why did Christ have to suffer death?

A. Because God's justice and truth require it:[1]
nothing else could pay for our sins
except the death of the Son of God.[2]

1. Gen. 2:17
2. Heb. 2:9, 15; **Phil. 2:8**

**4.041** 41 Q. **Why was he "buried"?**
A. His burial testifies
that he really died.[1]
1. Acts 13:29; Matt. 27:60; Luke 23:50[–53]; John 19:38[–42]

**4.042** 42 Q. **Since Christ has died for us,
why do we still have to die?**

A. Our death does not pay the debt of our sins.
Rather, it puts an end to our sinning
and is our entrance into eternal life.[1]
1 John 5:24; Phil. 1:23; Rom. 7:24 [21–25]

**4.043** 43 Q. **What further benefit do we receive
from Christ's sacrifice and death on the cross?**
A. By Christ's power
our old selves are crucified, put to death, and buried with him,[1]
so that the evil desires of the flesh
may no longer rule us,[2]
but that instead we may offer ourselves
as a sacrifice of gratitude to him.[3]
1. Rom. 6:6-8, 11–12; *Col. 2[:11–12]*
2. Rom. 6:12
3. Rom. 12:1

**4.044** 44 Q. **Why does the creed add,
"He descended to hell"?**
A. To assure me during attacks of deepest dread and temptation
that Christ my Lord,
by suffering unspeakable anguish, pain, and terror of soul,
on the cross but also earlier,
has delivered me from hellish anguish and torment.[1]
1. Isa. 53:10; Matt. 27:46

**LORD'S DAY 17**

**4.045** 45 Q. **How does Christ's resurrection
benefit us?**
A. First, by his resurrection he has overcome death,
so that he might make us share in the righteousness
he obtained for us by his death.[1]

Second, by his power we too
are already raised to a new life.[2]

Third, Christ's resurrection
is a sure pledge to us of our blessed resurrection.[3]
1. 1 Cor. 15:17, 54–55; Rom. 4:25; 1 Pet. 1:3, 21
2. Rom. 6:4; Col. 3:1–5; Eph. 2:5
3. 1 Cor. 15:12; Rom. 8:11

## LORD'S DAY 18

**4.046** 46 Q. **What do you mean by saying, "He ascended to heaven"?**

A. That Christ,
    while his disciples watched,
was taken up from the earth into heaven[1]
and remains there on our behalf[2]
until he comes again
    to judge the living and the dead.[3]

1. Acts 1:9; Matt. 26[:64]; Mark 16[:19]; Luke 24[:51]
2. Heb. 4:14; 7:15[–25]; 9:11; Rom. 8:34; Eph. 4:10; Col. 3:1
3. Acts 1:11; Matt. 24:30

**4.047** 47 Q. **But isn't Christ with us until the end of the world as he promised us?**[1]

A. Christ is true human and true God.
    In his human nature Christ is not now on earth;[2]
but in his divinity, majesty, grace, and Spirit
he is never absent from us.[3]

1. Matt. 28:20
2. Matt. 26:11; John 16:28; 17:11; Acts 3:21
3. John 14:17[-19]; 16:13; Matt. 28:20; Eph. 4:8, 12; also cited: **Augustine,** *Tractates on the Gospel of John 50*

**4.048** 48 Q. **If his humanity is not present wherever his divinity is, then aren't the two natures of Christ separated from each other?**

A. Certainly not.
Since divinity
    is not limited
    and is present everywhere,[1]
it is evident that
    Christ's divinity is surely beyond the bounds of
        the humanity that has been taken on,
but at the same time his divinity is in
and remains personally united to
    his humanity.[2]

1. Acts 7:49; **17:28**; Jer. 23:24
2. Col. 2:9; John 3:13; 11:15; Matt. 28:6

**4.049** 49 Q. **How does Christ's ascension to heaven benefit us?**

A. First, he is our advocate
    in heaven
    in the presence of his Father.[1]

Second, we have our own flesh in heaven
    as a sure pledge that Christ our head
    will also take us, his members,
    up to himself.[2]

Third, he sends his Spirit to us on earth
    as a corresponding pledge.[3]
  By the Spirit's power
    we seek not earthly things
    but the things above, where Christ is,
        sitting at God's right hand.[4]

1. 1 John 2:1-2; Rom. 8:34
2. John 14:2; 20:17; Eph. 2:6
3. John 14:16; **16:7**; Acts 2; 2 Cor. 1:22; 5:5
4. Col. 3:1; Phil. 3:14

## LORD'S DAY 19

**4.050**    50 Q. **Why the next words:
"and is seated at the right hand of God"?**

    A. Because Christ ascended to heaven
      to show there that he is head of his church,[1]
        the one through whom the Father rules all things.[2]

1. Eph. 1:20–23; **5:23**; Col. 1:18
2. Matt. 28:18; John 5:22

**4.051**    51 Q. **How does this glory of Christ our head
benefit us?**

A. First, through his Holy Spirit
he pours out gifts from heaven
upon us his members.[1]
Second, by his power
he defends us and keeps us safe
from all enemies.[2]

    1. Eph. 4:10
    2. Ps. 2:9; **110:1-2**; John 10:28; Eph. 4:8

**4.052**    52 Q. **How does Christ's return
"to judge the living and the dead"
comfort you?**

    A. In all distress and persecution,
      with uplifted head,
      I confidently await the very judge
        who has already offered himself to the judgment of God
        in my place and removed the whole curse from me.[1]
    Christ will cast all his enemies and mine

>       into everlasting condemnation,[2]
>   but will take me and all his chosen ones
>       to himself
>           into the joy and glory of heaven.[3]

1. Luke 21:28; Rom. 8:23, 33; Phil. 3:20; Titus 2:13
2. 2 Thess. 1:6–7; 1 Thess. 4:16; Matt. 25:41
3. Matt. 25:34

### *God the Holy Spirit*

**LORD'S DAY 20**

**4.053**  53  Q. **What do you believe concerning "the Holy Spirit"?**

> A. First, that the Spirit, with the Father and the Son,
>       is eternal God.[1]
>   Second, that the Spirit is given also to me,[2]
>       so that, through true faith,
>       he makes me share in Christ and all his benefits,[3]
>       comforts me,[4]
>       and will remain with me forever.[5]

1. Gen. 1:2; Isa. 48:16; 1 Cor. 3:16; 6:19; Acts 5:3–4
2. Matt. 28:19; 2 Cor. 1:21–22
3. Gal. 3:14; 1 Pet. 1:2; 1 Cor. 6:17
4. Acts 9:31
5. John 14:16; 1 Pet. 4:14

**LORD'S DAY 21**

**4.054**  54  Q. **What do you believe concerning "the holy catholic church"?**

> A. I believe that the Son of God[1]
>       through his Spirit and Word,[2]
>       out of the entire human race,[3]
>       from the beginning of the world to its end,[4]
>   gathers, protects, and preserves for himself,[5]
>       a community chosen for eternal life[6]
>           and united in true faith.[7]
>   And of this community I am[8] and always will be[9]
>       a living member.

1. John 10:11
2. Isa. 59:21; Rom. 1:16; 10:14, 17; **Eph. 5:26**
3. Gen. 26:4
4. Ps. 71:18; 1 Cor. 11:26
5. Matt. 16:18; John 10:28–30; 1 Cor. 1:8
6. Rom. 8:29–30; Eph. 1:10–13
7. **Acts 2:46**; Eph. 4:3–5
8. 1 John 3:21; **2 Cor. 13:5**
9. 1 John 2:19

4.055 55 Q. **What do you understand by "the communion of saints"?**

A. First, that believers one and all,
as members of this community,
share in Christ
and in all his treasures and gifts.[1]

Second, that each member
should consider it a duty
to use these gifts
    readily and joyfully
      for the service and enrichment
        of the other members.[2]

1. 1 John 1:3; 1 Cor. 1:9; Rom. 8:32
2. **1 Cor.6:17**; 12:12–21; 13:5; Phil. 2:4–6

4.056 56 Q. **What do you believe concerning "the forgiveness of sins"?**

A. I believe that God,
    because of Christ's satisfaction,[1]
will no longer remember
    any of my sins
    or my sinful nature
      which I need to struggle against all my life.[2]

Rather, by grace
    God grants me the righteousness of Christ
    to free me forever from judgment.[3]

1. 1 John 2:2; 2 Cor. 5:19, 21
2. Jer. 31:34; Ps. 103:3, 10–12; Rom. 7:24–25; 8:1–3
3. John 3:18

## LORD'S DAY 22

4.057 57 Q. **How does "the resurrection of the body" comfort you?**

A. Not only will my soul
    be taken immediately after this life
    to Christ its head,[1]
but also my very flesh will be
    raised by the power of Christ,
    reunited with my soul,
    and made like Christ's glorious body.[2]

1. Luke 23:43; Phil. 1:23
2. 1 Cor. 15:53–54; Job 19:25–26; 1 John 3:2; Phil. 3:21

4.058 58 Q. **How does the article concerning "life everlasting" comfort you?**

A. Even as I already now
　　experience in my heart
　　　the beginning of eternal joy,[1]
so after this life I will have
　　perfect blessedness such as
　　　　no eye has seen,
　　　　no ear has heard,
　　　　no human heart has ever imagined:[2]
a blessedness in which to praise God forever.[3]

1. 2 Cor. 5:2–3
2. 1 Cor. 2:9
3. *John 17*

### LORD'S DAY 23

4.059 59 Q. **What good does it do you, however, to believe all this?**

A. In Christ I am righteous before God
and heir to life everlasting.[1]

1. Hab. 2:4; Rom. 1:17; John 3:36

4.060 60 Q. **How are you righteous before God?**

A. Only by true faith in Jesus Christ.[1]

Even though my conscience accuses me
　　of having grievously sinned against all God's
　　　commandments,
　　of never having kept any of them,[2]
　　and of still being inclined toward all evil,[3]
nevertheless,
　　without any merit of my own,[4]
　　out of sheer grace,[5]
God grants and credits to me[6]
the perfect satisfaction,[7] righteousness, and holiness of Christ,[8]
　　as if I had never sinned nor been a sinner,
　　and as if I had been as perfectly obedient
　　　as Christ was obedient for me.[9]
All I need to do
is accept this gift with a believing heart.[10]

1. Rom. 3:21–28, **5:1**; Gal. 2:16; Eph. 2:8–9; Phil. 3:9
2. Rom. 3:9[–18]
3. Rom. 7:23
4. 2 Tim. 3:5
5. Rom. 3:24; Eph. 2:8

6. Rom. 4:4; 2 Cor. 5:19
7. 1 John 2:2
8. 1 John 2:1
9. 2 Cor. 5:21
10. Rom. 3:22; John 3:18

**4.061** 61 Q. **Why do you say that
through faith alone
you are righteous?**

A. Not because I please God
   by the worthiness of my faith.
It is because only Christ's satisfaction, righteousness, and holiness
   make me righteous before God,[1]
and because I can accept this righteousness and make it mine
   in no other way
   than through faith.[2]

1. 1 Cor. 1:30; 2:2
2. 1 John 5:10

## LORD'S DAY 24

**4.062** 62 Q. **Why can't our good works
be our righteousness before God,
or at least a part of our righteousness?**

A. Because the righteousness
   which can pass God's judgment
      must be entirely perfect
      and must in every way measure up to the divine law.[1]
But even our best works in this life
   are imperfect
   and stained with sin.[2]

1. Gal. 3:10; Deut. 27:26
2. Isa. 64:6

**4.063** 63 Q. **How can our good works
be said to merit nothing
when God promises to reward them
in this life and the next?**

A. This reward is not earned;
   it is a gift of grace.[1]

1. Luke 17:10

**4.064** 64 Q. **But doesn't this teaching
make people indifferent and wicked?**

A. No.
  It is impossible
    for those grafted into Christ through true faith
    not to produce fruits of gratitude.[1]
  1. Matt. [7]:18

*The Holy Sacraments*

**LORD'S DAY 25**

4.065 65 Q. **It is through faith alone
that we share in Christ and all his benefits:
where then does that faith come from?**
A. The Holy Spirit produces it in our hearts[1]
    by the preaching of the holy gospel,
  and confirms it
    by the use of the holy sacraments.[2]
  1. Eph. 2:8; John 3:5
  2. Matt. 28:19–20; 1 Pet. 1:22–23

4.066 66 Q. **What are sacraments?**
A. Sacraments are visible, holy signs and seals.
  They were instituted by God so that
    by our use of them
  he might make us understand more clearly
    the promise of the gospel,
  and seal that promise.

  And this is God's gospel promise:
    to grant us forgiveness of sins and eternal life
      by grace
      because of Christ's one sacrifice
      accomplished on the cross.[1]
  1. Gen. 17:11; Rom. 4:11; Deut. 30:6; Lev. 6:25; Heb. 9:8–9, [11–]24; Ezek. 20:12; **1 Sam. 17:36[–37]; Isa. 6:6–7**

4.067 67 Q. **Are both the word and the sacraments then
intended to focus our faith
on the sacrifice of Jesus Christ on the cross
as the only ground of our salvation?**
A. Yes!
  In the gospel the Holy Spirit teaches us
  and by the holy sacraments confirms
    that our entire salvation
    rests on Christ's one sacrifice for us on the cross.[1]
  1. Rom. 6:3; Gal. 3:27

**4.068 68 Q. How many sacraments did Christ institute in the New Testament?**

A. Two: holy baptism and the holy supper.

*Holy Baptism*

**LORD'S DAY 26**

**4.069 69 Q. How does baptism remind and assure you that Christ's one sacrifice on the cross benefits you personally?**

A. In this way:
Christ instituted this outward washing
and with it promised that,
> as surely as water washes away the dirt from the body,
> so certainly his blood and his Spirit
> wash away my soul's impurity,
>> that is, all my sins.[1]

1. Mark 1:4; Luke 3:3

**4.070 70 Q. What does it mean to be washed with Christ's blood and Spirit?**

A. To be washed with Christ's blood means
> that God, by grace, has forgiven our sins
> because of Christ's blood
> poured out for us in his sacrifice on the cross.[1]

To be washed with Christ's Spirit means
> that the Holy Spirit has renewed
> and sanctified us to be members of Christ,
>> so that more and more
>>> we become dead to sin
>>> and live holy and blameless lives.[2]

1. Heb. 12:24; 1 Pet. 1:2; Rev. 1:5; **22:14**; Zech. 13:1; Ezek. 36:25
2. John 1:33; 3:5; 1 Cor. 6:11; 12:13; Rom. 6.4; Col. 2:12

**4.071 71 Q. Where does Christ promise that we are washed with his blood and Spirit as surely as we are washed with the water of baptism?**

A. In the institution of baptism, where he says:

> "Go therefore and make disciples of all nations,
> baptizing them in the name of the Father
> and of the Son
> and of the Holy Spirit."[1]

"The one who believes and is baptized will be saved; but the one who does not believe will be condemned."[2]

This promise is repeated when Scripture calls baptism "the water of rebirth"[3] and the washing away of sins.[4]

1. Matt. 28:19
2. Mark 16:16
3. Titus 3:5
4. Acts 22:16

## LORD'S DAY 27

**4.072  72 Q. Does this outward washing with water itself wash away sins?**

A. No,[1] only Jesus Christ's blood and the Holy Spirit cleanse us from all sins.[2]

1. Matt. 3:11; 1 Pet. 3:21; Eph. 5:26
2. 1 John 1:7; 1 Cor. 6:11

**4.073  73 Q. Why then does the Holy Spirit call baptism the water of rebirth and the washing away of sins?**

A. God has good reason for these words.
To begin with, God wants to teach us that
the blood and Spirit of Christ take away our sins
just as water removes dirt from the body.[1]
But more important,
God wants to assure us, by this divine pledge and sign,
that we are as truly washed of our sins spiritually
as our bodies are washed with water physically.[2]

1. Rev. 1:5; 7:14; 1 Cor. 6:11
2. Mark 16:16; Gal. 3:[2]7

**4.074  74 Q. Should infants also be baptized?**

A. Yes.
Infants as well as adults
are included in God's covenant and people,[1]
and they, no less than adults, are promised
deliverance from sin through Christ's blood[2]
and the Holy Spirit who produces faith.[3]

Therefore, by baptism, the sign of the covenant,
they too should be incorporated into the Christian church
and distinguished from the children
of unbelievers.[4]
This was done in the Old Testament by circumcision,[5]
which was replaced in the New Testament by baptism.[6]

1. Gen. 17:7
2. Matt. 19:14
3. Luke 1:15, [4]4; Ps. 22:[9–]11; Isa. 46:1–5; Acts 2:39
4. Acts 10:47
5. Gen. 17:[9–]14
6. Col. 2:11–13

## *The Holy Supper of Jesus Christ*

### LORD'S DAY 28

4.075  75  Q. How does the holy supper
remind and assure you
that you share in
Christ's one sacrifice on the cross
and in all his benefits?

A. In this way:
Christ has commanded me and all believers
to eat this broken bread and to drink this cup
in remembrance of him.
With this command come these promises:

First,
as surely as I see with my eyes
the bread of the Lord broken for me
and the cup shared with me,
so surely
his body was offered and broken for me
and his blood poured out for me
on the cross.

Second,
as surely as
I receive from the hand of the one who serves,
and taste with my mouth
the bread and cup of the Lord,
given me as sure signs of Christ's body and blood,
so surely
he nourishes and refreshes my soul for eternal life
with his crucified body and poured-out blood.

4.076  76  Q. What does it mean
to eat the crucified body of Christ
and to drink his poured-out blood?

A. It means
to accept with a believing heart
the entire suffering and death of Christ
and thereby
to receive forgiveness of sins and eternal life.[1]

But it means more.
> Through the Holy Spirit, who lives both in Christ and in us,
>> we are united more and more to Christ's blessed body.[2]
>>> And so, although he is in heaven[3] and we are on earth,
>>> we are flesh of his flesh and bone of his bone.[4]
>>>> And we forever live on and are governed by one Spirit,
>>>> as the members of our body are by one soul.[5]

1. John 6:35, 40, 47–48, 50–54
2. John 6:55–56
3. Acts 1:9; 3:21; 1 Cor. 11:26
4. Eph. 3:17; 5:29–32; 1 Cor. 6:15, 17–19; 1 John 3:24; 4:13; John 14:23
5. John 6:56–58; 15:1–6; Eph. 4:15–16

**4.077 77 Q. Where does Christ promise
to nourish and refresh believers
with his body and blood
as surely as
they eat this broken bread
and drink this cup?**

A. In the institution of the Lord's Supper:[1]

> "The Lord Jesus, on the night when he was betrayed,
> took a loaf of bread, and when he had given thanks,
> he broke it and said,
>> 'This is my body that is [broken]* for you.'
>
> In the same way he took the cup also, after supper, saying,
>> 'This cup is the new covenant in my blood;[2]
>> do this, as often as you drink it,
>> in remembrance of me.'[3]
>
> For as often as you eat this bread and drink the cup,
> you proclaim the Lord's death
> until he comes."

This promise is repeated by Paul in these words:

> "The cup of blessing that we bless,
>> is it not a sharing in the blood of Christ?
>
> The bread that we break,
>> is it not a sharing in the body of Christ?
>
> Because there is one bread, we who are many are one body,
> for we all partake of the one bread."[4]

1. 1 Cor. 11:23[–26]; Matt. 26:26[–29]; Mark 14:22[–25]; Luke 22:17[–20]
2. **Exod. 24:8; Heb. 9:20**
3. **Exod. 13:9**
4. 1 Cor. 10:16–17

*The word "broken" does not appear in the NRSV text, but it was present in the original German of the Heidelberg Catechism.

## LORD'S DAY 29

**4.078**    **78 Q. Do the bread and wine become the real body and blood of Christ?**

     A. No.
>Just as the water of baptism
>>is not changed into Christ's blood
>>and does not itself wash away sins
>>>but is simply a divine sign and assurance of these things,[1]
>
>so too the holy bread of the Lord's Supper
>>does not become the actual body of Christ,[2]
>>even though it is called the body of Christ
>>>in keeping with the nature and language of sacraments.[3]

1. Matt. 26:[28–]29; Mark 14:24
2. 1 Cor. 10:16–17; 11:26–28
3. Gen. 17:10, 14–19; Exod. 12:27, 43–48; **13:9**; **24:8**; **29:36**; **Acts 7:8**; **22:16**; **Lev. 16:10**; **17:11**; **Isa. 6:6–7**; Titus 3:5; 1 Pet. 3:21; 1 Cor. 10:1–4

**4.079**    **79 Q. Why then does Christ call the bread his body and the cup his blood, or the new covenant in his blood, and Paul use the words, a participation in Christ's body and blood?**

     A. Christ has good reason for these words.
>He wants to teach us that
>>just as bread and wine nourish the temporal life,
>>so too his crucified body and poured-out blood
>>are the true food and drink of our souls for eternal life.[1]

>But more important,
>he wants to assure us, by this visible sign and pledge,
>>that we, through the Holy Spirit's work,
>>>share in his true body and blood
>>>as surely as our mouths
>>>>receive these holy signs in his remembrance,[2]
>>
>>and that all of his suffering and obedience
>>>are as definitely ours
>>>as if we personally
>>>>had suffered and made satisfaction for our sins.

1. John 6:51, 55
2. 1 Cor. 10:16–17

## LORD'S DAY 30

**4.080**    **80\* Q. How does the Lord's Supper differ from the Roman Catholic Mass?**

A. The Lord's Supper declares to us
>that all our sins are completely forgiven
>through the one sacrifice of Jesus Christ,
>which he himself accomplished on the cross once for all.[1]

It also declares to us
>that the Holy Spirit grafts us into Christ,[2]
>who with his true body
>is now in heaven at the right hand of the Father[3]
>where he wants us to worship him.[4]

But the Mass teaches
>that the living and the dead
>do not have their sins forgiven
>through the suffering of Christ
>unless Christ is still offered for them daily by the priests.

It also teaches
>that Christ is bodily present
>under the form of bread and wine
>where Christ is therefore to be worshiped.

Thus the Mass is basically
>nothing but a denial
>of the one sacrifice and suffering of Jesus Christ
>and a condemnable idolatry.

1. Heb. 7:27; 9:12, 26–28; 10:10, 12–14; John 19:30; Matt. 26:28; Luke 22:19–20
2. 1 Cor. 6:17; 10:16; **12:13**
3. Heb. 1:3; 8:1
4. John 4:21–23; 20:17; Luke 24:52; Acts 7:55–56; Col. 3:1; Phil. 3:20; 1 Thess. 1:10

*Question and Answer 80 reflects the polemical debates of the Reformation and was added in the second German edition of 1563. The second and fourth sentences of the Answer, as well as the concluding phrase, were added in the third German edition of 1563. After the fourth sentence, the third German and Latin texts have a note to the section on consecration in the Canon of the Mass.

As detailed in the preface to *The Book of Confessions*, these condemnations and characterizations of the Catholic Church are not the position of the Presbyterian Church (U.S.A.) and are not applicable to current relationships between the Presbyterian Church (U.S.A.) and the Catholic Church.

**4.081**  81  Q. **Who should come to the Lord's table?**

A. Those who are displeased with themselves
>because of their sins,
>but who nevertheless trust
>>that their sins are pardoned
>>and that their remaining weakness is covered
>>>by the suffering and death of Christ,

and who also desire more and more
> to strengthen their faith
> and to lead a better life.
>
> Hypocrites and those who are unrepentant, however,
> eat and drink judgment on themselves.[1]

1. 1 Cor. 10:21; 11:28[–29]

**4.082** **82 Q. Should those be admitted
to the Lord's Supper
who show by what they profess and how they live
that they are unbelieving and ungodly?**

**A.** No, that would dishonor God's covenant
and bring down God's wrath upon the entire congregation.[1]
Therefore, according to the instruction of Christ
> and his apostles,
> the Christian church is duty-bound to exclude such people,
> > by the official use of the keys of the kingdom,
> until they reform their lives.

1. 1 Cor. 11:20, 34; Isa. 1:11; 66:3; Jer. 7:21[–26]; Ps. 50:16

## LORD'S DAY 31

**4.083** **83 Q. What are the keys of the kingdom?**

**A.** The preaching of the holy gospel
and Christian discipline toward repentance.
Both of them
> open the kingdom of heaven to believers
> and close it to unbelievers.

**4.084** **84 Q. How does preaching the holy gospel
open and close the kingdom of heaven?**

**A.** According to the command of Christ:

The kingdom of heaven is opened
by proclaiming and publicly declaring
> to all believers, each and every one, that,
> as often as they accept the gospel promise in true faith,
> God, because of Christ's merit,
> truly forgives all their sins.

The kingdom of heaven is closed, however,
by proclaiming and publicly declaring
> to unbelievers and hypocrites that,
> as long as they do not repent,
> the wrath of God and eternal condemnation
> rest on them.[1]

God's judgment, both in this life and in the life to come,
is based on this gospel testimony.

1. John 20:21–23; Matt. 16:19

**4.085** 85 Q. **How is the kingdom of heaven
closed and opened by Christian discipline?**

A. According to the command of Christ:

Those who, though called Christians,
        profess unchristian teachings or live unchristian lives,
and who after repeated personal and loving admonitions,
        refuse to abandon their errors and evil ways,
and who after being reported to the church, that is,
        to those ordained by the church for that purpose,
    fail to respond also to the church's admonitions—
such persons the church excludes
    from the Christian community
    by withholding the sacraments from them,
and God also excludes them from the kingdom of Christ.

Such persons,
    when promising and demonstrating genuine reform,
are received again
    as members of Christ
    and of his church.[1]

1. Matt. 18:15–18; 1 Cor. 5; 2 Thess. 3:14–15; *John 2[:13–22]*; **2 John 10–11**

*Part III: Gratitude*

**LORD'S DAY 32**

**4.086** 86 Q. **Since we have been delivered
from our misery
by grace through Christ
without any merit of our own,
why then should we do good works?**

A. Because Christ, having redeemed us by his blood,
is also restoring us by his Spirit into his image,
    so that with our whole lives
        we may show that we are thankful to God
            for his benefits,[1]
    so that he may be praised through us,[2]
    so that we may be assured of our faith by its fruits,[3]
    and so that by our godly living
        our neighbors may be won over to Christ.[4]

1. Rom. 6:13; 12:1–2; 1 Pet. 2:5-10; 1 Cor. 6:20
2. Matt. 5:16; 1 Pet. 2:12
3. 1 Pet. 1:[6–]10; Matt. 7:17; Gal. 5:6, 22
4. 1 Pet. 3:1–2; Rom. 14:19

4.087 87 Q. Can those be saved
who do not turn to God
from their ungrateful
and unrepentant ways?

A. By no means.
Scripture tells us that
no unchaste person,
no idolater, adulterer, thief,
no covetous person,
no drunkard, slanderer, robber,
or the like
will inherit the kingdom of God.[1]

1. 1 Cor. 6:9–10; Eph. 5:5–6; 1 John 3:14

**LORD'S DAY 33**

4.088 88 Q. What is involved
in genuine repentance or conversion?

A. Two things:
the dying-away of the old self,[1]
and the rising-to-life of the new.

1. Rom. 6:4–6; Eph. 4:22–24; Col. 3:5–10; 1 Cor. 5:7

4.089 89 Q. What is the dying-away of the old self?

A. To be genuinely sorry for sin
and more and more to hate
and run away from it.[1]

1. Rom. 8:13; Joel 2:13

4.090 90 Q. What is the rising-to-life of the new self?

A. Wholehearted joy in God through Christ[1]
and a love and delight to live
according to the will of God
by doing every kind of good work.[2]

1. Rom. 5:1; 14:17; Isa. 57:15
2. Rom. 6:10–11; Gal. 2:20

4.091 91 Q. What are good works?

A. Only those which
are done out of true faith,[1]
conform to God's law,[2]
and are done for God's glory;[3]
and not those based
on our own opinion
or human tradition.[4]

1. Rom. 14:23
2. *1 Sam. 11*; **1 Sam. [15]:22**; Eph. 2:10

3. 1 Cor. 10:31
4. Deut. 12:32; Ezek. 20:18–19; Isa. 29:13; Matt. 15:9

*The Ten Commandments*

**LORD'S DAY 34**

4.092 92 **Q. What is God's law?**

**A.** God spoke all these words:

> THE FIRST COMMANDMENT
> "I am the LORD your God,
>   who brought you out of the land of Egypt,
>   out of the house of slavery;
> you shall have no other gods before me."
>
> THE SECOND COMMANDMENT
> "You shall not make for yourself an idol,
>   whether in form of anything that is in heaven above,
>   or that is on the earth beneath,
>   or that is in the water under the earth.
> You shall not bow down to them or worship them;
>   for I the LORD your God am a jealous God,
>   punishing children for the iniquity of parents,
>     to the third and fourth generation
>     of those who reject me,
>   but showing love to the thousandth generation of those
>     who love me and keep my commandments."
>
> THE THIRD COMMANDMENT
> "You shall not make wrongful use of the name of the
> LORD your God,
>   for the LORD will not acquit anyone
>   who misuses his name."
>
> THE FOURTH COMMANDMENT
> "Remember the Sabbath day and keep it holy.
> Six days you shall labor and do all your work.
> But the seventh day is a Sabbath to the LORD your God;
> you shall not do any work—
>   you, your son or your daughter,
>   your male or female slave,
>   your livestock,
>   or the alien resident in your towns.
> For in six days the LORD made
>   the heaven and earth, the sea,
>   and all that is in them,
> but rested the seventh day;
> therefore the LORD blessed the Sabbath day
> and consecrated it."

### THE FIFTH COMMANDMENT
"Honor your father and your mother,
so that your days may be long
in the land that the LORD your God is giving to you."

### THE SIXTH COMMANDMENT
"You shall not murder."

### THE SEVENTH COMMANDMENT
"You shall not commit adultery."

### THE EIGHTH COMMANDMENT
"You shall not steal."

### THE NINTH COMMANDMENT
"You shall not bear false witness
against your neighbor."

### THE TENTH COMMANDMENT
"You shall not covet your neighbor's house;
you shall not covet your neighbor's wife,
or male or female slave,
or ox, or donkey,
or anything that belongs to your neighbor."[1]

1. *Exod. 20[:1–17]; Deut. 5[:6–21]*

**93 Q. How are these commandments divided?**

**A.** Into two tables.[1]
The first has four commandments,
teaching us how we ought to live in relation to God.
The second has six commandments,
teaching us what we owe our neighbor.[2]

1. Exod. 34:28; Deut. 4:13; 10:3–4
2. Matt. 22:37–39

**94 Q. What does the Lord require
in the first commandment?**

**A.** That I, not wanting to endanger my own salvation,
avoid and shun
all idolatry,[1] sorcery, superstitious rites,[2]
and prayer to saints or to other creatures.[3]
That I rightly know the only true God,[4]
trust him alone,[5]
and look to God for every good thing[6]
humbly[7] and patiently,[8]
and love,[9] fear,[10] and honor[11] God
with all my heart.
In short,
that I give up anything
rather than go against God's will in any way.[12]

1. 1 Cor. 6:9–10; 10:7, 14
2. Lev. 19:31; Deut. 18:11
3. Matt. 4:10; Rev. 19:10; 22:[8]–9
4. John 17:3
5. Jer. 17:5
6. Ps. 104: 27–30; Isa. 45:7; James 1:17
7. 1 Pet. 5:5–6
8. Heb. 10:36; Col. 1:11; Rom. 5:3–4; 1 Cor. 10:10; Phil. 2:14
9. Deut. 6:5; Matt. 22:37
10. Deut. 6:2; Ps. 111:10; Prov. 1:7; 9:10; Matt. 10:28
11. Matt. 4:10; Deut. 10:20
12. Matt. 5:29–30; 10:37; Acts 5:29

4.095 95 Q. **What is idolatry?**

A. Idolatry is
having or inventing something in which one trusts
in place of or alongside of the only true God,
who has revealed himself in the Word.[1]

1. Eph. 5:5; 1 Chron. 16:26; Phil. 3:19; Gal. 4:8; Eph. 2:12; 1 John 2:23; 2 John 9; John 5:23

## LORD'S DAY 35

4.096 96 Q. **What is God's will for us in the second commandment?**

A. That we in no way make any image of God[1]
nor worship him in any other way
than has been commanded in God's Word.[2]

1. Deut. 4:15[–19]; Isa. 40:18; Rom. 1:23; Acts 17:29
2. 1 Sam. 15:23; Deut. 12:30; Matt. 15:9

4.097 97 Q. **May we then not make any image at all?**

A. God can not and may not
be visibly portrayed in any way.

Although creatures may be portrayed,
yet God forbids making or having such images
if one's intention is to worship them
or to serve God through them.[1]

1. Exod. 23:24; 34:13; Num. 33:52; Deut. 7:5; 12:3; 16:22; 2 Kings 18:4

4.098 98 Q. **But may not images be permitted in churches in place of books for the unlearned?**

A. No, we should not try to be wiser than God.
God wants the Christian community instructed
by the living preaching of his Word—[1]
not by idols that cannot even talk.[2]

1. 2 Tim. 3:16–17; 2 Pet. 1:19
2. Jer. 10:8; Hab. 2:18–19

## LORD'S DAY 36

**4.099** **99 Q. What is the aim of the third commandment?**

**A.** That we neither blaspheme nor misuse the name of God
by cursing, perjury,[1] or unnecessary oaths,[2]
nor share in such horrible sins
by being silent bystanders.

In summary,
we should use the holy name of God
only with reverence and awe,[3]
so that we may properly
confess God,[4]
pray to God,[5]
and glorify God in all our words and works.[6]

1. Lev. 24:11[–16]; 19:12
2. Matt. 5:37; James 5:12
3. Isa. 45:23
4. Matt. 10:32
5. 1 Tim. 2:8
6. Rom. **2:24**; 1 Tim. 6:1; Col. 3:16

**4.100** **100 Q. Is blasphemy of God's name by swearing and cursing really such serious sin that God is angry also with those who do not do all they can to help prevent and forbid it?**

**A.** Yes, indeed.[1]
No sin is greater
or provokes God's wrath more
than blaspheming his name.
That is why God commanded it to be punished with death.[2]

1. Lev. 5:1
2. Lev. 24:15–16

## LORD'S DAY 37

**4.101** **101 Q. But may we swear an oath in God's name if we do it reverently?**

**A.** Yes, when the government demands it,
or when necessity requires it,
in order to maintain and promote truth and trustworthiness
for God's glory and our neighbor's good.
Such oaths are grounded in God's Word[1]
and were rightly used by the people of God
in the Old and New Testaments.[2]

1. Deut. 6:13; 10:20; Isa. 48:1; Heb. 6:16
2. Gen. 21:24; 31:53; Josh. 9:15, 19; 1 Sam.24:[21–22]; 2 Sam. 3:35; 1 Kings 1:29; Rom. 1:9; 2 Cor. 1:23

**4.102** 102 Q. **May we also swear by saints or other creatures?**
    A. No.
       A legitimate oath means calling upon God
       as the only one who knows my heart
          to witness to my truthfulness
            and to punish me if I swear falsely.[1]
       No creature is worthy of such honor.[2]

    1. 2 Cor. 1:23
    2. Matt. 5:34–36; James 5:12

## LORD'S DAY 38

**4.103** 103 Q. **What is God's will for you in the fourth commandment?**

    A. First,
       that the gospel ministry and education for it be maintained,[1]
       and that, especially on the festive day of rest,
       I diligently attend the assembly of God's people[2]
          to learn what God's Word teaches,[3]
          to participate in the sacraments,[4]
          to pray to God publicly,[5]
          and to bring Christian offerings for the poor.[6]

    Second,
       that every day of my life
          I rest from my evil ways,
            let the Lord work in me through his Spirit,
       and so begin in this life
       the eternal Sabbath.[7]

    1. Titus 1:5; 1 Tim. 3[:1]; 4:13; 5:17; 1 Cor. 9:11, 13–14; 2 Tim. 2:2; 3:15
    2. Ps. 68:27; 40:10–11; Acts [2]:42, 46
    3. 1 Cor. 14:19, 29, 31
    4. 1 Cor. 11:33
    5. 1 Tim. 2:1–3, 8–9; 1 Cor. 14:16
    6. 1 Cor. 16:2
    7. Isa. 66:23

## LORD'S DAY 39

**4.104** 104 Q. **What is God's will for you in the fifth commandment?**

    A. That I honor, love, and be loyal
       to my father and mother
       and all those in authority over me;[1]
    that I submit myself with proper obedience
       to all their good teaching and discipline;

and also that I be patient with their failings—[2]
for through them God chooses to rule us.[3]

1. Eph. 6:1[–9]; Col. 3:18, 20–24; Eph. 5:22; Prov. 1:8; 4:1; 15:20; 20:20; Exod. 21:17; Rom. 13:[1–5]
2. Prov. 23:22; Gen. 9:25; 1 Pet. 2:18
3. Eph. 6:4, 9; Col. 3:19, 21; Rom. 13:[1–5]; Matt. 22:21

## LORD'S DAY 40

**4.105** 105 Q. **What is God's will for you in the sixth commandment?**

A. I am not to belittle, hate, insult, or kill my neighbor—
not by my thoughts, my words, my look or gesture,
and certainly not by actual deeds—[1]
and I am not to be party to this in others;
rather, I am to put away all desire for revenge.[2]

I am not to harm or recklessly endanger myself either.[3]

Prevention of murder is also why
government is armed with the sword.[4]

1. Matt. 5:21–22; Gen. 9:6; Matt. 26:52
2. Eph. 4:26; Rom. 12:19; Matt. 5:25; 18:35
3. Rom. 13:14; Col. 2:23; Sirach 3:27*; Matt. 4:7
4. Gen. 9:6; Exod. 21:14; Matt. 26:52; Rom. 13:4

*Sirach is a deutero-canonical book, treated with respect but not as canonical by the 16th century reformers.

**4.106** 106 Q. **Does this commandment refer only to murder?**

A. By forbidding murder God teaches us
that he hates the root of murder:
envy,[1] hatred,[2] anger,[3] vindictiveness.

In God's sight all such are disguised forms of murder.[4]

1. Rom. 1:29
2. 1 John 2:9, 11
3. *James 2:[13]*; **1:20**; Gal. 5:20
4. 1 John 3:15

**4.107** 107 Q. **Is it enough then that we do not murder our neighbor in any such way?**

A. No.
By condemning envy, hatred, and anger
God wants us
to love our neighbors as ourselves,[1]
to be patient, peace-loving, gentle,[2]
merciful,[3] and friendly toward them,[4]
to protect them from harm as much as we can,[5]
and to do good even to our enemies.[6]

1. Matt. 22:39; 7:12
2. Eph. 4:2; Gal. 6:1–2; Matt. 5:9; Rom. 12:18
3. Matt. 5:7; Luke 6:36
4. Rom. 12:10
5. Exod. 23:5
6. Matt. 5:44–45; Rom. 12:20–21

### LORD'S DAY 41

4.108 108 Q. **What does the seventh commandment teach us?**

A. That God condemns all unchastity,[1]
and that therefore we should thoroughly detest it[2]
and live decent and chaste lives,[3]
within or outside of the holy state of marriage.[4]

1. Lev. 18:27–28
2. Jude 23
3. 1 Thess. 4:3–5
4. Heb. 13:4; 1 Cor. 7

4.109 109 Q. **Does God, in this commandment, forbid only such scandalous sins as adultery?**

A. We are temples of the Holy Spirit, body and soul,
and God wants both to be kept clean and holy.
That is why God forbids
all unchaste actions, looks, talk,[1] thoughts, or desires,[2]
and whatever may incite someone to them.[3]

1. Eph. 5:3–4; 1 Cor. 6:18–20
2. Matt. 5:[27–28]
3. Eph. 5:18; 1 Cor. 15:33

### LORD'S DAY 42

4.110 110 Q. **What does God forbid in the eighth commandment?**

A. God forbids not only outright theft[1] and robbery,[2]
punishable by law.

But in God's sight theft also includes
all scheming and swindling
in order to get our neighbor's goods for ourselves,
whether by force or means that appear legitimate,[3]
such as
inaccurate measurements of weight,[4] size, or volume;[5]
fraudulent merchandising;
counterfeit money;
excessive interest;[6]
or any other means forbidden by God.

In addition God forbids all greed⁷
and pointless squandering of his gifts.⁸

1. 1 Cor. 6:10
2. 1 Cor. 5:10
3. Luke 3:14; 1Thess. 4:6
4. Prov. 11:1; 16:11
5. Ezek. 45:9[–11]; Deut. 25:13[–16]
6. Ps. 15:5; Luke 6:35
7. 1 Cor. 6:10
8. Prov. 5:16

**4.111  111 Q. What does God require of you in this commandment?**

A. That I do whatever I can
   for my neighbor's good,
that I treat others
   as I would like them to treat me,¹
and that I work faithfully
   so that I may share with those in need.²

1. Matt. 7:12
2. Eph. 4:28

### LORD'S DAY 43

**4.112  112 Q. What is the aim of the ninth commandment?**

A. That I
   never give false testimony against anyone,¹
   twist no one's words,²
   not gossip or slander,³
   nor join in condemning anyone
   rashly or without a hearing.⁴
Rather, in court and everywhere else,
I should avoid lying and deceit of every kind;⁵
   these are the very devices the devil uses,⁶
   and they would call down on me God's intense wrath.
I should love the truth,
   speak it candidly,
   and openly acknowledge it.⁷
And I should do what I can
   to guard and advance my neighbor's good name.⁸

1. Prov. 19:5, 9; 21:28
2. Ps. 15:3
3. Rom. 1:29–30
4. Matt. 7:1[–2]; Luke 6:37
5. Prov. 12:22; 13:5
6. John 8:44
7. 1 Cor. 13:6; Eph. 4:25
8. 1 Pet. 4:8

### LORD'S DAY 44

**4.113** **113 Q. What is the aim of the tenth commandment?**

A. That not even the slightest desire or thought
   contrary to any one of God's commandments
   should ever arise in our hearts.

Rather, with all our hearts
   we should always hate sin
   and take pleasure in whatever is right.[1]

1. Rom. 7:7

**4.114** **114 Q. But can those converted to God obey these commandments perfectly?**

A. No.
In this life even the holiest
   have only a small beginning of this obedience.[1]

Nevertheless, with all seriousness of purpose,
   they do begin to live
   according to all, not only some,
   of God's commandments.[2]

1. 1 John 1:8–10; Rom. 7:14–15; Eccl. 7:[20]
2. Rom. 7:22; James 2:10

**4.115** **115 Q. Since no one in this life can obey the Ten Commandments perfectly, why does God want them preached so pointedly?**

A. First, so that the longer we live
      the more we may come to know our sinfulness[1]
      and the more eagerly look to Christ
         for forgiveness of sins and righteousness.[2]

Second, so that,
we may never stop striving,
and never stop praying to God for the grace of the Holy Spirit,
   to be renewed more and more after God's image,
until after this life we reach our goal:
   perfection.[3]

1. 1 John 1:9; Ps. 32:5
2. Rom. 7:24–25
3. 1 Cor. 9:24; Phil. 3:11–14

*The Lord's Prayer*

### LORD'S DAY 45

**4.116** **116 Q. Why do Christians need to pray?**

A. Because prayer is the most important part
   of the thankfulness God requires of us.[1]

And also because God gives his grace and Holy Spirit
only to those who pray continually and groan inwardly,
    asking God for these gifts
    and thanking God for them.[2]

1. Ps. 50:14–15
2. Matt. 7:7[–8]; Luke 11:9–13; Matt. 13:12; Ps. 50:15

**117 Q. What is the kind of prayer
that pleases God and that he listens to?**

A. First, we must pray from the heart
    to no other than the one true God,
    revealed to us in his Word,[1]
    asking for everything God has commanded us to ask for.[2]

Second, we must fully recognize our need and misery,[3]
    so that we humble ourselves in God's majestic presence.[4]

Third, we must rest on this unshakable foundation:[5]
    even though we do not deserve it,
    God will surely listen to our prayer
        because of Christ our Lord.[6]
That is what God promised us in his Word.[7]

1. John 4:22
2. Rom. 8:26; 1 John 5:14; John 4:23–24; Ps. 145:18
3. 2 Chron. 20:12
4. Ps 2:11, 34:19; Isa 66:2
5. Rom 10:[13]; 8:15; James 1:6
6. John 14:13–15; 15:16; 16:23; Dan 9:17–18
7. Matt 7:8; Ps 143:1

**118 Q. What did God command us to pray for?**

A. Everything we need, spiritually and physically,[1]
    as embraced in the prayer
    Christ our Lord himself taught us.

1. James 1:17; Matt. 6:33

**119 Q. What is this prayer?**

A. Our Father in heaven,
hallowed be your name.
Your kingdom come.
Your will be done,
    on earth as it is in heaven.
Give us this day our daily bread.
And forgive us our debts,
    as we also have forgiven our debtors.
And do not bring us to the time of trial,
    but rescue us from the evil one.
For the kingdom

and the power
and the glory are yours forever.
Amen.[1]

1. Matt. 6:9[–13]; Luke 11:2[–4]

## LORD'S DAY 46

**4.120 120 Q. Why did Christ command us to call God "our Father"?**

A. To awaken in us
at the very beginning of our prayer
what should be basic to our prayer—
a childlike reverence and trust
that through Christ God has become our Father,
and that just as our parents do not refuse us
the things of this life,
even less will God our Father refuse to give us
what we ask in faith.[1]

1. Matt. 7:9–11; Luke 11:11–13

**4.121 121 Q. Why the words "in heaven"?**

A. These words teach us
not to think of God's heavenly majesty
as something earthly,[1]
and to expect everything
needed for body and soul
from God's almighty power.[2]

1. Jer. 23:23–24; Acts 17:24–25, 27
2. Rom. 10:12

## LORD'S DAY 47

**4.122 122 Q. What does the first petition mean?**

A. "Hallowed be your name" means:

Help us to truly know you,[1]
to honor, glorify, and praise you
for all your works
and for all that shines forth from them:
your almighty power, wisdom, kindness,
justice, mercy, and truth.[2]

And it means,

Help us to direct all our living—
what we think, say, and do—
so that your name will never be blasphemed because of us
but always honored and praised.[3]

1. John 17:3; Matt. 16:17; James 1:5; Ps. 119:105
2. Ps. 119:137; **Luke 1:46[–55], 68[–79]; Ps. 145:8–9, 17; Exod. 34:6–7; Ps 143:1–2, 5, 10–12; Jer. 32:18–19; 33:11, 20–21; Matt. 19:17;** Rom. 11:22, 33[–36]
3. Ps. 115:1; 71:8

### LORD'S DAY 48

4.123  123 Q. **What does the second petition mean?**

A. "Your kingdom come" means:

Rule us by your Word and Spirit in such a way
that more and more we submit to you.[1]

Preserve your church and make it grow.[2]

Destroy the devil's work;
destroy every force which revolts against you
and every conspiracy against your holy Word.[3]

Do this until your kingdom fully comes,[4]
when you will be
all in all.[5]

1. Matt. 6:33; Ps. 119:5; 143:10
2. Ps. 51:18; 122:6
3. 1 John 3:8; Rom. 16:20
4. Rev. 22:17, 20; Rom. 8:22–23
5. 1 Cor. 15:28

### LORD'S DAY 49

4.124  124 Q. **What does the third petition mean?**

A. "Your will be done, on earth as it is in heaven" means:

Help us and all people
to reject our own wills[1]
and to obey your will without any back talk.[2]
Your will alone is good.

Help us one and all to carry out the work we are called to,[3]
as willingly and faithfully as the angels in heaven.[4]

1. Matt.16:24; Titus 2:12
2. Luke 22:42
3. 1 Cor. 7:24
4. Ps. 103:20–21

### LORD'S DAY 50

4.125  125 Q. **What does the fourth petition mean?**

A. "Give us this day our daily bread" means:

Do take care of all our physical needs[1]
so that we come to know
that you are the only source of everything good,[2]
and that neither our work and worry

> nor your gifts
> can do us any good without your blessing.³
>
> And so help us to give up our trust in creatures
> and trust in you alone.⁴

1. Ps. 145:15; 104:27[–28]; Matt. 6:25[–34]
2. Acts 17:27; 14:17
3. 1 Cor. 15:58; Deut. 8:3; Ps. 37:16–17
4. Ps. 62:11; 55:23

## LORD'S DAY 51

**4.126** **126 Q. What does the fifth petition mean?**

**A.** "Forgive us our debts,
as we also have forgiven our debtors" means:

> Because of Christ's blood,
> do not hold against us, poor sinners that we are,
> any of the sins we do
> or the evil that constantly clings to us.¹
>
> Forgive us just as we are fully determined,
> as evidence of your grace in us,
> to forgive our neighbors.²

1. Ps. 51:1[–7]; 143:2; 1 John 2:1–2
2. Matt. 6:14–15

## LORD'S DAY 52

**4.127** **127 Q. What does the sixth petition mean?**

**A.** "And do not bring us to the time of trial,
but rescue us from the evil one" means:

> By ourselves we are too weak
> to hold our own even for a moment.¹
>
> And our sworn enemies—
> the devil,² the world,³ and our own flesh—⁴
> never stop attacking us.
>
> And so, Lord,
> uphold us and make us strong
> with the strength of your Holy Spirit,
> so that we may not go down to defeat
> in this spiritual struggle,⁵
> but may firmly resist our enemies
> until we finally win the complete victory.⁶

1. John 15:5; Ps. 103:14
2. 1 Pet. 5:8; Eph. 6:12
3. John 15:19
4. Rom. 7:23; Gal. 5:17

5. Matt. 26:41; Mark 13:33
6. 1 Thess. 3:13; 5:23

**4.128 128 Q. What does your conclusion to this prayer mean?**

A. "For the kingdom
and the power
and the glory are yours forever" means:

We have made all these petitions of you
because, as our all-powerful king,
    you are both willing and able
    to give us all that is good;[1]
and because your holy name,
    and not we ourselves,
should receive all the praise, forever.[2]

1. Rom. 10:11–12; 2 Pet. 2:9
2. John 14:13; Ps. 115:1; **Jer. 33:8–9**

**4.129 129 Q. What does that little word "Amen" express?**

A. "Amen" means:

This shall truly and surely be!

It is even more sure
    that God listens to my prayer
than that I really desire
    what I pray for.[1]

1. 2 Cor. 1:20; 2 Tim. 2:13

# THE SECOND HELVETIC CONFESSION
[TEXT]

## The Second Helvetic Confession

The word "Helvetic" is Latin for "Swiss." The setting of the Second Helvetic Confession is Swiss-German Reformed Protestantism.

After the great Reformer Ulrich Zwingli died in battle in 1531, Heinrich Bullinger succeeded him as minister of the church in Zurich. Bullinger was a model Reformed minister. A preacher, he expounded Scripture at least twice a week. A scholar, he wrote Latin commentaries on many books of the Old Testament and on every book of the New Testament except Revelation. An educator, he initiated a system of schools for Zurich and was rector of the Carolinum, a theological academy. A person with ecumenical and political concerns, he was in correspondence with leaders of the Reformation and with rulers throughout Europe. A pastor, he welcomed religious refugees into his own home. When the plague swept through Zurich in 1564, he insisted upon ministering to the afflicted, even though he knew he might become infected and die.

In 1561, Bullinger composed the document that later became known as the Second Helvetic Confession. He intended to attach it to his last will and testament to the Zurich church, but events in Germany soon brought it into the public arena.

The publication of the Heidelberg Catechism created trouble for the man who had ordered its preparation. Lutherans considered it too Reformed in spirit, and they demanded that Frederick the Elector, governor of the Palatinate, be brought to trial for heresy. Not a theologian himself, Frederick turned to Bullinger, who offered Frederick this confession as the basis for his defense. When the Imperial Diet, the ruling body of Germany, met for trial in 1566, Frederick was exonerated.

Meanwhile, the churches of Switzerland adopted Bullinger's confession as their new confession of faith. Soon finding wide acceptance throughout Europe and beyond, it was translated into French, English, Dutch, Polish, Hungarian, Italian, Arabic, and Turkish.

Reflecting the theological maturity of the Reformed churches, the Second Helvetic Confession is moderate in tone and catholic in spirit. From the opening paragraphs it emphasizes the church and its life and affirms the authority of the Scriptures for the church's government and reformation. By including an article on predestination, the confession asks the church to trust in God's free and gracious election of its membership in Jesus Christ. At the same time, the confession addresses the practical life of the gathered community, detailing matters of worship, church order and conflict, ministry, the sacraments, and marriage.

# THE SECOND HELVETIC CONFESSION[1]
## CHAPTER I
### Of the Holy Scripture
### Being the True Word of God

5.001 CANONICAL SCRIPTURE. We believe and confess the canonical Scriptures of the holy prophets and apostles of both Testaments to be the true Word of God, and to have sufficient authority of themselves, not of men. For God himself spoke to the fathers, prophets, apostles, and still speaks to us through the Holy Scriptures.

5.002 And in this Holy Scripture, the universal Church of Christ has the most complete exposition of all that pertains to a saving faith, and also to the framing of a life acceptable to God; and in this respect it is expressly commanded by God that nothing be either added to or taken from the same.

5.003 SCRIPTURE TEACHES FULLY ALL GODLINESS. We judge, therefore, that from these Scriptures are to be derived true wisdom and godliness, the reformation and government of churches; as also instruction in all duties of piety; and, to be short, the confirmation of doctrines, and the rejection of all errors, moreover, all exhortations according to that word of the apostle, "All Scripture is inspired by God and profitable for teaching, for reproof," etc. (II Tim. 3:16–17). Again, "I am writing these instructions to you," says the apostle to Timothy, "so that you may know how one ought to behave in the household of God," etc. (I Tim. 3:14–15). SCRIPTURE IS THE WORD OF GOD. Again, the selfsame apostle to the Thessalonians: "When," says he, "you received the Word of God which you heard from us, you accepted it, not as the word of men but as what it really is, the Word of God," etc. (I Thess. 2:13.) For the Lord himself has said in the Gospel, "It is not you who speak, but the Spirit of my Father speaking through you"; therefore "he who hears you hears me, and he who rejects me rejects him who sent me" (Matt. 10:20; Luke 10:16; John 13:20).

5.004 THE PREACHING OF THE WORD OF GOD IS THE WORD OF GOD. Wherefore when this Word of God is now preached in the church by preachers lawfully called, we believe that the very Word of God is proclaimed, and received by the faithful; and that neither any other Word of God is to be invented nor is to be expected from heaven: and that now the Word itself which is preached is to be regarded, not the minister that preaches; for even if he be evil and a sinner, nevertheless the Word of God remains still true and good.

---

[1] Reprinted from *Reformed Confessions of the 16th Century* by Arthur C. Cochrane. Copyright MCMLXVI W. L. Jenkins. The Westminster Press. Used by permission.

**5.005** Neither do we think that therefore the outward preaching is to be thought as fruitless because the instruction in true religion depends on the inward illumination of the Spirit, or because it is written "And no longer shall each man teach his neighbor ..., for they shall all know me" (Jer. 31:34), and "Neither he who plants nor he who waters is anything, but only God who gives the growth" (I Cor. 3:7). For although "no one can come to Christ unless he be drawn by the Father" (John 6:44), and unless the Holy Spirit inwardly illumines him, yet we know that it is surely the will of God that his Word should be preached outwardly also. God could indeed, by his Holy Spirit, or by the ministry of an angel, without the ministry of St. Peter, have taught Cornelius in the Acts; but, nevertheless, he refers him to Peter, of whom the angel speaking says, "He shall tell you what you ought to do."

**5.006** INWARD ILLUMINATION DOES NOT ELIMINATE EXTERNAL PREACHING. For he that illuminates inwardly by giving men the Holy Spirit, the same one, by way of commandment, said unto his disciples, "Go into all the world, and preach the Gospel to the whole creation" (Mark 16:15). And so in Philippi, Paul preached the Word outwardly to Lydia, a seller of purple goods; but the Lord inwardly opened the woman's heart (Acts 16:14). And the same Paul, after a beautiful development of his thought, in Rom. 10:17 at length comes to the conclusion, "So faith comes from hearing, and hearing from the Word of God by the preaching of Christ."

**5.007** At the same time we recognize that God can illuminate whom and when he will, even without the external ministry, for that is in his power; but we speak of the usual way of instructing men, delivered unto us from God, both by commandment and examples.

**5.008** HERESIES. We therefore detest all the heresies of Artemon, the Manichaeans, the Valentinians, of Cerdon, and the Marcionites, who denied that the Scriptures proceeded from the Holy Spirit; or did not accept some parts of them, or interpolated and corrupted them.

**5.009** APOCRYPHA. And yet we do not conceal the fact that certain books of the Old Testament were by the ancient authors called *Apocryphal*, and by others *Ecclesiastical*; inasmuch as some would have them read in the churches, but not advanced as an authority from which the faith is to be established. As Augustine also, in his *De Civitate Dei*, book 18, ch. 38, remarks that "in the books of the Kings, the names and books of certain prophets are cited"; but he adds that "they are not in the canon"; and that "those books which we have suffice unto godliness."

## CHAPTER II

## Of Interpreting the Holy Scriptures; and of Fathers, Councils, and Traditions

**5.010** THE TRUE INTERPRETATION OF SCRIPTURE. The apostle Peter has said that the Holy Scriptures are not of private interpretation (II Peter 1:20), and thus we do not allow all possible interpretations. Nor consequently do we acknowledge as the true or genuine interpretation of the Scriptures what is called the conception of the Roman Church, that is, what the defenders of the Roman Church plainly maintain should be thrust upon all for acceptance. But we hold that interpretation of the Scripture to be orthodox and genuine which is gleaned from the Scriptures themselves (from the nature of the language in which they were written, likewise according to the circumstances in which they were set down, and expounded in the light of like and unlike passages and of many and clearer passages) and which agree with the rule of faith and love, and contributes much to the glory of God and man's salvation.

**5.011** INTERPRETATIONS OF THE HOLY FATHERS. Wherefore we do not despise the interpretations of the holy Greek and Latin fathers, nor reject their disputations and treatises concerning sacred matters as far as they agree with the Scriptures; but we modestly dissent from them when they are found to set down things differing from, or altogether contrary to, the Scriptures. Neither do we think that we do them any wrong in this matter; seeing that they all, with one consent, will not have their writings equated with the canonical Scriptures, but command us to prove how far they agree or disagree with them, and to accept what is in agreement and to reject what is in disagreement.

**5.012** COUNCILS. And in the same order also we place the decrees and canons of councils.

**5.013** Wherefore we do not permit ourselves, in controversies about religion or matters of faith, to urge our case with only the opinions of the fathers or decrees of councils; much less by received customs, or by the large number of those who share the same opinion, or by the prescription of a long time. WHO IS THE JUDGE? Therefore, we do not admit any other judge than God himself, who proclaims by the Holy Scriptures what is true, what is false, what is to be followed, or what to be avoided. So we do assent to the judgments of spiritual men which are drawn from the Word of God. Certainly Jeremiah and other prophets vehemently condemned the assemblies of priests which were set up against the law of God; and diligently admonished us that we should not listen to the fathers, or tread in their path who, walking in their own inventions, swerved from the law of God.

**5.014** TRADITIONS OF MEN. Likewise we reject human traditions, even if they be adorned with high-sounding titles, as though they were divine and apostolical, delivered to the Church by the living voice of the apostles, and, as it were, through the hands of apostolical men to succeeding bishops which, when compared with the Scriptures, disagree with them; and by their disagreement show that they are not apostolic at all. For as the apostles did not contradict themselves in doctrine, so the apostolic men did not set forth things contrary to the apostles. On the contrary, it would be wicked to assert that the apostles by a living voice delivered anything contrary to their writings. Paul affirms expressly that he taught the same things in all churches (I Cor. 4:17). And, again, "For we write you nothing but what you can read and understand." (II Cor. 1:13). Also, in another place, he testifies that he and his disciples—that is, apostolic men—walked in the same way, and jointly by the same Spirit did all things (II Cor. 12:18). Moreover, the Jews in former times had the traditions of their elders; but these traditions were severely rejected by the Lord, indicating that the keeping of them hinders God's law, and that God is worshipped in vain by such traditions (Matt. 15:1 ff.; Mark 7:1 ff.).

## CHAPTER III*

### Of God, His Unity and Trinity

**5.015** GOD IS ONE. We believe and teach that God is one in essence or nature, subsisting in himself, all sufficient in himself, invisible, incorporeal, immense, eternal, Creator of all things both visible and invisible, the greatest good, living, quickening and preserving all things, omnipotent and supremely wise, kind and merciful, just and true. Truly we detest many gods because it is expressly written: "The Lord your God is one Lord" (Deut. 6:4). "I am the Lord your God. You shall have no other gods before me" (Ex. 20:2–3). "I am the Lord, and there is no other god besides me. Am I not the Lord, and there is no other God beside me? A righteous God and a Savior; there is none besides me" (Isa. 45:5, 21). "The Lord, the Lord, a God merciful and gracious, slow to anger, and abounding in steadfast love and faithfulness" (Ex. 34:6).

**5.016** GOD IS THREE. Notwithstanding we believe and teach that the same immense, one and indivisible God is in person inseparably and without confusion distinguished as Father, Son and Holy Spirit so, as the Father has begotten the Son from eternity, the Son is begotten by an ineffable generation, and the Holy Spirit truly proceeds from them both, and the same from eternity and is to be worshipped with both.

---

* See Preface for discussion of our current understanding of such condemnations.

**5.017** Thus there are not three gods, but three persons, consubstantial, coeternal, and coequal; distinct with respect to hypostases, and with respect to order, the one preceding the other yet without any inequality. For according to the nature or essence they are so joined together that they are one God, and the divine nature is common to the Father, Son and Holy Spirit.

**5.018** For Scripture has delivered to us a manifest distinction of persons, the angel saying, among other things, to the Blessed Virgin, "The Holy Spirit will come upon you, and the power of the Most High will overshadow you; therefore the child to be born will be called holy, the Son of God" (Luke 1:35). And also in the baptism of Christ a voice is heard from heaven concerning Christ, saying, "This is my beloved Son" (Matt. 3:17). The Holy Spirit also appeared in the form of a dove (John 1:32). And when the Lord himself commanded the apostles to baptize, he commanded them to baptize "in the name of the Father, and the Son, and the Holy Spirit" (Matt. 28:19). Elsewhere in the Gospel he said: "The Father will send the Holy Spirit in my name" (John 14:26), and again he said: "When the Counselor comes, whom I shall send to you from the Father, even the Spirit of truth, who proceeds from the Father, he will bear witness to me," etc. (John 15:26). In short, we receive the Apostles' Creed because it delivers to us the true faith.

**5.019** HERESIES. Therefore we condemn the Jews and Mohammedans, and all those who blaspheme that sacred and adorable Trinity. We also condemn all heresies and heretics who teach that the Son and Holy Spirit are God in name only, and also that there is something created and subservient, or subordinate to another in the Trinity, and that there is something unequal in it, a greater or a less, something corporeal or corporeally conceived, something different with respect to character or will, something mixed or solitary, as if the Son and Holy Spirit were the affections and properties of one God the Father, as the Monarchians, Noëtiani, Praxeas, Patripassians, Sabellius, Paul of Samosata, Aëtius, Macedonius, Anthropomorphites, Arius, and such like, have thought.

## CHAPTER IV

### Of Idols or Images of God, Christ and the Saints

**5.020** IMAGES OF GOD. Since God as Spirit is in essence invisible and immense, he cannot really be expressed by any art or image. For this reason we have no fear pronouncing with Scripture that images of God are mere lies. Therefore we reject not only the idols of the Gentiles, but also the images of Christians. IMAGES OF CHRIST. Although Christ assumed human nature, yet he did not on that account assume it in order to provide a model for carvers and painters. He denied that he had come "to abolish the law and the prophets" (Matt. 5:17). But images are forbidden by the law and the prophets (Deut. 4:15; Isa. 44:9). He denied that his bodily presence would be profitable for the Church, and promised that he would be near us by his Spirit forever (John 16:7). Who, therefore, would believe that a shadow or likeness of his body would contribute any benefit to the pious? (II Cor. 5:5). Since he abides in us by his Spirit, we are therefore the temple of God (I Cor. 3:16). But "what agreement has the temple of God with idols?" (II Cor. 6:16). IMAGES OF SAINTS. And since the blessed spirits and saints in heaven, while they lived here on earth, rejected all worship of themselves (Acts 3:12f.; 14:11ff.; Rev. 14:7; 22:9) and condemned images, shall anyone find it likely that the heavenly saints and angels are pleased with their own images before which men kneel, uncover their heads, and bestow other honors?

5.021 But in fact in order to instruct men in religion and to remind them of divine things and of their salvation, the Lord commanded the preaching of the Gospel (Mark 16:15)—not to paint and to teach the laity by means of pictures. Moreover, he instituted sacraments, but nowhere did he set up images. THE SCRIPTURES OF THE LAITY. Furthermore, wherever we turn our eyes, we see the living and true creatures of God which, if they be observed, as is proper, make a much more vivid impression on the beholders than all the images or vain, motionless, feeble and dead pictures made by men, of which the prophet truly said: "They have eyes, but do not see" (Ps. 115:5).

5.022 LACTANTIUS. Therefore we approved the judgment of Lactantius, an ancient writer, who says: "Undoubtedly no religion exists where there is an image." EPIPHANIUS AND JEROME. We also assert that the blessed bishop Epiphanius did right when, finding on the doors of a church a veil on which was painted a picture supposedly of Christ or some saint, he ripped it down and took it away, because to see a picture of a man hanging in the Church of Christ was contrary to the authority of Scripture. Wherefore he charged that from henceforth no such veils, which were contrary to our religion, should be hung in the Church of Christ, and that rather such questionable things, unworthy of the Church of Christ and the faithful people, should be removed. Moreover, we approve of this opinion of St. Augustine concerning true religion: "Let not the worship of the works of men be a religion for us. For the artists themselves who make such things are better; yet we ought not to worship them" (*De Vera Religione*, cap. 55).

## CHAPTER V

### Of the Adoration, Worship and Invocation of God Through the Only Mediator Jesus Christ

5.023 GOD ALONE IS TO BE ADORED AND WORSHIPPED. We teach that the true God alone is to be adored and worshipped. This honor we impart to none other, according to the commandment of the Lord, "You shall worship the Lord your God and him only shall you serve" (Matt. 4:10). Indeed, all the prophets severely inveighed against the people of Israel whenever they adored and worshipped strange gods, and not the only true God. But we teach that God is to be adored and worshipped as he himself has taught us to worship, namely, "in spirit and in truth" (John 4:23 f.), not with any superstition, but with sincerity, according to his Word; lest at any time he should say to us: "Who has required these things from your hands?" (Isa. 1:12; Jer. 6:20). For Paul also says: "God is not served by human hands, as though he needed anything," etc. (Acts 17:25).

5.024 GOD ALONE IS TO BE INVOKED THROUGH THE MEDIATION OF CHRIST ALONE. In all crises and trials of our life we call upon him alone, and that by the mediation of our only mediator and intercessor, Jesus Christ. For we have been explicitly commanded: "Call upon me in the day of trouble; I will deliver you, and you shall glorify me" (Ps. 1:15). Moreover, we have a most generous promise from the Lord who said: "If you ask anything of the Father, he will give it to you" (John 16:23), and: "Come to me, all who labor and are heavy laden and I will give you rest" (Matt 11:28). And since it is written: "How are men to call upon him in whom they have not believed?" (Rom. 10:14), and since we do believe in God alone, we assuredly call upon him alone, and we do so through Christ. For as the apostle says, "There is one God and there is one mediator between God and men, the man Christ Jesus" (I Tim. 2:5), and, "If any one does sin, we have an advocate with the Father, Jesus Christ the righteous," etc. (I John 2:1).

5.025 THE SAINTS ARE NOT TO BE ADORED, WORSHIPPED OR INVOKED. For this reason we do not adore, worship, or pray to the saints in heaven, or to other gods, and we do not acknowledge them as our intercessors or mediators before the Father in heaven. For God and Christ the Mediator are sufficient for us; neither do we give to others the honor that is due to God alone and to his Son, because he has expressly said: "My glory I give to no other" (Isa. 42:8), and because Peter has said: "There is no other name under heaven given among men by which we must be saved," except the name of Christ (Acts 4:12). In him, those who give their assent by faith do not seek anything outside Christ.

5.026 THE DUE HONOR TO BE RENDERED TO THE SAINTS. At the same time we do not despise the saints or think basely of them. For we acknowledge them to be living members of Christ and friends of God who have gloriously overcome the flesh and the world. Hence we love them as brothers, and also honor them; yet not with any kind of worship but by an honorable opinion of them and just praises of them. We also imitate them. For with ardent longings and supplications we earnestly desire to be imitators of their faith and virtues, to share eternal salvation with them, to dwell eternally with them in the presence of God, and to rejoice with them in Christ. And in this respect we approve of the opinion of St. Augustine in *De Vera Religione*: "Let not our religion be the cult of men who have died. For if they have lived holy lives, they are not to be thought of as seeking such honors; on the contrary, they want us to worship him by whose illumination they rejoice that we are fellow-servants of his merits. They are therefore to be honored by way of imitation, but not to be adored in a religious manner," etc.

5.027 RELICS OF THE SAINTS. Much less do we believe that the relics of the saints are to be adored and reverenced. Those ancient saints seemed to have sufficiently honored their dead when they decently committed their remains to the earth after the spirit had ascended on high. And they thought that the most noble relics of their ancestors were their virtues, their doctrine, and their faith. Moreover, as they commend these "relics" when praising the dead, so they strive to copy them during their life on earth.

5.028 SWEARING BY GOD'S NAME ALONE. These ancient men did not swear except by the name of the only God, Yahweh, as prescribed by the divine law. Therefore, as it is forbidden to swear by the names of strange gods (Ex. 23:13; Deut. 10:20), so we do not perform oaths to the saints that are demanded of us. We therefore reject in all these matters a doctrine that ascribes much to the saints in heaven.

## CHAPTER VI
### Of The Providence of God

5.029 ALL THINGS ARE GOVERNED BY THE PROVIDENCE OF GOD. We believe that all things in heaven and on earth, and in all creatures, are preserved and governed by the providence of this wise, eternal and almighty God. For David testifies and says: "The Lord is high above all nations, and his glory above the heavens! Who is like the Lord our God, who is seated on high, who looks far down upon the heavens and the earth?" (Ps. 113:4 ff.). Again: "Thou searchest out ... all my ways. Even before a word is on my tongue, lo, O Lord, Thou knowest it altogether" (Ps. 139:3 f.). Paul also testifies and declares: "In him we live and move and have our being" (Acts 17:28), and "from him and through him and to him are all things" (Rom. 11:36). Therefore Augustine most truly and according to Scripture declared in his book *De Agone Christi*, cap. 8, "The Lord said, 'Are not two sparrows sold for a penny? And not one of them will fall to the ground without your Father's will'" (Matt. 10:29). By speaking thus, he wanted to show that what men regard as of least value is governed by God's omnipotence. For he who is the truth says that the birds of the air are fed by him and the lilies of the field are clothed by him; he also says that the hairs of our head are numbered (Matt. 6:26 ff.).

**5.030** THE EPICUREANS. We therefore condemn the Epicureans who deny the providence of God, and all those who blasphemously say that God is busy with the heavens and neither sees nor cares about us and our affairs. David, the royal prophet, also condemned this when he said: "O Lord, how long shall the wicked exult? They say, 'The Lord does not see; the God of Jacob does not perceive.' Understand, O dullest of the people! Fools, when will you be wise? He who planted the ear, does he not hear? He who formed the eye, does he not see?" (Ps. 94:3, 7–9).

**5.031** MEANS NOT TO BE DESPISED. Nevertheless, we do not spurn as useless the means by which divine providence works, but we teach that we are to adapt ourselves to them in so far as they are recommended to us in the Word of God. Wherefore we disapprove of the rash statements of those who say that if all things are managed by the providence of God, then our efforts and endeavors are in vain. It will be sufficient if we leave everything to the governance of divine providence, and we will not have to worry about anything or do anything. For although Paul understood that he sailed under the providence of God who had said to him: "You must bear witness also at Rome" (Acts 23:11), and in addition had given him the promise, "There will be no loss of life among you ... and not a hair is to perish from the head of any of you" (Acts 27:22, 34), yet when the sailors were nevertheless thinking about abandoning ship the same Paul said to the centurion and the soldiers: "Unless these men stay in the ship, you cannot be saved" (Acts 27:31). For God, who has appointed to everything its end, has ordained the beginning and the means by which it reaches its goal. The heathen ascribe things to blind fortune and uncertain chance. But St. James does not want us to say: "Today or tomorrow we will go into such and such a town and trade," but adds: "Instead you ought to say, 'If the Lords wills, we shall live and we shall do this or that'" (James 4:13, 15). And Augustine says: "Everything which to vain men seems to happen in nature by accident, occurs only by his Word, because it happens only at his command" (*Enarrationes in Psalmos* 148). Thus it seemed to happen by mere chance when Saul, while seeking his father's asses, unexpectedly fell in with the prophet Samuel. But previously the Lord had said to the prophet: "Tomorrow I will send to you a man from the land of Benjamin" (I Sam. 9:16).

## CHAPTER VII
### Of the Creation of All Things:
### Of Angels, the Devil, and Man

**5.032** GOD CREATED ALL THINGS. This good and almighty God created all things, both visible and invisible, by his co-eternal Word, and preserves them by his co-eternal Spirit, as David testified when he said: "By the word of the Lord the heavens were made, and all their host by the breath of his mouth" (Ps. 33:6). And, as Scripture says, everything that God had made was very good, and was made for the profit and use of man. Now we assert that all those things proceed from one beginning.

MANICHAEANS AND MARCIONITES. Therefore, we condemn the Manichaeans and Marcionites who impiously imagined two substances and natures, one good, the other evil; also two beginnings and two gods contrary to each other, a good and an evil one.

5.033 OF ANGELS AND THE DEVIL. Among all creatures, angels and men are most excellent. Concerning angels, Holy Scripture declares: "Who makest the winds thy messengers, fire and flame thy ministers" (Ps. 104:4). Also it says: "Are they not all ministering spirits sent forth to serve, for the sake of those who are to obtain salvation?" (Heb. 1:14). Concerning the devil, the Lord Jesus himself testifies: "He was a murderer from the beginning, and has nothing to do with the truth, because there is no truth in him. When he lies, he speaks according to his own nature, for he is a liar and the father of lies" (John 8:44). Consequently we teach that some angels persisted in obedience and were appointed for faithful service to God and men, but others fell of their own free will and were cast into destruction, becoming enemies of all good and of the faithful, etc.

5.034 OF MAN. Now concerning man, Scripture says that in the beginning he was made good according to the image and likeness of God[2]; that God placed him in Paradise and made all things subject to him (Gen., ch. 2). This is what David magnificently sets forth in Psalm 8. Moreover, God gave him a wife and blessed them. We also affirm that man consists of two different substances in one person: an immortal soul which, when separated from the body, neither sleeps nor dies, and a mortal body which will nevertheless be raised up from the dead at the last judgment, in order that then the whole man, either in life or in death, abide forever.

5.035 THE SECTS. We condemn all who ridicule or by subtle arguments cast doubt upon the immortality of souls, or who say that the soul sleeps or is a part of God. In short, we condemn all opinions of all men, however many, that depart from what has been delivered unto us by the Holy Scriptures in the apostolic Church of Christ concerning creation, angels, and demons, and man.

## CHAPTER VIII

### Of Man's Fall, Sin and the Cause of Sin

5.036 THE FALL OF MAN. In the beginning, man was made according to the image of God, in righteousness and true holiness, good and upright. But when at the instigation of the serpent and by his own fault he abandoned goodness and righteousness, he became subject to sin, death and various

---

[2] *Ad imaginem et simulitudinem Dei.*

calamities. And what he became by the fall, that is, subject to sin, death and various calamities, so are all those who have descended from him.

**5.037** SIN. By sin we understand that innate corruption of man which has been derived or propagated in us all from our first parents, by which we, immersed in perverse desires and averse to all good, are inclined to all evil. Full of all wickedness, distrust, contempt and hatred of God, we are unable to do or even to think anything good of ourselves. Moreover, even as we grow older, so by wicked thoughts, words and deeds committed against God's law, we bring forth corrupt fruit worthy of an evil tree (Matt. 12:33 ff.). For this reason by our own deserts, being subject to the wrath of God, we are liable to just punishment, so that all of us would have been cast away by God if Christ, the Deliverer, had not brought us back.

**5.038** DEATH. By death we understand not only bodily death, which all of us must once suffer on account of sins, but also eternal punishment due to our sins and corruption. For the apostle says: "We were dead through trespasses and sins ... and were by nature children of wrath, like the rest of mankind. But God, who is rich in mercy ... even when we were dead through our trespasses, made us alive together with Christ" (Eph. 2:1 ff.). Also: "As sin came into the world through one man and death through sin, and so death spread to all men because all men sinned" (Rom. 5:12).

**5.039** ORIGINAL SIN. We therefore acknowledge that there is original sin in all men. ACTUAL SINS. We acknowledge that all other sins which arise from it are called and truly are sins, no matter by what name they may be called, whether mortal, venial or that which is said to be the sin against the Holy Spirit which is never forgiven (Mark 3:29; I John 5:16). We also confess that sins are not equal; although they arise from the same fountain of corruption and unbelief, some are more serious than others. As the Lord said, it will be more tolerable for Sodom than for the city that rejects the word of the Gospel (Matt. 10:14 f.; 11:20 ff.).

**5.040** THE SECTS. We therefore condemn all who have taught contrary to this, especially Pelagius and all Pelagians, together with the Jovinians who, with the Stoics, regard all sins as equal. In this whole matter we agree with St. Augustine who derived and defended his view from Holy Scriptures. Moreover, we condemn Florinus and Blastus, against whom Irenaeus wrote, and all who make God the author of sin.

**5.041** GOD IS NOT THE AUTHOR OF SIN, AND HOW FAR HE IS SAID TO HARDEN. It is expressly written: "Thou art not a God who delights in wickedness. Thou hatest all evildoers. Thou destroyest those who speak lies" (Ps. 5:4 ff.). And again: "When the devil lies, he speaks according to his own nature, for he is a liar and the father of lies" (John 8:44). Moreover, there is enough sinfulness and corruption in us that it is not necessary for God to infuse into us a new or still greater perversity.

When, therefore, it is said in Scripture that God hardens, blinds and delivers up to a reprobate mind, it is to be understood that God does it by a just judgment as a just Judge and Avenger. Finally, as often as God in Scripture is said or seems to do something evil, it is not thereby said that man does not do evil, but that God permits it and does not prevent it, according to his just judgment, who could prevent it if he wished, or because he turns man's evil into good, as he did in the case of the sin of Joseph's brethren, or because he governs sins lest they break out and rage more than is appropriate. St. Augustine writes in his *Enchiridion*: "What happens contrary to his will occurs, in a wonderful and ineffable way, not apart from his will. For it would not happen if he did not allow it. And yet he does not allow it unwillingly but willingly. But he who is good would not permit evil to be done, unless, being omnipotent, he could bring good out of evil." Thus wrote Augustine.

**5.042** CURIOUS QUESTIONS. Other questions, such as whether God willed Adam to fall, or incited him to fall, or why he did not prevent the fall, and similar questions, we reckon among curious questions (unless perchance the wickedness of heretics or of other churlish men compels us also to explain them out of the Word of God, as the godly teachers of the Church have frequently done), knowing that the Lord forbade man to eat of the forbidden fruit and punished his transgression. We also know that what things are done are not evil with respect to the providence, will, and power of God, but in respect of Satan and our will opposing the will of God.

## CHAPTER IX

### Of Free Will, and Thus of Human Powers

**5.043** In this matter, which has always produced many conflicts in the Church, we teach that a threefold condition or state of man is to be considered. WHAT MAN WAS BEFORE THE FALL. There is the state in which man was in the beginning before the fall, namely, upright and free, so that he could both continue in goodness and decline to evil. However, he declined to evil, and has involved himself and the whole human race in sin and death, as has been said already. WHAT MAN WAS AFTER THE FALL. Then we are to consider what man was after the fall. To be sure, his reason was not taken from him, nor was he deprived of will, and he was not entirely changed into a stone or a tree. But they were so altered and weakened that they no longer can do what they could before the fall. For the understanding is darkened, and the will which was free has become an enslaved will. Now it serves sin, not unwillingly but willingly. And indeed, it is called a will, not an unwill (ing).[3]

---

[3] *Etenim voluntas, non noluntas dicitur.*

**5.044** MAN DOES EVIL BY HIS OWN FREE WILL. Therefore, in regard to evil or sin, man is not forced by God or by the devil but does evil by his own free will, and in this respect he has a most free will. But when we frequently see that the worst crimes and designs of men are prevented by God from reaching their purpose, this does not take away man's freedom in doing evil, but God by his own power prevents what man freely planned otherwise. Thus Joseph's brothers freely determined to get rid of him, but they were unable to do it because something else seemed good to the counsel of God.

**5.045** MAN IS NOT CAPABLE OF GOOD *PER SE*. In regard to goodness and virtue man's reason does not judge rightly of itself concerning divine things. For the evangelical and apostolic Scripture requires regeneration of whoever among us wishes to be saved. Hence our first birth from Adam contributes nothing to our salvation. Paul says: "The unspiritual man does not receive the gifts of the Spirit of God," etc. (I Cor. 2:14). And in another place he denies that we of ourselves are capable of thinking anything good (II Cor. 3:5). Now it is known that the mind or intellect is the guide of the will, and when the guide is blind, it is obvious how far the will reaches. Wherefore, man not yet regenerate has no free will for good, no strength to perform what is good. The Lord says in the Gospel: "Truly, truly, I say to you, everyone who commits sin is a slave to sin" (John 8:34). And the apostle Paul says: "The mind that is set on the flesh is hostile to God; it does not submit to God's law, indeed it cannot" (Rom. 8:7). Yet in regard to earthly things, fallen man is not entirely lacking in understanding.

**5.046** UNDERSTANDING OF THE ARTS. For God in his mercy has permitted the powers of the intellect to remain, though differing greatly from what was in man before the fall. God commands us to cultivate our natural talents, and meanwhile adds both gifts and success. And it is obvious that we make no progress in all the arts without God's blessing. In any case, Scripture refers all the arts to God; and, indeed, the heathen trace the origin of the arts to the gods who invented them.

**5.047** OF WHAT KIND ARE THE POWERS OF THE REGENERATE, AND IN WHAT WAY THEIR WILLS ARE FREE. Finally, we must see whether the regenerate have free wills, and to what extent. In regeneration the understanding is illumined by the Holy Spirit in order that it may understand both the mysteries and the will of God. And the will itself is not only changed by the Spirit, but it is also equipped with faculties so that it wills and is able to do the good of its own accord (Rom. 8:1 ff.) Unless we grant this, we will deny Christian liberty and introduce a legal bondage. But the prophet has God saying: "I will put my law within them, and I will write it upon their hearts" (Jer. 31:33; Ezek. 36:26 f.). The Lord also says in the Gospel: "If the Son makes you free, you will be free indeed" (John 8:36). Paul also writes to the Philippians: "It has been granted to you that for the sake of Christ you should not only believe in him but also suffer for his sake" (Phil. 1:29). Again: "I am sure that he who began a good work in you will bring it to completion at the day of Jesus Christ" (v. 6). Also: "God is at work in you, both to will and to work for his good pleasure" (ch. 2:13).

**5.048** THE REGENERATE WORK NOT ONLY PASSIVELY BUT ACTIVELY. However, in this connection we teach that there are two things to be observed: First, that the regenerate, in choosing and doing good, work not only passively but actively. For they are moved by God that they may do themselves what they do. For Augustine rightly adduces the saying that "God is said to be our helper. But no one can be helped unless he does something." The Manichaeans robbed man of all activity and made him like a stone or a block of wood.

**5.049** THE FREE WILL IS WEAK IN THE REGENERATE. Secondly, in the regenerate a weakness remains. For since sin dwells in us, and in the regenerate the flesh struggles against the Spirit till the end of our lives, they do not easily accomplish in all things what they had planned. These things are confirmed by the apostle in Rom., ch. 7, and Gal., ch. 5. Therefore that free will is weak in us on account of the remnants of the old Adam and of innate human corruption remaining in us until the end of our lives. Meanwhile, since the powers of the flesh and the remnants of the old man are not so efficacious that they wholly extinguish the work of the Spirit, for that reason the faithful are said to be free, yet so that they acknowledge their infirmity and do not glory at all in their free will. For believers ought always to keep in mind what St. Augustine so many times inculcated according to the apostle: "What have you that you did not receive? If then you received it, why do you boast as if it were not a gift?" To this he adds that what we have planned does not immediately come to pass. For the issue of things lies in the hand of God. This is the reason Paul prayed to the Lord to prosper his journey (Rom. 1:10). And this also is the reason the free will is weak.

**5.050** IN EXTERNAL THINGS THERE IS LIBERTY. Moreover, no one denies that in external things both the regenerate and the unregenerate enjoy free will. For man has in common with other living creatures (to which he is not inferior) this nature to will some things and not to will others. Thus he is able to speak or to keep silent, to go out of his house or to remain at home, etc. However, even here God's power is always to be observed, for it was the cause that Balaam could not go as far as he wanted (Num., ch. 24), and Zacharias upon returning from the temple could not speak as he wanted (Luke, ch. 1).

**5.051** HERESIES. In this matter we condemn the Manichaeans who deny that the beginning of evil was for man [created] good, from his free will. We also condemn the Pelagians who assert that an evil man has sufficient free will to do the good that is commanded. Both are refuted by Holy Scripture which says to the former, "God made man upright" and to the latter, "If the Son makes you free, you will be free indeed" (John 8:36).

## CHAPTER X

### Of the Predestination of God and the Election of the Saints

5.052 GOD HAS ELECTED US OUT OF GRACE. From eternity God has freely, and of his mere grace, without any respect to men, predestinated or elected the saints whom he wills to save in Christ, according to the saying of the apostle, "God chose us in him before the foundation of the world" (Eph. 1:4). And again: "Who saved us and called us with a holy calling, not in virtue of our works but in virtue of his own purpose and the grace which he gave us in Christ Jesus ages ago, and now has manifested through the appearing of our Savior Christ Jesus" (II Tim. 1:9 f.).

5.053 WE ARE ELECTED OR PREDESTINATED IN CHRIST. Therefore, although not on account of any merit of ours, God has elected us, not directly, but in Christ, and on account of Christ, in order that those who are now ingrafted into Christ by faith might also be elected. But those who were outside Christ were rejected, according to the word of the apostle, "Examine yourselves, to see whether you are holding to your faith. Test yourselves. Do you not realize that Jesus Christ is in you?—unless indeed you fail to meet the test!" (II Cor. 13:5).

5.054 WE ARE ELECTED FOR A DEFINITE PURPOSE. Finally, the saints are chosen in Christ by God for a definite purpose, which the apostle himself explains when he says, "He chose us in him for adoption that we should be holy and blameless before him in love. He destined us for adoption to be his sons through Jesus Christ that they should be to the praise of the glory of his grace" (Eph. 1:4 ff.).

5.055 WE ARE TO HAVE A GOOD HOPE FOR ALL. And although God knows who are his, and here and there mention is made of the small number of elect, yet we must hope well of all, and not rashly judge any man to be a reprobate. For Paul says to the Philippians, "I thank my God for you all" (now he speaks of the whole Church in Philippi), "because of your fellowship in the Gospel, being persuaded that he who began a good work in you will bring it to completion at the day of Jesus Christ. It is also right that I have this opinion of you all" (Phil. 1:3 ff.).

5.056 WHETHER FEW ARE ELECT. And when the Lord was asked whether there were few that should be saved, he does not answer and tell them that few or many should be saved or damned, but rather he exhorts every man to "strive to enter by the narrow door" (Luke 13:24): as if he should say, It is not for you curiously to inquire about these matters, but rather to endeavor that you may enter into heaven by the straight way.

**5.057** WHAT IN THIS MATTER IS TO BE CONDEMNED. Therefore we do not approve of the impious speeches of some who say, "Few are chosen, and since I do not know whether I am among the number of the few, I will enjoy myself." Others say, "If I am predestinated and elected by God, nothing can hinder me from salvation, which is already certainly appointed for me, no matter what I do. But if I am in the number of the reprobate, no faith or repentance will help me, since the decree of God cannot be changed. Therefore all doctrines and admonitions are useless." Now the saying of the apostle contradicts these men: "The Lord's servant must be ready to teach, instructing those who oppose him, so that if God should grant that they repent to know the truth, they may recover from the snare of the devil, after being held captive by him to do his will" (II Tim. 2:23 ff.).

**5.058** ADMONITIONS ARE NOT IN VAIN BECAUSE SALVATION PROCEEDS FROM ELECTION. Augustine also shows that both the grace of free election and predestination, and also salutary admonitions and doctrines, are to be preached (*Lib. de Dono Perseverantiae*, cap. 14 ff.).

**5.059** WHETHER WE ARE ELECTED. We therefore find fault with those who outside of Christ ask whether they are elected.[4] And what has God decreed concerning them before all eternity? For the preaching of the Gospel is to be heard, and it is to be believed; and it is to be held as beyond doubt that if you believe and are in Christ, you are elected. For the Father has revealed unto us in Christ the eternal purpose of his predestination, as I have just now shown from the apostle in II Tim. 1:9–10. This is therefore above all to be taught and considered, what great love of the Father toward us is revealed to us in Christ. We must hear what the Lord himself daily preaches to us in the Gospel, how he calls and says: "Come to me all who labor and are heavy-laden, and I will give you rest" (Matt. 11:28). "God so loved the world, that he gave his only Son, that whoever believes in him should not perish, but have eternal life" (John 3:16). Also, "It is not the will of my Father that one of these little ones should perish" (Matt. 18:14).

**5.060** Let Christ, therefore be the looking glass, in whom we may contemplate our predestination. We shall have a sufficiently clear and sure testimony that we are inscribed in the Book of Life if we have fellowship with Christ, and he is ours and we are his in true faith.

**5.061** TEMPTATION IN REGARD TO PREDESTINATION. In the temptation in regard to predestination, than which there is scarcely any other more dangerous, we are confronted by the fact that God's promises apply to all the faithful, for he says: "Ask, and everyone who seeks, shall receive" (Luke 11:9 f.). This finally we pray, with the whole Church of God, "Our Father who art in heaven" (Matt. 6:9), both because by bap-

---

[4] Ed. 1568 reads: "whether they are elected from eternity?"

tism we are ingrafted into the body of Christ, and we are often fed in his Church with his flesh and blood unto life eternal. Thereby, being strengthened, we are commanded to work out our salvation with fear and trembling, according to the precept of Paul.

## CHAPTER XI

### Of Jesus Christ, True God and Man, the Only Savior of the World

5.062 CHRIST IS TRUE GOD. We further believe and teach that the Son of God, our Lord Jesus Christ, was predestinated or foreordained from eternity by the Father to be the Savior of the world. And we believe that he was born, not only when he assumed flesh of the Virgin Mary, and not only before the foundation of the world was laid, but by the Father before all eternity in an inexpressible manner. For Isaiah said: "Who can tell his generation?" (Ch. 53:8). And Micah says: "His origin is from of old, from ancient days" (Micah 5:2). And John said in the Gospel: "In the beginning was the Word, and the Word was with God, and the Word was God," etc. (Ch. 1:1). Therefore, with respect to his divinity the Son is coequal and consubstantial with the Father; true God (Phil. 2:11), not only in name or by adoption or by any merit, but in substance and nature, as the apostle John has often said: "This is the true God and eternal life" (I John 5:20). Paul also says: "He appointed the Son the heir of all things, through whom also he created the world. He reflects the glory of God and bears the very stamp of his nature, upholding all things by his word of power" (Heb. 1:2 f.). For in the Gospel the Lord himself said: "Father, glorify Thou me in Thy own presence with the glory which I had with Thee before the world was made" (John 17:5). And in another place in the Gospel it is written: "The Jews sought all the more to kill him because he ... called God his Father, making himself equal with God" (John 5:18).

5.063 THE SECTS. We therefore abhor the impious doctrine of Arius and the Arians against the Son of God, and especially the blasphemies of the Spaniard, Michael Servetus, and all his followers, which Satan through them has, as it were, dragged up out of hell and has most audaciously and impiously spread abroad in the world.

5.064 CHRIST IS TRUE MAN, HAVING REAL FLESH. We also believe and teach that the eternal Son of the eternal God was made the Son of man, from the seed of Abraham and David, not from the coitus of a man, as the Ebionites said, but was most chastely conceived by the Holy Spirit and born of the ever virgin Mary, as the evangelical history carefully explains to us (Matt., ch. 1). And Paul says: "He took not on him the nature of angels, but of the seed of Abraham." Also the apostle John says that whoever does not believe that Jesus Christ has come in the flesh, is not of

God. Therefore, the flesh of Christ was neither imaginary nor brought from heaven, as Valentinus and Marcion wrongly imagined.

**5.065** A RATIONAL SOUL IN CHRIST. Moreover, our Lord Jesus Christ did not have a soul bereft of sense and reason, as Apollinaris thought, nor flesh without a soul, as Eunomius taught, but a soul with its reason, and flesh with its senses, by which in the time of his passion he sustained real bodily pain, as he himself testified when he said: "My soul is very sorrowful, even to death" (Matt. 26:38). And, "Now is my soul troubled" (John 12:27).

**5.066** TWO NATURES IN CHRIST. We therefore acknowledge two natures or substances, the divine and the human, in one and the same Jesus Christ our Lord (Heb., ch. 2). And we say that these are bound and united with one another in such a way that they are not absorbed, or confused, or mixed, but are united or joined together in one person—the properties of the natures being unimpaired and permanent.

**5.067** NOT TWO BUT ONE CHRIST. Thus we worship not two but one Christ the Lord. We repeat: one true God and man. With respect to his divine nature he is consubstantial with the Father, and with respect to the human nature he is consubstantial with us men, and like us in all things, sin excepted (Heb. 4:15).

**5.068** THE SECTS. And indeed we detest the dogma of the Nestorians who make two of the one Christ and dissolve the unity of the Person. Likewise we thoroughly execrate the madness of Eutyches and of the Monothelites or Monophysites who destroy the property of the human nature.

**5.069** THE DIVINE NATURE OF CHRIST IS NOT PASSIBLE, AND THE HUMAN NATURE IS NOT EVERYWHERE. Therefore, we do not in anyway teach that the divine nature in Christ has suffered or that Christ according to his human nature is still in this world and thus is everywhere. For neither do we think or teach that the body of Christ ceased to be a true body after his glorification, or was deified, and deified in such a way that it laid aside its properties as regards body and soul, and changed entirely into a divine nature and began to be merely one substance.

**5.070** THE SECTS. Hence we by no means approve of or accept the strained, confused and obscure subtleties of Schwenkfeldt and of similar sophists with their self-contradictory arguments; neither are we Schwenkfeldians.

**5.071** OUR LORD TRULY SUFFERED. We believe, moreover, that our Lord Jesus Christ truly suffered and died for us in the flesh, as Peter says (I Peter 4:1). We abhor the most impious madness of the Jacobites and all the Turks who execrate the suffering of the Lord. At the same time we do not deny that the Lord of glory was crucified for us, according to Paul's words (I Cor. 2:8).

**5.072** IMPARTATION OF PROPERTIES. We piously and reverently accept and use the impartation of properties which is derived from Scripture and which has been used by all antiquity in explaining and reconciling apparently contradictory passages.

**5.073** CHRIST IS TRULY RISEN FROM THE DEAD. We believe and teach that the same Jesus Christ our Lord, in his true flesh in which he was crucified and died, rose again from the dead, and that not another flesh was raised other than the one buried, or that a spirit was taken up instead of the flesh, but that he retained his true body. Therefore, while his disciples thought they saw the spirit of the Lord, he showed them his hands and feet which were marked by the prints of the nails and wounds, and added: "See my hands and my feet, that it is I myself; handle me, and see, for a spirit has not flesh and bones as you see that I have" (Luke 24:39).

**5.074** CHRIST IS TRULY ASCENDED INTO HEAVEN. We believe that our Lord Jesus Christ, in his same flesh, ascended above all visible heavens into the highest heaven, that is, the dwelling-place of God and the blessed ones, at the right hand of God the Father. Although it signifies an equal participation in glory and majesty, it is also taken to be a certain place about which the Lord, speaking in the Gospel, says: "I go to prepare a place for you" (John 14:2). The apostle Peter also says: "Heaven must receive Christ until the time of restoring all things" (Acts 3:21). And from heaven the same Christ will return in judgment, when wickedness will then be at its greatest in the world and when the Antichrist, having corrupted true religion, will fill up all things with superstition and impiety and will cruelly lay waste the Church with bloodshed and flames (Dan., ch. 11). But Christ will come again to claim his own, and by his coming to destroy the Antichrist, and to judge the living and the dead (Acts 17:31). For the dead will rise again (I Thess. 4:14 ff.), and those who on that day (which is unknown to all creatures [Mark 13:32]) will be alive will be changed "in the twinkling of an eye," and all the faithful will be caught up to meet Christ in the air, so that then they may enter with him into the blessed dwelling-places to live forever (I Cor. 15:51 f.). But the unbelievers and ungodly will descend with the devils into hell to burn forever and never to be redeemed from torments (Matt. 25:46).

**5.075** THE SECTS. We therefore condemn all who deny a real resurrection of the flesh (II Tim. 2:18), or who with John of Jerusalem, against whom Jerome wrote, do not have a correct view of the glorification of bodies. We also condemn those who thought that the devil and all the ungodly would at some time be saved, and that there would be an end to punishments. For the Lord has plainly declared: "Their fire is not quenched, and their worm does not die" (Mark 9:44). We further condemn Jewish dreams that there will be a golden age on earth before the Day of Judgment, and that the pious, having subdued all their godless enemies, will possess all the kingdoms of the earth. For evangelical truth in Matt., chs. 24 and 25, and Luke, ch. 18, and apostolic teaching in II Thess., ch. 2, and II Tim., chs. 3 and 4, present something quite different.

**5.076** THE FRUIT OF CHRIST'S DEATH AND RESURRECTION. Further by his passion and death and everything which he did and endured for our sake by his coming in the flesh, our Lord reconciled all the faithful to the heavenly Father, made expiation for sins, disarmed death, overcame damnation and hell, and by his resurrection from the dead brought again and restored life and immortality. For he is our righteousness, life and resurrection, in a word, the fulness and perfection of all the faithful, salvation and all sufficiency. For the apostle says: "In him all the fulness of God was pleased to dwell," and, "You have come to fulness of life in him" (Col. chs. 1 and 2).

**5.077** JESUS CHRIST IS THE ONLY SAVIOR OF THE WORLD, AND THE TRUE AWAITED MESSIAH. For we teach and believe that this Jesus Christ our Lord is the unique and eternal Savior of the human race, and thus of the whole world, in whom by faith are saved all who before the law, under the law, and under the Gospel were saved, and however many will be saved at the end of the world. For the Lord himself says in the Gospel: "He who does not enter the sheepfold by the door but climbs in by another way, that man is a thief and a robber. ... I am the door of the sheep" (John 10:1 and 7). And also in another place in the same Gospel he says: "Abraham saw my day and was glad" (ch. 8:56). The apostle Peter also says: "There is salvation in no one else, for there is no other name under heaven given among men by which we must be saved." We therefore believe that we will be saved through the grace of our Lord Jesus Christ, as our fathers were (Acts 4:12, 10:43; 15:11). For Paul also says: "All our fathers ate the same spiritual food, and all drank the same spiritual drink. For they drank from the spiritual Rock which followed them, and the Rock was Christ" (I Cor. 10:3 f.). And thus we read that John says: "Christ was the Lamb which was slain from the foundation of the world" (Rev. 13:8), and John the Baptist testified that Christ is that "Lamb of God, who takes away the sin of the world" (John 1:29). Wherefore, we quite openly profess and preach that Jesus Christ is the sole Redeemer and Savior of the world, the King and High Priest, the true and awaited Messiah, that holy and blessed one whom all the types of the law and predictions of the prophets prefigured and promised; and that God appointed him beforehand and sent him to us, so that we are not now to look for any other. Now there only remains for all of us to give all glory to Christ, believe in him, rest in him alone, despising and rejecting all other aids in life. For however many seek salvation in any other than in Christ alone, have fallen from the grace of God and have rendered Christ null and void for themselves (Gal. 5:4).

**5.078** THE CREEDS OF FOUR COUNCILS RECEIVED. And, to say many things with a few words, with a sincere heart we believe, and freely confess with open mouth, whatever things are defined from the Holy Scriptures concerning the mystery of the incarnation of our Lord Jesus Christ, and are summed up in the Creeds and decrees of the first four most excellent synods convened at Nicaea, Constantinople, Ephesus and Chalcedon—together with the Creed of blessed Athanasius,[5] and all similar symbols; and we condemn everything contrary to these.

**5.079** THE SECTS. And in this way we retain the Christian, orthodox and catholic faith whole and unimpaired; knowing that nothing is contained in the aforesaid symbols which is not agreeable to the Word of God, and does not altogether make for a sincere exposition of the faith.

## CHAPTER XII
## Of the Law of God

**5.080** THE WILL OF GOD IS EXPLAINED FOR US IN THE LAW OF GOD. We teach that the will of God is explained for us in the law of God, what he wills or does not will us to do, what is good and just, or what is evil and unjust. Therefore, we confess that the law is good and holy.

**5.081** THE LAW OF NATURE. And this law was at one time written in the hearts of men by the finger of God (Rom. 2:15), and is called the law of nature (*the law of Moses is in two Tables*), and at another it was inscribed by his finger on the two Tables of Moses, and eloquently expounded in the books of Moses (Ex. 20:1 ff.; Deut. 5:6 ff.). For the sake of clarity we distinguish the moral law which is contained in the Decalogue or two Tables and expounded in the books of Moses, the ceremonial law which determines the ceremonies and worship of God, and the judicial law which is concerned with political and domestic matters.

**5.082** THE LAW IS COMPLETE AND PERFECT. We believe that the whole will of God and all necessary precepts for every sphere of life are taught in this law. For otherwise the Lord would not have forbidden us to add or to take away anything from this law; neither would he have commanded us to walk in a straight path before this law, and not to turn aside from it by turning to the right or to the left (Deut. 4:2; 12:32).

**5.083** WHY THE LAW WAS GIVEN. We teach that this law was not given to men that they might be justified by keeping it, but that rather from what it teaches we may know (our) weakness, sin and condemnation, and, despairing of our strength, might be converted to Christ in faith. For the apostle openly declares: "The law brings wrath," and, "Through

---

[5] The so-called Athanasian Creed was not written by Athanasius but dates from the ninth century. It is also called the "Quicunque" from the opening word of the Latin text.

the law comes knowledge of sin" (Rom. 4:15; 3:20), and, "If a law had been given which could justify or make alive, then righteousness would indeed be by the law. But the Scripture (that is, the law) has concluded all under sin, that the promise which was of the faith of Jesus might be given to those who believe ... Therefore, the law was our schoolmaster unto Christ, that we might be justified by faith" (Gal. 3:21 ff.).

5.084 THE FLESH DOES NOT FULFIL THE LAW. For no flesh could or can satisfy the law of God and fulfil it, because of the weakness in our flesh which adheres and remains in us until our last breath. For the apostle says again: "God has done what the law, weakened by the flesh, could not do: sending his own Son in the likeness of sinful flesh and for sin" (Rom. 8:3). Therefore, Christ is the perfecting of the law and our fulfilment of it (Rom. 10:4), who, in order to take away the curse of the law, was made a curse for us (Gal. 3:13). Thus he imparts to us through faith his fulfilment of the law, and righteousness and obedience are imputed to us.

5.085 HOW FAR THE LAW IS ABROGATED. The law of God is therefore abrogated to the extent that it no longer condemns us, nor works wrath in us. For we are under grace and not under the law. Moreover, Christ has fulfilled all the figures of the law. Hence, with the coming of the body, the shadows ceased, so that in Christ we now have the truth and all fulness. But yet we do not on that account contemptuously reject the law. For we remember the words of the Lord when he said: "I have not come to abolish the law and the prophets but to fulfil them" (Matt. 5:17). We know that in the law is delivered to us the patterns of virtues and vices. We know that the written law when explained by the Gospel is useful to the Church, and that therefore its reading is not to be banished from the Church. For although Moses' face was covered with a veil, yet the apostle says that the veil has been taken away and abolished by Christ. THE SECTS. We condemn everything that heretics old and new have taught against the law.

## CHAPTER XIII
### Of the Gospel of Jesus Christ,
### of the Promises, and of the Spirit and Letter

5.086 THE ANCIENTS HAD EVANGELICAL PROMISES. The Gospel is, indeed, opposed to the law. For the law works wrath and announces a curse, whereas the Gospel preaches grace and blessing. John says: "For the law was given through Moses; grace and truth came through Jesus Christ" (John 1:17). Yet notwithstanding it is most certain that those who were before the law and under the law, were not altogether destitute of the Gospel. For they had extraordinary evangelical promises such as these are: "The seed of the woman shall bruise the serpent's head" (Gen. 3:15). "In thy seed shall all the nations of the earth be blessed" (Gen. 22:18). "The scepter shall not depart from Judah ... until he comes" (Gen. 49:10). "The Lord will raise up a prophet from among his own brethren" (Deut. 18:15; Acts 3:22), etc.

**5.087** THE PROMISES TWOFOLD. And we acknowledge that two kinds of promises were revealed to the fathers, as also to us. For some were of present or earthly things, such as the promises of the Land of Canaan and of victories, and as the promise today still of daily bread. Others were then and are still now of heavenly and eternal things, namely, divine grace, remission of sins, and eternal life through faith in Jesus Christ.

**5.088** THE FATHERS ALSO HAD NOT ONLY CARNAL BUT SPIRITUAL PROMISES. Moreover, the ancients had not only external and earthly but also spiritual and heavenly promises in Christ. Peter says: "The prophets who prophesied of the grace that was to be yours searched and inquired about this salvation" (I Peter 1:10). Wherefore the apostle Paul also said: "The Gospel of God was promised beforehand through his prophets in the holy scriptures" (Rom. 1:2). Thereby it is clear that the ancients were not entirely destitute of the whole Gospel.

**5.089** WHAT IS THE GOSPEL PROPERLY SPEAKING? And although our fathers had the Gospel in this way in the writings of the prophets by which they attained salvation in Christ through faith, yet the Gospel is properly called glad and joyous news, in which, first by John the Baptist, then by Christ the Lord himself, and afterwards by the apostles and their successors, is preached to us in the world that God has now performed what he promised from the beginning of the world, and has sent, nay more, has given us his only Son and in him reconciliation with the Father, the remission of sins, all fulness and everlasting life. Therefore, the history delineated by the four Evangelists and explaining how these things were done or fulfilled by Christ, what things Christ taught and did, and that those who believe in him have all fulness, is rightly called the Gospel. The preaching and writings of the apostles, in which the apostles explain for us how the Son was given to us by the Father, and in him everything that has to do with life and salvation, is also rightly called evangelical doctrine, so that not even today, if sincerely preached, does it lose its illustrious title.

**5.090** OF THE SPIRIT AND THE LETTER. That same preaching of the Gospel is also called by the apostle "the spirit" and "the ministry of the spirit" because by faith it becomes effectual and living in the ears, nay more, in the hearts of believers through the illumination of the Holy Spirit (II Cor. 3:6). For the letter, which is opposed to the Spirit, signifies everything external, but especially the doctrine of the law which, without the Spirit and faith, works wrath and provokes sin in the minds of those who do not have a living faith. For this reason the apostle calls it "the ministry of death." In this connection the saying of the apostle is pertinent: "The letter kills, but the Spirit gives life." And false apostles preached a corrupted Gospel, having combined it with the law, as if Christ could not save without the law.

**5.091** THE SECTS. Such were the Ebionites said to be, who were descended from Ebion the heretic, and the Nazarites who were formerly called Mineans. All these we condemn, while preaching the pure Gospel and teaching that believers are justified by the Spirit alone,[6] and not by the law. A more detailed exposition of this matter will follow presently under the heading of justification.

**5.092** THE TEACHING OF THE GOSPEL IS NOT NEW, BUT MOST ANCIENT DOCTRINE. And although the teaching of the Gospel, compared with the teaching of the Pharisees concerning the law, seemed to be a new doctrine when first preached by Christ (which Jeremiah also prophesied concerning the New Testament), yet actually it not only was and still is an old doctrine (even if today it is called new by the Papists when compared with the teaching now received among them), but is the most ancient of all in the world. For God predestinated from eternity to save the world through Christ, and he has disclosed to the world through the Gospel this his predestination and eternal counsel (II Tim. 2:9 f.). Hence it is evident that the religion and teaching of the Gospel among all who ever were, are and will be, is the most ancient of all. Wherefore we assert that all who say that the religion and teaching of the Gospel is a faith which has recently arisen, being scarcely thirty years old, err disgracefully and speak shamefully of the eternal counsel of God. To them applies the saying of Isaiah the prophet: "Woe to those who call evil good and good evil, who put darkness for light and light for darkness, who put bitter for sweet and sweet for bitter!" (Isa. 5:20).

## CHAPTER XIV

### Of Repentance and the Conversion of Man

**5.093** The doctrine of repentance is joined with the Gospel. For so has the Lord said in the Gospel: "Repentance and forgiveness of sins should be preached in my name to all nations" (Luke 24:27). WHAT IS REPENTANCE? By repentance we understand (1) the recovery of a right mind in sinful man awakened by the Word of the Gospel and the Holy Spirit, and received by true faith, by which the sinner immediately acknowledges his innate corruption and all his sins accused by the Word of God; and (2) grieves for them from his heart, and not only bewails and frankly confesses them before God with a feeling of shame, but also (3) with indignation abominates them; and (4) now zealously considers the amendment of his ways and constantly strives for innocence and virtue in which conscientiously to exercise himself all the rest of his life.

---

[6] The original manuscript has "Christ" instead of "Spirit."

**5.094** TRUE REPENTANCE IS CONVERSION TO GOD. And this is true repentance, namely, a sincere turning to God and all good, and earnest turning away from the devil and all evil. 1. REPENTANCE IS A GIFT OF GOD. Now we expressly say that this repentance is a sheer gift of God and not a work of our strength. For the apostle commands a faithful minister diligently to instruct those who oppose the truth, if "God may perhaps grant that they will repent and come to know the truth" (II Tim. 2:25). 2. LAMENTS SINS COMMITTED. Now that sinful woman who washed the feet of the Lord with her tears, and Peter who wept bitterly and bewailed his denial of the Lord (Luke 7:38; 22:62) show clearly how the mind of a penitent man ought to be seriously lamenting the sins he has committed. 3. CONFESSES SINS TO GOD. Moreover, the prodigal son and the publican in the Gospel, when compared with the Pharisee, present us with the most suitable pattern of how our sins are to be confessed to God. The former said: " 'Father, I have sinned against heaven and before you; I am no longer worthy to be called your son; treat me as one of your hired servants' " (Luke 15:8 ff.). And the latter, not daring to raise his eyes to heaven, beat his breast, saying, "God be merciful to me a sinner" (ch. 18:13). And we do not doubt that they were accepted by God into grace. For the apostle John says: "If we confess our sins, he is faithful and just, and will forgive our sins and cleanse us from all unrighteousness. If we say we have not sinned, we make him a liar, and his word is not in us" (I John 1:9 f.).

**5.095** SACERDOTAL CONFESSION AND ABSOLUTION. But we believe that this sincere confession which is made to God alone, either privately between God and the sinner, or publicly in the Church where the general confession of sins is said, is sufficient, and that in order to obtain forgiveness of sins it is not necessary for anyone to confess his sins to a priest, murmuring them in his ears, that in turn he might receive absolution from the priest with his laying on of hands, because there is neither a commandment nor an example of this in Holy Scriptures. David testifies and says: "I acknowledged my sin to thee, and did not hide my iniquity; I said, 'I will confess my transgressions to the Lord'; then thou didst forgive the guilt of my sin" (Ps. 32:5). And the Lord who taught us to pray and at the same time to confess our sins said: "Pray then like this: Our Father, who art in heaven, ... forgive us our debts, as we also forgive our debtors" (Matt. 6:12). Therefore it is necessary that we confess our sins to God our Father, and be reconciled with our neighbor if we have offended him. Concerning this kind of confession, the Apostle James says: "Confess your sins to one another" (James 5:16). If, however, anyone is overwhelmed by the burden of his sins and by perplexing temptations, and will seek counsel, instruction and comfort privately, either from a minister of the Church, or from any other brother who is instructed in God's law, we do not disapprove; just as we also fully approve of that general and public confession of sins which is usually said in Church and in meetings for worship, as we noted above, inasmuch as it is agreeable to Scripture.

**5.096** OF THE KEYS OF THE KINGDOM OF HEAVEN. Concerning the keys of the Kingdom of Heaven which the Lord gave to the apostles, many babble many astonishing things, and out of them forge swords, spears, scepters and crowns, and complete power over the greatest kingdoms, indeed, over souls and bodies. Judging simply according to the Word of the Lord, we say that all properly called ministers possess and exercise the keys or the use of them when they proclaim the Gospel; that is, when they teach, exhort, comfort, rebuke, and keep in discipline the people committed to their trust.

**5.097** OPENING AND SHUTTING (THE KINGDOM). For in this way they open the Kingdom of Heaven to the obedient and shut it to the disobedient. The Lord promised these keys to the apostles in Matt., ch. 16, and gave them in John, ch. 20, Mark, ch. 16, and Luke, ch. 24, when he sent out his disciples and commanded them to preach the Gospel in all the world, and to remit sins.

**5.098** THE MINISTRY OF RECONCILIATION. In the letter to the Corinthians the apostle says that the Lord gave the ministry of reconciliation to his ministers (II Cor. 5:18 ff.). And what this is he then explains, saying that it is the preaching or teaching of reconciliation. And explaining his words still more clearly he adds that Christ's ministers discharge the office of an ambassador in Christ's name, as if God himself through ministers exhorted the people to be reconciled to God, doubtless by faithful obedience. Therefore, they exercise the keys when they persuade [men] to believe and repent. Thus they reconcile men to God.

**5.099** MINISTERS REMIT SINS. Thus they remit sins. Thus they open the Kingdom of Heaven, and bring believers into it: very different from those of whom the Lord said in the Gospel, "Woe to you lawyers! for you have taken away the key of knowledge; you did not enter yourselves, and you hindered those who were entering."

**5.100** HOW MINISTERS ABSOLVE. Ministers, therefore, rightly and effectually absolve when they preach the Gospel of Christ and thereby the remission of sins, which is promised to each one who believes, just as each one is baptized, and when they testify that it pertains to each one peculiarly. Neither do we think that this absolution becomes more effectual by being murmured in the ear of someone or by being murmured singly over someone's head. We are nevertheless of the opinion that the remission of sins in the blood of Christ is to be diligently proclaimed, and that each one is to be admonished that the forgiveness of sins pertains to him.

**5.101** DILIGENCE IN THE RENEWAL OF LIFE. But the examples in the Gospel teach us how vigilant and diligent the penitent ought to be in striving for newness of life and in mortifying the old man and quickening the new. For the Lord said to the man he healed of palsy: "See, you are well! Sin no more, that nothing worse befall you" (John 5:14). Likewise to the adulteress whom he set free he said: "Go, and sin no more" (ch. 8:11). To be sure, by these words he did not mean that any man, as long as he lived in the flesh, could not sin; he simply recommends diligence and a careful devotion, so that we should strive by all means, and beseech God in prayers lest we fall back into sins from which, as it were, we have been resurrected, and lest we be overcome by the flesh, the world and the devil. Zacchaeus the publican, whom the Lord had received back into favor, exclaims in the Gospel: "Behold, Lord, the half of my goods I give to the poor; and if I have defrauded any one of anything, I restore it fourfold" (Luke 19:8). Therefore, in the same way we preach that restitution and compassion, and even almsgiving, are necessary for those who truly repent, and we exhort all men everywhere in the words of the apostle: "Let not sin therefore reign in your mortal bodies, to make you obey their passions. Do not yield your members to sin as instruments of wickedness, but yield yourselves to God as men who have been brought from death to life, and your members to God as instruments of righteousness" (Rom. 6:12 f.).

**5.102** ERRORS. Wherefore we condemn all impious utterances of some who wrongly use the preaching of the Gospel and say that it is easy to return to God. Christ has atoned for all sins. Forgiveness of sins is easy. Therefore, what harm is there in sinning? Nor need we be greatly concerned about repentance, etc. Notwithstanding we always teach that an access to God is open to all sinners, and that he forgives all sinners of all sins except the one sin against the Holy Spirit (Mark 3:29).

**5.103** THE SECTS. Wherefore we condemn both old and new Navatianos and Catharists.

**5.104** PAPAL INDULGENCES. We especially condemn the lucrative doctrine of the Pope concerning penance, and against his simony and his simoniacal indulgences we avail ourselves of Peter's judgment concerning Simon: "Your silver perish with you, because you thought you could obtain the gift of God with money! You have neither part nor lot in this matter, for your heart is not right before God" (Acts 8:20 f.).

**5.105** SATISFACTIONS. We also disapprove of those who think that by their own satisfactions they make amends for sins committed. For we teach that Christ alone by his death or passion is the satisfaction, propitiation or expiation of all sins (Isa., ch. 53; I Cor. 1:30). Yet as we have already said, we do not cease to urge the mortification of the flesh. We add, however, that this mortification is not to be proudly obtruded upon God as a satisfaction for sins, but is to be performed humbly, in keeping with the nature of the children of God, as a new obedience out of gratitude for the deliverance and full satisfaction obtained by the death and satisfaction of the Son of God.

## CHAPTER XV

### Of the True Justification of the Faithful

**5.106** WHAT IS JUSTIFICATION? According to the apostle in his treatment of justification, to justify means to remit sins, to absolve from guilt and punishment, to receive into favor, and to pronounce a man just. For in his epistle to the Romans the apostle says: "It is God who justifies; who is to condemn?" (Rom. 8:33). To justify and to condemn are opposed. And in The Acts of the Apostles the apostle states: "Through Christ forgiveness of sins is proclaimed to you, and by him everyone that believes is freed from everything from which you could not be freed by the law of Moses" (Acts 13:38 f.). For in the Law and also in the Prophets we read: "If there is a dispute between men, and they come into court ... the judges decide between them, acquitting the innocent and condemning the guilty" (Deut. 25:1). And in Isa., ch. 5: "Woe to those ... who acquit the guilty for a bribe."

**5.107** WE ARE JUSTIFIED ON ACCOUNT OF CHRIST. Now it is most certain that all of us are by nature sinners and godless, and before God's judgment-seat are convicted of godlessness and are guilty of death, but that, solely by the grace of Christ and not from any merit of ours or consideration for us, we are justified, that is, absolved from sin and death by God the Judge. For what is clearer than what Paul said: "Since all have sinned and fall short of the glory of God, they are justified by his grace as a gift, through the redemption which is in Christ Jesus" (Rom. 3:23 f.).

**5.108** IMPUTED RIGHTEOUSNESS. For Christ took upon himself and bore the sins of the world, and satisfied divine justice. Therefore, solely on account of Christ's sufferings and resurrection God is propitious with respect to our sins and does not impute them to us, but imputes Christ's righteousness to us as our own (II Cor. 5:19 ff.; Rom. 4:25), so that now we are not only cleansed and purged from sins or are holy, but also, granted the righteousness of Christ, and so absolved from sin, death and condemnation, are at last righteous and heirs of eternal life. Properly speaking, therefore, God alone justifies us, and justifies only on account of Christ, not imputing sins to us but imputing his righteousness to us.

**5.109** WE ARE JUSTIFIED BY FAITH ALONE. But because we receive this justification, not through any works, but through faith in the mercy of God and in Christ, we therefore teach and believe with the apostle that sinful man is justified by faith alone in Christ, not by the law or any works. For the apostle says: "We hold that a man is justified by faith apart from works of law" (Rom. 3:28). Also: "If Abraham was justified by works, he has something to boast about, but not before God. For what does the scripture say? Abraham believed God, and it was reckoned to him as righteousness. ... And to one who does not work but believes in him who justified the ungodly, his faith is reckoned as righteousness" (Rom. 4:2 ff.; Gen. 15:6). And again: "By grace you have been saved through faith; and this is not your own doing, it is the gift of God—not because of works, lest any man should boast," etc. (Eph. 2:8 f.). Therefore, because faith receives Christ our righteousness and attributes everything to the grace of God in Christ, on that account justification is attributed to faith, chiefly because of Christ and not therefore because it is our work. For it is the gift of God.

**5.110** WE RECEIVE CHRIST BY FAITH. Moreover, the Lord abundantly shows that we receive Christ by faith, in John, ch. 6, where he puts eating for believing, and believing for eating. For as we receive food by eating, so we participate in Christ by believing. JUSTIFICATION IS NOT ATTRIBUTED PARTLY TO CHRIST OR TO FAITH, PARTLY TO US. Therefore, we do not share in the benefit of justification partly because of the grace of God or Christ, and partly because of ourselves, our love, works or merit, but we attribute it wholly to the grace of God in Christ through faith. For our love and our works could not please God if performed by unrighteous men. Therefore, it is necessary for us to be righteous before we may love and do good works. We are made truly righteous, as we have said, by faith in Christ purely by the grace of God, who does not impute to us our sins, but the righteousness of Christ, or rather, he imputes faith in Christ to us for righteousness. Moreover, the apostle very clearly derives love from faith when he says: "The aim of our command is love that issues from a pure heart, a good conscience, and a sincere faith" (I Tim. 1:5).

**5.111** JAMES COMPARED WITH PAUL. Wherefore, in this matter we are not speaking of a fictitious, empty, lazy and dead faith, but of a living, quickening faith. It is and is called a living faith because it apprehends Christ who is life and makes alive, and shows that it is alive by living works. And so James does not contradict anything in this doctrine of ours. For he speaks of an empty, dead faith of which some boasted but who did not have Christ living in them by faith (James 2:14 ff.). James said that works justify, yet without contradicting the apostle (otherwise he would have to be rejected) but showing that Abraham proved his living and justifying faith by works. This all the pious do, but they trust in Christ alone and not in their own works. For again the apostle said: "It is no longer I who live, but Christ who lives in me; and the life I now live in the flesh I live by faith in the Son of God,[7] who loved me and gave himself for me. I do not reject the grace of God; for if justification were through the law, then Christ died to no purpose," etc. (Gal. 2:20 f.).

---

[7] The Latin reads: "by the faith of the Son of God."

## CHAPTER XVI

## Of Faith and Good Works, and of Their Reward, and of Man's Merit

**5.112** WHAT IS FAITH? Christian faith is not an opinion or human conviction, but a most firm trust and a clear and steadfast assent of the mind, and then a most certain apprehension of the truth of God presented in the Scriptures and in the Apostles' Creed, and thus also of God himself, the greatest good, and especially of God's promise and of Christ who is the fulfilment of all promises.

**5.113** FAITH IS THE GIFT OF GOD. But this faith is a pure gift of God which God alone of his grace gives to his elect according to his measure when, to whom and to the degree he wills. And he does this by the Holy Spirit by means of the preaching of the Gospel and steadfast prayer. THE INCREASE OF FAITH. This faith also has its increase, and unless it were given by God, the apostles would not have said: "Lord, increase our faith" (Luke 17:5). And all these things which up to this point we have said concerning faith, the apostles have taught before us. For Paul said: "For faith is the ὑπόστασις or sure subsistence, of things hoped for, and the ἔλεγχος, that is, the clear and certain apprehension" (Heb. 11:1). And again he says that all the promises of God are Yes through Christ and through Christ are Amen (II Cor. 1:20). And to the Philippians he said that it has been given to them to believe in Christ (Phil. 1:29). Again, God assigned to each the measure of faith (Rom. 12:3). Again: "Not all have faith" and, "Not all obey the Gospel" (II Thess. 3:2; Rom. 10:16). But Luke also bears witness, saying: "As many as were ordained to life believed" (Acts 13:48). Wherefore Paul also calls faith "the faith of God's elect" (Titus 1:1), and again: "Faith comes from hearing, and hearing comes by the Word of God" (Rom. 10:17). Elsewhere he often commands men to pray for faith.

**5.114** FAITH EFFICACIOUS AND ACTIVE. The same apostle calls faith efficacious and active through love (Gal. 5:6). It also quiets the conscience and opens a free access to God, so that we may draw near to him with confidence and may obtain from him what is useful and necessary. The same [faith] keeps us in the service we owe to God and our neighbor, strengthens our patience in adversity, fashions and makes a true confession, and in a word, brings forth good fruit of all kinds, and good works.

**5.115** CONCERNING GOOD WORKS. For we teach that truly good works grow out of a living faith by the Holy Spirit and are done by the faithful according to the will or rule of God's Word. Now the apostle Peter says: "Make every effort to supplement your faith with virtue, and virtue with knowledge, and knowledge with self-control," etc. (II Peter 1:5 ff.). But we have said above that the law of God, which is his will, prescribes for us the pattern of good works. And the apostle says: "This is the will of

God, your sanctification, that you abstain from immorality ... that no man transgress, and wrong his brother in business" (I Thess. 4:3 ff.).

**5.116** WORKS OF HUMAN CHOICE. And indeed works and worship which we choose arbitrarily are not pleasing to God. These Paul calls θλεέοθρησκείας (Col. 2:23—"self-devised worship"). Of such the Lord says in the Gospel: "In vain do they worship me, teaching as doctrines the precepts of men" (Matt. 15:9). Therefore, we disapprove of such works, and approve and urge those that are of God's will and commission.

**5.117** THE END OF GOOD WORKS. These same works ought not to be done in order that we may earn eternal life by them, for, as the apostle says, eternal life is the gift of God. Nor are they to be done for ostentation which the Lord rejects in Matt., ch. 6, nor for gain which he also rejects in Matt., ch. 23, but for the glory of God, to adorn our calling, to show gratitude to God, and for the profit of the neighbor. For our Lord says again in the Gospel: "Let your light so shine before men, that they may see your good works and give glory to your Father who is in heaven" (Matt. 5:16). And the apostle Paul says: "Lead a life worthy of the calling to which you have been called" (Eph. 4:1). Also: "And whatever you do, in word or deed, do everything in the name of the Lord Jesus, giving thanks to God and to the Father through him" (Col. 3:17), and, "Let each of you look not to his own interests, but to the interests of others" (Phil. 2:4), and, "Let our people learn to apply themselves to good deeds, so as to help cases of urgent need, and not to be unfruitful" (Titus 3:14).

**5.118** GOOD WORKS NOT REJECTED. Therefore, although we teach with the apostle that a man is justified by grace through faith in Christ and not through any good works, yet we do not think that good works are of little value and condemn them. We know that man was not created or regenerated through faith in order to be idle, but rather that without ceasing he should do those things which are good and useful. For in the Gospel the Lord says that a good tree brings forth good fruit (Matt. 12:33), and that he who abides in me bears much fruit (John 15:5). The apostle says: "For we are his workmanship, created in Christ Jesus for good works, which God prepared beforehand, that we should walk in them" (Eph. 2:10), and again: "Who gave himself for us to redeem us from all iniquity and to purify for himself a people of his own who are zealous for good deeds" (Titus 2:14). We therefore condemn all who despise good works and who babble that they are useless and that we do not need to pay attention to them.

**5.119** WE ARE NOT SAVED BY GOOD WORKS. Nevertheless, as was said above, we do not think that we are saved by good works, and that they are so necessary for salvation that no one was ever saved without them. For we are saved by grace and the favor of Christ alone. Works necessarily proceed from faith. And salvation is improperly attributed to them, but is most properly ascribed to grace. The apostle's sentence is well known: "If it is by grace, then it is no longer of works; otherwise grace would no longer be grace. But if it is of works, then it is no longer grace, because otherwise work is no longer work" (Rom. 11:6).

**5.120** GOOD WORKS PLEASE GOD. Now the works which we do by faith are pleasing to God and are approved by him. Because of faith in Christ, those who do good works which, moreover, are done from God's grace through the Holy Spirit, are pleasing to God. For St. Peter said: "In every nation any one who fears God and does what is right is acceptable to him" (Acts 10:35). And Paul said: "We have not ceased to pray for you ... that you may walk worthily of the Lord, fully pleasing to him, bearing fruit in every good work" (Col. 1:9 f.).

**5.121** WE TEACH TRUE, NOT FALSE AND PHILOSOPHICAL VIRTUES. And so we diligently teach true, not false and philosophical virtues, truly good works, and the genuine service of a Christian. And as much as we can we diligently and zealously press them upon all men, while censuring the sloth and hypocrisy of all those who praise and profess the Gospel with their lips and dishonor it by their disgraceful lives. In this matter we place before them God's terrible threats and then his rich promises and generous rewards—exhorting, consoling and rebuking.

**5.122** GOD GIVES A REWARD FOR GOOD WORKS. For we teach that God gives a rich reward to those who do good works, according to that saying of the prophet: "Keep your voice from weeping, ... for your work shall be rewarded" (Jer. 31:16; Isa., ch. 4). The Lord also said in the Gospel: "Rejoice and be glad, for your reward is great in heaven" (Matt. 5:12), and, "Whoever gives to one of these my little ones a cup of cold water, truly, I say to you, he shall not lose his reward" (ch. 10:42). However, we do not ascribe this reward, which the Lord gives, to the merit of the man who receives it, but to the goodness, generosity and truthfulness of God who promises and gives it, and who, although he owes nothing to anyone, nevertheless promises that he will give a reward to his faithful worshippers; meanwhile he also gives them that they may honor him. Moreover, in the works even of the saints there is much that is unworthy of God and very much that is imperfect. But because God receives into favor and embraces those who do works for Christ's sake, he grants to them the promised reward. For in other respects our righteousnesses are compared to a filthy wrap (Isa. 64:6). And the Lord says in the Gospel: "When you have done all that is commanded you, say, 'We are unworthy servants; we have only done what was our duty'" (Luke 17:10).

**5.123** THERE ARE NO MERITS OF MEN. Therefore, although we teach that God rewards our good deeds, yet at the same time we teach, with Augustine, that God does not crown in us our merits but his gifts. Accordingly we say that whatever reward we receive is also grace, and is more grace than reward, because the good we do, we do more through God than through ourselves, and because Paul says: "What have you that you did not receive? If then you received it, why do you boast as if you had not received it?" (I Cor. 4:7). And this is what the blessed martyr Cyprian concluded from this verse: We are not to glory in anything in us, since nothing is our own. We therefore condemn those who defend the merits of men in such a way that they invalidate the grace of God.

## CHAPTER XVII*
### Of the Catholic and Holy Church of God, and of the One Only Head of the Church

5.124 THE CHURCH HAS ALWAYS EXISTED AND IT WILL ALWAYS EXIST. But because God from the beginning would have men to be saved, and to come to the knowledge of the truth (I Tim. 2:4), it is altogether necessary that there always should have been, and should be now, and to the end of the world, a Church.

5.125 WHAT IS THE CHURCH? The Church is an assembly of the faithful called or gathered out of the world; a communion, I say, of all saints, namely, of those who truly know and rightly worship and serve the true God in Christ the Savior, by the Word and Holy Spirit, and who by faith are partakers of all benefits which are freely offered through Christ. CITIZENS OF ONE COMMONWEALTH. They are all citizens of the one city, living under the same Lord, under the same laws, and in the same fellowship of all good things. For the apostle calls them "fellow citizens with the saints and members of the household of God" (Eph. 2:19), calling the faithful on earth saints (I Cor. 4:1), who are sanctified by the blood of the Son of God. The article of the Creed, "I believe in the holy catholic Church, the communion of saints," is to be understood wholly as concerning these saints.

5.126 ONLY ONE CHURCH FOR ALL TIMES. And since there is always but one God, and there is one mediator between God and men, Jesus the Messiah, and one Shepherd of the whole flock, one Head of this body, and, to conclude, one Spirit, one salvation, one faith, one Testament or covenant, it necessarily follows that there is only one Church. THE CATHOLIC CHURCH. We, therefore, call this Church catholic because it is universal, scattered through all parts of the world, and extended unto all times, and is not limited to any times or places. Therefore, we condemn the Donatists who confined the Church to I know not what corners of Africa. Nor do we approve of the Roman clergy who have recently passed off only the Roman Church as catholic.

---

* See Preface for discussion of our current understanding of such condmenations.

5.127 PARTS OR FORMS OF THE CHURCH. The Church is divided into different parts or forms; not because it is divided or rent asunder in itself, but rather because it is distinguished by the diversity of the numbers that are in it. MILITANT AND TRIUMPHANT. For the one is called the Church Militant, the other the Church Triumphant. The former still wages war on earth, and fights against the flesh, the world, and the prince of this world, the devil; against sin and death. But the latter, having been now discharged, triumphs in heaven immediately after having overcome all those things and rejoices before the Lord. Notwithstanding both have fellowship and union one with another.

5.128 THE PARTICULAR CHURCH. Moreover, the Church Militant upon the earth has always had many particular churches. Yet all these are to be referred to the unity of the catholic Church. This [Militant] Church was set up differently before the Law among the patriarchs; otherwise under Moses by the Law; and differently by Christ through the Gospel.

5.129 THE TWO PEOPLES. Generally two peoples are usually counted, namely, the Israelites and Gentiles, or those who have been gathered from among Jews and Gentiles into the Church. There are also two Testaments, the Old and the New. THE SAME CHURCH FOR THE OLD AND THE NEW PEOPLE. Yet from all these people there was and is one fellowship, one salvation in the one Messiah; in whom, as members of one body under one Head, all united together in the same faith, partaking also of the same spiritual food and drink. Yet here we acknowledge a diversity of times, and a diversity in the signs of the promised and delivered Christ; and that now the ceremonies being abolished, the light shines unto us more clearly, and blessings are given to us more abundantly, and a fuller liberty.

5.130 THE CHURCH THE TEMPLE OF THE LIVING GOD. This holy Church of God is called the temple of the living God, built of living and spiritual stones and founded upon a firm rock, upon a foundation which no other can lay, and therefore it is called "the pillar and bulwark of the truth" (I Tim. 3:15). THE CHURCH DOES NOT ERR. It does not err as long as it rests upon the rock Christ, and upon the foundation of the prophets and apostles. And it is no wonder if it errs, as often as it deserts him who alone is the truth. THE CHURCH AS BRIDE AND VIRGIN. This Church is also called a virgin and the Bride of Christ, and even the only Beloved. For the apostle says: "I betrothed you to Christ to present you as a pure bride to Christ" (II Cor. 11:2). THE CHURCH AS A FLOCK OF SHEEP. The Church is called a flock of sheep under the one shepherd, Christ, according to Ezek., ch. 34, and John, ch. 10. THE CHURCH AS THE BODY. It is also called the body of Christ because the faithful are living members of Christ under Christ the Head.

5.131 CHRIST THE SOLE HEAD OF THE CHURCH. It is the head which has the preeminence in the body, and from it the whole body receives life; by its spirit the body is governed in all things; from it, also, the body receives increase, that it may grow up. Also, there is one head of the body, and it is suited to the body. Therefore the Church cannot have any other head besides Christ. For as the Church is a spiritual body, so it must also have a spiritual head in harmony with itself. Neither can it be governed by any other spirit than by the Spirit of Christ. Wherefore Paul says: "He is the head of the body, the church; he is the beginning, the firstborn from the dead, that in everything he might be preeminent" (Col. 1:18). And in another place: "Christ is the head of the church, his body, and is himself its Savior" (Eph. 5:23). And again: he is "the head over all things for the church, which is his body, the fulness of him who fills all in all" (Eph. 1:22 f.). Also: "We are to grow up in every way into him who is the head, into Christ, from whom the whole body, joined and knit together, makes bodily growth" (Eph. 4:15 f.). And therefore we do not approve of the doctrine of the Roman clergy, who make their Pope at Rome the universal shepherd and supreme head of the Church Militant here on earth, and so the very vicar of Jesus Christ, who has (as they say) all fulness of power and sovereign authority in the Church. CHRIST THE ONLY PASTOR OF THE CHURCH. For we teach that Christ the Lord is, and remains the only universal pastor, the highest Pontiff before God the Father; and that in the Church he himself performs all the duties of a bishop or pastor, even to the world's end; [*Vicar*] and therefore does not need a substitute for one who is absent. For Christ is present with his Church, and is its life-giving Head. NO PRIMACY IN THE CHURCH. He has strictly forbidden his apostles and their successors to have any primacy and dominion in the Church. Who does not see, therefore, that whoever contradicts and opposes this plain truth is rather to be counted among the number of those of whom Christ's apostles prophesied: Peter in II Peter, ch. 2, and Paul in Acts 20:2; II Cor. 11:2; II Thess., ch. 2, and also in other places?

**5.132** NO DISORDER IN THE CHURCH. However, by doing away with a Roman head we do not bring any confusion or disorder into the Church, since we teach that the government of the Church which the apostles handed down is sufficient to keep the Church in proper order. In the beginning when the Church was without any such Roman head as is now said to keep it in order, the Church was not disordered or in confusion. The Roman head does indeed preserve his tyranny and the corruption that has been brought into the Church, and meanwhile he hinders, resists, and with all the strength he can muster cuts off the proper reformation of the Church.

**5.133** DISSENSIONS AND STRIFE IN THE CHURCH. We are reproached because there have been manifold dissensions and strife in our churches since they separated themselves from the Church of Rome, and therefore cannot be true churches. As though there were never in the Church of Rome any sects, nor contentions and quarrels concerning religion, and indeed, carried on not so much in the schools as from pulpits in the midst of the people. We know, to be sure, that the apostle said: "God is not a God of confusion but of peace" (I Cor. 14:33), and, "While there is jealousy and strife among you, are you not of the flesh?" Yet we cannot deny that God was in the apostolic Church and that it was a true Church, even though there were wranglings and dissensions in it. The apostle Paul reprehended Peter, an apostle (Gal. 2:11 ff.), and Barnabas dissented from Paul. Great contention arose in the Church of Antioch between them that preached the one Christ, as Luke records in The Acts of the Apostles, ch. 15. And there have at all times been great contentions in the Church, and the most excellent teachers of the Church have differed among themselves about important matters without meanwhile the Church ceasing to be the Church because of these contentions. For thus it pleases God to use the dissensions that arise in the Church to the glory of his name, to illustrate the truth, and in order that those who are in the right might be manifest (I Cor. 11:19).

5.134  OF THE NOTES OR SIGNS OF THE TRUE CHURCH. Moreover, as we acknowledge no other head of the Church than Christ, so we do not acknowledge every church to be the true Church which vaunts herself to be such; but we teach that the true Church is that in which the signs or marks of the true Church are to be found, especially the lawful and sincere preaching of the Word of God as it was delivered to us in the books of the prophets and the apostles, which all lead us unto Christ, who said in the Gospel: "My sheep hear my voice, and I know them, and they follow me; and I give unto them eternal life. A stranger they do not follow, but they flee from him, for they do not know the voice of strangers" (John 10:5, 27, 28).

5.135  And those who are such in the Church have one faith and one spirit; and therefore they worship but one God, and him alone they worship in spirit and in truth, loving him alone with all their hearts and with all their strength, praying unto him alone through Jesus Christ, the only Mediator and Intercessor; and they do not seek righteousness and life outside Christ and faith in him. Because they acknowledge Christ the only head and foundation of the Church, and, resting on him, daily renew themselves by repentance, and patiently bear the cross laid upon them. Moreover, joined together with all the members of Christ by an unfeigned love, they show that they are Christ's disciples by persevering in the bond of peace and holy unity. At the same time they participate in the sacraments instituted by Christ, and delivered unto us by his apostles, using them in no other way than as they received them from the Lord. That saying of the apostle Paul is well known to all: "I received from the Lord what I also delivered to you" (I Cor. 11:23 ff.). Accordingly, we condemn all such churches as strangers from the true Church of Christ, which are not such as we have heard they ought to be, no matter how much they brag of a succession of bishops, of unity, and of antiquity. Moreover, we have a charge from the apostles of Christ "to shun the worship of idols" (I Cor. 10:14; I John 5:21), and "to come out of Babylon," and to have no fellowship with her, unless we want to be partakers with her of all God's plagues (Rev. 18:4; II Cor. 6:17).

**5.136** OUTSIDE THE CHURCH OF GOD THERE IS NO SALVATION. But we esteem fellowship with the true Church of Christ so highly that we deny that those can live before God who do not stand in fellowship with the true Church of God, but separate themselves from it. For as there was no salvation outside Noah's ark when the world perished in the flood; so we believe that there is no certain salvation outside Christ, who offers himself to be enjoyed by the elect in the Church; and hence we teach that those who wish to live ought not to be separated from the true Church of Christ.

**5.137** THE CHURCH IS NOT BOUND TO ITS SIGNS. Nevertheless, by the signs [of the true Church] mentioned above, we do not so narrowly restrict the Church as to teach that all those are outside the Church who either do not participate in the sacraments, at least not willingly and through contempt, but rather, being forced by necessity, unwillingly abstain from them or are deprived of them; or in whom faith sometimes fails, though it is not entirely extinguished and does not wholly cease; or in whom imperfections and errors due to weakness are found. For we know that God had some friends in the world outside the commonwealth of Israel. We know what befell the people of God in the captivity of Babylon, where they were deprived of their sacrifices for seventy years. We know what happened to St. Peter, who denied his Master, and what is wont to happen daily to God's elect and faithful people who go astray and are weak. We know, moreover, what kind of churches the churches in Galatia and Corinth were in the apostles' time, in which the apostle found fault with many serious offenses; yet he calls them holy churches of Christ (I Cor. 1:2; Gal. 1:2).

**5.138** THE CHURCH APPEARS AT TIMES TO BE EXTINCT. Yes, and it sometimes happens that God in his just judgment allows the truth of his Word, and the catholic faith, and the proper worship of God to be so obscured and overthrown that the Church seems almost extinct, and no more to exist, as we see to have happened in the days of Elijah (I Kings 19:10, 14), and at other times. Meanwhile God has in this world and in this darkness his true worshippers, and those not a few, but even seven thousand and more (I Kings 19:18; Rev. 7:3 ff.). For the apostle exclaims: "God's firm foundation stands, bearing this seal, 'The Lord knows those who are his,'" etc. (II Tim. 2:19). Whence the Church of God may be termed invisible; not because the men from whom the Church is gathered are invisible, but because, being hidden from our eyes and known only to God, it often secretly escapes human judgment.

**5.139** NOT ALL WHO ARE IN THE CHURCH ARE OF THE CHURCH. Again, not all that are reckoned in the number of the Church are saints, and living and true members of the Church. For there are many hypocrites, who outwardly hear the Word of God, and publicly receive the sacraments, and seem to pray to God through Christ alone, to confess Christ to be their only righteousness, and to worship God, and to exercise the duties of charity, and for a time to endure with patience in misfortune. And yet they are inwardly destitute of true illumination of the Spirit, of faith and sincerity of heart, and of perseverance to the end. But eventually the character of these men, for the most part, will be disclosed. For the apostle John says; "They went out from us, but they were not of us; for if they had been of us, they would indeed have continued with us" (I John 2:19). And although while they simulate piety they are not of the Church, yet they are considered to be in the Church, just as traitors in a state are numbered among its citizens before they are discovered; and as the tares or darnel and chaff are found among the wheat, and as swellings and tumors are found in a sound body, when they are rather diseases and deformities than true members of the body. And therefore the Church of God is rightly compared to a net which catches fish of all kinds, and to a field, in which both wheat and tares are found (Matt. 13:24 ff., 47 ff.).

**5.140** WE MUST NOT JUDGE RASHLY OR PREMATURELY. Hence we must be very careful not to judge before the time, nor undertake to exclude, reject or cut off those whom the Lord does not want to have excluded or rejected, and those whom we cannot eliminate without loss to the Church. On the other hand, we must be vigilant lest while the pious snore the wicked gain ground and do harm to the Church.

**5.141** THE UNITY OF THE CHURCH IS NOT IN EXTERNAL RITES. Furthermore, we diligently teach that care is to be taken wherein the truth and unity of the Church chiefly lies, lest we rashly provoke and foster schisms in the Church. Unity consists not in outward rites and ceremonies, but rather in the truth and unity of the catholic faith. The catholic faith is not given to us by human laws, but by Holy Scriptures, of which the Apostles' Creed is a compendium. And, therefore, we read in the ancient writers that there was a manifold diversity of rites, but that they were free, and no one ever thought that the unity of the Church was thereby dissolved. So we teach that the true harmony of the Church consists in doctrines and in the true and harmonious preaching of the Gospel of Christ, and in rites that have been expressly delivered by the Lord. And here we especially urge that saying of the apostle: "Let those of us who are perfect have this mind; and if in any thing you are otherwise minded, God will reveal that also to you. Nevertheless let us walk by the same rule according to what we have attained, and let us be of the same mind" (Phil. 3:15 f.).

## CHAPTER XVIII

### Of the Ministers of the Church, Their Institution and Duties

**5.142** GOD USES MINISTERS IN THE BUILDING OF THE CHURCH. God has always used ministers for the gathering or establishing of a Church for himself, and for the governing and preservation of the same; and still he does, and always will, use them so long as the Church remains on earth. Therefore, the first beginning, institution, and office of ministers is a most ancient arrangement of God himself, and not a new one of men. INSTITUTION AND ORIGIN OF MINISTERS. It is true that God can, by his power, without any means join to himself a Church from among men; but he preferred to deal with men by the ministry of men. Therefore ministers are to be regarded, not as ministers by themselves alone, but as the ministers of God, inasmuch as God effects the salvation of men through them.

**5.143** THE MINISTRY IS NOT TO BE DESPISED. Hence we warn men to beware lest we attribute what has to do with our conversion and instruction to the secret power of the Holy Spirit in such a way that we make void the ecclesiastical ministry. For it is fitting that we always have in mind the words of the apostle: "How are they to believe in him of whom they have not heard? And how are they to hear without a preacher? So faith comes from hearing, and hearing comes by the word of God" (Rom. 10:14, 17). And also what the Lord said in the Gospel: "Truly, truly, I say to you, he who receives any one whom I send receives me; and he who receives me receives him who sent me" (John 13:20). Likewise a man of Macedonia, who appeared to Paul in a vision while he was in Asia, secretly admonished him, saying: "Come over to Macedonia and help us" (Acts 16:9). And in another place the same apostle said: "We are fellow workmen for God; you are God's tillage, God's building" (I Cor. 3:9).

**5.144** Yet, on the other hand, we must beware that we do not attribute too much to ministers and the ministry; remembering here also the words of the Lord in the Gospel: "No one can come to me unless my Father draws him" (John 6:44), and the words of the apostle: "What then is Paul? What is Apollos? Servants through whom you believed, as the Lord assigned to each. I planted, Apollos watered, but only God gives the growth" (I Cor. 3:5 ff.). GOD MOVES THE HEARTS OF MEN. Therefore, let us believe that God teaches us by his word, outwardly through his ministers, and inwardly moves the hearts of his elect to faith by the Holy Spirit; and that therefore we ought to render all glory unto God for this whole favor. But this matter has been dealt with in the first chapter of this Exposition.

**5.145** WHO THE MINISTERS ARE AND OF WHAT SORT GOD HAS GIVEN TO THE WORLD. And even from the beginning of the world God has used the most excellent men in the whole world (even if many of them were simple in worldly wisdom or philosophy, but were outstanding in true theology), namely, the patriarchs, with whom he frequently spoke by angels. For the patriarchs were the prophets or teachers of their age whom God for this reason wanted to live for several centuries, in order that they might be, as it were, fathers and lights of the world. They were followed by Moses and the prophets renowned throughout all the world.

**5.146** CHRIST THE TEACHER. After these the heavenly Father even sent his only-begotten Son, the most perfect teacher of the world; in whom is hidden the wisdom of God, and which has come to us through the most holy, simple, and most perfect doctrine of all. For he chose disciples for himself whom he made apostles. These went out into the whole world, and everywhere gathered together churches by the preaching of the Gospel, and then throughout all the churches in the world they appointed pastors or teachers[8] according to Christ's command; through their successors he has taught and governed the Church unto this day. Therefore, as God gave unto his ancient people the patriarchs, together with Moses and the prophets, so also to his people of the New Testament he sent his only-begotten Son, and, with him, the apostles and teachers of the Church.

**5.147** MINISTERS OF THE NEW TESTAMENT. Furthermore, the ministers of the new people are called by various names. For they are called apostles, prophets, evangelists, bishops, elders, pastors, and teachers (I Cor. 12:28; Eph. 4:11). THE APOSTLES. The apostles did not stay in any particular place, but throughout the world gathered together different churches. When they were once established, there ceased to be apostles, and pastors took their place, each in his church. PROPHETS. In former times the prophets were seers, knowing the future; but they also interpreted the Scriptures. Such men are also found still today. EVANGELISTS. The writers of the history of the Gospel were called Evangelists; but they also were heralds of the Gospel of Christ; as Paul also commended Timothy: "Do the work of an evangelist" (II Tim. 4:5). BISHOPS. Bishops are the overseers and watchmen of the Church, who administer the food and needs of the life of the Church. PRESBYTERS. The presbyters are the elders and, as it were, senators and fathers of the Church, governing it with wholesome counsel. PASTORS. The pastors both keep the Lord's sheepfold, and also provide for its needs. TEACHERS. The teachers instruct and teach the true faith and godliness. Therefore, the ministers of the churches may now be called bishops, elders, pastors, and teachers.

**5.148** PAPAL ORDERS. Then in subsequent times many more names of ministers in the Church were introduced into the Church of God. For

---

[8] *Ordinarunt pastores, atque doctores.*

some were appointed patriarchs, others archbishops, others suffragans; also, metropolitans, archdeacons, deacons, subdeacons, acolytes, exorcists, cantors, porters, and I know not what others, as cardinals, provosts, and priors; greater and lesser fathers, greater and lesser orders. But we are not troubled about all these about how they once were and are now. For us the apostolic doctrine concerning ministers is sufficient.

5.149 CONCERNING MONKS. Since we assuredly know that monks, and the orders or sects of monks, are instituted neither by Christ nor by the apostles, we teach that they are of no use to the Church of God, nay rather, are pernicious. For, although in former times they were tolerable (when they were hermits, earning their living with their own hands, and were not a burden to anyone, but like the laity were everywhere obedient to the pastors of the churches), yet now the whole world sees and knows what they are like. They formulate I know not what vows; but they lead a life quite contrary to their vows, so that the best of them deserves to be numbered among those of whom the apostle said: "We hear that some of you are living an irregular life, mere busybodies, not doing any work" etc. (II Thess. 3:11). Therefore, we neither have such in our churches, nor do we teach that they should be in the churches of Christ.

5.150 MINISTERS ARE TO BE CALLED AND ELECTED. Furthermore, no man ought to usurp the honor of the ecclesiastical ministry; that is, to seize it for himself by bribery or any deceits, or by his own free choice. But let the ministers of the Church be called and chosen by lawful and ecclesiastical election; that is to say, let them be carefully chosen by the Church or by those delegated from the Church for that purpose in a proper order without any uproar, dissension and rivalry. Not any one may be elected, but capable men distinguished by sufficient consecrated learning, pious eloquence, simple wisdom, lastly, by moderation and an honorable reputation, according to that apostolic rule which is compiled by the apostle in I Tim., ch. 3, and Titus, ch. 1.

5.151 ORDINATION. And those who are elected are to be ordained by the elders with public prayer and laying on of hands. Here we condemn all those who go off of their own accord, being neither chosen, sent, nor ordained (Jer., ch. 23). We condemn unfit ministers and those not furnished with the necessary gifts of a pastor.

5.152 In the meantime we acknowledge that the harmless simplicity of some pastors in the primitive Church sometimes profited the Church more than the many-sided, refined and fastidious, but a little too esoteric learning of others. For this reason we do not reject even today the honest, yet by no means ignorant, simplicity of some.

5.153 PRIESTHOOD OF ALL BELIEVERS. To be sure, Christ's apostles call all who believe in Christ "priests," but not on account of an office, but because, all the faithful having been made kings and priests, we are able to offer up spiritual sacrifices to God through Christ (Ex. 19:6; I Peter 2:9;

Rev. 1:6). Therefore, the priesthood and the ministry are very different from one another. For the priesthood, as we have just said, is common to all Christians; not so is the ministry. Nor have we abolished the ministry of the Church because we have repudiated the papal priesthood from the Church of Christ.

5.154 PRIESTS AND PRIESTHOOD. Surely in the new covenant of Christ there is no longer any such priesthood as was under the ancient people; which had an external anointing, holy garments, and very many ceremonies which were types of Christ, who abolished them all by his coming and fulfilling them. But he himself remains the only priest forever, and lest we derogate anything from him, we do not impart the name of priest to any minister. For the Lord himself did not appoint any priests in the Church of the New Testament who, having received authority from the suffragan, may daily offer up the sacrifice, that is, the very flesh and blood of the Lord, for the living and the dead, but ministers who may teach and administer the sacraments.

5.155 THE NATURE OF THE MINISTERS OF THE NEW TESTAMENT. Paul explains simply and briefly what we are to think of the ministers of the New Testament or of the Christian Church, and what we are to attribute to them. "This is how one should regard us, as servants of Christ and stewards of the mysteries of God" (I Cor. 4:1). Therefore, the apostle wants us to think of ministers as ministers. Now the apostle calls them ὑπηρετας, rowers, who have their eyes fixed on the coxswain, and so men who do not live for themselves or according to their own will, but for others—namely, their masters, upon whose command they altogether depend. For in all his duties every minister of the Church is commanded to carry out only what he has received in commandment from his Lord, and not to indulge his own free choice. And in this case it is expressly declared who is the Lord, namely, Christ; to whom the ministers are subject in all the affairs of the ministry.

5.156 MINISTERS AS STEWARDS OF THE MYSTERIES OF GOD. Moreover, to the end that he might expound the ministry more fully, the apostle adds that ministers of the Church are administrators and stewards of the mysteries of God. Now in many passages, especially in Eph., ch. 3, Paul called the mysteries of God the Gospel of Christ. And the sacraments of Christ are also called mysteries by the ancient writers. Therefore for this purpose are the ministers of the Church called—namely, to preach the Gospel of Christ to the faithful, and to administer the sacraments. We read, also, in another place in the Gospel, of "the faithful and wise steward," whom "his master will set over his household, to give them their portion of food at the proper time" (Luke 12:42). Again, elsewhere in the Gospel a man takes a journey in a foreign country and, leaving his house, gives his substance and authority over it to his servants, and to each his work.

**5.157** THE POWER OF MINISTERS OF THE CHURCH. Now, therefore, it is fitting that we also say something about the power and duty of the ministers of the Church. Concerning this power some have argued industriously, and to it have subjected everything on earth, even the greatest things, and they have done so contrary to the commandment of the Lord who has prohibited dominion for his disciples and has highly commended humility (Luke 22:24 ff.; Matt. 18:3 f.; 20:25 ff.). There is, indeed, another power that is pure and absolute, which is called the power of right. According to this power all things in the whole world are subject to Christ, who is Lord of all, as he himself has testified when he said: "All authority in heaven and on earth has been given to me" (Matt. 28:18), and again, "I am the first and the last, and behold I am alive for evermore, and I have the keys of Hades and Death" (Rev. 1:18); also, "He has the key of David, which opens and no one shall shut, who shuts and no one opens" (Rev. 3:7).

**5.158** THE LORD RESERVES TRUE POWER FOR HIMSELF. This power the Lord reserves to himself, and does not transfer it to any other, so that he might stand idly by as a spectator while his ministers work. For Isaiah says, "I will place on his shoulder the key of the house of David" (Isa. 22:22), and again, "The government will be upon his shoulders" (Isa. 9:6). For he does not lay the government on other men's shoulders, but still keeps and uses his own power, governing all things.

**5.159** THE POWER OF THE OFFICE AND OF THE MINISTER. Then there is another power of an office or of ministry limited by him who has full and absolute power. And this is more like a service than a dominion. THE KEYS. For a lord gives up his power to the steward in his house, and for that cause gives him the keys, that he may admit into or exclude from the house those whom his lord will have admitted or excluded. In virtue of this power the minister, because of his office, does that which the Lord has commanded him to do; and the Lord confirms what he does, and wills that what his servant has done will be so regarded and acknowledged, as if he himself had done it. Undoubtedly, it is to this that these evangelical sentences refer: "I will give you the keys of the kingdom of heaven, and whatever you bind on earth shall be bound in heaven, and whatever you loose on earth shall be loosed in heaven" (Matt. 16:19). Again, "If you forgive the sins of any, they are forgiven; if you retain the sins of any, they are retained" (John 20:23). But if the minister does not carry out everything as the Lord has commanded him, but transgresses the bounds of faith, then the Lord certainly makes void what he has done. Wherefore the ecclesiastical power of the ministers of the Church is that function whereby they indeed govern the Church of God, but yet so do all things in the Church as the Lord has prescribed in his Word. When those things are done, the faithful esteem them as done by the Lord himself. But mention has already been made of the keys above.

**5.160** THE POWER OF MINISTERS IS ONE AND THE SAME, AND EQUAL. Now the one and an equal power or function is given to all ministers in the Church. Certainly, in the beginning, the bishops or presbyters governed the Church in common; no man lifted up himself above another, none usurped greater power or authority over his fellow-bishops. For remembering the words of the Lord: "Let the leader among you become as one who serves" (Luke 22:26), they kept themselves in humility, and by mutual services they helped one another in the governing and preserving of the Church.

**5.161** ORDER TO BE PRESERVED. Nevertheless, for the sake of preserving order some one of the ministers called the assembly together, proposed matters to be laid before it, gathered the opinions of the others, in short, to the best of man's ability took precaution lest any confusion should arise. Thus did St. Peter, as we read in The Acts of the Apostles, who nevertheless was not on that account preferred to the others, nor endowed with greater authority than the rest. Rightly then does Cyprian the Martyr say, in his *De Simplicitate Clericorum*: "The other apostles were assuredly what Peter was, endowed with a like fellowship of honor and power; but [his] primacy proceeds from unity in order that the Church may be shown to be one."

**5.162** WHEN AND HOW ONE WAS PLACED BEFORE THE OTHERS. St. Jerome also in his commentary upon The Epistle of Paul to Titus, says something not unlike this: "Before attachment to persons in religion was begun at the instigation of the devil, the churches were governed by the common consultation of the elders; but after every one thought that those whom he had baptized were his own, and not Christ's, it was decreed that one of the elders should be chosen, and set over the rest, upon whom should fall the care of the whole Church, and all schismatic seeds should be removed." Yet St. Jerome does not recommend this decree as divine; for he immediately adds: "As the elders knew from the custom of the Church that they were subject to him who was set over them, so the bishops knew that they were above the elders, more from custom than from the truth of an arrangement by the Lord, and that they ought to rule the Church in common with them." Thus far St. Jerome. Hence no one can rightly forbid a return to the ancient constitution of the Church of God, and to have recourse to it before human custom.

**5.163** THE DUTIES OF MINISTERS. The duties of ministers are various; yet for the most part they are restricted to two, in which all the rest are comprehended: to the teaching of the Gospel of Christ, and to the proper administration of the sacraments. For it is the duty of the ministers to gather together an assembly for worship in which to expound God's Word and to apply the whole doctrine to the care and use of the Church, so that what is taught may benefit the hearers and edify the faithful. It falls to ministers, I say, to teach the ignorant, and to exhort;

and to urge the idlers and lingerers to make progress in the way of the Lord. Moreover, they are to comfort and to strengthen the fainthearted, and to arm them against the manifold temptations of Satan; to rebuke offenders; to recall the erring into the way; to raise the fallen; to convince the gainsayers to drive the wolf away from the sheepfold of the Lord; to rebuke wickedness and wicked men wisely and severely; not to wink at nor to pass over great wickedness. And, besides, they are to administer the sacraments, and to commend the right use of them, and to prepare all men by wholesome doctrine to receive them; to preserve the faithful in a holy unity; and to check schisms; to catechize the unlearned, to commend the needs of the poor to the Church, to visit, instruct, and keep in the way of life the sick and those afflicted with various temptations. In addition, they are to attend to public prayers or supplications in times of need, together with common fasting, that is, a holy abstinence; and as diligently as possible to see to everything that pertains to the tranquility, peace and welfare of the churches.

5.164 But in order that the minister may perform all these things better and more easily, it is especially required of him that he fear God, be constant in prayer, attend to spiritual reading, and in all things and at all times be watchful, and by a purity of life to let his light to shine before all men.

5.165 DISCIPLINE. And since discipline is an absolute necessity in the Church and excommunication was once used in the time of the early fathers, and there were ecclesiastical judgments among the people of God, wherein this discipline was exercised by wise and godly men, it also falls to ministers to regulate this discipline for edification, according to the circumstances of the time, public state, and necessity. At all times and in all places the rule is to be observed that everything is to be done for edification, decently and honorably, without oppression and strife. For the apostle testifies that authority in the Church was given to him by the Lord for building up and not for destroying (II Cor. 10:8). And the Lord himself forbade the weeds to be plucked up in the Lord's field, because there would be danger lest the wheat also be plucked up with it (Matt. 13:29 f.).

5.166 EVEN EVIL MINISTERS ARE TO BE HEARD. Moreover, we strongly detest the error of the Donatists who esteem the doctrine and administration of the sacraments to be either effectual or not effectual, according to the good or evil life of the ministers. For we know that the voice of Christ is to be heard, though it be out of the mouths of evil ministers; because the Lord himself said: "Practice and observe whatever they tell you, but not what they do" (Matt. 23:3). We know that the sacraments are sanctified by the institution and the word of Christ, and that they are effectual to the godly, although they be administered by unworthy ministers. Concerning this matter, Augustine, the blessed servant of God, many times argued from the Scriptures against the Donatists.

**5.167** SYNODS. Nevertheless, there ought to be proper discipline among ministers. In synods the doctrine and life of ministers is to be carefully examined. Offenders who can be cured are to be rebuked by the elders and restored to the right way, and if they are incurable, they are to be deposed, and like wolves driven away from the flock of the Lord by the true shepherds. For, if they be false teachers, they are not to be tolerated at all. Neither do we disapprove of ecumenical councils, if they are convened according to the example of the apostles, for the welfare of the Church and not for its destruction.

**5.168** THE WORKER IS WORTHY OF HIS REWARD. All faithful ministers, as good workmen, are also worthy of their reward, and do not sin when they receive a stipend, and all things that be necessary for themselves and their family. For the apostle shows in I Cor., ch. 9, and in I Tim., ch. 5, and elsewhere that these things may rightly be given by the Church and received by ministers. The Anabaptists, who condemn and defame ministers who live from their ministry are also refuted by the apostolic teaching.

## CHAPTER XIX

### Of the Sacraments of the Church of Christ

**5.169** THE SACRAMENTS [ARE] ADDED TO THE WORD AND WHAT THEY ARE. From the beginning, God added to the preaching of his Word in his Church sacraments or sacramental signs. For thus does all Holy Scripture clearly testify. Sacraments are mystical symbols, or holy rites, or sacred actions, instituted by God himself, consisting of his Word, of signs and of things signified, whereby in the Church he keeps in mind and from time to time recalls the great benefits he has shown to men; whereby also he seals his promises, and outwardly represents, and, as it were, offers unto our sight those things which inwardly he performs for us, and so strengthens and increases our faith through the working of God's Spirit in our hearts. Lastly, he thereby distinguishes us from all other people and religions, and consecrates and binds us wholly to himself, and signifies what he requires of us.

**5.170** SOME ARE SACRAMENTS OF THE OLD, OTHERS OF THE NEW, TESTAMENTS. Some sacraments are of the old, others of the new, people. The sacraments of the ancient people were circumcision, and the Paschal Lamb, which was offered up; for that reason it is referred to the sacrifices which were practiced from the beginning of the world.

**5.171** THE NUMBER OF SACRAMENTS OF THE NEW PEOPLE. The sacraments of the new people are Baptism and the Lord's Supper. There are some who count seven sacraments of the new people. Of these we acknowledge that repentance, the ordination of ministers (not indeed the papal but apostolic ordination), and matrimony are profitable ordinances of God, but not sacraments. Confirmation and extreme unction are human inventions which the Church can dispense with without any loss, and indeed, we do not have them in our churches. For they contain some things of which we can by no means approve. Above all we detest all the trafficking in which the Papists engage in dispensing the sacraments.

**5.172** THE AUTHOR OF THE SACRAMENTS. The author of all sacraments is not any man, but God alone. Men cannot institute sacraments. For they pertain to the worship of God, and it is not for man to appoint and prescribe a worship of God, but to accept and preserve the one he has received from God. Besides, the symbols have God's promises annexed to them, which require faith. Now faith rests only upon the Word of God; and the Word of God is like papers or letters, and the sacraments are like seals which only God appends to the letters.

**5.173** CHRIST STILL WORKS IN SACRAMENTS. And as God is the author of the sacraments, so he continually works in the Church in which they are rightly carried out; so that the faithful, when they receive them from the ministers, know that God works in his own ordinance, and therefore they receive them as from the hand of God; and the minister's faults (even if they be very great) cannot affect them, since they acknowledge the integrity of the sacraments to depend upon the institution of the Lord.

**5.174** THE AUTHOR AND THE MINISTERS OF THE SACRAMENTS TO BE DISTINGUISHED. Hence in the administration of the sacraments they also clearly distinguish between the Lord himself and the ministers of the Lord, confessing that the substance of the sacraments is given them by the Lord, and the outward signs by the ministers of the Lord.

**5.175** THE SUBSTANCE OR CHIEF THING IN THE SACRAMENTS. But the principal thing which God promises in all sacraments and to which all the godly in all ages direct their attention (some call it the substance and matter of the sacraments) is Christ the Savior—that only sacrifice, and the Lamb of God slain from the foundation of the world; that rock, also, from which all our fathers drank, by whom all the elect are circumcised without hands through the Holy Spirit, and are washed from all their sins, and are nourished with the very body and blood of Christ unto eternal life.

**5.176** THE SIMILARITY AND DIFFERENCE IN THE SACRAMENTS OF OLD AND NEW PEOPLES. Now, in respect of that which is the principal thing and the matter itself in the sacraments, the sacraments of both peoples are equal. For Christ, the only Mediator and Savior of the faithful, is the chief thing and very substance of the sacraments in both; for the one God is the author of them both. They were given to both peoples as signs and seals of the grace and promises of God, which should call to mind and renew the memory of God's great benefits, and should distinguish the faithful from all the religions in the world; lastly, which should be received spiritually by faith, and should bind the receivers to the Church, and admonish them of their duty. In these and similar respects, I say, the sacraments of both people are not dissimilar, although in the outward signs they are different. And, indeed, with respect to the signs we make a great difference. For ours are more firm and lasting, inasmuch as they will never be changed to the end of the world. Moreover, ours testify that both the substance and the promise have been fulfilled or perfected in Christ; the former signified what was to be fulfilled. Ours are also more simple and less laborious, less sumptuous and involved with ceremonies. Moreover, they belong to a more numerous people, one that is dispersed throughout the whole earth. And since they are more excellent, and by the Holy Spirit kindle greater faith, a greater abundance of the Spirit also ensues.

5.177 OUR SACRAMENTS SUCCEED THE OLD WHICH ARE ABROGATED. But now since Christ the true Messiah is exhibited unto us, and the abundance of grace is poured forth upon the people of The New Testament, the sacraments of the old people are surely abrogated and have ceased; and in their stead the symbols of the New Testament are placed—Baptism in the place of circumcision, the Lord's Supper in place of the Paschal Lamb and sacrifices.

5.178 IN WHAT THE SACRAMENTS CONSIST. And as formerly the sacraments consisted of the word, the sign, and the thing signified; so even now they are composed, as it were, of the same parts. For the Word of God makes them sacraments, which before they were not. THE CONSECRATION OF THE SACRAMENTS. For they are consecrated by the Word, and shown to be sanctified by him who instituted them. To sanctify or consecrate anything to God is to dedicate it to holy uses; that is, to take it from the common and ordinary use, and to appoint it to a holy use. For the signs in the sacraments are drawn from common use, things external and visible. For in baptism the sign is the element of water, and that visible washing which is done by the minister; but the thing signified is regeneration and the cleansing from sins. Likewise, in the Lord's Supper, the outward sign is bread and wine, taken from things commonly used for meat and drink; but the thing signified is the body of Christ which was given, and his blood which was shed for us, or the communion of the body and blood of the Lord. Wherefore, the water, bread, and wine, according to their nature and apart from the divine institution and sacred use, are only that which they are called and we experience. But when the Word of God is added to them, together with invocation of the divine name, and the renewing of their first institution and sanctification, then these signs are consecrated, and shown to be sanctified by Christ. For Christ's first institution and consecration of the sacraments remains always effectual in the Church of God, so that those who do not celebrate the sacraments in any other way than the Lord himself instituted from the beginning still today enjoy that first and all-surpassing consecration. And hence in the celebration of the sacraments the very words of Christ are repeated.

**5.179** SIGNS TAKE NAME OF THINGS SIGNIFIED. And as we learn out of the Word of God that these signs were instituted for another purpose than the usual use, therefore we teach that they now, in their holy use, take upon them the names of things signified, and are no longer called mere water, bread or wine, but also regeneration or the washing of water, and the body and blood of the Lord or symbols and sacraments of the Lord's body and blood. Not that the symbols are changed into the things signified, or cease to be what they are in their own nature. For otherwise they would not be sacraments. If they were only the thing signified, they would not be signs.

**5.180** THE SACRAMENTAL UNION. Therefore the signs acquire the names of things because they are mystical signs of sacred things, and because the signs and the things signified are sacramentally joined together; joined together, I say, or united by a mystical signification, and by the purpose or will of him who instituted the sacraments. For the water, bread, and wine are not common, but holy signs. And he that instituted water in baptism did not institute it with the will and intention that the faithful should only be sprinkled by the water of baptism; and he who commanded the bread to be eaten and the wine to be drunk in the supper did not want the faithful to receive only bread and wine without any mystery as they eat bread in their homes; but that they should spiritually partake of the things signified, and by faith be truly cleansed from their sins, and partake of Christ.

**5.181** THE SECTS. And, therefore, we do not at all approve of those who attribute the sanctification of the sacraments to I know not what properties and formula or to the power of words pronounced by one who is consecrated and who has the intention of consecrating, and to other accidental things which neither Christ or the apostles delivered to us by word or example. Neither do we approve of the doctrine of those who speak of the sacraments just as common signs, not sanctified and effectual. Nor do we approve of those who despise the visible aspect of the sacraments because of the invisible, and so believe the signs to be superfluous because they think they already enjoy the thing themselves, as the Messalians are said to have held.

**5.182** THE THING SIGNIFIED IS NEITHER INCLUDED IN OR BOUND TO THE SACRAMENTS. We do not approve of the doctrine of those who teach that grace and the things signified are so bound to and included in the signs that whoever participate outwardly in the signs, no matter what sort of persons they be, also inwardly participate in the grace and things signified.

**5.183** However, as we do not estimate the value of the sacraments by the worthiness or unworthiness of the ministers, so we do not estimate it by the condition of those who receive them. For we know that the value of the sacraments depends upon faith and upon the truthfulness and pure goodness of God. For as the Word of God remains the true Word of God, in which, when it is preached, not only bare words are repeated, but at the same time the things signified or announced in words are offered by God, even if the ungodly and unbelievers hear and understand the words yet do not enjoy the things signified, because they do not receive them by true faith; so the sacraments, which by the Word consist of signs and the things signified, remain true and inviolate sacraments, signifying not only sacred things, but, by God offering, the things signified, even if unbelievers do not receive the things offered. This is not the fault of God who gives and offers them, but the fault of men who receive them without faith and illegitimately; but whose unbelief does not invalidate the faithfulness of God (Rom. 3:3 f.)

**5.184** THE PURPOSE FOR WHICH SACRAMENTS WERE INSTITUTED. Since the purpose for which sacraments were instituted was also explained in passing when right at the beginning of our exposition it was shown what sacraments are, there is no need to be tedious by repeating what once has been said. Logically, therefore, we now speak severally of the sacraments of the new people.

## CHAPTER XX*
### Of Holy Baptism

**5.185** THE INSTITUTION OF BAPTISM. Baptism was instituted and consecrated by God. First John baptized, who dipped Christ in the water in Jordan. From him it came to the apostles, who also baptized with water. The Lord expressly commanded them to preach the Gospel and to baptize "in the name of the Father and of the Son and of the Holy Spirit" (Matt. 28:19). And in The Acts, Peter said to the Jews who inquired what they ought to do: "Be baptized every one of you in the name of Jesus Christ for the forgiveness of your sins; and you shall receive the gift of the Holy Spirit" (Acts 2:37 f.). Hence by some baptism is called a sign of initiation for God's people, since by it the elect of God are consecrated to God.

**5.186** ONE BAPTISM. There is but one baptism in the Church of God; and it is sufficient to be once baptized or consecrated unto God. For baptism once received continues for all of life, and is a perpetual sealing of our adoption.

---

* See Preface for discussion of our current understanding of such condemnations.

5.187 WHAT IT MEANS TO BE BAPTIZED. Now to be baptized in the name of Christ is to be enrolled, entered, and received into the covenant and family, and so into the inheritance of the sons of God; yes, and in this life to be called after the name of God; that is to say, to be called a son of God; to be cleansed also from the filthiness of sins, and to be granted the manifold grace of God, in order to lead a new and innocent life. Baptism, therefore, calls to mind and renews the great favor God has shown to the race of mortal men. For we are all born in the pollution of sin and are the children of wrath. But God, who is rich in mercy, freely cleanses us from our sins by the blood of his Son, and in him adopts us to be his sons, and by a holy covenant joins us to himself, and enriches us with various gifts, that we might live a new life. All these things are assured by baptism. For inwardly we are regenerated, purified, and renewed by God through the Holy Spirit; and outwardly we receive the assurance of the greatest gifts in the water, by which also those great benefits are represented, and, as it were, set before our eyes to be beheld.

5.188 WE ARE BAPTIZED WITH WATER. And therefore we are baptized, that is, washed or sprinkled with visible water. For the water washes dirt away, and cools and refreshes hot and tired bodies. And the grace of God performs these things for souls, and does so invisibly or spiritually.

5.189 THE OBLIGATION OF BAPTISM. Moreover, God also separates us from all strange religions and peoples by the symbol of baptism, and consecrates us to himself as his property. We, therefore, confess our faith when we are baptized, and obligate ourselves to God for obedience, mortification of the flesh, and newness of life. Hence, we are enlisted in the holy military service of Christ that all our life long we should fight against the world, Satan, and our own flesh. Moreover, we are baptized into one body of the Church, that with all members of the Church we might beautifully concur in the one religion and in mutual services.

5.190 THE FORM OF BAPTISM. We believe that the most perfect form of baptism is that by which Christ was baptized, and by which the apostles baptized. Those things, therefore, which by man's device were added afterwards and used in the Church we do not consider necessary to the perfection of baptism. Of this kind is exorcism, the use of burning lights, oil, salt, spittle, and such other things as that baptism is to be celebrated twice every year with a multitude of ceremonies. For we believe that one baptism of the Church has been sanctified in God's first institution, and that it is consecrated by the Word and is also effectual today in virtue of God's first blessing.

5.191 THE MINISTER OF BAPTISM. We teach that baptism should not be administered in the Church by women or midwives. For Paul deprived women of ecclesiastical duties, and baptism has to do with these.

**5.192** ANABAPTISTS. We condemn the Anabaptists, who deny that newborn infants of the faithful are to be baptized. For according to evangelical teaching, of such is the Kingdom of God, and they are in the covenant of God. Why, then, should the sign of God's covenant not be given to them? Why should those who belong to God and are in his Church not be initiated by holy baptism? We condemn also the Anabaptists in the rest of their peculiar doctrines which they hold contrary to the Word of God. We therefore are not Anabaptists and have nothing in common with them.

## CHAPTER XXI

### Of the Holy Supper of the Lord

**5.193** THE SUPPER OF THE LORD. The Supper of the Lord (which is called the Lord's Table, and the Eucharist, that is, a Thanksgiving), is, therefore, usually called a supper, because it was instituted by Christ at his last supper, and still represents it, and because in it the faithful are spiritually fed and given drink.

**5.194** THE AUTHOR AND CONSECRATOR OF THE SUPPER. For the author of the Supper of the Lord is not an angel or any man, but the Son of God himself, our Lord Jesus Christ, who first consecrated it to his Church. And the same consecration or blessing still remains along all those who celebrate no other but that very Supper which the Lord instituted, and at which they repeat the words of the Lord's Supper, and in all things look to the one Christ by a true faith, from whose hands they receive, as it were, what they receive through the ministry of the ministers of the Church.

**5.195** A MEMORIAL OF GOD'S BENEFITS. By this sacred rite the Lord wishes to keep in fresh remembrance that greatest benefit which he showed to mortal men, namely, that by having given his body and shed his blood he has pardoned all our sins, and redeemed us from eternal death and the power of the devil, and now feeds us with his flesh, and give us his blood to drink, which, being received spiritually by true faith, nourish us to eternal life. And this so great a benefit is renewed as often as the Lord's Supper is celebrated. For the Lord said: "Do this in remembrance of me." This holy Supper also seals to us that the very body of Christ was truly given for us, and his blood shed for the remission of our sins, lest our faith should in any way waver.

**5.196** THE SIGN AND THING SIGNIFIED. And this is visibly represented by this sacrament outwardly through the ministers, and, as it were, presented to our eyes to be seen, which is invisibly wrought by the Holy Spirit inwardly in the soul. Bread is outwardly offered by the minister, and the words of the Lord are heard: "Take, eat; this is my body"; and, "Take and divide among you. Drink of it, all of you; this is my blood."

Therefore the faithful receive what is given by the ministers of the Lord, and they eat the bread of the Lord and drink of the Lord's cup. At the same time by the work of Christ through the Holy Spirit they also inwardly receive the flesh and blood of the Lord, and are thereby nourished unto life eternal. For the flesh and blood of Christ is the true food and drink unto life eternal; and Christ himself, since he was given for us and is our Savior, is the principal thing in the Supper, and we do not permit anything else to be substituted in his place.

5.197 But in order to understand better and more clearly how the flesh and blood of Christ are the food and drink of the faithful, and are received by the faithful unto eternal life, we would add these few things. There is more than one kind of eating. There is corporeal eating whereby food is taken into the mouth, is chewed with the teeth, and swallowed into the stomach. In times past the Capernaites thought that the flesh of the Lord should be eaten in this way, but they are refuted by him in John, ch. 6. For as the flesh of Christ cannot be eaten corporeally without infamy and savagery, so it is not food for the stomach. All men are forced to admit this. We therefore disapprove of that canon in the Pope's decrees, *Ego Berengarius* (*De Consecrat.*, Dist. 2). For neither did godly antiquity believe, nor do we believe, that the body of Christ is to be eaten corporeally and essentially with a bodily mouth.

5.198 SPIRITUAL EATING OF THE LORD. There is also a spiritual eating of Christ's body; not such that we think that thereby the food itself is to be changed into spirit, but whereby the body and blood of the Lord, while remaining in their own essence and property, are spiritually communicated to us, certainly not in a corporeal but in a spiritual way, by the Holy Spirit, who applies and bestows upon us these things which have been prepared for us by the sacrifice of the Lord's body and blood for us, namely, the remission of sins, deliverance, and eternal life; so that Christ lives in us and we live in him, and he causes us to receive him by true faith to this end that he may become for us such spiritual food and drink, that is, our life.

5.199 CHRIST AS OUR FOOD SUSTAINS US IN LIFE. For even as bodily food and drink not only refresh and strengthen our bodies, but also keeps them alive, so the flesh of Christ delivered for us, and his blood shed for us, not only refresh and strengthen our souls, but also preserve them alive, not in so far as they are corporeally eaten and drunken, but in so far as they are communicated unto us spiritually by the Spirit of God, as the Lord said: "The bread which I shall give for the life of the world is my flesh" (John 6:51), and "the flesh" (namely what is eaten bodily) "is of no avail; it is the spirit that gives life" (v. 63). And: "The words that I have spoken to you are spirit and life."

5.200 CHRIST RECEIVED BY FAITH. And as we must by eating receive food into our bodies in order that it may work in us, and prove its efficacy in us—since it profits us nothing when it remains outside us—so it is necessary that we receive Christ by faith, that he may become ours, and he may live in us and we in him. For he says: "I am the bread of life; he who comes to me shall not hunger, and he who believes in me shall never thirst" (John 6:35); and also, "He who eats me will live because of me ... he abides in me, I in him" (vs. 57, 56).

5.201  SPIRITUAL FOOD. From all this it is clear that by spiritual food we do not mean some imaginary food I know not what, but the very body of the Lord given to us, which nevertheless is received by the faithful not corporeally, but spiritually by faith. In this matter we follow the teaching of the Savior himself, Christ the Lord, according to John, ch. 6.

5.202  EATING NECESSARY FOR SALVATION. And this eating of the flesh and drinking of the blood of the Lord is so necessary for salvation that without it no man can be saved. But this spiritual eating and drinking also occurs apart from the Supper of the Lord, and as often and wherever a man believes in Christ. To which that sentence of St. Augustine's perhaps applies: "Why do you provide for your teeth and your stomach? Believe, and you have eaten."

5.203  SACRAMENTAL EATING OF THE LORD. Besides the higher spiritual eating there is also a sacramental eating of the body of the Lord by which not only spiritually and internally the believer truly participates in the true body and blood of the Lord, but also, by coming to the Table of the Lord, outwardly receives the visible sacrament of the body and blood of the Lord. To be sure, when the believer believed, he first received the life-giving food, and still enjoys it. But therefore, when he now receives the sacrament, he does not receive nothing. For he progresses in continuing to communicate in the body and blood of the Lord, and so his faith is kindled and grows more and more, and is refreshed by spiritual food. For while we live, faith is continually increased. And he who outwardly receives the sacrament by true faith, not only receives the sign, but also, as we said, enjoys the thing itself. Moreover, he obeys the Lord's institution and commandment, and with a joyful mind gives thanks for his redemption and that of all mankind, and makes a faithful memorial to the Lord's death, and gives a witness before the Church, of whose body he is a member. Assurance is also given to those who receive the sacrament that the body of the Lord was given and his blood shed, not only for men in general, but particularly for every faithful communicant, to whom it is food and drink unto eternal life.

5.204  UNBELIEVERS TAKE THE SACRAMENT TO THEIR JUDGMENT. But he who comes to this sacred Table of the Lord without faith, communicates only in the sacrament and does not receive the substance of the sacrament whence comes life and salvation; and such men unworthily eat of the Lord's Table. Whoever eats the bread or drinks the cup of the Lord in an unworthy manner will be guilty of the body and blood of the Lord, and eats and drinks judgment upon himself (I Cor. 11:26–29). For when they do not approach with true faith, they dishonor the death of Christ, and therefore eat and drink condemnation to themselves.

5.205 THE PRESENCE OF CHRIST IN THE SUPPER. We do not, therefore, so join the body of the Lord and his blood with the bread and wine as to say that the bread itself is the body of Christ except in a sacramental way; or that the body of Christ is hidden corporeally under the bread, so that it ought to be worshipped under the form of bread; or yet that whoever receives the sign, receives also the thing itself. The body of Christ is in heaven at the right hand of the Father; and therefore our hearts are to be lifted up on high, and not to be fixed on the bread, neither is the Lord to be worshipped in the bread. Yet the Lord is not absent from his Church when she celebrates the Supper. The sun, which is absent from us in the heavens, is notwithstanding effectually present among us. How much more is the Sun of Righteousness, Christ, although in his body he is absent from us in heaven, present with us, nor corporeally, but spiritually, by his vivifying operation, and as he himself explained at his Last Supper that he would be present with us (John, chs. 14; 15; and 16). Whence it follows that we do not have the Supper without Christ, and yet at the same time have an unbloody and mystical Supper, as it was universally called by antiquity.

5.206 OTHER PURPOSES OF THE LORD'S SUPPER. Moreover, we are admonished in the celebration of the Supper of the Lord to be mindful of whose body we have become members, and that, therefore, we may be of one mind with all the brethren, live a holy life, and not pollute ourselves with wickedness and strange religions; but, persevering in the true faith to the end of our life, strive to excel in holiness of life.

5.207 PREPARATION FOR THE SUPPER. It is therefore fitting that when we would come to the Supper, we first examine ourselves according to the commandment of the apostle, especially as to the kind of faith we have, whether we believe that Christ has come to save sinners and to call them to repentance, and whether each man believes that he is in the number of those who have been delivered by Christ and saved; and whether he is determined to change his wicked life, to lead a holy life, and with the Lord's help to persevere in the true religion and in harmony with the brethren, and to give due thanks to God for his deliverance.

5.208 THE OBSERVANCE OF THE SUPPER WITH BOTH BREAD AND WINE. We think that rite, manner, or form of the Supper to be the most simple and excellent which comes nearest to the first institution of the Lord and to the apostles' doctrine. It consists in proclaiming the Word of God, in godly prayers, in the action of the Lord himself, and its repetition, in the eating of the Lord's body and drinking of his blood; in a fitting remembrance of the Lord's death, and a faithful thanksgiving; and in a holy fellowship in the union of the body of the Church.

5.209 We therefore disapprove of those who have taken from the faithful one species of the sacrament, namely, the Lord's cup. For these seriously offend against the institution of the Lord who says: "Drink ye all of this"; which he did not so expressly say of the bread.

5.210 We are not now discussing what kind of mass once existed among the fathers, whether it is to be tolerated or not. But this we say freely that the mass which is now used throughout the Roman Church has been abolished in our churches for many and very good reasons which, for brevity's sake, we do not now enumerate in detail. We certainly could not approve of making a wholesome action into a vain spectacle and a means of gaining merit, and of celebrating it for a price. Nor could we approve of saying that in it the priest is said to effect the very body of the Lord, and really to offer it for the remission of the sins of the living and the dead, and in addition, for the honor, veneration and remembrance of the saints in heaven, etc.

## CHAPTER XXII
### Of Religious and Ecclesiastical Meetings

5.211 WHAT OUGHT TO BE DONE IN MEETINGS FOR WORSHIP. Although it is permitted all men to read the Holy Scriptures privately at home, and by instruction to edify one another in the true religion, yet in order that the Word of God may be properly preached to the people, and prayers and supplication publicly made, also that the sacraments may be rightly administered, and that collections may be made for the poor and to pay the cost of all the Church's expenses, and in order to maintain social intercourse, it is most necessary that religious or Church gatherings be held. For it is certain that in the apostolic and primitive Church, there were such assemblies frequented by all the godly.

5.212 MEETINGS FOR WORSHIP NOT TO BE NEGLECTED. As many as spurn such meetings and stay away from them, despise true religion, and are to be urged by the pastors and godly magistrates to abstain from stubbornly absenting themselves from sacred assemblies.

5.213 MEETINGS ARE PUBLIC. But Church meetings are not to be secret and hidden, but public and well attended, unless persecution by the enemies of Christ and the Church does not permit them to be public. For we know how under the tyranny of the Roman emperors the meetings of the primitive Church were held in secret places.

5.214 DECENT MEETING PLACES. Moreover, the places where the faithful meet are to be decent, and in all respects fit for God's Church. Therefore, spacious buildings or temples are to be chosen, but they are to be purged of everything that is not fitting for a church. And everything is to be arranged for decorum, necessity, and godly decen-

**5.215** MODESTY AND HUMILITY TO BE OBSERVED IN MEETINGS. And as we believe that God does not dwell in temples made with hands, so we know that on account of God's Word and sacred use places dedicated to God and his worship are not profane, but holy, and that those who are present in them are to conduct themselves reverently and modestly, seeing that they are in a sacred place, in the presence of God and his holy angels.

**5.216** THE TRUE ORNAMENTATION OF SANCTUARIES. Therefore, all luxurious attire, all pride, and everything unbecoming to Christian humility, discipline and modesty, are to be banished from the sanctuaries and places of prayers of Christians. For the true ornamentation of churches does not consist in ivory, gold, and precious stones, but in the frugality, piety, and virtues of those who are in the Church. Let all things be done decently and in order in the church, and finally, let all things be done for edification.

**5.217** WORSHIP IN THE COMMON LANGUAGE. Therefore, let all strange tongues keep silence in gatherings for worship, and let all things be set forth in a common language which is understood by the people gathered in that place.

## CHAPTER XXIII

### Of the Prayers of the Church, of Singing, and of Canonical Hours

**5.218** COMMON LANGUAGE. It is true that a man is permitted to pray privately in any language that he understands, but public prayers in meetings for worship are to be made in the common language known to all. PRAYER. Let all the prayers of the faithful be poured forth to God alone, through the mediation of Christ only, out of faith and love. The priesthood of Christ the Lord and true religion forbid the invocation of saints in heaven or to use them as intercessors. Prayer is to be made for magistracy, for kings, and all that are placed in authority, for ministers of the Church, and for all needs of churches. In calamities, especially of the Church, unceasing prayer is to be made both privately and publicly.

**5.219** FREE PRAYER. Moreover, prayer is to be made voluntarily, without constraint or for any reward. Nor is it proper for prayer to be superstitiously restricted to one place, as if it were not permitted to pray anywhere except in a sanctuary. Neither is it necessary for public prayers to be the same in all churches with respect to form and time. Each Church is to exercise its own freedom. Socrates, in his history, says, "In all regions of the world you will not find two churches which wholly agree in prayer"

(*Hist. ecclesiast.* V.22, 57). The authors of this difference, I think, were those who were in charge of the Churches at particular times. Yet if they agree, it is to be highly commended and imitated by others.

5.220 THE METHOD TO BE EMPLOYED IN PUBLIC PRAYERS. As in everything, so also in public prayers there is to be a standard lest they be excessively long and irksome. The greatest part of meetings for worship is therefore to be given to evangelical teaching, and care is to be taken lest the congregation is wearied by too lengthy prayers and when they are to hear the preaching of the Gospel they either leave the meeting or, having been exhausted, want to do away with it altogether. To such people the sermon seems to be overlong, which otherwise is brief enough. And therefore it is appropriate for preachers to keep to a standard.

5.221 SINGING. Likewise moderation is to be exercised where singing is used in a meeting for worship. That song which they call the Gregorian Chant has many foolish things in it; hence it is rightly rejected by many of our churches. If there are churches which have a true and proper sermon[9] but no singing, they ought not to be condemned. For all churches do not have the advantage of singing. And it is well known from testimonies of antiquity that the custom of singing is very old in the Eastern Churches whereas it was late when it was at length accepted in the West.

5.222 CANONICAL HOURS. Antiquity knew nothing of canonical hours, that is, prayers arranged for certain hours of the day, and sung or recited by the Papists, as can be proved from their breviaries and by many arguments. But they also have not a few absurdities, of which I say nothing else; accordingly they are rightly omitted by churches which substitute in their place things that are beneficial for the whole Church of God.

## CHAPTER XXIV

### Of Holy Days, Fasts and the Choice of Foods

5.223 THE TIME NECESSARY FOR WORSHIP. Although religion is not bound to time, yet it cannot be cultivated and exercised without a proper distribution and arrangement of time. Every Church, therefore, chooses for itself a certain time for public prayers, and for the preaching of the Gospel, and for the celebration of the sacraments; and no one is permitted to overthrow this appointment of the Church at his own pleasure. For unless some due time and leisure is given for the outward exercise of religion, without doubt men would be drawn away from it by their own affairs.

---

[9] The Latin has *orationem* which has been rendered as "prayer." But from the context it would seem that the word should be given its usual classical meaning of a "speech."

**5.224** THE LORD'S DAY. Hence we see that in the ancient churches there were not only certain set hours in the week appointed for meetings, but that also the Lord's Day itself, ever since the apostles' time, was set aside for them and for a holy rest, a practice now rightly preserved by our Churches for the sake of worship and love.

**5.225** SUPERSTITION. In this connection we do not yield to the Jewish observance and to superstitions. For we do not believe that one day is any holier than another, or think that rest in itself is acceptable to God. Moreover, we celebrate the Lord's Day and not the Sabbath as a free observance.

**5.226** THE FESTIVALS OF CHRIST AND THE SAINTS. Moreover, if in Christian liberty the churches religiously celebrate the memory of the Lord's nativity, circumcision, passion, resurrection, and of his ascension into heaven, and the sending of the Holy Spirit upon his disciples, we approve of it highly. But we do not approve of feasts instituted for men and for saints. Holy days have to do with the first Table of the Law and belong to God alone. Finally, holy days which have been instituted for the saints and which we have abolished, have much that is absurd and useless, and are not to be tolerated. In the meantime, we confess that the remembrance of saints, at a suitable time and place, is to be profitably commended to the people in sermons, and the holy examples of the saints set forth to be imitated by all.

**5.227** FASTING. Now, the more seriously the Church of Christ condemns surfeiting, drunkenness, and all kinds of lust and intemperance, so much the more strongly does it commend to us Christian fasting. For fasting is nothing else than the abstinence and moderation of the godly, and a discipline, care and chastisement of our flesh undertaken as a necessity for the time being, whereby we are humbled before God, and we deprive the flesh of its fuel so that it may the more willingly and easily obey the Spirit. Therefore, those who pay no attention to such things do not fast, but imagine that they fast if they stuff their stomachs once a day, and at a certain or prescribed time abstain from certain foods, thinking that by having done this work they please God and do something good. Fasting is an aid to the prayers of the saints and for all virtues. But as is seen in the books of the prophets, the fast of the Jews who fasted from food but not from wickedness did not please God.

**5.228** PUBLIC AND PRIVATE FASTING. Now there is a public and a private fasting. In olden times they celebrated public fasts in calamitous times and in the affliction of the Church. They abstained altogether from food till the evening, and spent all that time in holy prayers, the worship of God, and repentance. These differed little from mourning, and there is frequent mention of them in the Prophets and espccially by Joel in Ch. 2. Such a fast should be kept at this day, when the Church is in distress. Private fasts are undertaken by each one of us, as he feels himself withdrawn from the Spirit. For in this manner he withdraws the flesh from its fuel.

**5.229** CHARACTERISTICS OF FASTING. All fasts ought to proceed from a free and willing spirit, and from genuine humility, and not feigned to gain the applause or favor of men, much less that a man should wish to merit righteousness by them. But let every one fast to this end, that he may deprive the flesh of its fuel in order that he may the more zealously serve God.

**5.230** LENT. The fast of Lent is attested by antiquity but not at all in the writings of the apostles. Therefore it ought not, and cannot, be imposed on the faithful. It is certain that formerly there were various forms and customs of fasting. Hence, Irenaeus, a most ancient writer, says: "Some think that a fast should be observed one day only, others two days, but others more, and some forty days. This diversity in keeping this fast did not first begin in our times, but long before us by those, as I suppose, who did not simply keep to what had been delivered to them from the beginning, but afterwards fell into another custom either through negligence or ignorance" (*Fragm. 3*, ed. Stieren, I. 824 f.). Moreover, Socrates, the historian says: "Because no ancient text is found concerning this matter, I think the apostles left this to every man's own judgment, that every one might do what is good without fear or constraint" (*Hist. ecclesiast.* V.22, 40).

**5.231** CHOICE OF FOOD. Now concerning the choice of foods, we think that in fasting all things should be denied to the flesh whereby the flesh is made more insolent, and by which it is greatly pleased, and by which it is inflamed with desire whether by fish or meat or spices or delicacies and excellent wines. Moreover, we know that all the creatures of God were made for the use of service of men. All things which God made are good, and without distinction are to be used in the fear of God and with proper moderation (Gen. 2:15 f.). For the apostle says: "To the pure all things are pure" (Titus 1:15), and also: "Eat whatever is sold in the meat market without raising any question on the ground of conscience" (I Cor. 10:25). The same apostle calls the doctrine of those who teach to abstain from meats "the doctrine of demons"; for "God created foods to be received with thanksgiving by those who believe and know this truth that everything created by God is good, and nothing is to be rejected if it is received with thanksgiving" (I Tim. 4:1 ff.). The same apostle, in the epistle to the Colossians, reproves those who want to acquire a reputation for holiness by excessive abstinence (Col. 2:18 ff.).

**5.232** SECTS. Therefore we entirely disapprove of the Tatians and the Encratites, and all the disciples of Eustathius, against whom the Gangrian Synod was called.

## CHAPTER XXV
## Of Catechizing and of Comforting and Visiting the Sick

5.233 YOUTH TO BE INSTRUCTED IN GODLINESS. The Lord enjoined his ancient people to exercise the greatest care that young people, even from infancy, be properly instructed. Moreover, he expressly commanded in his law that they should teach them, and that the mysteries of the sacraments should be explained. Now since it is well known from the writings of the Evangelists and apostles that God has no less concern for the youth of his new people, when he openly testifies and says: "Let the children come to me; for to such belongs the kingdom of heaven" (Mark 10:14), the pastors of the churches act most wisely when they early and carefully catechize the youth, laying the first grounds of faith, and faithfully teaching the rudiments of our religion by expounding the Ten Commandments, the Apostles' Creed, the Lord's Prayer, and the doctrine of the sacraments, with other such principles and chief heads of our religion. Here let the Church show her faith and diligence in bringing the children to be catechized, desirous and glad to have her children well instructed.

5.234 THE VISITATION OF THE SICK. Since men are never exposed to more grievous temptations than when they are harassed by infirmities, are sick and are weakened by diseases of both soul and body, surely it is never more fitting for pastors of churches to watch more carefully for the welfare of their flocks than in such diseases and infirmities. Therefore let them visit the sick soon, and let them be called in good time by the sick, if the circumstance itself would have required it. Let them comfort and confirm them in the true faith, and then arm them against the dangerous suggestions of Satan. They should also hold prayer for the sick in the home and, if need be, prayers should also be made for the sick in the public meeting; and they should see that they happily depart this life. We said above that we do not approve of the Popish visitation of the sick with extreme unction because it is absurd and is not approved by canonical Scriptures.

## CHAPTER XXVI
## Of the Burial of the Faithful, and of the Care to Be Shown for the Dead; of Purgatory, and the Appearing of Spirits

5.235 THE BURIAL OF BODIES. As the bodies of the faithful are the temples of the Holy Spirit which we truly believe will rise again at the Last Day, Scriptures command that they be honorably and without superstition committed to the earth, and also that honorable mention be made of those saints who have fallen asleep in the Lord, and that all duties of familial piety be shown to those left behind, their widows and orphans. We do not teach that any other care be taken for the dead. Therefore, we greatly disapprove of the Cynics, who neglected the bodies of the dead or most carelessly and disdainfully cast them into the earth, never saying a good word about the deceased, or caring a bit about those whom they left behind them.

**5.236** THE CARE FOR THE DEAD. On the other hand, we do not approve of those who are overly and absurdly attentive to the deceased; who, like the heathen, bewail their dead (although we do not blame that moderate mourning which the apostle permits in I Thess. 4:13, judging it to be inhuman not to grieve at all); and who sacrifice for the dead, and mumble certain prayers for pay, in order by such ceremonies to deliver their loved ones from the torments in which they are immersed by death, and then think they are able to liberate them by such incantations.

**5.237** THE STATE OF THE SOUL DEPARTED FROM THE BODY. For we believe that the faithful, after bodily death, go directly to Christ, and, therefore, do not need the eulogies and prayers of the living for the dead and their services. Likewise we believe that unbelievers are immediately cast into hell from which no exit is opened for the wicked by any services of the living.

**5.238** PURGATORY. But what some teach concerning the fire of purgatory is opposed to the Christian faith, namely, "I believe in the forgiveness of sins, and the life everlasting," and to the perfect purgation through Christ, and to these words of Christ our Lord: "Truly, truly, I say to you, he who hears my word and believes him who sent me, has eternal life; he shall not come into judgment, but has passed from death to life" (John 5:24). Again: "He who has bathed does not need to wash, except for his feet, but he is clean all over, and you are clean" (John 13:10).

**5.239** THE APPARITION OF SPIRITS. Now what is related of the spirits or souls of the dead sometimes appearing to those who are alive, and begging certain duties of them whereby they may be set free, we count those apparitions among the laughingstocks, crafts, and deceptions of the devil, who, as he can transform himself into an angel of light, so he strives either to overthrow the true faith or to call it into doubt. In the Old Testament the Lord forbade the seeking of the truth from the dead, and any sort of commerce with spirits (Deut. 18:11). Indeed, as evangelical truth declares, the glutton, being in torment, is denied a return to his brethren, as the divine oracle declares in the words: "They have Moses and the prophets; let them hear them. If they hear not Moses and the prophets, neither will they be convinced if some one should rise from the dead" (Luke 16:29 ff.).

## CHAPTER XXVII

### Of Rites, Ceremonies and Things Indifferent

**5.240** CEREMONIES AND RITES. Unto the ancient people were given at one time certain ceremonies, as a kind of instruction for those who were kept under the law, as under a schoolmaster or tutor. But when Christ, the Deliverer, came and the law was abolished, we who believe are no more under the law (Rom. 6:14), and the ceremonies have disappeared; hence the apostles did not want to retain or to restore them in Christ's Church to such a degree that they openly testified that they did not wish to impose any burden upon the Church. Therefore, we would seem to be bringing in and restoring Judaism if we were to increase ceremonies and rites in Christ's Church according to the custom in the ancient Church. Hence, we by no means approve of the opinion of those who think that the Church of Christ must be held in check by many different rites, as if by some kind of training. For if the apostles did not want to impose upon Christian people ceremonies or rites which were appointed by God, who, I pray, in his right mind would obtrude upon them the inventions devised by man? The more the mass of rites is increased in the Church, the more is detracted not only from Christian liberty, but also from Christ, and from faith in him, as long as the people seek those things in ceremonies which they should seek in the only Son of God, Jesus Christ, through faith. Wherefore a few moderate and simple rites, that are not contrary to the Word of God, are sufficient for the godly.

**5.241** DIVERSITY OF RITES. If different rites are found in churches, no one should think for this reason the churches disagree. Socrates says: "It would be impossible to put together in writing all the rites of churches throughout cities and countries. No religion observes the same rites, even though it embraces the same doctrine concerning them. For those who are of the same faith disagree among themselves about rites" (*Hist. ecclesiast.* V.22, 30, 62). This much says Socrates. And we, today, having in our churches different rites in the celebration of the Lord's Supper and in some other things, nevertheless do not disagree in doctrine and faith; nor is the unity and fellowship of our churches thereby rent asunder. For the churches have always used their liberty in such rites, as being things indifferent. We also do the same thing today.

**5.242** THINGS INDIFFERENT. But at the same time we admonish men to be on guard lest they reckon among things indifferent what are in fact not indifferent, as some are wont to regard the mass and the use of images in places of worship as things indifferent. "Indifferent," wrote Jerome to Augustine, "is that which is neither good nor bad, so that, whether you do it or not, you are neither just nor unjust." Therefore, when things indifferent are wrested to the confession of faith, they cease to be free; as Paul shows that it is lawful for a man to eat flesh if someone does not remind him that it was offered to idols, for then it is unlawful, because he who eats it seems to approve idolatry by eating it (I Cor. 8:9 ff.; 10:25 ff.).

## CHAPTER XXVIII

### Of the Possessions of the Church

**5.243** THE POSSESSIONS OF THE CHURCH AND THEIR PROPER USE. The Church of Christ possesses riches through the munificence of princes and the liberality of the faithful who have given their means to the Church. For the Church has need of such resources and from ancient time has had resources for the maintenance of things necessary for the Church. Now the true use of the Church's wealth was, and is now, to maintain teaching in schools and in religious meetings, along with all the worship, rites, and buildings of the Church; finally, to maintain teachers, scholars, and ministers, with other necessary things, and especially for the succor and relief of the poor. MANAGEMENT. Moreover, God-fearing and wise men, noted for the management of domestic affairs, should be chosen to administer properly the Church's possessions.

**5.244** THE MISUSE OF THE CHURCH'S POSSESSIONS. But if through misfortune or through the audacity, ignorance or avarice of some persons the Church's wealth is abused, it is to be restored to a sacred use by godly and wise men. For neither is an abuse, which is the greatest sacrilege, to be winked at. Therefore, we teach that schools and institutions which have been corrupted in doctrine, worship and morals must be reformed, and that the relief of the poor must be arranged dutifully, wisely, and in good faith.

## CHAPTER XXIX

### Of Celibacy, Marriage and the Management of Domestic Affairs

**5.245** SINGLE PEOPLE. Those who have the gift of celibacy from heaven, so that from the heart or with their whole soul are pure and continent and are not aflame with passion, let them serve the Lord in that calling, as long as they feel endued with that divine gift; and let them not lift up themselves above others, but let them serve the Lord continuously in simplicity and humility (I Cor. 7:7 ff.). For such are more apt to attend to divine things than those who are distracted with the private affairs of a family. But if, again, the gift be taken away, and they feel a continual burning, let them call to mind the words of the apostle: "It is better to marry than to be aflame" (I Cor. 7:9).

**5.246** MARRIAGE. For marriage (which is the medicine of incontinency, and continency itself) was instituted by the Lord God himself, who blessed it most bountifully, and willed man and woman to cleave one to the other inseparably, and to live together in complete love and concord (Matt. 19:4 ff). Whereupon we know that the apostle said: "Let marriage be held in honor among all, and let the marriage bed be undefiled" (Heb. 13:4). And again: "If a girl marries, she does not sin" (I Cor. 7:28). THE SECTS. We therefore condemn polygamy, and those who condemn second marriages.

5.247 HOW MARRIAGES ARE TO BE CONTRACTED. We teach that marriages are to be lawfully contracted in the fear of the Lord, and not against the laws which forbid certain degrees of consanguinity, lest the marriages should be incestuous. Let marriages be made with consent of the parents, or of those who take the place of parents, and above all for that purpose for which the Lord instituted marriages. Moreover, let them be kept holy with the utmost faithfulness, piety, love and purity of those joined together. Therefore let them guard against quarrels, dissensions, lust and adultery.

5.248 MATRIMONIAL FORUM. Let lawful courts be established in the Church, and holy judges who may care for marriages, and may repress all unchastity and shamefulness, and before whom matrimonial disputes may be settled.

5.249 THE REARING OF CHILDREN. Children are to be brought up by the parents in the fear of the Lord; and parents are to provide for their children, remembering the saying of the apostle: "If anyone does not provide for his relatives, he has disowned the faith and is worse than an unbeliever" (I Tim. 5:8). But especially they should teach their children honest trades or professions by which they may support themselves. They should keep them from idleness and in all these things instill in them true faith in God, lest through a lack of confidence or too much security or filthy greed they become dissolute and achieve no success.

5.250 And it is most certain that those works which are done by parents in true faith by way of domestic duties and the management of their households are in God's sight holy and truly good works. They are no less pleasing to God than prayers, fasting and almsgiving. For thus the apostle has taught in his epistles, especially in those to Timothy and Titus. And with the same apostle we account the doctrine of those who forbid marriage or openly castigate or indirectly discredit it, as if it were not holy and pure, among the doctrine of demons.

5.251 We also detest an impure single life, the secret and open lusts and fornications of hypocrites pretending to be continent when they are the most incontinent of all. All these God will judge. We do not disapprove of riches or rich men, if they be godly and use their riches well. But we reject the sect of the Apostolicals, etc.[10]

---

[10] The Apostolicals were followers of a religious fanatic, Gherado Segarelli, of Parma, who in the thirteenth century wanted to restore the poverty of the apostolic life.

## CHAPTER XXX
## Of the Magistracy

**5.252**  THE MAGISTRACY IS FROM GOD. Magistracy of every kind is instituted by God himself for the peace and tranquillity of the human race, and thus it should have the chief place in the world. If the magistrate is opposed to the Church, he can hinder and disturb it very much; but if he is a friend and even a member of the Church, he is a most useful and excellent member of it, who is able to benefit it greatly, and to assist it best of all.

**5.253**  THE DUTY OF THE MAGISTRATE. The chief duty of the magistrate is to secure and preserve peace and public tranquillity. Doubtless he will never do this more successfully than when he is truly God-fearing and religious; that is to say, when, according to the example of the most holy kings and princes of the people of the Lord, he promotes the preaching of the truth and sincere faith, roots out lies and all superstition, together with all impiety and idolatry, and defends the Church of God. We certainly teach that the care of religion belongs especially to the holy magistrate.

**5.254**  Let him, therefore, hold the Word of God in his hands, and take care lest anything contrary to it is taught. Likewise let him govern the people entrusted to him by God with good laws made according to the Word of God, and let him keep them in discipline, duty and obedience. Let him exercise judgment by judging uprightly. Let him not respect any man's person or accept bribes. Let him protect widows, orphans and the afflicted. Let him punish and even banish criminals, impostors and barbarians. For he does not bear the sword in vain (Rom. 13:4).

**5.255**  Therefore, let him draw this sword of God against all malefactors, seditious persons, thieves, murderers, oppressors, blasphemers, perjured persons, and all those whom God has commanded him to punish and even to execute. Let him suppress stubborn heretics (who are truly heretics), who do not cease to blaspheme the majesty of God and to trouble, and even to destroy the Church of God.

**5.256**  WAR. And if it is necessary to preserve the safety of the people by war, let him wage war in the name of God; provided he has first sought peace by all means possible, and cannot save his people in any other way except by war. And when the magistrate does these things in faith, he serves God by those very works which are truly good, and receives a blessing from the Lord.

**5.257**  We condemn the Anabaptists, who, when they deny that a Christian may hold the office of a magistrate, deny also that a man may be justly put to death by the magistrate, or that the magistrate may wage war, or that oaths are to be rendered to a magistrate, and such like things.

**5.258** THE DUTY OF SUBJECTS. For as God wants to effect the safety of his people by the magistrate, whom he has given to the world to be, as it were, a father, so all subjects are commanded to acknowledge this favor of God in the magistrate. Therefore let them honor and reverence the magistrate as the minister of God; let them love him, favor him, and pray for him as their father; and let them obey all his just and fair commands. Finally, let them pay all customs and taxes, and all other such dues faithfully and willingly. And if the public safety of the country and justice require it, and the magistrate of necessity wages war, let them even lay down their life and pour out their blood for the public safety and that of the magistrate. And let them do this in the name of God willingly, bravely and cheerfully. For he who opposes the magistrate provokes the severe wrath of God against himself.

**5.259** SECTS AND SEDITIONS. We, therefore, condemn all who are contemptuous of the magistrate—rebels, enemies of the state, seditious villains, finally, all who openly or craftily refuse to perform whatever duties they owe.

**5.260** We beseech God, our most merciful Father in heaven, that he will bless the rulers of the people, and us, and his whole people, through Jesus Christ, our only Lord and Savior; to whom be praise and glory and thanksgiving, for all ages. Amen.

# THE WESTMINSTER CONFESSION OF FAITH
[TEXT]

## The Westminster Standards

In 1643, the English House of Commons adopted an ordinance calling for the "settling of the government and liturgy of the Church of England (in a manner) most agreeable to God's Holy Word and most apt to procure the peace of the church at home and nearer abroad." After the ordinance passed the House of Lords, an assembly to accomplish this work convened in Westminster Abbey.

The Parliament nominated one hundred fifty-one persons to the assembly. Thirty were members of Parliament; the others were "learned, godly, and judicious divines." Five Scottish clergymen were in attendance and had the right of discussion but not vote. Churches in Holland, Belgium, France, Switzerland, and the American colonies were invited to send delegates, though none came. The assembly held 1,163 sessions, finally concluding in 1649.

The Westminster Assembly conducted its work in a crisis atmosphere. Internal conflicts had nearly torn apart both England and the English church. Political and religious problems were inseparable. Who should rule the church? Who should rule the state? What power should the king have? What power Parliament, local councils, and assemblies? The Anglican party stood for royal rule in England with the sovereign also head of the church's government. The Presbyterian party sought to vest authority in elected representatives of the people, both in Parliament and in church presbyteries. An emerging third party, soon led by Oliver Cromwell, wanted local autonomy for churches and limited powers for both king and Parliament.

Even before the assembly met, civil war broke out between the contending parties. But the assembly went to work and eventually completed the "Form of Presbyterian Church Government," a "Directory of Public Worship," "The Confession of Faith," "The Larger Catechism," and "The Shorter Catechism." Each document was approved by the English Parliament, which asked the assembly to add scriptural proofs.

Cromwell's ascendancy precipitated the end of the assembly. In 1648, Pride's Purge forcibly excluded Presbyterian members from Parliament. With the execution of King Charles I in 1649, English Puritanism split into "Presbyterians," who protested the regicide, and "Independents," who supported it and aligned themselves with Cromwell.

In 1647, the Scottish General Assembly adopted the Westminster Standards for use in the kirk, replacing the Scots Confession of 1560 and the Heidelberg Catechism. The standards came to New England with the Puritans (Independents) and to the Middle Atlantic states with the Scotch-Irish Presbyterians. In 1729, the standards were adopted as the confessional position of the newly organized Presbyterian synod in the colonies and have played a formative role in American Presbyterianism ever since. The Westminster Standards represent the fruits of a Protestant scholasticism that refined and systematized the teachings of the Reformation. The standards lift up the truth and authority of the Scriptures, as immediately inspired in Hebrew and Greek, kept pure in all ages, and known through the internal witness of the Holy Spirit. Divine sovereignty and double predestination are also emphasized. In appealing to Scripture to formulate a covenant theology, the standards had important implications for political thought and practice, reminding both ruler and people of their duties to God and to each other.

## The Westminster Confession of Faith

The Westminster Confession affirms God's work from its beginning in creation to its end in resurrection and last judgment. God is first, last, and preeminent in all things. God's people are to understand and bring their lives into accord with God's wondrous ways and magnificent will.

The confession begins with God's self-revelation in Scripture: God is the "one living and true God, infinite in being and perfection, invisible, immutable, immense, eternal, incomprehensible, almighty, most wise, most holy, most free, most absolute." Out of nothing, God created all that is, including humans, whom God upholds, directs, and governs. Humans, however, did not remain in blessed harmony with God's will. Sin's intervention, which God permitted but did not cause, resulted in corruption of the human condition and of humans' relationship to God. Yet, God has made a covenant of grace with humans; through Christ, relationship to God is restored. The Christian life—nurtured by prayer, preaching, and the sacraments, and lived in grace and glory—prepares for God's predetermined end of mercy (salvation of the elect) and of justice (damnation of the reprobate).

## The Westminster Catechisms

The Larger Catechism, written primarily by Dr. Anthony Tuckney, professor of divinity and vice-chancellor of Cambridge University, was designed for public exposition from the pulpit. The Shorter Catechism, primarily the work of the Reverend John Wallis, an eminent mathematician who later became professor of geometry at Oxford University, was written for the education of children. Both deal with questions of God, Christ, the Christian life, the Ten Commandments, the sacraments, and the Lord's Prayer; unlike most earlier catechisms, neither contains a section on the Apostles' Creed. Especially famous are the first question and answer of the Shorter Catechism. "What is the chief end of man? Man's chief end is to glorify God and enjoy Him forever."

# THE WESTMINSTER CONFESSION OF FAITH[a]

Presbyterian Church in the United States

The United Presbyterian Church in the United States of America

CHAPTER I

CHAPTER I

## Of the Holy Scripture

**6.001** 1. Although the light of nature, and the works of creation and providence, do so far manifest the goodness, wisdom, and power of God, as to leave men inexcusable;[1] yet are they[b] not sufficient to give that knowledge of God, and of his will, which is necessary unto salvation;[2] therefore it pleased the Lord, at sundry times, and in divers manners, to reveal himself, and to declare that his will unto his Church;[3] and afterwards for the better preserving and propagating of the truth, and for the more sure establishment and comfort of the Church against the corruption of the flesh, and the malice of Satan and of the world, to commit the same wholly unto writing;[4] which maketh the Holy Scripture to be most necessary;[5] those former ways of God's revealing his will unto his people being now ceased.[6]

**6.002** 2. Under the name of Holy Scripture, or the Word of God written, are now contained all the books of the Old and New Testaments, which are these:

### Of the Old Testament

| | | | |
|---|---|---|---|
| Genesis | II Samuel | Proverbs | Amos |
| Exodus | I Kings | Ecclesiastes | Obadiah |
| Leviticus | II Kings | The Song of Songs | Jonah |
| Numbers | I Chronicles | Isaiah | Micah |
| Deuteronomy | II Chronicles | Jeremiah | Nahum |
| Joshua | Ezra | Lamentations | Habakkuk |
| Judges | Nehemiah | Ezekiel | Zephaniah |
| Ruth | Esther | Daniel | Haggai |
| I Samuel | Job | Hosea | Zechariah |
| | Psalms | Joel | Malachi |

---

[a] The text of the Westminster Confession of Faith is that adopted by The United Presbyterian Church in the United States of America in 1958. Footnotes have been added to show how the text of 1958 differs from that of the 1647 edition of the Confession published under the title *The Humble Advice of the Assembly of Divines, Now by Authority of Parliament Sitting at Westminster, Concerning a Confession of Faith: with the Quotations and Text of Scripture Annexed. Presented by Them Lately to Both Houses of Parliament*. No attempt is made to trace the various amendments leading to the text of 1958. The footnotes use the punctuation, spelling, and capitalization of 1647. On the organization of the Presbyterian Church in the United States in 1861, it adopted the Standards of the Presbyterian Church in the United States of America from which its constituents had withdrawn. The only amendment in the Confession since 1861, by this Church, has been in striking out the clause in Chapter XXIV, Section 4, making it unlawful to marry a deceased wife's sister.

[b] UPCUSA ed. reads: "they are."

Presbyterian Church  
in the United States

The United Presbyterian Church  
in the United States of America

### Of the New Testament

| Matthew | Ephesians | Hebrews |
| Mark | Philippians | James |
| Luke | Colossians | I Peter |
| John | I Thessalonians | II Peter |
| Acts of the Apostles | II Thessalonians | I John |
| Romans | I Timothy | II John |
| I Corinthians | II Timothy | III John |
| II Corinthians | Titus | Jude |
| Galatians | Philemon | Revelation[c] |

All which are given by inspiration of God, to be the rule of faith and life.

**6.003**     3. The books commonly called Apocrypha, not being of divine inspiration, are no part of the canon of the Scripture; and therefore are of no authority in the Church of God, nor to be any otherwise approved, or made use of, than other human writings.[7]

**6.004**     4. The authority of the Holy Scripture, for which it ought to be believed and obeyed, dependeth not upon the testimony of any man or church, but wholly upon God (who is truth itself), the author thereof; and therefore it is to be received, because it is the Word of God.[8]

**6.005**     5. We may be moved and induced by the testimony of the Church to an high and reverent esteem for[d] the Holy Scripture; and the heavenliness of the matter, the efficacy of the doctrine, the majesty of the style, the consent of all the parts, the scope of the whole (which is to give all glory to God), the full discovery it makes of the only way of man's salvation, the many other incomparable excellencies, and the entire perfection thereof, are arguments whereby it doth abundantly evidence itself to be the Word of God; yet, notwithstanding, our full persuasion and assurance of the infallible truth and divine authority thereof, is from the inward work of the Holy Spirit, bearing witness by and with the Word in our hearts.[9]

**6.006**     6. The whole counsel of God, concerning all things necessary for his own glory, man's salvation, faith, and life, is either expressly set down in Scripture, or by good and necessary consequence may be deduced from Scripture:[10] unto which nothing at any time is to be added, whether by new revelations of the Spirit, or traditions of men.[11] Nevertheless we acknowledge the inward illumination of the Spirit of

---

[c] Ed. 1647 includes "of John."  
[d] UPCUSA ed. reads: "of."

God to be necessary for the saving understanding of such things as are revealed in the Word;[12] and that[e] there are some circumstances concerning the worship of God, and government of the Church, common to human actions and societies, which are to be ordered by the light of nature and Christian prudence, according to the general rules of the Word, which are always to be observed.[13]

6.007  7. All things in Scripture are not alike plain in themselves, nor alike clear unto all;[14] yet those things which are necessary to be known, believed, and observed, for salvation, are so clearly propounded and opened in some place of Scripture or other, that not only the learned, but the unlearned, in a due use of the ordinary means, may attain unto a sufficient understanding of them.[15]

6.008  8. The Old Testament in Hebrew (which was the native language of the people of God of old), and the New Testament in Greek (which at the time of the writing of it was most generally known to the nations), being immediately inspired by God,[16] and by his singular care and providence kept pure in all ages, are therefore authentical; so as in all controversies of religion the Church is finally to appeal unto them.[17] But because these original tongues are not known to all the people of God who have right unto, and interest in, the Scriptures, and are commanded, in the fear of God, to read and search them,[18] therefore they are to be translated into the[f] language of every people unto which they come, that the Word of God dwelling plentifully in all, they may worship him in an acceptable manner, and, through patience and comfort of the Scriptures, may have hope.[19]

6.009  9. The infallible rule of interpretation of Scripture, is the Scripture itself; and therefore, when there is a question about the true and full sense of any scripture (which is not manifold, but one), it may be searched and known by other places that speak more clearly.[20]

6.010  10. The Supreme Judge, by which[g] all controversies of religion are to be determined, and all decrees of councils, opinions of ancient writers, doctrines of men, and private spirits, are to be examined, and in whose sentence we are to rest, can be no other but the Holy Spirit speaking in the Scripture.[21]

## CHAPTER II

### Of God, and of the Holy Trinity

6.011  1. There is but one only living and true God,[1] who is infinite in being and perfection,[2] a most pure spirit,[3] invisible,[4] without body, parts, or passions,[5] immutable,[6] immense,[7] eternal,[8] incomprehensible,[9]

---

[e] UPCUSA ed. reads: "and there are."
[f] Ed. 1647 reads: "the vulgar language of every nation."
[g] UPCUSA ed. reads: "whom."

almighty;[10] most wise,[11] most holy,[12] most free,[13] most absolute,[14] working all things according to the counsel of his own immutable and most righteous will,[15] for his own glory;[16] most loving,[17] gracious, merciful, long-suffering, abundant in goodness and truth, forgiving iniquity, transgression, and sin;[18] the rewarder of them that diligently seek him;[19] and withal[h] most just and terrible in his judgments;[20] hating all sin,[21] and who will by no means clear the guilty.[22]

**6.012**   2. God hath all life, glory, goodness, blessedness, in and of himself;[23] and is alone in and unto himself all-sufficient, not standing in need of any creatures which he hath made, nor deriving any glory from them, but only manifesting his own glory in, by, unto, and upon them:[24] he is the alone fountain of all being, of whom, through whom, and to whom, are all things;[25] and hath most sovereign dominion over them, to do by them, for them, or[i] upon them, whatsoever himself pleaseth.[26] In his sight all things are open and manifest;[27] his knowledge is infinite, infallible, and independent upon the creature;[28] so as nothing is to him contingent or uncertain.[29] He is most holy in all his counsels, in all his works, and in all his commands.[30] To him is due from angels and men, and every other creature, whatsoever worship, service, or obedience he is pleased to require of them.[31]

**6.013**   3. In the unity of the Godhead there be three Persons of one substance, power, and eternity: God the Father, God the Son, and God the Holy Ghost.[32] The Father is of none, neither begotten nor proceeding; the Son is eternally begotten of the Father;[33] the Holy Ghost eternally proceeding from the Father and the Son.[34]

CHAPTER III                                                         CHAPTER III[j]

**Of God's Eternal Decrees[k]**

**6.014**   1. God from all eternity did by the most wise and holy counsel of his own will, freely and unchangeably ordain whatsoever comes to pass;[1] yet so as thereby neither is God the author of sin;[2] nor is violence offered to the will of the creatures, nor is the liberty or contingency of second causes taken away, but rather established.[3]

**6.015**   2. Although God knows whatsoever may or can come to pass, upon all supposed conditions;[4] yet hath he not decreed anything because he foresaw it as future, or as that which would come to pass, upon such conditions.[5]

---

[h] Ed. 1647 reads: "with all."
[i] UPCUSA ed. reads: "and."
[j] See Declaratory Statement at end of Confession of Faith. The Declaratory Statement is the authoritative interpretation of Chapter III.
[k] UPCUSA ed. reads: "Decree."

Presbyterian Church  in the United States

The United Presbyterian Church  in the United States of America

**6.016**     3. By the decree of God, for the manifestation of his glory, some men and angels are predestinated unto everlasting life,[6] and others fore-ordained to everlasting death.[7]

**6.017**     4. These angels and men, thus predestinated and fore-ordained, are particularly and unchangeably designed; and their number is so certain and definite that it cannot be either increased or diminished.[8]

**6.018**     5. Those of mankind that are predestinated unto life, God, before the foundation of the world was laid,[9] according to his eternal and immutable purpose,[10] and the secret counsel and good pleasure of his will,[11] hath chosen in Christ,[12] unto everlasting glory,[13] out of his[m] free grace and love alone, without any foresight of faith or good works, or perseverance in either of them, or any other thing in the creature, as conditions, or causes moving him thereunto;[14] and all to the praise of his glorious grace.[15]

**6.019**     6. As God hath appointed the elect unto glory, so hath he, by the eternal and most free purpose of his will, fore-ordained all the means thereunto.[16] Wherefore they who are elected being fallen in Adam are redeemed by Christ,[17] are effectually called unto faith in Christ by his Spirit working in due season;[18] are justified,[19] adopted,[20] sanctified,[21] and kept by his power through faith unto salvation.[22] Neither are any other redeemed by Christ, effectually called, justified, adopted, sanctified, and saved, but the elect only.[23]

**6.020**     7. The rest of mankind, God was pleased, according to the unsearchable counsel of his own will, whereby he extendeth or withholdeth mercy as he pleaseth, for the glory of his sovereign power over his creatures, to pass by,[24] and to ordain them to dishonour and wrath for their sin,[25] to the praise of his glorious justice.[26]

**6.021**     8. The doctrine of this high mystery of predestination is to be handled with special prudence and care, that men attending the will of God revealed in his Word, and yielding obedience thereunto, may, from the certainty of their effectual vocation, be assured of their eternal election. So shall this doctrine afford matter of praise, reverence, and admiration of God; and of humility, diligence, and abundant consolation to all that sincerely obey the gospel.[27]

CHAPTER IV

**Of Creation**

**6.022**     1. It pleased God the Father, Son, and Holy Ghost, for the manifestation of the glory of his eternal power, wisdom, and goodness, in the beginning, to create or make of nothing the world, and all things

---

[m] Ed. 1647 reads: "his meer grace and love."

therein, whether visible or invisible, in the space of six days, and all very good.[1]

**6.023** 2. After God had made all other creatures, he created man, male and female,[2] with reasonable and immortal souls,[3] endued with knowledge, righteousness, and true holiness after his own image,[4] having the law of God written in their hearts,[5] and power to fulfill it; and yet under a possibility of transgressing, being left to the liberty of their own will, which was subject unto change.[6] Besides this law written in their hearts, they received a command not to eat of the tree of the knowledge of good and evil;[7] which while they kept they were happy in their communion with God,[8] and had dominion over the creatures.[9]

CHAPTER V                                                                 CHAPTER V

**Of Providence**

**6.024** 1. God, the great Creator of all things, doth uphold, direct, dispose, and govern all creatures, actions, and things, from the greatest even to the least,[1] by his most wise and holy providence,[2] according to his infallible foreknowledge,[3] and the free and immutable counsel of his own will,[4] to the praise of the glory of his wisdom, power, justice, goodness, and mercy.[5]

**6.025** 2. Although in relation to the foreknowledge and decree of God, the first cause, all things come to pass immutably and infallibly,[6] yet, by the same providence, he ordereth them to fall out according to the nature of second causes, either necessarily,[7] freely, or contingently.[8]

**6.026** 3. God, in his ordinary providence, maketh use of means,[9] yet is free to work without,[10] above,[11] and against them, at his pleasure.[12]

**6.027** 4. The almighty power, unsearchable wisdom, and infinite goodness of God, so far manifest themselves in his providence, that it extendeth itself even to the first Fall,[13] and all other sins of angels and men,[14] and that not by a bare permission, but such as hath joined with it a most wise and powerful bounding,[15] and otherwise ordering and governing of them, in a manifold dispensation, to his own holy ends;[16] yet so, as the sinfulness thereof proceedeth only from the creature, and not from God; who being most holy and righteous, neither is nor can be the author or approver of sin.[17]

**6.028** 5. The most wise, righteous, and gracious God, doth often-times leave for a season his own children to manifold temptations and the corruption of their own hearts, to chastise them for their former sins, or to discover unto them the hidden strength of corruption and deceitfulness of their hearts, that they[n] be humbled;[18] and to raise them to a more close and constant dependence for their support upon himself, and to make them more watchful against all future occasions of sin, and for sundry other just and holy ends.[19]

6.029   6. As for those wicked and ungodly men whom God, as a righteous judge, for former sins, doth blind and harden;[20] from them he not only withholdeth his grace, whereby they might have been enlightened in their understandings, and wrought upon in their hearts,[21] but sometimes also withdraweth the gifts which they had;[22] and exposeth them to such objects as their corruption makes occasion of sin;[23] and withal, giveth[o] them over to their own lusts, the temptations of the world, and the power of Satan;[24] whereby it cometh[p] to pass that they harden themselves, even under those means which God useth for the softening of others.[25]

6.030   7. As the providence of God doth, in general, reach to all creatures; so, after a most special manner, it taketh care of his Church, and disposeth all things to the good thereof.[26]

## CHAPTER VI

### Of the Fall of Man, of Sin, and of the Punishment Thereof

6.031   1. Our first parents, being seduced by the subtilty and temptation of Satan, sinned in eating the forbidden fruit.[1] This their sin God was pleased, according to his wide and holy counsel, to permit, having purposed to order it to his own glory.[2]

6.032   2. By this sin they fell from their original righteousness and communion with God,[3] and so became dead in sin,[4] and wholly defiled in all the faculties and parts of soul and body.[5]

6.033   3. They being the root of all mankind, the guilt of this sin was imputed,[6] and the same death in sin and corrupted nature conveyed to all their posterity, descending from them by ordinary generation.[7]

6.034   4. From this original corruption, whereby we are utterly indisposed, disabled, and made opposite to all good, and wholly inclined to all evil,[8] do proceed all actual transgressions.[9]

6.035   5. This corruption of nature, during this life, doth remain in those that are regenerated:[10] and although it be through Christ pardoned and mortified, yet both itself, and all the motions thereof, are truly and properly sin.[11]

---

[n] UPCUSA ed. reads: "they may be."
[o] UPCUSA ed. reads: "gives."
[p] UPCUSA ed. reads: "comes."

**6.036** 6. Every sin, both original and actual, being a transgression of the righteous law of God, and contrary thereunto, doth, in its own nature, bring guilt upon the sinner,[12] whereby he is bound over to the wrath of God,[13] and curse of the law,[14] and so made subject to death[15] with all miseries spiritual, temporal, and eternal.[16]

CHAPTER VII

### Of God's Covenant with Man

**6.037** 1. The distance between God and the creature is so great, that although reasonable creatures do owe obedience unto him as their Creator, yet they could never have any fruition of him, as their blessedness and reward, but by some voluntary condescension on God's part, which he hath been pleased to express by way of covenant.[1]

**6.038** 2. The first covenant made with man was a covenant of works,[2] wherein life was promised to Adam, and in him to his posterity, upon condition of perfect and personal obedience.[3]

**6.039** 3. Man, by his Fall, having made himself incapable of life by that covenant, the Lord was pleased to make a second, commonly called the covenant of grace:[4] wherein he freely offered[q] unto sinners life and salvation by Jesus Christ, requiring of them faith in him, that they may be saved,[5] and promising to give unto all those that are ordained unto life, his Holy Spirit, to make them willing and able to believe.[6]

**6.040** 4. This covenant of grace is frequently set forth in the Scripture by the name of a testament, in reference to the death of Jesus Christ, the testator, and to the everlasting inheritance, with all things belonging to it, therein bequeathed.

**6.041** 5. This covenant was differently administered in the time of the law, and in the time of the gospel:[7] under the law it was administered by promises, prophecies, sacrifices, circumcision, the paschal lamb, and other types and ordinances delivered to the people of the Jews, all foresignifying Christ to come,[8] which were for that time sufficient and efficacious, through the operation of the Spirit, to instruct and build up the elect in faith in the promised Messiah,[9] by whom they had full remission of sins, and eternal salvation; and is called the Old Testament.[10]

---

[q] UPCUSA ed. reads: "offereth."

**6.042**        6. Under the gospel, when Christ the substance was exhibited, the ordinances in which this covenant is dispensed, are the preaching of the Word, and the administration of the sacraments of Baptism and the Lord's Supper;[11] which, though fewer in number, and administered with more simplicity and less outward glory, yet in them it is held forth in more fullness, evidence, and spiritual efficacy,[12] to all nations, both Jews and Gentiles;[13] and is called the New Testament. There are not, therefore, two covenants of grace differing in substance, but one and the same under various dispensations.[14]

CHAPTER VIII                          CHAPTER VIII

**Of Christ the Mediator**

**6.043**        1. It pleased God, in his eternal purpose, to choose and ordain the Lord Jesus, his only begotten Son, to be the Mediator between God and man,[1] the prophet,[2] priest,[3] and king;[4] the head and Savior of his Church,[5] the heir of all things,[6] and judge of the world;[7] unto whom he did, from all eternity, give a people to be his seed,[8] and to be by him in time redeemed, called, justified, sanctified, and glorified.[9]

**6.044**        2. The Son of God, the second Person in the Trinity, being very and eternal God, of one substance, and equal with the Father, did, when the fullness of time was come, take upon him man's nature,[10] with all the essential properties and common infirmities thereof; yet without sin:[11] being conceived by the power of the Holy Ghost, in the womb of the Virgin Mary, of her substance.[12] So that two whole, perfect, and distinct natures, the Godhead and the manhood, were inseparably joined together in one person, without conversion, composition, or confusion.[13] Which person is very God and very man, yet one Christ, the only Mediator between God and man.[14]

**6.045**        3. The Lord Jesus in his human nature thus united to the divine, was sanctified and anointed with the Holy Spirit above measure;[15] having in him all the treasures of wisdom and knowledge,[16] in whom it pleased the Father that all fullness should dwell:[17] to the end that being holy, harmless, undefiled, and full of grace and truth, he might be thoroughly furnished to execute the office of a Mediator and Surety.[18] Which office he took not unto himself, but was thereunto called by his Father;[19] who put all power and judgment into his hand, and gave him commandment to execute the same.[20]

**6.046**        4. This office the Lord Jesus did most willingly undertake,[21] which, that he might discharge, he was made under the law,[22] and did perfectly fulfill it;[23] endured most grievous torments immediately in his soul,[24] and most painful sufferings in his body;[25] was crucified and

Presbyterian Church in the United States

The United Presbyterian Church in the United States of America

died,[26] was buried, and remained under the power of death, yet saw no corruption.[27] On the third day he arose from the dead,[28] with the same body in which he suffered;[29] with which also he ascended into heaven, and there sitteth at the right hand of his Father,[30] making intercession;[31] and shall return to judge men and angels, at the end of the world.[32]

**6.047** 5. The Lord Jesus, by his perfect obedience and sacrifice of himself, which he through the eternal Spirit once offered up unto God, hath fully satisfied the justice of his Father;[33] and purchased not only reconciliation, but an everlasting inheritance in the kingdom of heaven, for all those whom the Father hath given unto him.[34]

**6.048** 6. Although the work of redemption was not actually wrought by Christ till after his incarnation, yet the virtue, efficacy, and benefits thereof were communicated unto the elect, in all ages successively from the beginning of the world, in and by those promises, types, and sacrifices wherein he was revealed, and signified to be the seed of the woman, which should bruise the serpent's head, and the Lamb slain from the beginning of the world, being yesterday and today the same and for ever.[35]

**6.049** 7. Christ, in the work of mediation, acteth according to both natures; by each nature doing that which is proper to itself;[36] yet by reason of the unity of the person, that which is proper to one nature is sometimes, in Scripture, attributed to the person denominated by the other nature.[37]

**6.050** 8. To all those for whom Christ hath purchased redemption, he doth certainly and effectually apply and communicate the same;[38] making intercession for them,[39] and revealing unto them, in and by the Word, the mysteries of salvation;[40] effectually persuading them by his Spirit to believe and obey; and governing their hearts by his Word and Spirit;[41] overcoming all their enemies by his almighty power and wisdom, in such manner and ways as are most consonant to his wonderful and unsearchable dispensation.[42]

CHAPTER IX

**Of the Holy Spirit**

**6.051** 1. The Holy Spirit, the third Person in the Trinity, proceeding from the Father and the Son, of the same substance and equal in power and glory, is, together with the Father and the Son, to be believed in, loved, obeyed, and worshipped throughout all ages.[1]

**6.052**  2. He is the Lord and Giver of life, everywhere present, and is the source of all good thoughts, pure desires, and holy counsels in men. By him the prophets were moved to speak the Word of God, and all the writers of the Holy Scriptures inspired to record infallibly the mind and will of God. The dispensation of the gospel is especially committed to him. He prepares the way for it, accompanies it with his persuasive power, and urges its message upon the reason and conscience of men, so that they who reject its merciful offer are not only without excuse, but are also guilty of resisting the Holy Spirit.[2]

**6.053**  3. The Holy Spirit, whom the Father is ever willing to give to all who ask him, is the only efficient agent in the application of redemption. He regenerates men by his grace, convicts them of sin, moves them to repentance, and persuades and enables them to embrace Jesus Christ by faith. He unites all believers to Christ, dwells in them as their Comforter and Sanctifier, gives to them the spirit of Adoption and Prayer, and performs all those gracious offices by which they are sanctified and sealed unto the day of redemption.[3]

**6.054**  4. By the indwelling of the Holy Spirit all believers being vitally united to Christ, who is the Head, are thus united one to another in the Church, which is his body. He calls and anoints ministers for their holy office, qualifies all other officers in the Church for their special work, and imparts various gifts and graces to its members. He gives efficacy to the Word and to the ordinances of the gospel. By him the Church will be preserved, increased, purified, and at last made perfectly holy in the presence of God.[4]

## CHAPTER X

### Of the Gospel

**6.055** 1. God in infinite and perfect love, having provided in the covenant of grace, through the mediation and sacrifice of the Lord Jesus Christ, a way of life and salvation, sufficient for and adapted to the whole lost race of man, doth freely offer this salvation to all men in the gospel.[1]

**6.056** 2. In the gospel God declares his love for the world and his desire that all men should be saved; reveals fully and clearly the only way of salvation; promises eternal life to all who truly repent and believe in Christ; invites and commands all to embrace the offered mercy; and by his Spirit accompanying the Word pleads with men to accept his gracious invitation.[2]

**6.057** 3. It is the duty and privilege of everyone who hears the gospel immediately to accept its merciful provisions; and they who continue in impenitence and unbelief incur aggravated guilt and perish by their own fault.[3]

THE WESTMINSTER CONFESSION OF FAITH 6.058–.062

Presbyterian Church  
in the United States

The United Presbyterian Church  
in the United States of America

**6.058** 4. Since there is no other way of salvation than that revealed in the gospel, and since in the divinely established and ordinary method of grace faith cometh by hearing the Word of God, Christ hath commissioned his Church to go into all the world and to make disciples of all nations. All believers are, therefore, under obligation to sustain the ordinances of the Christian religion where they are already established, and to contribute by their prayers, gifts, and personal efforts to the extension of the Kingdom of Christ throughout the whole earth.[4]

CHAPTER XI                                                               CHAPTER IX

**Of Free Will**

**6.059** 1. God hath endued the will of man with that natural liberty, that it is neither forced, nor by any absolute necessity of nature determined to[r] good or evil.[1]

**6.060** 2. Man, in his state of innocency, had freedom and power to will and to do that which is[s] good and well-pleasing to God;[2] but yet mutably, so that he might fall from it.[3]

**6.061** 3. Man, by his Fall into a state of sin, hath wholly lost all ability of will to any spiritual good accompanying salvation;[4] so as a natural man, being altogether averse from that good,[5] and dead in sin,[6] is not able, by his own strength, to convert himself, or to prepare himself thereunto.[7]

**6.062** 4. When God converteth[t] a sinner and translateth[u] him into the state of grace, he freeth him from his natural bondage under sin, and, by his grace alone, enableth[v] him freely to will and to do that which is spiritually good;[8] yet so as that, by reason of his remaining corruption,

---

[r] Ed. 1647 includes: "do."  
[s] Ed. 1647 reads: "was."  
[t] UPCUSA ed. reads: "converts."  
[u] UPCUSA ed. reads: "translates."  
[v] UPCUSA ed. reads: "enables."

Presbyterian Church in the United States / The United Presbyterian Church in the United States of America

he doth not perfectly, nor only, will that which is good, but doth also will that which is evil.⁹

**6.063** 5. The will of man is made perfectly and immutably free to good alone, in the state of glory¹⁰ only.¹¹

CHAPTER XII  CHAPTER X

**Of Effectual Calling**

**6.064** 1. All those whom God hath predestinated unto life, and those only, he is pleased, in his appointed and accepted time, effectually to call, by his Word and Spirit, out of that state of sin and death in which they are by nature, to grace and salvation by Jesus Christ:¹ enlightening their minds, spiritually and savingly, to understand the things of God,² taking away their heart of stone, and giving unto them an heart of flesh;³ renewing their wills, and by his almighty power determining them to that which is good;⁴ and effectually drawing them to Jesus Christ;⁵ yet so as they come most freely, being made willing by his grace.⁶

**6.065** 2. This effectual call is of God's free and special grace alone, not from anything at all foreseen in man,⁷ who is altogether passive therein, until, being quickened and renewed by the Holy Spirit,⁸ he is thereby enabled to answer this call, and to embrace the grace offered and conveyed in it.⁹

**6.066** ᵃ3. Elect infants, dying in infancy, are regenerated and saved by Christ through the Spirit, who worketh when, and where, and how he pleaseth. So also are all other elect persons who are incapable of being outwardly called by the ministry of the Word.¹⁰

**6.067** 4. Others, not elected, although they may be called by the ministry of the Word, and may have some common operations of the Spirit, yet they never truly come to Christ, and therefore cannot be saved:¹¹ much less can men, not professing the Christian religion, be saved in any other way whatsoever,ᵇ ¹² be they never so diligent to frame their lives according to the light of nature, and the law of that religion they do profess; and to assert and maintain that they mayᶜ is without warrant of the Word of God.¹³

---

ᵃ See Declaratory Statement at end of the Confession of Faith. The Declaratory Statement is the authoritative interpretation of Chapter X, Section 3, in the UPCUSA ed.
ᵇ UPCUSA ed. includes: "than by Christ"; Ed. 1647 lacks: "than by Christ."
ᶜ Ed.1647 reads: "is very pernicious, and to be detested."

Presbyterian Church in the United States

The United Presbyterian Church in the United States of America

CHAPTER XIII

CHAPTER XI

**Of Justification**

**6.068**     1. Those whom God effectually calleth, he also freely justifieth:[1] not by infusing righteousness into them, but by pardoning their sins, and by accounting and accepting their persons as righteous; not for anything wrought in them, or done by them, but for Christ's sake alone; not[d] by imputing faith itself, the act of believing, or any other evangelical obedience to them, as their righteousness; but by imputing the obedience and satisfaction of Christ unto them,[2] they receiving and resting on him and his righteousness by faith; which faith they have not of themselves, it is the gift of God.[3]

**6.069**     2. Faith, thus receiving and resting on Christ and his righteousness, is the alone instrument of justification;[4] yet is it not alone in the person justified, but is ever accompanied with all other saving graces, and is no dead faith, but worketh by love.[5]

**6.070**     3. Christ, by his obedience and death, did fully discharge the debt of all those that are thus justified, and did make a proper, real, and full satisfaction to his Father's justice in their behalf.[6] Yet inasmuch as he was given by the Father for them,[7] and his obedience and satisfaction accepted in their stead,[8] and both freely, not for anything in them, their justification is only of free grace;[9] that both the exact justice and rich grace of God might be glorified in the justification of sinners.[10]

**6.071**     4. God did, from all eternity, decree to justify all the elect;[11] and Christ did, in the fullness of time, die for their sins and rise again for their justification:[12] nevertheless they are not justified until the Holy Spirit doth, in due time, actually apply Christ unto them.[13]

**6.072**     5. God doth continue to forgive the sins of those that are justified;[14] and although they can never fall from the state of justification,[15] yet they may by their sins fall under God's Fatherly displeasure, and not have the light of his countenance restored unto them, until they humble themselves, confess their sins, beg pardon, and renew their faith and repentance.[16]

**6.073**     6. The justification of believers under the Old Testament was, in all these respects, one and the same with the justification of believers under the New Testament.[17]

---

[d] Ed. reads: "nor."

Presbyterian Church in the United States

The United Presbyterian Church in the United States of America

CHAPTER XIV

CHAPTER XII

### Of Adoption

**6.074** 1. All those that are justified, God vouchsafeth, in and for his only Son Jesus Christ, to make partakers of the grace of adoption:[1] by which they are taken into the number, and enjoy the liberties and privileges of the children of God;[2] have his name put upon them;[3] receive the Spirit of adoption;[4] have access to the throne of grace with boldness;[5] are enabled to cry, Abba, Father;[6] are pitied,[7] protected,[8] provided for,[9] and chastened by him as by a father;[10] yet never cast off,[11] but sealed to the day of redemption,[12] and inherit the promises,[13] as heirs of everlasting salvation.[14]

CHAPTER XV

CHAPTER XIII

### Of Sanctification

**6.075** 1. They who are effectually called and regenerated, having a new heart and a new spirit created in them, are further sanctified, really and personally, through the virtue of Christ's death and resurrection, by his Word and Spirit dwelling in them;[1] the dominion of the whole body of sin is destroyed,[2] and the several lusts thereof are more and more weakened and mortified,[3] and they more and more quickened and strengthened, in all saving graces,[4] to the practice of true holiness, without which no man shall see the Lord.[5]

**6.076** 2. This sanctification is throughout in the whole man,[6] yet imperfect in this life: there abideth still some remnants of corruption in every part, whence ariseth a continual and irreconcilable war, the flesh lusting against the Spirit, and the Spirit against the flesh.[7]

**6.077** 3. In which war, although the remaining corruption for a time may much prevail,[8] yet, through the continual supply of strength from the sanctifying Spirit of Christ, the regenerate part doth overcome:[9] and so the saints grow in grace,[10] perfecting holiness in the fear of God.[11]

CHAPTER XVI

CHAPTER XIV

### Of Saving Faith

**6.078** 1. The grace of faith, whereby the elect are enabled to believe to the saving of their souls, is the work of the Spirit of Christ in their hearts;[1] and is ordinarily wrought by the ministry of the Word:[2] by which also, and by the administration of the sacraments, and prayer, it is increased and strengthened.[3]

Presbyterian Church  
in the United States

The United Presbyterian Church  
in the United States of America

**6.079**      2. By this faith, a Christian believeth to be true whatsoever is revealed in the Word, for the authority of God himself speaking therein;[4] and acteth differently, upon that which each particular passage thereof containeth; yielding obedience to the commands, trembling at the threatenings, and embracing the promises of God for this life, and that which is to come. But the principal acts of saving faith are, accepting, receiving, and resting upon Christ alone for justification, sanctification, and eternal life, by virtue of the covenant of grace.

**6.080**      3. This faith is different in degrees, weak or strong;[5] may be often and many ways assailed and weakened, but gets the victory;[6] growing up in many to the attainment of a full assurance through Christ,[7] who is both the author and finisher of our faith.[8]

CHAPTER XVII                                  CHAPTER XV

**Of Repentance Unto Life**

**6.081**      1. Repentance unto life is an evangelical grace,[1] the doctrine whereof is to be preached by every minister of the gospel, as well as that of faith in Christ.[2]

**6.082**      2. By it a sinner, out of the sight and sense, not only of the danger, but also of the filthiness and odiousness of his sins, as contrary to the holy nature and righteous law of God, and upon the apprehension of his mercy in Christ to such as are penitent, so grieves for, and hates his sins, as to turn from them all unto God,[3] purposing and endeavoring to walk with him in all the ways of his commandments.[4]

**6.083**      3. Although repentance be not to be rested in as any satisfaction for sin, or any cause of the pardon thereof,[5] which is the act of God's free grace in Christ;[6] yet is it of such necessity to all sinners, that none may expect pardon without it.[7]

**6.084**      4. As there is no sin so small but it deserves damnation;[8] so there is no sin so great that it can bring damnation upon those who truly repent.[9]

**6.085**      5. Men ought not to content themselves with a general repentance, but it is every man's duty to endeavor to repent of his particular sins, particularly.[10]

**6.086**      6. As every man is bound to make private confession of his sins to God, praying for the pardon thereof,[11] upon which, and the forsaking of them, he shall find mercy:[12] so he that scandalizeth his brother, or the church of Christ, ought to be willing, by a private or public confession and sorrow for his sin, to declare his repentance to those that are offended;[13] who are thereupon to be reconciled to him, and in love to receive him.[14]

CHAPTER XVIII / CHAPTER XVI

### Of Good Works

**6.087** 1. Good works are only such as God hath commanded in his holy Word,[1] and not such as, without the warrant thereof, are devised by men out of blind zeal, or upon any pretense of good intention.[2]

**6.088** 2. These good works, done in obedience to God's commandments, are the fruits and evidences of a true and lively faith:[3] and by them believers manifest their thankfulness,[4] strengthen their assurance,[5] edify their brethren,[6] adorn the profession of the gospel,[7] stop the mouths of the adversaries,[8] and glorify God,[9] whose workmanship they are, created in Christ Jesus thereunto,[10] that, having their fruit unto holiness, they may have the end, eternal life.[11]

**6.089** 3. Their ability to do good works is not at all of themselves, but wholly from the Spirit of Christ.[12] And that they may be enabled thereunto, besides the graces they have already received, there is required an actual influence of the same Holy Spirit to work in them to will and to do of his good pleasure;[13] yet are they not hereupon to grow negligent, as if they were not bound to perform any duty unless upon a special motion of the Spirit; but they ought to be diligent in stirring up the grace of God that is in them.[14]

**6.090** 4. They, who in their obedience, attain to the greatest height which is possible in this life, are so far from being able to supererogate and to do more than God requires, that they fall short of much which in duty they are bound to do.[15]

**6.091** 5. We cannot, by our best works, merit pardon of sin, or eternal life, at the hand of God, because[e] of the great disproportion that is between them and the glory to come, and the infinite distance that is between us and God, whom by them we can neither profit, nor satisfy for the debt of our former sins;[16] but when we have done all we can, we have done but our duty, and are unprofitable servants:[17] and because, as they are good, they proceed from his Spirit;[18] and as they are wrought by us, they are defiled and mixed with so much weakness and imperfection that they cannot endure the severity of God's judgment.[19]

---

[e] UPCUSA reads: "by reason."

Presbyterian Church in the United States / The United Presbyterian Church in the United States of America

**6.092**    6. Yet notwithstanding, the persons of believers being accepted through Christ, their good works also are accepted in him,[20] not as though they were in this life wholly unblamable and unreprovable in God's sight;[21] but that he, looking upon them in his Son, is pleased to accept and reward that which is sincere, although accompanied with many weaknesses and imperfections.[22]

**6.093**    7. Works done by unregenerate men, although for the matter of them they may be things which God commands, and of good use both to themselves and others,[23] yet because they proceed not from a heart purified by faith;[24] nor are done in a right manner, according to the Word;[25] nor to a right end, the glory of God;[26] they are therefore sinful, and cannot please God, or make a man meet to receive grace from God.[27] And yet their neglect of them is more sinful, and displeasing unto God[28]

7. [f]Works done by unregenerate men, although for the matter of them they they may be things which God commands, and in themselves praiseworthy and useful, and although the neglect of such things is sinful and displeasing unto God; yet, because they proceed not from a heart purified by faith; nor are done in a right manner, according to his Word; nor to a right end, the glory of God; they come short of what God requires, and do not make any man meet to receive the grace of God.

## CHAPTER XIX / CHAPTER XVII

### Of the Perseverance of the Saints

**6.094**    1. They whom God hath accepted in his Beloved, effectually called and sanctified by his Spirit, can neither totally nor finally fall away from the state of grace: but shall certainly persevere therein to the end, and be eternally saved.[1]

**6.095**    2. This perseverance of the saints depends, not upon their own free-will, but upon the immutability of the decree of election, flowing from the free and unchangeable love of God the Father;[2] upon the efficacy of the merit and intercession of Jesus Christ;[3] the abiding of the Spirit and of the seed of God within them;[4] and the nature of the covenant of grace;[5] from all which ariseth also the certainty and infallibility thereof.[6]

---

[f] Ed. 1647 reads: "VII. Works done by unregenerate men, although, for the matter of them, they may bee things which God commands, and of good use both to themselves, and others: yet, because they proceed not from an heart purified by faith; nor are done in a right manner, according to the Word; nor, to a right end, the glory of God; they are therefore sinfull, and cannot please God, or make a man meet to receive grace from God. And yet, their neglect of them is more sinfull, and displeasing unto God."

Presbyterian Church
in the United States

The United Presbyterian Church
in the United States of America

**6.096**     3. Nevertheless they may, through the temptations of Satan and of the world, the prevalency of corruption remaining in them, and the neglect of the means of their preservation, fall into grievous sins; and for a time continue therein:[7] whereby they incur God's displeasure,[8] and grieve his Holy Spirit;[9] come to be deprived of some measure of their graces and comforts;[10] have their hearts hardened,[11] and their consciences wounded;[12] hurt and scandalize others,[13] and bring temporal judgments upon themselves.[14]

CHAPTER XX                                                CHAPTER XVIII

### Of the Assurance of Grace and Salvation

**6.097**     1. Although hypocrites, and other unregenerate men, may vainly deceive themselves with false hopes and carnal presumptions: of being in the favor of God and estate of salvation;[1] which hope of theirs shall perish:[2] yet such as truly believe in the Lord Jesus, and love him in sincerity, endeavoring to walk in all good conscience before him, may in this life be certainly assured that they are in a state of grace,[3] and may rejoice in the hope of the glory of God: which hope shall never make them ashamed.[4]

**6.098**     2. This certainty is not a bare conjectural and probable persuasion, grounded upon a fallible hope; but an infallible assurance of faith,[5] founded upon the divine truth of the promises of salvation,[6] the inward evidence of those graces unto which these promises are made,[7] the testimony of the Spirit of adoption witnessing with our spirits that we are the children of God;[8] which Spirit is the earnest of our inheritance, whereby we are sealed to the day of redemption.[9]

**6.099**     3. This infallible assurance doth not so belong to the essence of faith but that a true believer may wait long and conflict with many difficulties before he be partaker of it:[10] yet, being enabled by the Spirit to know the things which are freely given him to God, he may, without extraordinary revelation, in the right use of ordinary means, attain thereunto.[11] And therefore it is the duty of everyone to give all diligence to make his calling and election sure; that thereby his heart may be enlarged in peace and joy in the Holy Ghost, in love and thankfulness to God, and in strength and cheerfulness in the duties of obedience, the proper fruits of this assurance: so far is it from inclining men to looseness.[12]

**6.100**     4. True believers may have the assurance of their salvation divers ways shaken, diminished, and intermitted; as, by negligence in preserving of it; by falling into some special sin, which woundeth the conscience, and grieveth the Spirit; by some sudden or vehement

Presbyterian Church in the United States / The United Presbyterian Church in the United States of America

temptation; by God's withdrawing the light of his countenance and suffering even such as fear him to walk in darkness and to have no light:[13] yet are they never utterly destitute of that seed of God, and life of faith, that love of Christ and the brethren, that sincerity of heart and conscience of duty, out of which, by the operation of the Spirit, this assurance may in due time be revived,[14] and by the which, in the meantime, they are supported from utter despair.[15]

CHAPTER XXI                              CHAPTER XIX

**Of the Law of God**

**6.101**  1. God gave to Adam a law, as a covenant of works, by which he bound him and all his posterity to personal, entire, exact, and perpetual obedience; promised life upon the fulfilling, and threatened death upon the breach of it; and endued him with power and ability to keep it.

**6.102**  2. This law, after his Fall, continued to be a perfect rule of righteousness; and, as such, was delivered by God upon mount Sinai in ten commandments, and written in two tables;[1] the first four commandments containing our duty toward God, and the other six our duty to man.[2]

**6.103**  3. Besides this law, commonly called moral, God was pleased to give to the people of Israel, as a Church under age, ceremonial laws, containing several typical ordinances, partly of worship, prefiguring Christ, his graces, actions, sufferings, and benefits;[3] and partly holding forth divers instructions of moral duties.[4] All which ceremonial laws are now abrogated under the New Testament.[5]

**6.104**  4. To them also, as a body politic, he gave sundry judicial laws, which expired together with the state of that people, not obliging any other, now, further than the general equity thereof may require.[6]

**6.105**  5. The moral law doth forever bind all, as well justified persons as others, to the obedience thereof; and that not only in regard of the matter contained in it, but also in respect of the authority of God the Creator who gave it.[7] Neither doth Christ in the gospel any way dissolve, but much strengthen, this obligation.[8]

**6.106**  6. Although true believers be not under the law as a covenant of works, to be thereby justified or condemned;[9] yet is it of great use to them, as well as to others; in that, as a rule of life, informing them of the will of God and their duty, it directs and binds them to walk accordingly;[10] discovering also the sinful pollutions of their nature, hearts, and lives;[11] so as, examining themselves thereby, they may come to further conviction of, humiliation for, and hatred against sin;[12] together with a clearer sight of the need they have of Christ, and the perfection of his obedience.[13] It is likewise of use to the regenerate, to restrain their corruptions, in that it forbids sin,[14] and the threatenings of it serve to show what even their sins deserve, and what afflictions in this life they may expect for them, although freed from the curse thereof threatened in the law.[15] The promises of it, in like manner, show them God's approbation of obedience, and what blessings they may expect upon the performance thereof;[16] although not as due to them by the law as a covenant of works: so as a man's doing good, and refraining from evil, because the law encourageth to the one, and deterreth from the other, is no evidence of his being under the law, and not under grace.[17]

**6.107**      7. Neither are the forementioned uses of the law contrary to the grace of the gospel, but do sweetly comply with it:[18] the Spirit of Christ subduing and enabling the will of man to do that freely and cheerfully, which the will of God, revealed in the law, requireth to be done.[19]

CHAPTER XXII      CHAPTER XX

**Of Christian Liberty, and Liberty of Conscience**

**6.108**      1. The liberty which Christ hath purchased for believers under the gospel consists in their freedom from the guilt of sin, the condemning wrath of God, the curse of the moral law;[1] and in their being delivered from this present evil world, bondage to Satan, and dominion of sin,[2] from the evil of afflictions, the sting of death, the victory of the grave, and everlasting damnation;[3] as also in their free access to God,[4] and their yielding obedience unto him, not out of slavish fear, but a childlike love, and a willing mind.[5] All which were common also to believers under the law;[6] but under the New Testament, the liberty of Christians is further enlarged in their freedom from the yoke of the ceremonial law, to which the Jewish church was subjected;[7] and in greater boldness of access to the throne of grace,[8] and in fuller[g] communications of the free Spirit of God, than believers under the law did ordinarily partake of.[9]

---

[g] UPCUSA ed. reads: "full."

**6.109** 2. God alone is Lord of the conscience, and hath left it free from the doctrines and commandments of men which are in anything contrary to his Word, or beside it in matters of faith or worship.[10] So that to believe such doctrines, or to obey such commandments out of conscience, is to betray true liberty of conscience;[11] and the requiring an implicit faith, and an absolute and blind obedience, is to destroy liberty of conscience, and reason also.[12]

**6.110** 3. They who, upon pretense of Christian liberty, do practice any sin, or cherish any lust, do thereby destroy the end of Christian liberty; which is, that, being delivered out of the hands of our enemies, we might serve the Lord without fear, in holiness and righteousness before him, all the days of our life.[13]

**6.111** 4. And because the power which God hath ordained, and the liberty which Christ hath purchased, are not intended by God to destroy, but mutually to uphold and preserve one another; they who, upon pretense of Christian liberty, shall oppose any lawful power, or the lawful exercise of it, whether it be civil or ecclesiastical, resist the ordinance of God.[14] And for their publishing of such opinions, or maintaining of such practices, as are contrary to the light of nature, or to the known principles of Christianity, whether concerning faith, worship, or conversation; or to the power of godliness; or such erroneous opinions or practices as, either in their own nature, or in the manner of publishing or maintaining them, are destructive to the external peace and order which Christ hath established in the church; they may lawfully be called to account, and proceeded against by the censures of the Church.[h15]

CHAPTER XXIII / CHAPTER XXI

### Of Religious Worship and the Sabbath Day

**6.112** 1. The light of nature showeth that there is a God, who hath lordship and sovereignty over all; is good, and doeth good unto all; and is therefore to be feared, loved, praised, called upon, trusted in, and served with all the heart, and with all the soul, and with all the might.[1] But the acceptable way of worshipping the true God is instituted by himself, and so limited by his own revealed will, that he may not be worshipped according to the imaginations and devices of men, or the suggestions of Satan, under any visible representation or any other way not prescribed in the Holy Scripture.[2]

---

[h] Ed. 1647 includes: "and by the Power of the Civil Magistrate."

Presbyterian Church
in the United States

The United Presbyterian Church
in the United States of America

**6.113**      2. Religious worship is to be given to God, the Father, Son, and Holy Ghost; and to him alone:[3] not to angels, saints, or any other creature:[4] and since the Fall, not without a Mediator; nor in the mediation of any other but of Christ alone.[5]

**6.114**      3. Prayer with thanksgiving, being one special part of religious worship,[6] is by God required of all men;[7] and that it may be accepted, it is to be made in the name of the Son,[8] by the help of his Spirit,[9] according to his will,[10] with understanding, reverence, humility, fervency, faith, love, and perseverance;[11] and, if vocal, in a known tongue.[12]

**6.115**      4. Prayer is to be made for things lawful,[13] and for all sorts of men living, or that shall live hereafter,[14] but not for the dead.[i][15]

**6.116**      5. The reading of the Scriptures with godly fear;[17] the sound preaching,[18] and conscionable hearing of the Word, in obedience unto God with understanding, faith, and reverence;[19] singing of psalms with grace in the heart;[20] as, also, the due administration and worthy receiving of the sacraments instituted by Christ; are all parts of the ordinary religious worship of God:[21] besides religious oaths,[22] and[j] vows,[23] solemn fastings,[24] and thanksgivings upon special occasion;[25] which are, in their several times and seasons, to be used in an holy and religious manner.[26]

**6.117**      6. Neither prayer, nor any other part of religious worship, is now, under the gospel, either tied unto, or made more acceptable by, any place in which it is performed, or towards which it is directed:[27] but God is to be worshipped everywhere[28] in spirit and in[k] truth;[29] as in private families[30] daily,[31] and in secret each one by himself,[32] so more solemnly in the public assemblies, which are not carelessly or willfully to be neglected or forsaken, when God, by his Word or providence, calleth thereunto.[33]

**6.118**      7. As it is of the law of nature that, in general, a due proportion of time be set apart for the worship of God; so, in his Word, by a positive, moral, and perpetual commandment, binding all men in all ages, he hath particularly appointed one day in seven for a Sabbath, to be kept holy unto him:[34] which, from the beginning of the world to the resurrection of Christ, was the last day of the week; and from the resurrection of Christ, was changed into the first day of the week, which in Scripture is called the Lord's Day, and is to be continued to the end of the world as the Christian Sabbath.[35]

---

[i] Ed. 1647 includes: "nor for those of whom it may be known, that they have sinned the sin unto death."
[j] Ed. 1647 lacks: "and."
[k] Ed. 1647 lacks: "in."

Presbyterian Church in the United States

The United Presbyterian Church in the United States of America

**6.119** 8. This Sabbath is then kept holy unto the Lord when men, after a due preparing of their hearts, and ordering of their common affairs beforehand, do not only observe an holy rest all the day from their own works, words, and thoughts about their worldly employments and recreations;[36] but also are taken up the whole time in the public and private exercises of his worship, and in the duties of necessity and mercy.[37]

CHAPTER XXIV / CHAPTER XXII

### Of Lawful Oaths and Vows

**6.120** 1. A lawful oath is a part of religious worship,[1] wherein upon just occasion, the person swearing solemnly calleth God to witness what he asserteth or promiseth; and to judge him according to the truth or falsehood of what he sweareth.[2]

**6.121** 2. The name of God only is that by which men ought to swear, and therein it is to be used with all holy fear and reverence,[3] therefore to swear vainly or rashly by that glorious and dreadful name, or to swear at all by any other thing, is sinful, and to be abhorred.[4] Yet, as, in matters of weight and moment, an oath is warranted by the Word of God, under the New Testament, as well as under the Old, so a lawful oath, being imposed by lawful authority, in such matters ought to be taken.[5]

**6.122** 3. Whosoever taketh an oath ought duly to consider the weightiness of so solemn an act, and therein to avouch nothing but what he is fully persuaded is the truth. Neither may any man bind himself by oath to anything but what is good and just, and what he believeth so to be, and what he is able and resolved to perform. Yet it is a sin to refuse an oath touching anything that is good and just, being imposed by lawful authority.[6]

3. Whosoever taketh an oath ought duly to consider the weightiness of so solemn an act, and therein to avouch nothing but what he is fully persuaded is the truth. Neither may any man bind himself by oath to anything but what is good and just, and what he believeth so to be, and what he is able and resolved to perform.[m]

**6.123** 4. An oath is to be taken in the plain and common sense of the words, without equivocation or mental reservation.[7] It cannot oblige to sin; but in anything not sinful, being taken, it binds to performance, although to a man's own hurt:[8] nor is it to be violated, although made to heretics or infidels.[9]

---

[m] Ed. 1647 continues: "Yet is it a sin, to refuse an Oath touching any thing that is good and just, being imposed by lawfull Authority."

Presbyterian Church  
in the United States

The United Presbyterian Church  
in the United States of America

**6.124**      5. A vow is of the like nature with a promissory oath, and ought to be made with the like religious care, and to be performed with the like faithfulness.[10]

**6.125**      6. It is not to be made to any creature, but to God alone:[11] and that it may be accepted, it is to be made voluntarily, out of faith and conscience of duty, in way of thankfulness for mercy received, or for obtaining of what we want; whereby we more strictly bind ourselves to necessary duties, or to other things, so far and so long as they may fitly conduce thereunto.[12]

**6.126**      7. No man may vow to do anything forbidden in the Word of God, or what would hinder any duty therein commanded, or which is not in his own power, and for the performance whereof he hath no promise or ability from God.[13] In which respects,[n] monastical vows of perpetual single life, professed poverty, and regular obedience, are so far from being degrees of higher perfection, that they are superstitious and sinful snares, in which no Christian may entangle himself.

CHAPTER XXV                                              CHAPTER XXIII

### Of the Civil Magistrate

**6.127**      1. God, the Supreme Lord and King of all the world, hath ordained civil magistrates to be under him over the people, for his own glory and the public good; and to this end, hath armed them with the power of the sword, for the defense and encouragement of them that are good, and for the punishment of evildoers.[1]

**6.128**      2. It is lawful for Christians to accept and execute the office of a magistrate, when called thereunto;[2] in the managing whereof, as they ought especially to maintain piety, justice, and peace, according to the wholesome laws of each commonwealth,[3] so, for that end, they may lawfully, now under the New Testament, wage war upon just and necessary occasions.[4]

---

[n] Ed. 1647 includes: "Popish."

Presbyterian Church  
in the United States

The United Presbyterian Church  
in the United States of America

**6.129**     3. °Civil magistrates may not assume to themselves the administration of the Word and Sacraments; or the power of the keys of the kingdom of heaven; or, in the least, interfere in matters of faith.[5] Yet, as nursing fathers, it is the duty of civil magistrates to protect the church of our common Lord, without giving the preference to any denomination of Christians above the rest, in such a manner that all ecclesiastical persons whatever shall enjoy the full, free, and unquestioned liberty of discharging every part of their sacred functions, without violence or danger. And, as Jesus Christ hath appointed a regular government and discipline in his church, no law of any commonwealth should interfere with, let, or hinder, the due exercise thereof, among the voluntary members of any denomination of Christians, according to their own profession and belief. It is the duty of civil magistrates to protect the person and good name of all their people, in such an effectual manner as that no person be suffered, either upon pretense of religion or infidelity, to offer any indignity, violence, abuse, or injury to any other person whatsoever: and to take order, that all religious and ecclesiastical assemblies be held without molestation or disturbance.[6]

**6.130**     4. It is the duty of the people to pray for magistrates,[7] to honor their persons,[8] to pay them tribute and other dues,[9] to obey their lawful commands, and to be subject to their authority, for conscience' sake.[10] Infidelity, or difference in religion, doth not make void the magistrate's just and legal authority, nor free the people from their due obedience to him:[11] from which ecclesiastical persons are not exempted;[12] much less hath the Pope any power or[p] jurisdiction over them in their dominions, or over any of their people; and least of all to deprive them of their dominions or lives, if he shall judge them to be heretics, or upon any other pretense whatsoever.[13]

---

° Ed. 1647 reads: "III. The Civill Magistrate may not assume to himself the administration of the Word and Sacraments, or the power of the Keyes of the Kingdome of Heaven: yet, he hath Authoritie, and it is his duetie, to take order, that Unitie and Peace be preserved in the Church, that the Truth of God be kept pure, and intire, that all Blasphemies and Heresies be suppressed, all corruptions and abuses in Worship and Discipline prevented, or reformed; and all the Ordinances of God duely settled, administered, and observed. For the better effecting whereof, he hath power to call Synods, to be present at them, and to provide that whatsoever is transacted in them, be according to the minde of God."

[p] Ed. 1647 reads: "and"

Presbyterian Church in the United States  
The United Presbyterian Church in the United States of America

## CHAPTER XXIV[q]

### Of Marriage and Divorce

**6.131** 1. Christian marriage is an institution ordained of God, blessed by our Lord Jesus Christ, established and sanctified for the happiness and welfare of mankind, into which spiritual and physical union one man and one woman enter, cherishing a mutual esteem and love, bearing with each other's infirmities and weaknesses, comforting each other in trouble, providing in honesty and industry for each other and for their household, praying for each other, and living together the length of their days as heirs of the grace of life.

**6.132** 2. Because the corruption of man is apt unduly to put asunder those whom God hath joined

---

[q] Ed.1647, Chapter XXIV reads:

"I. Marriage is to be between one Man and one Woman: neither is it lawfull for any Man to have more then one Wife, nor for any Woman to have more then one Husband, at the same time.

"II. Marriage was ordained for the mutuall help of Husband and Wife, for the increase of man-kinde with a legitimate issue, and of the Church with an holy seed and, for preventing of uncleannesse.

"III. It is lawful for all sorts of people to marry, who are able with judgement, to give their consent. Yet, is it the duty of Christians to marry onely in the Lord: And therefore such as professe the true reformed Religion, should not marry with Infidels, Papists or other Idolaters: Neither should such as are godly be unequally yoked, by marrying with such as are notoriously wicked in their life, or maintaine damnable Heresies.

"IV. Marriage ought not be within the degrees of Consanguinity or Affinity forbidden in the Word: Nor can such incestuous marriages ever be made lawfull by any Law of man, or consent of Parties, so as those persons may live together as man and wife. The man may not marry any of his wives kindred, nearer in blood, then he may of his own: nor the woman of her husbands kindred, then of her own.

"V. Adultery, or fornication committed after a Contract, being detected before marriage, giveth just occasion to the innocent party to dissolve that Contract. In the case of Adultery after marriage, it is lawfull for the innocent party to sue out a Divorce: And after the Divorce, to marry another, as if the offending party were dead.

"VI. Although the corruption of man be such as is apt to study arguments, unduely to put asunder those whom God hath joyned together in marriage: yet, nothing but Adultery, or such wilfull desertion as can no way be remedied, by the Church, or Civil Magistrate, is cause sufficient of dissolving the bond of Marriage: Wherein, a publicke and orderly course of proceeding is to be observed: And the Persons concerned in it, not left to their own wills and discretion, in their owne case."

Presbyterian Church in the United States / The United Presbyterian Church in the United States of America

together in marriage, and because the Church is concerned with the establishment of marriage in the Lord as Scripture sets it forth, and with the present penitence as well as with the past innocence or guilt of those whose marriage has been broken; therefore as a breach of that holy relation may occasion divorce, so remarriage after a divorce granted on grounds explicitly stated in Scripture or implicit in the gospel of Christ may be sanctioned in keeping with his redemptive gospel, when sufficient penitence for sin and failure is evident, and a firm purpose of and endeavor after Christian marriage is manifest.

## CHAPTER XXVI

### Of Marriage and Divorce

6.133    1. Marriage is a union between one man and one woman, designed of God to last so long as they both shall live.[1]

6.134    2. Marriage is designed for the mutual help of husband and wife;[2] for the safeguarding, undergirding, and development of their moral and spiritual character;[3] for the propagation of children and the rearing of them in the discipline and instruction of the Lord.[4]

6.135    3. All persons who are able with judgment to give their consent may marry,[5] except within the limits of blood relationship forbidden by Scripture,[6] and such marriages are valid before God in the eyes of the church.[7] But no

Presbyterian Church
in the United States

marriage can be fully and securely Christian in spirit or in purpose unless both partners are committed to a common Christian faith and to a deeply shared intention of building a Christian home. Evangelical Christians should seek as partners in marriage only persons who hold in common a sound basis of evangelical faith.[8]

**6.136** 4. Marriage for the Christian has religious as well as civil significance.[9] The distinctive contribution of the church in performing the marriage ceremony is to affirm the divine institution of marriage;[10] to invoke God's blessing upon those who enter into the marital relationship in accordance with his word;[11] to hear the vows of those who desire to be married; and to assure the married partners of God's grace within their new relationship.[12]

**6.137** 5. It is the divine intention that persons entering the marriage covenant become inseparably united, thus allowing for no dissolution save that caused by the death of either husband or wife.[13] However, the weaknesses of one or both partners may lead to gross and persistent denial of the marriage vows so that marriage dies at the heart and the union becomes intolerable; yet only in cases of extreme, unrepented-of, and irremediable unfaithfulness (physical or spiritual) should separation or divorce be considered. Such separation or divorce is accepted as permissible only because of the failure of one or both

Presbyterian Church in the United States | The United Presbyterian Church in the United States of America

of the partners, and does not lessen in any way the divine intention for indissoluble union.[14]

**6.138** 6. The remarriage of divorced persons may be sanctioned by the church, in keeping with the redemptive gospel of Christ, when sufficient penitence for sin and failure is evident, and a firm purpose of and endeavor after Christian marriage is manifested.[15]

**6.139** 7. Divorced persons should give prayerful thought to discover if God's vocation for them is to remain unmarried, since one failure in this realm raises serious question as to the rightness and wisdom of undertaking another union.[16]

CHAPTER XXVII       CHAPTER XXV

**Of the Church**

**6.140** 1. The catholic or universal church, which is invisible, consists of the whole number of the elect, that have been, are, or shall be gathered into one, under Christ the head thereof, and is the spouse, the body, the fullness of Him that filleth all in all.[1]

**6.141** 2. The visible Church, which is also catholic or universal under the gospel (not confined to one nation as before under the law), consists of all those throughout the world that profess the true religion,[r][2] together with their children;[3] and is the Kingdom of the Lord Jesus Christ;[4] the house and family of God,[s][5] through which men are ordinarily saved and union with which is essential to their best growth and service.[6]

**6.142** 3. Unto this catholic visible Church, Christ hath given the ministry, oracles, and ordinances of God, for the gathering and perfecting of the saints, in this life, to the end of the world: and doth by his own presence and Spirit, according to his promise, make them effectual thereunto.[7]

---

[r] Ed. 1647 reads: "and of their children."
[s] Ed. 1647 reads: "out of which, there is no ordinary possibility of Salvation."

| Presbyterian Church in the United States | The United Presbyterian Church in the United States of America |

**6.143**     4. This catholic Church hath been sometimes more, sometimes less, visible.[8] And particular churches, which are members thereof, are more or less pure, according as the doctrine of the gospel is taught and embraced, ordinances administered, and public worship performed more or less purely in them.[9]

**6.144**     5. The purest churches under heaven are subject both to mixture and error:[10] and some have so degenerated as to become[t] apparently no churches of Christ.[11] Nevertheless, there shall be always a Church on earth, to worship God according to his will.[12]

**6.145**

| | |
|---|---|
| 6. The Lord Jesus Christ is the only head of the Church,[13] and the claim of any man to be the vicar of Christ and the head of the Church is without warrant in fact or in Scripture, even anti-Christian, a usurpation dishonoring to the Lord Jesus Christ. | 6. [u]The Lord Jesus Christ is the only head of the Church, and the claim of any man to be the vicar of Christ and the head of the Church is unscriptural, without warrant in fact, and is a usurpation dishonoring to the Lord Jesus Christ. |

CHAPTER XXVIII            CHAPTER XXVI

### Of the Communion of Saints

**6.146**     1. All saints being[v] united to Jesus Christ their head, by his Spirit and by faith, have fellowship with him in his graces, sufferings, death, resurrection, and glory:[1] and, being united to one another in love, they have communion in each other's gifts and graces,[2] and are obliged to the performance of such duties, public and private, as to conduce to their mutual good, both in the inward and outward man.[3]

**6.147**     2. Saints by their[w] profession are bound to maintain an holy fellowship and communion in the worship of God, and in performing such other spiritual services as tend to their mutual edification;[4] as also in relieving each other in outward things, according to their several abilities and necessities. Which communion, as God offereth opportunity, is to be extended unto all those who, in every place, call upon the name of the Lord Jesus.[5]

---

[t] Ed. 1647 reads: "no Churches of Christ, but Synagogues of Satan."
[u] Ed. 1647 reads: "VI. There is no other Head of the Church, but the Lord Jesus Christ: Nor can the Pope of Rome, in any sense be head thereof: but is, that Antichrist, that Man of sin and Son of Perdition, that exalteth himself, in the Church, against Christ, and all that is called God."
[v] UPCUSA ed. reads: "that are."
[w] UPCUSA ed. reads: "by profession."

Presbyterian Church  
in the United States

The United Presbyterian Church  
in the United States of America

**6.148**     3. This communion which the saints have with Christ, doth not make them in any wise partakers of the substance of his Godhead, or to be equal with Christ in any respect: either of which to affirm, is impious and blasphemous.[6] Nor doth their communion one with another as saints, take away or infringe the title or property which each man hath in his goods and possessions.[7]

CHAPTER XXIX                         CHAPTER XXVII

### Of the Sacraments

**6.149**     1. Sacraments are holy signs and seals of the covenant of grace, immediately instituted by God,[1] to represent Christ and his benefits, and to confirm our interest in him:[2] as also to put a visible difference between those that belong unto the church, and the rest of the world;[3] and solemnly to engage them to the service of God in Christ, according to his Word.[4]

**6.150**     2. There is in every sacrament a spiritual relation, or sacramental union, between the sign and the thing signified; whence it comes to pass that the names and effects of the one are attributed to the other.[5]

**6.151**     3. The grace which is exhibited in or by the sacraments, rightly used, is not conferred by any power in them; neither doth the efficacy of a sacrament depend upon the piety or intention of him that doth administer it, but upon the work of the Spirit,[6] and the word of institution, which contains, together with a precept authorizing the use thereof, a promise of benefit to worthy receivers.[7]

**6.152**     4. There be only two sacraments ordained by Christ our Lord in the gospel, that is to say, baptism and the supper of the Lord:[8] neither of which may be dispensed by any but by a minister of the Word, lawfully ordained.[9]

**6.153**     5. The sacraments of the Old Testament, in regard of the spiritual things thereby signified and exhibited, were, for substance, the same with those of the New.[10]

CHAPTER XXX                         CHAPTER XXVIII

### Of Baptism

**6.154**     1. Baptism is a sacrament of the New Testament, ordained by Jesus Christ,[1] not only for the solemn admission of the party baptized into the visible Church,[2] but also to be unto him a sign and seal of the covenant of grace,[3] of his ingrafting into Christ,[4] of regeneration,[5] of remission of sins,[6] and of his giving up unto God, through Jesus Christ, to walk in newness of life:[7] which sacrament is, by Christ's own appointment, to be continued in his church until the end of the world.[8]

Presbyterian Church in the United States / The United Presbyterian Church in the United States of America

**6.155**     2. The outward element to be used in this sacrament is water, wherewith the party is to be baptized in the name of the Father, and of the Son, and of the Holy Ghost,[9] by a minister of the gospel, lawfully called thereunto.[10]

**6.156**     3. Dipping of the person into the water is not necessary, but baptism is rightly administered by pouring or sprinkling water upon the person.[11]

**6.157**     4. Not only those that do actually profess faith in and obedience unto Christ,[12] but also the infants of one or both believing parents are to be baptized.[13]

**6.158**     5. Although it be a great sin to contemn or neglect this ordinance,[14] yet grace and salvation are not so inseparably annexed unto it as that no person can be regenerated or saved without it,[15] or that all that are baptized are undoubtedly regenerated.[16]

**6.159**     6. The efficacy of Baptism is not tied to that moment of time wherein it is administered;[17] yet, notwithstanding, by the right use of this ordinance the grace promised is not only offered, but really exhibited and conferred by the Holy Ghost, to such (whether of age or infants) as that grace belongeth unto, according to the counsel of God's own will, in his appointed time.[18]

**6.160**     7. The sacrament of Baptism is but once to be administered to any person.[19]

CHAPTER XXXI                                              CHAPTER XXIX

**Of the Lord's Supper**

**6.161**     1. Our Lord Jesus, in the night wherein he was betrayed, instituted the sacrament of his body and blood, called the Lord's Supper, to be observed in his Church unto the end of the world; for the perpetual remembrance of the sacrifice of himself in his death, the sealing all benefits thereof unto true believers, their spiritual nourishment and growth in him, their further engagement in and to all duties which they owe unto him; and to be a bond and pledge of their communion with him, and with each other, as members of his mystical body.[1]

**6.162**     2. In this sacrament Christ is not offered up to his Father, nor any real sacrifice made at all for remission of sins of the quick or dead, but[x]

---

[x] Ed. 1647 reads: "... but onely a Commemoration of that one offering up of Himselfe, by Himselfe, upon the Crosse, once for all: and, a spirituall Oblation of all possible praise unto God, for the same: So that, the Popish Sacrifice of the masse (as they call it) is most abominably injurious to Christs one, onely Sacrifice, the alone Propitation for all the sins of the Elect."

| Presbyterian Church in the United States | The United Presbyterian Church in the United States of America |

a commemoration of that one[y] offering up of himself, by himself, upon the cross, once for all, and a spiritual oblation of all possible praise unto God for the same; so that the so-called sacrifice of the mass is most contradictory to Christ's one[z] sacrifice, the only propitiation for all the sins of the elect.[2]

**6.163** 3. The Lord Jesus hath, in this ordinance, appointed his ministers to declare his word of institution to the people, to pray, and bless the elements of bread and wine, and thereby to set them apart from a common to an holy use; and to take and break the bread, to take the cup, and (they communicating also themselves) to give both to the communicants.[3]

3. The Lord hath, in this ordinance, appointed his ministers to declare his word of institution to the people, to pray, and bless the elements of bread and wine, and thereby to set them apart from a common to an holy use; and to take and break the bread, to take cup, and (they communicating also themselves) to give both to the communicants; but to none who are not then present in the congregation.

**6.164** 4. Private masses, or receiving this sacrament by a priest, or any other, alone; as likewise the denial of the cup to the people; worshipping the elements, the lifting them up, or carrying them about for adoration, and the reserving them for any pretended religious use, are all contrary to the nature of this sacrament, and to the institution of Christ.[4]

**6.165** 5. The outward elements in this sacrament, duly set apart to the uses ordained by Christ, have such relation to him crucified, as that truly, yet sacramentally only, they are sometimes called by the name of the things they represent, to wit, the body and blood of Christ;[5] albeit, in substance and nature, they still remain truly, and only, bread and wine, as they were before.[6]

**6.166** 6. That doctrine which maintains a change of the substance of bread and wine, into the substance of Christ's body and blood (commonly called transubstantiation) by consecration of a priest, or by any other way, is repugnant, not to Scripture alone, but even to common sense and reason; overthroweth the nature of the sacrament; and hath been, and is, the cause of manifold superstitions, yea, of gross idolatries.[7]

**6.167** 7. Worthy receivers, outwardly partaking of the visible elements in this sacrament, do then also inwardly by faith, really and indeed, yet not carnally and corporally, but spiritually, receive and feed upon Christ cru-

---

[y] UPCUSA ed. reads: "once."
[z] UPCUSA ed. reads: "own."

**6.167–.170**

Presbyterian Church in the United States / The United Presbyterian Church in the United States of America

cified, and all benefits of his death: the body and blood of Christ being then not corporally or carnally in, with, or under the bread and wine; yet as really, but spiritually, present to the faith of believers in that ordinance, as the elements themselves are to their outward senses.[8]

**6.168**

*Presbyterian Church in the United States:*

8. Although ignorant and wicked men receive the outward elements in this sacrament, yet they receive not the thing signified thereby; but by their unworthy coming thereunto are guilty of the body and blood of the Lord, and bring judgement of themselves.[9]

*The United Presbyterian Church in the United States of America:*

8. Although ignorant and wicked men receive the outward elements in this sacrament, yet they receive not the thing signified thereby; but by their unworthy coming thereunto are guilty of body and blood of the Lord,[a] and bring judgement on themselves. Wherefore all ignorant and ungodly persons, as they are unfit to enjoy communion with him, so are they unworthy of the Lord's Table, and cannot, without great sin against Christ, while they remain such, partake of these holy mysteries, or be admitted thereunto.

CHAPTER XXXII / CHAPTER XXX

**Of Church Censures**

**6.169** 1. The Lord Jesus, as king and head of his Church, hath therein appointed a government in the hand of Church officers, distinct from the civil magistrate.[1]

**6.170** 2. To these officers the keys of the Kingdom of Heaven are committed, by virtue whereof they have power respectively to retain and remit sins, to shut that kingdom against the impenitent, both by the word and censures; and to open it unto penitent sinners, by the ministry of the gospel, and by absolution from censures, as occasion shall require.[2]

---

[a] Ed. 1647 reads: "… to their own damnation."

Presbyterian Church  
in the United States

The United Presbyterian Church  
in the United States of America

**6.171**     3. Church censures are necessary for the reclaiming and gaining of offending brethren; for deterring of others from like offenses; for purging out of that leaven which might infect the whole lump; for vindicating the honor of Christ, and the holy profession of the gospel; and for preventing the wrath of God, which might justly fall upon the Church, if they should suffer his covenant, and the seals thereof, to be profaned by notorious and obstinate offenders.³

**6.172**     4. For the better attaining of these ends, the officers of the church are to proceed by admonition, suspension from the sacrament of the Lord's Supper for a season, by excommunication from the Church, according to the nature of the crime, and demerit of the person.⁴

CHAPTER XXXIII

CHAPTER XXXI

**Of Synods and Councils**

**6.173**     1. For the better government and further edification of the Church, there ought to be such assemblies as are commonly called synods or councils:ᵇ and it belongeth to the overseers and other rulers of the particular churches, by virtue of their office, and the power which Christ hath given them for edification, and not for destruction, to appoint such assemblies; and to convene together in them, as often as they shall judge it expedient for the good of the Church.¹

**6.174**     2.ᶜ It belongeth to synods and councils, ministerially, to determine controversies of faith, and cases of conscience; to set down rules and directions for the better ordering of the public worship of God, and government of his Church; to receive complaints in cases of maladministration, and authoritatively to determine the same: which decrees and determinations, if consonant to the Word of God, are to be received with reverence and submission, not only for their agreement with the Word, but also for the power whereby they are made, as being an ordinance of God, appointed thereunto in his Word.²

**6.175**     3. All synods or councils since the apostles' times, whether general or particular, may err, and many have erred; therefore they are not to be made the rule of faith or practice, but to be used as a help in both.³

---

ᵇ Remainder of this section added in 1788.

ᶜ Ed. 1647 reads: "II. As Magistrates may lawfully call a Synod of Ministers, and other fit Persons, to consult and advise with, about matters of Religion: So, if Magistrates be open enemies to the Church, the Ministers of Christ, of themselves, by vertue of their Office, or, they, with other fit persons, upon delegation from their Churches, may meet together in such Assemblies."

Sections 3–5 renumbered as 2–4 in 1788.

Presbyterian Church in the United States / The United Presbyterian Church in the United States of America

**6.176**     4. Synods and councils are to handle or conclude nothing but that which is ecclesiastical; and are not to intermeddle with civil affairs which concern the commonwealth unless by way of humble petition in cases extraordinary; or by way of advice for satisfaction of conscience, if they be thereunto required by the civil magistrate.[4]

CHAPTER XXXIV     CHAPTER XXXII

### Of the State of Man After Death, and of the Resurrection of the Dead

**6.177**     1. The bodies of men, after death, return to dust, and see corruption;[1] but their souls (which neither die nor sleep), having an immortal subsistence, immediately return to God who gave them.[2] The souls of the righteous, being then made perfect in holiness, are received into the highest heavens, where they behold the face of God in light and glory, waiting for the full redemption of their bodies;[3] and the souls of the wicked are cast into hell, where they remain in torments and utter darkness, reserved to the judgment of the great day.[4] Besides these two places for souls separated from their bodies, the Scripture acknowledgeth none.

**6.178**     2. At the last day, such as are found alive shall not die, but be changed:[5] and all the dead shall be raised up with the self-same bodies, and none other, although with different qualities, which shall be united again to their souls for ever.[6]

**6.179**     3. The bodies of the unjust shall, by the power of Christ, be raised to dishonor; the bodies of the just, by his Spirit, unto honor, and be made conformable to his own glorious body.[7]

CHAPTER XXXV     CHAPTER XXXIII

### Of the Last Judgement

**6.180**     1. God hath appointed a day, wherein he will judge the world in righteousness by Jesus Christ,[1] to whom all power and judgment is given of the Father.[2] In which day, not only the apostate angels shall be judged; but likewise all persons, that have lived upon earth, shall appear before the tribunal of Christ, to give an account of their thoughts, words, and deeds; and to receive according to what they have done in the body, whether good or evil.[3]

**6.181**     2. The end of God's appointing this day, is for the manifestation of the glory of his mercy in the eternal salvation of the elect;[4] and of his justice in the damnation of the reprobate, who are wicked and disobedient.[5] For then shall the righteous go into everlasting life, and receive that fullness of joy and refreshing which shall come from the presence

Presbyterian Church in the United States / The United Presbyterian Church in the United States of America

of the Lord:⁶ but the wicked, who know not God, and obey not the gospel of Jesus Christ, shall be cast into eternal torments, and punished with everlasting destruction from the presence of the Lord, and from the glory of his power.⁷

**6.182** 3. As Christ would have us to be certainly persuaded that there shall be a day of judgment, both to deter all men from sin, and for the greater consolation of the godly in their adversity;⁸ so will he have that day unknown to men, that they may shake off all carnal security, and be always watchful, because they know not at what hour the Lord will come; and may be ever prepared to say, Come Lord Jesus, come quickly.⁹ Amen.

## CHAPTER XXXIV ᵈ

### Of the Holy Spirit

**6.183** 1. The Holy Spirit, the third Person in the Trinity, proceeding from the Father and the Son, of the same substance and equal in power and glory, is, together with the Father and the Son, to be believed in, loved, obeyed, and worshiped throughout all ages.

**6.184** 2. He is the Lord and Giver of life, everywhere present, and is the source of all good thoughts, pure desires, and holy counsels in men. By him the prophets were moved to speak the Word of God, and all the writers of the Holy Scriptures inspired to record infallibly the mind and will of God. The dispensation of the gospel is especially committed to him. He prepares the way for it, accompanies it with his persuasive power, and urges its message upon the reason and conscience of men, so that they who reject its merciful offer are not only without excuse, but are also guilty of resisting the Holy Spirit.

---

ᵈ Added 1903.

**6.185**

3. The Holy Spirit, whom the Father is ever willing to give to all who ask him, is the only efficient agent in the application of redemption. He regenerates men by his grace, convicts them of sin, moves them to repentance, and persuades and enables them to embrace Jesus Christ by faith. He unites all believers to Christ, dwells in them as their Comforter and Sanctifier, gives to them the Spirit of adoption and prayer, and performs all these gracious offices by which they are sanctified and sealed unto the day of redemption.

**6.186**

4. By the indwelling of the Holy Spirit all believers being vitally united to Christ, who is the head, are thus united one to another in the Church, which is his body. He calls and anoints ministers for their holy office, qualifies all other officers in the Church for their special work, and imparts various gifts and graces to its members. He gives efficacy to the Word and to the ordinances of the gospel. By him the Church will be preserved, increased, purified, and at last made perfectly holy in the presence of God.

CHAPTER XXXV[e]

**Of the Gospel of the Love of God and Missions**

**6.187**

1. God in infinite and perfect love, having provided in the covenant of grace, through the mediation and sacrifice of the Lord Jesus Christ, a way of life

---

[e] Added 1903.

| Presbyterian Church in the United States | The United Presbyterian Church in the United States of America |

and salvation, sufficient for and adapted to the whole lost race of man, doth freely offer this salvation to all men in the gospel.

**6.188**

2. In the gospel God declares his love for the world and his desire that all men should be saved; reveals fully and clearly the only way of salvation; promises eternal life to all who truly repent and believe in Christ; invites and commands all to embrace the offered mercy; and by his Spirit accompanying the Word pleads with men to accept his gracious invitation.

**6.189**

3. It is the duty and privilege of everyone who hears the gospel immediately to accept its merciful provisions; and they who continue in impenitence and unbelief incur aggravated guilt and perish by their own fault.

**6.190**

4. Since there is no other way of salvation than that revealed in the gospel, and since in the divinely established and ordinary method of grace faith cometh by hearing the Word of God, Christ hath commissioned his Church to go into all the world and to make disciples of all nations. All believers are, therefore, under obligation to sustain the ordinance of the Christian religion where they are already established, and to contribute by their prayers, gifts, and personal efforts to the extension of the Kingdom of Christ throughout the whole earth.

Presbyterian Church
in the United States

The United Presbyterian Church
in the United States of America

**Declaratory Statement**[f]

6.191 While the ordination vow of ministers, ruling elders, and deacons, as set forth in the Form of Government, requires the reception and adoption of the Confession of Faith only as containing the system of doctrine taught in the Holy Scriptures, nevertheless, seeing that the desire has been formally expressed for a disavowal by the Church of certain inferences drawn from statements in the Confession of Faith, and also for a declaration of certain aspects of revealed truth which appear at the present time to call for more explicit statement, therefore The United Presbyterian Church in the United States of America does authoritatively declare as follows:

6.192 *First*, with reference to Chapter III of the Confession of Faith: that concerning those who are saved in Christ, the doctrine of God's eternal decree is held in harmony with the doctrine of his love to all mankind, his gift of his Son to be the propitiation for the sins of the whole world, and his readiness to bestow his saving grace on all who seek it; that concerning those who perish, the doctrine of God's eternal decree is held in harmony with the doctrine that God desires not the death of any sinner, but has provided in Christ a salvation sufficient for all, adapted to all, and freely offered in the gospel to all; that men are fully responsible for their

---

[f] Added 1903.

| Presbyterian Church in the United States | The United Presbyterian Church in the United States of America |

treatment of God's gracious offer; that his decree hinders no man from accepting that offer; and that no man is condemned except on the ground of his sin.

**6.193**     *Second*, with reference to Chapter X, Section 3, of the Confession of Faith, that it is not to be regarded as teaching that any who die in infancy are lost. We believe that all dying in infancy are included in the election of grace, and are regenerated and saved by Christ through the Spirit, who works when and where and how he pleases.

# ENDNOTES

GENERAL NOTE: At several points the Confession of Faith is more specific in its statements than the Scriptures. These statements are inferences drawn from the Scriptures or from statements based on the Scriptures, or from the experience and observation of the Church. In such cases no texts are cited, but reference is made to this General Note.

Chapter I
1. Rom. 1:19, 20; 2:14, 15; 1:32.
2. I Cor. 1:21; 2:13, 14; 2:9–12; Acts 4:12; Rom. 10:13, 14.
3. Heb. 1:1, 2; Gal. 1:11, 12; Deut. 4:12–14.
4. Luke 24:27; II Tim. 3:16; Rom 15:4; II Peter 3:15, 16.
5. Luke 16:29–31; Heb. 2:1–3; II Tim. 3:15, 16; II Peter 1:10.
6. See General Note.
7. The Canon of Scripture is not established by explicit passages, but by the testimony of Jesus and His Apostles; of ancient manuscripts and versions; of ancient Christian writers and church councils, and by the internal evidence exhibited in the separate books.
8. I Thess. 2:13; II Tim. 3:16; II Peter 1:21; Gal. 1:11, 12.
9. I Cor. 2:10, 11; John 16:13, 14; I Cor. 2:6–9.
10. Mark 7:5–7.
11. This statement is an inference from the sufficiency of the Scriptures.
12. John 6:45; I Cor. 2:9, 10, 12.
13. I Cor. 14:26, 40; 11:13, 14.
14. II Peter 3:16; John 16:17; 6:60.
15. Ps 119:105, 130; Acts 17:11, 12.
16. See Note under Section 3, figure 9 above.
17. Isaiah 8:20; Acts 15:14–18.
18. John 5:39; II Tim. 3:14, 15; II Peter 1:19.
19. I Cor. 14:6, 9, 11, 12, 24, 27, 28; Matt. 28:19, 20; Col. 3:16; Rom. 15:4.
20. Matt. 4:5–7; 12:1–7.
21. Matt. 22:29, 31; Acts 28:25; Luke 10:26.

Chapter II
1. Deut. 6:4; I Cor. 8:4, 6; I Thess. 1:9; Jer. 10:10.
2. Jer. 23:24; Ps. 147:5; I Kings 8:27; Ps. 139.
3. John 4:24.
4. I Tim. 1:17.
5. Luke 24:39; Deut. 4:15, 16.
6. James 1:17; Mal. 3:6.
7. I Kings 8:27; Jer. 23:23, 24.
8. Ps. 90:2, I Tim. 1:17.
9. Rom 11:33; Ps. 145:3.
10. Rev. 4:8.
11. Rom 16:27.
12. Isa. 6:3; Rev. 4:8.
13. Ps. 115:3.
14. Isa. 44:6; Acts 17:24, 25.
15. Eph. 1:11.
16. Rom. 11:36; Rev. 4:11.
17. I John 4:8–10.
18. Exod. 34:6, 7.
19. Heb. 11:6.
20. Neh. 9:32, 33.
21. Hab. 1:13; Ps. 5:5, 6.
22. Exod. 34:7; Nahum 1:2, 3.
23. John 5:26; Acts 7:2, Ps. 119:68; I Tim. 6:15; Rom. 9:5.
24. Acts 17:24, 25.
25. Rom. 11:36; Isa. 40:12–17.
26. Dan. 4:25; Eph. 1:11.
27. Heb. 4:13.
28. Rom. 11:33; Ps. 147:5.
29. Isa. 46:9–11; Acts 15:18; Ezek. 11:5.
30. Ps. 145:17; Rom 7:12.
31. Rev. 7:11, 12; Rev. 5:12–14.
32. Matt. 28:19; II Cor. 13:14; Matt. 3:16, 17.
33. John 1:14, 18; 17:24.
34. Gal. 4:6; John 15:26.

## Chapter III

1. Eph. 1:11; Acts 4:27, 28: Matt. 10:29, 30; Eph. 2:10.
2. James 1:13; I John 1:5.
3. Acts 2:23; Matt. 17:12; Acts 4:27, 28; John 19:11; Prov. 16:33; Acts 27:23, 24, 34, 44.
4. I Sam. 23:11, 12; Matt 11:21, 23; Ps. 139:1–4.
5. Rom. 9:11, 13, 16, 18; II Tim. 1:9; Eph. 1:4, 5.
6. I Tim. 5:21; Acts 13:48; Rom. 8:29, 30; John 10:27–29.
7. Matt 25:41; Rom 9:22, 23; Jude 4.
8. John 10:14–16, 27–29; 6:37–39; 13:18; Acts 13:48; II Tim. 2:19.
9. Eph. 1:4.
10. Eph. 1:11.
11. Eph. 1:9.
12. II Tim. 1:9.
13. Rom. 8:30; I Peter 5:10.
14. II Tim. 1:9; Eph. 1:6, 2:8, 9.
15. Eph. 1:5, 6, 12.
16. Eph. 2:10; II Thess. 2:13; I Peter 1:2; Eph. 1:4.
17. Rom. 5:19; I Thess. 5:9, 10; Titus 2:14.
18. Rom 9:11; II Thess. 2:13, 14; I Cor. 1:9.
19. Rom 8:30.
20. Eph. 1:5.
21. Eph. 1:4; I Thess. 4:3; II Thess. 2:13.
22. I Peter 1:5; John 10:28.
23. John 17:9; 6:64, 65; 8:47; 10:26; Acts 13:48; I John 2:19.
24. Matt. 11:25, 26.
25. Rom. 2:8, 9; II Thess. 2:10–12; Rom. 9:14–22.
26. Rev. 15:3, 4.
27. See General Note.

## Chapter IV

1. Gen. 1:1–3; Exod 20:11; Jer. 10:12; Col. 1:16; John 1:2, 3; Heb. 1:2; 11:3; Ps. 104:24; Gen 1.
2. Gen. 1:27.
3. Ps. 8:5, 6; Gen. 2:19, 20; Luke 23:43; Matt. 10:28.
4. Gen. 1:26; Col. 3:10; Eph. 4:24.
5. Rom. 2:14, 15.
6. Gen. 2:16, 17, 3:6, 17.
7. Gen. 2:16, 17.
8. Gen. 2:17; 3:8–11, 23.
9. Gen. 1:28; Ps. 8:6–8.

## Chapter V

1. Neh. 9:6; Heb. 1:3; Ps. 135:6; Matt. 10:29–31; Acts 17:25, 28; Matt. 6:26, 30; Job, Chapters 38–41.
2. Prov. 15:3; II Chron. 16:9; Ps. 145:17; 104:24.
3. Acts 15:18.
4. Eph. 1:11; Ps. 33:11.
5. Eph. 3:10; Rom. 9:17; Ps. 145.
6. Acts 2:23. See under figures 3 and 4 above.
7. Gen. 8:22; Jer. 31–35.
8. Exod. 21:13; Gen 50:19, 20; I Kings 22:34; Isa. 10:6–7.
9. Acts 27:24, 31, 44; Isa. 55:10, 11.
10. Hos. 1:7.
11. Rom. 4:19–21.
12. II Kings 6:6; Dan. 3:27.
13. This statement is sustained by the doctrines of God's decrees and providence. See citations under Chapter III and Chapter V. Sections 1, 2, 3.
14. Rom. 11:32, 33; II Sam. 24:1; Acts 4:27, 28. See citations under Chapter III and Chapter V, Sections 1, 2, 3.
15. II Kings 19:28; Isa. 10:5–7, 12, 15.
16. Gen. 50:20. See under figure 15 above.
17. I John 2:16; Ps. 50:21; James 1:13, 14.
18. Deut. 8:2; II Chron 32:25, 26, 31.
19. II Cor. 12:7–9; Ps. 73; 77:1–12; Mark 14:66–72; John 21:15–17.

20. Rom. 1:24, 26, 28; 11:7, 8; II Thess. 2:11, 12.
21. Deut. 29:4; Mark 4:11, 12.
22. Matt. 13:12; 25:29.
23. II Kings 8:12, 13.
24. Ps. 81:11, 12; II Thess. 2:10–12.
25. Exod. 8:15, 32; II Cor. 2:15, 16; Isa. 8:14; Exod. 7:3; I Peter 2:7, 8; Isa. 6:9, 10; Acts 28:26, 27.
26. Amos 9:8, 9; Rom. 8:28; Eph. 1:22.

## Chapter VI

1. Gen. 3:13; II Cor. 11:3; Gen. 3:1–14.
2. Rom. 5:19–21.
3. Gen. 3:7, 8; 2:17.
4. Rom. 5:12; Eph. 2:3.
5. Gen. 6:5; Jer. 17:9; Rom. 3:10–19; 8:6–8; Ps. 58:1–5.
6. Acts 17:26. Compare Gen. 2:16, 17, with Rom. 5:12, 15–19; I Cor. 15:21, 22, 45, 49.
7. Ps. 51:5; Gen. 5:3; John 3:6; Rom. 3:10–18.
8. Rom. 5:6; 8:7; John 3:6; Rom. 7:18; Gen. 8:21; Rom. 8:7.
9. James 1:14, 15; Matt 15:19.
10. Rom. 7:14, 17, 18, 23.
11. Rom. 7:5, 7, 8, 25.
12. Rom. 3:19; 2:15; I John 3:4.
13. Eph. 2:3; Rom. 5:12.
14. Gal. 3:10.
15. Rom. 6:23; Gen. 2:17.
16. Eph. 4:18; Matt. 25:41; II Thess. 1:9; Rom. 1:21–28; Lev. 26:14ff; Deut. 28:15ff.

## Chapter VII

1. See General Note.
2. Gen. 2:16, 17; Gal. 3:10; Hosea 6:7; Rom. 5:12, 19; I Cor. 15:22, 47.
3. Compare Gen. 2:16, 17, with Rom. 5:12–14; Rom. 10:5; Luke 10:25–28; and with the covenants made with Noah and Abraham.
4. Matt. 26:28; Gal. 3:21; Rom. 8:3; Isa. 42:6; Gen. 3:15; Heb. 10:5–10.
5. John 3:16; Acts 16:30, 31.
6. John 3:5–8; 6:37–44; Ezek. 36:26, 27.
7. Heb. 1:1, 2; II Cor. 3:6–9.
8. Rom. 4:11; Heb., Chapters 8, 9, 10.
9. Heb. 11:13; John 8:56, Gal. 3:6–8.
10. Acts 15:11; Rom. 3:30; Gal. 3:8, 9, 14.
11. Matt. 28:19, 20; I Cor. 11:23–25.
12. Heb. 8:6–13; II Cor. 3:9–11.
13. Eph. 2:15–19. See under figure 11 above.
14. Gal. 3:17, 29. See context and citations under figure 10 above.

## Chapter VIII

1. Isa. 42:1; I Peter 1:19, 20; I Tim. 2:5; John 3:16.
2. Acts 3:22; Deut. 18:15.
3. Heb. 5:5, 6.
4. Ps. 2:6; Luke 1:33; Isa 9:6, 7.
5. Eph. 5:23.
6. Heb. 1:2.
7. Acts 17:31; II Cor. 5:10.
8. John 17:6; Eph. 1:4; John 6:37, 39; Isa. 53:10.
9. I Tim. 2:5, 6; Mark 10:45; I Cor. 1:30; Rom 8:30.
10. John 1:1, 14; I John 5:20; Phil. 2:6; Gal. 4:4; Heb. 2:14.
11. Heb. 2:17; 4:15.
12. Luke 1:27, 31, 35; Ga. 4:4. See under figure 10 above.
13. Col. 2:9; Rom. 9:5. See under figure 12 above.
14. Rom. 1:3, 4; 1 Tim 2:5.
15. Luke 4:18, 19, 21; Acts 10:38.
16. Col. 2:3.
17. Col. 1:19.
18. Heb. 7:26; John 1:14; Luke 4:18–21.
19. Heb. 5:4, 5.
20. John 5:22, 27; Matt 28:18.
21. Ps. 40:7, 8; Phil. 2:5–8.
22. Gal. 4:4.
23. Matt. 3:15; John 17:4.

24. Matt. 26:37, 38; Luke 22:44; Matt. 27:46.
25. Matt., Chapters 26 and 27.
26. Phil. 2:8.
27. Acts 2:24, 27; 13:37.
28. I Cor. 15:4.
29. John 20:25, 27.
30. Luke 24:50, 51; Acts 1:9; Acts 2:33–36.
31. Rom. 8:34; Heb. 7:25.
32. Acts 10:42; Matt. 13:40–42; 16:27; 25:31–33; II Tim. 4:1.
33. Rom. 5:19; Heb. 9:14; Rom. 3:25, 26; Heb. 10:14; Eph. 5:2.
34. Eph. 1:11, 14; John 17:2; Rom. 5:10, 11; Heb. 9:12, 15.
35. Gen. 3:15; Rev. 13:8; Heb. 13:8.
36. I Peter 3:18; Heb. 9:14; John 10:17, 18.
37. Acts 20:28; John 3:13; I John 3:16.
38. John 6:37, 39; 10:16.
39. I John 2:1; Rom. 8:34.
40. John 15:15; 17:6; Gal. 1:11, 12; Eph. 1:7–9.
41. Rom. 8:9, 14; Titus 3:4, 5; Rom. 15:18, 19; John 17:17.
42. Ps. 110:1; I Cor. 15:25, 26; Mal. 4:2, 3: Col. 2:15.

Chapter IX (PCUS)
1. *Paragraph 1:* II Cor. 13:14; John 15:26; Matt. 28:19; 3:16; Luke 1:35; Eph. 4:30; Heb. 10:29; I Cor. 10:10, 11; Rev. 22:17; Eph. 2:18–20, 22; John 14:26; 16:7; Gal. 4:6; Acts 5:3, 4; 16:6, 7; Mark 3:29; Rom. 8:26, 27; I John 2:20–27.
2. *Paragraph 2:* Eph. 4:30; 5:9; Gen. 1:2; John 3:5; Acts 2:1–21; Gal. 5:22–25; John 16:8–11; II Peter 1:21; II Tim. 3:16; I Cor. 2:10; I Peter 1:11; John 16:13–15; Acts 7:51; I Thess. 5:19; Eph. 4:30; Ps. 104:30.
3. *Paragraph 3:* John 3:1–8; Acts 2:38; Luke 11:13; I Cor. 12:3; John 7:37–39; 16:13; 16:7–11; Rev. 22:17; Titus 3:5–7; II Thess. 2:13; Gal. 4:6; I John 4:2; Rom. 8:14, 17, 26, 27; Eph. 4:30; I Cor. 2:13, 14.
4. *Paragraph 4:* Eph. 2:14–18; 4:1–6; 5:18; Acts 2:4; 13:2; I Cor. 12; II Peter 1:19–21; I Thess. 1:5, 6; John 20:22, 23; Matt. 28:19, 20.

Chapter X (PCUS)
1. *Paragraph 1:* Rev. 22:17; John 3:16; I John 2:1, 2; Acts 2:38, 39; Matt. 11:28–30; II Cor. 5:14–19; Titus 2:11; Heb. 2:9; Luke 24:46, 47.
2. *Paragraph 2:* Matt. 28:19, 20; Acts 4:12; John 6:37–40; 17:3; Acts 16:31; 2:38; Gal. 2:16–20; Rom. 1:16, 17; 4:5; Acts 13:38, 39, 48; II Peter 3:9; Matt. 11:28–30; Mark 1:14, 15; Acts 17:30; Rev. 22:17; Ezek. 33:11; Isa. 1:18; Luke 13:34.
3. *Paragraph 3:* Heb. 2:3; 12:25; Acts 12:46; Matt. 10:32, 33; Luke 12:47, 48; Heb. 10:29.
4. *Paragraph 4:* Acts 4:12; Matt. 28:19, 20; Acts 1:8; Rom. 10:13–15; Heb. 10:19–25; Gal. 3:28; I Cor. 16:1, 2; Matt. 9:36–38; Acts 13:2–4; Col. 3:16; Rev. 22:17; Col. 1:28, 29.

Chapter XI (PCUS)
1. Deut. 30:19; John 7:17; Rev. 22:17; James 1:14; John 5:40.
2. Gen. 1:26. See under figure 1 above.
3. Gen 2:16, 17; 3:6.
4. Rom. 5:6, 8:7; John 15:5.
5. Rom. 3:10, 12; 8:7.
6. Eph. 2:1, 5; Col. 2:13.
7. John 6:44, 65; I Cor. 2:14; Rom. 8:8; Eph. 2:2–5; Titus 3:3–5.

8. Col. 1:13; John 8:34, 36; Phil 2:13; Rom. 6:18, 22.
9. Gal. 5:17; Rom. 7:15.
10. I John 3:2; Rev. 22:3, 4.
11. II Chron. 6:36; I John 1:8–10; 2:1–6; Ps. 17:15.

Chapter XII (PCUS)
1. Rom. 11:7; 8:30; II Thess. 2:13, 14; Rom. 8:2; II Tim. 1:9, 10.
2. Acts 26:18; I Cor. 2:10, 12.
3. Ezek. 36:26.
4. Ezek. 11:19; 36:27; Phil. 2:13; 4:13; Deut. 30:6.
5. John 6:44, 45.
6. John 6:37. See under figure 5 above.
7. II Tim. 1:9; Titus 3:4, 5; Rom. 9:11; Eph. 2:4, 5, 8, 9.
8. I Cor. 2:14; Rom. 8:7; Eph. 2:5.
9. John 6:37; Ezek. 36:27; John 5:25.
10. Acts 4:12; John 3:8.
11. Matt. 22:14; 13:20, 21; John 6:64–66; 8:24; I John 2:19; Heb. 6:4–6.
12. Acts 4:12; John 14:6; John 17:3.
13. II John 9–11; Gal. 1:8.

Chapter XIII (PCUS)
1. Rom. 8:30; 3:24.
2. Rom. 4:5–8; II Cor. 5:19, 21; Titus 3:5, 7; Eph. 1:7; Jer. 23:6; Rom. 3:22, 24, 25, 27, 28; I Cor. 1:30, 31; Rom. 5:17–19.
3. Phil. 3:9; Eph. 2:8; Acts 13:38, 39.
4. John 1:12; Rom. 3:28; 5:1.
5. James 2:17, 22, 26; Gal. 5:6.
6. Rom. 5:8–10, 19; I Cor. 15:3; II Cor. 5:21; I Peter 2:24; 3:18; Heb. 10:10, 14; Isa. 53.
7. Rom. 8:32; John 3:16.
8. II Cor. 5:21; Isa. 53:6.
9. Rom. 3:24; 6:23; Eph. 1:7, 2:6–9.
10. Rom. 3:26; Eph. 2:7.
11. I Peter 1:2, 19, 20; Rom. 8:30.
12. Gal. 4:4; I Tim. 2:6; Rom. 4:25.
13. John 3:5, 18, 36; Gal. 2:16; Titus 3:4–7.
14. Matt 6:12; I John 1:9; 2:1.
15. Luke 22:32; John 10:28; Heb. 10:14; Phil. 1:6; I John 2:19.
16. Ps. 89:31–33; 32:5; Matt. 26:75; Ps. 51:7–12; I Cor. 11:30, 32.
17. Heb. 11:13; John 8:56; Gal. 3:6–8; Acts 15:11; Rom. 3:30; Gal. 3:8, 9, 14.

Chapter XIV (PCUS)
1. Eph. 1:5; Gal. 4:4, 5.
2. John 1:12; Rom 8:17.
3. Rev. 3:12.
4. Rom. 8:15.
5. Eph. 3:12; Heb. 4:16; Rom. 5:2.
6. Gal. 4:6.
7. Ps. 103:13.
8. Prov. 14:26; Ps. 27:1–3.
9. Matt. 6:30, 32; I Peter 5:7.
10. Heb. 12:6.
11. Lam. 3:31; Heb. 13:5.
12. Eph. 4:30.
13. Heb. 6:12.
14. I Peter 1:4; Heb. 1:14.

Chapter XV (PCUS)
1. Acts 20:32; Rom. 6:5, 6; John 17:17; Eph. 5:26; II Thess. 2:13.
2. Rom. 6:6, 14.
3. Rom. 8:13; Gal. 5:24; Col 3:5.
4. Col 1:11; II Peter 3:13, 14; Eph. 3:16–19.
5. II Cor. 7:1; Heb. 12:14.
6. I Thess. 5:23.
7. I John 1:10; Phil. 3:12; Gal. 5:17; Rom. 7:18, 23.
8. Rom. 7:23.
9. Rom. 6:14, I John 5:4; Eph. 4:16.
10. II Peter 3:18; II Cor. 3:18.
11. II Cor. 7:1.

Chapter XVI (PCUS)
1. I Cor. 12:3; Eph. 2:8; Heb. 12:2.

2. Rom. 10:14, 17.
3. I Peter 2:2, Acts 20:32; Matt. 28:19; I Cor. 11:23–29; II Cor. 12:8–10.
4. I Thess. 2:13; I John 5:10; Acts 24:14.
5. Matt. 6:30; Matt 8:10; Rom. 4:19, 20.
6. Luke 22:31, 32; I Cor. 10:13.
7. Heb. 6:11, 12; Heb. 10:22; II Tim. 1:12.
8. Heb. 12:2.

Chapter XVII (PCUS)
1. Acts 11:18.
2. Luke 24:47; Mark 1:15; Acts 20:21.
3. Ezek. 18:30, 31; Ezek. 36:31; Ps. 51:4; Jer. 31:18, 19; II Cor. 7:11.
4. Ps. 119:59, 106; John 14:23.
5. Titus 3:5; Acts 5:31.
6. Rom. 3:24; Eph. 1:7.
7. Luke 13:3; Acts 17:30.
8. Rom. 6:23; Matt. 12:36; James 2:10.
9. Isa. 55:7; Rom. 8:1; Isa. 1:18.
10. Ps. 19:13; Luke 19:8; I Tim. 1:13, 15; Dan. 9; Neh. 9.
11. Ps. 32:5, 6; Ps. 51:4, 5, 7, 9, 14.
12. Prov. 28:13; I John 1:9.
13. James 5:16; Luke 17:3, 4; Josh. 7:19; Ps. 51.
14. II Cor. 2:7, 8; Gal. 6:1, 2.

Chapter XVIII (PCUS)
1. Deut. 12:32; Ps. 119:9; Matt. 28:20; Luke 10:25, 26; II Peter 1:19.
2. Matt. 15:9; Isa. 29:13; John 16:2; I Sam. 15:22, 23; Col. 2:20–23.
3. James 2:18, 22.
4. Ps. 116:12, 13; Col. 3:17; I Chron. 29:6–9.
5. I John 2:3, 5; II Peter 1:5–10.
6. II Cor. 9:2; Matt. 5:16.
7. Titus 2:5; I Tim. 6:1; Titus 2:9–12.
8. I Peter 2:15.
9. I Peter 2:12; Phil. 1:11; John 15:8.
10. Eph. 2:10.
11. Rom. 6:22.
12. John 15:5, 6; Ezek. 36:26, 27.
13. Phil. 2:13; Phil. 4:13; II Cor. 3:5.
14. Phil. 2:12; Heb. 6:11, 12; Isa. 64:7; II Peter 1:3, 5, 10, 11; II Tim. 1:6; Jude 20, 21.
15. Luke 17:10; Gal. 5:17.
16. Rom. 3:20; Rom. 4:2, 4, 6; Eph. 2:8, 9; Titus 3:5–7; Rom. 8:18.
17. See citations under 15 above.
18. Gal. 5:22, 23.
19. Isa. 64:6; Ps. 143:2; Ps. 130:3; Gal. 5:17; Rom. 7:15, 18.
20. Eph. 1:6; I Peter 2:5; Gen. 4:4; Heb. 11:4.
21. I Cor. 4:3, 4; Ps. 143:2.
22. II Cor. 8:12; Heb. 6:10.
23. II Kings 10:30, 31; Phil. 1:15, 16, 18.
24. Heb. 11:4, 6; Gen. 4:3–5.
25. I Cor. 13:3; Isa. 1:12.
26. Matt. 6:2, 5, 16; Rom. 14:23.
27. Titus 1:15; Prov. 15:8; Prov. 28:9.
28. Matt. 25:24–28; Matt. 25:41–45; Matt. 23:23.

Chapter XIX (PCUS)
1. Phil. 1:6; John 10:28, 29; Jer. 32:40; I John 3:9; I Peter 1:5, 9.
2. II Tim. 2:19; Jer. 31:3; Eph. 1:4, 5; John 13:1; Rom. 8:35–39.
3. Heb. 10:10, 14; John 17:11, 24; Heb. 7:25; Heb. 9:12–15; Rom. 8:32–39; Luke 22:32.
4. John 14:16, 17; I John 2:27; I John 3:9.
5. Jer. 32:40; Heb. 8:10–12.
6. II Thess. 3:3; I John 2:19; John 10:28; I Thess. 5:23, 24; Heb. 6:17–20.
7. Matt. 26:70, 72, 74; II Sam. 12:9, 13.
8. Isa. 64:7, 9; II Sam. 11:27.
9. Eph. 4:30.
10. Ps. 51:8, 10, 12; Rev. 2:4.

11. Mark 6:52; Ps. 95:8.
12. Ps. 32:3, 4; Ps. 51:8.
13. II Sam. 12:14; Ezek. 16:54.
14. II Sam. 12:10; Ps. 89:31, 32; I Cor. 11:32.

Chapter XX (PCUS)
1. Deut. 29:19; John 8:41.
2. Matt. 7:22, 23.
3. II Tim. 1:12; I John 2:3; I John 5:13; I John 3:14, 18, 19, 21, 24.
4. Rom. 5:2, 5. See citations under 3 above.
5. Heb. 6:11, 12. See citations under 3 and 4 above.
6. Heb. 6:17, 18; II Peter 1:4, 5.
7. II Peter 1:10, 11; I John 3:14.
8. Rom. 8:15, 16.
9. Eph. 1:13, 14; II Cor. 1:21, 22.
10. Isa. 50:10; I John 5:13; Ps. 73; 77; 88.
11. I Cor. 2:12; I John 4:13; Ps. 77:10–20; Ps. 73. See citations under Section 2 above.
12. II Peter 1:10; Rom. 6:1, 2; Titus 2:11, 12, 14.
13. Ps. 51:8, 12, 14; Eph. 4:30; Ps.77:1–10; Matt. 26:69–72; Ps. 31:22; Ps. 88; Isa. 50:10.
14. I John 3:9; Luke 22:32; Ps. 73:15; Ps. 51:8, 12; Isa. 50:10.
15. Micah 7:7–9.

Chapter XXI (PCUS)
1. Gal. 3:12; Hos. 6:7 (A.S.V.); Gen. 2:16, 17. Compare Rom. 5:12–14; I Cor. 15:22; Luke 10:25–28, and the covenants made with Noah and Abraham; Gen. 1:26; Deut. 30:19; John 7:17; Rev. 22:17; James 1:14; James 1:25; James 2:8, 10; Rom. 3:19; Deut. 5:32; Deut. 10:4; Exod. 34:1; Rom. 13:8, 9.
2. Matt. 22:37–40; Exod. 20:3–18.
3. Heb. 10:1; Gal. 4:1–3; Col. 2:17; Heb. 9.
4. See Lev. 5:1–6; 6:1–7, and similar passages.
5. Mark 7:18, 19 (A.S.V.); Gal. 2:4; Col. 2:17; Eph. 2:15, 16.
6. Matt. 5:38, 39; I Cor. 9:8–10; Exod. Chapters 21 and 22.
7. Rom. 13:8, 9; I John 2:3, 4, 7; Rom. 3:31; Rom. 6:15. See citations under Section 2 above.
8. Matt. 5:18, 19; James 2:8; Rom. 3:31.
9. Rom. 6:14; Rom. 8:1; Gal. 4:4, 5; Acts 13:39.
10. Rom. 7:12; Ps. 119:5; I Cor. 7:19; Gal. 5:14, 18, 23.
11. Rom. 7:7; Rom. 3:20.
12. Rom. 7:9, 14, 24.
13. Gal. 3:24; Rom. 8:3, 4; Rom. 7:24, 25.
14. James 2:11; Ps. 119:128.
15. Ezra 9:13, 14; Ps. 89:30–34.
16. Ps. 37:11; Ps. 19:11; Lev. 26:3–13; Eph. 6:2; Matt. 5:5.
17. Rom. 6:12, 14; Heb. 12:28, 29; I Peter 3:8–12; Ps. 34:12–16.
18. See citations under Section 6 above.
19. See citations under Chapter X, Section 1; Gal. 3:13.

Chapter XXII (PCUS)
1. Titus 2:14; I Thess. 1:10.
2. Gal. 1:4; Acts 26:18; Col. 1:13; Rom. 6:14.
3. Ps. 119:71; I Cor. 15:56, 57; Rom. 8:1.
4. Rom. 5:2.
5. Rom. 8:14, 15; Eph. 2:18; Gal. 4:6; Heb. 10:19; I John 4:18.
6. Gal. 3:9, 14. See citations under Chapter VIII, Section 6.
7. Gal. 5:1; Acts 15:10; Gal. 4:1–3, 6.
8. Heb. 4:14, 16; Heb. 10:19, 20.
9. John 7:38, 39; II Cor. 3:13, 17, 18.
10. Rom. 14:4; Acts 4:19; Acts 5:29; I Cor. 7:23; Matt. 23:8–10; II Cor. 1:24; Matt. 15:19.
11. Gal. 2:3, 4; Col. 2:20, 22, 23; Gal. 5:1.

12. Hosea 5:11; Rev. 13:12, 16, 17.
13. Gal. 5:13; I Peter 2:16; Luke 1:74, 75; II Peter 2:19; John 8:34.
14. I Peter 2:13, 14, 16; Heb. 13:17; Rom. 13:1–8.
15. I Cor. 5:1, 5, 11, 13; Titus 1:13; Matt. 18:17, 18; II Thess. 3:14; Titus 3:10.

Chapter XXIII (PCUS)
1. Rom. 1:19, 20; Jer. 10:7; Ps. 19:1–6.
2. Deut. 12:32; Matt. 15:9; Matt. 4:9, 10; Acts 17:24, 25; Exod. 20:4–6; Deut. 4:15–20; Col. 2:20–23.
3. John 5:23; II Cor. 13:14; Matt. 4:10; Rev. 5:11–13.
4. Col. 2:18; Rev. 19:10; Rom. 1:25.
5. John 14:6; I Tim. 2:5; Eph. 2:18.
6. Phil. 4:6.
7. Luke 18:1; I Tim. 2:8.
8. John 14:13, 14.
9. Rom. 8:26.
10. I John 5:14.
11. Ps. 47:7; Heb. 12:28; Gen. 18:27; James 5:16; Eph. 6:18; James 1:6, 7; Mark 11:24; Matt. 6:12, 14, 15; Col. 4:2.
12. I Cor. 14:14.
13. I John 5:14.
14. I Tim. 2:1, 2; John 17:20; II Sam. 7:29.
15. This statement is based on the absence of any command to pray for the dead, and of any example in the Scripture of such prayer. I John 5:14.
16. Original note 16 removed by amendment enacted by the General Assembly in 1939.
17. Acts 15:21; Acts 17:11; Rev. 1:3.
18. II Tim. 4:2.
19. James 1:22; Acts 10:33; Heb. 4:2; Matt. 13:19; Isa. 66:2.
20. Col. 3:16; Eph. 5:19; James 5:13.
21. Matt. 28:19; Acts 2:42; I Cor. 11:23–29.
22. Deut. 6:13.
23. Ps. 116:14; Isa. 19:21; Neh. 10:29.
24. Joel 2:12; Matt. 9:15; I Cor. 7:5; Esther 4:16.
25. Ps. 107.
26. John 4:24; Heb. 10:22.
27. John 4:21.
28. Mal. 1:11; I Tim. 2:8.
29. John 4:23, 24.
30. Deut. 6:7; Job 1:5; Acts 10:2.
31. Matt. 6:11.
32. Matt. 6:6; Eph. 6:18.
33. Isa. 56:7; Heb. 10:25; Acts 2:42; Luke 4:16; Acts 13:42.
34. Exod. 20:8–11; Isa. 56:2, 4, 6.
35. I Cor. 16:1, 2; Acts 20:7. These texts are cited in connection with the example of the apostles and the early church.
36. Exod. 16:23, 25, 26, 29, 30; Exod. 31:15, 16; Isa. 58:13; Neh. 13:15–22; Luke 23:56.
37. Isa. 58:13; Matt. 12:1–13.

Chapter XXIV (PCUS)
1. Deut. 10:20.
2. II Cor. 1:23; II Chron. 6:22, 23; Exod. 20:7.
3. Deut. 6:13.
4. Jer. 5:7; James 5:12; Matt. 5:37; Exod. 20:7.
5. I Kings 8:31; Ezra 10:5; Matt. 26:63, 64.
6. See citations under Section 2, above.
7. Ps. 24:4; Jer. 4:2.
8. Ps. 15:4.
9. Ezek. 17:16, 18; Josh. 9:18, 19; II Sam. 21:1.
10. Ps. 66:13, 14; Ps. 61:8; Deut. 23:21, 23.
11. Ps. 76:11; Jer. 44:25, 26.
12. Ps. 50:14; Gen. 28:20–22. Compare with the above I Sam. 1:11; Ps. 132:2–5.
13. Num. 30:5, 8, 12, 13.

## Chapter XXV (PCUS)

1. Rom. 13:1, 3, 4; I Peter 2:13, 14.
2. Prov. 8:15, 16. See citations under Section 1, above.
3. Ps. 82:3, 4; I Peter 2:13. See citations under Section 1, above.
4. Rom. 13:1–4; Luke 3:14, Matt. 8:9; Acts 10:1, 2.
5. Matt. 16:19; I Cor. 4:1; John 18:36; Eph. 4:11, 12; II Chron. 26:18.
6. See General Note.
7. I Tim. 2:1, 2.
8. I Peter 2:17.
9. Rom. 13:6, 7.
10. Rom. 13:5; Titus 3:1.
11. This is an inference from the duties just stated.
12. Rom. 13:1; Acts 25:10, 11.
13. This is an inference from the doctrine of the civil magistrate, and from duties incumbent on believers with respect to him.

## Chapter XXVI (PCUS)

1. Gen. 2:23, 24; I Cor. 7:2, 39; Matt. 19:4–6; Eph. 5:28, 31, 33; I Cor.13:8, 13; Matt. 5:31, 32; Mark 10:5–9; Rom. 7:2, 3.
2. Gen. 2:18, 24.
3. Gen. 1:27, 28; Eph. 5:22, 23; Col. 3:18, 19; Gen. 2:18–25; I Cor. 7:3–5, 9, 36.
4. Gen. 1:27, 28; Gen. 9:1; Mal. 2:15; Matt. 18:5, 6, 10, 14; Matt. 19:14; Eph. 6:1–4; Col. 3:20, 21; Mark 10:13–16; Luke 18:15–17.
5. Gen. 1:27, 28.
6. Mark 6:18; I Cor. 5:1; Lev. 18:6–18.
7. Mark 1:30; John 2:1, 2; I Tim. 5:14; Heb. 13:4; I Cor. 7:7, 36; I Cor. 9:5; I Tim. 4:3.
8. I Cor. 7 especially v. 39; II Cor. 6:14, 15.
9. Prov. 18:22; Matt. 19:6; Eph. 5:29, 30, 32; Mark 10:9, 11, 12.
10. Gen. 1:27, 28.
11. Mark 10:9.
12. Eph. 5:22, 23.
13. Gen. 2:23, 24; Matt. 5:31, 32; Mark 10:5–9; Rom. 7:2, 3; I Cor. 7:2, 10, 11, 39; Eph. 5:28, 31, 33; Matt. 19:4–9; I Cor. 13:4–13.
14. Mark 10:4–9; I Cor. 7:12, 13, 15; Matt. 19:7–9.
15. II Sam. 12:13; Neh. 9:17; Ps. 32:5; Ps. 130:4; Matt. 12:31a; Matt. 21:31, 32; John 8:3, 11; Rom. 3:23; Gal. 6:1; I Tim. 2:4; Heb. 7:25; I John 1:9; I John 2:1, 2; Luke 7:36–50; Luke 15:11–32; John 3:16, 17; Rom. 10:9, 10.
16. Matt. 5:31, 32; I Cor. 7:10, 11, 20, 32–35; Mark 10:11; Luke 16:18.

## Chapter XXVII (PCUS)

1. Eph. 1:22, 23; Col. 1:18; Eph. 5:23, 27, 32.
2. I Cor. 1:2; I Cor. 12:12, 13; Rom 15:9–12.
3. Gen. 17:7. See context. Compare Gal. 3:7, 9, 14; Rom. 4; Acts 2:39; I Cor. 7:14; Mark 10:13–16.
4. Matt. 13:47; Col. 1:13; Isa. 9:7.
5. Eph. 2:19.
6. Matt. 28:19; Acts 2:38; I Cor. 12:13; Matt. 26:26–28.
7. Eph. 4:11–13; Isa. 59:21; Matt. 28:19, 20.
8. Rom. 11:3, 4; Acts 9:31.
9. I Cor. 5:6, 7; Rev. 2, 3.
10. Matt. 13:24–30, 47, 48.
11. Rom. 11:18–22; Rev. 18:2.

12. Matt. 16:18; Ps. 102:28; Matt. 28:19, 20.
13. Col. 1:18.

Chapter XXVIII (PCUS)
1. I John 1:3; Eph. 3:16–19; John 1:16; Phil. 3:10; Rom. 6:5, 6; Rom. 8:17.
2. Eph. 4:15, 16; I John 1:3, 7.
3. I Thess. 5:11, 14; Gal. 6:10; I John 3:16–18.
4. Heb. 10:24, 25; Acts 2:42, 46; I Cor. 11:20.
5. I John 3:17; Acts 11:29, 30; II Cor., Chapters 8 and 9.
6. Col. 1:18; I Cor. 8:6; Ps. 14:7.
7. Acts 5:4.

Chapter XXIX (PCUS)
1. Gen. 17:9–11; Exod. 13:9, 10; Rom. 4:11; Exod. 12:3–20.
2. I Cor. 10:16; I Cor. 11:25, 26; Gal. 3:27.
3. Exod. 12:48; Heb. 13:10; I Cor. 11:27–29.
4. Rom. 6:3, 4; I Cor. 10:14–16. See context.
5. Gen. 17:10; Matt. 26:27, 28; Titus 3:5.
6. Rom. 2:28, 29; I Cor. 3:7; I Cor. 6:11; John 3:5; Acts 8:13–23.
7. John 6:63.
8. Matt. 28:19; I Cor. 11:20, 23.
9. See General Note.
10. Col. 2:11, 12; I Cor. 5:7, 8.

Chapter XXX (PCUS)
1. Matt. 28:19.
2. Acts 2:41; Acts 10:47.
3. Rom. 4:11. Compare with Gal. 3:29; Col. 2:11, 12.
4. Gal. 3:27; Rom. 6:3, 4.
5. Titus 3:5.
6. Acts 2:38; Mark 1:4; Acts 22:16.
7. Rom. 6:3, 4.
8. Matt. 28:19, 20.
9. Acts 10:47; Acts 8:36, 38; Matt. 28:19; Eph. 4:11–13.
10. See General Note.
11. Mark 7:4; Acts 1:5; Acts 2:3, 4, 17; Acts 11:15, 16; Heb. 9:10, 19–21.
12. See citations under Section 1 above.
13. Gen. 17:7, 9–10; Gal. 3:9, 14; Rom. 4:11, 12; Acts 2:38, 39; Acts 16:14, 15, 33; Col. 2:11, 12; I Cor. 7:14; Mark 10:13–16; Luke 18:15, 16.
14. Luke 7:30; Gen. 17:14.
15. Rom. 4:11; Luke 23:40–43; Acts 10:45–47.
16. Acts 8:13, 23.
17. John 3:5, 8; Rom. 4:11.
18. Gal. 3:27, Eph. 1:4, 5; Eph. 5:25, 26; Acts 2:38–41; Acts 16:31, 33.
19. There is no command, and no adequate example for the repetition of baptism.

Chapter XXXI (PCUS)
1. I Cor. 11:23–26; Matt. 26:26, 27; Luke 22:19, 20; I Cor. 10:16, 17, 21; I Cor. 12:13.
2. Heb. 9:22, 25, 26, 28; Matt. 26:26, 27; Luke 22:19, 20; Heb. 10:11, 12, 14, 18.
3. See citations under Sections 1, 2.
4. Matt. 15:9. Note—There is not the least appearance of a warrant for any of these things, either in precept or example, in any part of the Word of God. See all the places in which the ordinance is mentioned.
5. Matt. 26:26–28.
6. I Cor. 11:26, 27.
7. These statements are inferences from the doctrine of the sacraments, and do not require specific Scripture proofs.
8. I Cor. 10:16; John 6:53–58. See Note under Section 6, above.
9. I Cor. 11:27, 29; I Cor. 10:21; I Cor. 5:6, 7, 13; II Thess. 3:6, 14, 15.

# ENDNOTES FOR 6.169–.182

Chapter XXXII (PCUS)
1. John 18:36; Isa. 9:6, 7; I Cor. 12:28; I Tim. 5:17.
2. Matt. 16:19; Matt. 18:17, 18; John 20:21–23; II Cor. 2:6–8.
3. I Tim. 5:20; I Tim. 1:20; Jude 23; I Cor. 5; I Cor. 11:27–34; II Sam. 12:14.
4. I Thess. 5:12; II Thess. 3:6, 14; I Cor. 5:4, 5, 13; Matt. 18:17; Titus 3:10.

Chapter XXXIII (PCUS)
1. Acts 15.
2. Acts 16:4; Acts 15:15, 19, 24, 27–31; Matt. 18:17–20.
3. See General Note.
4. Luke 12:13, 14; John 18:36; Matt. 22:21.

Chapter XXXIV (PCUS)
1. Gen. 3:19; Acts 13:36.
2. Luke 23:43; Phil. 1:23; II Cor. 5:6–8.
3. Luke 16:23; Rom. 8:23. See under figure 2 above.
4. Luke 16:23, 24; II Peter 2:9.
5. I Thess. 4:17; I Cor. 15:51, 52.
6. I Cor. 15:42–44. See preceding context.
7. Acts 24:15; John 5:28, 29; Phil. 3:21.

Chapter XXXV (PCUS)
1. Acts 17:31; Matt. 25:31–34.
2. John 5:22, 27.
3. Jude 6; II Peter 2:4; II Cor. 5:10; Rom. 2:16; Rom. 14:10, 12; Matt. 12:36, 37; I Cor. 3:13–15.
4. Rom. 9:23; Eph. 2:4–7.
5. Rom 2:5, 6; II Thess. 1:7, 8.
6. Matt. 25:31–34; II Thess. 1:7; Ps. 16:11.
7. Matt. 25:41, 46; II Thess. 1:9; Mark 9:47, 48.
8. II Cor. 5:11; I Thess. 1:5–7; Luke 21:27, 28; II Peter 3:11, 14.
9. Mark 13:35–37; Luke 12:35, 36; Rev. 22:20. See Matt. 24:36, 42–44.

# *THE* SHORTER CATECHISM
[TEXT]

For the prologue to the Westminster Catechism (Shorter Catechism), see pages 146–48.

## THE SHORTER CATECHISM

**7.001**      Q. 1. **What is the chief end of man?**
A. Man's chief end is to glorify God,[1] and to enjoy him forever.[2]

**7.002**      Q. 2. **What rule hath God given to direct us how we may glorify and enjoy him?**
A. The Word of God which is contained in the Scriptures of the Old and New Testaments is the only rule to direct us how we may glorify and enjoy him.[1]

**7.003**      Q. 3. **What do the Scriptures principally teach?**
A. The Scriptures principally teach what man is to believe concerning God, and what duty God requires of man.[1]

**7.004**      Q. 4. **What is God?**
A. God is a Spirit,[1] infinite, eternal and unchangeable, in his being,[2] wisdom,[3] power,[4] holiness,[5] justice,[6] goodness,[7] and truth.[8]

**7.005**      Q. 5. **Are there more Gods than one?**
A. There is but one only, the living and true God.[1]

**7.006**      Q. 6. **How many Persons are there in the Godhead?**
A. There are three Persons in the Godhead: the Father, the Son, and the Holy Ghost; and these three are one God, the same in substance, equal in power and glory.[1]

**7.007**      Q. 7. **What are the decrees of God?**
A. The decrees of God are his eternal purpose, according to the counsel of his will, whereby, for his own glory, he hath foreordained whatsoever comes to pass.[1]

**7.008**      Q. 8. **How doth God execute his decrees?**
A. God executeth his decrees in the works of creation and providence.[1]

**7.009**      Q. 9. **What is the work of creation?**
A. The work of creation is God's making all things of nothing, by the word of his power, in the space of six days, and all very good.[1]

**7.010**      Q. 10. **How did God create man?**
A. God created man male and female, after his own image,[1] in knowledge, righteousness, and holiness,[2] with dominion over the creatures.[3]

**7.011**      Q. 11. **What are God's works of providence?**
A. God's works of providence are his most holy,[1] wise,[2] and powerful preserving[3] and governing all his creatures, and all their actions.[4]

**7.012**      Q. 12. **What special act of providence did God exercise towards man, in the estate wherein he was created?**
A. When God created man, he entered into a covenant of life with him, upon condition of perfect obedience;[1] forbidding him to eat of the tree of knowledge of good and evil, upon the pain of death.[2]

**7.013** Q. 13. Did our first parents continue in the estate wherein they were created?

A. Our first parents, being left to the freedom of their own will, fell from the estate wherein they were created, by sinning against God.[1]

**7.014** Q. 14. What is sin?

A. Sin is any want of conformity unto, or transgression of, the law of God.[1]

**7.015** Q. 15. What was the sin whereby our first parents fell from the estate wherein they were created?

A. The sin whereby our first parents fell from the estate wherein they were created was their eating the forbidden fruit.[1]

**7.016** Q. 16. Did all mankind fall in Adam's first transgression?

A. The covenant being made with Adam, not only for himself, but for his posterity,[1] all mankind, descending from him by ordinary generation, sinned in him, and fell with him, in his first transgression.[2]

**7.017** Q. 17. Into what estate did the Fall bring mankind?

A. The Fall brought mankind into an estate of sin and misery.[1]

**7.018** Q. 18. Wherein consists the sinfulness of that estate whereinto man fell?

A. The sinfulness of that estate whereinto man fell consists in: the guilt of Adam's first sin,[1] the want of original righteousness, and the corruption of his whole nature, which is commonly called original sin;[2] together with all actual transgressions which proceed from it.[3]

**7.019** Q. 19. What is the misery of that estate whereinto man fell?

A. All mankind, by their fall, lost communion with God,[1] are under his wrath and curse,[2] and so made liable to all miseries of this life, to death itself, and to the pains of hell forever.[3]

**7.020** Q. 20. Did God leave all mankind to perish in the estate of sin and misery?

A. God, having out of his mere good pleasure, from all eternity, elected some to everlasting life,[1] did enter into a covenant of grace, to deliver them out of the estate of sin and misery, and to bring them into an estate of salvation by a Redeemer.[2]

**7.021** Q. 21. Who is the Redeemer of God's elect?

A. The only Redeemer of God's elect is the Lord Jesus Christ,[1] who, being the eternal Son of God, became man,[2] and so was, and continueth to be, God and man, in two distinct natures, and one Person forever.[3]

**7.022** Q. 22. How did Christ, being the Son of God, become man?

A. Christ, the Son of God, became man, by taking to himself a true body and a reasonable soul,[1] being conceived by the power of the Holy Ghost, in the womb of the Virgin Mary, and born of her,[2] yet without sin.[3]

**7.023 Q. 23. What offices doth Christ execute as our Redeemer?**
A. Christ, as our Redeemer, executeth the offices of a prophet,[1] of a priest,[2] and of a king, both in his estate of humiliation and exaltation.[3]

**7.024 Q. 24. How doth Christ execute the office of a prophet?**
A. Christ executeth the office of a prophet in revealing to us,[1] by his Word and Spirit, the will of God for our salvation.[2]

**7.025 Q. 25. How doth Christ execute the office of a priest?**
A. Christ executeth the office of a priest in his once offering up of himself a sacrifice to satisfy divine justice,[1] and reconcile us to God,[2] and in making continual intercession for us.[3]

**7.026 Q. 26. How doth Christ execute the office of a king?**
A. Christ executeth the office of a king in subduing us to himself,[1] in ruling and defending us,[2] and in restraining and conquering all his and our enemies.[3]

**7.027 Q. 27. Wherein did Christ's humiliation consist?**
A. Christ's humiliation consisted in his being born, and that in a low condition,[1] made under the law,[2] undergoing the miseries of this life,[3] the wrath of God,[4] and the cursed death of the cross;[5] in being buried, and continuing under the power of death for a time.[6]

**7.028 Q. 28. Wherein consisteth Christ's exaltation?**
A. Christ's exaltation consisteth in his rising again from the dead on the third day,[1] in ascending up into heaven, in sitting at the right hand of God the Father,[2] and in coming to judge the world at the last day.[3]

**7.029 Q. 29. How are we made partakers of the redemption purchased by Christ?**
A. We are made partakers of the redemption purchased by Christ by the effectual application of it to us by his Holy Spirit.[1]

**7.030 Q. 30. How doth the Spirit apply to us the redemption purchased by Christ?**
A. The Spirit applieth to us the redemption purchased by Christ by working faith in us,[1] and thereby uniting us to Christ in our effectual calling.[2]

**7.031 Q. 31. What is effectual calling?**
A. Effectual calling is the work of God's Spirit,[1] whereby, convincing us of our sin and misery,[2] enlightening our minds in the knowledge of Christ,[3] and renewing our wills,[4] he doth persuade and enable us to embrace Jesus Christ, freely offered to us in the gospel.[5]

**7.032 Q. 32. What benefits do they that are effectually called partake of in this life?**
A. They that are effectually called do in this life partake of justification,[1] adoption,[2] sanctification, and the several benefits which, in this life, do either accompany or flow from them.[3]

**7.033** **Q. 33. What is justification?**
A. Justification is an act of God's free grace, wherein he pardoneth all our sins,[1] and accepteth us as righteous in his sight,[2] only for the righteousness of Christ imputed to us,[3] and received by faith alone.[4]

**7.034** **Q. 34. What is adoption?**
A. Adoption is an act of God's free grace,[1] whereby we are received into the number, and have a right to all privileges, of the sons of God.[2]

**7.035** **Q. 35. What is sanctification?**
A. Sanctification is the work of God's free grace,[1] whereby we are renewed in the whole man after the image of God,[2] and are enabled more and more to die unto sin and live unto righteousness.[3]

**7.036** **Q. 36. What are the benefits which in this life do accompany or flow from justification, adoption, and sanctification?**
A. The benefits which in this life do accompany or flow from justification, adoption, and sanctification are: assurance of God's love, peace of conscience, joy in the Holy Ghost,[1] increase of grace,[2] and perseverance therein to the end.[3]

**7.037** **Q. 37. What benefits do believers receive from Christ at death?**
A. The souls of believers are at their death made perfect in holiness, and do immediately pass into glory;[1] and their bodies, being still united to Christ,[2] do rest in their graves till the resurrection.[3]

**7.038** **Q. 38. What benefits do believers receive from Christ at the resurrection?**
A. At the resurrection, believers, being raised up in glory,[1] shall be openly acknowledged and acquitted in the Day of Judgment,[2] and made perfectly blessed in the full enjoying of God[3] to all eternity.[4]

**7.039** **Q. 39. What is the duty which God requireth of man?**
A. The duty which God requireth of man is obedience to his revealed will.[1]

**7.040** **Q. 40. What did God at first reveal to man for the rule of his obedience?**
A. The rule which God at first revealed to man for his obedience was the moral law.[1]

**7.041** **Q. 41. Where is the moral law summarily comprehended?**
A. The moral law is summarily comprehended in the Ten Commandments.[1]

**7.042** **Q. 42. What is the sum of the Ten Commandments?**
A. The sum of the Ten Commandments is: to love the Lord our God with all our heart, with all our soul, with all our strength, and with all our mind; and our neighbor as ourselves.[1]

**7.043**     **Q. 43. What is the preface to the Ten Commandments?**
A. The preface to the Ten Commandments is in these words: "I am the Lord thy God, which have brought thee out of the land of Egypt, out of the house of bondage."[1]

**7.044**     **Q. 44. What doth the preface to the Ten Commandments teach us?**
A. The preface to the Ten Commandments teacheth us that because God is the Lord, and our God and Redeemer, therefore we are bound to keep all his commandments.

**7.045**     **Q. 45. Which is the First Commandment?**
A. The First Commandment is, "Thou shalt have no other gods before me."[1]

**7.046**     **Q. 46. What is required in the First Commandment?**
A. The First Commandment requireth us[1] to know and acknowledge God to be the only true God, and our God;[2] and to worship and glorify him accordingly.[3]

**7.047**     **Q. 47. What is forbidden in the First Commandment?**
A. The First Commandment forbiddeth the denying,[1] or not worshiping and glorifying, the true God as God,[2] and our God;[3] and the giving of that worship and glory to any other which is due to him alone.[4]

**7.048**     **Q. 48. What are we specially taught by these words, "before me," in the First Commandment?**
A. These words, "before me," in the First Commandment teach us that God, who seeth all things, taketh notice of, and is much displeased with, the sin of having any other god.[1]

**7.049**     **Q. 49. What is the Second Commandment?**
A. The Second Commandment is, "Thou shalt not make unto thee any graven image, or any likeness of any thing that is in heaven above, or that is in the earth beneath, or that is in the water under the earth: thou shalt not bow down thyself to them, nor serve them: for I the Lord thy God am a jealous God, visiting the iniquity of the fathers upon the children unto the third and fourth generation of them that hate me; and showing mercy unto thousands of them that love me, and keep my commandments."[1]

**7.050**     **Q. 50. What is required in the Second Commandment?**
A. The Second Commandment requireth the receiving, observing, and keeping pure and entire all such religious worship and ordinances as God hath appointed in his Word.[1]

**7.051**     **Q. 51. What is forbidden in the Second Commandment?**
A. The Second Commandment forbiddeth the worshiping of God by images,[1] or any other way not appointed in his Word.[2]

**7.052**     Q. 52. What are the reasons annexed to the Second Commandment?

A. The reasons annexed to the Second Commandment are: God's sovereignty over us,?[1] his propriety in us,[2] and the zeal he hath to his own worship.[3]

**7.053**     Q. 53. Which is the Third Commandment?

A. The Third Commandment is, "Thou shalt not take the name of the Lord thy God in vain: for the Lord will not hold him guiltless that taketh his name in vain."[1]

**7.054**     Q. 54. What is required in the Third Commandment?

A. The Third Commandment requireth the holy and reverent use of God's names,[1] titles, attributes,[2] ordinances,[3] Word,[4] and works.[5]

**7.055**     Q. 55. What is forbidden in the Third Commandment?

A. The Third Commandment forbiddeth all profaning or abusing of anything whereby God maketh himself known.[1]

**7.056**     Q. 56. What is the reason annexed to the Third Commandment?

A. The reason annexed to the Third Commandment is that, however the breakers of this commandment may escape punishment from men, yet the Lord our God will not suffer them to escape his righteous judgment.[1]

**7.057**     Q. 57. Which is the Fourth Commandment?

A. The Fourth Commandment is, "Remember the Sabbath day, to keep it holy. Six days shalt thou labor, and do all thy work: but the seventh day is the Sabbath of the Lord thy God: in it thou shall not do any work, thou, nor thy son, nor thy daughter, thy manservant, nor thy maidservant, nor thy cattle, nor thy stranger that is within thy gates: for six days the Lord made heaven and earth, the sea, and all that in them is, and rested the seventh day: wherefore the Lord blessed the Sabbath day, and hallowed it."[1]

**7.058**     Q. 58. What is required in the Fourth Commandment?

A. The Fourth Commandment requireth the keeping holy to God such set times as he hath appointed in his Word; expressly one whole day in seven, to be a holy Sabbath to himself.[1]

**7.059**     Q. 59. Which day of the seven hath God appointed to be the weekly Sabbath?

A. From the beginning of the world to the resurrection of Christ, God appointed the seventh day of the week to be the weekly Sabbath;[1] and the first day of the week ever since, to continue to the end of the world, which is the Christian Sabbath.[2]

**7.060**     Q. 60. How is the Sabbath to be sanctified?

A. The Sabbath is to be sanctified by a holy resting all that day, even from such worldly employments and recreations as are lawful on other days;[1] and spending the whole time in the public and private exercises of God's worship,[2] except so much as is to be taken up in the works of necessity and mercy.[3]

**7.061**   Q. 61. What is forbidden in the Fourth Commandment?

A. The Fourth Commandment forbiddeth the omission, or careless performance, of the duties required,[1] and the profaning the day by idleness, or doing that which is in itself sinful,[2] or by unnecessary thoughts, words, or works, about our worldly employments or recreations.[3]

**7.062**   Q. 62. What are the reasons annexed to the Fourth Commandment?

A. The reasons annexed to the Fourth Commandment are: God's allowing us six days of the week for our own employments,[1] his challenging a special propriety in the seventh,[2] his own example,[3] and his blessing the Sabbath Day.[4]

**7.063**   Q. 63. Which is the Fifth Commandment?

A. The Fifth Commandment is, "Honor thy father and thy mother: that thy days may be long upon the land which the Lord thy God giveth thee."[1]

**7.064**   Q. 64. What is required in the Fifth Commandment?

A. The Fifth Commandment requireth the preserving the honor, and performing the duties, belonging to everyone in their several places and relations, as superiors, inferiors, or equals.[1]

**7.065**   Q. 65. What is forbidden in the Fifth Commandment?

A. The Fifth Commandment forbiddeth the neglecting of, or doing anything against, the honor and duty which belongeth to everyone in their several places and relations.[1]

**7.066**   Q. 66. What is the reason annexed to the Fifth Commandment?

A. The reason annexed to the Fifth Commandment is a promise of long life and prosperity (as far as it shall serve for God's glory, and their own good) to all such as keep this commandment.[1]

**7.067**   Q. 67. What is the Sixth Commandment?

A. The Sixth Commandment is, "Thou shall not kill."[1]

**7.068**   Q. 68. What is required in the Sixth Commandment?

A. The Sixth Commandment requireth all lawful endeavors to preserve our own life,[1] and the life of others.[2]

**7.069**   Q. 69. What is forbidden in the Sixth Commandment?

A. The Sixth Commandment forbiddeth the taking away of our own life,[1] or the life of our neighbor unjustly,[2] or whatsoever tendeth thereunto.[3]

**7.070**   Q. 70. Which is the Seventh Commandment?

A. The Seventh Commandment is, "Thou shalt not commit adultery."[1]

**7.071**   Q. 71. What is required in the Seventh Commandment?

A. The Seventh Commandment requireth the preservation of our own[1] and our neighbor's chastity,[2] in heart,[3] speech,[4] and behavior.[5]

| 7.072 | Q. 72. What is forbidden in the Seventh Commandment? |

A. The Seventh Commandment forbiddeth all unchaste thoughts,[1] words,[2] and actions.[3]

| 7.073 | Q. 73. Which is the Eighth Commandment? |

A. The Eighth Commandment is, "Thou shalt not steal."[1]

| 7.074 | Q. 74. What is required in the Eighth Commandment? |

A. The Eighth Commandment requireth the lawful procuring and furthering the wealth and outward estate of ourselves[1] and others.[2]

| 7.075 | Q. 75. What is forbidden in the Eighth Commandment? |

A. The Eighth Commandment forbiddeth whatsoever doth, or may, unjustly hinder our own,[1] or our neighbor's, wealth or outward estate.[2]

| 7.076 | Q. 76. Which is the Ninth Commandment? |

A. The Ninth Commandment is, "Thou shalt not bear false witness against thy neighbor."[1]

| 7.077 | Q. 77. What is required in the Ninth Commandment? |

A. The Ninth Commandment requireth the maintaining and promoting of truth between man and man,[1] and of our own[2] and our neighbor's good name,[3] especially in witness-bearing.[4]

| 7.078 | Q. 78. What is forbidden in the Ninth Commandment? |

A. The Ninth Commandment forbiddeth whatsoever is prejudicial to truth,[1] or injurious to our own or our neighbor's good name.[2]

| 7.079 | Q. 79. Which is the Tenth Commandment? |

A. The Tenth Commandment is, "Thou shalt not covet thy neighbor's house, thou shalt not covet thy neighbor's wife, nor his manservant, nor his maidservant, nor his ox, nor his ass, nor any thing that is thy neighbor's."[1]

| 7.080 | Q. 80. What is required in the Tenth Commandment? |

A. The Tenth Commandment requireth full contentment with our own condition,[1] with a right and charitable frame of spirit toward our neighbor and all that is his.[2]

| 7.081 | Q. 81. What is forbidden in the Tenth Commandment? |

A. The Tenth Commandment forbiddeth all discontentment with our own estate,[1] envying or grieving at the good of our neighbor,[2] and all inordinate motions and affections to anything that is his.[3]

| 7.082 | Q. 82. Is any man able perfectly to keep the commandments of God? |

A. No mere man, since the Fall, is able, in this life, perfectly to keep the commandments of God,[1] but doth daily break them, in thought,[2] word,[3] and deed.[4]

| 7.083 | Q. 83. Are all transgressions of the law equally heinous? |

A. Some sins in themselves, and by reason of several aggravations, are more heinous in the sight of God than others.[1]

**7.084** Q. 84. What doth every sin deserve?

A. Every sin deserveth God's wrath and curse, both in this life and that which is to come.[1]

**7.085** Q. 85. What doth God require of us, that we may escape his wrath and curse, due to us for sin?

A. To escape the wrath and curse of God, due to us for sin, God requireth of us faith in Jesus Christ, repentance unto life,[1] with the diligent use of all the outward means whereby Christ communicateth to us the benefits of redemption.[2]

**7.086** Q. 86. What is faith in Jesus Christ?

A. Faith in Jesus Christ is a saving grace,[1] whereby we receive[2] and rest upon him alone for salvation,[3] as he is offered to us in the gospel.[4]

**7.087** Q. 87. What is repentance unto life?

A. Repentance unto life is a saving grace,[1] whereby a sinner, out of a true sense of his sin,[2] and apprehension of the mercy of God in Christ,[3] doth, with grief and hatred of his sin, turn from it unto God,[4] with full purpose of, and endeavor after, new obedience.[5]

**7.088** Q. 88. What are the outward means whereby Christ communicateth to us the benefits of redemption?

A. The outward and ordinary means whereby Christ communicateth to us the benefits of redemption are his ordinances, especially the Word, sacraments, and prayer,[1] all which are made effectual to the elect for salvation.

**7.089** Q. 89. How is the Word made effectual to salvation?

A. The Spirit of God maketh the reading, but especially the preaching, of the Word an effectual means of convincing and converting sinners,[1] and of building them up in holiness and comfort, through faith unto salvation.[2]

**7.090** Q. 90. How is the Word to be read and heard, that it may become effectual to salvation?

A. That the Word may become effectual to salvation we must attend thereunto with diligence,[1] preparation,[2] and prayer;[3] receive it with faith[4] and love;[5] lay it up in our hearts;[6] and practice it in our lives.[7]

**7.091** Q. 91. How do the sacraments become effectual means of salvation?

A. The sacraments become effectual means of salvation, not from any virtue in them, or in him that doth administer them, but only by the blessing of Christ, and the working of his Spirit in them that by faith receive them.[1]

**7.092** Q. 92. What is a sacrament?

A. A sacrament is a holy ordinance instituted by Christ, wherein, by sensible signs, Christ and the benefits of the new covenant are represented,[1] sealed, and applied to believers.[2]

**7.093** **Q. 93. Which are the sacraments of the New Testament?**
A. The sacraments of the New Testament are Baptism[1] and the Lord's Supper.[2]

**7.094** **Q. 94. What is Baptism?**
A. Baptism is a sacrament, wherein the washing with water, in the name of the Father, and of the Son, and of the Holy Ghost,[1] doth signify and seal our ingrafting into Christ, and partaking of the benefits of the covenant of grace,[2] and our engagement to be the Lord's.[3]

**7.095** **Q. 95. To whom is Baptism to be administered?**
A. Baptism is not to be administered to any that are out of the visible Church, till they profess their faith in Christ and obedience to him;[1] but the infants of such as are members of the visible Church are to be baptized.[2]

**7.096** **Q. 96. What is the Lord's Supper?**
A. The Lord's Supper is a sacrament, wherein by giving and receiving bread and wine, according to Christ's appointment, his death is showed forth;[1] and the worthy receivers are, not after a corporal and carnal manner, but by faith, made partakers of his body and blood, with all his benefits, to their spiritual nourishment and growth in grace.[2]

**7.097** **Q. 97. What is required to the worthy receiving of the Lord's Supper?**
A. It is required of them that would worthily partake of the Lord's Supper that they examine themselves, of their knowledge to discern the Lord's body,[1] of their faith to feed upon him,[2] of their repentance,[3] love,[4] and new obedience;[5] lest, coming unworthily, they eat and drink judgment to themselves.[6]

**7.098** **Q. 98. What is prayer?**
A. Prayer is an offering up of our desires unto God,[1] for things agreeable to his will,[2] in the name of Christ,[3] with confession of our sins,[4] and thankful acknowledgment of his mercies.[5]

**7.099** **Q. 99. What rule hath God given for our direction in prayer?**
A. The whole Word of God is of use to direct us in prayer;[1] but the special rule of direction is that form of prayer which Christ taught his disciples, commonly called "the Lord's Prayer."[2]

**7.100** **Q. 100. What doth the preface of the Lord's Prayer teach us?**
A. The preface of the Lord's Prayer, which is, "Our Father which art in heaven," teacheth us to draw near to God with all holy reverence and confidence, as children to a father, able and ready to help us;[1] and that we should pray with and for others.[2]

**7.101** **Q. 101. What do we pray for in the first petition?**
A. In the first petition, which is, "Hallowed be thy name," we pray that God would enable us, and others, to glorify him in all that whereby he maketh himself known,[1] and that he would dispose all things to his own glory.[2]

**7.102**     **Q. 102. What do we pray for in the second petition?**

A. In the second petition, which is, "Thy kingdom come," we pray that Satan's kingdom may be destroyed,[1] and that the Kingdom of grace may be advanced, ourselves and others brought into it, and kept in it,[2] and that the Kingdom of glory may be hastened.[3]

**7.103**     **Q. 103. What do we pray for in the third petition?**

A. In the third petition, which is, "Thy will be done in earth, as it is in heaven," we pray that God, by his grace, would make us able and willing to know, obey, and submit to his will in all things,[1] as the angels do in heaven.[2]

**7.104**     **Q. 104. What do we pray for in the fourth petition?**

A. In the fourth petition, which is, "Give us this day our daily bread," we pray that, of God's free gift, we may receive a competent portion of the good things of this life,[1] and enjoy his blessing with them.[2]

**7.105**     **Q. 105. What do we pray for in the fifth petition?**

A. In the fifth petition, which is, "And forgive us our debts, as we forgive our debtors," we pray that God, for Christ's sake, would freely pardon all our sins;[1] which we are then rather encouraged to ask because by his grace we are enabled from the heart to forgive others.[2]

**7.106**     **Q. 106. What do we pray for in the sixth petition?**

A. In the sixth petition, which is, "And lead us not into temptation, but deliver us from evil," we pray that God would either keep us from being tempted to sin[1] or support and deliver us when we are tempted.[2]

**7.107**     **Q. 107. What doth the conclusion of the Lord's Prayer teach us?**

A. The conclusion of the Lord's Prayer, which is, "For thine is the kingdom, and the power, and the glory, forever. Amen," teacheth us to take our encouragement in prayer from God only,[1] and in our prayers to praise him, ascribing Kingdom, power, and glory to him;[2] and in testimony of our desire and assurance to be heard, we say, "Amen."[3]

**7.108**     **THE TEN COMMANDMENTS**
                        EXODUS, CH. 20

God spake all these words, saying, I am the Lord thy God, which have brought thee out of the land of Egypt, out of the house of bondage.

    I. Thou shalt have no other gods before me.

    II. Thou shalt not make unto thee any graven image, or any likeness of any thing that is in heaven above, or that is in the earth beneath, or that is in the water under the earth: thou shalt not bow down thyself to them, nor serve them: for I the Lord thy God am a jealous God, visiting the iniquity of the fathers upon the children unto the third and fourth generation of them that hate me; and showing mercy unto thousands of them that love me, and keep my commandments.

III. Thou shalt not take the name of the Lord thy God in vain: for the Lord will not hold him guiltless that taketh his name in vain.

IV. Remember the Sabbath day, to keep it holy. Six days shalt thou labor, and do all thy work: but the seventh day is the Sabbath of the Lord thy God: in it thou shalt not do any work, thou, nor thy son, nor thy daughter, thy manservant, nor thy maidservant, nor thy cattle, nor thy stranger that is within thy gates: for in six days the Lord made heaven and earth, the sea, and all that in them is, and rested the seventh day: wherefore the Lord blessed the seventh day, and hallowed it.

V. Honor thy father and thy mother: that thy days may be long upon the land which the Lord thy God giveth thee.

VI. Thou shalt not kill.

VII. Thou shalt not commit adultery.

VIII. Thou shalt not steal.

IX. Thou shalt not bear false witness against thy neighbor.

X. Thou shalt not covet thy neighbor's house, thou shalt not covet thy neighbor's wife, nor his manservant, nor his maidservant, nor his ox, nor his ass, nor any thing that is thy neighbor's.

**7.109**
### THE LORD'S PRAYER
MATTHEW, CH. 6

Our Father which art in heaven, hallowed be thy name. Thy kingdom come. Thy will be done in earth, as it is in heaven. Give us this day our daily bread. And forgive us our debts, as we forgive our debtors. And lead us not into temptation, but deliver us from evil: For thine is the kingdom, and the power, and the glory, forever. Amen.

**7.110**
### THE APOSTLES' CREED

I BELIEVE in God the Father Almighty, Maker of heaven and earth;

And in Jesus Christ his only Son our Lord; who was conceived by the Holy Ghost, born of the Virgin Mary, suffered under Pontius Pilate, was crucified, dead, and buried; he descended into hell;[1] the third day he rose again from the dead; he ascended into heaven, and sitteth on the right hand of God the Father Almighty; from thence he shall come to judge the quick and the dead.

I believe in the Holy Ghost; the holy catholic Church; the communion of saints; the forgiveness of sins; the resurrection of the body; and the life everlasting. Amen.

# ENDNOTES FOR 7.001–.021

Q. 1.
1. I Cor. 10:31; Rom. 11:36.
2. Ps. 73:24–26; John 17:22, 24.

Q. 2.
1. Gal. 1:8, 9; Isa. 8:20; Luke 16:29, 31; II Tim. 3:15–17.

Q. 3.
1. Micah 6:8; John 20:31; John 3:16.

Q. 4.
1. John 4:24.
2. Ps. 90:2; Mal. 3:6; James 1:17; I Kings 8:27; Jer. 23:24; Isa. 40:22.
3. Ps. 147:5; Rom. 16:27.
4. Gen. 17:1; Rev. 19:16.
5. Isa. 57:15; John 17:11; Rev. 4:8.
6. Deut. 32:4.
7. Ps. 100:5; Rom. 2:4.
8. Exod. 34:6; Ps. 117:2.

Q. 5.
1. Deut. 6:4; Jer. 10:10.

Q. 6.
1. II Cor. 13:14; Matt. 28:19; Matt. 3:16, 17.

Q. 7.
1. Eph. 1:11; Acts 4:27, 28; Ps. 33:11; Eph. 2:10; Rom. 9:22, 23; 11:33.

Q. 8.
1. Rev. 4:11; Eph. 1:11.

Q. 9.
1. Heb. 11:3; Rev. 4:11; Gen. 1:1–31.

Q. 10.
1. Gen. 1:27.
2. Col. 3:10; Eph. 4:24.
3. Gen. 1:28.

Q. 11.
1. Ps. 145:17.
2. Ps. 104:24.
3. Heb. 1:3.
4. Ps. 103:19; Matt. 10:29, 30; Job, Chapters 38–41.

Q. 12.
1. Compare Gen. 2:16, 17 with Rom. 5:12–14; Rom. 10:5; Luke 10:25–28, and with the covenants made with Noah and Abraham.
2. Gen. 2:17.

Q. 13.
1. Gen. 3:6–8, 13; II Cor. 11:3.

Q. 14.
1. I John 3:4; James 4:17; Rom. 3:23.

Q. 15.
1. See proof to Answer 13. Gen 3:6.

Q. 16.
1. Acts 17:26. See under Question 12.
2. Gen. 2:17. Compare Rom. 5:12–20; I Cor. 15:21, 22.

Q. 17.
1. Rom. 5:12; Gal. 3:10.

Q. 18.
1. Rom. 5:12, 19; I Cor. 15:22.
2. Rom. 5:6; Eph. 2:1–3; Rom 8:7, 8; Gen. 6:5; Rom. 3:10–20; Ps. 51:5; 58:3.
3. James 1:14, 15; Matt. 15:19.

Q. 19.
1. Gen. 3:8, 24.
2. Eph. 2:3.
3. Rom. 5:14; Rom 6:23.

Q. 20.
1. Eph. 1:4–7.
2. Titus 3:4–7; Titus 1:2; Gal. 3:21; Rom. 3:20–22.

Q. 21.
1. I Tim. 2:5.
2. John 1:1, 14; John 10:30; Phil. 2:6; Gal. 4:4.
3. See texts just cited; also Phil. 2:5–11.

Q. 22.
1. John 1:14; Heb. 2:14; Matt. 26:38.
2. Luke 1:31, 35, 41, 42; Gal. 4:4.
3. Heb. 4:15; Heb. 7:26.

Q. 23.
1. Acts 3:22; Luke 4:18, 21.
2. Heb. 5:5, 6; Heb. 4:14, 15.
3. Rev. 19:16; Isa. 9:6, 7; Ps. 2:6.

Q. 24.
1. John 1:1, 4.
2. John 15:15; John 20:31; II Peter 1:21; John 14:26.

Q. 25.
1. Heb. 9:14, 28; Rom. 3:26; Rom. 10:4.
2. Heb. 2:17.
3. Heb. 7:25.

Q. 26.
1. Ps. 110:3.
2. Isa. 33:22.
3. I Cor. 15:25; Acts 12:17; 18:9, 10.

Q. 27.
1. Luke 2:7; Phil. 2:6–8; II Cor. 8:9.
2. Gal. 4:4.
3. Isa. 53:3.
4. Matt. 27:46; Luke 22:41–44.
5. Gal. 3:13; Phil. 2:8.
6. I Cor. 15:3, 4.

Q. 28.
1. See last quoted text.
2. Acts 1:9; Eph. 1:19, 20.
3. Acts 1:11; Acts 17:31.

Q. 29.
1. John 1:12, 13; John 3:5, 6; Titus 3:5, 6.

Q. 30.
1. Eph. 2:8.
2. John 15:5; I Cor. 6:17; I Cor. 1:9; I Peter 5:10.

Q. 31.
1. II Tim. 1:8, 9; Eph. 1:18–20.
2. Acts 2:37.
3. Acts 26:18.
4. Ezek. 11:19; Ezek. 36:26, 27.
5. John 6:44, 45; Phil. 2:13; Deut. 30:6; Eph. 2:5.

Q. 32.
1. Rom. 8:30.
2. Eph. 1:5.
3. I Cor. 1:30.

Q. 33.
1. Eph. 1:7.
2. II Cor. 5:19, 21; Rom. 4:5; Rom. 3:22, 24, 25.
3. Rom. 5:17–19; Rom. 4:6–8.
4. Rom. 5:1; Acts 10:43; Gal. 2:16; Phil. 3:9.

Q. 34.
1. I John 3:1.
2. John 1:12; Rom. 8:17.

Q. 35.
1. II Thess. 2:13.
2. Eph. 4:23, 24.
3. Rom. 6:4, 6, 14; Rom. 8:4.

Q. 36.
1. Rom. 5:1, 2, 5; Rom. 14:17.
2. Col. 1:10, 11; Prov. 4:18; Eph. 3:16–18; II Peter 3:18.
3. Jer. 32:40; I John 2:19, 27; Rev. 14:12; I Peter 1:5; I John 5:13.

Q. 37.
1. Luke 23:43; Luke 16:23; Phil. 1:23; II Cor. 5:6–8.
2. I Thess. 4:14.
3. Rom. 8:23; I Thess. 4:14.

Q. 38.
1. I Cor. 15:42, 43.
2. Matt. 25:33, 34; Matt. 10:32.
3. Ps. 16:11; I Cor. 2:9.
4. I Thess. 4:17. See preceding context.

Q. 39.
1. Deut. 29:29; Micah 6:8; I Sam. 15:22.

Q. 40.
1. Rom. 2:14, 15; Rom. 10:5.

Q. 41.
1. Matt. 19:17–19.

Q. 42.
1. Matt. 22:37–40

Q. 43.
1. Exod. 20:2.

Q. 45.
1. Exod. 20:3.

# ENDNOTES FOR 7.046–.071

Q. 46.
1. The exposition of the Ten Commandments found in answers to Questions 46–81 are deductions from the commandments themselves and the rules set forth in the Larger Catechism, Q.99. The texts under the specifications are given to show that they are in accord with the general teaching of the Scriptures.
2. I Chron. 28:9; Deut. 26:17.
3. Matt. 4:10; Ps. 95:6, 7; Ps. 29:2.

Q. 47.
1. Ps. 14:1.
2. Rom. 1:20, 21.
3. Ps. 81:11.
4. Rom. 1:25.

Q. 48.
1. I Chron. 28:9; Ps. 44:20, 21.

Q. 49.
1. Exod. 20:4–6.

Q. 50.
1. Deut. 12:32; Duet. 32:46; Matt. 28:20.

Q. 51.
1. Deut. 4:15, 16; See verses 17–19; Acts 17:29.
2. Deut. 12:30–32.

Q. 52.
1. Ps. 95:2, 3.
2. Ps. 45:11.
3. Exod. 34:14.

Q. 53.
1. Exod. 20:7.

Q. 54.
1. Ps. 29:2; Matt. 6:9.
2. Rev. 15:3, 4.
3. Mal. 1:14.
4. Ps. 138:2.
5. Ps. 107:21, 22.

Q. 55.
1. Mal. 2:2; Isa. 5:12.

Q. 56.
1. Deut. 28:58, 59.

Q. 57.
1. Exod. 20:8–11.

Q. 58.
1. Lev. 19:30; Deut. 5:12; Isa. 56:2–7.

Q. 59.
1. Gen. 2:3; Luke 23:56.
2. Acts 20:7; I Cor. 16:1, 2; John 20:19–26.

Q. 60.
1. Lev. 23:3; Exod. 16:25–29; Jer. 17:21, 22.
2. Ps. 92:1, 2. (A Psalm or Song for the sabbath day.) Luke 4:16; Isa. 58:13; Acts 20:7.
3. Matt. 12:11, 12. See context.

Q. 61.
1. Ezek. 22:26; Mal. 1:13; Amos 8:5.
2. Ezek. 23:38.
3. Isa. 58:13; Jer. 17:24, 27.

Q. 62.
1. Exod. 31:15, 16.
2. Lev. 23:3.
3. Exod. 31:17.
4. Gen. 2:3.

Q. 63.
1. Exod. 20:12.

Q. 64.
1. Eph. 5:21, 22; Eph. 6:1, 5, 9; Rom. 13:1; Rom. 12:10.

Q. 65.
1. Rom. 13:7, 8.

Q. 66.
1. Eph. 6:2, 3.

Q. 67.
1. Exod. 20:13.

Q. 68.
1. Eph. 5:29; Matt. 10:23.
2. Ps. 82:3, 4; Job 29:13; I Kings 18:4.

Q. 69.
1. Acts 16:28.
2. Gen. 9:6.
3. Matt. 5:22; I John 3:15; Gal. 5:15; Prov. 24:11, 12; Exod. 21:18–32.

Q. 70.
1. Exod. 20:14.

Q. 71.
1. I Thess. 4:4, 5.
2. I Cor. 7:2; Eph. 5:11, 12.
3. Matt. 5:28.
4. Eph. 4:29; Col. 4:6.
5. I Peter 3:2.

Q. 72.
1. Matt. 5:28.
2. Eph. 5:4.
3. Eph. 5:3.

Q. 73.
1. Exod. 20:15.

Q. 74.
1. II Thess. 3:10–12; Rom. 12:17; Prov. 27:23.
2. Lev. 25:35; Phil. 2:4; Prov. 13:4; Prov. 20:4; Prov. 24:30–34.

Q. 75.
1. I Tim. 5:8.
2. Eph. 4:28; Prov. 21:16; II Thess. 3:7–10.

Q. 76.
1. Exod. 20:16.

Q. 77.
1. Zech. 8:16.
2. I Peter 3:16; Acts 25:10.
3. III John 12.
4. Prov. 14:5, 25.

Q. 78.
1. Prov. 19:5; Prov. 6:16–19.
2. Luke 3:14; Ps. 15:3.

Q. 79.
1. Exod. 20:17.

Q. 80.
1. Heb. 13:5.
2. Rom. 12:15; Phil. 2:4; I Cor. 13:4–6.

Q. 81.
1. I Cor. 10:10.
2. Gal. 5:26.
3. Col. 3:5.

Q. 82.
1. I Kings 8:46; I John 1:8–2:6.
2. Gen. 8:21.
3. James 3:8.
4. James 3:2.

Q. 83.
1. Ps. 19:13; John 19:11.

Q. 84.
1. Gal. 3:10; Matt. 25:41.

Q. 85.
1. Acts 20:21; Mark 1:15; John 3:18.
2. See under Question 88 below.

Q. 86.
1. Heb. 10:39.
2. John 1:12.
3. Phil. 3:9.
4. John 6:40.

Q. 87.
1. Acts 11:18.
2. Acts 2:37.
3. Joel 2:13.
4. II Cor. 7:11; Jer. 31:18, 19; Acts 26:18.
5. Ps. 119:59.

Q. 88.
1. Matt. 28:19, 20; Acts 2:41, 42.

Q. 89.
1. Ps. 19:7, Ps. 119:130; Heb. 4:12.
2. I Thess. 1:6; Rom. 1:16; Rom. 16:25; Acts 20:32.

Q. 90.
1. Prov. 8:34.
2. Luke 8:18; I Peter 2:1, 2.
3. Ps. 119:18.
4. Heb. 4:2.
5. II Thess. 2:10.
6. Ps. 119:11.
7. Luke 8:15; James 1:25.

Q. 91.
1. I Peter 3:21; Acts 8:13, 23. See intervening context. I Cor. 3:7; I Cor. 6:11; I Cor. 12:13.

Q. 92.
1. Matt. 28:19; Matt. 26:26–28.
2. Rom. 4:11.

Q. 93.
1. Matt. 28:19.
2. I Cor. 11:23.

Q. 94.
1. See Matt. 28:19 cited under Question 93 above.
2. Gal. 3:27; Rom. 6:3.
3. Rom. 6:4.

Q. 95.
1. Acts 2:41.
2. Gen. 17:7, 10; Gal. 3:17, 18, 29; Acts 2:38, 39.

Q. 96.
1. Matt. 26:26, 27; I Cor. 11:26.
2. I Cor. 10:16; Eph. 3:17.

Q. 97.
1. I Cor. 11:28, 29.
2. John 6:53–56.
3. Zech. 12:10.
4. I John 4:19; Gal. 5:6.
5. Rom. 6:4; Rom. 6:17–22.
6. I Cor. 11:27.

Q. 98.
1. Ps. 62:8; Ps. 10:17.
2. I John 5:14; Matt. 26:39; John 6:38.
3. John 16:23.
4. Dan. 9:4.
5. Phil. 4:6.

Q. 99.
1. II Tim. 3:16, 17; I John 5:14.
2. Matt. 6:9.

Q. 100.
1. Isa. 64:9; Luke 11:13; Rom. 8:15.
2. Eph. 6:18; Acts 12:5; Zech. 8:21.

Q. 101.
1. Ps. 67:1–3; II Thess. 3:1; Ps. 145.
2. Isa. 64:1, 2; Rom. 11:36.

Q. 102.
1. Ps. 68:1.
2. II Thess. 3:1; Ps. 51:18; 67:1–3; Rom. 10:1.
3. Rev. 22:20; II Peter 3:11–13.

Q. 103.
1. Ps. 119:35–36; Acts 21:14.
2. Ps. 103:20–22.

Q. 104.
1. Prov. 30:8.
2. I Tim. 4:4, 5; Prov. 10:22.

Q. 105.
1. Ps. 51:1; Rom 3:24, 25.
2. Luke 11:4; Matt. 18:35; Matt. 6:14, 15.

Q. 106.
1. Matt. 26:41; Ps. 19:13.
2. I Cor. 10:13; Ps. 51:10, 12.

Q. 107.
1. Dan. 9:18, 19.
2. I Chron. 29:11–13.
3. Rev. 22:20, 21; I Cor. 14:16.

THE APOSTLES' CREED

1. *I.e.* Continued in the state of the dead, and under the power of death, until the third day. See the answer to Question 50 in the Larger Catechism.

# *THE* LARGER CATECHISM
[TEXT]

For the prologue to the Westminster Catechism
(Larger Catechism), see pages 146–48.

# THE LARGER CATECHISM

**7.111**     **Q. 1. What is the chief and highest end of man?**
A. Man's chief and highest end is to glorify God,[1] and fully to enjoy him forever.[2]

**7.112**     **Q. 2. How doth it appear that there is a God?**
A. The very light of nature in man, and the works of God, declare plainly that there is a God;[1] but his Word and Spirit only, do sufficiently and effectually reveal him unto men for their salvation.[2]

**7.113**     **Q. 3. What is the Word of God?**
A. The holy Scriptures of the Old and New Testaments are the Word of God, the only rule of faith and obedience.[1]

**7.114**     **Q. 4. How doth it appear that the Scriptures are the Word of God?**
A. The Scriptures manifest themselves to be the Word of God, by their majesty and purity; by the consent of all the parts, and the scope of the whole, which is to give all glory to God; by their light and power to convince and convert sinners, to comfort and build up believers unto salvation.[1] But the Spirit of God, bearing witness by and with the Scriptures in the heart of man, is alone able fully to persuade it that they are the very word of God.[2]

**7.115**     **Q. 5. What do the Scriptures principally teach?**
A. The Scriptures principally teach, what man is to believe concerning God, and what duty God requires of man.[1]

*What Man Ought to Believe Concerning God*

**7.116**     **Q. 6. What do the Scriptures make known of God?**
A. The Scriptures make known what God is,[1] the persons in the Godhead,[2] his decrees,[3] and the execution of his decrees.[4]

**7.117**     **Q. 7. What is God?**
A. God is a Spirit,[1] in and of himself infinite in being,[2] glory, blessedness, and perfection;[3] all-sufficient,[4] eternal,[5] unchangeable,[6] incomprehensible,[7] everywhere present,[8] almighty;[9] knowing all things,[10] most wise,[11] most holy,[12] most just,[13] most merciful and gracious, long-suffering, and abundant in goodness and truth.[14]

**7.118**     **Q. 8. Are there more Gods than one?**
A. There is but one only, the living and true God.[1]

**7.119**     **Q. 9. How many persons are there in the Godhead?**
A. There be three persons in the Godhead: the Father, the Son, and the Holy Ghost; and these three are one true, eternal God, the same in substance, equal in power and glory; although distinguished by their personal properties.[1]

7.120 **Q. 10. What are the personal properties of the three persons in the Godhead?**

A. It is proper to the Father to beget his Son,[1] and to the Son to be begotten of the Father,[2] and to the Holy Ghost to proceed from the Father and the Son, from all eternity.[3]

7.121 **Q. 11. How doth it appear that the Son and the Holy Ghost are equal with the Father?**

A. The Scriptures manifest that the Son and the Holy Ghost are God equal with the Father, ascribing unto them such names,[1] attributes,[2] works,[3] and worship,[4] as are proper to God only.

7.122 **Q. 12. What are the decrees of God?**

A. God's decrees are the wise, free, and holy acts of the counsel of his will, whereby, from all eternity, he hath, for his own glory, unchangeably foreordained whatsoever comes to pass in time,[1] especially concerning angels and men.

7.123 **Q. 13. What hath God especially decreed concerning angels and men?**

A. God, by an eternal and immutable decree, out of his mere love, for the praise of his glorious grace, to be manifested in due time, hath elected some angels to glory;[1] and, in Christ, hath chosen some men to eternal life, and the means thereof;[2] and also, according to his sovereign power, and the unsearchable counsel of his own will (whereby he extendeth or withholdeth favor as he pleaseth) hath passed by, and foreordained the rest to dishonor and wrath, to be for their sin inflicted, to the praise of the glory of his justice.[3]

7.124 **Q. 14. How doth God execute his decrees?**

A. God executeth his decrees in the works of creation and providence, according to his infallible foreknowledge, and the free and immutable counsel of his own will.[1]

7.125 **Q. 15. What is the work of creation?**

A. The work of creation is that wherein God did in the beginning, by the word of his power, make of nothing, the world and all things therein for himself, within the space of six days, and all very good.[1]

7.126 **Q. 16. How did God create angels?**

A. God created all the angels, spirits,[1] immortal,[2] holy,[3] excelling in knowledge,[4] mighty in power,[5] to execute his commandments, and to praise his name,[6] yet subject to change.[7]

7.127 **Q. 17. How did God create man?**

A. After God had made all other creatures, he created man, male and female;[1] formed the body of the man of the dust of the ground,[2] and the woman of the rib of man;[3] endued them with living, reasonable, and immortal souls;[4] made them after his own image,[5] in knowledge,[6] righteousness and holiness,[7] having the law of God written in their hearts,[8] and power to fulfill it, with dominion over the creatures;[9] yet subject to fall.[10]

**7.128 Q. 18. What are God's works of providence?**

A. God's works of providence are his most holy,[1] wise,[2] and powerful preserving,[3] and governing all his creatures;[4] ordering them, and all their actions,[5] to his own glory.[6]

**7.129 Q. 19. What is God's providence toward the angels?**

A. God by his providence permitted some of the angels, willfully and irrecoverably, to fall into sin and damnation,[1] limiting and ordering that, and all their sins, to his own glory;[2] and established the rest in holiness and happiness;[3] employing them all, at his pleasure, in the administrations of his power, mercy, and justice.[4]

**7.130 Q. 20. What was the providence of God toward man in the estate in which he was created?**

A. The providence of God toward man in the estate in which he was created was, the placing him in paradise, appointing him to dress it, giving him liberty to eat of the fruit of the earth,[1] putting the creatures under his dominion,[2] ordaining marriage for his help,[3] affording him communion with himself,[4] and instituting the Sabbath;[5] entering into a covenant of life with him, upon condition of personal, perfect, and perpetual obedience,[6] of which the tree of life was a pledge; and forbidding to eat of the tree of the knowledge of good and evil, upon the pain of death.[7]

**7.131 Q. 21. Did man continue in that estate wherein God at first created him?**

A. Our first parents, being left to the freedom of their own will, through the temptation of Satan, transgressed the commandment of God, in eating the forbidden fruit, and thereby fell from the estate of innocency wherein they were created.[1]

**7.132 Q. 22. Did all mankind fall in that first transgression?**

A. The covenant being made with Adam, as a public person, not for himself only, but for his posterity, all mankind, descending from him by ordinary generation,[1] sinned in him, and fell with him in that first transgression.[2]

**7.133 Q. 23. Into what estate did the Fall bring mankind?**

A. The Fall brought mankind into an estate of sin and misery.[1]

**7.134 Q. 24. What is sin?**

A. Sin is any want of conformity unto, or transgression of, any law of God, given as a rule to the reasonable creature.[1]

**7.135 Q. 25. Wherein consists the sinfulness of that estate whereinto man fell?**

A. The sinfulness of that estate whereinto man fell, consisteth in the guilt of Adam's first sin,[1] the want of that righteousness wherein he was created, and the corruption of his nature, whereby he is utterly indisposed, disabled, and made opposite unto all that is spiritually good, and wholly inclined to all evil, and that continually;[2] which is commonly called original sin, and from which do proceed all actual transgressions.[3]

**7.136** Q. 26. How is original sin conveyed from our first parents unto their posterity?

A. Original sin is conveyed from our first parents unto their posterity by natural generation, so as all that proceed from them in that way, are conceived and born in sin.[1]

**7.137** Q. 27. What misery did the Fall bring upon mankind?

A. The Fall brought upon mankind the loss of communion with God,[1] his displeasure and curse; so as we are by nature children of wrath,[2] bondslaves to Satan,[3] and justly liable to all punishments in this world and that which is to come.[4]

**7.138** Q. 28. What are the punishments of sin in this world?

A. The punishments of sin in this world, are either inward, as blindness of mind,[1] a reprobate sense,[2] strong delusions,[3] hardness of heart,[4] horror of conscience,[5] and vile affections;[6] or outward, as the curse of God upon the creatures for our sake,[7] and all other evils that befall us in our bodies, names, estates, relations, and employments;[8] together with death itself.[9]

**7.139** Q. 29. What are the punishments of sin in the world to come?

A. The punishments of sin in the world to come are everlasting separation from the comfortable presence of God, and most grievous torments in soul and body, without intermission, in hell fire forever.[1]

**7.140** Q. 30. Doth God leave all mankind to perish in the estate of sin and misery?

A. God doth not leave all men to perish in the estate of sin and misery, into which they fell by the breach of the first covenant, commonly called the covenant of works;[1] but of his mere love and mercy delivereth his elect out of it, and bringeth them into an estate of salvation by the second covenant, commonly called the covenant of grace.[2]

**7.141** Q. 31. With whom was the covenant of grace made?

A. The covenant of grace was made with Christ as the second Adam, and in him with all the elect as his seed.[1]

**7.142** Q. 32. How is the grace of God manifested in the second covenant?

A. The grace of God is manifested in the second covenant, in that he freely provideth and offereth to sinners a mediator,[1] and life and salvation by him;[2] and requiring faith as the condition to interest them in him,[3] promiseth and giveth his Holy Spirit to all his elect, to work in them that faith, with all other saving graces;[4] and to enable them unto all holy obedience,[5] as the evidence of the truth of their faith[6] and of their thankfulness to God,[7] and as the way which he hath appointed them to salvation.[8]

**7.143 Q. 33. Was the covenant of grace always administered after one and the same manner?**
A. The covenant of grace was not always administered after the same manner, but the administrations of it under the Old Testament were different from those under the New.[1]

**7.144 Q. 34. How was the covenant of grace administered under the Old Testament?**
A. The covenant of grace was administered under the Old Testament, by promises,[1] prophecies,[2] sacrifices,[3] circumcision,[4] the passover,[5] and other types and ordinances; which did all foresignify Christ then to come, and were for that time sufficient to build up the elect in faith in promised Messiah,[6] by whom they then had full remission of sin and eternal salvation.[7]

**7.145 Q. 35. How is the covenant of grace administered under the New Testament?**
A. Under the New Testament, when Christ the substance was exhibited, the same covenant of grace was, and still is to be, administered in the preaching of the Word,[1] and the administration of the sacraments of Baptism,[2] and the Lord's Supper;[3] in which grace and salvation are held forth in more fullness, evidence, and efficacy to all nations.[4]

**7.146 Q. 36. Who is the Mediator of the covenant of grace?**
A. The only Mediator of the covenant of grace is the Lord Jesus Christ,[1] who being the eternal Son of God, of one substance and equal with the Father, in the fullness of time became man, and so was, and continues to be, God and man, in two entire distinct natures, and one person, forever.[2]

**7.147 Q. 37. How did Christ, being the Son of God, become man?**
A. Christ, the Son of God, became man by taking to himself a true body, and a reasonable soul,[1] being conceived by the power of the Holy Ghost, in the womb of the Virgin Mary, of her substance, and born of her,[2] yet without sin.[3]

**7.148 Q. 38. Why was it requisite that the Mediator should be God?**
A. It was requisite that the Mediator should be God; that he might sustain and keep the human nature from sinking under the infinite wrath of God, and the power of death; give worth and efficacy to his sufferings, obedience, and intercession; and to satisfy God's justice, procure his favor, purchase a peculiar people, give his Spirit to them, conquer all their enemies, and bring them to everlasting salvation.[1]

**7.149** **Q. 39. Why was it requisite that the Mediator should be man?**
A. It was requisite that the Mediator should be man; that he might advance our nature, perform obedience to the law,[1] suffer and make intercession for us in our nature,[2] have a fellow feeling of our infirmities;[3] that we might receive the adoption of sons,[4] and have comfort and access with boldness unto the throne of grace.[5]

**7.150** **Q. 40. Why was it requisite that the Mediator should be God and man in one person?**
A. It was requisite that the Mediator who was to reconcile God and man, should himself be both God and man, and this in one person; that the proper works of each nature might be accepted of God for us, and relied on by us, as the works of the whole person.[1]

**7.151** **Q. 41. Why was our Mediator called Jesus?**
A. Our Mediator was called Jesus, because he saveth his people from their sins.[1]

**7.152** **Q. 42. Why was our Mediator called Christ?**
A. Our Mediator was called Christ, because he was anointed with the Holy Ghost above measure;[1] and so set apart, and fully furnished with all authority and ability,[2] to execute the office of prophet,[3] priest,[4] and king of his Church, in the estate both of his humiliation and exaltation.[5]

**7.153** **Q. 43. How doth Christ execute the office of a prophet?**
A. Christ executeth the office of a prophet, in his revealing to the Church in all ages,[1] by his Spirit and Word,[2] in divers ways of administration, the whole will of God, in all things concerning their edification and salvation.[3]

**7.154** **Q. 44 How doth Christ execute the office of a priest?**
A. Christ executeth the office of a priest, in his once offering himself a sacrifice without spot to God,[1] to be a reconciliation for the sins of his people;[2] and in making continual intercession for them.[3]

**7.155** **Q. 45. How doth Christ execute the office of a king?**
A. Christ executeth the office of a king, in calling out of the world a people to himself;[1] and giving them officers,[2] laws,[3] and censures, by which he visibly governs them;[4] in bestowing saving grace upon his elect,[5] rewarding their obedience,[6] and correcting them for their sins,[7] preserving and supporting them under all their temptations and sufferings;[8] restraining and overcoming all their enemies,[9] and powerfully ordering all things for his own glory,[10] and their good;[11] and also in taking vengeance on the rest, who know not God, and obey not the gospel.[12]

**7.156** **Q. 46. What was the estate of Christ's humiliation?**
A. The estate of Christ's humiliation was that low condition, wherein he, for our sakes, emptying himself of his glory, took upon him the form of a servant, in his conception and birth, life, death, and after his death until his resurrection.[1]

**7.157** **Q. 47. How did Christ humble himself in his conception and birth?**

A. Christ humbled himself in his conception and birth, in that, being from all eternity the Son of God in the bosom of the Father, he was pleased in the fullness of time to become the Son of man, made of a woman of low estate, and to be born to her, with divers circumstances of more than ordinary abasement.[1]

**7.158** **Q. 48. How did Christ humble himself in his life?**

A. Christ humbled himself in his life, by subjecting himself to the law,[1] which he perfectly fulfilled,[2] and by conflicting with the indignities of the world,[3] temptations of Satan,[4] and infirmities in his flesh; whether common to the nature of man, or particularly accompanying that his low condition.[5]

**7.159** **Q. 49. How did Christ humble himself in his death?**

A. Christ humbled himself in his death, in that having been betrayed by Judas,[1] forsaken by his disciples,[2] scorned and rejected by the world,[3] condemned by Pilate, and tormented by his persecutors;[4] having also conflicted with the terrors of death and the powers of darkness, felt and borne the weight of God's wrath,[5] he laid down his life an offering for sin,[6] enduring the painful, shameful, and cursed death of the cross.[7]

**7.160** **Q. 50. Wherein consisted Christ's humiliation after his death?**

A. Christ's humiliation after his death consisted in his being buried,[1] and continuing in the state of the dead, and under the power of death till the third day,[2] which hath been otherwise expressed in these words: "He descended into hell."

**7.161** **Q. 51. What was the estate of Christ's exaltation?**

A. The estate of Christ's exaltation comprehendeth his resurrection,[1] ascension,[2] sitting at the right hand of the Father,[3] and his coming again to judge the world.[4]

**7.162** **Q. 52. How was Christ exalted in his resurrection?**

A. Christ was exalted in his resurrection, in that, not having seen corruption in death (of which it was not possible for him to be held),[1] and having the very same body in which he suffered, with the essential properties thereof[2] (but without mortality and other common infirmities belonging to this life), really united to his soul,[3] he rose again from the dead the third day by his own power;[4] whereby he declared himself to be the Son of God,[5] to have satisfied divine justice,[6] to have vanquished death and him that had the power of it,[7] and to be Lord of quick and dead.[8] All which he did as a public person,[9] the head of his Church,[10] for their justification,[11] quickening in grace,[12] support against enemies,[13] and to assure them of their resurrection from the dead at the last day.[14]

7.163 Q. 53. **How was Christ exalted in his ascension?**
A. Christ was exalted in his ascension, in that having, after his resurrection, often appeared unto, and conversed with his apostles, speaking to them of the things pertaining to the Kingdom of God,[1] and giving them commission to preach the gospel to all nations;[2] forty days after his resurrection, he, in our nature, and as our head, triumphing over enemies, visibly went up into the highest heavens,[3] there to receive gifts for men,[4] to raise up our affections thither,[5] and to prepare a place for us,[6] where himself is, and shall continue till his second coming at the end of the world.[7]

7.164 Q. 54. **How is Christ exalted in his sitting at the right hand of God?**
A. Christ is exalted in his sitting at the right hand of God, in that as God-man he is advanced to the highest favor with God the Father,[1] with all fullness of joy,[2] glory,[3] and power over all things in heaven and earth;[4] and doth gather and defend his Church, and subdue their enemies; furnisheth his ministers and people with gifts and graces,[5] and maketh intercession for them.[6]

7.165 Q. 55. **How doth Christ make intercession?**
A. Christ maketh intercession, by his appearing in our nature continually before the Father in heaven,[1] in the merit of his obedience and sacrifice on earth;[2] declaring his will to have it applied to all believers;[3] answering all accusations against them;[4] and procuring for them quiet of conscience, notwithstanding daily failings,[5] access with boldness to the throne of grace,[6] and acceptance of their persons[7] and services.[8]

7.166 Q. 56. **How is Christ to be exalted in his coming again to judge the world?**
A. Christ is to be exalted in his coming again to judge the world, in that he, who was unjustly judged and condemned by wicked men, shall come again at the last day in great power, and in the full manifestation of his own glory, and of his Father's, with all his holy angels, with a shout, with the voice of the archangel, and with the trumpet of God, to judge the world in righteousness.[1]

7.167 Q. 57. **What benefits hath Christ procured by his mediation?**
A. Christ by his mediation hath procured redemption, with all other benefits of the covenant of grace.[1]

7.168 Q. 58. **How do we come to be made partakers of the benefits which Christ hath procured?**
A. We are made partakers of the benefits which Christ hath procured, by the application of them unto us, which is the work especially of God the Holy Ghost.[1]

**7.169** Q. 59. Who are made partakers of redemption through Christ?

A. Redemption is certainly applied, and effectually communicated, to all those for whom Christ hath purchased it;[1] who are in time by the Holy Ghost enabled to believe in Christ, according to the gospel.[2]

**7.170** Q. 60. Can they who have never heard the gospel, and so know not Jesus Christ nor believe in him, be saved by their living according to the light of nature?

A. They who having never heard the gospel, know not Jesus Christ, and believe not in him, cannot be saved,[1] be they never so diligent to frame their lives according to the light of nature,[2] or the laws of that religion which they profess;[3] neither is there salvation in any other, but in Christ alone,[4] who is the Saviour only of his body the Church.[5]

**7.171** Q. 61. Are all they saved who hear the gospel, and live in the Church?

A. All that hear the gospel, and live in the visible Church, are not saved; but only they who are true members of the Church invisible.[1]

**7.172** Q. 62. What is the visible Church?

A. The visible Church is a society made up of all such as in all ages and places of the world do profess the true religion,[1] and of their children.[2]

**7.173** Q. 63. What are the special privileges of the visible Church?

A. The visible Church hath the privilege of being under God's special care and government;[1] of being protected and preserved in all ages, notwithstanding the opposition of all enemies;[2] and of enjoying the communion of saints, the ordinary means of salvation,[3] and offers of grace by Christ, to all members of it, in the ministry of the gospel, testifying that whosoever believes in him shall be saved,[4] and excluding none that will come unto him.[5]

**7.174** Q. 64. What is the invisible Church?

A. The invisible Church is the whole number of the elect, that have been, are, or shall be gathered into one under Christ the head.[1]

**7.175** Q. 65. What special benefits do the members of the invisible Church enjoy by Christ?

A. The members of the invisible Church, by Christ, enjoy union and communion with him in grace and glory.[1]

**7.176** Q. 66. What is that union which the elect have with Christ?

A. The union which the elect have with Christ is the work of God's grace,[1] whereby they are spiritually and mystically, yet really and inseparably, joined to Christ as their head and husband;[2] which is done in their effectual calling.[3]

**7.177** Q. 67. What is effectual calling?

A. Effectual calling is the work of God's almighty power and grace,[1] whereby (out of his free and especial love to his elect, and from nothing in them moving him thereunto)[2] he doth in his accepted time invite and draw them to Jesus Christ, by his Word and Spirit;[3] savingly enlightening their minds,[4] renewing and powerfully determining their wills,[5] so as they (although in themselves dead in sin) are hereby made willing and able, freely to answer his call, and to accept and embrace the grace offered and conveyed therein.[6]

**7.178** Q. 68. Are the elect only effectually called?

A. All the elect, and they only, are effectually called;[1] although others may be, and often are, outwardly called by the ministry of the Word,[2] and have some common operations of the Spirit,[3] who, for their willful neglect and contempt of the grace offered to them, being justly left in their unbelief, do never truly come to Jesus Christ.[4]

**7.179** Q. 69. What is the communion in grace, which the members of the invisible Church have with Christ?

A. The communion in grace, which the members of the invisible Church have with Christ, is their partaking of the virtue of his mediation, in their justification,[1] adoption,[2] sanctification, and whatever else in this life manifests their union with him.[3]

**7.180** Q. 70. What is justification?

A. Justification is an act of God's free grace unto sinners, in which he pardoneth all their sin, accepteth and accounteth their persons righteous in his sight;[1] not for anything wrought in them, or done by them,[2] but only for the perfect obedience and full satisfaction of Christ, by God imputed to them[3] and received by faith alone.[4]

**7.181** Q. 71. How is justification an act of God's free grace?

A. Although Christ by his obedience and death, did make a proper, real, and full satisfaction to God's justice in the behalf of them that are justified: yet inasmuch as God accepteth the satisfaction from a surety, which he might have demanded of them; and did provide this surety, his only Son, imputing his righteousness to them, and requiring nothing of them for their justification, but faith, which also is his gift, their justification is to them of free grace.[1]

**7.182** Q. 72. What is justifying faith?

A. Justifying faith is a saving grace,[1] wrought in the heart of a sinner, by the Spirit and the Word of God;[2] whereby he, being convinced of his sin and misery, and of the disability in himself and all other creatures to recover him out of his lost condition,[3] not only assenteth to the truth of the promise of the gospel,[4] but receiveth and resteth upon Christ and his righteousness therein held forth, for pardon of sin,[5] and for the accepting and accounting of his person righteous in the sight of God for salvation.[6]

7.183 Q. 73. **How doth faith justify a sinner in the sight of God?**

A. Faith justifies a sinner in the sight of God, not because of those other graces which do always accompany it, or of good works that are the fruits of it;[1] nor as if the grace of faith, or any act thereof, were imputed to him for justification;[2] but only as it is an instrument, by which he receiveth and applieth Christ and his righteousness.[3]

7.184 Q. 74. **What is adoption?**

A. Adoption is an act of the free grace of God,[1] in and for his only Son Jesus Christ,[2] whereby all those that are justified are received into the number of his children,[3] have his name put upon them,[4] the Spirit of his Son given to them,[5] are under his Fatherly care and dispensations,[6] admitted to all the liberties and privileges of the sons of God, made heirs of all the promises, and fellow heirs with Christ in glory.[7]

7.185 Q. 75. **What is sanctification?**

A. Sanctification is a work of God's grace, whereby they, whom God hath, before the foundation of the world, chosen to be holy, are, in time, through the powerful operation of his Spirit, applying the death and resurrection of Christ unto them, renewed in their whole man after the image of God;[1] having the seeds of repentance unto life, and all other saving graces, put into their hearts,[2] and those graces so stirred up, increased and strengthened,[3] as that they more and more die unto sin, and rise into newness of life.[4]

7.186 Q. 76. **What is repentance unto life?**

A. Repentance unto life is a saving grace,[1] wrought in the heart of a sinner by the Spirit and Word of God,[2] whereby out of the sight and sense, not only of the danger,[3] but also of the filthiness and odiousness of his sins,[4] and upon the apprehension of God's mercy in Christ to such as are penitent,[5] he so grieves for, and hates his sins,[6] as that he turns from them all to God,[7] purposing and endeavoring constantly to walk with him in all the ways of new obedience.[8]

7.187 Q. 77. **Wherein do justification and sanctification differ?**

A. Although sanctification be inseparably joined with justification,[1] yet they differ in that God, in justification, imputeth the righteousness of Christ;[2] in sanctification, his Spirit infuseth grace, and enableth to the exercise thereof;[3] in the former, sin is pardoned;[4] in the other, it is subdued;[5] the one doth equally free all believers from the revenging wrath of God, and that perfectly in this life, that they never fall into condemnation;[6] the other is neither equal in all,[7] nor in this life perfect in any,[8] but growing up to perfection.[9]

7.188 Q. 78. **Whence ariseth the imperfection of sanctification in believers?**

A. The imperfection of sanctification in believers ariseth from the remnants of sin abiding in every part of them, and the perpetual lusting of the flesh against the Spirit; whereby they are often foiled with temptations, and fall into many sins,[1] are hindered in all their spiritual service,[2] and their best works are imperfect and defiled in the sight of God.[3]

**7.189 Q. 79. May not true believers, by reason of their imperfections, and the many temptations and sins they are overtaken with, fall away from the state of grace?**

A. True believers, by reason of the unchangeable love of God,[1] and his decree and covenant to give them perseverance,[2] their inseparable union with Christ,[3] his continual intercession for them,[4] and the Spirit and seed of God abiding in them,[5] can neither totally nor finally fall away from the state of grace, but are kept by the power of God through faith unto salvation.[6]

**7.190 Q. 80. Can true believers be infallibly assured that they are in the estate of grace, and that they shall persevere therein unto salvation?**

A. Such as truly believe in Christ, and endeavor to walk in all good conscience before him, may, without extraordinary revelation, by faith grounded upon the truth of God's promises, and by the Spirit enabling them to discern in themselves those graces to which the promises of life are made, and bearing witness with their spirits that they are the children of God, be infallibly assured that they are in the estate of grace, and shall persevere therein unto salvation.[1]

**7.191 Q. 81. Are all true believers at all times assured of their present being in the estate of grace, and that they shall be saved?**

A. Assurance of grace and salvation not being of the essence of faith, true believers may wait long before they obtain it;[1] and, after the enjoyment thereof, may have it weakened and intermitted, through manifold distempers, sins, temptations, and desertions;[2] yet are they never left without such a presence and support of the Spirit of God, as keeps them from sinking into utter despair.[3]

**7.192 Q. 82. What is the communion in glory which the members of the invisible Church have with Christ?**

A. The communion in glory which the members of the invisible Church have with Christ, is in this life,[1] immediately after death,[2] and at last perfected at the resurrection and day of judgment.[3]

**7.193 Q. 83. What is the communion in glory with Christ, which the members of the invisible Church enjoy in this life?**

A. The members of the invisible Church have communicated to them, in this life, the first fruits of glory with Christ, as they are members of him their head, and so in him are interested in that glory which he is fully possessed of;[1] and as an earnest thereof, enjoy the sense of God's love,[2] peace of conscience, joy in the Holy Ghost, and hope of glory.³ As, on the contrary, the sense of God's revenging wrath, horror of conscience, and a fearful expectation of judgment, are to the wicked the beginning of the torment which they shall endure after death.⁴

7.194 Q. 84. Shall all men die?
A. Death being threatened as the wages of sin,¹ it is appointed unto all men once to die;² for that all have sinned.³

7.195 Q. 85. Death being the wages of sin, why are not the righteous delivered from death, seeing all their sins are forgiven in Christ?
A. The righteous shall be delivered from death itself at the last day, and even in death are delivered from the sting and curse of it;¹ so that although they die, yet it is out of God's love,² to free them perfectly from sin and misery,³ and to make them capable of further communion with Christ in glory, which they then enter upon.⁴

7.196 Q. 86. What is the communion in glory with Christ, which the members of the invisible Church enjoy immediately after death?
A. The communion in glory with Christ, which the members of the invisible Church enjoy immediately after death, is in that their souls are then made perfect in holiness, and received into the highest heavens, where they behold the face of God in light and glory;¹ waiting for the full redemption of their bodies,² which even in death continue united to Christ,³ and rest in their graves as in their beds, till at the last day they be again united to their souls.⁴ Whereas the souls of the wicked are at their death cast into hell, where they remain in torments and utter darkness; and their bodies kept in their graves, as in their prisons, until the resurrection and judgment of the great day.⁵

7.197 Q. 87. What are we to believe concerning the resurrection?
A. We are to believe that, at the last day, there shall be a general resurrection of the dead, both of the just and unjust;¹ when they that are then found alive shall in a moment be changed; and the selfsame bodies of the dead which are laid in the grave, being then again united to their souls forever, shall be raised up by the power of Christ.² The bodies of the just, by the Spirit of Christ, and by virtue of his resurrection as their head, shall be raised in power, spiritual, and incorruptible, and made like to his glorious body:³ and the bodies of the wicked shall be raised up in dishonor by him as an offended judge.⁴

7.198 Q. 88. What shall immediately follow after the resurrection?
A. Immediately after the resurrection shall follow the general and final judgment of angels and men,¹ the day and hour whereof no man knoweth, that all may watch and pray, and be ever ready for the coming of the Lord.²

7.199 Q. 89. What shall be done to the wicked at the day of judgment?

A. At the day of judgment, the wicked shall be set on Christ's left hand,[1] and upon clear evidence, and full conviction of their own consciences,[2] shall have the fearful but just sentence of condemnation pronounced against them;[3] and thereupon shall be cast out from the favorable presence of God, and the glorious fellowship with Christ, his saints, and all his holy angels, into hell, to be punished with unspeakable torments both of body and soul, with the devil and his angels forever.[4]

7.200 Q. 90. **What shall be done to the righteous at the day of judgment?**
A. At the day of judgment, the righteous, being caught up to Christ in the clouds,[1] shall be set on his right hand, and, there openly acknowledged and acquitted,[2] shall join with him in the judging of reprobate angels and men;[3] and shall be received into heaven,[4] where they shall be fully and forever freed from all sin and misery;[5] filled with inconceivable joy;[6] made perfectly holy and happy both in body and soul, in the company of innumerable saints and angels,[7] but especially in the immediate vision and fruition of God the Father, of our Lord Jesus Christ, and of the Holy Spirit, to all eternity.[8] And this is the perfect and full communion, which the members of the invisible Church shall enjoy with Christ in glory, at the resurrection and day of judgment.

Having Seen What the Scriptures Principally Teach Us to Believe Concerning God, It Follows to Consider What They Require as the Duty of Man

7.201 Q. 91. **What is the duty which God requireth of man?**
A. The duty which God requireth of man is obedience to his revealed will.[1]

7.202 Q. 92. **What did God at first reveal unto man as the rule of his obedience?**
A. The rule of obedience revealed to Adam in the estate of innocence, and to all mankind in him, besides a special command, not to eat of the fruit of the tree of knowledge of good and evil, was the moral law.[1]

7.203 Q. 93. **What is the moral law?**
A. The moral law is the declaration of the will of God to mankind, directing and binding everyone to personal, perfect, and perpetual conformity and obedience thereunto, in the frame and disposition of the whole man, soul and body, and in performance of all those duties of holiness and righteousness which he oweth to God and man:[1] promising life upon the fulfilling, and threatening death upon the breach of it.[2]

7.204 Q. 94. **Is there any use of the moral law to man since the Fall?**
A. Although no man since the Fall can attain to righteousness and life by the moral law,[1] yet there is great use thereof, as well common to all men, as peculiar either to the unregenerate, or the regenerate.[2]

7.205 Q. 95. **Of what use is the moral law to all men?**

A. The moral law is of use to all men, to inform them of the holy nature and will of God,[1] and of their duty binding them to walk accordingly;[2] to convince them of their disability to keep it, and of the sinful pollution of their nature, hearts, and lives,[3] to humble them in the sense of their sin and misery,[4] and thereby help them to a clearer sight of the need they have of Christ,[5] and of the perfection of his obedience.

**Q. 96. What particular use is there of the moral law to unregenerate men?**

A. The moral law is of use to unregenerate men, to awaken their consciences to flee from the wrath to come,[1] and to drive them to Christ;[2] or, upon their continuance in the estate and way of sin, to leave them inexcusable,[3] and under the curse thereof.[4]

**Q. 97. What special use is there of the moral law to the regenerate?**

A. Although they that are regenerate and believe in Christ be delivered from the moral law as a covenant of works, so as thereby they are neither justified nor condemned: yet, besides the general uses thereof common to them with all men, it is of special use to show them how much they are bound to Christ for his fulfilling it, and enduring the curse thereof, in their stead and for their good;[1] and thereby to provoke them to more thankfulness, and to express the same in their greater care to conform themselves thereunto as the rule of their obedience.[2]

**Q. 98. Wherein is the moral law summarily comprehended?**

A. The moral law is summarily comprehended in the Ten Commandments,[1] which were delivered by the voice of God upon Mount Sinai, and written by him on two tables of stone;[2] and are recorded in the twentieth chapter of Exodus; the first four commandments containing our duty to God, and the other six our duty to man.

**Q. 99. What rules are to be observed for the right understanding of the Ten Commandments?**

A. For the right understanding of the Ten Commandments, these rules are to be observed:

1. That the law is perfect, and bindeth everyone to full conformity in the whole man unto the righteousness thereof, and unto entire obedience forever; so as to require the utmost perfection of every duty, and to forbid the least degree of every sin.[1]

2. That it is spiritual, and so reacheth the understanding, will, affections, and all other powers of the soul; as well as words, works, and gestures.[1]

3. That one and the same thing, in divers respects, is required or forbidden in several commandments.[1]

4. That as, where a duty is commanded, the contrary sin is forbidden;[1] and where a sin is forbidden, the contrary duty is commanded;[2]

so, where a promise is annexed, the contrary threatening is included;[3] and where a threatening is annexed, the contrary promise is included.[4]

5. That what God forbids, is at no time to be done;[1] what he commands is always our duty;[2] and yet every particular duty is not to be done at all times.[3]

6. That, under one sin or duty, all of the same kind are forbidden or commanded; together with all the causes, means, occasions, and appearances thereof, and provocations thereunto.[1]

7. That what is forbidden or commanded to ourselves, we are bound, according to our places, to endeavor that it may be avoided or performed by others, according to the duty of their places.[1]

8. That in what is commanded to others, we are bound, according to our places and callings, to be helpful to them:[1] and to take heed of partaking with others in what is forbidden them.[2]

7.210 **Q. 100. What special things are we to consider in the Ten Commandments?**

A. We are to consider in the Ten Commandments: the preface, the substances of the commandments themselves, and the several reasons annexed to some of them the more to enforce them.

7.211 **Q. 101. What is the preface to the Ten Commandments?**

A. The preface to the Ten Commandments is contained in these words: "I am the Lord thy God, which have brought thee out of the land of Egypt, out of the house of bondage."[1] Wherein God manifesteth his sovereignty, as being Jehovah, the eternal, immutable, and almighty God; having his being in and of himself, and giving being to all his words and works; and that he is a God in covenant, as with Israel of old, so with all his people; who as he brought them out of their bondage in Egypt, so he delivered us from our spiritual thralldom; and that therefore we are bound to take him for our God alone, and to keep all his commandments.

7.212 **Q. 102. What is the sum of the four Commandments which contain our duty to God?**

A. The sum of the four Commandments containing our duty to God is, to love the Lord our God with all our heart, and with all our soul, and with all our strength, and with all our mind.[1]

7.213 **Q. 103. Which is the First Commandment?**

A. The First Commandment is, "Thou shalt have no other gods before me."[1]

7.214 **Q. 104. What are the duties required in the First Commandment?**

A. The duties required in the First Commandment[1] are: the knowing and acknowledging of God to be the only true God, and our God;[2] and to worship and glorify him accordingly;[3] by thinking,[4] meditating,[5] remembering,[6] highly esteeming,[7] honoring,[8] adoring,[9] choosing,[10] loving,[11] desiring,[12] fearing of him;[13] believing him;[14] trusting,[15] hoping,[16] delighting,[17] rejoicing in him;[18] being zealous for him;[19] calling upon him, giving all praise and thanks,[20] and yielding all obedience and submission to him with the whole man;[21] being careful in all things to please him,[22] and sorrowful when in anything he is offended;[23] and walking humbly with him.[24]

7.215  Q. 105. What are the sins forbidden in the First Commandment?

A. The sins forbidden in the First Commandment are: atheism, in denying or not having a God;[1] idolatry, in having or worshiping more gods than one, or any with, or instead of the true God;[2] the not having and vouching him for God, and our God;[3] the omission or neglect of anything due to him, required in this commandment;[4] ignorance,[5] forgetfulness,[6] misapprehensions, false opinions,[7] unworthy and wicked thoughts of him;[8] bold and curious searchings into his secrets;[9] all profaneness,[10] hatred of God,[11] self-love,[12] self-seeking,[13] and all other inordinate and immoderate setting of our mind, will, or affections upon other things, and taking them off from him in whole or in part;[14] vain credulity,[15] unbelief,[16] heresy,[17] misbelief,[18] distrust,[19] despair,[20] incorrigibleness, and insensibleness under judgments,[21] hardness of heart,[22] pride,[23] presumption,[24] carnal security,[25] tempting of God;[26] using unlawful means,[27] and trusting in lawful means;[28] carnal delights and joys,[29] corrupt, blind, and indiscreet zeal;[30] lukewarmness,[31] and deadness in the things of God;[32] estranging ourselves, and apostatizing from God;[33] praying or giving any religious worship to saints, angels, or any other creatures;[34] all compacts and consulting with the devil,[35] and hearkening to his suggestions;[36] making men the lords of our faith and conscience;[37] slighting and despising God, and his commands;[38] resisting and grieving of his Spirit,[39] discontent and impatience at his dispensations, charging him foolishly for the evils he inflicts on us;[40] and ascribing the praise of any good, we either are, have, or can do, to fortune, idols,[41] ourselves,[42] or any other creature.[43]

7.216  Q. 106. What are we especially taught by these words "before me," in the First Commandment?

A. These words "before me," or "before my face," in the First Commandment, teach us, that God, who seeth all things, taketh special notice of, and is much displeased with, the sin of having any other God; that so it may be an argument to dissuade from it, and to aggravate it as a most impudent provocation;[1] as also to persuade us to do as in his sight, whatever we do in his service.[2]

7.217  Q. 107. Which is the Second Commandment?

A. The Second Commandment is, "Thou shalt not make unto thee any graven image, or any likeness of any thing that is in heaven above, or that is in the earth beneath, or that is in the water under the earth: thou shalt not bow down thyself to them, nor serve them: for I the Lord thy God am a jealous God, visiting the iniquity of the fathers upon the children unto the third and fourth generation of them that hate me; and shewing mercy unto thousands of them that love me, and keep my commandments."[1]

7.218 Q. 108. **What are the duties required in the Second Commandment?**

A. The duties required in the Second Commandment are: the receiving, observing, and keeping pure and entire, all such religious worship and ordinances as God hath instituted in his Word;[1] particularly prayer and thanksgiving in the name of Christ;[2] the reading, preaching, and hearing of the Word;[3] the administration and receiving of the sacraments;[4] church government and discipline;[5] the ministry and maintenance thereof;[6] religious fasting;[7] swearing by the name of God;[8] and vowing unto him:[9] as also the disapproving, detesting, opposing all false worship;[10] and, according to each one's place and calling, removing it, and all monuments of idolatry.[11]

7.219 Q. 109. **What are the sins forbidden in the Second Commandment?**

A. The sins forbidden in the Second Commandment are: all devising,[1] counseling,[2] commanding,[3] using,[4] and any wise approving any religious worship not instituted by God himself;[5] the making any representation of God, of all, or of any of the three Persons, either inwardly in our mind, or outwardly in any kind of image or likeness of any creature whatsoever;[6] all worshiping of it,[7] or God in it or by it;[8] the making of any representation of feigned deities,[9] and all worship of them, or service belonging to them;[10] all superstitious devices,[11] corrupting the worship of God,[12] adding to it, or taking from it,[13] whether invented and taken up of ourselves,[14] or received by tradition from others,[15] though under the title of antiquity,[16] custom,[17] devotion,[18] good intent, or any other pretense whatsoever;[19] simony,[20] sacrilege;[21] all neglect,[22] contempt,[23] hindering,[24] and opposing the worship and ordinances which God hath appointed.[25]

7.220 Q. 110. **What are the reasons annexed to the Second Commandment, the more to enforce it?**

A. The reasons annexed to the Second Commandment, the more to enforce it, contained in these words, "For I the Lord thy God am a jealous God, visiting the iniquity of the fathers upon the children unto the third and fourth generation of them that hate me; and shewing mercy unto thousands of them that love me, and keep my commandments;"[1] are, besides God's sovereignty over us, and propriety in us, his revengeful indignation against all false worship,[2] as being a spiritual whoredom;[3] accounting the breakers of this Commandment such as hate him, and threatening to punish them unto divers generations,[4] and esteeming the observers of it such as love him and keep his commandments, and promising mercy to them unto many generations.[5]

7.221 **Q. 111. What is the Third Commandment?**
A. The Third Commandment is, "Thou shalt not take the name of the Lord thy God in vain; for the Lord will not hold him guiltless that taketh his name in vain."[1]

7.222 **Q. 112. What is required in the Third Commandment?**
A. The Third Commandment requires, that the name of God, his titles, attributes,[1] ordinances,[2] the word,[3] sacraments,[4] prayer,[5] oaths,[6] vows,[7] lots,[8] his works,[9] and whatsoever else there is whereby he makes himself known, be holily and reverently used in thought,[10] meditation,[11] word,[12] and writing;[13] by an holy profession,[14] and answerable conversation,[15] to the glory of God,[16] and the good of ourselves[17] and others.[18]

7.223 **Q. 113. What are the sins forbidden in the Third Commandment?**
A. The sins forbidden in the Third Commandment are: the not using of God's name as is required;[1] and the abuse of it in an ignorant,[2] vain,[3] irreverent, profane,[4] superstitious,[5] or wicked mentioning or otherwise using the titles, attributes,[6] ordinances,[7] or works;[8] by blasphemy;[9] perjury;[10] all sinful cursing,[11] oaths,[12] vows,[13] and lots;[14] violating our oaths and vows, if lawful;[15] and fulfilling them, if of things unlawful;[16] murmuring and quarreling at,[17] curious prying into,[18] and misapplying of God's decrees[19] and providence;[20] misinterpreting,[21] misapplying,[22] or any way perverting the Word, or any part of it,[23] to profane jests,[24] curious and unprofitable questions, vain janglings, or the maintaining of false doctrines;[25] abusing it, the creatures, or anything contained under the name of God, to charms,[26] or sinful lusts and practices;[27] the maligning,[28] scorning,[29] reviling,[30] or any way opposing of God's truth, grace, and ways;[31] making profession of religion in hypocrisy, or for sinister ends;[32] being ashamed of it,[33] or a shame to it, by uncomfortable,[34] unwise,[35] unfruitful,[36] and offensive walking[37] or backsliding from it.[38]

7.224 **Q. 114. What reasons are annexed to the Third Commandment?**
A. The reasons annexed to the Third Commandment, is these words, "the Lord thy God," and, "for the Lord will not hold him guiltless that taketh his name in vain,"[1] are because he is the Lord and our God, therefore his name is not to be profaned, or any way abused by us;[2] especially because he will be so far from acquitting and sparing the transgressors of this Commandment, as that he will not suffer them to escape his righteous judgment,[3] albeit many such escape the censures and punishments of men.[4]

7.225 **Q. 115. Which is the Fourth Commandment?**
A. The Fourth Commandment is, "Remember the sabbath day, to keep it holy. Six days shalt thou labour, and do all thy work: but the seventh day is the sabbath of the Lord thy God: in it thou shalt not do any work, thou, nor thy son, nor thy daughter, thy manservant, nor thy maidservant, nor thy cattle, nor thy stranger that is within thy gates; for

in six days the Lord made heaven and earth, the sea, and all that in them is, and rested the seventh day: wherefore the Lord blessed the sabbath day, and hallowed it."[1]

**7.226 Q. 116. What is required in the Fourth Commandment?**

A. The Fourth Commandment requireth of all men the sanctifying or keeping holy to God such set times as he hath appointed in his Word, expressly one whole day in seven;[1] which was the seventh from the beginning of the world to the resurrection of Christ,[2] and the first day of the week ever since, and so to continue to the end of the world; which is the Christian Sabbath,[3] and in the New Testament called "the Lord's Day."

**7.227 Q. 117. How is the Sabbath or Lord's Day to be sanctified?**

A. The Sabbath, or Lord's Day, is to be sanctified by an holy resting all that day,[1] not only from such works as are at all times sinful, but even from such worldly employments and recreations as are on other days lawful;[2] and making it our delight to spend the whole time (except so much of it as is to be taken up in works of necessity and mercy)[3] in the public and private exercise of God's worship.[4] And, to that end, we are to prepare our hearts, and with such foresight, diligence, and moderation, to dispose, and seasonably to dispatch our worldly business, that we may be the more free and fit for the duties of the day.[5]

**7.228 Q. 118. Why is the charge of keeping the Sabbath more specially directed to governors of families and other superiors?**

A. The charge of keeping the Sabbath is more specially directed to governors of families and other superiors, because they are bound not only to keep it themselves, but to see that it be observed by all those that are under their charge; and because they are prone ofttimes to hinder them by employments of their own.[1]

**7.229 Q. 119. What are the sins forbidden in the Fourth Commandment?**

A. The sins in the Fourth Commandment are: all omissions of the duties required,[1] all careless, negligent, and unprofitable performing of them, and being weary of them;[2] all profaning the day by idleness, and doing that which is in itself sinful;[3] and by all needless works, words, and thoughts about our worldly employments and recreations.[4]

**7.230 Q. 120. What are the reasons annexed to the Fourth Commandment, the more to enforce it?**

A. The reasons annexed to the Fourth Commandment, the more to enforce it, are taken from the equity of it, God allowing us six days of seven for our own affairs, and reserving but one for himself, in these words, "Six days shalt thou labour, and do all thy work;"[1] from God's challenging a special propriety in that day. "The seventh day is the sabbath of the Lord thy God;"[2] from the example of God who "in six days ... made heaven and earth, the sea, and all that in them is, and rested the seventh day"; and from that blessing which God put upon that day, not only in sanctifying it to be a holy day for his service, but in ordaining it to be a means of blessing to us in our sanctifying it, "wherefore the Lord blessed the sabbath day, and hallowed it."[3]

**7.231 Q. 121. Why is the word "remember" set in the beginning of the Fourth Commandment?**

A. The word "remember" is set in the beginning of the Fourth Commandment,[1] partly because of the great benefit of remembering it, we being thereby helped in our preparation to keep it;[2] and, in keeping it, better to keep all the rest of the Commandments[3] and to continue a thankful remembrance of the two great benefits of creation and redemption, which contain a short abridgement of religion:[4] and partly because we are ready to forget it,[5] for that there is less light of nature for it, and yet it restraineth our natural liberty in things at other times lawful;[6] that it cometh but once in seven days, and many worldly businesses come between, and too often take off our minds from thinking of it, either to prepare for it, or to sanctify it;[7] and that Satan with his instruments much labor to blot out the glory, and even the memory of it, and to bring in all irreligion and impiety.[8]

**7.232 Q. 122. What is the sum of the six Commandments which contain our duty to man?**

A. The sum of the six Commandments which contain our duty to man is, to love our neighbor as ourselves,[1] and to do to others what we would have them to do to us.[2]

**7.233 Q. 123. Which is the Fifth Commandment?**

A. The Fifth Commandment is, "Honour thy father and thy mother: that thy days may be long upon the land which the Lord thy God giveth thee."[1]

**7.234 Q. 124. Who are meant by "father" and "mother," in the Fifth Commandment?**

A. By "father" and "mother" in the Fifth Commandment, are meant not only natural parents, but all superiors in age[1] and gifts;[2] and especially such as by God's ordinance are over us in place of authority, whether in family,[3] church,[4] or commonwealth.[5]

**7.235 Q. 125. Why are superiors styled "father" and "mother"?**

A. Superiors are styled "father" and "mother" both to teach them in all duties towards their inferiors, like natural parents, to express love and tenderness to them, according to their several relations,[1] and to work inferiors to a greater willingness and cheerfulness in performing their duties to their superiors, as to their parents.[2]

7.236   Q. 126. What is the general scope of the Fifth Commandment?
A. The general scope of the Fifth Commandment is, the performance of those duties which we mutually owe in our several relations, as inferiors, superiors, or equals.[1]

7.237   Q. 127. What is the honor which inferiors owe to superiors?
A. The honor which inferiors owe to their superiors is: all due reverence in heart,[1] word,[2] and behavior;[3] prayer and thanksgiving for them;[4] imitation of their virtues and graces;[5] willing obedience to their lawful commands and counsels,[6] due submission to their corrections;[7] fidelity to,[8] defense and maintenance of their persons and authority, according to their several ranks, and the nature of their places;[9] bearing with their infirmities, and covering them in love,[10] that so they may be an honor to them and to their government.[11]

7.238   Q. 128. What are the sins of inferiors against their superiors?
A. The sins of inferiors against their superiors are: all neglect of the duties required toward them;[1] envying at,[2] contempt of,[3] and rebellion[4] against their persons[5] and places,[6] in their lawful counsels,[7] commands, and corrections;[8] cursing, mocking,[9] and all such refractory and scandalous carriage, as proves a shame and dishonor to them and their government.[10]

7.239   Q. 129. What is required of superiors towards their inferiors?
A. It is required of superiors, according to that power they receive from God, and that relation wherein they stand, to love,[1] pray for,[2] and bless their inferiors;[3] to instruct,[4] counsel, and admonish them;[5] countenancing,[6] commending, and rewarding such as do well;[7] and discountenancing,[8] reproving, and chastising such as do ill;[9] protecting, and providing for them all things necessary for soul and body;[10] and, by grave, wise, holy, and exemplary carriage, to procure glory to God,[11] honor to themselves,[12] and so to preserve that authority which God hath put upon them.[13]

7.240   Q. 130. What are the sins of superiors?
A. The sins of superiors are, besides the neglect of the duties required of them[1] an inordinate seeking of themselves,[2] their own glory,[3] ease, profit or pleasure;[4] commanding things unlawful,[5] or not in the power of inferiors to perform;[6] counseling,[7] encouraging,[8] or favoring them in that which is evil;[9] dissuading, discouraging, or discountenancing them in that which is good;[10] correcting them unduly;[11] careless exposing or leaving them to wrong, temptation, and danger;[12] provoking them to wrath;[13] or any way dishonoring themselves, or lessening their authority, by an unjust, indiscreet, rigorous, or remiss behavior.[14]

7.241   Q. 131. What are the duties of equals?
A. The duties of equals are: to regard the dignity and worth of each other,[1] in giving honor to go one before another,[2] and to rejoice in each other's gifts and advancement as their own.[3]

**7.242**     **Q. 132. What are the sins of equals?**
A. The sins of equals are, besides the neglect of the duties required,[1] the undervaluing of the worth,[2] envying the gifts,[3] grieving at the advancement or prosperity one of another,[4] and usurping preeminence one over another.[5]

**7.243**     **Q. 133. What is the reason annexed to the Fifth Commandment the more to enforce it?**
A. The reason annexed to the Fifth Commandment in these words, "that thy days may be long upon the land which the Lord thy God giveth thee,"[1] is an express promise of long life and prosperity, as far as it shall serve for God's glory and their own good, to all such as keep this Commandment.[2]

**7.244**     **Q. 134. Which is the Sixth Commandment?**
A. The Sixth Commandment is, "Thou shalt not kill."[1]

**7.245**     **Q. 135. What are the duties required in the Sixth Commandment?**
A. The duties required in the Sixth Commandment are: all careful studies and lawful endeavors, to preserve the life of ourselves[1] and others,[2] by resisting all thoughts and purposes,[3] subduing all passions,[4] and avoiding all occasions,[5] temptations,[6] and practices, which tend to the unjust taking away the life of any;[7] by just defense thereof against violence;[8] patient bearing of the hand of God,[9] quietness of mind,[10] cheerfulness of spirit,[11] a sober use of meat,[12] drink,[13] physic,[14] sleep,[15] labor,[16] and recreation;[17] by charitable thoughts,[18] love,[19] compassion,[20] meekness, gentleness, kindness;[21] peaceable,[22] mild, and courteous speeches and behavior,[23] forbearance, readiness to be reconciled, patient bearing and forgiving of injuries, and requiting good for evil;[24] comforting and succoring the distressed, and protecting and defending the innocent.[25]

**7.246**     **Q. 136. What are the sins forbidden in the Sixth Commandment?**
A. The sins forbidden in the Sixth Commandment are: all taking away the life of ourselves,[1] or of others,[2] except in case of public justice,[3] lawful war,[4] or necessary defense;[5] the neglecting or withdrawing the lawful or necessary means of preservation of life;[6] sinful anger,[7] hatred,[8] envy,[9] desire of revenge;[10] all excessive passions;[11] distracting cares;[12] immoderate use of meat, drink,[13] labor,[14] and recreation;[15] provoking words;[16] oppression,[17] quarreling,[18] striking, wounding,[19] and whatsoever else tends to the destruction of the life of any.[20]

**7.247**     **Q. 137. Which is the Seventh Commandment?**
A. The Seventh Commandment is, "Thou shalt not commit adultery."[1]

**7.248** Q. 138. What are the duties required in the Seventh Commandment?

A. The duties required in the Seventh Commandment are: chastity in body, mind, affections,[1] words,[2] and behavior,[3] and the preservation of it in ourselves and others;[4] watchfulness over the eyes and all the senses;[5] temperance,[6] keeping of chaste company,[7] modesty in apparel,[8] marriage by those that have not the gift of continency,[9] conjugal love,[10] and cohabitation;[11] diligent labor in our callings;[12] shunning of all occasions of uncleanness, and resisting temptations thereunto.[13]

**7.249** Q. 139. What are the sins forbidden in the Seventh Commandment?

A. The sins forbidden in the Seventh Commandment, besides the neglect of the duties required,[1] are: adultery, fornication,[2] rape, incest,[3] sodomy, and all unnatural lusts;[4] all unclean imaginations, thoughts, purposes, and affections;[5] all corrupt or filthy communications, or listening thereunto;[6] wanton looks,[7] impudent or light behavior, immodest apparel,[8] prohibiting of lawful,[9] and dispensing with unlawful marriages;[10] allowing, tolerating, keeping of stews, and resorting to them;[11] entangling vows of single life,[12] undue delay of marriage;[13] having more wives or husbands than one at the same time;[14] unjust divorce[15] or desertion;[16] idleness, gluttony, drunkenness,[17] unchaste company;[18] lascivious songs, books, pictures, dancings, stageplays,[19] and all other provocations to, or acts of, uncleanness either in ourselves or others.[20]

**7.250** Q. 140. Which is the Eighth Commandment?

A. The Eighth Commandment is, "Thou shalt not steal."[1]

**7.251** Q. 141. What are the duties required in the Eighth Commandment?

A. The duties required in the Eighth Commandment are: truth, faithfulness, and justice in contracts and commerce between man and man;[1] rendering to everyone his due;[2] restitution of goods unlawfully detained from the right owners thereof;[3] giving and lending freely, according to our abilities, and the necessities of others;[4] moderation of our judgments, wills, and affections, concerning worldly goods;[5] a provident care and study to get,[6] keep, use, and dispose of those things which are necessary and convenient for the sustentation of our nature, and suitable to our condition;[7] a lawful calling,[8] and a diligence in it;[9] frugality;[10] avoiding unnecessary lawsuits,[11] and suretyship, or other like engagements;[12] and an endeavor by all just and lawful means to procure, preserve, and further the wealth and outward estate of others, as well as our own.[13]

**7.252** Q. 142. What are the sins forbidden in the Eighth Commandment?

A. The sins forbidden in the Eighth Commandment besides the neglect of duties required,[1] are: theft,[2] robbery,[3] man-stealing,[4] and receiving anything that is stolen;[5] fraudulent dealing,[6] false weights and measures,[7] removing landmarks,[8] injustice and unfaithfulness in contracts between man and man,[9] or in matters of trust;[10] oppression,[11] extortion, usury,[12] bribery,[13] vexatious lawsuits,[14] unjust enclosures and depopulations;[15] engrossing commodities to enhance the price,[16] unlawful callings,[17] and all other unjust or sinful ways of taking or withholding from our neighbor what belongs to him, or of enriching ourselves;[18] covetousness,[19] inordinate prizing and affecting worldly goods;[20] distrustful and distracting cares and studies in getting, keeping, and using them;[21] envying at the prosperity of others;[22] as likewise idleness,[23] prodigality, wasteful gaming, and all other ways whereby we do unduly prejudice our own outward estate;[24] and defrauding ourselves of the due use and comfort of that estate which God hath given us.[25]

7.253 Q. 143. Which is the Ninth Commandment?
A. The Ninth Commandment is, "Thou shalt not bear false witness against thy neighbour."[1]

7.254 Q. 144. What are the duties required in the Ninth Commandment?
A. The duties required in the Ninth Commandment are: the preserving and promoting of truth between man and man,[1] and the good name of our neighbor, as well as our own;[2] appearing and standing for the truth;[3] and from the heart, sincerely,[4] freely,[5] clearly,[6] and fully,[7] speaking the truth, and only the truth, in matters of judgment and justice,[8] and in all other things whatsoever;[9] a charitable esteem of our neighbors,[10] loving, desiring, and rejoicing in their good name;[11] sorrowing for,[12] and covering of their infirmities;[13] freely acknowledging of their gifts and graces,[14] defending their innocency;[15] a ready receiving of good report,[16] and unwillingness to admit of an evil report concerning them;[17] discouraging talebearers,[18] flatterers,[19] and slanderers;[20] love and care of our own good name, and defending it when need requireth;[21] keeping of lawful promises;[22] studying and practicing of whatsoever things are true, honest, lovely, and of good report.[23]

7.255 Q. 145. What are the sins forbidden in the Ninth Commandment?
A. The sins forbidden in the Ninth Commandment are: all prejudicing of the truth, and the good name of our neighbors as well as our own,[1] especially in public judicature;[2] giving false evidence,[3] suborning false witnesses,[4] wittingly appearing and pleading for an evil cause, outfacing and overbearing the truth;[5] passing unjust sentence,[6] calling evil good, and good evil; rewarding the wicked according to the work of the righteous, and the righteous according to the work of the wicked;[7] forgery,[8] concealing the truth, undue silence in a just cause,[9] and holding our peace when iniquity calleth for either a reproof from ourselves,[10] or complaint to others;[11] speaking the truth unseasonably,[12] or maliciously to a wrong end,[13] or perverting it to a wrong meaning,[14] or

in doubtful and equivocal expression, to the prejudice of truth or justice;[15] speaking untruth,[16] lying,[17] slandering,[18] backbiting,[19] detracting,[20] talebearing,[21] whispering,[22] scoffing,[23] reviling;[24] rash,[25] harsh,[26] and partial censuring;[27] misconstruing intentions, words, and actions;[28] flattering,[29] vainglorious boasting,[30] thinking or speaking too highly or too meanly of ourselves or others; denying the gifts and graces of God;[31] aggravating smaller faults;[32] hiding, excusing, or extenuating of sins, when called to a free confession;[33] unnecessarily discovering of infirmities;[34] raising false rumors;[35] receiving and countenancing evil reports,[36] and stopping our ears against just defense;[37] evil suspicion;[38] envying or grieving at the deserved credit of any;[39] endeavoring or desiring to impair it,[40] rejoicing in their disgrace and infamy;[41] scornful contempt,[42] fond admiration,[43] breach of lawful promises;[44] neglecting such things as are of good report;[45] and practicing or not avoiding ourselves, or not hindering what we can in others, such things as procure an ill name.[46]

7.256    Q. 146. Which is the Tenth Commandment?

A. The Tenth Commandment is, "Thou shalt not covet thy neighbour's house, thou shalt not covet thy neighbour's wife, nor his manservant, nor his maidservant, nor his ox, nor his ass, nor any thing that is thy neighbour's."[1]

7.257    Q. 147. What are the duties required in the Tenth Commandment?

A. The duties required in the Tenth Commandment are: such a full contentment with our own condition,[1] and such a charitable frame of the whole soul towards our neighbor, as that all our inward motions and affections touching him, tend unto and further all that good which is his.[2]

7.258    Q. 148. What are the sins forbidden in the Tenth Commandment?

A. The sins forbidden in the Tenth Commandment are: discontentment with our own estate;[1] envying,[2] and grieving at the good of our neighbor,[3] together with all inordinate motions and affections to anything that is his.[4]

7.259    Q. 149. Is any man able perfectly to keep the Commandments of God?

A. No man is able, either of himself,[1] or by any grace received in this life, perfectly to keep the Commandments of God;[2] but doth daily break them in thought,[3] word, and deed.[4]

7.260    Q. 150. Are all transgressions of the law of God equally heinous in themselves, and in the sight of God?

A. All transgressions of the law of God are not equally heinous; but some sins in themselves, and by reason of several aggravations, are more heinous in the sight of God than others.[1]

7.261 Q. 151. **What are those aggravations that make some sins more heinous than others?**

A. Sins receive their aggravations,

1. From the persons offending:[1] if they be of riper age, greater experience, or grace;[2] eminent for profession,[3] gifts,[4] place, office,[5] guides to others,[6] and whose example is likely to be followed by others.[7]

2. From the parties offended:[8] if immediately against God,[9] his attributes,[10] and worship;[11] against Christ, and his grace:[12] the Holy Spirit, his witness, and workings;[13] against superiors, men of eminency,[14] and such as we stand especially related and engaged unto;[15] against any of the saints,[16] particularly weak brethren, the souls of them or any other;[17] and the common good of all or many.[18]

3. From the nature and quality of the offense:[19] if it be against the express letter of the law,[20] break many commandments, contain in it many sins:[21] if not only conceived in the heart, but break forth in words and actions,[22] scandalize others,[23] and admit no reparation:[24] if against means,[25] mercies,[26] judgments,[27] light of nature,[28] conviction of conscience,[29] public or private admonition,[30] censures of the church,[31] civil punishments;[32] and our prayers, purposes, promises, vows, covenants, and engagements to God or men:[33] if done deliberately, willfully,[34] presumptuously, impudently, boastingly,[35] maliciously,[36] frequently,[37] obstinately,[38] with light,[39] continuance,[40] or relapsing after repentance.[41]

4. From circumstances of time,[42] and place:[43] if on the Lord's Day,[44] or other times of divine worship;[45] or immediately before,[46] or after these,[47] or other helps to prevent or remedy such miscarriages;[48] if in public, or in the presence of others, who are thereby likely to be provoked or defiled.[49]

7.262 Q. 152. **What doth every sin deserve at the hands of God?**

A. Every sin, even the least,[1] being against the sovereignty,[2] goodness,[3] and holiness of God,[4] and against his righteous law,[5] deserveth his wrath and curse,[6] both in this life,[7] and that which is to come;[8] and cannot be expiated but by the blood of Christ.[9]

7.263 Q. 153. **What doth God require of us, that we may escape his wrath and curse due to us by reason of the transgression of the law?**

A. That we may escape the wrath and curse of God due to us by reason of the transgression of the law, he requireth of us repentance towards God, and faith towards our Lord Jesus Christ,[1] and the diligent use of the outward means whereby Christ communicates to us the benefits of his mediation.[2]

7.264 Q. 154. **What are the outward means whereby Christ communicates to us the benefits of his mediation?**

A. The outward and ordinary means, whereby Christ communicates to his Church the benefits of his mediation, are all his ordinances, especially the Word, sacraments, and prayer, all which are made effectual to the elect for their salvation.[1]

**Q. 155. How is the Word made effectual to salvation?**
A. The Spirit of God maketh the reading, but especially the preaching of the Word, an effectual means of enlightening, convincing, and humbling sinners,[1] of driving them out of themselves, and drawing them unto Christ,[2] of conforming them to his image,[3] and subduing them to his will;[4] of strengthening them against temptations and corruptions;[5] of building them up in grace,[6] and establishing their hearts in holiness and comfort through faith unto salvation.[7]

**Q. 156. Is the Word of God to be read by all?**
A. Although all are not permitted to read the Word publicly to the congregation, yet all sorts of people are bound to read it apart by themselves,[1] and with their families;[2] to which end, the Holy Scriptures are to be translated out of the original into the language of every people unto whom they come.[3]

**Q. 157. How is the Word of God to be read?**
A. The Holy Scriptures are to be read with an high and reverent esteem of them;[1] with a firm persuasion that they are the very Word of God,[2] and that he only can enable us to understand them;[3] with desire to know, believe, and obey, the will of God revealed in them;[4] with diligence,[5] and attention to the matter and scope of them;[6] with meditation,[7] application,[8] self-denial,[9] and prayer.[10]

**Q. 158. By whom is the Word of God to be preached?**
A. The Word of God is to be preached only by such as are sufficiently gifted,[1] and also duly approved and called to that office.[2]

**Q. 159. How is the Word of God to be preached by those that are called thereunto?**
A. They that are called to labor in the ministry of the Word are to preach sound doctrine,[1] diligently, in season, and out of season,[2] plainly,[3] not in the enticing word of man's wisdom, but in demonstration of the Spirit, and of power;[4] faithfully,[5] making known the whole counsel of God;[6] wisely,[7] applying themselves to the necessities and capacities of the hearers;[8] zealously,[9] with fervent love to God,[10] and the souls of his people;[11] sincerely,[12] aiming at his glory,[13] and their conversion,[14] edification,[15] and salvation.[16]

**Q. 160. What is required of those that hear the Word preached?**
A. It is required of those that hear the Word preached, that they attend upon it with diligence,[1] preparation,[2] and prayer;[3] examine what they hear by the Scriptures;[4] receive the truth with faith,[5] love,[6] meekness,[7] and readiness of mind,[8] as the Word of God;[9] meditate,[10] and confer of it;[11] hide it in their hearts,[12] and bring forth the fruit of it in their lives.[13]

**7.271**   Q. 161. How do the sacraments become effectual means of salvation?

A. The sacraments become effectual means of salvation, not by any power in themselves or any virtue derived from the piety or intention of him by whom they are administered; but only by the working of the Holy Ghost, and the blessing of Christ by whom they are instituted.[1]

**7.272**   Q. 162. What is a sacrament?

A. A sacrament is an holy ordinance instituted by Christ in his Church,[1] to signify, seal and exhibit[2] unto those that are within the covenant of grace,[3] the benefits of his mediation;[4] to strengthen and increase their faith and all other graces;[5] to oblige them to obedience;[6] to testify and cherish their love and communion one with another,[7] and to distinguish them from those that are without.[8]

**7.273**   Q. 163. What are the parts of a sacrament?

A. The parts of a sacrament are two: the one, an outward and sensible sign used according to Christ's own appointment; the other, an inward and spiritual grace thereby signified.[1]

**7.274**   Q. 164. How many sacraments hath Christ instituted under the New Testament?

A. Under the New Testament Christ hath instituted in his Church only two sacraments, Baptism, and the Lord's Supper.[1]

**7.275**   Q. 165. What is Baptism?

A. Baptism is a sacrament of the New Testament, wherein Christ hath ordained the washing with water in the name of the Father, and of the Son, and of the Holy Ghost,[1] to be a sign and seal of ingrafting into himself,[2] of remission of sins by his blood,[3] and regeneration by his Spirit;[4] of adoption,[5] and resurrection unto everlasting life:[6] and whereby the parties baptized are solemnly admitted into the visible Church,[7] and enter into an open and professed engagement to be wholly and only the Lord's.[8]

**7.276**   Q. 166. Unto whom is Baptism to be administered?

A. Baptism is not to be administered to any that are out of the visible Church, and so strangers from the covenant of promise, till they profess their faith in Christ, and obedience to him;[1] but infants descending from parents, either both or but one of them, professing faith in Christ, and obedience to him, are, in that respect, within the covenant, and are to be baptized.[2]

**7.277**   Q. 167. How is our Baptism to be improved by us?

A. The needful but much neglected duty of improving our Baptism, is to be performed by us all our life long, especially in the time of temptation,[1] and when we are present at the administration of it to others, by serious and thankful consideration of the nature of it and of the ends for which Christ instituted it, the privileges and benefits conferred and sealed thereby, and our solemn vow made therein;[2] by being humbled for our sinful defilement, our falling short of, and walking contrary to, the grace of Baptism and our engagements;[3] by growing up to assurance of pardon of sin, and of all other blessings sealed to us in that sacrament;[4] by drawing strength from the death and resurrection of Christ, into whom we are baptized, for the mortifying of sin, and quickening of grace;[5] and by endeavoring to live by faith,[6] to have our conversation in holiness and righteousness,[7] as those that have therein given up their names to Christ, and to walk in brotherly love, as being baptized by the same Spirit into one body.[8]

7.278 Q. 168. **What is the Lord's Supper?**

A. The Lord's Supper is a sacrament of the New Testament, wherein by giving and receiving bread and wine according to the appointment of Jesus Christ, his death is showed forth;[1] and they that worthily communicate, feed upon his body and blood to their spiritual nourishment and growth in grace;[2] have their union and communion with him confirmed; testify and renew their thankfulness and engagement to God,[3] and their mutual love and fellowship each with other, as members of the same mystical body.[4]

7.279 Q. 169. **How hath Christ appointed bread and wine to be given and received in the sacrament of the Lord's Supper?**

A. Christ hath appointed the ministers of his Word in the administration of this sacrament of the Lord's Supper, to set apart the bread and wine from common use by the word of institution, thanksgiving, and prayer; to take and break the bread, and to give both the bread and the wine to the communicants; who are by the same appointment to take and eat the bread, and to drink the wine; in thankful remembrance that the body of Christ was broken and given, and his blood shed for them.[1]

7.280 Q. 170. **How do they that worthily communicate in the Lord's Supper feed upon the body and blood of Christ therein?**

A. As the body and the blood of Christ are not corporally or carnally present in, with, or under the bread and wine in the Lord's Supper;[1] and yet are spiritually present to the faith of the receiver, no less truly and really than the elements themselves are to their outward senses;[2] so they that worthily communicate in the sacrament of the Lord's Supper, do therein feed upon the body and blood of Christ, not after a corporal or carnal, but in a spiritual manner; yet truly and really,[3] while by faith they receive and apply unto themselves Christ crucified, and all the benefits of his death.[4]

7.281 Q. 171. **How are they that receive the sacrament of the Lord's Supper to prepare themselves before they come unto it?**

A. They that receive the sacrament of the Lord's Supper are, before they come, to prepare themselves thereunto; by examining themselves,[1] of their being in Christ,[2] of their sins and wants;[3] of the truth and measure of their knowledge,[4] faith,[5] repentance,[6] love to God and the brethren,[7] charity to all men,[8] forgiving those that have done them wrong;[9] of their desires after Christ,[10] and of their new obedience;[11] and by renewing the exercise of these graces,[12] by serious meditation,[13] and fervent prayer.[14]

7.282 Q. 172. **May one who doubteth of his being in Christ, or of his due preparation, come to the Lord's Supper?**

A. One who doubteth of his being in Christ, or of his due preparation to the sacrament of the Lord's Supper, may have true interest in Christ, though he be not yet assured thereof;[1] and in God's account hath it, if he be duly affected with the apprehension of the want of it,[2] and unfeignedly desirous to be found in Christ,[3] and to depart from iniquity;[4] in which case (because promises are made, and this sacrament is appointed, for the relief even of weak and doubting Christians)[5] he is to bewail his unbelief,[6] and labor to have his doubts resolved;[7] and so doing, he may and ought to come to the Lord's Supper, that he may be further strengthened.[8]

7.283 Q. 173. **May any who profess the faith, and desire to come to the Lord's Supper, be kept from it?**

A. Such as are found to be ignorant or scandalous, notwithstanding their profession of the faith, and desire to come to the Lord's Supper, may and ought to be kept from that sacrament by the power which Christ hath left in his Church,[1] until they receive instruction, and manifest their reformation.[2]

7.284 Q. 174. **What is required of them that receive the sacrament of the Lord's Supper in the time of the administration of it?**

A. It is required of them that receive the sacrament of the Lord's Supper that, during the time of the administration of it, with all holy reverence and attention, they wait upon God in that ordinance; diligently observe the sacramental elements and actions;[1] heedfully discern the Lord's body,[2] and affectionately meditate upon his death and sufferings,[3] and thereby stir up themselves to a vigorous exercise of their graces; in judging themselves,[4] and sorrowing for sin;[5] in earnest hungering and thirsting after Christ,[6] feeding on him by faith,[7] receiving of his fullness,[8] trusting in his merits,[9] rejoicing in his love,[10] giving thanks for his grace;[11] in renewing of their covenant with God,[12] and love to all the saints.[13]

7.285 Q. 175. **What is the duty of Christians after they have received the sacrament of the Lord's Supper?**

A. The duty of Christians after they have received the sacrament of the Lord's Supper, is seriously to consider how they have behaved themselves therein, and with what success;[1] if they find quickening and comfort, to bless God for it,[2] beg the continuance of it, watch against relapse,³ fulfill their vows,⁴ and encourage themselves to a frequent attendance on that ordinance:⁵ but if they find no present benefit, more exactly to review their preparation to, and carriage at, the sacrament;⁶ in both which if they can approve themselves to God and their own consciences, they are to wait for the fruit of it in due time;⁷ but if they see that they have failed in either, they are to be humbled,⁸ and to attend upon it afterward with more care and diligence.⁹

**7.286**    **Q. 176. Wherein do the sacraments of Baptism and the Lord's Supper agree?**
A. The sacraments of Baptism and the Lord's Supper agree, in that the author of both is God;¹ the spiritual part of both is Christ and his benefits;² both are seals of the same covenant,³ are to be dispensed by ministers of the gospel and by none other,⁴ and to be continued in the Church of Christ until his second coming.⁵

**7.287**    **Q. 177. Wherein do the sacraments of Baptism and the Lord's Supper differ?**
A. The sacraments of Baptism and the Lord's Supper differ, in that Baptism is to be administered but once, with water, to be a sign and seal of our regeneration and ingrafting into Christ,¹ and that even to infants;² whereas the Lord's Supper is to be administered often, in the elements of bread and wine, to represent and exhibit Christ as spiritual nourishment to the soul,³ and to confirm our continuance and growth in him,⁴ and that only to such as are of years and ability to examine themselves.⁵

**7.288**    **Q. 178. What is prayer?**
A. Prayer is an offering up of our desires unto God,¹ in the name of Christ,² by the help of his Spirit,³ with confession of our sins,⁴ and thankful acknowledgment of his mercies.⁵

**7.289**    **Q. 179. Are we to pray unto God only?**
A. God only being able to search the heart,¹ hear the requests,² pardon the sins,³ and fulfill the desires of all,⁴ and only to be believed in,⁵ and worshiped with religious worship;⁶ prayer, which is a special part thereof,⁷ is to be made by all to him alone, and to none other.⁸

**7.290**    **Q. 180. What is it to pray in the name of Christ?**
A. To pray in the name of Christ is, in obedience to his command, and in confidence on his promises, to ask mercy for his sake;¹ not by bare mentioning of his name;² but by drawing our encouragement to pray, and our boldness, strength, and hope of acceptance in prayer, from Christ and his mediation.³

**7.291**    **Q. 181. Why are we to pray in the name of Christ?**
A. The sinfulness of man, and his distance from God by reason thereof, being so great, as that we can have no access into his presence without a mediator, and there being none in heaven or earth appointed

to, or fit for, that glorious work but Christ alone, we are to pray in no other name but his only.[1]

7.292 Q. 182. How doth the Spirit help us to pray?
A. We not knowing what to pray for as we ought, the Spirit helpeth our infirmities, by enabling us to understand both for whom, and what, and how prayer is to be made; and by working and quickening in our hearts (although not in all persons, nor at all times in the same measure) those apprehensions, affections, and graces, which are requisite for the right performance of that duty.[1]

7.293 Q. 183. For whom are we to pray?
A. We are to pray for the whole Church of Christ upon earth,[1] for magistrates,[2] and ministers,[3] for ourselves,[4] our brethren,[5] yea, our enemies,[6] and for all sorts of men living,[7] or that shall live hereafter;[8] but not for the dead.[9]

7.294 Q. 184. For what things are we to pray?
A. We are to pray for all things tending to the glory of God,[1] the welfare of the church,[2] our own[3] or others' good;[4] but not for anything that is unlawful.[5]

7.295 Q. 185. How are we to pray?
A. We are to pray with an awful apprehension of the majesty of God,[1] and deep sense of our own unworthiness,[2] necessities,[3] and sins;[4] with penitent,[5] thankful,[6] and enlarged hearts;[7] with understanding,[8] faith,[9] sincerity,[10] fervency,[11] love,[12] and perseverance,[13] waiting upon him[14] with humble submission to his will.[15]

7.296 Q. 186. What rule hath God given for our direction in the duty of prayer?
A. The whole Word of God is of use to direct us in the duty of praying;[1] but the special rule of direction is that form of prayer which our Saviour Christ taught his disciples, commonly called, "the Lord's Prayer."[2]

7.297 Q. 187. How is the Lord's Prayer to be used?
A. The Lord's Prayer is not only for direction, as a pattern according to which we are to make other prayers; but may be also used as a prayer so that it be done with understanding, faith, reverence, and other graces necessary to the right performance of the duty of prayer.[1]

7.298 Q. 188. Of how many parts doth the Lord's Prayer consist?
A. The Lord's Prayer consists of three parts; a preface, petitions, and a conclusion.

7.299 Q. 189. What doth the preface of the Lord's Prayer teach us?
A. The preface of the Lord's Prayer (contained in these words, "Our Father which art in heaven")[1] teacheth us, when we pray, to draw near to God with confidence of his fatherly goodness, and our interest

therein;[2] with reverence, and all other childlike dispositions,[3] heavenly affections,[4] and due apprehensions of his sovereign power, majesty, and gracious condescension:[5] as also to pray with and for others.[6]

**7.300  Q. 190. What do we pray for in the first petition?**

A. In the first petition (which is, "Hallowed be thy name"),[1] acknowledging the utter inability and indisposition that is in ourselves and all men to honor God aright,[2] we pray; that God would by his grace enable and incline us and others to know, to acknowledge, and highly esteem him,[3] his titles,[4] attributes,[5] ordinances, word,[6] works, and whatsoever he is pleased to make himself known by;[7] and to glorify him in thought, word,[8] and deed;[9] that he would prevent and remove atheism,[10] ignorance,[11] idolatry,[12] profaneness,[13] and whatsoever is dishonorable to him;[14] and by his overruling providence, direct and dispose of all things to his own glory.[15]

**7.301  Q. 191. What do we pray for in the second petition?**

A. In the second petition (which is, "Thy Kingdom come"),[1] acknowledging ourselves and all mankind to be by nature under the dominion of sin and Satan,[2] we pray: that the kingdom of sin and Satan may be destroyed,[3] the gospel propagated throughout the world,[4] the Jews called,[5] the fullness of the Gentiles brought in;[6] that the church may be furnished with all gospel-officers and ordinances,[7] purged from corruption,[8] countenanced and maintained by the civil magistrate; that the ordinances of Christ may be purely dispensed, and made effectual to the converting of those that are yet in their sins, and the confirming, comforting, and building up of those that are already converted;[9] that Christ would rule in our hearts here,[10] and hasten the time of his second coming, and our reigning with him forever;[11] and that he would be pleased so to exercise the Kingdom of his power in all the world, as may best conduce to these ends.[12]

**7.302  Q. 192. What do we pray for in the third petition?**

A. In the third petition (which is, "Thy will be done on earth as it is in heaven"),[1] acknowledging that by nature we and all men are not only utterly unable and unwilling to know and do the will of God,[2] but prone to rebel against his Word,[3] to repine and murmur against his providence,[4] and wholly inclined to do the will of the flesh, and of the devil:[5] we pray that God would by his Spirit take away from ourselves and others all blindness,[6] weakness,[7] indisposedness,[8] and perverseness of heart,[9] and by his grace make us able and willing to know, do, and submit to his will in all things,[10] with the like humility,[11] cheerfulness,[12] faithfulness,[13] diligence,[14] zeal,[15] sincerity,[16] and constancy,[17] as the angels do in heaven.[18]

**7.303  Q. 193. What do we pray for in the fourth petition?**

A. In the fourth petition (which is, "Give us this day our daily bread"),[1] acknowledging that in Adam, and by our own sin, we have forfeited our right to all the outward blessings of this life, and deserve to be wholly deprived of them by God, and to have them cursed to us in the use of them;[2] and that neither they of themselves are able to sustain us,[3] nor we to merit,[4] or by our own industry to procure them,[5] but prone to desire,[6] get,[7] and use them unlawfully:[8] we pray for ourselves and others, that both they and we, waiting upon the providence of God from day to day in the use of lawful means may, of his free gift, and as to his fatherly wisdom shall seem best, enjoy a competent portion of them,[9] and have the same continued and blessed unto us in our holy and comfortable use of them,[10] and contentment in them;[11] and be kept from all things that are contrary to our temporal support and comfort.[12]

7.304 **Q. 194. What do we pray for in the fifth petition?**

A. In the fifth petition (which is, "Forgive us our debts, as we forgive our debtors"),[1] acknowledging that we and all others are guilty both of original and actual sin, and thereby become debtors to the justice of God, and neither we nor any other creature can make the least satisfaction for that debt:[2] we pray for ourselves and others, that God of his free grace would, through the obedience and satisfaction of Christ apprehended and applied by faith, acquit us both from the guilt and punishment of sin,[3] accept us in his Beloved,[4] continue his favor and grace to us,[5] pardon our daily failings,[6] and fill us with peace and joy, in giving us daily more and more assurance of forgiveness;[7] which we are the rather emboldened to ask, and encouraged to expect, when we have this testimony in ourselves, that we from the heart forgive others their offenses.[8]

7.305 **Q. 195. What do we pray for in the sixth petition?**

A. In the sixth petition (which is, "And lead us not into temptation, but deliver us from evil"),[1] acknowledging that the most wise, righteous, and gracious God, for divers holy and just ends, may so order things that we may be assaulted, foiled, and for a time led captive by temptations;[2] that Satan,[3] the world,[4] and the flesh, are ready powerfully to draw us aside and ensnare us;[5] and that we, even after the pardon of our sins, by reason of our corruption,[6] weakness, and want of watchfulness,[7] are not only subject to be tempted, and forward to expose ourselves unto temptations,[8] but also of ourselves unable and unwilling to resist them, to recover out of them, and to improve them;[9] and worthy to be left under the power of them;[10] we pray: that God would so overrule the world and all in it,[11] subdue the flesh,[12] and restrain Satan,[13] order all things,[14] bestow and bless all means of grace,[15] and quicken us to watchfulness in the use of them, that we and all his people may by his providence be kept from being tempted to sin;[16] or, if tempted, that by his Spirit we may be powerfully supported and enabled to stand in the hour of temptation;[17] or, when fallen, raised again and recovered out of it,[18] and have a sanctified use and improvement thereof;[19] that our sanctification and salvation may be perfected,[20] Satan trodden under our feet,[21] and we fully freed from sin, temptation, and all evil forever.[22]

**7.306**     **Q. 196. What doth the conclusion of the Lord's Prayer teach us?**

A. The conclusion of the Lord's Prayer (which is, "For thine is the Kingdom, and the power, and the glory, for ever. Amen."),[1] teacheth us to enforce our petitions with arguments,[2] which are to be taken, not from any worthiness in ourselves, or in any other creature, but from God;[3] and with our prayers to join praises,[4] ascribing to God alone eternal sovereignty, omnipotency, and glorious excellency;[5] in regard whereof, as he is able and willing to help us,[6] so we by faith are emboldened to plead with him that he would,[7] and quietly to rely upon him that he will, fulfill our requests.[8] And to testify our desires and assurance, we say, "Amen."[9]

# ENDNOTES FOR 7.111–.128

Q. 1. General Note.—At several points the Larger Catechism is more specific in its statements than in Scriptures. These statements are inferences from the Scriptures, or from statements based on the Scriptures, or from the experience and observation of the church. In such cases no texts are cited; but reference is made to this general note.
  1. Rom. 11:36; I Cor. 10:31.
  2. Ps. 73:24–26; John 17:22, 24.

Q. 2.
  1. Rom. 1:19, 20; Ps. 19:1–4.
  2. I Cor. 1:21; I Cor. 2:9, 10.

Q. 3.
  1. Gal. 1:8, 9; Isa. 8:20; Luke 16:29, 31; II Tim. 3:15–17.

Q. 4.
  1. See General Note.
  2. John 16:13, 14; I Cor. 2:6–9.

Q. 5.
  1. See General Note.

Q. 6.
  1. John 4:24; Exod. 34:6, 7.
  2. Matt. 28:19; II Cor. 13:14.
  3. Eph. 1:11. See the context.
  4. Acts 4:27, 28; Isa. 42:9.

Q. 7.
  1. John 4:24.
  2. I Kings 8:27; Isa. 40:20.
  3. See General Note.
  4. Acts 17:24, 25.
  5. Ps. 90:2.
  6. Mal. 3:6; James 1:17.
  7. Rom. 11:33.
  8. Jer. 23:24; Ps. 139.
  9. Rev. 4:8.
  10. Heb. 4:13; Ps. 147:5.
  11. Rom. 16:27.
  12. Isa. 6:3; Rev. 15:4.
  13. Deut. 32:4.
  14. Exod. 34:6.

Q. 8.
  1. Deut. 6:4; I Cor. 8:4, 6; Jer. 10:10.

Q. 9.
  1. Matt. 3:16, 17; Matt. 28:19; II Cor. 13:14.

Q. 10.
  1. Heb. 1:5.
  2. John 1:14.
  3. Gal. 4:6; John 15:26.

Q. 11.
  1. Jer. 23:6; I John 5:20; Ps. 45:6; Acts 5:3, 4.
  2. John 1:1; Isa. 9:6; John 2:24, 25; I Cor. 2:10, 11; Heb. 9:14.
  3. Col. 1:16; Gen. 1:2; Ps. 104:30; John 1:3.
  4. Matt. 28:19; II Cor. 13:14.

Q. 12.
  1. Eph. 1:4, 11; Acts 4:27, 28; Ps. 33:11.

Q. 13.
  1. I Tim. 5:21.
  2. Eph. 1:4–6; II Thess. 2:13, 14; I Peter 1:2.
  3. Rom. 9:17, 18, 21, 22; Jude 4; Matt. 11:25, 26; II Tim. 2:20.

Q. 14.
  1. Eph. 1:11; I Peter 1:1, 2.

Q. 15.
  1. Heb. 11:3; Rev. 4:11; Gen. 1.

Q. 16.
  1. Ps. 104:4; Col. 1:16.
  2. Luke 20:36.
  3. Gen. 1:31.
  4. Matt. 24:36.
  5. II Thess. 1:7.
  6. Ps. 103:20, 21.
  7. II Peter 2:4.

Q. 17.
  1. Gen. 1:27.
  2. Gen. 2:7.
  3. Gen. 2:22.
  4. Gen. 2:7; Matt. 10:28; Luke 23:43.
  5. Gen. 1:27.
  6. Col. 3:10; Gen. 2:19, 20.
  7. Eph. 4:24.
  8. Rom. 2:14, 15.
  9. Rom. 1:28.
  10. Gen. 2:16, 17; Gen. 3:6.

Q. 18.
  1. Ps. 145:17.
  2. Ps. 104:24; Isa. 28:29.
  3. Heb. 1:3.
  4. Ps. 103:19; Job Chapters 38–41.

ENDNOTES FOR 7.128–.146

  5. Matt. 10:29, 30; Gen. 45:7; Ps. 135:6.
  6. Rom. 11:36; Isa. 63:14.
Q. 19.
  1. Jude 6; II Peter 2:4.
  2. Job 1:12; Luke 10:17; Matt. 8:31.
  3. I Tim. 5:21; Mark 8:38; Heb. 12:22.
  4. Ps. 104:4; Heb. 1:14.
Q. 20.
  1. Gen. 2:8; Gen. 2:15, 16.
  2. Gen. 1:28.
  3. Gen. 2:18.
  4. Gen. 1:27, 28.
  5. Gen. 2:3.
  6. Compare Gen. 2:16, 17, with Rom. 5:12–14; 10:5; Luke 10:25–28, and with the covenants made with Noah and Abraham.
  7. Gen. 2:17.
Q. 21.
  1. Gen. 3:6–8, 13; II Cor.11:3.
Q. 22.
  1. Acts 17:16. See under figure 6 above.
  2. Gen. 2:17. Compare with Rom. 5:12–20, and with I Cor. 15:21, 22.
Q. 23.
  1. Rom. 5:12; Gal. 3:10.
Q. 24.
  1. Rom. 3:23; I John 3:4; James 4:17.
Q. 25.
  1. Rom. 5:12, 19; I Cor. 15:22.
  2. Rom. 5:6; Eph. 2:1–3; Rom. 8:7, 8; Gen. 6:5; Rom. 3:10–20; Ps. 51:5; 58:3.
  3. James 1:14, 15; Matt. 15:19.
Q. 26.
  1. Ps. 51:5; John 3:6.
Q. 27.
  1. Gen. 3:8, 24.
  2. Eph. 2:2, 3.
  3. II Tim. 2:26; Luke 11:21, 22; Heb. 2:14.
  4. Rom. 6:23; Rom. 5:14.
Q. 28.
  1. Eph. 4:18.

  2. Rom. 1:28.
  3. II Thess. 2:11.
  4. Rom. 2:5.
  5. Isa. 33:14; Gen. 4:13; Matt. 27:4; Heb. 10:27.
  6. Rom. 1:26.
  7. Gen. 3:17.
  8. Deut. 28:15–68.
  9. Rom. 6:21, 23.
Q. 29.
  1. II Thess. 1:9; Mark 9:43, 44; Luke 16:24, 26; Matt. 25:41, 46; Rev. 14:11; John 3:36.
Q. 30.
  1. I Thess. 5:9.
  2. Titus 3:4–7; Titus 1:2; Gal. 3:21; Rom. 3:20–22.
Q. 31.
  1. I Cor. 15:22, 45; Eph. 1:4, II Tim. 1:9; Isa. 53:10, 11; Heb. 2:10, 11, 14.
Q. 32.
  1. I Tim. 2:5.
  2. I John 5:11, 12.
  3. John 3:16; John 1:12; John 3:36.
  4. John 1:12, 13; John 3:5, 6, 8; Gal. 5:22, 28.
  5. Ezek. 36:27.
  6. James 2:18, 22.
  7. II Cor. 5:14, 15.
  8. Eph. 2:10, Titus 2:24; 3:8.
Q. 33.
  1. II Cor. 3:6; Heb. 1:1, 2; 8:7,8 ff.
Q. 34.
  1. Rom. 15:8; Acts 3:20.
  2. Acts 3:20, 24.
  3. Heb. 10:1.
  4. Rom. 4:11.
  5. I Cor. 5:7; Exod. 12:14, 17, 24.
  6. Heb. 11:13.
  7. Gal. 3:7–9; Heb. 11.
Q. 35.
  1. Matt. 28:19, 20.
  2. Matt. 28:19.
  3. I Cor. 11:23–26.
  4. Heb. 8:6, 7.
Q. 36.
  1. I Tim. 2:5.

## ENDNOTES FOR 7.146–.162

    2. John 1:1; John 10:30; Phil. 2:6; Gal. 4:4; Col. 2:9; Phil. 2:5–11.

Q. 37.
1. John 1:14; Matt. 26:38.
2. Luke 1:31, 35, 42; Gal. 4:4.
3. Heb. 4:15.

Q. 38.
1. See General Note.

Q. 39.
1. Rom. 5:19; Gal. 4:4, 5.
2. Heb. 2:14; Heb. 7:24, 25.
3. Heb. 4:15.
4. Gal. 4:5.
5. Heb. 4:14–16.

Q. 40.
1. See General Note.

Q. 41.
1. Matt. 1:21.

Q. 42.
1. John 3:34; Luke 4:18–21.
2. Luke 4:14; Heb. 9:14; Matt. 28:18–20.
3. Acts 3:22; Luke 4:18, 21.
4. Heb. 5:5, 6; Heb. 4:14, 15.
5. Rev. 19:16; Isa. 9:6, 7; Ps. 2:6.

Q. 43.
1. John 1:1, 4.
2. II Peter 1:21; II Cor. 2:9, 10.
3. Eph. 4:11–13; John 20:31.

Q. 44.
1. Heb. 9:14, 28.
2. Heb. 2:17.
3. Heb. 7:25.

Q. 45.
1. John 10:16, 27; Isa. 55:5.
2. I Cor. 12:28; Eph. 4:11, 12.
3. Matt. 28:19, 20.
4. Matt. 18:17, 18; I Cor. 5:4, 5; I Tim. 5:20; Titus 3:10.
5. Acts 5:31.
6. Rev. 22:12; Matt. 25:34–36; Rom. 2:7.
7. Rev. 3:19; Heb. 12:6, 7.
8. II Cor. 12:9, 10; Rom. 8:35–39.
9. I Cor. 15:25; Acts 12:17; Acts 18:9, 10.
10. Rom. 14:11; Col. 1:18; Matt. 28:19, 20.

    11. Rom. 8:28.
    12. II Thess. 1:8; Ps. 2:9.

Q. 46.
1. Phil. 2:6–8; II Cor. 8:9; Gal. 4:4.

Q. 47.
1. John 1:18. See citations under Q. 46 above.

Q. 48.
1. Gal. 4:4.
2. Matt. 3:15; John 19:30; Rom. 5:19.
3. Heb. 12:2, 3; Isa. 53:2, 3; Ps. 22:6.
4. Matt. 4:1. See verses 2:12; Luke 4:1–14.
5. Heb. 2:17, 18; Heb. 4:15; Isa. 52:13, 14.

Q. 49.
1. Matt. 27:4.
2. Matt. 26:56.
3. Luke 18:32, 33; Isa. 53:3.
4. Matt. 27:26; John 19:34; Luke 22:63, 64.
5. Luke 22:44; Matt. 27:46; Rom. 8:32.
6. Rom. 4:25; I Cor. 15:3, 4; Isa. 53:10.
7. Phil. 2:8; Heb. 12:2; Gal. 3:13.

Q. 50.
1. I Cor. 15:3, 4.
2. Matt. 12:40; Luke 18:33.

Q. 51.
1. I Cor. 15:4.
2. Luke 24:51; Acts 1:9–11.
3. Eph. 1:20.
4. Acts 1:11; Acts 17:31.

Q. 52.
1. Acts 2:24; Ps. 16:10.
2. Luke 24:39.
3. Rev. 1:18.
4. John 10:18.
5. Rom. 1:4.
6. Rom. 4:25; I Cor. 15:17.
7. Heb. 2:14; Rev. 1:18.
8. Rom. 14:9.
9. I Cor. 15:21, 22.
10. Eph. 1:22, 23; Col. 1:18.
11. Rom. 4:25.
12. Eph. 2:5, 6; Col. 2:12.

13. I Cor. 15:25, 26; Acts 12:17; Acts 18:9, 10.
14. I Cor. 15:20; I Thess. 4:13–18.

Q. 53.
1. Acts 1:2, 3.
2. Matt. 28:19, 20; Acts 1:8.
3. Heb. 6:20; Eph. 4:8; Acts 1:9.
4. Ps. 68:18.
5. Col. 3:1, 2.
6. John 14:2.
7. Acts 3:21.

Q. 54.
1. Phil. 2:9.
2. Acts 2:28. Compare Ps. 16:11.
3. John 17:5.
4. Eph. 1:22; I Peter 3:22.
5. Eph. 4:11, 12. See citations under Q. 45.
6. Rom. 8:34. See citations under Q. 44.

Q. 55.
1. Heb. 9:24.
2. Heb. 1:3.
3. John 17:9, 20, 24.
4. Rom. 8:33, 34.
5. Rom. 5:1, 2.
6. Heb. 4:16.
7. Eph. 1:6.
8. I Peter 2:5; Rev. 8:3, 4.

Q. 56.
1. Matt. 24:30; Luke 9:26; I Thess. 4:16; Acts 17:31; Matt. 25:31.

Q. 57.
1. Heb. 9:12; I Cor. 1:30; Rom. 8:32; II Cor. 1:20.

Q. 58.
1. John 1:12, 13; John 3:5, 6; Titus 3:5, 6.

Q. 59.
1. John 6:37, 39; John 10:15, 16; Rom. 8:29, 30.
2. I Peter 1:2; II Thess. 2:13.

Q. 60.
1. Rom. 10:14; II Thess. 1:8, 9; Acts 4:12; Rom. 1:18–32.
2. I Cor. 1:21; Rom. 1:18–32; Rom. 3:9–19.
3. John 4:22; Phil. 3:4–10.
4. Acts 4:12.
5. John 6:39, 44; John 17:9.

Q. 61.
1. Rom. 9:6; Matt. 7:21; Matt. 13:41, 42.

Q. 62.
1. I Cor. 1:2; I Cor. 12:12, 13; Rom. 15:1–12.
2. Gen. 17:7. (See the context.) Compare Gal. 3:7, 9, 14; Rom. 4; Acts 2:39; I Cor. 7:14; Mark 10:13–16.

Q. 63.
1. I Cor. 12:28; Eph. 4:11, 12; Acts 13:1, 2; Isa. 49:14–16.
2. Matt. 16:18; Isa. 31:4, 5; Ps. 115:9–18.
3. Acts 2:42; Rom. 3:1, 2.
4. Ps. 147:19, 20; Rom. 9:4; Acts 16:31; Rev. 22:17.
5. John 6:37.

Q. 64.
1. John 11:52; John 10:16; Eph. 1:10, 22, 23.

Q. 65.
1. John 17:21; Eph. 2:5, 6; I John 1:3; John 17:24.

Q. 66.
1. Eph. 2:8. (See context.)
2. I Cor. 6:17; John 10:28; Eph. 5:23, 30; John 15:1–5.
3. I Cor. 1:9; I Peter 5:10.

Q. 67.
1. Eph. 1:18–20; II Tim. 1:9.
2. Titus 3:4, 5; Rom. 9–11; Eph. 2:4–10.
3. II Cor. 5:20; John 6:44; II Thess. 2:13, 14.
4. Acts 26:18.
5. Ezek. 11:19; Ezek. 36:26, 27.
6. John 6:45; Phil. 2:13; Deut. 30:6; Eph. 2:5.

Q. 68.
1. Acts 13:48; John 6:39, 44; John 17:9.
2. Matt. 22:14.
3. Matt. 13:20, 21; Heb. 6:4–6.
4. Ps. 81:11, 12; John 12:38–40; Acts 28:25–27; John 6:64, 65; Prov. 1:24–32; Ps. 95:9–11.

Q. 69.
1. Rom. 8:30.
2. Eph. 1:5.

3. I Cor. 1:30.
Q. 70.
1. II Cor. 5:19, 21; Rom. 3:22, 24, 25; Rom. 4:5.
2. Eph. 1:6, 7; Rom. 3:28.
3. Rom. 3:24, 25; Rom. 5:17–19; Rom. 4:6–8.
4. Rom. 5:1; Acts 10:43; Gal. 2:16; Phil. 3:9; Rom. 3:25, 26.
Q. 71.
1. See citations under Question 70.
Q. 72.
1. Heb. 10:39.
2. Rom. 10:14, 17; II Thess. 2:13.
3. John 16:8, 9; Acts 16:30; Acts 2:37; Eph. 2:1; Acts 4:12; Rom. 7:9.
4. Rom. 10:8–10.
5. Acts 10:43; Gal. 2:15, 16; Acts 16:31.
6. Phil. 3:19; Acts 15:11.
Q. 73.
1. Gal. 3:11; Rom. 3:28.
2. Titus 3:5–7; Rom. 4:5–8.
3. Phil. 3:9.
Q. 74.
1. I John 3:1.
2. Eph. 1:5; Gal. 4:4, 5.
3. John 1:12.
4. Rev. 3:12; II Cor. 6:18.
5. Gal. 4:6.
6. Ps. 103:13; Prov. 14:26; Matt. 6:32.
7. Rom. 8:17; Heb. 6:12.
Q. 75.
1. Eph. 1:4; I Cor. 6:11; II Thess. 2:13.
2. Rom. 6:4–6; Eph. 4:23, 24; Phil. 3:10.
3. Acts 11:18; I John 3:9.
4. Jude 20; Eph. 3:16–18; Col. 1:10, 11; Rom. 6:4, 6, 14.
Q. 76.
1. II Tim. 2:25; Luke 24:47.
2. Acts 11:18, 20, 21; Zech. 12:10; Acts 2:37.
3. Ezek. 18:30, 32; Luke 15:17, 18; Hos. 2:6, 7.
4. Ezek. 36:31; Ezek. 16:61, 63; Isa. 30:22.
5. Luke 22:61, 62; Zech. 12:10.
6. II Cor. 7:11; Acts 2:37.
7. Acts 26:18; Ezek. 14:6; I Kings 8:47, 48; I Sam. 7:3.
8. Ps. 119:59, 128.
Q. 77.
1. I Cor. 6:11; I Cor. 1:30; Rom. 8:30.
2. Rom. 4:6, 8; Phil. 3:8, 9; II Cor. 5:21.
3. Ezek. 36: 27.
4. Rom. 3:24, 25.
5. Rom. 6:6, 14.
6. Rom. 8:1, 33, 34.
7. I Cor. 3:1, 2; Mark 4:8, 28.
8. I John 1:8, 10.
9. II Cor. 7:1; Phil. 3:12–14; Eph. 4:11–15.
Q. 78.
1. Rom. 7:18, 23.
2. Gal. 5:17; Heb. 12:1.
3. Exod. 28:38; Rom. 7:18, 23.
Q. 79.
1. Jer. 31:3; John 13:1.
2. I Cor. 1:8; Heb. 6:17; Heb. 13:20, 21; Isa. 54:10.
3. I Cor. 12:27. Compare with Rom. 8:35–39.
4. Heb. 7:25; Luke 22:32.
5. I John 3:9; I John 2:27.
6. Jer. 32:40; John 10:28; I Peter 1:5; Phil. 1:6.
Q. 80.
1. I John 2:3; I Cor. 2:12; I John 4:13, 16; I John 3:14, 18, 19, 21, 24; Rom. 8:16; I John 5:13.
Q. 81.
1. Isa. 50:10; Ps. 88.
2. Ps. 31:22; Ps. 77:1–12; Ps. 30:6, 7; Ps. 51:8, 12.
3. Job 13:15; Ps. 73:13–15, 23; I John 3:9; Isa 54:7–11.
Q. 82.
1. II Cor. 3:18.
2. Luke 23:43.
3. I John 3:2; I Thess. 4:17; Rev. 22:3–5.

Q. 83.
1. Eph. 2:4–6.
2. Rom. 5:5; II Cor. 1:22.
3. Rom. 5:1, 2; Rom. 14:17.
4. Gen. 4:13; Matt. 27:3–5; Heb. 10:27; Mark 9:44; Rom. 2:9.

Q. 84.
1. Rom. 6:23.
2. Heb. 9:27.
3. Rom. 5:12.

Q. 85.
1. I Cor. 15:26, 55–57; Heb. 2:15.
2. Isa. 57:1, 2; II Kings 22:20.
3. Luke 16:25; II Cor. 5:1–8.
4. Luke 23:43; Phil. 1:23.

Q. 86.
1. Luke 16:23; Luke 23:43; Phil. 1:23; II Cor. 5:6–8.
2. Rom. 8:23; Ps. 16:9.
3. I Thess. 4:14.
4. Rom. 8:23.
5. Luke 16:23, 24; Acts 1:25; Jude 6.

Q. 87.
1. Acts 24:15.
2. I Cor. 15:51–53; I Thess. 4:15–17; John 5:28, 29.
3. I Cor. 15:21–23, 42–44 [It is evidently the scope of the apostle's argument in this passage, to prove, that as all the natural seed of Adam, their covenant-head, were subjected to death by his offence; so all the spiritual seed of Christ, their new covenant-head, shall be raised from death, to an immortal life of glory and blessedness, by virtue of his resurrection. It is therefore a perversion of the Scripture, to adduce this text as a proof of universal redemption.] Phil 3:21.
4. John 5:28, 29; Dan. 12:2; Matt. 25:33.

Q. 88.
1. II Peter 2:4; Rev. 20:11–13.
2. Matt. 24:36, 42, 44; Luke 21:35, 36.

Q. 89.
1. Matt. 25:33.
2. Rom. 2:15, 16. (See the context.)
3. Matt. 25:41, 42.
4. Matt. 25:46; II Thess. 1:8, 9; Luke 16:26; Mark 9:43, 44; Mark 14:21.

Q. 90.
1. I Thess. 4:17.
2. Matt. 25:33; Matt. 10:32.
3. I Cor. 6:2, 3.
4. Matt. 25:34, 46.
5. Eph. 5:27; Rev. 7:17.
6. Ps. 16:11, I Cor. 2:9.
7. Heb. 12:22, 23.
8. I John 3:2; I Cor. 13:12; I Thess. 4:17, 18; Rev. 22:3–5.

Q. 91.
1. Deut. 29:29; Micah 6:8; I Sam. 15:22.

Q. 92.
1. Rom. 10:5; Rom. 2:14, 15; Gen. 2:17.

Q. 93.
1. James 2:10; Deut. 5:1, 31, 33; Luke 10:26, 27; I Thess. 5:23.
2. Rom. 10:5; Gal. 3:10.

Q. 94.
1. Rom. 8:3; Gal. 2:16.
2. I Tim. 1:8; Gal. 3:19, 24.

Q. 95.
1. Rom. 7:12.
2. Micah 6:8, Luke 10:26, 28, 37.
3. Ps. 19:11, 12; Rom. 3:20; Rom. 7:7.
4. Rom. 3:9, 23; Rom. 7:9, 13.
5. Gal. 3:21, 22.

Q. 96.
1. Rom. 7:9; I Tim. 1:9, 10.
2. Gal. 3:24.
3. Rom. 1:20. (Compare Rom. 2:15.)
4. Gal. 3:10.

Q. 97.
1. Rom. 7:4, 6; Rom. 6:14; Rom. 3:20; Rom. 8:1, 34; Gal. 3:13, 14; Rom. 8:3, 4; II Cor. 5:21.
2. Col. 1:12–14; Rom. 7:22; Titus 2:11–14.

Q. 98.
   1. Matt. 19:17–19.
   2. Deut. 10:4; Exod. 34:1–4.

Q. 99.
  Rule 1.
   1. Ps. 19:7; James 2:10; Matt. 5:22, 28, 37, 44.
  Rule 2.
   1. Rom. 7:14; Deut. 6:5; Matt. 22:37–39; Matt. 12:36, 37. See citations under Rule 1 above.
  Rule 3.
   1. Col. 3:5; I Tim. 6:10; Exod. 20:3–5; Amos 8:5.
  Rule 4.
   1. Isa. 58:13; Matt. 15:4–6; Deut. 6:12. Compare with Matt. 4:9, 10.
   2. Eph. 4:18.
   3. Exod. 20:12. Compare with Prov. 30:17.
   4. Jer. 18:7, 8; Exod. 20:7. Compare with Ps. 15:1, 4, 5; Ps. 24:4, 5.
  Rule 5.
   1. Rom. 3:8; Heb. 11:25.
   2. Deut. 4:9.
   3. Matt. 12:7; Mark 14:7.
  Rule 6.
   1. I Thess. 5:22; Gal. 5:26; Heb. 10:24; Col. 3:21.
  Rule 7.
   1. Exod. 20:10; Deut. 6:6, 7; Josh. 24:15.
  Rule 8.
   1. Heb. 10:24.
   2. I Tim. 5:22; Eph. 5:11.

Q. 101.
   1. Exod. 20:2.

Q. 102.
   1. Luke 10:27.

Q. 103.
   1. Exod. 20:3.

Q. 104.
   1. The exposition of the Ten Commandments contained in the answers to Questions 104 to 148 are deduced from the Commandments themselves, and from the "Rules" set forth in Question 99. Texts under the specifications are given in order to show that the specifications are in accord with the general teaching of the Scriptures.
   2. I Chron. 28:9; Deut. 26:17; Isa. 43:10; Jer. 14:22.
   3. Ps. 95:6, 7; Matt. 4:10; Ps. 29:2.
   4. Mal. 3:16.
   5. Ps. 63:6.
   6. Eccl. 12:1.
   7. Ps. 18:1, 2.
   8. Mal. 1:6.
   9. Isa. 45:23; Ps. 96.
   10. Josh. 24:22.
   11. Deut. 6:5.
   12. Ps. 73:25.
   13. Isa. 8:13.
   14. Exod. 14:31; Rom. 10:11; Acts 10:43.
   15. Isa. 26:4; Ps. 40:4.
   16. Ps. 130:7.
   17. Ps. 37:4.
   18. Ps. 32:11.
   19. Rom. 12:11; Rev. 3:19; Num. 25:11.
   20. Phil. 4:6.
   21. Jer. 7:23; James 4:7; Rom. 12:1.
   22. I John 3:22.
   23. Neh. 13:8; Ps. 73:21; Ps. 119:136; Jer. 31:18, 19.
   24. Micah 6:8.

Q. 105.
   1. Ps. 14:1.
   2. Jer. 2:27, 28. Compare I Thess. 1:9.
   3. Ps. 81:11.
   4. Isa. 43:22, 23.
   5. Jer. 4:22; Hos. 4:1, 6.
   6. Jer. 2:32; Ps. 50:22.
   7. Acts 17:23, 29.
   8. Ps. 50:21.
   9. Deut. 29:29.
   10. Titus 1:16; Heb. 12:16.
   11. Rom. 1:30.
   12. II Tim. 3:2.
   13. Phil. 2:21.
   14. I John 2:15; I Sam. 2:29; Col. 3:2, 5.
   15. I John 4:1.

16. Heb. 3:12.
17. Gal. 5:20; Titus 3:10.
18. Acts 26:9.
19. Ps. 78:22.
20. Ezek. 37:11.
21. Jer. 5:3.
22. Rom. 2:5.
23. Jer. 13:15.
24. Ps. 19:13.
25. Zeph. 1:12.
26. Matt. 4:7.
27. Rom. 3:8.
28. Jer. 17:5.
29. II Tim. 3:4.
30. Gal. 4:17; Rom. 10:2; John 16:2; Luke 9:54, 55.
31. Rev. 3:16.
32. Rev. 3:1.
33. Ezek. 14:5; Isa. 1:4, 5.
34. Hos. 4:12; Rev. 19:10; Col. 2:18; Rom. 1:25.
35. Lev. 20:6; I Sam. 28:7–11. Compare I Chron. 10:13, 14.
36. Acts 5:3.
37. Matt. 23:9.
38. Deut. 32:15; Prov. 13:13; II Sam. 12:9.
39. Acts 7:51; Eph. 4:30.
40. Ps. 73:2, 3. See verses 13–15, 22.
41. Dan. 5:23.
42. Deut. 8:17; Dan. 4:30.
43. Hab. 1:16.

Q. 106.
1. Ps. 44:20, 21; Ezek. 8:15–18.
2. I Chron. 28:9.

Q. 107.
1. Exod. 20:4–6.

Q. 108.
1. Deut. 32:46; Matt. 28:20; I Tim. 6:13, 14; Acts 2:42.
2. Phil. 4:6; Eph. 5:20.
3. Deut. 17:18, 19; Acts 15:21; II Tim. 4:2; James 1:21; Acts 10:33.
4. Matt. 28:19; I Cor. 11:23–30.
5. Matt. 16:19; Matt. 18:17; I Cor. 5; I Cor. 12:28; John 20:23.
6. Eph. 4:11, 12; I Tim. 5:17, 18; I Cor. 9:1–15.
7. Joel 2:12; I Cor. 7:5.
8. Deut. 6:13.
9. Ps. 76:11; Isa. 19:21; Ps. 116:14, 18.
10. Acts 17:16, 17; Ps. 16:4.
11. Deut. 7:5; Isa. 30:22.

Q. 109.
1. Num. 15:39.
2. Deut. 13:6, 8.
3. Hos. 5:11; Micah 6:16.
4. I Kings 11:33; I Kings 12:33.
5. Deut. 12:30, 32.
6. Deut. 4:15, 16; Acts 17:29; Rom. 1:21–25.
7. Gal. 4:8; Dan. 3:18.
8. Exod. 32:5.
9. Exod. 32:8.
10. I Kings 18:26, 28; Isa. 65:11.
11. Acts 19:19.
12. Mal. 1:7, 8, 14.
13. Deut. 4:2.
14. Ps. 106:39.
15. Matt. 15:9.
16. I Peter 1:18.
17. Jer. 44:17.
18. Isa. 65:3–5; Gal. 1:13, 14.
19. I Sam. 13:12; I Sam. 15:21.
20. Acts 8:18.
21. Rom. 2:22; Mal. 3:8.
22. Exod. 4:24–26.
23. Matt. 22:25; Mal. 1:7, 12, 13.
24. Matt. 23:13.
25. Acts 13:45; I Thess. 2:15, 16.

Q. 110.
1. Exod. 20:5, 6.
2. Exod. 34:13, 14.
3. I Cor. 10:20–22; Deut. 32:16–19; Jer. 7:18–20; Ezek. 16:26, 27.
4. Hos. 2:2–4.
5. Deut. 5:29.

Q. 111.
1. Exod. 20:7.

Q. 112.
1. Matt. 6:9; Deut. 28:58; Ps. 68:4; Ps. 29:2; Rev. 15:3, 4.
2. Mal. 1:14.
3. Ps. 138:2.
4. I Cor. 11:28, 29. See context.

5. I Tim. 2:8.
6. Jer. 4:2.
7. Ps. 76:11.
8. Acts 1:24, 26.
9. Ps. 107:21, 22.
10. Mal. 3:16.
11. Ps. 8.
12. Ps. 105:2, 5; Col. 3:17.
13. Ps. 102:18.
14. I Peter 3:15; Micah 4:5.
15. Phil. 1:27.
16. I Cor. 10:31.
17. Jer. 32:39.
18. I Peter 2:12.

Q. 113.
1. Mal. 2:2.
2. Acts 17:23.
3. Prov. 30:9.
4. Mal. 1:6, 7, 12; Mal. 3:14.
5. Jer. 7:4. See context. Col. 2:20–22.
6. Exod. 5:2; Ps. 139:20.
7. Ps. 50:16, 17.
8. Isa. 5:12.
9. II Kings 19:22; Lev. 24:11.
10. Zech. 5:4.
11. Rom. 12:14; I Sam. 17:43; II Sam. 16:5.
12. Jer. 5:7; Jer. 23:10.
13. Deut. 23:18; Acts 23:12.
14. Esth. 3:7; Esth. 9:24.
15. Ps. 24:4; Ezek. 17:19. See context.
16. Mark 6:26; I Sam. 25:22, 32–34.
17. Rom. 9:14, 19, 20.
18. Deut. 29:29.
19. Rom. 3:5, 7. See context.
20. Ps. 73:12, 13.
21. Matt. 5:21–48.
22. Ezek. 13:22.
23. II Peter 3:16; Matt. 22:29. See context, verses 23–32.
24. Eph. 5:4.
25. I Tim. 6:4, 5, 20; II Tim. 2:14; Titus 3:9.
26. Deut. 18:10, 11. See context. Acts 19:13.
27. II Tim. 4:3, 4; Jude 4; Rom 13:13, 14; I Kings 21:9, 10.
28. Acts 13:45.
29. II Peter 3:3; Ps. 1:1.
30. I Peter 4:4.
31. Acts 13:50. See verses 45, 46; Acts 4:18; Acts 19:9; I Thess. 2:16, Heb. 10:29.
32. II Tim. 3:5; Matt. 23:14; Matt. 6:1–3, 5, 16.
33. Mark 8:38.
34. Ps. 73:14, 15.
35. Eph. 5:15, 17; I Cor. 6:5, 6.
36. Isa. 5:4; II Peter 1:8, 9.
37. Rom. 2:23, 24.
38. Gal. 3:1, 3; Heb. 6:6.

Q. 114.
1. Exod. 20:7.
2. Lev. 19:12.
3. Deut. 28:58, Zech. 5:2–4; Ezek. 36:21–23.
4. I Sam. 2:12, 17, 22.

Q. 115.
1. Exod. 20:8–11.

Q. 116.
1. Isa. 56:2, 4, 6, 7.
2. Gen. 2:3; Luke 23:56.
3. I Cor. 16:2; Acts 20:7; John 20:19–27.

Q. 117.
1. Exod. 20:8, 10.
2. Jer. 17:21, 22; Exod. 16:25–29; Neh. 13:15–22.
3. Matt. 12:1–14.
4. Lev. 23:3; Isa. 58:13; Luke 4:16; Acts 20:7.
5. Exod. 20:8; Luke 23:54, 56; Neh. 13:19.

Q. 118.
1. These statements are necessary inferences from the relations which exist between governors and the governed.

Q. 119.
1. Ezek. 22:26.
2. Ezek. 33:31, 32; Mal 1:13; Amos 8:5.
3. Ezek. 23:38.
4. Jer. 17:27. See context. Isa. 58:13, 14.

Q. 120.
1. Exod. 20:9.
2. Exod. 20:10.
3. Exod. 20:11.

Q. 121.
 1. Exod. 20:8.
 2. Exod. 16:23; Luke 23:54. Compare Mark 15:42; Neh. 13:19.
 3. Ezek. 20:12, 20.
 4. Gen. 2:2, 3; Ps. 118:22, 24; Heb. 4:9.
 5. Num. 15:37, 38, 40. See context.
 6. Exod. 34:21.
 7. See citation under figure 5 above.
 8. Lam. 1:7; Neh. 13:15–23; Jer. 17:21–23.

Q. 122.
 1. Matt. 22:39.
 2. Matt. 7:12.

Q. 123.
 1. Exod. 20:12.

Q. 124.
 1. I Tim. 5:1, 2.
 2. Gen. 4:20, 21; Gen. 45:8.
 3. II Kings 5:13.
 4. Gal. 4:19; II Kings 2:12; II Kings 13:14.
 5. Isa. 49:23.

Q. 125.
 1. Eph. 6:4; I Thess. 2:7, 8, 11; Num. 11:11, 12, 16.
 2. I Cor. 4:14–16.

Q. 126.
 1. Eph. 5:21; I Peter 2:17; Rom. 12:10.

Q. 127.
 1. Mal. 1:6; Lev. 19:3.
 2. Prov. 31:28; I Peter 3:6.
 3. Lev. 19:32; I Kings 2:19.
 4. I Tim. 2:1, 2.
 5. Heb. 13:7; Phil. 3:17.
 6. Eph. 6:1, 5–7; I Peter 2:13, 14; Rom. 13:1–6; Heb. 13:17; Prov. 4:3, 4; Prov. 23:22.
 7. Heb. 12:9; I Peter 2:18–20.
 8. Titus 2:9, 10.
 9. Matt. 22:21; Rom. 13:6, 7; I Tim. 5:17, 18; Gal. 6:6; Gen. 45:11; Gen 47:12.
 10. Gen. 9:23; I Peter 2:18; Prov. 23:22.
 11. Ps. 127:3, 5; Prov. 31:23.

Q. 128.
 1. Matt. 15:5, 6.
 2. Ps. 106:16.
 3. I Sam. 8:7; Isa. 3:5.
 4. II Sam. 15:1–12.
 5. Exod. 21:15.
 6. I Sam. 10:27.
 7. I Sam. 2:25.
 8. Deut. 21:18, 20, 21.
 9. Prov. 30:11, 17.
 10. Prov. 19:26.

Q. 129.
 1. Col. 3:19; Titus 2:4.
 2. I Sam. 12:23; Job. 1:5.
 3. I Kings 8:55, 56; Gen. 49:28.
 4. Deut. 6:6, 7.
 5. Eph. 6:4.
 6. I Peter 3:7.
 7. Rom. 13:3; I Peter 2:14.
 8. Rom. 13:4.
 9. Prov. 29:15; Rom 13:4.
 10. I Tim. 5:8; Isa. 1:10, 17; Eph. 6:4.
 11. I Tim. 4:12; Titus 2:2–14.
 12. I Kings 3:28.
 13. Titus 2:15.

Q. 130.
 1. Ezek. 34:2, 4.
 2. Phil. 2:21.
 3. John 5:44, John 7:18.
 4. Isa. 56:10, 11; Deut. 17:17.
 5. Acts 4:18; Dan. 3:4–6.
 6. Exod. 5:10–19; Matt. 23:2, 4.
 7. Matt. 14:8. Compare with Mark 6:24.
 8. Jer. 5:30, 32; II Sam. 13:28.
 9. Jer. 6:13, 14; Ezek. 13:9, 10.
 10. John 7:46–49; John 9:28.
 11. I Peter 2:19, 20; Heb. 12:10; Deut. 25:3.
 12. Lev. 19:29; Isa. 58:7; Gen. 38:11, 26.
 13. Eph. 6:4.
 14. Gen. 9:21; I Kings 12:13, 14; I Kings 1:6; I Sam. 3:13.

Q. 131.
 1. I Peter 2:17.
 2. Rom. 12:10; Phil. 2:3.
 3. Rom. 12:15, 16; Phil. 2:4.

Q. 132.
 1. Rom. 13:8.

2. Prov. 14:21; Isa. 65:5; II Tim. 3:3.
 3. Acts 7:9; Gal. 5:26.
 4. I John 3:12; Matt. 20:15; Num. 12:2; Luke 15:28, 29.
 5. Matt. 20:25–27; III John 9; Luke 22:24–26.

Q. 133.
 1. Exod. 20:12.
 2. Eph. 6:2, 3; Deut. 5:16; I Kings 8:25.

Q. 134.
 1. Exod. 20:13.

Q. 135.
 1. Eph. 5:29; Matt. 10:23.
 2. Ps. 82:4; Deut. 22:8.
 3. Matt. 5:22; Jer. 26:15, 16.
 4. Eph. 4:26.
 5. Prov. 22:24, 25; I Sam. 25:32, 33; Deut. 22:8.
 6. Prov. 1:10, 11, 15; Matt. 4:6, 7.
 7. I Kings 21:9, 10, 19; Gen. 37:21, 22; I Sam. 24:12 and 26:9–11.
 8. Prov. 24:11, 12; I Sam. 14:45.
 9. Luke 21:19; James 5:8; Heb. 12:5.
 10. Ps. 37:8, 11; I Peter 3:3, 4.
 11. Prov. 17:22; I Thess. 5:16.
 12. Prov. 23:20; Prov. 25:16.
 13. Prov. 23:29, 30; I Tim. 5:23.
 14. Matt. 9:12; Isa. 38:21.
 15. Ps. 127:2.
 16. II Thess. 3:10, 12.
 17. Mark 6:31; I Tim. 4:8.
 18. I Cor. 13:4, 5; I Sam. 19:4, 5.
 19. Rom. 13:10; Prov. 10:12.
 20. Zech. 7:9; Luke 10:33, 34.
 21. Col. 3:12.
 22. Rom. 12:18.
 23. I Peter 3:8, 9; I Cor. 4:12, 13.
 24. Col. 3:13; James 3:17; I Peter 2:20; Rom. 12:20, 21; Matt. 5:24.
 25. I Thess. 5:14; Matt. 25:35, 36; Prov. 31:8, 9; Isa. 58:7.

Q. 136.
 1. Acts 16:28; Prov. 1:18.
 2. Gen. 9:6.
 3. Exod. 21:14; Num. 35:31, 33.
 4. Deut. 20:1; Heb. 11:32–34; Jer. 48:10.
 5. Exod. 22:2.
 6. Matt. 25:42, 43; James 2:15, 16.
 7. Matt. 5:22.
 8. I John 3:15; Prov. 10:12; Lev. 19:17.
 9. Prov. 14:30.
 10. Rom. 12:19.
 11. James 4:1; Eph. 4:31.
 12. Matt. 6:34.
 13. Luke 21:34.
 14. Exod. 20:9, 10.
 15. I Peter 4:3, 4.
 16. Prov. 15:1; Prov. 12:18.
 17. Isa. 3:15; Exod. 1:14.
 18. Gal. 5:15.
 19. Num. 35:16.
 20. Prov. 28:17; Exod. 21:18–36.

Q. 137.
 1. Exod. 20:14.

Q. 138.
 1. I Thess. 4:4, 5.
 2. Eph. 4:29; Col. 4:6.
 3. I Peter 3:2.
 4. I Cor. 7:2; Titus 2:4, 5.
 5. Matt. 5:28.
 6. Prov. 23:31, 33; Jer. 5:7.
 7. Prov. 2:16, 20; I Cor. 5:9.
 8. I Tim. 2:9.
 9. I Cor. 7:9.
 10. Prov. 5:18, 19.
 11. I Peter 3:7; I Cor. 7:5.
 12. I Tim. 5:13, 14; Prov. 31:27.
 13. Prov. 5:8.

Q. 139.
 1. Prov. 5:7; Prov. 4:23, 27.
 2. Heb. 13:4; Eph. 5:5; Gal. 5:19.
 3. II Sam. 13:14; Mark 6:18; I Cor. 5:1, 13.
 4. Rom. 1:26, 27; Lev. 20:15, 16.
 5. Matt. 15:19; Col. 3:5; Matt. 5:28.
 6. Eph. 5:3, 4; Prov. 7:5, 21; Prov. 19:27.
 7. Isa. 3:16; II Peter 2:14.
 8. Prov. 7:10, 13.
 9. I Tim. 4:3.
 10. Lev. 18:1–21.

11. II Kings 23:7; Lev. 19:29; Jer. 5:7.
12. Matt. 19:10–12.
13. I Tim. 5:14, 15; Gen. 38:26.
14. Matt. 19:5; I Cor. 7:2.
15. Matt. 5:32; Mal. 2:16.
16. See citations under Question 138. I Cor. 7:12, 13.
17. Ezek. 16:49; Jer. 5:7.
18. Eph. 5:11; Prov. 5:8.
19. Rom. 13:13; I Peter 4:3; Mark 6:22.
20. Rom. 13:14; II Peter 2:17, 18.

Q. 140.
1. Exod. 20:15.

Q. 141.
1. Ps. 15:2, 4; Micah 6:8; Zech. 8:16.
2. Rom. 13:7.
3. Lev. 6:4, 5; Luke 19:8.
4. Deut. 15:7, 8, 10; Gal. 6:10; Luke 6:30, 38.
5. I Tim. 6:8, 9.
6. I Tim. 5:8.
7. Prov. 27:23, 24; I Tim. 6:17, 18.
8. Eph. 4:28; Rom. 12:5–8.
9. Prov. 10:4; Rom 12:11.
10. Prov. 12:27; Prov. 21:20; John 6:12.
11. I Cor. 6:7.
12. Prov. 11:15; Prov. 6:1–5.
13. Lev. 25:35; Phil. 2:4; Deut. 22:1–4; Exod. 23:4, 5.

Q. 142.
1. Prov. 23:21; I John 3:17; James 2:15, 16.
2. Eph. 4:28.
3. Ps. 62:10.
4. I Tim. 1:10; Exod. 21:16.
5. Prov. 29:24; Ps. 50:18.
6. I Thess. 4:6.
7. Prov. 11:1; Prov. 20:10.
8. Deut. 19:14; Prov. 23:10.
9. Amos 8:5; Ps. 37:21.
10. Luke 16:11.
11. Ezek. 22:29; Lev. 25:17.
12. Matt. 23:25; Ezek. 22:12.
13. Isa. 33:15.
14. Prov. 3:30; I Cor. 6:7.
15. Isa. 5:8; Micah 2:2.

16. Prov. 11:26.
17. Acts 19:19. See context.
18. James 5:4; Prov. 21:6.
19. Luke 12:15; Prov. 1:19.
20. I John 2:15, 16; Prov. 23:5; Ps. 62:10.
21. Matt. 6:25, 34.
22. Ps. 73:3; James 5:9.
23. II Thess. 3:11; Prov. 18:9.
24. Prov. 21:17; Prov. 23:20, 21; Prov. 28:19.
25. Deut. 12:7; Deut. 16:14.

Q. 143.
1. Exod. 20:16.

Q. 144.
1. Eph. 4:25.
2. III John 12.
3. Prov. 31:9.
4. Ps. 15:2.
5. Jer. 9:3.
6. Jer. 42:4; Acts 20:20.
7. Acts 20:27.
8. Lev. 19:15; Prov. 14:15.
9. Isa. 63:8; Col. 3:9; II Cor. 1:17.
10. Heb. 6:9; I Cor. 13:4, 5.
11. III John 4; Rom. 1:8.
12. II Cor. 12:21; Ps. 119:158.
13. Prov. 17:9; I Peter 4:8.
14. I Cor. 1:4, 5; II Tim. 1:4, 5.
15. Ps. 82:3.
16. I Cor. 13:4, 6, 7.
17. Ps. 15:3.
18. Prov. 25:23.
19. Prov. 26:24, 25.
20. Ps. 101:5.
21. II Cor. 11:18, 23; Prov. 22:1; John 8:49.
22. Ps. 15:4.
23. Phil. 4:8.

Q. 145.
1. Luke 3:14.
2. Lev. 19:15; Hab. 1:4.
3. Prov. 19:5; Prov. 6:16, 19.
4. Acts 6:13.
5. Jer. 9:3; Ps. 12:3, 4; Ps. 52:1–4.
6. Prov. 17:15.
7. Isa. 5:23.
8. I Kings 21:8.
9. Lev. 5:1; Acts 5:3.

10. Lev. 19:17; Isa. 58:1.
11. Isa. 59:4.
12. Prov. 29:11.
13. I Sam. 22:9, 10; Ps. 52:1.
14. Ps. 56:5; Matt. 26:60, 61. Compare John 2:19.
15. Gen. 3:5; Gen 26:7, 9.
16. Isa. 59:13.
17. Col. 3:9; Lev. 19:11.
18. Ps. 50:20.
19. Ps. 15:3; Rom. 1:30.
20. James 4:11; Titus 3:2.
21. Lev. 19:16.
22. Rom. 1:29; Prov. 16:28.
23. Isa. 28:22; Gen. 21:9; Gal. 4:29.
24. I Cor. 6:10.
25. Matt. 7:1.
26. James 2:13.
27. John 7:24; Rom 2:1.
28. Rom. 3:8; Ps. 69:10.
29. Ps. 12:2, 3.
30. II Tim. 3:2.
31. Luke 18:11; Gal. 5:26; Exod. 4:10, 14; Acts 12:22.
32. Isa. 29:20, 21; Matt. 7:3.
33. Gen. 3:12, 13; Prov. 28:13; Gen. 4:9.
34. Prov. 25:9; Gen. 9:22.
35. Exod. 23:1.
36. Jer. 20:10; Prov. 29:12.
37. Acts 7:57.
38. I Cor. 13:4, 5; I Tim. 6:4.
39. Matt. 21:15; Num. 11:29.
40. Dan. 6:3, 4; Ezra 4:12, 13.
41. Jer. 48:27.
42. Matt. 27:28, 29; Ps. 35:15, 16.
43. I Cor. 3:21; Jude 16; Acts 12:22.
44. Rom. 1:31; II Tim. 3:3.
45. II Sam. 12:14; I Sam. 2:24.
46. Phil. 3:18, 19; II Peter 2:2; II Sam. 12:13, 14.

Q. 146.
1. Exod. 20:17.

Q. 147.
1. Heb. 13:5; I Tim. 6:6.
2. Rom. 12:15; Phil. 2:4; I Tim. 1:5.

Q. 148.
1. I Cor. 10:10.
2. Gal. 5:26; James 3:14, 16.
3. Ps. 112:9, 10; Neh. 2:10.
4. Rom. 7:7; Deut. 5:21; Col. 3:5; Rom. 13:9.

Q. 149.
1. James 3:2; John 15:5.
2. I Kings 8:46; Ps. 17:15; I John 1:8–2:6.
3. Gen. 8:21; James 1:14; Gen. 6:5. See citations under figure 2 above.
4. Ps. 19:12; James 3:2, 8.

Q. 150.
1. Heb. 2:2, 3; Ezra 9:14; Ps. 78:17, 32, 56.

Q. 151.
1. Jer. 2:8.
2. I Kings 11:9.
3. II Sam. 12:14; I Cor. 5:1.
4. James 4:17; Luke 12:47.
5. John 3:10; Jer. 5:4, 5; II Sam. 12:7–9; Ezek. 8:11, 12.
6. Rom. 2:21, 23, 24.
7. Gal. 2:14; II Peter 2:2.
8. I John 5:10; Matt. 21:38, 39.
9. I Sam. 2:25; Acts 5:4.
10. Rom. 2:4.
11. Mal. 1:14; I Cor. 10:21, 22.
12. John 3:18, 36; Heb. 12:25.
13. Heb. 6:4–6; Heb. 10:29; Matt. 12:31, 32; Eph. 4:30.
14. Num. 12:8; Jude 8.
15. Prov. 30:17; Ps. 41:9; Ps. 55:12–14.
16. Zech. 2:8.
17. I Cor. 8:11, 12; Rom. 14:13, 15, 21.
18. I Thess. 2:15, 16; Matt. 23:34–38.
19. Isa. 3:9.
20. Ezek. 20:12, 13.
21. Col. 3:5; I Tim. 6:10.
22. Micah 2:1, 2.
23. Rom. 2:23, 24; Matt. 18:7.
24. Prov. 6:32–35; Matt. 16:26.
25. Matt. 11:21–24; John 15:22.
26. Deut. 32:6; Isa. 1:2, 3; Ezra 9:13, 14.
27. Jer. 5:3; Amos 4:8–11.
28. Rom. 1:20, 21.
29. Rom. 1:32; Dan. 5:22.

30. Prov. 29:1.
31. Matt. 18:17; Titus 3:10.
32. Rom. 13:1–5.
33. Ps. 78:34, 36, 37; Jer. 42:5, 6, 20–22; Prov. 20:25; Lev. 26:25; Jer. 31:32; Prov. 2:17; Ezek. 17:18.
34. Ps. 36:4; Jer. 6:16.
35. Num. 15:30; Jer. 6:15; Ps. 52:1.
36. Ezek. 35:5, 6; III John 10.
37. Num. 14:22.
38. Zech. 7:11, 12.
39. Prov. 2:14.
40. Jer. 9:3, 5; Isa. 57:17.
41. II Peter 2:20, 21; Heb. 6:4, 6.
42. Isa. 22:12–14; II Kings 5:26.
43. Jer. 7:10, 11.
44. Ezek. 23:38.
45. Isa. 58:3, 4.
46. I Cor. 11:20, 21; Jer. 7:9, 10.
47. Prov. 7:14, 15.
48. Neh. 9:13–16; II Chron. 36:15, 16.
49. Isa. 3:9; I Sam. 2:22–24.

Q. 152.
1. James 2:10, 11.
2. Mal. 1:14.
3. Deut. 32:6.
4. Hab. 1:13; I Peter 1:15, 16; Lev. 11:45.
5. I John 3:4; Rom. 7:12.
6. Gal. 3:10; Eph. 5:6.
7. Deut. 28:15; Prov. 13:21.
8. Matt. 25:41; Rom. 6:21, 23.
9. Heb. 9:22; I John 1:7; I Peter 1:18, 19.

Q. 153.
1. Acts 20:21; Mark 1:15; John 3:18.
2. See texts cited under Q. 154.

Q. 154.
1. Matt. 28:19, 20; Acts 2:42, 46; I Tim. 4:16; I Cor. 1:21; Eph. 5:19, 20; Eph. 6:17, 18.

Q. 155.
1. Jer. 23:28, 29; Heb. 4:12; Acts 17:11, 12; Acts 26:18.
2. Acts 2:37, 41; Acts 8:27–38.
3. II Cor. 3:18; Col. 1:27.
4. II Cor. 10:4, 5; Rom. 6:17.
5. Ps. 19:11; Col. 1:28; Eph. 6:16, 17; Matt. 4:7, 10.
6. Eph. 4:11, 12; Acts 20:32; II Tim. 3:15, 16; I Cor. 3:9–11.
7. Rom. 16:25; I Thess. 3:2, 13; Rom. 10:14–17.

Q. 156.
1. Deut. 17:18, 19; Isa. 34:16; John 5:39; Rev. 1:3.
2. Deut. 6:6, 7; Ps. 78:5, 6.
3. I Cor. 14:18, 19. See context.

Q. 157.
1. Ps. 119:97; Neh. 8:5; Isa. 66:2.
2. I Thess. 2:13; II Peter 1:16–21.
3. Ps. 119:18; Luke 24:44–48.
4. James 1:21, 22; I Peter 2:2; Mark 4:20.
5. Acts 17:11; Deut. 11:13.
6. Acts 8:30, 34; Matt. 13:23.
7. Ps. 1:2; Ps. 119:97.
8. Acts 2:38, 39; II Sam. 12:7; II Chron. 34:21.
9. Gal. 1:15, 16; Prov. 3:5.
10. Ps. 119:18; Luke 24:45.

Q. 158.
1. I Tim. 3:2, 6; II Tim. 2:2; Mal. 2:7.
2. Rom. 10:15; I Tim. 4:14.

Q. 159.
1. Titus 2:1, 8.
2. Acts 18:25; II Tim. 4:2.
3. I Cor. 14:9.
4. I Cor. 2:4.
5. Jer. 23:28; I Cor. 4:1, 2; Matt. 24:45–47.
6. Acts 20:27.
7. Col. 1:28; II Tim. 2:15.
8. I Cor. 3:2; Heb. 5:12–14; I Thess. 2:7; Luke 12:42.
9. Acts 18:25; II Tim. 4:5.
10. II Cor. 5:13, 14; Phil. 1:15–17.
11. II Cor. 12:15; I Thess. 3:12.
12. II Cor. 4:2; II Cor. 2:17.
13. John 7:18; I Thess. 2:4–6.
14. I Cor. 9:19–22.
15. II Cor. 12:19; Eph. 4:12.
16. I Tim. 4:16; II Tim. 2:10; Acts 26:16–18.

- Q. 160.
  1. Ps. 84:1, 2, 4; Ps. 27:4; Prov. 8:34.
  2. Luke 8:18; I Peter 2:1, 2; James 1:21.
  3. Ps. 119:18; Eph. 6:18, 19.
  4. Acts 17:11.
  5. Heb. 4:2.
  6. II Thess. 2:10.
  7. James 1:21; Ps. 25:9.
  8. Acts 17:11; Acts 2:41.
  9. I Thess. 2:13.
  10. Heb. 2:1.
  11. Deut. 6:6, 7.
  12. Ps. 119:11; Prov. 2:1–5.
  13. Luke 8:15; James 1:25.
- Q. 161.
  1. I Peter 3:21; Acts 8:13, 23; I Cor. 3:7; I Cor. 6:11.
- Q. 162.
  1. Matt. 28:19; Matt. 26:26, 27.
  2. Rom. 4:11; I Cor. 11:24, 25.
  3. Rom. 9:8; Gal. 3:27, 29; Gal. 5:6; Gal. 6:15.
  4. Acts 2:38; I Cor. 10:16; Acts 22:16.
  5. I Cor. 11:24–26.
  6. Rom. 6:4; I Cor. 10:21.
  7. I Cor. 12:13; I Cor. 10:17; Eph. 4:3–5.
  8. I Cor. 10:21.
- Q. 163.
  1. See Confession of Faith, Chapter XXIX, Section 2, and passages there cited.
- Q. 164.
  1. Matt. 28:19; Matt. 26:26, 27; I Cor. 11:23–26.
- Q. 165.
  1. Matt. 28:19.
  2. Gal. 3:27; Rom. 6:3.
  3. Acts 22:16; Mark 1:4; Rev. 1:5.
  4. John 3:5; Titus 3:5.
  5. Gal. 3:26, 27.
  6. I Cor. 15:29.
  7. Acts 2:41.
  8. Rom. 6:4.
- Q. 166.
  1. Acts 2:41.
  2. Acts 2:38, 39; I Cor. 7:14; Luke 18:16; Rom. 11:16; Gen. 17:7–9, compare with Col. 2:11, 12; Gal. 3:17, 18, 29.
- Q. 167.
  1. Ps. 22:10, 11.
  2. Rom. 6:3–5.
  3. Rom. 6:2, 3; I Cor. 1:11–13.
  4. I Peter 3:21; Rom. 4:11, 12.
  5. Rom. 6:2–4.
  6. Gal. 3:26, 27.
  7. Rom. 6:22.
  8. I Cor. 12:13, 25, 26. See context.
- Q. 168.
  1. I Cor. 11:26.
  2. Matt. 26:26, 27; I Cor. 11:23–27.
  3. I Cor. 10:16, 21.
  4. I Cor. 10:17.
- Q. 169.
  1. See General Note.
- Q. 170.
  1. The specifications enumerated in answers to Questions 170–175 are deduced from the nature of the Lord's Supper as set forth in the New Testament. The texts are given to show that these specifications are in accord with the general tenor of the Scriptures. Acts 3:21.
  2. Gal. 3:1; Heb. 11:1.
  3. John 6:51, 53. See context.
  4. I Cor. 10:16.
- Q. 171.
  1. I Cor. 11:28.
  2. II Cor. 13:5.
  3. I Cor. 5:7. Compare Exod. 12:15.
  4. I Cor. 11:29.
  5. II Cor. 13:5. See citation under figure 2 above.
  6. I Cor. 11:31.
  7. I Cor. 10:17.
  8. I Cor. 5:8; I Cor. 11:18, 20.
  9. Matt. 5:23, 24.
  10. John 7:37; Luke 1:53; Isa. 55:1.
  11. I Cor. 5:8.

12. Heb. 10:21, 22, 24; Ps. 26:6.
13. I Cor. 11:24.
14. Matt. 26:26; II Chron. 30:18, 19.

Q. 172.
1. Isa. 50:10.
2. Isa. 54:7, 8, 10; Matt. 5:3, 4; Ps. 31:22.
3. Ps. 42:11.
4. II Tim. 2:19; Rom. 7:24, 25.
5. Matt. 26:28; Matt. 11:28; Isa. 4:11, 29, 31.
6. Mark 9:24.
7. Acts 16:30; Acts 9:6.
8. I Cor. 11:28; Matt. 11:28.

Q. 173.
1. I Cor. 11:29; I Cor. 5:11; Matt. 7:6.
2. I Cor. 5:4, 5; II Cor. 2:5–8.

Q. 174.
1. Gal. 3:1.
2. I Cor. 11:29.
3. Luke 22:19.
4. I Cor. 11:31.
5. Zech. 12:10.
6. Ps. 63:1, 2.
7. Gal. 2:20; John 6:35.
8. John 1:16; Col. 1:19.
9. Phil. 3:9.
10. I Peter 1:8; I Chron. 30:21.
11. Ps. 22:26.
12. Jer. 50:5; Ps. 50:5.
13. I Cor. 10:17; Acts 2:42.

Q. 175.
1. I Cor. 11:17, 30, 31.
2. II Cor. 2:14; Acts 2:42, 46, 47.
3. I Cor. 10:12; Rom. 11:20.
4. Ps. 50:14.
5. I Cor. 11:25, 26; Ps. 27:4; Acts 2:42.
6. Ps. 77:6; Ps. 139:23, 24.
7. Ps. 123:1, 2; Isa. 8:17.
8. Hos. 14:2; Hos. 6:1, 2.
9. II Cor. 7:11; I Chron. 15:12–14.

Q. 176.
1. Matt. 28:19; I Cor. 11:23.
2. Rom. 6:3, 4; I Cor. 10:16.
3. Col. 2:11, 12. Compare with Rom. 4:11. Matt. 26:27, 28.
4. See General Note.
5. Matt. 28:20; I Cor. 11:26.

Q. 177.
1. Matt. 3:11; Gal. 3:27; Titus 3:5.
2. Acts 2:38, 39; I Cor. 7:14. See citations under Q. 166, figure 2.
3. I Cor. 11:26; Col. 2:19.
4. I Cor. 10:16; John 6:51–53.
5. I Cor. 11:28.

Q. 178.
1. Ps. 62:8.
2. John 16:23, 24.
3. Rom. 8:26.
4. Dan. 9:4; Ps. 32:5, 6.
5. Phil. 4:6.

Q. 179.
1. I Kings 8:39; Acts 1:24; Rom. 8:27.
2. Ps. 65:2.
3. Micah 7:18.
4. Ps. 145:16, 19.
5. II Sam. 22:32; John 14:1.
6. Matt. 4:10.
7. I Cor. 1:2.
8. Luke 4:8; Isa. 42:8; Jer. 3:23.

Q. 180.
1. John 14:13, 14; Dan. 9:17.
2. Luke 6:46; Matt. 7:21.
3. Heb. 4:14–16; I John 5:13–15.

Q. 181.
1. John 14:6; Eph. 3:12; I Tim. 2:5; John 6:27; Col. 3:17; Heb. 7:25–27; 13:15.

Q. 182.
1. Rom. 8:26; Ps. 80:18; Ps. 10:17; Zech. 12:10.

Q. 183.
1. Eph. 6:18; Ps. 28:9.
2. I Tim. 2:1, 2.
3. II Thess. 3:1; Col 4:3.
4. Gen. 32:11.
5. James 5:16; II Thess. 1:11.
6. Matt. 5:44.
7. I Tim. 2:1, 2. See under figure 2 above.
8. John 17:20; II Sam. 7:29.
9. This statement is based on the absence of any command to pray for the dead, and of any example in the Scriptures of such prayer.

# ENDNOTES FOR 7.294–.303

Q. 184.
1. Matt. 6:9.
2. Ps. 51:18; Ps. 122:6.
3. Matt. 7:11.
4. Ps. 125:4; I Thess. 5:23; II Thess. 3:16.
5. I John 5:14; James 4:3.

Q. 185.
1. Ps. 33:8; Ps. 95:6.
2. Gen. 18:27; Ps. 144:3.
3. Ps. 86:1; Luke 15:17–19.
4. Ps. 130:3; Luke 18:13.
5. Ps. 51:17; Zech. 12:10–14.
6. Phil. 4:6; I Thess. 5:18.
7. Ps. 81:10; Eph. 3:20, 21.
8. I Cor. 14:15.
9. Heb. 10:22; James 1:6.
10. Heb. 10:22; Ps. 145:18; Ps. 17:1; John 4:24.
11. James 5:16.
12. I Tim. 2:8; Matt. 5:23, 24.
13. Eph. 6:18.
14. Micah 7:7.
15. Matt. 26:39.

Q. 186.
1. II Tim. 3:16, 17; I John 5:14.
2. Matt. 6:9–13; Luke 11:2–4.

Q. 187.
1. Matt. 6:9; Luke 11:2.

Q. 189.
1. Matt. 6:9.
2. Luke 11:13; Rom. 8:15.
3. Ps. 95:6, 7; Isa. 64:9.
4. Ps. 123:1; Lam. 3:41.
5. Ps. 104:1; Isa. 63:15; Ps. 113:4–6.
6. Acts 12:5; Zech. 8:21.

Q. 190.
1. Matt. 6:9.
2. II Cor. 3:5; Ps. 51:15.
3. Ps. 67:2, 3; Ps. 72:19; Eph. 3:20, 21.
4. Ps. 83:18.
5. Ps. 145:6–8; Ps. 86:10–15.
6. II Thess. 3:1; Ps. 107:32; II Cor. 2:14.
7. Ps. 8 and 145, throughout.
8. Ps. 19:14.
9. Phil. 1:11.
10. Ps. 79:10; Ps. 67:1–4.
11. Eph. 1:17, 18.
12. Ps. 97:7.
13. Ps. 74:18, 22.
14. Jer. 14:21; II Kings 19:16.
15. Isa. 64:1, 2; II Chron. 20:6, 10–12.

Q. 191.
1. Matt. 6:10.
2. Eph. 2:2, 3.
3. Ps. 68:1; Rev. 12:9.
4. II Thess. 3:1.
5. Rom. 10:1; Ps. 67:2.
6. Rom. 11:25; Ps. 67:1–7.
7. Matt. 9:38.
8. Eph. 5:26, 27; Mal. 1:11.
9. II Cor. 4:2; Acts 26:18; II Thess. 2:16, 17.
10. Eph. 3:14, 17.
11. Rev. 22:20.
12. Isa. 64:1, 2; II Chron. 20:6, 10–12.

Q. 192.
1. Matt. 6:10.
2. I Cor. 2:14; Rom. 8:5, 8.
3. Rom. 8:7.
4. Matt. 20:11, 12; Ps. 73:3.
5. Titus 3:3; Eph. 2:2, 3. See Q. 191 under figure 2.
6. Eph. 1:17, 18.
7. Eph. 3:16.
8. Matt. 26:40, 41; Rom. 7:24, 25.
9. Ezek. 11:19; Jer. 31:18.
10. Ps. 119:35; Acts 21:14; I Sam. 3:18.
11. Ps. 123:2; Ps. 131:2; Micah 6:8.
12. Ps. 100:2.
13. Isa. 38:3; Eph. 6:6.
14. Ps. 119:4.
15. Rom. 12:11.
16. II Cor. 1:12.
17. Ps. 119:112; Rom. 2:7.
18. Ps. 103:20–22; Dan. 7:10.

Q. 193.
1. Matt. 6:11.
2. Gen. 3:17; Lam. 3:22; Deut. 28:15–68.
3. Deut. 8:3.
4. Gen. 32:10.
5. Deut. 8:18; Prov. 10:22.
6. Luke 12:15; Jer. 6:13.

7. Hos. 12:7.
8. James 4:3.
9. Gen. 28:20, 21; James 4:13, 15; Ps. 90:17; Ps. 144:12–15.
10. I Tim. 4:4, 5; Prov. 10:22.
11. I Tim.6:6, 8.
12. Prov. 30:8, 9.

Q. 194.
1. Matt. 6:12.
2. Matt. 18:24; Rom. 5:19; Rom. 3:9, 19. See context. Ps. 130:3; Micah 6:6, 7.
3. Rom. 5:19; Rom. 3:24, 25; Acts. 13:39.
4. Eph. 1:6.
5. II Peter 1:2.
6. Hos. 14:2; Ps. 143:2; Ps. 130:3.
7. Rom. 15:13; Rom. 5:1, 2; Ps. 51:7–12.
8. Luke 11:4; Matt. 18:35; Matt. 6:14, 15.

Q. 195.
1. Matt. 6:13.
2. II Chron. 32:31; Job 2:6.
3. I Peter 5:8; Job 2:2.
4. Luke 21:34; Mark 4:19.
5. James 1:14.
6. Gal. 5:17; Rom. 7:18.
7. Matt. 26:41.
8. I Tim. 6:9; Prov. 7:22.
9. Rom. 7:18, 19.
10. Ps. 81:11, 12.
11. John 17:15; Rom. 8:28.
12. Ps. 51:10; Ps. 119:133.
13. Heb. 2:18; I Cor. 10:13; II Cor. 12:8.
14. Rom. 8:28.
15. Heb. 13:20, 21; Eph. 4:11, 12.
16. Matt. 26:41; Ps. 19:13.
17. I Cor. 10:13; Eph. 3:14–16.
18. Ps. 51:12.
19. I Peter 5:10; I Peter 1:6, 7.
20. I Thess. 3:13.
21. Rom. 16:20.
22. I Thess. 5:23.

Q. 196.
1. Matt. 6:13.
2. Job. 23:3, 4; Jer. 14:20, 21.
3. Dan. 9:4, 7–9, 16, 19.
4. Phil. 4:6.
5. I Chron. 29:10–13.
6. Eph. 3:20, 21; Luke 11:13; Ps. 84:11.
7. Eph. 3:12; Heb. 10:19–22.
8. I John 5:14; Rom. 8:32.
9. I Cor. 14:16; Rev. 22:20, 21.

# THE THEOLOGICAL DECLARATION OF BARMEN

[TEXT]

# The Theological Declaration of Barmen

The Theological Declaration of Barmen was written by a group of church leaders in Germany to help Christians withstand the challenges of the Nazi party and of the so-called "German Christians," a popular movement that saw no conflict between Christianity and the ideals of Hitler's National Socialism.

In January 1933, after frustrating years in which no government in Germany was able to solve problems of economic depression and mass unemployment, Adolph Hitler was named chancellor. By playing on people's fear of communism and Bolshevism, he was able to persuade the Parliament to allow him to rule by edict. As he consolidated his power, Hitler abolished all political rights and democratic processes: police could detain persons in prison without a trial, search private dwellings without a warrant, seize property, censor publications, tap telephones, and forbid meetings. He soon outlawed all political parties except his own, smashed labor unions, purged universities, replaced the judicial system with his own "People's Courts," initiated a systematic terrorizing of Jews, and obtained the support of church leaders allied with or sympathetic to the German Christians.

Most Germans took the union of Christianity, nationalism, and militarism for granted, and patriotic sentiments were equated with Christian truth. The German Christians exalted the racially pure nation and the rule of Hitler as God's will for the German people.

Nonetheless, some in the churches resisted. Among those few determined church leaders who did oppose the church's captivity to National Socialism were pastors Hans Asmussen, Karl Koch, Karl Iraruer, and Martin Niemoller, and theologian Karl Barth. Following a number of regional meetings, these men assembled representatives of Lutheran, Reformed, and United churches in Gemarke Church, Barmen, in the city of Wupperthal, May 29–31, 1934. Among the one hundred thirty-nine delegates were ordained ministers, fifty-three church members, and six university professors.

The chief item of business was discussion of a declaration to appeal to the Evangelical churches of Germany to stand firm against the German Christian accommodation to National Socialism. The Theological Declaration of Barmen contains six propositions, each quoting from Scripture, stating its implications for the present day, and rejecting the false doctrine of the German Christians. The declaration proclaims the church's freedom in Jesus Christ who is Lord of every area of life. The church obeys him as God's one and only Word who determines its order, ministry, and relation to the state.

The declaration was debated and adopted without amendment, and the Confessing Church, that part of the church that opposed the German Christians, rallied around it.

# THE THEOLOGICAL DECLARATION OF BARMEN[1]

## I. An Appeal to the Evangelical Congregations and Christians in Germany

**8.01** The Confessional Synod of the German Evangelical Church met in Barmen, May 29–31, 1934. Here representatives from all the German Confessional churches met with one accord in a confession of the one Lord of the one, holy, apostolic Church. In fidelity to their Confession of Faith, members of Lutheran, Reformed, and United Churches sought a common message for the need and temptation of the Church in our day. With gratitude to God they are convinced that they have been given a common word to utter. It was not their intention to found a new church or to form a union. For nothing was farther from their minds than the abolition of the confessional status of our churches. Their intention was, rather, to withstand in faith and unanimity the destruction of the Confession of Faith, and thus of the Evangelical Church in Germany. In opposition to attempts to establish the unity of the German Evangelical Church by means of false doctrine, by the use of force and insincere practices, the Confessional Synod insists that the unity of the Evangelical Churches in Germany can come only from the Word of God in faith through the Holy Spirit. Thus alone is the Church renewed.

**8.02** Therefore the Confessional Synod calls upon the congregations to range themselves behind it in prayer, and steadfastly to gather around those pastors and teachers who are loyal to the Confessions.

**8.03** Be not deceived by loose talk, as if we meant to oppose the unity of the German nation! Do not listen to the seducers who pervert our intentions, as if we wanted to break up the unity of the German Evangelical Church or to forsake the Confessions of the Fathers!

**8.04** Try the spirits whether they are of God! Prove also the words of the Confessional Synod of the German Evangelical Church to see whether they agree with Holy Scripture and with the Confessions of the Fathers. If you find that we are speaking contrary to Scripture, then do not listen to us! But if you find that we are taking our stand upon Scripture, then let no fear or temptation keep you from treading with us the path of faith and obedience to the Word of God, in order that God's people be of one mind upon earth and that we in faith experience what he himself has said: "I will never leave you, nor forsake you." Therefore, "Fear not, little flock, for it is your Father's good pleasure to give you the kingdom."

---

[1] Reprinted from *The Church's Confessions Under Hitler* by Arthur C. Cochrane. Philadelphia: Westminster Press, 1962, pp. 237–242. Used by permission.

## II. Theological Declaration Concerning the Present Situation of the German Evangelical Church

**8.05** According to the opening words of its constitution of July 11, 1933, the German Evangelical Church is a federation of Confessional churches that grew out of the Reformation and that enjoy equal rights. The theological basis for the unification of these churches is laid down in Article 1 and Article 2(1) of the constitution of the German Evangelical Church that was recognized by the Reich Government on July 14, 1933:

> Article 1. The inviolable foundation of the German Evangelical Church is the gospel of Jesus Christ as it is attested for us in Holy Scripture and brought to light again in the Confessions of the Reformation. The full powers that the Church needs for its mission are hereby determined and limited.
>
> Article 2(1). The German Evangelical Church is divided into member Churches" (*Landeskirchen*).

**8.06** We, the representatives of Lutheran, Reformed, and United Churches, of free synods, church assemblies, and parish organizations united in the Confessional Synod of the German Evangelical Church, declare that we stand together on the ground of the German Evangelical Church as a federation of German Confessional churches. We are bound together by the confession of the one Lord of the one, holy, catholic, and apostolic Church.

**8.07** We publicly declare before all evangelical churches in Germany that what they hold in common in this Confession is grievously imperiled, and with it the unity of the German Evangelical Church. It is threatened by the teaching methods and actions of the ruling church party of the "German Christians" and of the church administration carried on by them. These have become more and more apparent during the first year of the existence of the German Evangelical Church. This threat consists in the fact that the theological basis, in which the German Evangelical Church is united, has been continually and systematically thwarted and rendered ineffective by alien principles, on the part of the leaders and spokesmen of the "German Christians" as well as on the part of the church administration. When these principles are held to be valid, then, according to all the Confessions in force among us, the church ceases to be the church and the German Evangelical Church, as a federation of Confessional churches, becomes intrinsically impossible.

**8.08** As members of Lutheran, Reformed, and United churches, we may and must speak with one voice in this matter today. Precisely because we want to be and to remain faithful to our various Confessions, we may not keep silent, since we believe that we have been given a common message to utter in a time of common need and temptation. We commend to God what this may mean for the interrelations of the Confessional churches.

**8.09** In view of the errors of the "German Christians" of the present Reich Church government which are devastating the Church and are also thereby breaking up the unity of the German Evangelical Church, we confess the following evangelical truths:

**8.10** 1. "I am the way, and the truth, and the life: no one comes to the Father, but by me." (John 14:6). "Truly, truly, I say to you, he who does not enter the sheepfold by the door but climbs in by another way, that man is a thief and a robber. ... I am the door; if anyone enters by me, he will be saved." (John 10:1, 9.)

**8.11** Jesus Christ, as he is attested for us in Holy Scripture, is the one Word of God which we have to hear and which we have to trust and obey in life and in death.

**8.12** We reject the false doctrine, as though the church could and would have to acknowledge as a source of its proclamation, apart from and besides this one Word of God, still other events and powers, figures and truths, as God's revelation.

**8.13** 2. "Christ Jesus, whom God made our wisdom, our righteousness and sanctification and redemption." (I Cor. 1:30.)

**8.14** As Jesus Christ is God's assurance of the forgiveness of all our sins, so in the same way and with the same seriousness is he also God's mighty claim upon our whole life. Through him befalls us a joyful deliverance from the godless fetters of this world for a free, grateful service to his creatures.

**8.15** We reject the false doctrine, as though there were areas of our life in which we would not belong to Jesus Christ, but to other lords—areas in which we would not need justification and sanctification through him.

**8.16** 3. "Rather, speaking the truth in love, we are to grow up in every way into him who is the head, into Christ, from whom the whole body [is] joined and knit together." (Eph. 4:15, 16.)

**8.17** The Christian Church is the congregation of the brethren in which Jesus Christ acts presently as the Lord in Word and Sacrament through the Holy Spirit. As the Church of pardoned sinners, it has to testify in the midst of a sinful world, with its faith as with its obedience, with its message as with its order, that it is solely his property, and that it lives and wants to live solely from his comfort and from his direction in the expectation of his appearance.

**8.18** We reject the false doctrine, as though the church were permitted to abandon the form of its message and order to its own pleasure or to changes in prevailing ideological and political convictions.

**8.19** 4. "You know that the rulers of the Gentiles lord it over them, and their great men exercise authority over them. It shall not be so among you; but whoever would be great among you must be your servant." (Matt. 20:25, 26.)

**8.20** The various offices in the church do not establish a dominion of some over the others; on the contrary, they are for the exercise of the ministry entrusted to and enjoined upon the whole congregation.

**8.21** We reject the false doctrine, as though the church, apart from this ministry, could and were permitted to give to itself, or allow to be given to it, special leaders vested with ruling powers.

**8.22** 5. "Fear God. Honor the emperor." (I Peter 2:17.)

Scripture tells us that, in the as yet unredeemed world in which the Church also exists, the State has by divine appointment the task of providing for justice and peace. [It fulfills this task] by means of the threat and exercise of force, according to the measure of human judgment and human ability. The church acknowledges the benefit of this divine appointment in gratitude and reverence before him. It calls to mind the Kingdom of God, God's commandment and righteousness, and thereby the responsibility both of rulers and of the ruled. It trusts and obeys the power of the Word by which God upholds all things.

**8.23** We reject the false doctrine, as though the State, over and beyond its special commission, should and could become the single and totalitarian order of human life, thus fulfilling the church's vocation as well.

**8.24** We reject the false doctrine, as though the church, over and beyond its special commission, should and could appropriate the characteristics, the tasks, and the dignity of the State, thus itself becoming an organ of the State.

**8.25** 6. "Lo, I am with you always, to the close of the age." (Matt. 28:20.) "The word of God is not fettered." (II Tim. 2:9.)

**8.26** The church's commission, upon which its freedom is founded, consists in delivering the message of the free grace of God to all people in Christ's stead, and therefore in the ministry of his own Word and work through sermon and Sacrament.

**8.27** We reject the false doctrine, as though the church in human arrogance could place the Word and work of the Lord in the service of any arbitrarily chosen desires, purposes, and plans.

**8.28** The Confessional Synod of the German Evangelical Church declares that it sees in the acknowledgment of these truths and in the rejection of these errors the indispensable theological basis of the German Evangelical Church as a federation of Confessional churches. It invites all who are able to accept its declaration to be mindful of these theological principles in their decisions in church politics. It entreats all whom it concerns to return to the unity of faith, love, and hope.

# THE CONFESSION OF 1967
[TEXT]

## The Confession of 1967

In approving the Confession of 1967, the United Presbyterian Church in the United States of America adopted its first new confession of faith in three centuries. The turbulent decade of the 1960s challenged churches everywhere to restate their faith. While the Second Vatican Council was reformulating Roman Catholic thought and practice, Presbyterians were developing the Confession of 1967.

The 168th General Assembly (1956) of the Presbyterian Church in the United States of America (PCUSA) received an overture asking that the Westminster Shorter Catechism be revised. The 170th General Assembly (1958) proposed instead that the church draw up a "brief contemporary statement of faith." A committee labored at the task seven years.

The 177th General Assembly (1965) (UPCUSA) vigorously discussed the committee's proposal and sent an amended draft to the church for study. Sessions, congregations, and presbyteries suggested changes and additions. In response, a newly appointed Committee of Fifteen made revisions. The 178th General Assembly (1966) (UPCUSA) debated this draft, accepted it, and forwarded it to the presbyteries for final ratification. After extensive debate, more than 90 percent of the presbyteries voted approval. Final adoption came at the 179th General Assembly (1967) (UPCUSA).

Modestly titled, the Confession of 1967 is built around a single passage of Scripture: "In Christ God was reconciling the world to himself..." (2 Cor. 5:19, NRSV). The first section, "God's Work of Reconciliation," is divided into three parts: the grace of the Lord Jesus Christ, the love of God, and the communion of the Holy Spirit. The second section, "The Ministry of Reconciliation," has two parts: the mission of and the equipment of the church. The last section, "The Fulfillment of Reconciliation," affirms the church's hope in God's ultimate triumph.

The Confession of 1967 addresses the church's role in the modern world. Responsive to developments in biblical scholarship, it asks the church to "approach the Scriptures with literary and historical understanding" (paragraph 9.29). It calls the church to obedient action, particularly in response to social problems such as racial discrimination, nationalistic arrogance, and family and class conflict. It sees the life, death, resurrection, and promised coming of Jesus Christ as the pattern for the church's mission today and calls on all Christians to be reconciled to God and to one another.

With the Confession of 1967, the church also adopted a *Book of Confessions* that placed creeds from the early Christian church (the Nicene and the Apostles' Creeds) and from the Reformation (the Scots Confession, the Heidelberg Catechism, and the Second Helvetic Confession) alongside the Westminster Confession and Catechisms, adding two documents from the twentieth century (the Theological Declaration of Barmen and the Confession of 1967).

# THE CONFESSION OF 1967

## PREFACE

**9.01** The church confesses its faith when it bears a present witness to God's grace in Jesus Christ.

**9.02** In every age the church has expressed its witness in words and deeds as the need of the time required. The earliest examples of confession are found within the Scriptures. Confessional statements have taken such varied forms as hymns, liturgical formulas, doctrinal definitions, catechisms, theological systems in summary, and declarations of purpose against threatening evil.

**9.03** Confessions and declarations are subordinate standards in the church, subject to the authority of Jesus Christ, the Word of God, as the Scriptures bear witness to him. No one type of confession is exclusively valid, no one statement is irreformable. Obedience to Jesus Christ alone identifies the one universal church and supplies the continuity of its tradition. This obedience is the ground of the church's duty and freedom to reform itself in life and doctrine as new occasions, in God's providence, may demand.

**9.04** The United Presbyterian Church in the United States of America acknowledges itself aided in understanding the gospel by the testimony of the church from earlier ages and from many lands. More especially it is guided by the Nicene and Apostles' Creeds from the time of the early church; the Scots Confession, the Heidelberg Catechism, the Second Helvetic Confession from the era of the Reformation; the Westminster Confession and Shorter Catechism from the seventeenth century; and the Theological Declaration of Barmen from the twentieth century.

**9.05** The purpose of the Confession of 1967 is to call the church to that unity in confession and mission which is required of disciples today. This Confession is not a "system of doctrine," nor does it include all the traditional topics of theology. For example, the Trinity and the Person of Christ are not redefined but are recognized and reaffirmed as forming the basis and determining the structure of the Christian faith.

**9.06** God's reconciling work in Jesus Christ and the mission of reconciliation to which he has called his church are the heart of the gospel in any age. Our generation stands in peculiar need of reconciliation in Christ. Accordingly this Confession of 1967 is built upon that theme.

## THE CONFESSION

**9.07** In Jesus Christ, God was reconciling the world to himself. Jesus Christ is God with man. He is the eternal Son of the Father, who became man and lived among us to fulfill the work of reconciliation. He is present in the church by the power of the Holy Spirit to continue and complete his mission. This work of God, the Father, Son, and Holy Spirit, is the foundation of all confessional statements about God, man, and the world. Therefore the church calls men to be reconciled to God and to one another.

## PART I
## GOD'S WORK OF RECONCILIATION

### Section A. The Grace of Our Lord Jesus Christ

1. JESUS CHRIST

**9.08** In Jesus of Nazareth true humanity was realized once for all. Jesus, a Palestinian Jew, lived among his own people and shared their needs, temptations, joys, and sorrows. He expressed the love of God in word and deed and became a brother to all kinds of sinful men. But his complete obedience led him into conflict with his people. His life and teaching judged their goodness, religious aspirations, and national hopes. Many rejected him and demanded his death. In giving himself freely for them he took upon himself the judgment under which all men stand convicted. God raised him from the dead, vindicating him as Messiah and Lord. The victim of sin became victor, and won the victory over sin and death for all men.

**9.09** God's reconciling act in Jesus Christ is a mystery which the Scriptures describe in various ways. It is called the sacrifice of a lamb, a shepherd's life given for his sheep, atonement by a priest; again it is ransom of a slave, payment of debt, vicarious satisfaction of a legal penalty, and victory over the powers of evil. These are expressions of a truth which remains beyond the reach of all theory in the depths of God's love for man. They reveal the gravity, cost, and sure achievement of God's reconciling work.

**9.10** The risen Christ is the Savior for all men. Those joined to him by faith are set right with God and commissioned to serve as his reconciling community. Christ is head of this community, the church, which began with the apostles and continues through all generations.

**9.11** The same Jesus Christ is the judge of all men. His judgment discloses the ultimate seriousness of life and gives promise of God's final victory over the power of sin and death. To receive life from the risen Lord is to have life eternal; to refuse life from him is to choose the death which is separation from God. All who put their trust in Christ face divine judgment without fear, for the judge is their redeemer.

2. THE SIN OF MAN

**9.12** The reconciling act of God in Jesus Christ exposes the evil in men as sin in the sight of God. In sin, men claim mastery of their own lives, turn against God and their fellow men, and become exploiters and despoilers of the world. They lose their humanity in futile striving and are left in rebellion, despair, and isolation.

**9.13** Wise and virtuous men through the ages have sought the highest good in devotion to freedom, justice, peace, truth, and beauty. Yet all human virtue, when seen in the light of God's love in Jesus Christ, is found to be infected by self-interest and hostility. All men, good and bad alike, are in the wrong before God and helpless without his forgiveness. Thus all men fall under God's judgment. No one is more subject to that judgment than the man who assumes that he is guiltless before God or morally superior to others.

**9.14** God's love never changes. Against all who oppose him, God expresses his love in wrath. In the same love, God took on himself judgment and shameful death in Jesus Christ, to bring men to repentance and new life.

### Section B. The Love of God

**9.15** God's sovereign love is a mystery beyond the reach of man's mind. Human thought ascribes to God superlatives of power, wisdom, and goodness. But God reveals his love in Jesus Christ by showing power in the form of a servant, wisdom in the folly of the cross, and goodness in receiving sinful men. The power of God's love in Christ to transform the world discloses that the Redeemer is the Lord and Creator who made all things to serve the purpose of his love.

**9.16** God has created the world of space and time to be the sphere of his dealings with men. In its beauty and vastness, sublimity and awfulness, order and disorder, the world reflects to the eye of faith the majesty and mystery of its Creator.

**9.17** God has created man in a personal relation with himself that man may respond to the love of the Creator. He has created male and female and given them a life which proceeds from birth to death in a succession of generations and in a wide complex of social relations. He has endowed man with capacities to make the world serve his needs and to enjoy its good things. Life is a gift to be received with gratitude and a task to be pursued with courage. Man is free to seek his life within the purpose of God: to develop and protect the resources of nature for the common welfare, to work for justice and peace in society, and in other ways to use his creative powers for the fulfillment of human life.

**9.18** God expressed his love for all mankind through Israel, whom he chose to be his covenant people to serve him in love and faithfulness. When Israel was unfaithful, he disciplined the nation with his judgments and maintained his cause through prophets, priests, teachers, and true believers. These witnesses called all Israelites to a destiny in which they would serve God faithfully and become a light to the nations. The same witnesses proclaimed the coming of a new age, and a true servant of God in whom God's purpose for Israel and for mankind would be realized.

**9.19** Out of Israel God in due time raised up Jesus. His faith and obedience were the response of the perfect child of God. He was the fulfillment of God's promise to Israel, the beginning of the new creation, and the pioneer of the new humanity. He gave history its meaning and direction and called the church to be his servant for the reconciliation of the world.

**Section C. The Communion of the Holy Spirit**

**9.20** God the Holy Spirit fulfills the work of reconciliation in man. The Holy Spirit creates and renews the church as the community in which men are reconciled to God and to one another. He enables them to receive forgiveness as they forgive one another and to enjoy the peace of God as they make peace among themselves. In spite of their sin, he gives them power to become representatives of Jesus Christ and his gospel of reconciliation to all men.

1. THE NEW LIFE

**9.21** The reconciling work of Jesus was the supreme crisis in the life of mankind. His cross and resurrection become personal crisis and present hope for men when the gospel is proclaimed and believed. In this experience the Spirit brings God's forgiveness to men, moves them to respond in faith, repentance, and obedience, and initiates the new life in Christ.

**9.22** The new life takes shape in a community in which men know that God loves and accepts them in spite of what they are. They therefore accept themselves and love others, knowing that no man has any ground on which to stand, except God's grace.

**9.23** The new life does not release a man from conflict with unbelief, pride, lust, fear. He still has to struggle with disheartening difficulties and problems. Nevertheless, as he matures in love and faithfulness in his life with Christ, he lives in freedom and good cheer, bearing witness on good days and evil days, confident that the new life is pleasing to God and helpful to others.

**9.24** The new life finds its direction in the life of Jesus, his deeds and words, his struggles against temptation, his compassion, his anger, and his willingness to suffer death. The teaching of apostles and prophets guides men in living this life, and the Christian community nurtures and equips them for their ministries.

**9.25** The members of the church are emissaries of peace and seek the good of man in cooperation with powers and authorities in politics, culture, and economics. But they have to fight against pretensions and injustices when these same powers endanger human welfare. Their strength is in their confidence that God's purpose rather than man's schemes will finally prevail.

**9.26** Life in Christ is life eternal. The resurrection of Jesus is God's sign that he will consummate his work of creation and reconciliation beyond death and bring to fulfillment the new life begun in Christ.

2. THE BIBLE

**9.27** The one sufficient revelation of God is Jesus Christ, the Word of God incarnate, to whom the Holy Spirit bears unique and authoritative witness through the Holy Scriptures, which are received and obeyed as the word of God written. The Scriptures are not a witness among others, but the witness without parallel. The church has received the books of the Old and New Testaments as prophetic and apostolic testimony in which it hears the word of God and by which its faith and obedience are nourished and regulated.

**9.28** The New Testament is the recorded testimony of apostles to the coming of the Messiah, Jesus of Nazareth, and the sending of the Holy Spirit to the Church. The Old Testament bears witness to God's faithfulness in his covenant with Israel and points the way to the fulfillment of his purpose in Christ. The Old Testament is indispensable to understanding the New, and is not itself fully understood without the New.

**9.29** The Bible is to be interpreted in the light of its witness to God's work of reconciliation in Christ. The Scriptures, given under the guidance of the Holy Spirit, are nevertheless the words of men, conditioned by the language, thought forms, and literary fashions of the places and times at which they were written. They reflect views of life, history, and the cosmos which were then current. The church, therefore, has an obligation to approach the Scriptures with literary and historical understanding. As God has spoken his word in diverse cultural situations, the church is confident that he will continue to speak through the Scriptures in a changing world and in every form of human culture.

**9.30** God's word is spoken to his church today where the Scriptures are faithfully preached and attentively read in dependence on the illumination of the Holy Spirit and with readiness to receive their truth and direction.

PART II
THE MINISTRY OF RECONCILIATION

### Section A. The Mission of the Church

1. DIRECTION

**9.31** To be reconciled to God is to be sent into the world as his reconciling community. This community, the church universal, is entrusted with

God's message of reconciliation and shares his labor of healing the enmities which separate men from God and from each other. Christ has called the church to this mission and given it the gift of the Holy Spirit. The church maintains continuity with the apostles and with Israel by faithful obedience to his call.

**9.32** The life, death, resurrection, and promised coming of Jesus Christ has set the pattern for the church's mission. His life as man involves the church in the common life of men. His service to men commits the church to work for every form of human well-being. His suffering makes the church sensitive to all the sufferings of mankind so that it sees the face of Christ in the faces of men in every kind of need. His crucifixion discloses to the church God's judgment on man's inhumanity to man and the awful consequences of its own complicity in injustice. In the power of the risen Christ and the hope of his coming, the church sees the promise of God's renewal of man's life in society and of God's victory over all wrong.

**9.33** The church follows this pattern in the form of its life and in the method of its action. So to live and serve is to confess Christ as Lord.

2. FORMS AND ORDERS

**9.34** The institutions of the people of God change and vary as their mission requires in different times and places. The unity of the church is compatible with a wide variety of forms, but it is hidden and distorted when variant forms are allowed to harden into sectarian divisions, exclusive denominations, and rival factions.

**9.35** Wherever the church exists, its members are both gathered in corporate life and dispersed in society for the sake of mission in the world.

**9.36** The church gathers to praise God, to hear his word for mankind, to baptize and to join in the Lord's Supper, to pray for and present the world to him in worship, to enjoy fellowship, to receive instruction, strength, and comfort, to order and organize its own corporate life, to be tested, renewed, and reformed, and to speak and act in the world's affairs as may be appropriate to the needs of the time.

**9.37** The church disperses to serve God wherever its members are, at work or play, in private or in the life of society. Their prayer and Bible study are part of the church's worship and theological reflection. Their witness is the church's evangelism. Their daily action in the world is the church in mission to the world. The quality of their relation with other persons is the measure of the church's fidelity.

**9.38** Each member is the church in the world, endowed by the Spirit with some gift of ministry and is responsible for the integrity of his witness in his own particular situation. He is entitled to the guidance and support of the Christian community and is subject to its advice and correction. He in turn, in his own competence, helps to guide the church.

**9.39** In recognition of special gifts of the Spirit and for the ordering of its life as a community, the church calls, trains, and authorizes certain members for leadership and oversight. The persons qualified for these duties in accordance with the polity of the church are set apart by ordination or other appropriate act and thus made responsible for their special ministries.

**9.40** The church thus orders its life as an institution with a constitution, government, officers, finances, and administrative rules. These are instruments of mission, not ends in themselves. Different orders have served the gospel, and none can claim exclusive validity. A presbyterian polity recognizes the responsibility of all members for ministry and maintains the organic relation of all congregations in the church. It seeks to protect the church from exploitation by ecclesiastical or secular power and ambition. Every church order must be open to such reformation as may be required to make it a more effective instrument of the mission of reconciliation.

3. REVELATION AND RELIGION

**9.41** The church in its mission encounters the religions of men and in that encounter becomes conscious of its own human character as a religion. God's revelation to Israel, expressed within Semitic culture, gave rise to the religion of the Hebrew people. God's revelation in Jesus Christ called forth the response of Jews and Greeks and came to expression within Judaism and Hellenism as the Christian religion. The Christian religion, as distinct from God's revelation of himself, has been shaped throughout its history by the cultural forms of its environment.

**9.42** The Christian finds parallels between other religions and his own and must approach all religions with openness and respect. Repeatedly God has used the insight of non-Christians to challenge the church to renewal. But the reconciling word of the gospel is God's judgment upon all forms of religion, including the Christian. The gift of God in Christ is for all men. The church, therefore, is commissioned to carry the gospel to all men whatever their religion may be and even when they profess none.

4. RECONCILIATION IN SOCIETY

**9.43** In each time and place there are particular problems and crises through which God calls the church to act. The church, guided by the Spirit, humbled by its own complicity and instructed by all attainable knowledge, seeks to discern the will of God and learn how to obey in these concrete situations. The following are particularly urgent at the present time.

**9.44** a. God has created the peoples of the earth to be one universal family. In his reconciling love, he overcomes the barriers between brothers and breaks down every form of discrimination based on racial or ethnic difference, real or imaginary. The church is called to bring all men to receive and uphold one another as persons in all relationships of life: in employment, housing, education, leisure, marriage, family, church, and the exercise of political rights. Therefore, the church labors for the abolition of all racial discrimination and ministers to those injured by it. Congregations, individuals, or groups of Christians who exclude, dominate, or patronize their fellowmen, however subtly, resist the Spirit of God and bring contempt on the faith which they profess.

**9.45** b. God's reconciliation in Jesus Christ is the ground of the peace, justice, and freedom among nations which all powers of government are called to serve and defend. The church, in its own life, is called to practice the forgiveness of enemies and to commend to the nations as practical politics the search for cooperation and peace. This search requires that the nations pursue fresh and responsible relations across every line of conflict, even at risk to national security, to reduce areas of strife and to broaden international understanding. Reconciliation among nations becomes peculiarly urgent as countries develop nuclear, chemical, and biological weapons, diverting their manpower and resources from constructive uses and risking the annihilation of mankind. Although nations may serve God's purposes in history, the church which identifies the sovereignty of any one nation or any one way of life with the cause of God denies the Lordship of Christ and betrays its calling.

**9.46** c. The reconciliation of man through Jesus Christ makes it plain that enslaving poverty in a world of abundance is an intolerable violation of God's good creation. Because Jesus identified himself with the needy and exploited, the cause of the world's poor is the cause of his disciples. The church cannot condone poverty, whether it is the product of unjust social structures, exploitation of the defenseless, lack of national resources, absence of technological understanding, or rapid expansion of populations. The church calls every man to use his abilities, his possessions, and the fruits of technology as gifts entrusted to him by God for the maintenance of his family and the advancement of the common welfare. It encourages those forces in human society that raise men's hopes for better conditions and provide them with opportunity for a decent living. A church that is indifferent to poverty, or evades responsibility in economic affairs, or is open to one social class only, or expects gratitude for its beneficence makes a mockery of reconciliation and offers no acceptable worship to God.

**9.47** d. The relationship between man and woman exemplifies in a basic way God's ordering of the interpersonal life for which he created mankind. Anarchy in sexual relationships is a symptom of man's alienation from God, his neighbor, and himself. Man's perennial confusion about the meaning of sex has been aggravated in our day by the availability of new means of birth control and the treatment of infection, by the pressures of urbanization, by the exploitation of sexual symbols in mass communication, and by world overpopulation. The church, as the household of God, is called to lead men out of this alienation into the responsible freedom of the new life in Christ. Reconciled to God, each person has joy in and respect for his own humanity and that of other persons; a man and woman are enabled to marry, to commit themselves to a mutually shared life, and to respond to each other in sensitive and lifelong concern; parents receive the grace to care for children in love and to nurture their individuality. The church comes under the judgment of God and invites rejection by man when it fails to lead men and women into the full meaning of life together, or withholds the compassion of Christ from those caught in the moral confusion of our time.

### Section B. The Equipment of the Church

**9.48** Jesus Christ has given the church preaching and teaching, praise and prayer, and Baptism and the Lord's Supper as means of fulfilling its service of God among men. These gifts remain, but the church is obliged to change the forms of its service in ways appropriate to different generations and cultures.

1. PREACHING AND TEACHING

**9.49** God instructs his church and equips it for mission through preaching and teaching. By these, when they are carried on in fidelity to the Scriptures and dependence upon the Holy Spirit, the people hear the word of God and accept and follow Christ. The message is addressed to men in particular situations. Therefore, effective preaching, teaching, and personal witness require disciplined study of both the Bible and the contemporary world. All acts of public worship should be conducive to men's hearing of the gospel in a particular time and place and responding with fitting obedience.

2. PRAISE AND PRAYER

**9.50** The church responds to the message of reconciliation in praise and prayer. In that response, it commits itself afresh to its mission, experiences a deepening of faith and obedience, and bears open testimony to the gospel. Adoration of God is acknowledgment of the Creator by the creation. Confession of sin is admission of all men's guilt before God and of their need for his forgiveness. Thanksgiving is rejoicing in God's goodness to all men and in giving for the needs of others. Petitions and intercessions are addressed to God for the continuation of his goodness, the healing of men's ills, and their deliverance from every form of oppression. The arts, especially music and architecture, contribute to the praise and prayer of a Christian congregation when they help men to look beyond themselves to God and to the world which is the object of his love.

3. BAPTISM

**9.51** By humble submission to John's baptism, Christ joined himself to men in their need and entered upon his ministry of reconciliation in the power of the spirit. Christian baptism marks the receiving of the same Spirit by all his people. Baptism with water represents not only cleansing from sin but a dying with Christ and a joyful rising with him to new life. It commits all Christians to die each day to sin and to live for righteousness. In baptism the church celebrates the renewal of the covenant with which God has bound his people to himself. By baptism, individuals are publicly received into the church to share in its life and ministry, and the church becomes responsible for their training and support in Christian discipleship. When those baptized are infants, the congregation, as well as the parents, has a special obligation to nurture them in the Christian life, leading them to make, by a public profession, a personal response to the love of God shown forth in their baptism.

4. THE LORD'S SUPPER

**9.52** The Lord's Supper is a celebration of the reconciliation of men with God and with one another, in which they joyfully eat and drink together at the table of their Savior. Jesus Christ gave his church this remembrance of his dying for sinful men so that by participation in it they have communion with him and with all who shall be gathered to him. Partaking in him as they eat the bread and drink the wine in accordance with Christ's appointment, they receive from the risen and living Lord the benefits of his death and resurrection. They rejoice in the foretaste of the kingdom which he will bring to consummation at his promised coming, and go out from the Lord's Table with courage and hope for the service to which he has called them.

## PART III
## THE FULFILLMENT OF RECONCILIATION

**9.53** God's redeeming work in Jesus Christ embraces the whole of man's life: social and cultural, economic and political, scientific and technological, individual and corporate. It includes man's natural environment as exploited and despoiled by sin. It is the will of God that his purpose for human life shall be fulfilled under the rule of Christ and all evil be banished from his creation.

**9.54** Biblical visions and images of the rule of Christ, such as a heavenly city, a father's house, a new heaven and earth, a marriage feast, and an unending day culminate in the image of the kingdom. The kingdom represents the triumph of God over all that resists his will and disrupts his creation. Already God's reign is present as a ferment in the world, stirring hope in men and preparing the world to receive its ultimate judgment and redemption.

**9.55** With an urgency born of this hope, the church applies itself to present tasks and strives for a better world. It does not identify limited progress with the kingdom of God on earth, nor does it despair in the face of disappointment and defeat. In steadfast hope, the church looks beyond all partial achievement to the final triumph of God.

**9.56** "Now to him who by the power at work within us is able to do far more abundantly than all we ask or think, to him be glory in the church and in Christ Jesus to all generations, forever and ever. Amen."

# CONFESSION OF BELHAR
[TEXT]

# CONFESSION OF BELHAR

How should the church respond when sin disrupts the church's unity, creates division among the children of God, and constructs unjust systems that steal life from God's creation? Members and leaders of the Dutch Reformed Mission Church in South Africa faced these questions under apartheid, a system of laws that separated people by race from 1948–1994.

Apartheid formed a racially stratified society. Those with the lightest skin tones were offered the greatest protection and opportunity. Non-"white" persons were separated into three categories; each skin tone step away from the "white" category represented a decrease in governmental protections and opportunities. Racial separation was established by law and enforced through violence. Non-white citizens lived with constant and intrusive police presence and interference in the daily functions of life. Those who protested risked punishment, imprisonment, and even death.

The roots of apartheid go back in South African culture and church for several centuries. The Dutch Reformed Church embodied racial separation when it formed three "mission" churches in the late nineteenth century, each categorized by its racial identity. The Dutch Reformed Mission Church was formed for people designated as "coloured" (biracial). The church's complicity with racial separation kept Christians from worshipping and coming to the Lord's Table together. The white Dutch Reformed Church (DRC) created an elaborate biblical interpretation and ideology that supported racial separation and then the formal apartheid policies.

The Dutch Reformed Church's active participation and theological defense of apartheid moved the global church to name apartheid a *status confessionis*—a conviction that the Gospel was at stake and thus the faith needed to be proclaimed. Leaders of the Dutch Reformed Mission Church wrestled with this situation theologically and practically. One outcome of their struggles was the emergence of the Confession of Belhar in the early 1980s.

The Uniting Reformed Church of Southern Africa (URCSA), the church that succeeded the Dutch Reformed Mission Church after apartheid, has offered the Confession of Belhar to the global Reformed family as a gift, believing that the themes of unity, reconciliation, and justice issue a call from God to the whole church toward holy action, transformation, and life.

The Special Committee on the Confession of Belhar recommended that the Presbyterian Church (U.S.A.) add Belhar as part of its Constitution because it believed the clarity of Belhar's witness to unity, reconciliation, and justice might help the PC(USA) speak and act with similar clarity at a time when it faces division, racism, and injustice.

The Presbyterian Church (U.S.A.) approved the Confession of Belhar as part of the *Book of Confessions* at the 222nd General Assembly (2016).

## CONFESSION OF BELHAR
September 1986[1]

**10.1**
Revelation 21:6–7

**We believe** in the triune God, Father, Son and Holy Spirit, who gathers, protects and cares for the church through Word and Spirit. This, God has done since the beginning of the world and will do to the end.

**10.2**
Matthew 28:19–20

**We believe** in one holy, universal Christian church, the communion of saints called from the entire human family.

**10.3**

**We believe**

Ephesians 2:13–20

- that Christ's work of reconciliation is made manifest in the church as the community of believers who have been reconciled with God and with one another;

Ephesians 4:11–16, Psalm 133

- that unity is, therefore, both a gift and an obligation for the church of Jesus Christ; that through the working of God's Spirit it is a binding force, yet simultaneously a reality which must be earnestly pursued and sought: one which the people of God must continually be built up to attain;

John 17:20–23

- that this unity must become visible so that the world may believe that separation, enmity and hatred between people and groups is sin which Christ has already conquered, and accordingly that anything which threatens this unity may have no place in the church and must be resisted;

John 13:34

- that this unity of the people of God must be manifested and be active in a variety of ways;

Colossians 3:12–16

* in that we love one another;

Philippians 2:1–5

* that we experience, practice and pursue community with one another;

1 Corinthians 1:10–13

* that we are obligated to give ourselves willingly and joyfully to be of benefit and blessing to one another;

---

[1] This is a translation of the original Afrikaans text of the confession as it was adopted by the synod of the Dutch Reformed Mission Church in South Africa in 1986. In 1994 the Dutch Reformed Mission Church and the Dutch Reformed Church in Africa united to form the Uniting Reformed Church in Southern Africa (URCSA). This inclusive language text was prepared by the Office of Theology and Worship, Presbyterian Church (U.S.A.).

| | | |
|---|---|---|
| Ephesians 4:1–6 | * | that we share one faith, have one calling, are of one soul and one mind; |
| 1 Corinthians 10:16–17 | * | have one God and Father, are filled with one Spirit, are baptized with one baptism, eat of one bread and drink of one cup, confess one name, are obedient to one Lord, work for one cause, and share one hope; |
| Ephesians 3:18–20 | * | together come to know the height and the breadth and the depth of the love of Christ; |
| | * | together are built up to the stature of Christ, to the new humanity; |
| Galatians 6:2 | * | together know and bear one another's burdens, thereby fulfilling the law of Christ; |
| 2 Corinthians 1:3–4 | * | that we need one another and upbuild one another, admonishing and comforting one another; |
| 1 Corinthians 12:24b–28, Ephesians 3:14–20 | * | that we suffer with one another for the sake of righteousness; pray together; together serve God in this world; and together fight against all which may threaten or hinder this unity; |
| 1 Corinthians 12:4–11, Romans 12:3–8 | • | that this unity can be established only in freedom and not under constraint; that the variety of spiritual gifts, opportunities, backgrounds, convictions, as well as the various languages and cultures, are by virtue of the reconciliation in Christ, opportunities for mutual service and enrichment within the one visible people of God; |
| Galatians 3:27–29 | • | that true faith in Jesus Christ is the only condition for membership of this church; |

**10.4** **Therefore, we reject any doctrine**

- which absolutizes either natural diversity or the sinful separation of people in such a way that this absolutization hinders or breaks the visible and active unity of the church, or even leads to the establishment of a separate church formation;
- which professes that this spiritual unity is truly being maintained in the bond of peace while believers of the same confession are in effect alienated from one another for the sake of diversity and in despair of reconciliation;
- which denies that a refusal earnestly to pursue this visible unity as a priceless gift is sin;

- which explicitly or implicitly maintains that descent or any other human or social factor should be a consideration in determining membership of the church.

**10.5** **We believe**

2 Corinthians 5:17–21
- that God has entrusted the church with the message of reconciliation in and through Jesus Christ;

Matthew 5:9, 13–16; 2 Peter 3:13; Revelation 21:1–5
- that the church is called to be the salt of the earth and the light of the world, that the church is called blessed because it is a peacemaker, that the church is witness both by word and by deed to the new heaven and the new earth in which righteousness dwells;

Romans 6:12–14, Colossians 1:11–14
- that God's life-giving Word and Spirit has conquered the powers of sin and death, and therefore also of irreconciliation and hatred, bitterness and enmity, that God's life-giving Word and Spirit will enable the church to live in a new obedience which can open new possibilities of life for society and the world;

James 2:8–9
- that the credibility of this message is seriously affected and its beneficial work obstructed when it is proclaimed in a land which professes to be Christian, but in which the enforced separation of people on a racial basis promotes and perpetuates alienation, hatred and enmity;

- that any teaching which attempts to legitimate such forced separation by appeal to the gospel, and is not prepared to venture on the road of obedience and reconciliation, but rather, out of prejudice, fear, selfishness and unbelief, denies in advance the reconciling power of the gospel, must be considered ideology and false doctrine.

**10.6** **Therefore, we reject any doctrine** which, in such a situation sanctions in the name of the gospel or of the will of God the forced separation of people on the grounds of race and color and thereby in advance obstructs and weakens the ministry and experience of reconciliation in Christ.

## 10.7 We believe

- Isaiah 42:1–7 — that God has revealed God's self as the one who wishes to bring about justice and true peace among people;
- Luke 6:20–26 — that God, in a world full of injustice and enmity, is in a special way the God of the destitute, the poor and the wronged
- Luke 4:16–19 — that God calls the church to follow God in this; for God brings justice to the oppressed and gives bread to the hungry;
- Luke 7:22 — that God frees the prisoner and restores sight to the blind;
- Psalm 146 — that God supports the downtrodden, protects the stranger, helps orphans and widows and blocks the path of the ungodly;
- James 1:27 — that for God pure and undefiled religion is to visit the orphans and the widows in their suffering;
- Micah 6:8 — that God wishes to teach the church to do what is good and to seek the right;
- Amos 5:14–15, 23–24 — that the church must therefore stand by people in any form of suffering and need, which implies, among other things, that the church must witness against and strive against any form of injustice, so that justice may roll down like waters, and righteousness like an ever-flowing stream;
- Psalm 82:1–5 — that the church as the possession of God must stand where the Lord stands, namely against injustice and with the wronged;
- Leviticus 19:15 — that in following Christ the church must witness against all the powerful and privileged who selfishly seek their own interests and thus control and harm others.

## 10.8 Therefore, we reject any ideology

- which would legitimate forms of injustice and any doctrine which is unwilling to resist such an ideology in the name of the gospel.

**10.9**
Acts 5:29–32;
1 Peter 3:15–18

**We believe** that, in obedience to Jesus Christ, its only head, the church is called to confess and to do all these things, even though the authorities and human laws might forbid them and punishment and suffering be the consequence.

Jesus is Lord.

To the one and only God, Father, Son and Holy Spirit, be the honor and the glory for ever and ever.

### Accompanying Letter to the Confession of Belhar[2]

*This letter was a statement made upon the adoption of the Confession of Belhar by the Uniting Reformed Church in Southern Africa*

1. We are deeply conscious that moments of such seriousness can arise in the life of the Church that it may feel the need to confess its faith anew in the light of a specific situation. We are aware that such an act of confession is not lightly undertaken, but only if it is considered that the heart of the gospel is so threatened as to be at stake. In our judgment, the present church and political situation in our country and particularly within the Dutch Reformed church family calls for such a decision. Accordingly, we make this confession not as a contribution to a theological debate nor as a new summary of our beliefs, but as a cry from the heart, as something we are obliged to do for the sake of the gospel in view of the times in which we stand. Along with many, we confess our guilt, in that we have not always witnessed clearly enough in our situation and so are jointly responsible for the way in which those things which were experienced as sin and confessed to be sin have grown in time to seem self-evidently right and to be ideologies foreign to the Scriptures. As a result many have been given the impression that the gospel was not really at stake. We make this confession because we are convinced that all sorts of theological arguments have contributed to so disproportionate an emphasis on some aspects of the truth that it has in effect become a lie.

2. We are aware that the only authority for such a confession and the only grounds on which it may be made are the Holy Scriptures as the Word of God. Being fully aware of the risk involved in taking this step, we are nevertheless convinced that we have no alternative. Furthermore, we are aware that no other motives or convictions, however valid they may be, would give us the right to confess in this way. An act of confession may only be made by the Church for the sake of its purity and credibility and that of its message. As solemnly as we are able, we hereby declare before men that our only motive lies in our fear that the truth and power of the gospel itself is threatened in this situation. We do not wish to serve any group interests, advance the cause of any factions, promote any theologies, or achieve any ulterior purposes. Yet, having said this, we know that our deepest intentions may only be judged at their true value by him before whom all is revealed. We do not make this confession from his throne and from on high, but before his throne and before men. We plead, therefore, that this confession would not be misused by anyone with ulterior motives and also that it should not be resisted to serve such motives. Our earnest desire is to lay

---

[2] While not of constitutional character, the following letter accompanies the Confession of Belhar to explain the context of the confession.

no false stumbling blocks in the way, but to point to the true stumbling block, Jesus Christ the rock.

3. This confession is not aimed at specific people or groups of people or a church or churches. We proclaim it against a false doctrine, against an ideological distortion which threatens the gospel itself in our church and our country. Our heartfelt longing is that no one will identify himself with this objectionable doctrine and that all who have been wholly or partially blinded by it will turn themselves away from it. We are deeply aware of the deceiving nature of such a false doctrine and know that many who have been conditioned by it have to a greater or lesser extent learnt to take a half-truth for the whole. For this reason we do not doubt the Christian faith of many such people, their sincerity, honor, integrity, and good intentions and their in many ways estimable practice and conduct. However, it is precisely because we know the power of deception that we know we are not liberated by the seriousness, sincerity, or intensity of our certainties, but only by the truth in the Son. Our church and our land have an intense need of such liberation. Therefore it is that we speak pleadingly rather than accusingly. We plead for reconciliation, that true reconciliation which follows on conversion and change of attitudes and structures. And while we do so we are aware that an act of confession is a two-edged sword, that none of us can throw the first stone, and none is without a beam in his own eye. We know that the attitudes and conduct which work against the gospel are present in all of us and will continue to be so. Therefore this confession must be seen as a call to a continuous process of soul searching together, a joint wrestling with the issues, and a readiness to repent in the name of our Lord Jesus Christ in a broken world. It is certainly not intended as an act of self-justification and intolerance, for that would disqualify us in the very act of preaching to others.

4. Our prayer is that this act of confession will not place false stumbling blocks in the way and thereby cause and foster false divisions, but rather that it will be reconciling and uniting. We know that such an act of confession and process of reconciliation will necessarily involve much pain and sadness. It demands the pain of repentance, remorse, and confession; the pain of individual and collective renewal and a changed way of life. It places us on a road whose end we can neither foresee nor manipulate to our own desire. On this road we shall unavoidably suffer intense growing pains while we struggle to conquer alienation, bitterness, irreconciliation, and fear. We shall have to come to know and encounter both ourselves and others in new ways. We are only too well aware that this confession calls for the dismantling of structures of thought, of church, and of society which have developed over many years. However, we confess that for the sake of the gospel, we have no other choice. We pray that our brothers and sisters throughout the Dutch Reformed church family, but also outside it, will want to make this new beginning with us, so that we can be free together and together may walk the road of reconciliation and justice. Accordingly, our prayer is that the pain and sadness we speak of will be pain and sadness that lead to salvation. We believe that this is possible in the power of our Lord and by his Spirit. We believe that the gospel of Jesus Christ offers hope, liberation, salvation, and true peace to our country.

# A BRIEF STATEMENT OF FAITH—PRESBYTERIAN CHURCH (U.S.A.)
## [TEXT]

## A Brief Statement of Faith

In 1983, the Presbyterian Church (U.S.A.) was formed by the reunion of the United Presbyterian Church in the United States of America and the Presbyterian Church in the United States. Integral to reunion was the preparation of a brief statement of faith. While recognizing realities of diversity and disagreement in both the church and the world, members of the drafting committee sought to articulate Presbyterians' common identity.

Early in its discussions, the committee decided to write a statement of faith that could be used in worship. The committee drew extensively on the documents in the *Book of Confessions* and on Scripture for its formulations, and arranged them within a trinitarian framework.

The Brief Statement of Faith (statement) is distinctive in several respects. Unlike the Apostles' and Nicene Creeds, which move directly from Jesus' birth to his death, the statement emphasizes the significance of Jesus' ministry in Judea and Galilee. The Brief Statement of Faith emphasizes gender-inclusiveness. It underscores the role of both men and women in God's covenant, uses feminine as well as masculine imagery of God, and affirms ordination of both women and men. The statement also expresses concern for the integrity of God's creation.

Affirming at its beginning that "In life and death we belong to God" (11.1, line 1) and, at its end, that "nothing in life or in death can separate us from the love of God in Jesus Christ our Lord," (11.05, lines 78, 79) the Brief Statement of Faith concludes liturgically with the church's familiar doxology of praise and thanksgiving.

# PREFACE[1] TO
# A BRIEF STATEMENT OF FAITH
# PRESBYTERIAN CHURCH (U.S.A.)

In 1983 the two largest Presbyterian churches in the United States reunited. *The Plan for Reunion* called for the preparation of a brief statement of the Reformed faith for possible inclusion in the *Book of Confessions*. This statement is therefore not intended to stand alone, apart from the other confessions of our church. It does not pretend to be a complete list of all our beliefs, nor does it explain any of them in detail. It is designed to be confessed by the whole congregation in the setting of public worship, and it may also serve pastors and teachers as an aid to Christian instruction. It celebrates our rediscovery that for all our undoubted diversity, we are bound together by a common faith and a common task.

The faith we confess unites us with the one, universal church. The most important beliefs of Presbyterians are those we share with other Christians, and especially with other evangelical Christians who look to the Protestant Reformation as a renewal of the gospel of Jesus Christ. Diversity remains. But we are thankful that in our time the many churches are learning to accept, and even to affirm, diversity without divisiveness, since the whole counsel of God is more than the wisdom of any individual or any one tradition. The Spirit of Truth gives new light to the churches when they are willing to become pupils together of the Word of God. This statement therefore intends to confess the catholic faith.

We are convinced that to the Reformed churches a distinctive vision of the catholic faith has been entrusted for the good of the whole church. Accordingly, "A Brief Statement of Faith" includes the major themes of the Reformed tradition (such as those mentioned in the *Book of Order*, The Foundations of Presbyterian Polity, Chapter 2),[2] without claiming them as our private possession, just as we ourselves hope to learn and to share the wisdom and insight given to traditions other than our own. And as a confession that seeks to be both catholic and Reformed, the statement (following the apostle's blessing in 2 Cor. 13:14) is a trinitarian confession in which the grace of Jesus Christ has first place as the foundation of our knowledge of God's sovereign love and our life together in the Holy Spirit.

No confession of faith looks merely to the past; every confession seeks to cast the light of a priceless heritage on the needs of the present moment, and so to shape the future. Reformed confessions, in particular, when necessary even reform the tradition itself in the light of the Word of God. From the first, the Reformed churches have insisted that the renewal of the church must become visible in the transformation of human lives and societies. Hence "A Brief Statement of Faith" lifts up concerns that call most urgently for the church's attention in our

---

[1] The preface and the appendix do not have confessional authority.

[2] The appendix provides cross-references that will enable the reader to place the affirmations of "A Brief Statement of Faith" in the context of the Reformed tradition.

time. The church is not a refuge from the world; an elect people is chosen for the blessing of the nations. A sound confession, therefore, proves itself as it nurtures commitment to the church's mission, and as the confessing church itself becomes the body by which Christ continues the blessing of his earthly ministry.

## THE STATEMENT

**11.1**

1      In life and in death we belong to God.
2          Through the grace of our Lord Jesus Christ,
3             the love of God,
4                and the communion of the Holy Spirit,
5      we trust in the one triune God, the Holy One of Israel,
6          whom alone we worship and serve.

**11.2**

7      We trust in Jesus Christ,
8          fully human, fully God.
9          Jesus proclaimed the reign of God:
10             preaching good news to the poor
11                and release to the captives,
12             teaching by word and deed
13                and blessing the children,
14             healing the sick
15                and binding up the brokenhearted,
16             eating with outcasts,
17             forgiving sinners,
18             and calling all to repent and believe the gospel.
19          Unjustly condemned for blasphemy and sedition,
20          Jesus was crucified,
21             suffering the depths of human pain
22             and giving his life for the sins of the world.
23          God raised this Jesus from the dead,
24             vindicating his sinless life,
25             breaking the power of sin and evil,
26             delivering us from death to life eternal.

**11.3**

27      We trust in God,
28          whom Jesus called Abba, Father.
29          In sovereign love God created the world good
30             and makes everyone equally in God's image,
31                male and female, of every race and people,
32             to live as one community.
33          But we rebel against God; we hide from our Creator.
34             Ignoring God's commandments.
35             we violate the image of God in others and ourselves,
36             accept lies as truth,
37             exploit neighbor and nature,
38             and threaten death to the planet entrusted to our care.
39             We deserve God's condemnation.
40          Yet God acts with justice and mercy to redeem creation.
41          In everlasting love,

|  |  |
|---|---|
| 42 | the God of Abraham and Sarah chose a covenant people |
| 43 | to bless all families of the earth. |
| 44 | Hearing their cry, |
| 45 | God delivered the children of Israel |
| 46 | from the house of bondage. |
| 47 | Loving us still, |
| 48 | God makes us heirs with Christ of the covenant. |
| 49 | Like a mother who will not forsake her nursing child, |
| 50 | like a father who runs to welcome the prodigal home, |
| 51 | God is faithful still. |

**11.4**

| | |
|---|---|
| 52 | We trust in God the Holy Spirit |
| 53 | everywhere the giver and renewer of life. |
| 54 | The Spirit justifies us by grace through faith, |
| 55 | sets us free to accept ourselves and to love God and neighbor, |
| 56 | and binds us together with all believers |
| 57 | in the one body of Christ, the Church. |
| 58 | The same Spirit |
| 59 | who inspired the prophets and apostles |
| 60 | rules our faith and life in Christ through Scripture, |
| 61 | engages us through the Word proclaimed, |
| 62 | claims us in the waters of baptism, |
| 63 | feeds us with the bread of life and the cup of salvation, |
| 64 | and calls women and men to all ministries of the Church. |
| 65 | In a broken and fearful world |
| 66 | the Spirit gives us courage |
| 67 | to pray without ceasing, |
| 68 | to witness among all peoples to Christ as Lord and Savior, |
| 69 | to unmask idolatries in Church and culture, |
| 70 | to hear the voices of peoples long silenced, |
| 71 | and to work with others for justice, freedom, and peace. |
| 72 | In gratitude to God, empowered by the Spirit, |
| 73 | we strive to serve Christ in our daily tasks |
| 74 | and to live holy and joyful lives, |
| 75 | even as we watch for God's new heaven and new earth, |
| 76 | praying, "Come, Lord Jesus!" |

**11.5**

| | |
|---|---|
| 77 | With believers in every time and place, |
| 78 | we rejoice that nothing in life or in death |
| 79 | can separate us from the love of God in Christ Jesus our Lord. |

**11.6**

| | |
|---|---|
| 80 | Glory be to the Father, and to the Son, and to the Holy Spirit. Amen.* |

---

\* Instead of saying this line, congregations may wish to sing a version of the Gloria.

A BRIEF STATEMENT OF FAITH

## APPENDIX TO
## A BRIEF STATEMENT OF FAITH
## PRESBYTERIAN CHURCH (U.S.A.)

Cross-Reference

The writers of "A Brief Statement of Faith" have endeavored to establish this confession on the broad base of Scripture as a whole and the consensus of Reformed theology, not upon isolated or particular texts either in Scripture or theology.

These cross-references identify sources that have significantly shaped the specific part of the faith being confessed at the lines indicated. They show the congruence of "A Brief Statement of Faith" with the teachings of the Scriptures and of earlier confessional documents. They point to only a selected few of the passages and contexts that congregations could study in comparing the ways the faith has been re-confessed in diverse historical situations.

The verse references and abbreviations for books of the Bible are based on the *Revised Standard Version*. Biblical passages are listed in the order of their occurrence in the English Bible, except that the parallel passages from the Synoptic Gospels (Matthew, Mark, and Luke) have been grouped together. Portions of the verses cited in italics are quoted or closely paraphrased in "A Brief Statement of Faith."

Documents in the *Book of Confessions* are abbreviated as follows: NC, Nicene Creed; AC, Apostles' Creed; SC, Scots Confession; HC, Heidelberg Catechism; SHC, Second Helvetic Confession; WCF, Westminster Confession of Faith [numbered according to the edition used by the former United Presbyterian Church (U.S.A.)]; WSC, Westminster Shorter Catechism; WLC, Westminster Larger Catechism; BD, Theological Declaration of Barmen; C67, Confession of 1967.

Citations are listed in the order of their occurrence in the *Book of Confessions*.

BOOK OF CONFESSIONS

### Lines 1–6

1 Scripture  Deut 7:6–11; Ps 100; 139:1–12; Is 43:1–9; Jer 31; Rom 8:31–39; 14:7–9; 2 Cor. 5:1–5.

Confessions  SC, 1; HC, q 1; WLC, q 1; BD, II, 1, 2.

2–6 Scripture  Ex 20:3–6; Deut 6:4–9; 11:16; 2 Kings 19:14–22; Ps 56:3–4; 62:1–8; 71:22–24; 103; Is 10:20; 12:5–6; 17:7–8; 43:14–15; 54:5; Jer 17:5–8; 25:5–6; Dan 3:28; Mt 28:16–20; Jn 3:16; 14:8–17; Acts 2:41–42; 27:21–26; 1 Cor 8:1–6; *2 Cor 13:14*; Eph 2:8–10; 1 Pet 1:2–9.

Confessions  NC; SC, I, IV; HC, q 25; SHC, III, V; WCF, II, VII, 5; WSC, q 6; WLC, qq 6–11; C67, "The Confession," IA–C.

### Lines 7–26

7–8 Scripture  Ps 86:1–2; Is 12:2; Mt 1:18–25; 11:27; Mk 8:27–30; 14:61–62; Lk 2:1–52; Jn 1:1–18; 5:1–18; 7:25–31; 10:30–39; Gal 4:1–7; Phil 2:5–11; Col 1:15–20; 2:8–10; Heb 1; 2:14–18; 4:14–15; 5:7–10; 13:8; 1 Jn 1:1–2.

Confessions  NC, 2nd art.; SC, VI; HC, qq 31, 35, 47; SHC, XI; WCF, VIII, 2; WSC, q 21; WLC, qq 36–42; C67, IA1.

9–18 Scripture  Ps 34:6–18; 146:5–9; 147:1–6; Is 42:1–7; *61:1–3*; Ezek 34:15–16; Zeph 3:19; Mt 4:23–25; 9:10–13; 13:1–58; 15:21–28; 18:21–35; 23:1–4; Mk *1:14–15*; 5:1–20; 6:30–44; 9:33–37; 10:13–16; Lk *4*:16–22 (*18*); 5:17–32; 6:17–36; 7:1–27, 33–50; 8:1–3; 10:38–42; 15:1–32; Jn 4:1–42; 8:1–11; 10:1–18; 11:1–44; 16:33; Acts 10:34–43.

Confessions  SC, XIV, XVI; HC, qq 1, 31, 74, 107; SHC, XIII–XV; WCF, VIII, XII, XXV; WSC, qq 21–30, I 36; WLC, qq 43–50, 135; BD, I; C67, IA1, IIA4c, III.

19–22 Scripture
Lines 19–20  Mt 26:57–68; Mk 14:53–65; Lk 22:63–71; Mt 27:32–37; Mk 15:21–26; Lk 23:32–35; Jn 10:22–39; 19:1–22; 1 Cor 1:20–25.

Lines 21–22  Ps 22; 88:1–9; Is 52:13–53:12; Mt 27:27–31, 39–50; Mk 15:16–20, 29–37; Lk 23:11, 39–46; Mk 8:31–35; 10:45; Lk 22:39–46; Jn 1:29–34; 3:16–18; 10:7–18; 19:28–37; Rom 5; 2 Cor 5:17–21; 1 Tim 2:5–6; Heb 2; 5:7–10; 9:11–22; 1 Pet 2:21–24; 3:18; 1 Jn 2:1–2; 4:9–10; Rev 5.

Confessions  SC, VIII, IX; HC, qq 29–44; SHC, XI; WCF, VIII; WSC, qq 28–31; WLC, qq 44, 49.

23–26 Scripture
Lines 23–24  Ps 24:4–5; 26:1; 37:5–6; Is 50:4–9; Matt 27:3–4; 28:1–17; Mk 16:1–8; Lk 24:1–47; Jn 20–21; Acts 2:22–36 (*32*); 17:16–34; Rom 1:1–7; 1 Cor 15:3–57; 1 Tim 3:14–16.

Lines 25–26  Ps 49:13–15; Is 25:6–8; Dan 12:2–3; Jn 3:16–18; 5:19–24; 11:17–27; Rom 4:24–25; 5:1–21; 6:1–23; 8:1–11; 1 Cor

314

## A BRIEF STATEMENT OF FAITH

|  |  |  |
|---|---|---|
|  |  | 15:20–28; Eph 2:1–7; Col 1:9–14; 2:8–15; 1 Thess 4:13–18; 2 Tim 1:10; Heb 13:20–21; Rev 21:3–4. |
|  | Confessions | SC, X; HC, qq 45–52; SHC, XI; WCF, VIII, 4–8; WLC, qq 52–56; BD, II, 2–4; C67, IA1. |

### Lines 27–51

| | | |
|---|---|---|
| 27–28 | Scripture | 2 Kings 18:5–6; Ps 28:6–7; 71:5–6; Prov 3:5–8; Mt 6:25–34; *Mk 14:32–36*; Lk 11:2–4; Rom 8:12–17; Gal 4:1–7. |
|  | Confessions | NC, 1st art.; AC, 1st art.; HC, qq 26–28; WCF, XII; WLC, q 100. |
| 29–32 | Scripture | |
|  | Line 29 | Gen 1:1–25; Ps 33:1–9; 104; Is 40:21–28; Jn 1:1–5; Col 1:15–20; 1 Tim 4:4. |
|  | Lines 30–32 | Gen 1:26–2:25; 5:1–32 (esp. 1–5, 32); 10:32–11:1; Lev 19:9–18; Ps 22:25–31; 67; 133; Is 56:3–8; 66:18–21; Mic 4:1–4; Lk 10:29–37; Acts 17:22–28: Eph 1:9–10; Rev 7:9–12; 22:1–2. |
|  | Confessions | HC, q 6; SHC, VII; WCF, IV, 1–2; WSC, qq 9, 10; WLC, qq 12–17; C67, IIA4a. |
| 33–38 | Scripture | |
|  | Line 33 | Gen 3:1–24; 4:1–6; Ex 3:6; 4:1–17; Judg 11:29–40; 1 Sam 10:20–24; Ps 2:1–3; 14:1–4; Is 1:1–6; Jer 5:20–25; 23:24; Jon 1:1–4; Mt 5:14–16; Mk 4:21–23; Lk 8:16–18; Mt 19:16–22; 25:14–30 (esp. 18, 24–25); Lk 8:43–48; 10:38–42 (Martha); Rom 1:16–3:26; Heb 4:13; Rev 2–3; 6:12–17. |
|  | Line 34 | Gen 1:28; 2:15–16; Ex 20:1–17; 21:1–23:19; Lev 19:1–37; Deut 6:4–9; 10:19; Neh 7:73b–8:18; Ps 119:169–176; Amos 5:24; Mic 6:8; Mt 5:17–6:21; 7:12; 22:34–40; Jn 13:34; 14:15; 15:12–17; Rom 13:8–10; 1 Cor 8; 1 Jn 2:3–11. |
|  | Line 35 | Gen 1:27; 4:8; 6:11–12; 16; 21:9–21; Judg 19; 2 Sam 11; 13:1–20; 18:5–15; Ps 14:1–4; Is 1:12–23; 59:1–8; Ezek 7:10–11; 45:9; Zeph 3:1–4; Mt 23:13–28; 25:31–46; Lk 16:19–31; Rom 1:28–32; Eph 4:17–22; Col 3:5–11; 2 Tim 3:1–9; Tit 1:15–16. |
|  | Line 36 | Gen 2:16–17; 3:1–4; Job 13:1–12; Ps 4:2; Is 5:20–21; 28:14–15; 59:3b, 12–15a; Jer 5:1–3; 14:13–14; Jn 8:42–45. |
|  | Lines 37–38 | Gen 2:15; Ps 8; Is 5:7–8; 24:4–6; 33:7–9; Jer 2:7–8; 9:4–6; Hos 4:1–3; Amos 2:6–8; Acts 16:16–24. |
|  | Confessions | SC, II; HC, qq 3–11, 106, 107; SHC, VIII, IX; WCF, VI; WSC, q 77; WLC, qq 22–28, 105, 131, 132, 136, 145, 149; C67, IA2. |
| 39 | Scripture | Gen 6:5–7; Deut 28:15–68; 30:15–20; 2 Sam 12:1–12; Is 1:24–25; 5:9–10, 24–25; 28:16–22; 59:9–11, 15b–19; Jer |

|  |  |  |
|---|---|---|
|  |  | 2:9; 9:7–11; 14:15–16; Amos 2:13–16; Jn 3:16–21; Rom 5:18–21; 8:1–4. |
|  | Confessions | SC, III, XV; HC, qq 10–12; SHC, XII, XIII; WCF, VI, 6; WSC, qq 82–85; WLC, q 27; C67, IA2. |
| 40 | Scripture | 2 Chron 7:11–14; Ps 34:22; 51; 78:36–39; 103:1–14; 130; 145:8–9; Is 2:2–4; 6:5–7; 11:1–9; 30:18; 51:4–6; Jer 31:20; Lam 3:22–33; Ezek 36:8–15; Hos 11:1–9; 14:4–8; Mt 1:18–21; Lk 1:67–79; 15:1–7; Jn 3:16–17; Rom 5:15–17; 8:18–25; Eph 2:4–7; 1 Pet 1:13–21. |
|  | Confessions | SC, I, IV; HC, qq 26–28; SHC, VI, X; WCF, V; WSC, q 31; WLC, q 30. |
| 41–51 | Scripture | |
|  | Lines 41–43 | Gen 12:1–7; 15; 17:1–21; 18:1–15; 21:1–7; 28:10–17; Deut 7:6–7; Neh 9:6–8; Ps 65:1–4; Is 41:8–10; 44:1–8; 51:1–2; Jer 31:3, 31–34; Mt 9:9–13; 26:26–28; Rom 4:13–25; 11; 1 Cor 1:26–29; Gal 3:6–9; Eph 1:3–10; 1 Thess 1; Heb 11:8–12; Jas 2:5; 1 Pet 2:9–10. |
|  | Lines 44–46 | Ex 2:23–3:10; 6:2–8; 15:1–21; 18:5–12; 20:1–2; 22:21–24; Deut 7:8; Judg 6:7–16; 10:10–16; 2 Chron 32:9–23; Ezra 9:6–9; Neh 9:9–15; Ps 18:1–19; 34; 77; 105:23–45; 107; 136; Is 40:3–5, 9–11; 43:14–21; 51:9–16; Dan 3; 6; Mic 6:4; Mt 6:13; 15:21–28; Mk 5:1–20; 2 Cor 1:8–11; Rev 1:4–11; 15:2–4. |
|  | Lines 47–48 | Ps 33:20–22; 36:7–9; Is 54:4–10; 63:7–9; Mic 7:18–20; Mt 26:26–29; *Rom 8:15–17*, 38–39; 1 Cor 11:23–26; Gal 3:15–29; 4:6–7, 21–31; Eph 1:3–6; 2:11–22; Heb 13:20–21; 1 Pet 1:1–9; 1 Jn 3:1–2. |
|  | Lines 49–51 | Gen 33:1–11; Deut 7:9; 32:10–12; Neh 9:16–23; Ps 27:7–10; 36:5–12; 91; 117; Is 42:14–16; 46:3–4; 49:7; *49:14–15*; 66:13; Jer 31:15–20; Lam 3:22–23; Hos 11:3–4; Lk 13:34–35; 15:11–32 (esp. 20); *1 Cor 1:9*; 1 Thess 5:23–24; 2 Thess 2:16–17. |
|  | Confessions | SC, IV, V; HC, qq 12–15, 18, 19, 34, 49, 51, 52, 54, 128; SHC, XIII, XVII–XIX; WCF, VI, 4, VII, VIII, 8, XVII, XVIII, XXXV, "Declaratory Statement" of 1903; WSC, q 36; WLC, qq 31–34, 74; BD, II, 2; C67, IB. |

### Lines 52–76

|  |  |  |
|---|---|---|
| 52–53 | Scripture | Gen 1:1–2; Ps 23; 139:1–12; Ezek 37:1–14; Lk 1:26–35; Jn 3:1–15; Acts 2:1–21; 10; Rom 8:1–11; 2 Cor 3. |
|  | Confessions | NC, 3rd art.; AC, 3rd art.; SC, XII; HC, q 53; WCF, XX, XXXIV; WLC, qq 58, 89, 182. |
| 54–57 | Scripture | |
|  | Line 54 | Gen 15:1–6; Hab 2:4; Rom 1:16–17; 3:21–28 (*24–25*); 4:1–5; 5:1–2; Gal 3:1–14; Eph 2:8–9; Tit 3:3–7. |
|  | Lines 55–57 | Lev 19:18; Deut 6:4–5; Mk 12:28–34; Lk 10:25–37; Jn 3:1–15; Rom 8:26–27; 12; 13:8–10; 1 Cor 12:1–31 (esp. |

## A BRIEF STATEMENT OF FAITH

|  |  |  |
|---|---|---|
|  |  | 13, 27); 13; 2 Cor 3:17–4:2; Gal 5; 6:1–10; Eph 2:11–22; 4:1–6; Phil 4:1–7; Col 1:24; 3:12–17; 1 Pet 4:8–11; 1 Jn 4:19–5:5. |
|  | Confessions | SC, XVI–XX; HC, qq 1, 21, 54, 55, 86, 87; SHC, XV–XVII; WCF, XI, XX, XXV, XXVI, XXXIV, XXXV; WSC, qq 29–36; WLC, qq 63–66, 70–73; BD, II, 1–3; C67, IC1. |
| 58–61 | Scripture | |
|  | Lines 58–59 | Num 11:24–30; Deut 18:15–22; 2 Chron 20:13–19; 24:20–22; Ezek 3:22–27; 8:1–4; 11:5–12; 13:3; Mic 3:5–8; Mk 12:35–37; Jn 20:19–23; Acts 1:1–9; 2:1–4; 9:17–19a; 1 Pet 1:10–11; 2 Pet 1:20–21. |
|  | Lines 60–61 | 2 Kings 22:8–13; 23:1–3; Ps 119:1–16; Zech 7:11–12; Mt 5:17; Mk 13:9–11; Lk 24:13–27, 44; Jn 5:30–47; 16:13; Acts 2:14–36; 4:13–20; 8:4–8; 9:17–22; 10:34–44; 13:4–5; 17:1–4; Rom 15:17–21; Eph 2:19–3:6; 2 Tim 1:11–14; 3:14–17; Heb 1:1–4; 3:7–11; 1 Pet 1:12; 2 Pet 1:16–19; 3:1–2; Rev 3:22. |
|  | Confessions | SC, XIX, XX; HC, qq 19–21; SHC, I, II; WCF, I, XXXIV, 2; WSC, qq 2, 3; WLC, qq 2–6, 108; BD, I, II, 1; C67, IC2, IIB1. |
| 62–64 | Scripture | |
|  | Line 62 | Mk 1:1–12; 6:30–52; Jn 1:19–34; 3:5; 7:37–39; Acts 2:38–42; 8:26–39; 9:10–19; 10:44–11:18; Rom 6:1–4; 1 Cor 12:12–13; Gal 3:27–28; Eph 1:13–14; Col 2:8–15; Tit 3:3–7; 1 Jn 5:6–8. |
|  | Line 63 | *Ps 116*:12–14 (*13*); Mt 26:17–29; Mk 14:22–25; Lk 22:14–20; 24:13–35; *Jn 6*:22–59 (*35, 48*); Acts 2:41–42; 1 Cor 10:16–17; 11:17–34; Heb 9:11–28. |
|  | Line 64 | Gen 1:26–27; Ex 15:1–21; Judg 4:4–10;2 Kings 22:8–20; Joel 2:28–32; Lk 1:46–55; 2:25–38; 8:1–3; 10:38–42; Jn 4:7–42; 20; Acts 1:12–2:47; 13:1–4; 16:1–15; 18:24–28; Rom 16:1–16; 1 Cor 12:4–7; 2 Cor 4–5; Gal 3:27–29; Eph 4:7–16; Phil 4:1–3; 1 Pet 2:9–10. |
|  | Confessions | SC, XVIII, XXI–XXIII; HC, qq 65–85; SHC, XVIII–XXVIII; WCF, XXVI–XXXI; WSC, qq 88–98; WLC, qq 157, 158, 164–177; BD, II, 1, 3–6; C67, IIA1–2, IIB. |
| 65–71 | Scripture | |
|  | Lines 65–66 | Gen 15:1; Ps 23:1–4; 27:1–6; 46:1–3; Is 41:8–10; Hag 2:4–5; Acts 4:13–31; Phil 1:19–20; 2 Cor 1:18–22. |
|  | Line 67 | Gen 18:16–33; 2 Sam 7:18–29; Dan 6; Mt 6:5–15; Mk 14:32–42; Lk 18:1–8; Jn 17; Rom 12:12; Eph 6:18–20; Col 1:3–14; 4:2; *1 Thess* 5:16–18 (*17*); Jas 5:13–18; Jude 20–21. |
|  | Line 68 | Is 60:1–3; Mt 28:19–20; Lk 24:45–47; Acts 1:8; 9:27–29; 23:11; Rom 1:1–6; 1 Thess 2:1–8; 2 Tim 1:8–14; 4:1–2. |

|  |  |  |
|---|---|---|
|  | Line 69 | Ex 20:2–6; 1 Kings 18:21–39; Ps 115:1–11; Is 31:1–3; 44:6–20; Jer 7:1–20; Zech 4:6; Mt 6:24; Lk 18:18–23; Acts 19:21–41; 1 Cor 8:1–6; Phil 3:18–19; Col 3:5; 1 Jn 5:20–21. |
|  | Line 70 | Gen 41:1–45; Ruth 1–4; 1 Kings 12:1–20; Jer 36; Zeph 3:1–2; Mt 15:21–28; Mk 5:15–20; 9:38–41; 16:9–11; Lk 7:36–50; 10:30–35; Jn 4:27–30, 39; 20:11–18; Acts 24; 1 Cor 14:33b–35; 1 Tim 2:11–12. |
|  | Line 71 | Lev 25:25–55; Deut 15:1–11; Ps 34:14; 72:1–4, 12–14; Is 58; Amos 5:11–24; Mic 6:6–8; Mt 5:9; 25:31–46; Rom 14:17–19; Gal 5:13–26; Heb 12:14; 13:1–3, 20–21; Jas 1:22–2:26. |
|  | Confessions | SC, XIII, XIV, XXIV; HC, qq 86–129; SHC, IV, XVII, XXIII, XXX; WCF, IX, XII, XIX–XXIII, XXV, XXXIV, 3, XXXV; WSC, qq 35, 36, 98–107; WLC, qq 75, 76, 91–148; BD, II; C67, IB, IIA1, 3, 4, IIB2. |
| 72–76 | Scripture Lines 72–74 | Lev 19:1–4; Neh 7:73b–8:12; Ps 68:32–35; 96; 100; Mt 13:44; Lk 9:23; 24:44–53; Jn 15:10–11; Acts 1:8, 13:52; Rom 7:4–6; 12:1–3, 9–21; 15:13; 1 Cor 3:16–17; 13; 2 Cor 1:12; Eph 1:3–2:21; 1 Thess 1:4–8; 5:16–18; 1 Pet 1:13–16. |
|  | Lines 75–76 | Is 65:17; 66:22–23; Mt 24:42–44; 25:1–13; Mk 13:32–37; Lk 14:15–24; 1 Cor 15:51–58; 16:21–24; 2 Pet 3; *Rev 21:1–22:5; 22:20.* |
|  | Confessions | HC, qq 31, 32, 86 and all of Part III; SHC, XIV, XVI, XXIX; WCF, VII, 5, XIII–XVI, XIX, XXI–XXIV, XXXIV; WSC, qq 39–82; WLC, qq 56, 175; BD, II, 2; C67, IB, IC1, IIA, III. |

**Lines 77–80**

|  |  |  |
|---|---|---|
| 77–80 | Scripture | Ps 27:1–10; 91; 118:1–6; 139:1–18; Is 25:6–9; Jn 3:16; *Rom 8*:31–*39*; Eph 2:1–10; 2 Tim 2:8–13; Jas 1:12; 1 Pet 1:3–9; 1 Jn 4:7–21. |
|  | Confessions | NC, 3rd art.; AC, 3rd art.; SC, XVI, XVII; HC, qq 1, 50–58; SHC, XXVI; WCF, XVII, XVIII; WLC, qq 67, 196; BD, II, 2; C67, IB, IC, IC1, III. |

# INDEX

# INDEX

| | Reference Numbers | Page Numbers |
|---|---|---|

## A

| | Reference Numbers | Page Numbers |
|---|---|---|
| AARON | 3.18 | 19 |
| ABBA | 11.3 | 311 |
| ABEL | 3.18 | 19 |
| ABILITY: | | |
|   Believer's | 6.089 | 166 |
|   Lost | 6.034 | 155 |
| | 6.061–.062 | 161–62 |
|   Original | 6.023 | 154 |
| | 6.060 | 161 |
| | 6.101 | 169 |
| | 7.127 | 226–27 |
| ABRAHAM | 3.04 | 12 |
| | 3.05 | 12 |
| | 11.3 | 312 |
|   Call of | 3.05 | 12 |
|   Children of | 3.05 | 12 |
|   Seed of | 5.064 | 93–94 |
| ABROGATION OF THE LAW OF GOD | 5.085 | 98 |
| ABSOLUTION | 6.170 | 184 |
|   By ministers | 5.100 | 102 |
|   Sacerdotal | 5.095 | 101–02 |
| ABSTENTION FROM MEAT | 5.231 | 136 |
| ABUNDANCE, WORLD | 9.46 | 294 |
| ABUSE | 11.3 | 311 |
| ACCEPTANCE: | | |
|   Of good works in Christ | 6.092 | 167 |
|   Grounds of | 6.068 | 163 |
| | 7.033 | 208 |
| | 7.180 | 234 |
| | 7.304 | 259 |
| | 11.3 | 311 |
|   Of prayer through Christ | 7.291 | 256–57 |
| ACCESS TO GOD: | | |
|   Through Christ | 6.112 | 171 |
| | 7.149 | 230 |
| | 7.165 | 232 |
| | 7.291 | 256–57 |
| | 11.1 | 311 |
|   Under New Testament | 6.108 | 170 |
| ACOLYTES | 5.148 | 116–17 |

BOOK OF CONFESSIONS

|  | Reference Numbers | Page Numbers |
|---|---|---|
| ACTIONS, GOVERNING OF | 6.024 | 154 |
|  | 7.011 | 205 |
|  | 7.128 | 227 |
| ADAM (See also Parents, First) | 3.04 | 12 |
|  | 3.05 | 12 |
|  | 4.007 | 33 |
|  | 5.045 | 89 |
|  | 5.049 | 90 |
|     Covenant with | 3.04 | 12 |
|  | 6.038 | 156 |
|  | 7.012 | 205 |
|  | 7.130 | 227 |
|  | 4.020 | 36 |
|     Fall of | 5.042 | 88 |
|  | 6.032 | 155 |
|  | 7.013 | 206 |
|  | 7.131 | 227 |
|     Original ability of | 6.023 | 154 |
|  | 6.101 | 169 |
|  | 7.127 | 226–27 |
|     As representative | 6.033 | 155 |
|  | 6.038 | 156 |
|  | 6.101 | 169 |
|  | 7.016 | 206 |
|  | 7.132–.133 | 227 |
|     Second | 7.141 | 228 |
|     Sin of | 3.08 | 13 |
|     Temptation of | 6.031 | 155 |
|  | 7.131 | 227 |
| ADMINISTRATION: |  |  |
|     Of baptism | 5.191 | 127 |
|  | 6.156 | 182 |
|     Of Lord's Supper | 7.096 | 214 |
|  | 7.279 | 254 |
|     Of sacraments | 3.18 | 19 |
|  | 3.22 | 23 |
|  | 5.173–.174 | 123 |
| ADMINISTRATIVE RULES, OF THE CHURCH | 9.40 | 293 |
| ADMINISTRATORS, MINISTERS AS | 5.156 | 118 |
| ADMISSION: |  |  |
|     To the Lord's Supper | 4.081–.082 | 56–57 |
|     To the visible church | 6.154 | 181 |
| ADMONITION, JUDICIAL | 6.172 | 185 |

# INDEX

| | Reference Numbers | Page Numbers |
|---|---|---|
| ADOPTION: | | |
| Assurance of | 6.099 | 168 |
| Benefits of | 7.036–.037 | 208 |
| | 7.193 | 236–37 |
| | 7.196 | 237 |
| Definition of | 6.074 | 164 |
| | 7.034 | 208 |
| | 7.184 | 235 |
| Holy Spirit and | 6.053 | 159 |
| | 6.185 | 188 |
| ADORATION: | | |
| Of God | 5.024 | 83 |
| | 7.214 | 240 |
| Of saints | 5.025 | 83 |
| ADULTERY | 5.247 | 141 |
| | 7.070 | 211 |
| | 7.247 | 247 |
| And salvation | 4.087 | 59 |
| | 4.109 | 66 |
| ADVICE, TO CIVIL MAGISTRATES | 6.176 | 186 |
| AETIUS, ERRORS OF | 5.019 | 81 |
| AFFAIRS, CHURCH AND THE WORLD'S | 9.36 | 292 |
| | 11.4 | 312 |
| AFFLICTED, THE | 5.254 | 142 |
| AFRICA | 5.126 | 109 |
| AGE: | | |
| Coming of the new | 9.18 | 289–90 |
| Golden | 5.075 | 95–96 |
| And sin | 7.261 | 251 |
| ALIENATION, FROM GOD, NEIGHBOR, SELF | 9.47 | 294–95 |
| | 10.4 | 302 |
| | 10.5 | 303 |
| | 11.3 | 311 |
| AMBASSADOR, MINISTER AS | 5.098 | 102 |
| AMBITION | 9.40 | 293 |
| AMEN, MEANING OF | 4.129 | 73 |
| | 7.107 | 215 |
| | 7.306 | 260 |
| ANABAPTISTS, ERRORS OF | 3.23 | 24 |
| | 5.168 | 122 |
| | 5.192 | 128 |
| | 5.257 | 142 |
| ANARCHY, IN SEXUAL RELATIONS | 9.47 | 294–95 |

| | Reference Numbers | Page Numbers |
|---|---|---|
| ANGELS: | | |
| Elect | 6.017 | 153 |
| | 7.123 | 226 |
| God's decree and | 6.016 | 153 |
| | 7.123 | 226 |
| Judgment of | 6.180 | 186 |
| Nature of | 5.033 | 86 |
| | 7.126 | 226 |
| Providence and | 6.027 | 154 |
| | 7.129 | 227 |
| Worship of | 6.113 | 172 |
| | 7.215 | 241 |
| ANGER | 7.246 | 247 |
| ANNIHILATION OF MANKIND | 9.45 | 294 |
| ANTHROPOMORPHITES, ERRORS OF | 5.019 | 81 |
| ANTICHRIST, THE | 5.074 | 95 |
| APOCRYPHA, STATUS OF | 5.009 | 78 |
| | 6.003 | 150 |
| APOLLINARIS, ERRORS OF | 5.065 | 94 |
| APOSTASY | 7.215 | 241 |
| APOSTLES, THE: | | |
| Definition of | 5.147 | 116 |
| Teaching of | 9.24 | 290 |
| Traditions of | 5.014 | 80 |
| APOSTLES' CREED | 5.112 | 106 |
| | 5.125 | 109 |
| | 5.141 | 114 |
| | 5.233 | 137 |
| | 9.04 | 287 |
| Articles of | 4.024 | 37 |
| Continuity with | 9.31 | 291–92 |
| Prologue | | 6 |
| Reception of | 5.018 | 81 |
| As summary of gospel | 4.022 | 36 |
| Text of | 2.1–2.3 | 7 |
| | 4.023 | 37 |
| | 7.110 | 216 |
| APOSTOLIC BENEDICTION | 9.56 | 297 |
| | 11.1 | 311 |
| APOSTOLICALS, ERRORS OF | 5.251 | 141 |
| APPARITION OF SPIRITS | 5.239 | 138 |
| APPEARANCE OF CHRIST, EXPECTATION OF | 8.17 | 283 |
| APPREHENSION, FAITH AS | 5.113 | 106 |
| ARCHBISHOPS | 5.148 | 116–17 |
| ARCHDEACONS | 5.148 | 116–17 |

# INDEX

| | Reference Numbers | Page Numbers |
|---|---|---|
| ARCHITECTURE | 9.50 | 295–96 |
| ARIANS, ERRORS OF | 5.063 | 93 |
| ARIUS, ERRORS OF | 3.06 | 13 |
| | 5.019 | 81 |
| | 5.063 | 93 |
| ARK, OF NOAH | 5.136 | 113 |
| ARTEMON, ERRORS OF | 5.008 | 78 |
| ARTS, THE | 5.046 | 89 |
| | 9.50 | 261 |
| ASCENSION OF CHRIST | 3.10 | 14 |
| | 4.046 | 44 |
| | 4.049–.050 | 44–45 |
| | 5.074 | 95 |
| | 7.163 | 232 |
|     Celebration of | 5.226 | 135 |
| ASSEMBLIES FOR WORSHIP: | | |
|     Freedom of | 6.129 | 175 |
|     Neglect of | 6.117 | 172 |
|     Protection of | 6.129 | 175 |
| ASSEMBLY, ORDERING OF | 5.161 | 120 |
| ASSURANCE OF GRACE AND SALVATION | 6.097–.100 | 168–69 |
| | 7.036 | 208 |
| | 7.190–.191 | 236 |
| | 11.3 | 311 |
| | 11.4 | 312 |
| ATHANASIUS, CREED OF | 5.078 | 97 |
| ATHEISM | 7.047 | 209 |
| | 7.215 | 241 |
| | 7.300 | 258 |
| ATONEMENT, DOCTRINE OF | 3.08–.09 | 13–14 |
| | 4.037 | 42 |
| | 9.08 | 288 |
| ATTRIBUTES OF GOD | 6.011–.013 | 151–52 |
| | 7.004 | 205 |
| | 7.117 | 225 |
| | 7.211 | 240 |
| | 11.3 | 311 |
| AUGUSTINE, ST., CITED | 5.009 | 78 |
| | 5.022 | 82 |
| | 5.026 | 83–84 |
| | 5.029 | 84 |
| | 5.031 | 85 |

|  | Reference Numbers | Page Numbers |
|---|---|---|
| AUGUSTINE, ST., CITED (*Continued*) | | |
| | 5.040 | 87 |
| | 5.041 | 87–88 |
| | 5.048 | 90 |
| | 5.049 | 90 |
| | 5.058 | 92 |
| | 5.123 | 108–09 |
| | 5.166 | 121 |
| | 5.202 | 130 |
| | 5.242 | 139 |
| AUTHOR OF THE SACRAMENTS | 5.172 | 123 |
| | 5.174 | 123 |
| AUTHORITATIVE WITNESS, SCRIPTURE AS | 9.27 | 291 |
| | 11.4 | 312 |
| AUTHORITY: | | |
| Of church | 5.165 | 121 |
| Of civil magistrates | 6.130 | 175 |
| Of Confessions | 9.03 | 287 |
| Of general councils | 3.20 | 20 |
| Of oaths | 6.121 | 173 |
| Parental | 4.104 | 64–65 |
| Of Scriptures | 3.19 | 20 |

**B**

|  | Reference Numbers | Page Numbers |
|---|---|---|
| BABYLON, CAPTIVITY IN | 5.137 | 113 |
| BACKSLIDING | 6.096 | 168 |
| | 6.100 | 168–69 |
| | 7.223 | 243 |
| BALAAM | 5.050 | 90 |
| BAPTISM | 3.21 | 21 |
| | 4.069–.074 | 51–53 |
| | 6.154–.160 | 181–82 |
| | 7.095 | 214 |
| | 7.275 | 253 |
| | 10.3 | 302 |
| | 11.4 | 312 |
| Administration of | 5.191 | 127 |
| | 7.277 | 253–54 |
| Of Christ | 5.018 | 81 |
| | 9.51 | 296 |
| And circumcision | 4.074 | 52–53 |
| | 5.177 | 124 |
| Elements in | 5.188 | 127 |
| Errors in | 5.190 | 127 |
| | 5.192 | 128 |

# INDEX

| | Reference Numbers | Page Numbers |
|---|---|---|
| **BAPTISM** (*Continued*) | | |
| Form of | 5.190 | 127 |
| And gathered church | 9.36 | 292 |
| Holy Spirit and | 11.4 | 312 |
| Infants | 4.074 | 52–53 |
| | 9.51 | 296 |
| Institution of | 4.071 | 51–52 |
| | 5.185 | 126 |
| By John | 9.51 | 296 |
| And Lord's Supper | 7.286–.287 | 256 |
| Meaning of | 5.187 | 127 |
| | 9.51 | 296 |
| Nature of | 4.069–.070 | 51 |
| | 7.275 | 253 |
| Obligations of | 5.189 | 127 |
| Recipients of | 3.23 | 24 |
| | 7.276 | 253 |
| For remission of sins | 1.3 | 3 |
| And sacrifice of Christ | 4.069 | 51 |
| Sufficiency of | 5.186 | 126 |
| Water in | 4.078 | 55 |
| | 5.188 | 127 |
| Waters of | 11.4 | 312 |
| **BAPTISMAL REGENERATION** | 6.158 | 182 |
| **BAPTIZED CHILDREN** | 6.141 | 179 |
| | 7.172 | 233 |
| **BARMEN:** | | |
| Confessional synod at | 8.01 | 281 |
| Theological declaration of | 8.01–.28 | 281–84 |
| | 9.04 | 287 |
| **BARNABAS** | 5.133 | 111–12 |
| **BEARING ONE ANOTHER'S BURDEN** | 10.3 | 302 |
| **BELHAR, CONFESSION OF** | 10.1-.9 | 301–5 |
| **BELIEF, CHRISTIAN** | 4.022 | 36 |
| **BELIEVERS:** | | |
| Adoption of | 6.074 | 164 |
| | 7.034 | 208 |
| | 7.184 | 235 |
| Backsliding of | 6.072 | 163 |
| | 6.089 | 166 |
| | 6.100 | 168–69 |
| Baptism of | 6.155–.157 | 182 |
| | 7.276 | 253 |

|  | Reference Numbers | Page Numbers |
|---|---|---|
| **BELIEVERS** (*Continued*) | | |
| Benefits to | 6.161 | 182 |
|  | 6.167 | 183–84 |
| Censures and | 6.169–.172 | 184–85 |
| And civil office | 6.128 | 174 |
| Communion of | 6.146–.148 | 180–81 |
|  | 6.161 | 182 |
|  | 7.278 | 254 |
| Confession by | 6.086 | 165–66 |
|  | 7.098 | 214 |
|  | 7.300–.305 | 258–59 |
| Conflict of | 6.076–.077 | 164 |
|  | 6.080 | 165 |
| Death of | 6.177 | 186 |
|  | 7.195–.196 | 237 |
| Distinguishing of | 6.149 | 181 |
|  | 7.272 | 253 |
| Duty of | 6.058 | 161 |
|  | 6.190 | 189 |
|  | 7.285 | 255–56 |
| Faith of | 6.078–.080 | 164 |
|  | 7.086 | 213 |
|  | 7.182 | 234 |
| Good works of | 6.088–.092 | 166–67 |
| Growth of | 6.077 | 164 |
|  | 7.036 | 208 |
| Intercession for | 6.050 | 158 |
|  | 7.165 | 232 |
| And judgment | 6.181 | 186–87 |
|  | 7.038 | 208 |
|  | 7.200 | 238 |
| Justification of | 6.068–.073 | 163 |
|  | 7.033 | 208 |
|  | 7.180 | 234 |
| Liberty of | 6.108–.111 | 170–71 |
| Moral law and | 6.105–.106 | 169–70 |
|  | 7.207 | 239 |
| Priesthood of | 5.154 | 118 |
| Repentance of | 7.073–.078 | 212 |
| Resurrection of | 6.178–.179 | 186 |
|  | 7.038 | 208 |
|  | 7.197 | 237 |
| Sanctification of | 6.075–.077 | 164 |
|  | 7.035 | 208 |
|  | 7.185 | 235 |

# INDEX

|  | Reference Numbers | Page Numbers |
|---|---|---|
| **BELIEVERS** (*Continued*) | | |
| Scriptures and | 6.001 | 149 |
|  | 7.114 | 225 |
| Sins of | 6.035 | 155 |
|  | 6.076 | 164 |
|  | 6.096 | 168 |
|  | 6.106 | 169–70 |
|  | 7.188 | 235–36 |
| Temporal judgment on | 6.096 | 168 |
|  | 6.106 | 169–70 |
| True | 6.078–.080 | 164–65 |
|  | 6.094–.096 | 167–68 |
|  | 6.097–.100 | 168–69 |
|  | 7.189–.191 | 236 |
| **BENEDICTION** | 5.260 | 143 |
|  | 9.56 | 297 |
| **BENEFITS:** | | |
| To believers | 7.037–.038 | 208 |
|  | 7.196 | 237 |
| In this life | 7.036 | 208 |
|  | 7.193 | 236–37 |
| To man, from Christ's death | 4.043 | 43 |
| Procured by Christ | 7.029 | 207 |
|  | 7.167–.169 | 232–33 |
| Of resurrection | 4.045 | 43 |
|  | 7.198 | 237 |
| To those called | 7.032 | 207 |
|  | 7.169 | 233 |
| **BENEVOLENCE, GRATITUDE FOR** | 9.46 | 294 |
| **BIBLE** (See also Scripture): | | |
| As guide | 7.099 | 214 |
|  | 7.296 | 257 |
| Interpretation of, for teaching | 6.010 | 151 |
| Study of | 9.37 | 292 |
|  | 9.49 | 295 |
| **BIBLICAL VISIONS AND IMAGES** | 9.54 | 296–97 |
| **BIOLOGICAL WEAPONS** | 9.45 | 294 |
| **BIRTH CONTROL** | 9.47 | 294–95 |
| **BIRTH OF NEW SELF** | 4.090 | 59 |
| **BISHOPS** | 5.160 | 120 |
| Definition of | 5.147 | 116 |
| Succession of | 5.135 | 112 |
| And tradition | 5.014 | 80 |
| **BLASPHEMERS** | 5.255 | 142 |

|  | Reference Numbers | Page Numbers |
|---|---|---|
| BLASPHEMY | 4.100 | 63 |
|  | 7.053 | 210 |
|  | 7.055 | 210 |
|  | 7.221 | 243 |
|  | 7.223 | 243 |
|  | 11.2 | 311 |
| BLASTUS, ERRORS OF | 5.040 | 87 |
| BLESSING ONE ANOTHER | 10.3 | 301 |
| BLESSINGS, PRAYERS FOR | 7.104 | 215 |
|  | 7.303 | 258–59 |
| BLINDNESS TO GOOD | 6.029 | 155 |
| BLOOD OF CHRIST: | | |
|     In baptism | 4.069–.074 | 51–53 |
|  | 7.275 | 253 |
|     Drinking of | 4.076 | 53–54 |
|  | 7.278–.280 | 254 |
|     In Lord's Supper | 6.167 | 183–84 |
|  | 7.096 | 214 |
|  | 7.280 | 254 |
|     And sin | 7.262 | 251 |
|     Symbol of | 6.165 | 183 |
|  | 7.096 | 214 |
| BOASTING | 7.255 | 249–50 |
| BODIES, OF MEN, AFTER DEATH | 6.177 | 186 |
|  | 7.037 | 208 |
|  | 7.196 | 237 |
| BODY OF CHRIST: | | |
|     Church as | 5.130 | 110 |
|     Crucified | 4.076 | 53–54 |
|     Eating of | 4.076 | 53–54 |
|     In Lord's Supper | 6.161 | 182 |
|  | 7.278–.280 | 254 |
|     Membership in | 6.161 | 182 |
|  | 7.278 | 254 |
|     Mystical | 6.140 | 179 |
|  | 7.176 | 233 |
|     Presence in Lord's Supper (See also Christ: Presence) | 6.167 | 183–84 |
|  | 7.096 | 214 |
|     Resurrection of (See also Resurrection of the Body) | 6.046 | 157–58 |
|  | 7.028 | 207 |
|  | 7.162 | 231 |
|     Symbol of | 6.165 | 183 |
|  | 7.096 | 214 |

INDEX

| | Reference Numbers | Page Numbers |
|---|---|---|
| BODY OF CHRIST (*Continued*) | | |
| True | 6.044 | 157 |
| | 7.147 | 229 |
| BODY AND SOUL | 5.034 | 86 |
| BODY, RESURRECTION OF | 7.197 | 237 |
| BOOK OF LIFE | 5.060 | 92 |
| BREAD: | | |
| Daily | 7.104 | 215 |
| | 7.303 | 258–59 |
| In Lord's Supper | 5.178–.180 | 124–25 |
| | 6.166 | 183 |
| BRIBERY | 7.252 | 248–49 |
| BRIDE, CHURCH AS | 5.130 | 110 |
| BRIEF STATEMENT OF FAITH, A | 11.1–.6 | 311–12 |
| BROKENHEARTED, BINDING UP | 11.2 | 311 |
| BROTHERHOOD OF CHRIST | 9.08 | 288 |
| BURIAL: | | |
| Of Christ | 4.041 | 43 |
| | 6.046 | 157–58 |
| | 7.027 | 207 |
| | 7.160 | 231 |
| Of the dead | 5.235–.236 | 137–38 |

## C

| | Reference Numbers | Page Numbers |
|---|---|---|
| CAIN | 3.18 | 19 |
| CALL: | | |
| Of women and men | 11.4 | 312 |
| CALL, EFFECTUAL | 6.064–.065 | 162 |
| | 7.031 | 207 |
| | 7.177 | 234 |
| CALLING, OF MINISTERS | 5.150 | 117 |
| | 7.268 | 252 |
| CANAAN, LAND OF | 3.05 | 12 |
| | 5.087 | 99 |
| CANON OF SCRIPTURE | 6.001–.003 | 149–50 |
| CANONICAL HOURS | 5.222 | 134 |
| CANONICAL SCRIPTURES | 5.001 | 77 |
| | 5.011 | 79 |
| CANONS OF COUNCILS | 5.012–.013 | 79 |
| CANTORS | 5.148 | 116–17 |
| CAPERNAITES, ERRORS OF | 5.197 | 129 |
| CARDINALS | 5.148 | 116–17 |
| CARES, DISTRACTING | 7.246 | 247 |
| CARNAL PROMISES | 5.087–.088 | 99 |

|  | Reference Numbers | Page Numbers |
|---|---|---|
| CARVERS, AND IMAGES | 5.020 | 81–82 |
| CATECHISMS: | | |
|    As Confessions | 9.02 | 287 |
|    Heidelberg, text | 4.001–.129 | 31–73 |
|    Westminster Larger, text | 7.111–.306 | 225–60 |
|    Westminster Shorter, text | 7.001–.110 | 205–16 |
| CATECHIZING OF YOUTH | 5.233 | 137 |
| CATHARISTS, ERRORS OF | 5.103 | 103 |
| CATHOLIC OR UNIVERSAL CHURCH (See also Church: Catholic; Roman Church) | 5.126 | 109 |
| CAUSES, SECOND | 6.014 | 152 |
| CELIBACY | 5.245 | 140 |
|  | 6.126 | 174 |
|  | 7.247 | 247 |
| CERDON, ERRORS OF | 5.008 | 78 |
| CEREMONIAL LAWS, OLD TESTAMENT | 6.103 | 169 |
| CEREMONIES | 3.20 | 20–21 |
|  | 5.240–.242 | 138–39 |
| CHALCEDON, CREED OF | 5.078 | 97 |
| CHANGE OF FORMS OF CHURCH SERVICE | 9.48 | 295 |
| CHARITY | 7.245 | 247 |
|  | 7.254 | 249 |
|  | 7.257 | 250 |
| CHEERFULNESS | 7.245 | 247 |
| CHEMICAL WEAPONS | 9.45 | 294 |
| CHILDREN: | | |
|    Baptism of | 4.074 | 52–53 |
|    Of believers | 3.16 | 18 |
|  | 6.042 | 157 |
|  | 7.095 | 214 |
|  | 7.276 | 253 |
|    Dying in infancy | 6.066 | 162 |
|  | 6.193 | 191 |
|    Of God | 6.074 | 164 |
|  | 7.034 | 208 |
|  | 7.184 | 235 |
|    Instruction of | 5.233 | 137 |
|    And parents | 9.47 | 294–95 |
|    Rearing of | 5.249–.250 | 141 |
| CHOSEN PEOPLE, PROMISE TO | 3.05 | 12 |

# INDEX

| | Reference Numbers | Page Numbers |
|---|---|---|
| **CHRIST:** | | |
| Adoption in and for | 6.074 | 164 |
| | 7.149 | 230 |
| Anointing of | 4.031 | 40 |
| | 6.045 | 157 |
| | 7.152 | 230 |
| Appearance of | 8.17 | 283 |
| Ascension of | 1.2 | 3 |
| | 2.2 | 7 |
| | 3.11 | 15 |
| | 4.046 | 44 |
| | 4.049–.050 | 44–45 |
| | 5.074 | 95 |
| | 6.046 | 157–58 |
| | 7.028 | 207 |
| | 7.163 | 232 |
| Atonement of | 3.08 | 13 |
| | 3.09 | 14 |
| | 4.037 | 42 |
| | 5.102 | 103 |
| | 9.08 | 288 |
| As author of faith | 6.080 | 165 |
| Baptism of | 5.018 | 81 |
| | 5.190 | 127 |
| | 9.51 | 296 |
| Begotten son | 4.033 | 40 |
| Body of | 4.076–.079 | 53–55 |
| Brotherhood with | 3.08 | 13 |
| | 9.08 | 288 |
| Burial of | 4.041 | 43 |
| Calling of | 6.045 | 157 |
| Church of | 6.140–.145 | 179–80 |
| Church government and discipline and | 6.129 | 175 |
| | 6.169 | 184 |
| | 7.155 | 230 |
| Church as property of | 8.17 | 283 |
| As comfort | 4.001 | 31 |
| | 8.17 | 283 |
| Coming of | 6.046 | 157–58 |
| | 6.180–.182 | 186–87 |
| Communion with | 7.179 | 234 |
| | 7.192–.193 | 236–37 |
| | 7.196 | 237 |
| | 7.200 | 238 |

|  | Reference Numbers | Page Numbers |
|---|---|---|
| **CHRIST** (*Continued*) | | |
| Conception of | 5.064 | 93–94 |
| As consummation of law | 3.15 | 17–18 |
| Creation of | 1.2 | 3 |
| | 5.016 | 80 |
| | 5.062 | 93 |
| | 9.19 | 290 |
| Crucifixion of | 6.046 | 157–58 |
| | 11.2 | 311 |
| Day of | 3.04 | 12 |
| Death of | 3.08 | 13 |
| | 3.09 | 14 |
| | 4.039–.040 | 42 |
| | 11.2 | 311 |
| Definition of | 9.07 | 287–88 |
| Denial of | 9.45 | 294 |
| Descent into hell | 4.044 | 43 |
| Dishonor to | 6.145 | 180 |
| Effect of spirit of | 6.087–.093 | 166–67 |
| And the elect | 6.018 | 153 |
| | 6.019 | 153 |
| | 6.043 | 157 |
| | 7.175–.176 | 233 |
| And election | 5.053 | 91 |
| | 5.059–.061 | 92–93 |
| | 7.123 | 226 |
| Eternally begotten | 6.012 | 152 |
| Exaltation of | 6.046 | 157–58 |
| | 7.028 | 207 |
| | 7.161–.166 | 231–32 |
| And faith | 5.110 | 105 |
| | 6.061 | 161 |
| | 7.085–.086 | 213 |
| | 7.263 | 251 |
| Festivals of | 5.226 | 135 |
| Flesh and blood of | 5.064 | 93–94 |
| | 5.196–.197 | 128–29 |
| | 5.199 | 129 |
| | 5.201–.203 | 130 |
| Fulfillment of law by | 6.046 | 157–58 |
| Fullness of Godhead in | 6.045 | 157 |
| Fully human, fully God | 11.2 | 311 |
| Functions of | 3.08 | 13 |

## INDEX

| | Reference Numbers | Page Numbers |
|---|---|---|
| **CHRIST** (*Continued*) | | |
| Gifts of............................................................... | 3.25 | 25 |
| | 6.142 | 179 |
| | 7.163–.164 | 232 |
| God and man united in................................... | 6.044 | 157 |
| | 6.045 | 157 |
| | 6.049 | 158 |
| | 7.022 | 206 |
| | 7.146 | 229 |
| And good works............................................ | 3.13 | 16 |
| | 6.089 | 166 |
| | 7.304 | 259 |
| Grace of ......................................................... | 5.107 | 104 |
| | 6.105–.107 | 169–70 |
| | 9.08–.14 | 288–89 |
| As head of the church ................................... | 4.050 | 45 |
| | 5.131 | 110–11 |
| | 6.043 | 157 |
| | 6.140 | 179 |
| | 6.145 | 180 |
| | 6.146 | 180 |
| | 7.162–.163 | 231–32 |
| | 7.174 | 233 |
| | 9.10 | 288 |
| | 10.9 | 305 |
| Honor of........................................................ | 6.171 | 185 |
| Human nature of ........................................... | 6.159 | 182 |
| Humiliation of............................................... | 6.044 | 157 |
| | 7.027 | 207 |
| | 7.156–.160 | 230–31 |
| Images of ...................................................... | 5.020–.022 | 81–82 |
| Incarnation of................................................ | 1.2 | 3 |
| | 2.2 | 7 |
| | 3.06 | 13 |
| | 3.08 | 13 |
| | 5.078 | 97 |
| | 11.2 | 311 |
| Infants and ................................................... | 6.066 | 162 |
| | 6.193 | 191 |
| Ingrafting into .............................................. | 6.154 | 181 |
| Innocence of ................................................ | 11.2 | 311 |
| Intercession of.............................................. | 6.046 | 157–58 |
| | 6.095 | 167 |
| | 7.028 | 207 |

BOOK OF CONFESSIONS

| | Reference Numbers | Page Numbers |
|---|---|---|
| **CHRIST** (*Continued*) | | |
| Intercession of (*Continued*) | | |
| | 7.164–.165 | 232 |
| | 7.189 | 236 |
| And Israel | 9.19 | 290 |
| As judge | 4.052 | 45–46 |
| Judgment by | 1.2 | 3 |
| | 2.2 | 7 |
| | 3.11 | 15 |
| | 7.152 | 230 |
| | 9.08 | 288 |
| | 9.11 | 288 |
| Keys of kingdom and | 6.170 | 184 |
| | 7.155 | 230 |
| As king | 6.169 | 184 |
| | 7.026 | 207 |
| | 7.155 | 230 |
| Kingdom of | 1.2 | 3 |
| | 6.141 | 179 |
| And law of God | 5.084 | 98 |
| Liberty through | 6.108 | 170 |
| Lord of living and dead | 7.162 | 231 |
| Love of | 6.100 | 168–69 |
| Manifestations of | 6.042 | 157 |
| | 7.145 | 229 |
| Meaning of name | 7.023 | 207 |
| | 7.151–.152 | 230 |
| As mediator | 3.07–.08 | 13 |
| | 5.024 | 83 |
| | 6.043–.050 | 157–58 |
| | 6.113 | 172 |
| | 7.021–.026 | 206–07 |
| | 7.029 | 207 |
| | 7.146–.155 | 229–30 |
| | 7.167–.169 | 232–33 |
| | 7.291 | 256–57 |
| Ministry of | 11.2 | 311 |
| Mission of | 9.07 | 287–88 |
| Names of | 4.029 | 39 |
| | 4.031 | 40 |
| | 4.033 | 40–41 |
| | 4.034 | 41 |
| | 7.023 | 207 |
| | 7.151–.152 | 230 |

# INDEX

| | Reference Numbers | Page Numbers |
|---|---|---|
| **CHRIST** (*Continued*) | | |
| Nature of | 1.2 | 3 |
| | 2.2 | 7 |
| | 3.06 | 13 |
| | 4.048 | 44 |
| | 5.069 | 94 |
| | 6.045 | 157 |
| | 6.049 | 158 |
| | 7.148–.150 | 229–30 |
| Obedience of | 6.047 | 158 |
| | 6.070–.071 | 163 |
| | 7.027 | 207 |
| | 7.029 | 207 |
| | 7.148–.149 | 229–30 |
| | 7.180–.181 | 234 |
| | 7.205 | 238–39 |
| | 7.304 | 259 |
| | 9.08 | 288 |
| Offering of | 6.162 | 182–83 |
| Ordinances of | 7.088 | 213 |
| | 7.263–.264 | 251 |
| Passion of | 1.2 | 3 |
| | 2.2 | 7 |
| As pastor | 5.131 | 110–11 |
| Peace and order and | 6.111 | 171 |
| Person of | 3.06 | 13 |
| | 5.066 | 94 |
| | 6.013 | 152 |
| | 6.044 | 157 |
| | 9.05 | 287 |
| Power of | 3.13 | 16 |
| | 5.158 | 119 |
| | 6.045 | 157 |
| | 7.152 | 230 |
| Prayer in name of | 6.114 | 172 |
| | 7.098 | 214 |
| | 7.288 | 256 |
| | 7.290–.291 | 256–57 |
| Predestination and foreordination of | 5.062 | 93 |
| Pre-existence of | 1.2 | 3 |
| Prefigured in Old Testament | 6.041 | 156 |
| | 6.048 | 158 |
| | 6.103 | 169 |
| | 7.144 | 229 |

|  | Reference Numbers | Page Numbers |
|---|---|---|
| **CHRIST** (*Continued*) | | |
| Presence of | 4.047 | 44 |
| | 5.205 | 131 |
| | 7.278–.279 | 254 |
| | 9.07 | 287–88 |
| Present witness to | 9.01 | 287 |
| As priest | 5.154 | 118 |
| | 6.043 | 157 |
| | 7.025 | 207 |
| | 7.154 | 230 |
| Proclaimer of the reign of God | 11.2 | 311 |
| And prophesy of Scripture | 1.2 | 3 |
| As prophet | 6.043 | 157 |
| | 7.024 | 207 |
| | 7.153 | 230 |
| Reception of | 5.110 | 105 |
| Reconciliation by | 5.076 | 96 |
| As redeemer | 7.021 | 206 |
| | 7.023 | 207 |
| | 7.151–.152 | 230 |
| | 9.11 | 288 |
| Redemption by | 6.047–.050 | 158 |
| | 7.030 | 207 |
| | 7.161–.162 | 231 |
| | 7.169 | 233 |
| Resurrection of | 3.10 | 14 |
| | 4.045 | 43 |
| | 5.073 | 95 |
| | 6.046 | 157–58 |
| | 7.028 | 207 |
| | 7.162 | 231 |
| | 9.08 | 288 |
| | 9.26 | 291 |
| | 11.2 | 311 |
| Return of | 11.4 | 312 |
| Rule of | 9.54 | 296–97 |
| Sacraments and | 6.149 | 181 |
| | 6.152 | 181 |
| | 6.154 | 181 |
| | 6.161 | 182 |
| | 7.091 | 213 |
| | 7.271 | 253 |
| Sacrifice of | 3.09 | 14 |
| | 3.22 | 23 |

# INDEX

| | Reference Numbers | Page Numbers |
|---|---|---|
| **CHRIST** (*Continued*) | | |
| Sacrifice of (*Continued*) | 4.066–.067 | 50 |
| | 6.047 | 158 |
| | 7.025 | 207 |
| | 7.154 | 230 |
| | 7.159–.160 | 231 |
| | 7.262 | 251 |
| Salvation through | 4.020 | 36 |
| | 6.039 | 156 |
| | 6.057 | 160 |
| | 6.189 | 189 |
| | 6.191 | 190 |
| | 7.031 | 207 |
| | 7.142 | 228–29 |
| | 7.170 | 233 |
| Sanctification by | 6.075 | 164 |
| | 7.185 | 235 |
| As Savior | 5.077 | 96 |
| | 6.043 | 157 |
| | 7.170 | 233 |
| | 9.10 | 288 |
| As second Adam | 7.141 | 228 |
| Second coming of | 1.2 | 3 |
| | 2.2 | 7 |
| | 7.028 | 207 |
| | 7.166 | 232 |
| | 8.17 | 283 |
| Service of | 9.32 | 292 |
| Sinless | 6.044 | 157 |
| | 6.045 | 157 |
| | 7.022 | 206 |
| | 7.147 | 229 |
| | 7.154 | 230 |
| Son | 6.155 | 182 |
| Son of God | 4.026–.052 | 37–46 |
| | 7.043–.044 | 209 |
| Son of man | 5.064 | 93–94 |
| Soul of | 5.065 | 94 |
| Spirit of | 3.12 | 15–16 |
| Spiritual eating of | 5.198 | 129 |
| As spiritual food | 5.199 | 129 |
| | 5.201 | 130 |

BOOK OF CONFESSIONS

| | Reference Numbers | Page Numbers |
|---|---|---|
| **CHRIST** (*Continued*) | | |
| Suffering of | 3.09 | 14 |
| | 4.037–.040 | 42 |
| | 5.071 | 94 |
| | 6.046 | 157–58 |
| | 7.027 | 207 |
| | 7.148 | 229 |
| | 7.159 | 231 |
| | 9.32 | 292 |
| As teacher | 5.146 | 116 |
| Temptation of | 7.158 | 231 |
| As testator of New Testament | 6.040 | 156 |
| Trust in | 11.2 | 311 |
| Two natures of | 5.066 | 94 |
| | 6.049 | 158 |
| | 7.148–.150 | 229–30 |
| Union with | 7.175–.176 | 233 |
| Unity of | 5.067 | 94 |
| Unity of God and man in | 3.07 | 13 |
| Vanquished death | 7.162 | 231 |
| Very God and very man | 1.2 | 3 |
| | 6.043–.044 | 157 |
| | 7.022 | 206 |
| | 7.121 | 226 |
| | 7.146–.147 | 229 |
| Virgin birth of | 1.2 | 3 |
| | 2.2 | 7 |
| | 3.06 | 13 |
| | 4.035–.036 | 41 |
| | 5.062 | 93 |
| | 7.022 | 206 |
| | 7.147 | 229 |
| As word of God | 8.11 | 283 |
| **CHRISTIAN, BELIEF OF** | 4.022 | 36 |
| **CHRISTIAN CHURCH, DEFINITION OF** | 8.17 | 283 |
| **CHRISTIAN FAITH, BASIS OF** | 9.05 | 287 |
| **CHRISTIAN LIBERTY** | 5.047 | 89–90 |
| | 6.108–.111 | 170–71 |
| **CHRISTIAN MARRIAGE:** | | |
| Definition of | 6.131 | 176 |
| | 6.133 | 177 |
| And remarriage | 6.132 | 176–77 |
| | 6.138 | 179 |
| **CHRISTIAN, MEANING OF THE NAME** | 4.032 | 40 |

340

# INDEX

| | Reference Numbers | Page Numbers |
|---|---|---|
| **CHRISTIANS:** | | |
| And civil office | 6.128 | 174 |
| And marriage | 6.131 | 176 |
| | 6.135 | 177–78 |
| **CHRISTIANITY AND OTHER RELIGIONS** | 9.41–.42 | 293 |
| **CHURCH:** | | |
| Administrative rules of | 9.40 | 293 |
| Apostolic | 1.3 | 3 |
| | 5.035 | 86 |
| | 8.01 | 281 |
| | 8.06 | 282 |
| Attendance at | 4.103 | 64 |
| Authority in | 5.165 | 121 |
| And baptism | 9.51 | 296 |
| Betrayal by | 9.45 | 294 |
| As body of Christ | 5.130 | 110 |
| | 6.054 | 159–60 |
| | 6.186 | 188 |
| As bride and virgin | 5.130 | 110 |
| Call of, to mission | 9.31 | 291–92 |
| Catholic or universal | 1.3 | 3 |
| | 2.3 | 7 |
| | 3.16 | 18 |
| | 4.054 | 46 |
| | 5.126 | 109 |
| | 6.140–.143 | 179–80 |
| | 8.06 | 282 |
| Ceasing to be the church | 8.07 | 282 |
| Censure | 6.169 | 184 |
| | 6.171–.172 | 185 |
| Christ and | 6.169 | 184 |
| Christian, definition of | 8.17 | 283 |
| And civil magistrates | 5.252–.258 | 142–43 |
| Commission of | 6.058 | 161 |
| | 6.190 | 189 |
| As commonwealth | 5.125 | 109 |
| As confessor | 10.9 | 305 |
| Constitution of | 9.40 | 293 |
| Continuance of | 3.05 | 12 |
| Corporate life of | 9.36 | 292 |
| Councils of | 5.012–.013 | 79 |
| Definition of | 5.125 | 109 |
| | 8.17 | 283 |
| Direction of | 9.31–.33 | 257–58 |

341

BOOK OF CONFESSIONS

|  | Reference Numbers | Page Numbers |
|---|---|---|
| CHURCH (*Continued*) | | |
| Discipline in | 5.165 | 121 |
|  | 6.121 | 173 |
| Disorder in | 5.132 | 111 |
| Dispersed | 9.35 | 292 |
|  | 9.37 | 292 |
| Dissension and strife in | 5.133 | 111–12 |
| Division in | 9.34 | 292 |
| Equality of people in | 9.44 | 294 |
| Equipment of | 9.48–.52 | 295–96 |
| Exclusion from | 4.085 | 58 |
| Exploitation of | 9.40 | 293 |
| False | 3.18 | 19 |
| Fathers of | 5.011 | 79 |
| Fidelity of | 9.37 | 292 |
| Finances | 9.40 | 293 |
| As flock | 5.130 | 110 |
| Forms of | 9.34 | 292 |
| Forms of service in | 9.48 | 295 |
| Gathered | 9.35–.36 | 292 |
| Gentiles and | 5.129 | 110 |
| German Evangelical | 8.01 | 281 |
|  | 8.03–.07 | 281–82 |
|  | 8.09 | 283 |
|  | 8.28 | 284 |
| Gifts of Christ to | 3.25 | 25 |
| Government of | 5.003 | 77 |
|  | 5.132 | 111 |
|  | 6.129 | 175 |
|  | 9.40 | 293 |
| Head of | 3.16 | 18 |
|  | 4.050 | 45 |
|  | 5.131 | 110–11 |
|  | 6.145 | 180 |
|  | 6.169 | 184 |
|  | 9.10 | 288 |
| Hear peoples long silenced | 11.4 | 312 |
| Holy Spirit and | 6.054 | 159–60 |
|  | 6.186 | 188 |
|  | 11.4 | 312 |
| As household of God | 9.47 | 294–95 |
| Images in | 4.098 | 62 |
| Increase and preservation of | 3.05 | 12 |
|  | 4.123 | 71 |

|  | Reference Numbers | Page Numbers |
|---|---|---|
| **CHURCH** (*Continued*) | | |
| Inerrancy of | 5.130 | 110 |
| As institution | 9.34 | 292 |
| Invisible | 3.16 | 18 |
| | 3.25 | 25 |
| | 5.138 | 113 |
| | 6.140 | 179 |
| | 7.174–.175 | 233 |
| Israelites or Jews and | 5.129 | 110 |
| Judgment of | 9.47 | 294–95 |
| As kingdom of Christ | 6.141 | 179 |
| Leadership and oversight of | 9.39 | 293 |
| And limited progress | 9.55 | 297 |
| Lutheran | 8.01 | 281 |
| | 8.06 | 282 |
| | 8.08 | 282 |
| As matrimonial forum | 5.248 | 141 |
| As meeting place | 5.214 | 132–33 |
| | 5.216 | 133 |
| Membership in | 4.054 | 46 |
| | 5.139 | 113–14 |
| | 9.25 | 290–91 |
| | 9.38 | 292–93 |
| Message of | 8.17 | 283 |
| Militant | 3.17 | 19 |
| | 5.127–.128 | 109–10 |
| Ministries of | 11.2 | 311 |
| | 11.4 | 312 |
| Mission of | 9.31–.46 | 257–60 |
| And national sovereignty | 9.45 | 294 |
| Nature of | 3.16 | 18 |
| Necessity of, for salvation | 3.16 | 18 |
| And non-Christians | 9.42 | 293 |
| Notes and signs of the true | 3.18 | 19 |
| Obedience of | 8.17 | 283 |
| Obligations concerning Scripture | 9.29 | 291 |
| Obscuring of | 5.138 | 113 |
| Officers of | 6.169–.170 | 184 |
| | 9.40 | 293 |
| Offices in | 8.20 | 284 |
| Order, reformation of | 9.40 | 293 |
| Origin of | 5.124 | 109 |
| Ornamentation of | 5.216 | 133 |

BOOK OF CONFESSIONS

|  | Reference Numbers | Page Numbers |
|---|---|---|
| CHURCH (*Continued*) | | |
| Particular | 6.143–.144 | 180 |
|  | 6.173 | 185 |
| Parts or forms of | 5.127 | 109–10 |
| Pastor of | 5.131 | 110–11 |
| And peace | 9.45 | 294 |
| Perpetuity of | 6.144 | 180 |
| Politics | 8.28 | 284 |
| Polity | 9.39 | 293 |
| As the possession of God | 10.7 | 304 |
| Possessions of | 5.243–.244 | 140 |
| Power of ministers in | 5.157 | 119 |
| Presence of Christ in | 9.07 | 287–88 |
| Primacy in | 5.131 | 110–11 |
| Proclamation of | 4.012 | 34 |
|  | 11.4 | 312 |
| Reconciling mission of | 9.06 | 287 |
|  | 9.31 | 257 |
| Reformation of | 5.003 | 77 |
| Reformed | 8.01 | 281 |
|  | 8.06 | 282 |
|  | 8.08 | 282 |
| Renewed | 8.01 | 281 |
| Revelation to | 6.001 | 149 |
| Rites of | 5.141 | 114 |
| Roman (See Roman Church) | 3.22 | 23 |
|  | 5.126 | 109 |
| Salvation and | 5.136–.137 | 113 |
|  | 7.171 | 233 |
| As servant | 9.19 | 290 |
| And state | 6.127–.130 | 174–75 |
|  | 8.22–.24 | 284 |
| Subordinate standards of | 9.03 | 287 |
| As temple of God | 5.130 | 110 |
| And testaments | 5.129 | 110 |
| Testimony of | 6.005 | 150 |
| Test of purity of | 6.143 | 180 |
| Triumphant | 3.16 | 18 |
|  | 5.127 | 109–10 |
| True | 3.18 | 19 |
|  | 5.134–.135 | 112 |
| United Germany | 8.01 | 281 |
|  | 8.06 | 282 |
|  | 8.08 | 282 |

344

# INDEX

|  | Reference Numbers | Page Numbers |
|---|---|---|
| **CHURCH** (*Continued*) | | |
| Unity of | 5.126 | 109 |
| | 5.129 | 110 |
| | 5.141 | 114 |
| | 9.34 | 292 |
| Universal | 5.002 | 77 |
| | 9.03 | 287 |
| Unmask idolatries in | 11.4 | 312 |
| Visible | 6.141 | 179 |
| | 6.154 | 181 |
| | 7.172–.173 | 233 |
| **CIRCUMCISION** | 5.170 | 122 |
| And baptism | 4.074 | 52–53 |
| | 5.177 | 124 |
| Of Christ, celebration of | 5.226 | 135 |
| **CIVIL MAGISTRATE** | 6.127–.130 | 174–75 |
| And the church | 5.252–.258 | 142–43 |
| Duties of | 5.253–.255 | 142 |
| Duties of subjects to | 5.258 | 143 |
| Origin of | 5.252 | 142 |
| Powers of | 3.24 | 24 |
| | 8.20–.24 | 284 |
| Prayer for | 5.260 | 143 |
| And true religion | 3.24 | 24 |
| And worship | 5.212 | 132 |
| **CIVIL PENALTIES** | 7.261 | 251 |
| **CLASS, SOCIAL** | 9.46 | 294 |
| **COHABITATION** | 7.248 | 248 |
| **COMFORT** | 10.3 | 302 |
| **COMFORT, IN LIFE AND DEATH** | 4.001 | 31 |
| | 11.1 | 311 |
| | 11.2 | 311 |
| | 11.5 | 312 |
| **COMING OF THE LORD** | 7.038 | 208 |
| | 7.198 | 237 |
| **COMMANDMENT, TEN** (See Ten Commandments) | | |
| **COMMISSION:** | | |
| Of church | 8.26 | 284 |
| Of service | 9.10 | 288 |
| Of state | 8.22–.24 | 284 |
| **COMMON LANGUAGE IN WORSHIP** | 5.217–.218 | 133 |
| **COMMONWEALTH, CHURCH AS** | 5.125 | 109 |

BOOK OF CONFESSIONS

|  | Reference Numbers | Page Numbers |
|---|---|---|
| COMMUNICANT: | | |
| Examination of | 3.23 | 24 |
| | 7.097 | 214 |
| | 7.281 | 254–55 |
| Requirements of | 7.097 | 214 |
| | 7.284 | 255 |
| Weak and doubting | 7.282 | 255 |
| COMMUNICATION: | | |
| In Lord's Supper | 7.097 | 214 |
| | 7.280 | 254 |
| Mass | 9.47 | 294–95 |
| COMMUNION (See also Lord's Supper): | | |
| Of body and blood of Christ | 3.21 | 21 |
| With Christ | 9.52 | 296 |
| In glory | 7.036–.038 | 208 |
| | 7.192–.193 | 236–37 |
| | 7.196 | 237 |
| | 7.200 | 238 |
| In grace | 7.179 | 234 |
| Lord's Supper and | 6.161 | 182 |
| Perfect and full | 7.038 | 208 |
| | 7.200 | 238 |
| Of saints | 2.3 | 7 |
| | 3.16 | 18 |
| | 4.055 | 47 |
| | 5.125 | 109 |
| | 6.146–.148 | 180–81 |
| | 10.2 | 301 |
| Unbelievers | 4.082 | 57 |
| COMMUNITY | 10.3 | 301 |
| Live as one | 11.3 | 311 |
| Members of | 4.055 | 47 |
| Nurture by | 9.24 | 290 |
| Reconciling | 9.31 | 257 |
| COMPANY: | | |
| Chaste | 7.248 | 248 |
| Unchaste | 7.249 | 248 |
| COMPASSION | 7.245 | 247 |
| COMPENDIUM OF FAITH | 5.141 | 114 |
| CONDUCT, IN WORSHIP | 5.215 | 133 |
| CONFESSION: | | |
| Definition of | 9.01 | 287 |
| Nature of | 9.33 | 292 |
| Sacerdotal | 5.095 | 101–02 |

# INDEX

| | Reference Numbers | Page Numbers |
|---|---|---|
| CONFESSION: (*Continued*) | | |
|     Unity in | 9.05 | 287 |
| | 10.3 | 301 |
| CONFESSION OF BELHAR | 10.1-.9 | 301–5 |
| CONFESSION OF FAITH: | | |
|     German | 8.01 | 281 |
|     And indifferent things | 5.242 | 139 |
|     Universal | 4.022 | 36 |
|     Westminster, text | 6.001–.193 | 149–91 |
| CONFESSION OF 1967: | | |
|     Prologue | | 286 |
|     Purpose of | 9.05 | 287 |
|     Text | 9.01–.56 | 287–97 |
|     Theme of | 9.06 | 287 |
| CONFESSION OF SINS | 5.094–.095 | 100–01 |
| | 6.108 | 170 |
| | 9.50 | 261 |
| CONFESSIONAL CHURCHES, FEDERATION OF | 8.05 | 282 |
| CONFESSIONAL STATEMENTS, FOUNDATION OF | 9.07 | 287–88 |
| CONFESSIONAL SYNOD, OF GERMAN EVANGELICAL CHURCH | 8.01–.02 | 281 |
| | 8.04 | 281 |
| | 8.06 | 282 |
| | 8.28 | 284 |
| CONFESSIONS: | | |
|     Authority of | 9.03 | 287 |
|     Examples of | 8.02 | 281 |
|     Of the fathers | 8.04 | 281 |
|     Loyalty to | 8.02 | 281 |
| CONFIDENCE IN GOD | 4.028 | 39 |
| CONFIRMATION | 5.171 | 122–23 |
| CONFLICT, IN MAN | 9.23 | 290 |
| CONSANGUINITY | 5.247 | 141 |
| CONSCIENCE: | | |
|     Cases of | 6.174 | 185 |
|     Liberty of | 6.109 | 171 |
|     Lord of | 6.109 | 171 |
| | 7.215 | 241 |
|     Sins against | 7.261 | 251 |
| CONSECRATION OF SACRAMENTS | 5.178 | 124–25 |
| CONSTANTINOPLE, CREED OF | 5.078 | 97 |
| CONSTITUTION, CHURCH | 9.40 | 293 |
| CONTEMPORARY WORLD, STUDY OF | 9.49 | 295 |
| CONTEMPT OF SUPERVISORS | 7.238 | 246 |

| | Reference Numbers | Page Numbers |
|---|---|---|
| CONTENTMENT | 7.257 | 250 |
| CONTINENCY | 5.246 | 140–41 |
| | 7.248 | 248 |
| CONTRACTS | 7.251 | 248 |
| CONTROVERSIES: | | |
|    Appeal in | 6.008 | 151 |
|    About religion | 5.013 | 79 |
|    Supreme judge in | 6.010 | 151 |
|    Synods and councils and | 6.174 | 185 |
| CONVERSION | 6.059–.063 | 161–62 |
|    Genuine | 4.088 | 59 |
|    Of man | 5.093–.105 | 100–03 |
|    And repentance | 5.094 | 101 |
| CONVICTIONS, IDEOLOGICAL AND POLITICAL | 8.18 | 283 |
| CORINTH, CHURCH IN | 3.18 | 19 |
| | 5.137 | 113 |
| CORNELIUS | 5.005 | 78 |
| CORPORATE LIFE OF THE CHURCH | 9.36 | 292 |
| | 9.53 | 296 |
| CORRUPTION OF HUMAN NATURE | 4.007 | 33 |
| | 6.032–.036 | 155 |
| | 6.062 | 161–62 |
| | 6.068–.069 | 163 |
| | 7.135–.136 | 227–28 |
| | 7.188 | 235–36 |
| | 7.301–.305 | 258–59 |
| COUNCILS: | | |
|    Decrees and canons of | 5.012–.013 | 79 |
|    Ecumenical | 5.167 | 122 |
|    General | 3.20 | 20 |
| COUNSEL: | | |
|    In Scripture | 6.006 | 150–51 |
|    Of superiors | 7.239 | 246 |
| COURTESY | 7.245 | 247 |
| COURTS, MATRIMONIAL | 5.248 | 141 |
| COVENANT: | | |
|    With Adam | 3.04 | 12 |
|    Baptism, sign of | 4.074 | 52–53 |
|    Essentially one | 6.042 | 157 |
|    First | 6.038 | 156 |
| | 7.012 | 205 |
| | 7.130 | 227 |
|    Of grace | 6.039 | 156 |
| | 6.040 | 156 |

INDEX

| | Reference Numbers | Page Numbers |
|---|---|---|
| **COVENANT** (*Continued*) | | |
| Of grace (*Continued*) | | |
| | 6.149 | 181 |
| | 6.154 | 181 |
| | 6.161 | 182 |
| | 7.021–.026 | 206–07 |
| | 7.142 | 228–29 |
| | 7.146–.155 | 229–30 |
|     Heirs with Christ | 10.3 | 301 |
|     With Israel | 9.18 | 289–90 |
| | 11.3 | 312 |
|     Man and | 6.037–.042 | 156–57 |
| | 7.141 | 228 |
|     New Testament | 4.074 | 52–53 |
| | 6.042 | 157 |
|     Old Testament | 4.074 | 52–53 |
| | 6.041 | 156 |
| | 11.3 | 312 |
|     Renewal of | 3.04 | 12 |
| | 9.51 | 296 |
|     Second | 6.039 | 156 |
| | 7.020 | 206 |
| | 7.140–.146 | 228–29 |
|     Of works | 6.038 | 156 |
| | 7.012 | 205 |
| | 7.130 | 227 |
| **COVETOUSNESS** | 7.079 | 212 |
| | 7.256 | 250 |
| **CREATION:** | | |
|     Of angels | 7.126 | 226 |
|     By God | 5.032–.034 | 85–86 |
| | 6.022 | 153–54 |
| | 7.009–.010 | 205 |
| | 7.124–.127 | 226–27 |
|     Of man | 6.023 | 154 |
| | 7.010 | 205 |
| | 7.127 | 226–27 |
|     Poverty and | 9.46 | 294 |
|     Providence and | 6.001 | 149 |
|     Redemption of | 11.3 | 311 |
|     Threatened | 11.3 | 311 |
|     Of the world | 6.022 | 153–54 |
| | 7.009 | 205 |
| | 7.125 | 226 |
| **CREDIBILITY** | 10.5 | 303 |
| **CREDULITY** | 7.215 | 241 |

|  | Reference Numbers | Page Numbers |
|---|---|---|
| CREED, APOSTLES' (See Apostles' Creed) | | |
| CREED OF CONSTANTINOPLE | 5.078 | 97 |
| CREED, NICENE (See Nicene Creed) | | |
| CREEDS, OF COUNCILS | 5.078 | 97 |
| CRISIS: | | |
|    Personal | 9.21 | 290 |
|    Supreme, for humanity | 9.21 | 290 |
| CROSS, OF CHRIST (See Sacrifice) | | |
| CULTURAL LIFE | 9.53 | 296 |
| CULTURES | 10.3 | 302 |
| CUP, DENIAL OF | 5.209 | 132 |
|  | 6.164 | 183 |
| CURSE: | | |
|    Of Christ | 7.027 | 207 |
|  | 7.159 | 231 |
|  | 7.207 | 239 |
|    Escape from | 7.085 | 213 |
|  | 7.263 | 251 |
|    Freedom from | 6.106 | 169–70 |
|  | 6.108 | 170 |
|    Of the law | 6.036 | 156 |
|  | 7.019 | 206 |
|  | 7.084 | 213 |
|  | 7.137 | 228 |
|  | 7.206 | 239 |
|  | 7.262 | 251 |
| CURSING | 4.099–.100 | 63 |
|  | 7.223 | 243 |
| CUSTOMS, PAYMENT OF | 5.258 | 143 |
| CYNICS, ERRORS OF | 5.235 | 137–38 |
| CYPRIAN, CITED | 5.161 | 120 |

## D

|  | Reference Numbers | Page Numbers |
|---|---|---|
| DAILY RESPONSE TO GOD'S GIFTS | 11.4 | 312 |
| DAMNATION, ETERNAL | 3.25 | 25 |
| DANCING | 7.249 | 248 |
| DAVID, REFERENCE TO | 3.04 | 12 |
|  | 3.05 | 12 |
|  | 3.06 | 13 |
|  | 5.029 | 84 |
|  | 5.030 | 85 |
|  | 5.032 | 85–86 |
|  | 5.034 | 86 |
|  | 5.064 | 93–94 |
| DAY OF JUDGMENT | 5.075 | 95–96 |

# INDEX

| | Reference Numbers | Page Numbers |
|---|---|---|
| DAY, LORD'S | 5.224–.225 | 135 |
| DEACONS | 5.148 | 116–17 |
| **DEAD:** | | |
|   Burial of | 5.235–.236 | 137–38 |
|   Prayers for | 6.115 | 172 |
|   Resurrection of the | 7.197 | 237 |
| *DE AGONE CHRIST*, AUGUSTINE | 5.029 | 84 |
| **DEATH:** | | |
|   Unto all men | 7.194 | 237 |
|   Benefits at | 7.037 | 208 |
| | 7.196 | 237 |
|   Of Christ | 3.08–.09 | 13–14 |
| | 4.039–.040 | 42 |
| | 6.046 | 157–58 |
| | 6.070–.071 | 163 |
| | 6.146 | 180 |
| | 6.161 | 182 |
| | 7.027 | 207 |
| | 7.096 | 214 |
| | 7.156 | 230 |
| | 7.159 | 231 |
| | 7.162 | 231 |
| | 7.278 | 254 |
| | 9.52 | 296 |
|     Definition of | 5.038 | 87 |
| | 9.11 | 288 |
|     Dominion of | 3.03 | 11 |
|     Nature of life after | 3.17 | 19 |
|     Our death, meaning of | 4.042 | 43 |
|     Of old self | 4.088–.089 | 59 |
|     Resurrection from | 6.178–.179 | 186 |
| | 7.197 | 237 |
|     Righteous at | 7.037 | 208 |
| | 7.195 | 237 |
|     In sin | 6.032–.033 | 155 |
| | 6.061 | 161 |
|     State of man after | 5.237–.239 | 138 |
| | 6.177–.179 | 186 |
| | 7.037 | 208 |
| | 7.196 | 237 |
|     Sting of | 6.108 | 170 |
| | 7.195 | 237 |
|     Vanquished by Christ | 7.162 | 231 |

|  | Reference Numbers | Page Numbers |
|---|---|---|
| **DEATH** (*Continued*) | | |
| Victory over | 10.5 | 303 |
| Wages of sin | 6.036 | 156 |
| | 7.012 | 205 |
| | 7.019 | 206 |
| | 7.130 | 227 |
| | 7.138 | 228 |
| | 7.194–.195 | 237 |
| | 7.203 | 238 |
| **DEBTS:** | | |
| Forgiveness of | 4.126 | 72 |
| Paying of | 7.251 | 248 |
| To God | 4.013 | 34 |
| DECALOGUE (See also Ten Commandments) | 5.081 | 97 |
| *DE CIVITATE DEI*, AUGUSTINE | 5.009 | 78 |
| DECLARATIONS, AS CONFESSIONS | 9.02 | 287 |
| **DECREES:** | | |
| Of councils | 5.012–.013 | 79 |
| | 6.174 | 185 |
| Of God (See also Eternal Decrees of God) | 3.07 | 13 |
| | 7.007–.008 | 205 |
| | 7.122–.124 | 226 |
| Of Synods | 6.174 | 185 |
| *DE DONO PERSEVERANTIAE*, AUGUSTINE | 5.058 | 92 |
| DELIVERANCE | 4.012–.025 | 34–37 |
| DELIVERANCE FROM THIS WORD | 8.14 | 283 |
| DENOMINATIONS, EXCLUSIVE | 9.34 | 292 |
| DESCENT OF CHRIST INTO HELL | 4.044 | 43 |
| DESERTION | 7.249 | 248 |
| *DE SIMPLICITATE CLERICORUM*, CYPRIAN | 5.161 | 120 |
| DESPAIR | 7.215 | 241 |
| *DE VERA RELIGIONE*, AUGUSTINE | 5.022 | 82 |
| | 5.026 | 83–84 |
| DEVIL, THE (See also Satan; Hell) | 5.033 | 86 |
| DILIGENCE | 7.251 | 248 |
| DIPPING, IN BAPTISM | 6.156 | 182 |
| DIRECTION, OF THE CHURCH | 9.31–.33 | 257–58 |
| DISCIPLINES, REQUIREMENTS OF | 9.05 | 287 |
| **DISCIPLINE:** | | |
| Christian | 4.085 | 58 |
| Ecclesiastical | 3.18 | 19 |
| Necessity of | 5.165 | 121 |
| And synods | 5.167 | 122 |

# INDEX

| | Reference Numbers | Page Numbers |
|---|---|---|
| DISCONTENT | 7.081 | 212 |
| | 7.215 | 241 |
| | 7.258 | 250 |
| DISCRIMINATION, RACIAL OR ETHNIC | 9.44 | 294 |
| DISHONOR TO CHRIST | 6.145 | 180 |
| DISOBEDIENCE, the first sin | 7.015 | 206 |
| | 7.131 | 227 |
| DISORDER IN THE CHURCH | 5.132 | 111 |
| DISPERSED CHURCH | 9.35 | 292 |
| | 9.37 | 292 |
| DISSENSIONS IN THE CHURCH | 5.133 | 111–12 |
| DISTRESSED, COMFORT OF | 7.245 | 247 |
| DIVERSITY OF RITES | 5.241 | 139 |
| DIVINE JUSTICE | 5.108 | 104 |
| DIVISION | 10.3 | 301 |
| DIVISION, SECTARIAN | 9.34 | 292 |
| DIVORCE | 6.132 | 176–77 |
| | 6.137–.139 | 178–79 |
| DOCTRINAL DEFINITIONS, AS CONFESSIONS | 9.02 | 287 |
| DOCTRINE: | | |
|     Confirmation of | 5.003 | 77 |
|     Evangelical | 5.089 | 99 |
|     Judge of | 3.18 | 19 |
|     In preaching | 7.269 | 252 |
|     Reformation in | 9.03 | 287 |
| DONATISTS, ERRORS OF | 5.126 | 109 |
| | 5.166 | 121 |
| DOUBTERS AND THE LORD'S SUPPER | 7.282 | 255 |
| DRUNKARD, AND SALVATION | 4.087 | 59 |
| DUTIES OF MAN | 6.004 | 150 |
| | 6.006 | 150–51 |
| | 6.112 | 171 |
| | 7.039 | 208 |
| | 7.111 | 225 |
| | 7.115 | 225 |
| | 7.201 | 238 |

## E

| | | |
|---|---|---|
| EARTH, GOD'S WILL IN | 7.103 | 215 |
| | 7.302 | 258 |
| EASTERN CHURCHES, MUSIC IN | 5.221 | 134 |
| EATING, SACRAMENTAL | 5.203 | 130 |
| EBION | 5.091 | 100 |
| EBIONITES, ERRORS OF | 5.064 | 93–94 |
| | 5.091 | 100 |

| | Reference Numbers | Page Numbers |
|---|---|---|
| ECCLESIASTICAL: | | |
| Discipline | 3.18 | 19 |
| Judgments | 5.165 | 121 |
| Matters | 6.176 | 186 |
| Persons, and civil magistrates | 6.130 | 175 |
| Power | 5.159 | 119 |
| | 9.40 | 293 |
| ECOLOGY | 11.3 | 311 |
| ECONOMIC AFFAIRS AND LIFE | 9.46 | 294 |
| | 9.53 | 296 |
| ECUMENICAL COUNCILS (See also General Councils) | 5.167 | 122 |
| ECUMENICITY: | | |
| And baptism | 6.160 | 182 |
| | 7.095 | 214 |
| | 7.276 | 253 |
| And church unity | 6.054 | 159–60 |
| | 6.186 | 188 |
| Communion of saints and | 6.146–.148 | 180–81 |
| Creedal basis of | 6.140 | 179 |
| Error in | 6.175 | 185 |
| Invisible Church | 7.174 | 233 |
| Kingship of Christ | 7.155 | 230 |
| Sacraments | 7.286 | 256 |
| Visible Church | 7.172 | 233 |
| EDUCATION (See also Instruction; Teaching) | 4.103 | 64 |
| | 9.44 | 294 |
| EFFECTUAL CALLING: | | |
| Assurance of | 6.099 | 168 |
| Benefits of | 6.068 | 163 |
| | 6.074 | 164 |
| | 6.075 | 164 |
| | 6.094 | 167 |
| | 7.032 | 207 |
| | 7.179 | 234 |
| Definition of | 7.031 | 207 |
| | 7.177 | 234 |
| Elect and | 6.019 | 153 |
| | 6.064 | 162 |
| | 7.178 | 234 |
| Source of | 6.065 | 162 |
| EFFICACY: | | |
| Of baptism | 6.159 | 182 |
| Of sacraments | 5.183 | 126 |
| *EGO BERENGARIUS*, PAPAL DECREE | 5.197 | 129 |
| ELDERS, OR PRESBYTERS, DEFINITION OF | 5.147 | 116 |

INDEX

|  | Reference Numbers | Page Numbers |
|---|---|---|
| ELECT, THE: | | |
| Assurance of | 6.098 | 168 |
| Calling of | 6.050 | 158 |
|  | 7.178 | 234 |
| Church and | 6.140 | 179 |
|  | 7.174 | 233 |
| Grace and | 6.016–.019 | 153 |
| Number of | 5.055–.056 | 91 |
|  | 6.017 | 153 |
| Perseverance of | 6.095–.096 | 167–68 |
| Sacrifice for | 6.162 | 182–83 |
| Sins of | 6.096 | 168 |
| Union with Christ | 7.175–.176 | 233 |
| ELECTION (See also Predestination): | | |
| Choice in | 6.018 | 153 |
|  | 7.020 | 206 |
|  | 7.123 | 226 |
| In Christ | 5.053 | 91 |
| Decree of | 6.016 | 153 |
| Determination of | 5.059 | 92 |
| Doctrine of | 3.08 | 13 |
|  | 5.052–.061 | 91–93 |
|  | 6.021 | 153 |
| Errors in doctrine of | 5.057 | 92 |
| Foreknowledge of | 6.015 | 152 |
| God and | 6.047 | 158 |
| Grace and love and | 6.018 | 153 |
|  | 7.020 | 206 |
|  | 7.123 | 226 |
| Hope of | 5.055 | 91 |
| Means of | 6.019 | 153 |
|  | 7.123 | 226 |
| Of ministers | 5.150 | 117 |
| Purpose of | 5.054 | 91 |
| And salvation | 5.058 | 92 |
| ELEGKOS: GREEK, CONVICTION | 5.113 | 106 |
| ELEMENTS, IN LORD'S SUPPER | 3.21 | 21 |
|  | 4.079 | 55 |
|  | 6.163–.165 | 183 |
|  | 7.096 | 214 |
|  | 7.279 | 254 |
| EMINENCE IN PROFESSION | 7.261 | 251 |
| EMPLOYMENT | 9.44 | 294 |
| Rest from | 6.119 | 173 |
|  | 7.061 | 211 |
|  | 7.227 | 244 |
|  | 7.229 | 244 |

|  | Reference Numbers | Page Numbers |
|---|---|---|
| *ENCHIRIDION*, AUGUSTINE | 5.041 | 87–88 |
| ENCRATITES, ERRORS OF | 5.232 | 136 |
| END OF THE WORLD | 6.161 | 182 |
| ENEMIES: | | |
|    Forgiveness of | 9.45 | 294 |
|    Prayer for | 7.293 | 257 |
| *ENNARATIONES IN PSALMOS*, AUGUSTINE | 5.031 | 85 |
| ENVY | 7.081 | 212 |
| | 7.238 | 246 |
| | 7.242 | 247 |
| | 7.252 | 248–49 |
| | 7.258 | 250 |
| EPHESUS | 3.18 | 19 |
|    Creed of | 5.078 | 97 |
| EPICUREANS, ERRORS OF | 5.030 | 85 |
| EPIPHANIUS, CITED | 5.022 | 82 |
| EQUALITY OF THE MINISTRY | 5.160 | 120 |
| EQUALS | 7.241–.242 | 246–47 |
| EQUIPMENT OF THE CHURCH | 9.48–.52 | 295–96 |
| ERRORS, REJECTION OF | 5.003 | 77 |
| ESAU | 3.18 | 19 |
| ETERNAL DECREE OF GOD: | | |
|    Assurance and | 6.097–.100 | 168–69 |
|    Baptism and | 6.159 | 182 |
|    Effectual calling and | 6.064–.067 | 162 |
|    Foreknowledge and | 6.015 | 152 |
|    Immutability of | 6.095 | 167 |
|    Justification and | 6.071 | 163 |
|    Perseverance of saints and | 6.095 | 167 |
| ETERNAL LIFE | 4.042 | 43 |
| | 4.048–.059 | 44–48 |
| | 4.076 | 53–54 |
| | 9.11 | 288 |
| | 9.26 | 291 |
|    And good works | 5.117 | 107 |
| ETERNITY OF GOD | 6.011 | 151–52 |
| | 7.004 | 205 |
| | 7.117 | 225 |
| ETHELOTHRASKEIA: GREEK, SELF-DEVISED WORSHIP | 5.116 | 107 |
| ETHNIC OR RACIAL DISCRIMINATION | 9.44 | 294 |
| EUCHARIST (See Lord's Supper) | | |
| EUNOMIUS, ERRORS OF | 5.065 | 94 |

# INDEX

| | Reference Numbers | Page Numbers |
|---|---|---|
| EUSTATHIUS, ERRORS OF | 5.232 | 136 |
| EUTYCHES, ERRORS OF | 3.06 | 13 |
| | 5.068 | 94 |
| **EVANGELICAL:** | | |
| Congregations and Christians in Germany | 8.01 | 281 |
| Doctrine | 5.089 | 99 |
| Promises | 5.086 | 98–99 |
| Truths | 8.09–.27 | 283–84 |
| **EVANGELISM:** | | |
| Dispersed church and | 9.37 | 292 |
| And fruits of faith | 4.086 | 58 |
| Of good works | 5.121 | 108 |
| **EVANGELISTS:** | | |
| Definition of | 5.147 | 116 |
| Four | 5.089 | 99 |
| EVE | 4.007 | 33 |
| EVIDENCE, FALSE | 7.255 | 249–50 |
| **EVIL:** | | |
| And creation of people | 4.006 | 32 |
| Deliverance from | 7.106 | 215 |
| | 7.305 | 259 |
| And good | 5.032 | 85–86 |
| EXALTATION OF CHRIST | 6.046 | 157–58 |
| | 7.028 | 207 |
| | 7.161–.166 | 231–32 |
| EXAMINATION OF COMMUNICANTS | 3.23 | 24 |
| EXAMPLE, POWER OF | 7.261 | 251 |
| EXCLUSION OF LORD'S SUPPER | 6.170 | 184 |
| | 7.283 | 255 |
| EXCLUDE FROM CHRISTIAN COMMUNITY | 4.085 | 58 |
| EXCOMMUNICATION | 4.085 | 58 |
| | 5.165 | 121 |
| | 6.172 | 185 |
| EXORCISTS | 5.148 | 116–17 |
| EXPERIENCE AGGRAVATES SIN | 7.261 | 251 |
| EXPIATION OF CHRIST FOR SINS | 5.076 | 96 |
| | 5.105 | 103–4 |
| | 7.262 | 251 |
| EXPLOITATION | 11.3 | 311 |
| Of nature | 11.3 | 311 |
| Of neighbor | 11.3 | 311 |
| EXTINCTION OF THE CHURCH | 5.138 | 113 |
| EXTORTION | 7.252 | 248–49 |
| EXTREME UNCTION | 5.171 | 122–23 |
| | 5.234 | 137 |

BOOK OF CONFESSIONS

|  | Reference Numbers | Page Numbers |
|---|---|---|
| **F** | | |
| FACTIONS, RIVAL IN THE CHURCH | 9.34 | 292 |
| FAITH: | | |
|   As apprehension | 5.113 | 106 |
|   Assured | 3.03 | 11 |
|   And Christ | 5.110 | 105 |
| | 7.085–.086 | 213 |
| | 7.263 | 251 |
|   Christian, basis of | 9.05 | 287 |
|   Compendium of | 5.141 | 114 |
|   Definition of | 5.112–.114 | 106 |
|   As gift of God | 5.113 | 106 |
| | 6.039 | 156 |
| | 6.068 | 163 |
| | 7.181 | 234 |
|   And good works | 5.115 | 106–7 |
| | 6.088 | 166 |
|   And grace | 6.039 | 156 |
| | 7.142 | 228–29 |
|   And the Holy Ghost | 3.12 | 15 |
|   Implicit | 6.109 | 171 |
|   Increase of | 5.113 | 106 |
| | 7.265 | 252 |
| | 7.272 | 253 |
|   Justification by | 5.109 | 104–5 |
| | 6.069 | 163 |
| | 7.033 | 208 |
| | 7.182–.183 | 234–35 |
|   And Lord's Supper | 5.200 | 129–30 |
|   And love | 5.114 | 106 |
|   Nature of | 5.111 | 105 |
|   Necessity of | 6.114 | 172 |
| | 6.116 | 172 |
| | 6.167 | 183–84 |
| | 7.090 | 213 |
| | 7.096–.098 | 214 |
| | 7.270 | 252 |
| | 7.280 | 254 |
| | 7.290 | 256 |
|   Origin of | 4.065 | 50 |
|   Orthodox and Catholic | 5.079 | 97 |
|   Righteousness by | 4.060–.062 | 48–49 |
|   Rule of | 5.010 | 79 |
| | 6.002 | 149–50 |

## INDEX

| | Reference Numbers | Page Numbers |
|---|---|---|
| **FAITH** (*Continued*) | | |
| Sacraments and | 7.091 | 213 |
| Saving | 6.068–.069 | 163 |
| | 6.078–.080 | 164–65 |
| | 6.099 | 168 |
| | 7.086 | 213 |
| | 7.089 | 213 |
| | 7.181–.182 | 234 |
| | 7.191 | 236 |
| Scripture and | 6.002 | 149–50 |
| Shared | 10.3 | 301–2 |
| As substance, hypostasis | 5.113 | 106 |
| True | 4.020–.021 | 36 |
| | 10.3 | 302 |
| **FALL OF ADAM AND EVE** | 4.007 | 33 |
| | 5.042 | 88 |
| **FALL OF MAN** | 4.007 | 33 |
| | 5.036 | 86–87 |
| | 7.131–.137 | 227–28 |
| Covenant of works and | 6.039 | 156 |
| Involvement in | 6.033 | 155 |
| | 7.016 | 206 |
| | 7.132 | 227 |
| Law of God and | 6.102 | 169 |
| Loss of will in | 6.061 | 161 |
| | 7.135 | 227–28 |
| Misery of | 7.019 | 206 |
| | 7.137 | 228 |
| Nature of | 6.031–.036 | 155–56 |
| | 7.013–.019 | 206 |
| | 7.131 | 227 |
| Permission of | 6.031 | 155 |
| Results of | 6.032 | 155 |
| | 7.017 | 206 |
| | 7.133 | 227 |
| **FALSE:** | | |
| Doctrine, and church unity | 8.01 | 281 |
| | 10.5 | 303 |
| Testimony | 4.112 | 67 |
| | 7.255 | 249–50 |
| Weights | 4.110 | 66–67 |
| **FALSE GODS REJECTED** | 11.1 | 311 |
| **FAMILY** | 7.228 | 244 |
| | 7.234 | 245 |
| | 7.239 | 246 |
| | 9.44 | 294 |

|  | Reference Numbers | Page Numbers |
|---|---|---|
| FAMILY (*Continued*) | | |
| Church as | 6.141 | 179 |
| Maintenance of | 9.46 | 294 |
| Of ministers | 5.168 | 122 |
| Universal, of man | 9.44 | 294 |
| FASTING | 5.227–.231 | 135–36 |
| FATHER: | | |
| Abba | 11.3 | 311 |
| Baptism in name of | 6.155 | 182 |
| In Godhead | 6.013 | 152 |
|  | 11.3 | 311 |
| And Mother | 7.064 | 211 |
|  | 7.234–.235 | 245 |
| FATHERHOOD OF GOD | 6.016 | 153 |
|  | 6.053 | 159 |
|  | 6.055–.056 | 160 |
|  | 6.185 | 188 |
|  | 6.187–.188 | 188–89 |
|  | 7.100 | 214 |
|  | 7.299 | 257–58 |
| FATHERS, GREEK AND LATIN | 5.011 | 79 |
| FEAR OF GOD | 7.214 | 240 |
| FELLOWSHIP: | | |
| Of believers (See Communion of Saints) | | |
| And the gathered church | 9.36 | 292 |
| FERVENCY IN PRAYER | 6.114 | 172 |
|  | 7.295 | 257 |
| FESTIVALS OF CHRIST AND THE SAINTS | 5.226 | 135 |
| FIDELITY OF THE CHURCH | 9.37 | 292 |
| FINANCES | 9.40 | 293 |
| FIRST PARENTS | 7.012 | 205 |
|  | 7.130 | 227 |
| FIRST TRANSGRESSION | 7.016 | 206 |
|  | 7.132 | 227 |
| FLATTERY | 7.254–.255 | 249–50 |
| FLESH: | | |
| And blood of Christ | 5.064 | 93–94 |
|  | 5.196–.197 | 128–29 |
|  | 5.199 | 129 |
|  | 5.201–.203 | 130 |
| And law of God | 5.084 | 98 |
| Resurrection of | 3.25 | 25 |
|  | 5.075 | 95–96 |
| And spirit | 3.13 | 16 |
|  | 6.076 | 164 |
| Temptations of | 7.305 | 259 |

# INDEX

|  | Reference Numbers | Page Numbers |
|---|---|---|
| FLOCK, CHURCH AS | 5.130 | 110 |
| FLORINUS, ERRORS OF | 5.040 | 87 |
| FOOD: | | |
|    Choice of, in fasting | 5.231 | 136 |
|    Spiritual | 5.199 | 129 |
| | 5.201 | 130 |
|    Temperate use of | 7.245–.246 | 247 |
| FORBEARANCE | 7.245 | 247 |
| FORCE, USE OF | 8.01 | 281 |
| FOREKNOWLEDGE OF GOD | 6.012 | 152 |
| | 6.015 | 152 |
| FOREORDINATION | 6.016–.020 | 153 |
| | 6.159 | 182 |
| | 6.191–.193 | 190–91 |
| FORGERY | 7.255 | 249–50 |
| FORGIVENESS | 7.105 | 215 |
| | 7.245 | 247 |
| | 7.304 | 259 |
|    Of debts | 4.126 | 72 |
|    Ease of | 5.012 | 79 |
|    Of enemies | 9.45 | 294 |
|    And the Holy Spirit | 9.21 | 290 |
|    Necessity of | 9.13 | 289 |
|    Of sinners | 11.2 | 311 |
|    Of sins | 2.3 | 7 |
| | 4.056 | 47 |
| | 4.070 | 51 |
| | 4.076 | 53–54 |
| | 5.095 | 101–02 |
| | 6.068–.069 | 163 |
| | 6.083 | 165 |
| | 7.033 | 208 |
| | 7.105 | 215 |
| | 7.180 | 234 |
| | 7.182 | 234 |
| | 7.304 | 259 |
| | 8.14 | 283 |
| FORNICATION | 7.249 | 248 |
| FORNICATORS, SALVATION OF | 4.087 | 59 |
| FORUM, MATRIMONIAL, CHURCH AS | 5.248 | 141 |
| *FRAGMENTA*, IRENAEUS | 5.230 | 136 |
| FRAUD | 7.252 | 248–49 |
| | 4.110 | 66 |
| FREEDOM | 10.3 | 302 |
| | 10.7 | 304 |

|  | Reference Numbers | Page Numbers |
|---|---|---|
| **FREEDOM** (*Continued*) | | |
| Of humankind | 5.043 | 88 |
| | 9.17 | 289 |
| | 9.23 | 290 |
| Work with others for | 11.4 | 312 |
| **FREE WILL** | 5.044 | 89 |
| | 6.059–.063 | 161–62 |
| | 6.095 | 167 |
| And good works | 3.13 | 16 |
| And the regenerate | 5.049 | 90 |
| **FRUGALITY** | 7.251 | 248 |
| **FULFILLMENT OF RECONCILIATION** | 9.53–.56 | 296–97 |
| **FUNERALS** | 5.235–.236 | 137–38 |

## G

|  | Reference Numbers | Page Numbers |
|---|---|---|
| **GALATIA, CHURCH IN** | 3.18 | 19 |
| | 5.137 | 113 |
| **GAMBLING** | 7.252 | 248–49 |
| **GANGRIAN SYNOD** | 5.232 | 136 |
| **GATHERED CHURCH** | 9.35–.36 | 292 |
| **GENERAL COUNCILS** | 3.20 | 20 |
| **GENEROSITY** | 10.3 | 301 |
| **GENTILES** | 5.020 | 81–82 |
| | 5.129 | 110 |
| **GENTLENESS** | 7.245 | 247 |
| **GERMAN CHRISTIANS** | 8.07 | 282 |
| | 8.09–.28. | 283–84 |
| **GERMAN CONFESSIONAL CHURCHES** | 8.06 | 282 |
| **GERMAN EVANGELICAL CHURCH** | 8.01 | 281 |
| | 8.03–.07 | 281–82 |
| | 8.09 | 283 |
| | 8.28 | 284 |
| **GERMAN NATION, UNITY OF** | 8.03 | 281 |
| **GHOST, HOLY** (See Holy Spirit) | | |
| **GIFTS:** | | |
| Of Christ to the church | 3.25 | 25 |
| Of God | 5.113 | 106 |
| | 7.261 | 251 |
| **GIVING** | 7.251 | 248 |
| **GLORIA PATRI** | 11.6 | 312 |
| **GLORY:** | | |
| Ascribed to God | 7.107 | 215 |
| | 7.306 | 260 |

## INDEX

| | Reference Numbers | Page Numbers |
|---|---|---|
| **GLORY** (*Continued*) | | |
| Communion in | 6.146 | 180 |
| | 7.038 | 208 |
| | 7.175 | 233 |
| | 7.192–.193 | 236–37 |
| | 7.196–.197 | 237 |
| | 7.200 | 238 |
| Of God | 6.005 | 150 |
| | 6.014–.015 | 152 |
| | 6.020 | 153 |
| | 6.022 | 153–54 |
| | 6.024 | 154 |
| | 6.031 | 155 |
| | 6.088 | 166 |
| | 6.093 | 167 |
| | 6.127 | 174 |
| | 6.180–.182 | 186–87 |
| | 7.001 | 205 |
| | 7.007 | 205 |
| | 7.046–.047 | 209 |
| | 7.066 | 211 |
| | 7.101 | 214 |
| | 7.111 | 225 |
| | 7.114 | 225 |
| | 7.122–.123 | 226 |
| | 7.128 | 227 |
| | 7.166 | 232 |
| | 7.222 | 243 |
| | 7.243 | 247 |
| | 7.269 | 252 |
| | 7.294 | 257 |
| | 7.300 | 258 |
| Hope of | 6.097 | 168 |
| Kingdom of | 7.102 | 215 |
| State of, and free will | 6.063 | 162 |
| **GOD:** | | |
| Abba, Father | 11.3 | 311 |
| Adoration of | 9.50 | 295–96 |
| Alienation from | 9.47 | 294–95 |
| All-sufficiency of | 6.012 | 152 |
| Ascription to | 7.107 | 215 |
| | 7.306 | 260 |
| | 9.15 | 289 |
| As author of Sacraments | 5.172 | 123 |
| Belief concerning | 4.026 | 37–38 |

363

|  | Reference Numbers | Page Numbers |
|---|---|---|
| **GOD** (*Continued*) | | |
| Care of | 4.001 | 31 |
| And Christ | 9.07 | 287–88 |
| Civil magistrate and | 6.127 | 174 |
| Commandments ignored | 11.3 | 311 |
| Covenant of | 6.037–.042 | 156–57 |
| | 7.012 | 205 |
| | 7.020 | 206 |
| | 7.130 | 227 |
| | 7.140–.146 | 228–29 |
| Creator | 1.1 | 3 |
| | 2.1 | 7 |
| | 3.01 | 11 |
| | 5.032–.034 | 85–86 |
| | 6.022 | 153–54 |
| | 6.023 | 154 |
| | 7.009–.010 | 205 |
| | 7.124–.127 | 226–27 |
| | 9.15–.17 | 289 |
| | 11.3 | 311 |
| Debt to | 4.013 | 34 |
| Decree of | 3.07 | 13 |
| | 6.014–.021 | 152–53 |
| | 7.007–.008 | 205 |
| | 7.122–.124 | 226 |
| Definition of | 6.011 | 151–52 |
| | 7.004 | 205 |
| | 7.117 | 225 |
| Disobedience and Rebellion | 4.010 | 33 |
| And election | 5.052 | 91 |
| Existence of | 7.112 | 225 |
| Faithfulness of | 11.3 | 311 |
| As father | 4.026–.028 | 37–39 |
| Like a father | 11.3 | 311 |
| Free grace of | 8.26 | 284 |
| And good works | 5.120 | 108 |
| Grace of | 4.060 | 48–49 |
| Gratitude to | 4.002 | 31 |
| Hardness of | 5.041 | 87–88 |
| Heavenly majesty of | 4.121 | 70 |
| Holy One of Israel | 11.1 | 311 |
| Household of | 9.47 | 294–95 |
| Illumination by | 5.007 | 78 |

# INDEX

|  | Reference Numbers | Page Numbers |
|---|---|---|
| **GOD** (*Continued*) | | |
| Image of | 3.03 | 11 |
|  | 4.006 | 32 |
|  | 4.115 | 68 |
|  | 5.034 | 86 |
|  | 6.023 | 154 |
|  | 7.010 | 205 |
|  | 7.035 | 208 |
|  | 7.127 | 226–27 |
|  | 7.185 | 235 |
|  | 11.3 | 311 |
| Image of violated | 11.3 | 311 |
| Images and portrayals | 4.096–.098 | 62 |
|  | 5.020–.022 | 81–82 |
| Initiative of | 11.1 | 311 |
| Invocation of | 5.024 | 83 |
| Judgment of | 4.038 | 42 |
|  | 4.084 | 57 |
|  | 5.013 | 79 |
|  | 5.041 | 87–88 |
|  | 9.13 | 289 |
|  | 9.32 | 292 |
| Justice of | 4.009–.011 | 33–34 |
|  | 11.3 | 311 |
| And justification | 5.108 | 104 |
| Law of | 3.14 | 17 |
|  | 4.003 | 32 |
| Love of (See also Love of God) | 6.056 | 160 |
|  | 6.188 | 189 |
|  | 11.1 | 311 |
|  | 11.3 | 311 |
| Mercy of | 4.011 | 34 |
|  | 11.3 | 311 |
| And ministers | 5.142 | 115 |
| Misuse of name of | 4.099 | 63 |
| Monotheism | 11.1 | 311 |
| Like a mother | 11.3 | 312 |
| Mysteries of | 5.156 | 118 |
| Name of, swearing by | 5.028 | 84 |
| Nature of | 3.01 | 11 |
|  | 4.026 | 37–38 |
|  | 5.015 | 80 |
| Payment to | 4.012–.014 | 34 |
| Person of | 5.016–.018 | 80–81 |
| Prayer to | 7.098 | 214 |
|  | 7.288–.289 | 256 |

|  | Reference Numbers | Page Numbers |
|---|---|---|
| **GOD** (*Continued*) | | |
| Providence of | 3.01 | 11 |
| | 4.027 | 38–39 |
| | 5.029–.031 | 84–85 |
| | 6.024–.030 | 154–55 |
| | 7.011–.012 | 205 |
| | 7.128–.130 | 227 |
| | 9.03 | 287 |
| Reconciliation and | 4.012 | 34 |
| | 9.06–.07 | 287–88 |
| Reign of | 11.2 | 311 |
| Requirements of | 7.039 | 208 |
| | 7.085 | 213 |
| | 7.201 | 238 |
| | 7.263 | 251 |
| Revelation of | 6.001 | 149 |
| Ruler and guide | 3.01 | 11 |
| Salvation and | 6.056 | 160 |
| | 6.188 | 189 |
| Service to | 3.01 | 11 |
| | 5.114 | 106 |
| Sin against | 7.084 | 213 |
| | 7.262 | 251 |
| As son | 4.029–.052 | 39–46 |
| Son of | 6.043–.050 | 157–58 |
| Sovereignty of | 3.01 | 11 |
| | 11.3 | 311 |
| Temple of | 5.130 | 110 |
| Three persons of | 3.01 | 11 |
| | 11.1 | 311 |
| Triumph of | 9.55 | 297 |
| Trust in | 3.01 | 11 |
| | 11.1 | 311 |
| Unity of | 5.015 | 80 |
| | 6.011–.013 | 151–52 |
| | 7.005 | 205 |
| | 7.118 | 225 |
| Vows to | 6.125 | 174 |
| Will of | 5.042 | 88 |
| Work of reconciliation of | 9.08–.30 | 288–91 |
| Worship and serve alone | 11.2 | 311 |
| Worship of | 3.01 | 11 |
| | 4.096 | 62 |
| | 5.023 | 82–83 |
| | 5.135 | 112 |

# INDEX

|  | Reference Numbers | Page Numbers |
|---|---|---|
| GOD (*Continued*) | | |
| Wrath of | 4.010 | 33 |
| | 4.014 | 34 |
| GODHEAD | 4.025 | 37 |
| | 5.016–.018 | 80–81 |
| | 6.013 | 152 |
| | 6.044 | 157 |
| | 6.051 | 158 |
| | 6.183 | 187 |
| | 7.006 | 205 |
| | 7.119–.121 | 225–26 |
| | 11.1 | 311 |
| | 11.3 | 311 |
| GODS: | | |
| And the arts | 5.046 | 89 |
| Many | 5.015 | 80 |
| GOLDEN AGE | 5.075 | 95–96 |
| GOOD: | | |
| And evil | 5.032 | 85–86 |
| And evil days | 9.23 | 290 |
| Highest | 9.13 | 289 |
| Man and | 5.045 | 89 |
| Name, of neighbor | 4.112 | 67 |
| Things of life | 7.104 | 215 |
| | 7.303 | 258–59 |
| GOODNESS OF GOD | 6.011 | 151–52 |
| | 7.004 | 205 |
| | 7.117 | 225 |
| GOOD WORKS | 5.110 | 105 |
| | 6.052 | 159 |
| | 6.068–.069 | 163 |
| | 6.087–.093 | 166–67 |
| | 6.184 | 187 |
| | 7.033 | 208 |
| | 7.082 | 212 |
| | 7.180 | 234 |
| | 7.183 | 235 |
| | 7.188 | 235–36 |
| | 7.302 | 258 |
| Approval of | 5.120 | 108 |
| Cause of | 3.13 | 16 |
| Definition of | 4.091 | 59–60 |
| And eternal life | 5.117 | 107 |

|  | Reference Numbers | Page Numbers |
|---|---|---|
| **GOOD WORKS** (*Continued*) | | |
| And faith | 5.115 | 106–7 |
| Necessity of | 4.086 | 58 |
| Purpose of | 5.117 | 107 |
| Reward of | 4.063 | 49 |
| | 5.122 | 108 |
| And righteousness | 4.062 | 49 |
| Salvation and | 5.119 | 107–8 |
| Value of | 5.118 | 107 |
| **GOSPEL:** | | |
| Christ in | 7.081 | 212 |
| | 7.086 | 213 |
| | 7.182 | 234 |
| Covenant of grace under | 6.042 | 157 |
| Definition of | 5.089 | 99 |
| Disobedience to | 7.155 | 230 |
| As foundation of German Evangelical Church | 8.05 | 282 |
| Great Commission of | 6.160 | 182 |
| | 7.163 | 232 |
| Grounds for divorce in | 6.132 | 176–77 |
| | 6.133 | 177 |
| Heart of | 9.06 | 287 |
| And law | 5.086 | 98–99 |
| Love of God in | 6.056 | 160 |
| | 6.188 | 189 |
| Minister of | 6.155 | 182 |
| | 7.286 | 256 |
| Ministry of | 7.173 | 233 |
| Moral law and | 6.105 | 169 |
| And the papists | 5.092 | 100 |
| Preaching of | 4.065 | 50 |
| Proclamation of | 9.21 | 290 |
| And repentance | 5.093 | 100 |
| Reconciling power of the | 10.5 | 303 |
| Revelation in | 4.019 | 35–36 |
| Sacraments in | 6.152 | 181 |
| And slander | 4.112 | 67 |
| Worship and | 6.117 | 172 |
| **GOVERNMENT, CHURCH** | 5.003 | 77 |
| | 5.132 | 111 |
| | 6.129 | 175 |
| | 6.169–.176 | 184–86 |
| | 7.155 | 230 |
| | 9.40 | 293 |

# INDEX

|  | Reference Numbers | Page Numbers |
|---|---|---|
| **GOVERNMENT, CIVIL:** | | |
| Arming of | 4.105 | 65 |
| Cooperation with | 9.25 | 290–91 |
| And oaths | 4.101 | 63 |
| And theft | 4.110 | 66–67 |
| **GRACE:** | | |
| Assurance of | 6.097 | 168 |
|  | 7.190–.191 | 236 |
| Of Christ | 5.107 | 104 |
|  | 9.08–.14 | 288–89 |
| Communion in | 7.179 | 234 |
| And election | 5.052 | 91 |
| Of faith | 6.078 | 164 |
|  | 7.086 | 213 |
|  | 7.182 | 234 |
| Free, of God | 6.018 | 153 |
|  | 6.062 | 161–62 |
|  | 6.065 | 162 |
|  | 6.068 | 163 |
|  | 6.074 | 164 |
|  | 6.083 | 165 |
|  | 7.033 | 208 |
|  | 7.034 | 208 |
|  | 7.087 | 213 |
|  | 7.180–.181 | 234 |
|  | 7.184 | 235 |
|  | 7.186 | 235 |
|  | 8.26 | 284 |
| God's covenant of | 6.039 | 156 |
|  | 7.020 | 206 |
|  | 7.140–.146 | 228–29 |
|  | 7.273 | 253 |
|  | 7.277 | 253–54 |
| Growth in | 6.077 | 164 |
| Means of | 6.078 | 164 |
|  | 7.088 | 213 |
|  | 7.264 | 251–52 |
| And sacraments | 6.149–.151 | 181 |
|  | 6.158 | 182 |
|  | 7.273 | 253 |
|  | 7.277 | 253–54 |
| Sanctification and | 6.077 | 164 |
|  | 7.035 | 208 |
|  | 7.185 | 235 |
| And sin | 7.261 | 251 |

|  | Reference Numbers | Page Numbers |
|---|---|---|
| **GRACE** (*Continued*) | | |
| State of | 6.094 | 167 |
| Withheld | 6.029 | 155 |
| **GRACES, SAVING** | 6.069 | 163 |
|  | 6.075 | 164 |
|  | 6.078 | 164 |
|  | 7.086–.087 | 213 |
|  | 7.182–.183 | 234–35 |
|  | 7.185 | 235 |
|  | 7.187 | 235 |
| **GRACIOUSNESS OF GOD** | 6.011 | 151–52 |
|  | 6.055–.056 | 160 |
|  | 6.187–.188 | 188–89 |
|  | 7.117 | 225 |
| **GRATITUDE:** | | |
| Fruits of | 4.064 | 49–50 |
| To God | 4.086–.115 | 58–68 |
|  | 4.116 | 68–69 |
|  | 11.4 | 312 |
| **GREAT COMMISSION** | 6.058 | 161 |
|  | 6.190 | 189 |
|  | 10.4 | 268 |
| **GREEKS** | 9.41 | 293 |
| **GREEK FATHERS AND THE SCRIPTURE** | 5.011 | 79 |
| **GREGORIAN CHANT** | 5.221 | 134 |
| **GUILT** | 6.033 | 155 |
|  | 6.074 | 164 |
|  | 6.108 | 170 |
|  | 7.018 | 206 |
|  | 7.135 | 227–28 |
|  | 7.304 | 259 |

# H

|  | | |
|---|---|---|
| **HANDS, LAYING ON OF** | 5.151 | 117 |
| **HATRED** | 10.5 | 303 |
| Of God | 7.215 | 241 |
| Of Man | 7.246 | 247 |
| **HEALING, LABOR OF** | 9.31 | 257 |
| **HEARERS OF THE GOSPEL** | 6.057 | 160 |
|  | 6.189 | 189 |

# INDEX

| | Reference Numbers | Page Numbers |
|---|---|---|
| HEARING: | | |
|     The Word | 6.057 | 160 |
| | 6.189 | 189 |
| | 7.090 | 213 |
| | 7.171 | 233 |
| | 7.218 | 242 |
| | 7.270 | 252 |
| | 11.4 | 312 |
|     Peoples long silenced | 11.4 | 312 |
| HEAVEN | 6.047 | 158 |
| | 6.177 | 186 |
| | 6.181 | 186–87 |
| | 7.103 | 215 |
| | 7.163 | 232 |
| | 7.200 | 238 |
| | 7.302 | 258 |
| HEAVEN, KINGDOM OF (See Kingdom of Heaven) | | |
| HEAVENLY MAJESTY OF GOD | 4.121–.122 | 70–71 |
| HEBREW PEOPLE, RELIGION OF | 9.41 | 293 |
| HEIDELBERG CATECHISM | 9.04 | 287 |
|     Prologue | | 28–29 |
|     Text | 4.001–.129 | 31–73 |
| HELL | 4.044 | 43 |
| | 6.177 | 186 |
| | 6.181 | 186–87 |
| | 7.019 | 206 |
| | 7.139 | 228 |
| | 7.196 | 237 |
| | 7.199 | 237–38 |
| HELLENISM | 9.41 | 293 |
| HERESY | 3.06 | 13 |
| | 3.20 | 20–21 |
| | 5.008 | 78 |
| | 5.019 | 81 |
| | 5.030 | 85 |
| | 5.068 | 94 |
| | 6.111 | 171 |
| | 7.215 | 241 |
| HERETICS | 5.255 | 142 |
| | 6.123 | 173 |
| HERMITS | 5.149 | 117 |
| HISTORIAE ECCLESIASTICAE, SOCRATES | 5.219 | 133–34 |
| | 5.230 | 136 |
| | 5.241 | 139 |

BOOK OF CONFESSIONS

|  | Reference Numbers | Page Numbers |
|---|---|---|
| HISTORY: | | |
|    Of the gospel | 5.089 | 99 |
|    Meaning and direction of | 9.19 | 290 |
| HOLINESS, OF GOD | 6.011–.012 | 151–52 |
| | 7.004 | 205 |
| | 7.117 | 225 |
| HOLY COMMUNION (See Lord's Supper) | | |
| HOLY GHOST (See also Holy Spirit) | 3.03 | 11 |
| | 3.12 | 15 |
| | 3.21 | 21–22 |
| | 6.155 | 182 |
| HOLY ONE OF ISRAEL | 11.1 | 311 |
| HOLY SCRIPTURES (See Scriptures) | | |
| HOLY SPIRIT | 11.4 | 312 |
|    Abiding in | 6.095 | 167 |
| | 7.189 | 236 |
|    As agent | 6.064–.066 | 162 |
| | 6.071 | 163 |
| | 6.074–.075 | 164 |
| | 6.098 | 168 |
| | 7.031 | 207 |
| | 7.177 | 234 |
| | 7.184–.185 | 235 |
| | 7.190 | 236 |
| | 7.275 | 253 |
|    Baptism and | 11.4 | 312 |
|    Calls men and women | 11.4 | 312 |
|    Christ and | 6.045 | 157 |
| | 6.047 | 158 |
| | 7.169 | 233 |
|    And the church | 11.4 | 312 |
|    Creation of | 1.3 | 3 |
| | 5.016 | 80 |
|    Definition of | 4.053 | 46 |
| | 6.051–.054 | 158–60 |
| | 6.183–.186 | 187–88 |
|    Dependence on | 9.49 | 295 |
|    Efficacy of | 6.041 | 156 |
| | 6.142 | 179 |
| | 6.159 | 182 |
| | 7.265 | 252 |
| | 7.271 | 253 |
|    Empowered by | 11.4 | 312 |
|    Eternal life of | 4.001 | 31 |
| | 6.013 | 152 |
| | 7.120 | 226 |

# INDEX

|  | Reference Numbers | Page Numbers |
|---|---|---|
| **HOLY SPIRIT** (*Continued*) | | |
| And faith | 4.065 | 50 |
|  | 6.039 | 156 |
|  | 6.050 | 158 |
|  | 6.078 | 164 |
|  | 7.030–.031 | 207 |
|  | 7.169 | 233 |
|  | 7.182 | 234 |
| And forgiveness | 9.21 | 290 |
| Freedom of | 11.4 | 312 |
| Giver and renewer of life | 11.4 | 312 |
| And Godhead | 1.3 | 3 |
|  | 2.3 | 7 |
| And good works | 6.062 | 161–62 |
|  | 6.089 | 166 |
| Illumination of | 6.006 | 150–51 |
|  | 7.265 | 252 |
| Justification by | 5.091 | 100 |
|  | 7.182 | 234 |
|  | 11.4 | 312 |
| And the Lord's Supper | 5.196 | 128–29 |
|  | 11.4 | 312 |
| New life in | 11.4 | 312 |
| And obedience | 6.050 | 158 |
|  | 6.107 | 170 |
|  | 7.186 | 235 |
| And prayer | 6.114 | 172 |
|  | 7.288 | 256 |
| And prophesy | 1.3 | 3 |
| Sacraments and | 11.4 | 312 |
| Sin against | 5.102 | 103 |
|  | 6.100 | 168–69 |
|  | 7.215 | 241 |
|  | 7.261 | 251 |
| As supreme judge | 6.010 | 151 |
| Temple of | 4.109 | 66 |
| Testimony of | 6.005 | 150 |
|  | 6.098 | 168 |
|  | 7.114 | 225 |
|  | 7.190–.191 | 236 |
| And trinity | 6.013 | 152 |
|  | 7.006 | 205 |
|  | 7.119 | 225–26 |
| Trust in | 11.4 | 312 |

|  | Reference Numbers | Page Numbers |
|---|---|---|
| HOLY SPIRIT (*Continued*) | | |
|     Work of | 6.064 | 162 |
| | 7.186 | 235 |
| | 11.4 | 312 |
|     Worshipped | 6.113 | 172 |
| HOLY TRINITY (See also Trinity): | | |
|     Baptism and | 6.155 | 182 |
|     Creation by | 6.022–.023 | 153–54 |
|     Named | 6.013 | 152 |
|     Persons of | 6.013 | 152 |
| | 6.044 | 157 |
| | 6.051 | 158 |
| | 6.071 | 163 |
| | 6.113 | 172 |
| | 6.183 | 187 |
| | 7.006 | 205 |
| | 7.119–.121 | 225–26 |
| | 10.1 | 301 |
|     Worship of | 6.113 | 172 |
| HOPE: | | |
|     And election | 5.055 | 91 |
|     Of glory | 6.097 | 168 |
| | 6.116 | 172 |
|     Present | 9.21 | 290 |
|     Shared | 10.3 | 302 |
| HOPES, FALSE | 6.097 | 168 |
| HOURS, CANONICAL | 5.222 | 134 |
| HOUSE OF GOD | 6.141 | 179 |
| HOUSEHOLD: | | |
|     Of faith | 3.23 | 24 |
|     Of God | 9.47 | 294–95 |
| HOUSING | 9.44 | 294 |
| HUMAN NATURE, CORRUPTION OF | 4.007 | 33 |
| HUMANITY, DOCTRINE OF | 11.3 | 311 |
| HUMANITY, NEW | 9.19 | 290 |
| | 10.3 | 302 |
| HUMILIATION OF CHRIST | 6.044 | 157 |
| | 6.046 | 157–58 |
| | 7.027 | 207 |
| | 7.147 | 229 |
| | 7.156–.160 | 230–31 |

INDEX

| | Reference Numbers | Page Numbers |
|---|---|---|
| HUMILITY, IN PRAYER | 6.114 | 172 |
| | 7.214 | 240 |
| | 7.295 | 257 |
| | 7.302 | 258 |
| HUSBAND, OF THE CHURCH | 6.140 | 179 |
| | 7.176 | 233 |
| HYMNS, AS CONFESSIONS | 9.02 | 287 |
| HYPERETAS: GREEK, ROWERS, MINISTERS AS | 5.155 | 118 |
| HYPOCRISY | 7.223 | 243 |
| HYPOCRITES, AND THE LORD'S SUPPER | 4.081 | 56–57 |
| HYPOSTASES, DISTINCT | 5.017 | 81 |
| HYPOTASIS: GREEK, SUBSTANCE, SUBSISTENCE, FAITH AS | 5.113 | 106 |

## I

| | | |
|---|---|---|
| IDLENESS | 7.061 | 211 |
| IDOLATERS, SALVATION OF | 4.087 | 59 |
| IDOLATRY | 7.045–.051 | 209 |
| | 7.213 | 240 |
| | 7.215 | 241 |
| | 7.217–.219 | 241–42 |
| | 7.300 | 258 |
|     Definition and discussion of | 4.094–.095 | 61–62 |
|     Of sacrifice in the mass | 4.080 | 55–56 |
|     Unmasking of | 11.4 | 312 |
| IDOLS, OF GOD | 5.020–.022 | 81–82 |
| IGNORANCE | 7.300 | 258 |
| IGNORANT AND SCANDALOUS, THE | 6.168 | 184 |
| IMAGE OF GOD | 3.03 | 11 |
| | 4.006 | 32 |
| | 4.115 | 68 |
| | 5.034 | 86 |
| | 6.023 | 154 |
| | 7.010 | 205 |
| | 7.035 | 208 |
| | 7.127 | 226–27 |
| | 7.185 | 235 |
| | 11.3 | 311 |
|     Makes everyone equally in | 11.3 | 311 |
| IMAGES: | | |
|     Biblical | 9.54 | 296–97 |
|     Of God | 4.097–.098 | 62–63 |
| | 5.020–.022 | 81–82 |

BOOK OF CONFESSIONS

| | Reference Numbers | Page Numbers |
|---|---|---|
| IMAGES (*Continued*) | | |
| Worship of | 7.049 | 209 |
| | 7.051 | 209 |
| | 7.217 | 241–42 |
| | 7.219 | 242 |
| IMMORTALITY OF THE SOUL | 3.17 | 19 |
| | 5.034–.035 | 86 |
| IMMUTABILITY OF GOD | 6.011 | 151–52 |
| | 7.004 | 205 |
| | 7.117 | 225 |
| IMPARTATION OF PROPERTIES | 5.072 | 95 |
| IMPATIENCE, AT GOD | 7.215 | 241 |
| IMPENITENT, THE | 6.057 | 160 |
| | 6.189 | 189 |
| And the Lord's Supper | 4.081 | 56–57 |
| Salvation of | 4.087 | 59 |
| IMPERFECTIONS OF BELIEVERS | 6.076 | 164 |
| IMPUTATION: | | |
| Of Adam's guilt | 6.033 | 155 |
| | 7.018 | 206 |
| | 7.135–.136 | 227–28 |
| Of righteousness | 5.108 | 104 |
| | 6.068 | 163 |
| | 7.033 | 208 |
| | 7.082 | 212 |
| | 7.181 | 234 |
| | 7.187 | 235 |
| INABILITY | 7.135 | 227–28 |
| | 7.205 | 238–39 |
| | 7.259 | 250 |
| | 7.302 | 258 |
| | 7.305 | 259 |
| INCARNATE WORD OF GOD | 9.27 | 291 |
| INCARNATION | 5.078 | 97 |
| | 6.044 | 157 |
| | 7.021–.022 | 206 |
| | 7.147 | 229 |
| | 7.149 | 230 |
| | 7.157 | 231 |
| INCEST | 7.249 | 248 |
| INCOMPREHENSIBILITY OF GOD | 6.011 | 151–52 |
| | 7.117 | 225 |

376

# INDEX

|  | Reference Numbers | Page Numbers |
|---|---|---|
| INDIFFERENT, DEFINITION OF THINGS | 5.242 | 139 |
| INDIVIDUAL LIFE | 9.53 | 296 |
| INDULGENCES, PAPAL | 5.104 | 103 |
| INFANTS: | | |
| Baptism of | 4.074 | 52–53 |
|  | 6.157 | 182 |
| Of believers | 6.157 | 182 |
| Dying in infancy | 6.066 | 162 |
|  | 6.193 | 191 |
| Elect | 6.142 | 179 |
|  | 6.193 | 191 |
| INFECTION, TREATMENT OF | 9.47 | 294–95 |
| INFERIORS | 7.237–.240 | 246 |
| INFIDELITY | 7.215 | 241 |
| INFIDELITY OF MAGISTRATE | 6.130 | 175 |
| INFIDELS, OATHS TO | 6.123 | 173 |
| INHERITANCE, EVERLASTING | 6.040 | 156 |
|  | 6.047 | 158 |
| INJUSTICE | 7.075 | 212 |
|  | 7.240 | 246 |
|  | 7.252 | 248–49 |
|  | 7.255 | 249–50 |
|  | 9.32 | 292 |
|  | 10.7 | 304 |
|  | 10.8 | 304 |
| INNOCENCY | 6.060 | 161 |
| INNOCENT | 7.245 | 247 |
| INSPIRATION OF SCRIPTURE | 6.002 | 149–50 |
| INSTITUTION: | | |
| Of baptism | 4.071 | 51–52 |
|  | 5.185 | 126 |
| Change in | 9.34 | 292 |
| Of Lord's Supper | 5.193 | 128 |
| Of Sacraments | 5.178 | 124–25 |
| INSTRUCTION (See also Education; Teaching): | | |
| Duty of | 7.239 | 246 |
| Gathered church and | 9.36 | 292 |
| And images | 5.020–.022 | 81–82 |
| Of youth | 5.233 | 137 |
| INSTRUMENTS OF MISSION | 9.40 | 293 |
| INTELLECT, POWERS OF | 5.046 | 89 |
| INTEMPERANCE | 7.246 | 247 |
|  | 7.249 | 248 |

377

BOOK OF CONFESSIONS

| | Reference Numbers | Page Numbers |
|---|---|---|
| INTERCESSION OF CHRIST | 6.046 | 157–58 |
| | 6.050 | 158 |
| | 6.095 | 167 |
| | 7.025 | 207 |
| | 7.148–.149 | 229–30 |
| | 7.154 | 230 |
| | 7.164–.165 | 232 |
| | 7.189 | 236 |
| INTERCESSION AND PETITIONS | 9.50 | 295–96 |
| INTEREST, EXCESSIVE | 4.110 | 66–67 |
| INTERPRETATION OF SCRIPTURES | 3.18 | 19 |
| | 5.010–.014 | 79–80 |
| INVISIBLE CHURCH | 5.138 | 113 |
| | 7.179 | 234 |
| | 7.192–.193 | 236–37 |
| | 7.196 | 237 |
| | 7.200 | 238 |
| INVOCATION: | | |
|    Of God alone | 5.024 | 83 |
|    Of saints | 5.025 | 83 |
| IRENAEUS, CITED | 5.040 | 87 |
| | 5.230 | 136 |
| IRREVERENCE | 7.055 | 210 |
| | 7.223 | 243 |
| ISAAC | 3.18 | 19 |
| ISAIAH | 3.14 | 17 |
| ISHMAEL | 3.18 | 19 |
| ISRAEL: | | |
|    And Christ | 9.19 | 290 |
|    Continuity with | 9.31 | 257 |
|    And the love of God | 9.18 | 289–90 |
|    Revelation to | 9.41 | 293 |
|    Worship in | 5.023 | 82–83 |
| ISRAELITES | 5.129 | 110 |

## J

| | | |
|---|---|---|
| JACOB | 3.18 | 19 |
| JACOBITES, ERRORS OF | 5.071 | 94 |
| JAMES, ST., CITED | 5.031 | 85 |
| JAMES AND PAUL | 5.111 | 105 |
| JEREMIAH, CITED | 5.013 | 79 |
| | 5.092 | 100 |

# INDEX

| | Reference Numbers | Page Numbers |
|---|---|---|
| JEROME, ST., CITED | 5.075 | 95–96 |
| | 5.162 | 120 |
| | 5.242 | 139 |
| JERUSALEM | 3.05 | 12 |
| | 3.10 | 14 |
| | 3.16 | 18 |
| | 3.18 | 19 |
| JERUSALEM, JOHN OF, ERRORS OF | 5.075 | 95–96 |
| JESTS | 7.223 | 243 |
| JESUS CHRIST (See Christ) | | |
| JESUS OF NAZARETH | 9.08 | 288 |
| JEW, JESUS AS A PALESTINIAN | 9.08 | 288 |
| JEWISH: | | |
|     Heresies | 5.075 | 95–96 |
|     Sabbath | 5.225 | 135 |
| JEWS | 9.41 | 293 |
|     And the church | 5.129 | 110 |
| | 7.301 | 258 |
|     Fasting of | 5.227 | 135 |
|     Heresies of | 5.019 | 81 |
|     Traditions of | 5.014 | 80 |
| JOHN THE BAPTIST | 5.077 | 96 |
| | 5.089 | 99 |
| | 9.51 | 296 |
| JOHN OF JERUSALEM, ERRORS OF | 5.075 | 95–96 |
| JORDAN RIVER | 5.185 | 126 |
| JOSEPH'S BROTHERS | 5.041 | 87–88 |
| | 5.044 | 89 |
| JOVIANS, ERRORS OF | 5.040 | 87 |
| JOY: | | |
|     In God | 7.214 | 240 |
|     Of heaven | 7.038 | 208 |
| | 7.200 | 238 |
|     In the Holy Spirit | 7.036 | 208 |
| | 7.193 | 236–37 |
|     Prayer for | 7.304 | 259 |
| JUDAISM | 5.240 | 138–39 |
| | 9.41 | 293 |
| JUDGE: | | |
|     Of doctrine | 3.18 | 19 |
|     Supreme | 6.010 | 151 |
| JUDGMENT: | | |
|     By Christ | 9.08 | 288 |
| | 9.11 | 288 |

BOOK OF CONFESSIONS

| | Reference Numbers | Page Numbers |
|---|---|---|
| JUDGMENT (*Continued*) | | |
| Of the church | 9.47 | 294–95 |
| By civil authorities and magistrates | 3.24 | 24 |
| | 5.254 | 142 |
| Day of | 5.075 | 95–96 |
| Ecclesiastical | 5.165 | 121 |
| Final | 7.038 | 208 |
| | 7.198–.200 | 237–38 |
| Of God | 4.038 | 42 |
| | 4.084 | 57 |
| | 5.013 | 79 |
| | 5.041 | 87–88 |
| | 9.13 | 289 |
| | 9.32 | 292 |
| Last | 3.11 | 15 |
| Private | 3.18 | 19 |
| | 6.109 | 171 |
| Rash or premature | 5.140 | 114 |
| Temporal | 6.096 | 168 |
| Of unbelievers | 5.204 | 130–31 |
| JUDICIAL LAWS OF OLD TESTAMENT | 6.104 | 169 |
| JURISDICTION: | | |
| Civil | 6.127 | 174 |
| Ecclesiastical | 6.129 | 175 |
| | 6.176 | 186 |
| JUSTICE | 10.7 | 304 |
| Civil | 6.128 | 174 |
| Divine | 5.108 | 104 |
| Of God | 4.009 | 33 |
| | 6.011 | 151–52 |
| | 6.047 | 158 |
| | 6.061 | 161 |
| | 7.004 | 205 |
| | 7.033 | 208 |
| | 7.148 | 229 |
| | 7.180 | 234 |
| | 7.187 | 235 |
| | 7.246 | 247 |
| In society | 9.17 | 289 |
| | 7.246 | 247 |
| | 7.251 | 248 |
| | 11.4 | 312 |
| JUSTIFICATION: | | |
| Adoption and | 6.074 | 164 |

# INDEX

| | Reference Numbers | Page Numbers |
|---|---|---|
| JUSTIFICATION (*Continued*) | | |
| Benefits of | 7.036–.037 | 208 |
| | 7.193 | 236–37 |
| | 7.196 | 237 |
| In Christ | 6.068 | 163 |
| | 6.083 | 165 |
| | 6.092 | 167 |
| | 7.033 | 208 |
| | 7.180–.181 | 234 |
| Definition and discussion of | 5.106 | 104 |
| | 6.068–.073 | 163 |
| | 7.033 | 208 |
| | 7.180 | 234 |
| Elect and | 6.019 | 153 |
| | 6.043 | 157 |
| | 6.059 | 161 |
| | 6.062 | 161–62 |
| By faith | 5.109 | 104–5 |
| | 7.182 | 234 |
| And grace | 6.068 | 163 |
| | 7.033 | 208 |
| | 7.180–.181 | 234 |
| | 7.187 | 235 |
| Need of | 8.15 | 283 |
| And sanctification | 6.075 | 164 |
| | 7.187 | 235 |

## K

| | Reference Numbers | Page Numbers |
|---|---|---|
| KERYGMA OF CHRIST (See also Gospel) | 6.055–.058 | 160–61 |
| | 6.187–.190 | 188–89 |
| KEYS: | | |
| Of the Kingdom | 4.082–.083 | 57 |
| | 5.096–.097 | 102 |
| | 5.159 | 119 |
| | 6.129 | 175 |
| | 6.170 | 184 |
| KILLING, LAW CONCERNING | 4.105–.107 | 65–66 |
| | 7.246 | 247 |
| KINDNESS | 7.245 | 247 |
| KING, CHRIST AS | 6.169 | 184 |
| | 7.026 | 207 |
| | 7.155 | 230 |

|  | Reference Numbers | Page Numbers |
|---|---|---|
| **KINGDOM:** | | |
| Of Christ | 6.058 | 161 |
|  | 6.141 | 179 |
|  | 6.190 | 189 |
|  | 7.102 | 215 |
|  | 7.301 | 258 |
| Of glory | 7.102 | 215 |
| Of God | 4.123 | 71 |
|  | 7.107 | 215 |
|  | 7.163 | 232 |
|  | 7.306 | 260 |
|  | 8.22 | 284 |
|  | 9.52 | 296 |
|  | 9.54 | 296–97 |
|  | 9.55 | 297 |
| Of grace | 7.102 | 215 |
| Of heaven | 4.084 | 57 |
|  | 5.096–.099 | 102 |
|  | 6.162 | 182–83 |
| Image of | 9.54 | 296–97 |
| **KIRK (See Church)** | | |
| **KNOWLEDGE:** | | |
| Of God | 6.001 | 149 |
|  | 6.112 | 171 |
|  | 7.112 | 225 |
| God's infinite | 6.102 | 169 |
|  | 7.117 | 225 |
| Improvement of | 6.112 | 171 |
| Necessary items of | 4.002 | 31 |
| Saving | 6.001 | 149 |
|  | 6.006–.007 | 150–51 |
|  | 7.046 | 209 |
|  | 7.103 | 215 |
|  | 7.214 | 240 |
|  | 7.300 | 258 |
|  | 7.302 | 258 |

## L

|  | | |
|---|---|---|
| LABOR | 7.245 | 247 |
|  | 7.248 | 248 |
| LACTANTIUS, CITED | 5.022 | 82 |
| LAMB, PASCHAL | 5.170 | 122 |
|  | 5.177 | 124 |
| LANDESKIRCHEN: GERMAN DISTRICT CHURCHES | 8.05 | 282 |
| LANDMARKS | 7.252 | 248–49 |

# INDEX

| | Reference Numbers | Page Numbers |
|---|---|---|
| LAND OF CANAAN | 5.087 | 99 |
| LANGUAGE | 10.3 | 302 |
|    Common, in worship | 5.217–.218 | 133 |
|    Of Scripture | 5.010 | 79 |
| | 6.008 | 151 |
| LARGER CATECHISM, THE WESTMINSTER: | | |
|    Prologue | | 146–48 |
|    Text | 7.111–.306 | 225–60 |
| LASCIVIOUSNESS | 7.249 | 248 |
| LAST DAY, THE | 5.235 | 137–38 |
| LAST JUDGMENT | 3.11 | 15 |
| | 6.180–.182 | 186–87 |
| LATIN FATHERS, AND SCRIPTURE | 5.011 | 79 |
| LAW: | | |
|    Of Christ | 10.3 | 302 |
|    Consummation of | 3.15 | 17–18 |
|    Of God (See Law of God) | | |
|    And gospel | 5.086 | 98–99 |
|    Holy | 3.14 | 17 |
|    Human | 10.9 | 305 |
|    Of Moses | 5.128 | 110 |
|    Of nature | 5.081 | 97 |
|    Obedience to | 3.15 | 17–18 |
|    Of patriarchs | 5.128 | 110 |
|    Perfection of | 3.15 | 17 |
|    Table of | 5.226 | 135 |
| LAW OF GOD, THE | 5.080–.085 | 97–98 |
|    Abrogation of | 5.085 | 98 |
|    Ceremonial | 6.103 | 169 |
| | 6.108 | 170 |
|    Christ and | 5.084 | 98 |
|    Completeness of | 5.082 | 97 |
|    Definition of | 4.092 | 60–61 |
|    And flesh | 5.084 | 98 |
|    Judicial | 6.104 | 169 |
|    Keeping of | 4.005 | 32 |
|    And misery | 4.003 | 32 |
|    Moral | 6.023 | 154 |
| | 6.036 | 156 |
| | 6.038 | 156 |
| | 6.046 | 157–58 |
| | 6.101–.107 | 169–70 |
| | 7.027 | 207 |
| | 7.039–.041 | 208 |
| | 7.127 | 226–27 |

## BOOK OF CONFESSIONS

| | Reference Numbers | Page Numbers |
|---|---|---|
| LAW OF GOD, THE (*Continued*) | | |
|   Moral (*Continued*) | 7.137 | 228 |
| | 7.201–.208 | 238–39 |
| | 7.260–.261 | 250–51 |
|     Purpose of | 5.083 | 97–98 |
|     Requirements of | 4.004 | 32 |
| | 4.009 | 33 |
|     Summary of | 4.004 | 32 |
|     And tradition | 5.014 | 80 |
|     And will of God | 5.080 | 97 |
| LAWFUL OATHS AND VOWS | 6.120–.126 | 173–74 |
| LAWFUL POWER | 6.111 | 171 |
| | 6.130 | 175 |
| LAWS OF THE CHURCH | 7.155 | 230 |
| LAWS OF THE STATE | 6.130 | 175 |
| | 7.234 | 245 |
| | 7.237 | 246 |
| LAWSUITS | 7.251 | 248 |
| LAYING ON OF HANDS | 5.151 | 117 |
| LEADERSHIP AND OVERSIGHT OF THE CHURCH | 9.39 | 293 |
| LEISURE | 9.44 | 294 |
| LENDING | 7.251 | 248 |
| LENT, FASTING IN | 5.230 | 136 |
| LETTER, AND SPIRIT | 5.090 | 99 |
| LIBERTY: | | |
|   Christian | 5.047 | 89–90 |
| | 6.108–.111 | 170–71 |
|   Of man | 3.15 | 17–18 |
| | 5.050 | 90 |
| LIFE: | | |
|   Benefits in this | 7.036 | 208 |
| | 7.193 | 236–37 |
|   Eternal | 1.3 | 3 |
| | 2.3 | 7 |
| | 3.25 | 25 |
| | 4.042 | 43 |
| | 4.058–.059 | 48 |
|   Gift of | 9.17 | 289 |
|   New, in Christ | 9.21–.26 | 290–91 |
|   Preservation of | 7.068–.069 | 211 |
| | 7.245–.246 | 247 |
|   Promise of long | 7.063 | 211 |
| | 7.066 | 211 |
| | 7.233 | 245 |
| | 7.243 | 247 |

# INDEX

| | Reference Numbers | Page Numbers |
|---|---|---|
| LIFE (*Continued*) | | |
|     Renewal of | 5.101 | 102–3 |
|     Repentance and | 7.085 | 213 |
| | 7.087 | 213 |
| | 7.186 | 235 |
| | 7.263 | 251 |
|     Rule of | 6.002 | 149–50 |
| LIFE EVERLASTING | 4.058–.059 | 48 |
| LIGHT OF NATURE | 6.001 | 149 |
| | 6.006 | 150–51 |
| | 6.067 | 162 |
| | 6.111 | 171 |
| | 6.112 | 171 |
| | 6.118 | 172 |
| | 7.112 | 225 |
| | 7.170 | 233 |
| | 7.261 | 251 |
| LIGHT OF THE WORLD, CHURCH CALLED TO BE... | 10.5 | 303 |
| LITERATURE, SCRIPTURE AS | 9.29 | 291 |
| LITURGICAL FORMULAS, AS CONFESSIONS | 9.02 | 287 |
| LIVING, PRAYER FOR THE | 6.115 | 172 |
| LORD, ONE, CONFESSION OF | 8.01 | 281 |
| | 8.06 | 282 |
| LORD'S DAY, THE | 5.224–.225 | 135 |
| LORDSHIP OF CHRIST, DENIAL OF | 9.45 | 294 |
| LORD'S PRAYER | 5.233 | 137 |
|     Discussion of | 4.120–.129 | 70–73 |
| | 7.009–.107 | 205–15 |
| | 7.296–.306 | 257–60 |
|     Parts | 7.100–.107 | 214–15 |
| | 7.298 | 257 |
|     Proper uses | 7.297 | 257 |
|     Rule in prayer | 7.099 | 214 |
| | 7.296 | 257 |
|     Text | 4.119 | 69–70 |
| | 7.109 | 216 |
|     Preface | 7.100 | 214 |
| | 7.299 | 257–58 |
|     First petition | 7.101 | 214 |
| | 7.300 | 258 |
|     Second petition | 7.102 | 215 |
| | 7.301 | 258 |
|     Third petition | 7.103 | 215 |
| | 7.302 | 258 |

# BOOK OF CONFESSIONS

| | Reference Numbers | Page Numbers |
|---|---|---|
| **LORD'S PRAYER** (*Continued*) | | |
| Fourth petition | 7.104 | 215 |
| | 7.303 | 258–59 |
| Fifth petition | 7.105 | 215 |
| | 7.304 | 259 |
| Sixth petition | 7.106 | 215 |
| | 7.305 | 259 |
| Conclusion | 7.107 | 215 |
| | 7.306 | 260 |
| **LORD'S SUPPER, THE** (See also Sacraments): | | |
| Administered by | 7.279 | 254 |
| Admission to | 3.23 | 24 |
| | 4.081–.082 | 56–57 |
| | 7.282 | 255 |
| Author of | 5.194 | 128 |
| And baptism | 7.286 | 256 |
| Communication in | 7.097 | 214 |
| | 7.280 | 254 |
| Definition and discussion of | 6.161–.168 | 182–84 |
| | 7.093 | 214 |
| | 7.096–.097 | 214 |
| | 7.278 | 254 |
| Duty after receiving | 7.285 | 255–56 |
| Effects of | 3.21 | 21–22 |
| Elements in | 4.075 | 53 |
| | 4.079 | 55 |
| | 5.208 | 131–32 |
| | 7.279 | 254 |
| | 9.52 | 296 |
| And faith | 5.200 | 129–30 |
| And gathered church | 9.36 | 292 |
| And the Holy Spirit | 5.196 | 128–29 |
| Institution of | 4.077 | 54 |
| | 5.193 | 128 |
| | 6.152 | 181 |
| And the mass | 4.080 | 55–56 |
| Meaning of | 4.075 | 53 |
| | 9.52 | 296 |
| As memorial | 5.195 | 128 |
| Nature of sacrifice in | 4.080 | 55–56 |
| Observance of | 5.208 | 131–32 |
| Outward sign in | 5.196–.197 | 128–29 |
| Participation in | 4.075 | 53 |
| And paschal lamb | 5.177 | 124 |

# INDEX

| | Reference Numbers | Page Numbers |
|---|---|---|
| **LORD'S SUPPER, THE** (See also Sacraments) (*Continued*) | | |
| Preparation for | 5.207 | 131 |
| | 7.281 | 254–55 |
| Presence of Christ in | 5.205 | 131 |
| Purpose of | 5.206 | 131 |
| Recipients of | 3.23 | 24 |
| | 7.284 | 255 |
| And reconciliation | 9.52 | 296 |
| And salvation | 5.202 | 130 |
| Spiritual eating and | 5.198 | 129 |
| Transubstantiation in | 5.210 | 132 |
| Unbelievers and | 5.204 | 130–31 |
| Unity in | 10.3 | 302 |
| Withholding of cup and | 5.209 | 132 |
| **LORD'S SUPPER AND THE HOLY SPIRIT** | 11.4 | 312 |
| **LORD'S TABLE** (See Lord's Supper) | | |
| **LOVE:** | | |
| Brotherly | 6.100 | 168–69 |
| | 6.146 | 180 |
| | 7.281 | 254–55 |
| | 7.284 | 255 |
| Of Christ | 6.097 | 168 |
| | 6.100 | 168–69 |
| | 7.284 | 255 |
| | 10.3 | 302 |
| Conjugal | 7.248 | 248 |
| As an expression of unity | 10.3 | 301 |
| Faith and | 5.114 | 106 |
| | 6.069 | 163 |
| God's | 7.036 | 208 |
| | 7.140 | 228 |
| | 7.177 | 234 |
| | 7.189 | 236 |
| | 7.193 | 236–37 |
| | 7.195 | 237 |
| | 11.3 | 312 |
| Of God (See Love of God) | | |
| Necessity of | 6.114 | 172 |
| | 7.097 | 214 |
| | 7.281 | 254–55 |
| | 7.295 | 257 |
| Toward God | 6.099 | 168 |
| | 6.108 | 170 |
| | 6.112 | 171 |
| | 7.042 | 208 |

|  | Reference Numbers | Page Numbers |
|---|---|---|
| LOVE (See also Sacraments) (*Continued*) | | |
|   Toward God (*Continued*) | 7.212 | 240 |
| | 7.214 | 240 |
| | 7.269 | 252 |
| | 7.281 | 254–55 |
|     Toward men | 7.042 | 208 |
| | 7.232 | 245 |
| | 7.245 | 247 |
| | 7.269 | 252 |
| | 7.281 | 254–55 |
|    And the word | 7.090 | 213 |
| | 7.269–.270 | 252 |
| LOVE OF GOD | 9.08 | 288 |
| | 9.14–.19 | 289–90 |
| | 11.3 | 312 |
|    And Israel | 9.18 | 289–90 |
|    And missions | 6.055–.058 | 160–61 |
| | 6.187–.190 | 188–89 |
|     As a mystery | 9.15 | 289 |
|     Power of | 9.15 | 289 |
|     Revelation of | 9.15 | 289 |
| LUSTS | 7.249 | 248 |
| LUTHERAN CHURCH | 8.01 | 281 |
| | 8.06 | 282 |
| | 8.08 | 282 |
| LYDIA | 5.006 | 78 |
| LYING | 7.076 | 212 |
| | 7.078 | 212 |
| | 7.253 | 249 |
| | 7.255 | 249–50 |

## M

|  | Reference Numbers | Page Numbers |
|---|---|---|
| MACEDONIA | 5.143 | 115 |
| MACEDONIUS, ERRORS OF | 5.019 | 81 |
| MAGISTRATE, CIVIL (See also civil magistrate) | 3.24 | 24 |
| | 6.111 | 171 |
| | 6.127–.130 | 174–75 |
| | 6.176 | 186 |
| | 7.239 | 246 |
| | 7.293 | 257 |
| MAJESTY OF GOD | 7.295 | 257 |
| MALEFACTORS | 5.255 | 142 |
| MALICE | 7.261 | 251 |

# INDEX

|  | Reference Numbers | Page Numbers |
|---|---|---|
| **MAN:** | | |
| And Adam | 3.02 | 11 |
| Annihilation of | 9.45 | 294 |
| Belief of | 7.005–.012 | 205 |
|  | 7.116–.130 | 225–27 |
| Benefits to | 4.043 | 43 |
|  | 4.045 | 43 |
|  | 4.049–.051 | 44–45 |
| Call to reconciliation of | 9.07 | 287–88 |
| Chief end of | 7.001 | 205 |
|  | 7.111 | 225 |
| Common life of | 9.32 | 292 |
| And conflict | 9.23 | 290 |
| Conversion of | 5.093–.105 | 100–03 |
|  | 6.062 | 161–62 |
| Corruption | 4.007 | 33 |
| Creation of | 3.02 | 11 |
|  | 4.006 | 32 |
|  | 6.023 | 154 |
|  | 7.010 | 205 |
|  | 7.127 | 226–27 |
| Crisis in the life of | 9.21 | 290 |
| Death of | 4.042 | 43 |
|  | 5.038 | 87 |
| Deliverance of | 4.012–.025 | 34–37 |
| Disobedience of | 4.009–.010 | 33 |
| Duty of | 7.039 | 208 |
|  | 7.201 | 238 |
| Effectual calling of | 6.064–.067 | 162 |
| Fall of | 3.02 | 11 |
|  | 5.036 | 86–87 |
|  | 7.013–.019 | 206 |
|  | 7.131–.137 | 227–28 |
| Freedom of | 5.043 | 88 |
|  | 9.17 | 289 |
|  | 9.23 | 290 |
| Free will of | 5.044 | 89 |
|  | 5.050 | 90 |
|  | 6.059 | 161 |
| God with | 9.07 | 287–88 |
| Goodness of | 5.045 | 89 |
| Ground of | 9.22 | 290 |
| And image of God | 3.03 | 11 |
|  | 5.034 | 86 |
| Imperfection of | 3.15 | 17–18 |

|  | Reference Numbers | Page Numbers |
|---|---|---|
| **MAN** (*Continued*) | | |
| Inheritance of | 3.02 | 11 |
| Judgment of | 9.08 | 288 |
| | 9.11 | 288 |
| Liberty of | 3.15 | 17–18 |
| | 5.050 | 90 |
| Life of | 9.53 | 296 |
| Merits of | 5.123 | 108–09 |
| Misery of | 4.003–.011 | 32–34 |
| Natural | 6.061 | 161 |
| Natural environment of | 9.53 | 296 |
| Nature of | 3.02 | 11 |
| | 4.005 | 32 |
| | 5.034 | 86 |
| | 5.107 | 104 |
| | 9.17 | 289 |
| Original state of | 4.006 | 32 |
| | 4.008 | 33 |
| | 5.034 | 86 |
| | 5.043 | 88 |
| Perfection of | 6.062–.063 | 161–62 |
| Physical needs of | 4.125 | 71–72 |
| Potential of | 4.009 | 33 |
| Providence and | 7.012 | 205 |
| | 7.130 | 227 |
| Purpose for | 9.53 | 296 |
| Rebirth of | 4.008 | 33 |
| Redemption of | 6.048 | 158 |
| Renewal of | 5.101 | 102–3 |
| | 9.32 | 292 |
| Repentance of | 4.088 | 59 |
| | 5.093–.105 | 100–03 |
| Righteousness of | 4.060–.062 | 48–49 |
| And Satan | 3.03 | 11 |
| Sin of | 5.037 | 87 |
| | 6.061 | 161 |
| | 9.12–.14 | 288–89 |
| Soul of | 4.057 | 47 |
| | 5.034 | 86 |
| State of | 6.060 | 161 |
| Talents of | 5.046 | 89 |
| Traditions of | 5.014 | 80 |
| Universal family of | 9.44 | 294 |

INDEX

|  | Reference Numbers | Page Numbers |
|---|---|---|
| MAN (*Continued*) | | |
|    And woman | 3.02 | 11 |
| | 5.034 | 86 |
| | 5.246 | 140–41 |
| | 9.17 | 289 |
| | 9.47 | 294–95 |
|    Works of | 5.116 | 107 |
| MANICHAEANS, ERRORS OF | 5.008 | 78 |
| | 5.032 | 85–86 |
| | 5.048 | 90 |
| | 5.051 | 90–91 |
| MANKIND, FALL OF | 7.016 | 206 |
| | 7.132 | 227 |
| MAN-STEALING | 7.252 | 248–49 |
| MARCION, ERRORS OF | 3.06 | 13 |
| | 5.064 | 93–94 |
| MARCIONITES, ERRORS OF | 5.008 | 78 |
| | 5.032 | 85–86 |
| MARRIAGE | 5.246–.248 | 140–41 |
| | 6.131–.139 | 176–79 |
| | 7.130 | 227 |
| | 9.44 | 294 |
| | 9.47 | 294–95 |
|    And chastity | 4.108–.109 | 66 |
|    Contracting of | 5.247 | 141 |
|    As an ordinance | 5.171 | 122–23 |
|    Second | 5.246 | 140–41 |
| MARY, VIRGIN | 5.062 | 93 |
| | 5.064 | 93–94 |
| MASS, ROMAN: | | |
|    Abolition of | 5.210 | 132 |
|    And Lord's Supper | 4.080 | 55–56 |
| | 6.162 | 182–83 |
|    Purpose of | 3.22 | 23 |
| MASS COMMUNICATION | 9.47 | 294–95 |
| MATRIMONIAL FORUM, CHURCH AS | 5.248 | 141 |
| MEANS OF GRACE: | | |
|    Administration of | 7.143–.145 | 229 |
|    Enumeration of | 7.088 | 213 |
| | 7.145 | 229 |
| | 7.264 | 251–52 |
|    Sacraments as | 7.091 | 213 |
| | 7.271 | 253 |
|    Sins against | 7.261 | 251 |
|    Word as | 7.089 | 213 |
| | 7.265 | 252 |

|  | Reference Numbers | Page Numbers |
|---|---|---|
| MEASUREMENTS, INACCURATE | 4.110 | 66–67 |
| MEAT, ABSTENTION FROM | 5.231 | 136 |
| MEDIATOR, CHRIST AS | 4.015–.018 | 35 |
|  | 5.024 | 83 |
|  | 6.045 | 157 |
|  | 7.021–.026 | 206–07 |
|  | 7.146–.155 | 229–30 |
|  | 7.167 | 232 |
| MEDITATION UPON GOD | 7.214 | 240 |
| MEEKNESS | 7.245 | 247 |
| MEETING PLACES FOR WORSHIP | 5.214–.216 | 132–33 |
| MEETINGS, FOR WORSHIP | 5.211–.217 | 132–33 |
| MEMBERS, CHURCH (See also Church Member) | 5.139 | 113–14 |
|  | 9.25 | 290–91 |
|  | 9.38 | 292–93 |
| MEMBERSHIP, CHURCH | 4.054 | 46 |
|  | 10.3 | 302 |
|  | 10.4 | 303 |
| MEMORIAL, LORD'S SUPPER AS | 5.195 | 128 |
| MEN AND MORAL LAW | 7.205 | 238–39 |
| MEN, PRAYER, FOR ALL | 6.115 | 172 |
|  | 7.293 | 257 |
| MERCY: |  |  |
|     Of God | 4.011 | 34 |
|  | 6.011 | 151–52 |
|  | 6.074 | 164 |
|  | 6.075 | 164 |
|  | 6.086 | 165–66 |
|  | 6.125 | 174 |
|  | 7.087 | 213 |
|  | 7.117 | 225 |
|  | 7.140 | 228 |
|  | 7.180 | 234 |
|  | 7.261 | 251 |
|  | 7.288 | 256 |
|     Works of | 6.119 | 173 |
|  | 7.060 | 210 |
|  | 7.227 | 244 |
| MERIT | 6.091 | 166 |
|  | 7.303 | 258–59 |
|     Effect of | 4.063 | 49 |
|     Human | 5.123 | 108–09 |
|     And justification | 5.107 | 104 |

# INDEX

|  | Reference Numbers | Page Numbers |
|---|---|---|
| MESSALIANS, ERRORS OF | 5.181 | 125 |
| METROPOLITANS | 5.148 | 116–17 |
| MILITANT CHURCH | 5.127–.128 | 109–10 |
| MINISTERS: | | |
| And absolution | 5.100 | 102 |
| And administration of Sacraments | 3.22 | 23 |
|  | 5.166 | 121 |
|  | 5.174 | 123 |
|  | 7.279 | 254 |
| And baptism | 5.191 | 127 |
| Calling and anointing of | 5.150 | 117 |
|  | 6.054 | 159–60 |
|  | 6.186 | 188 |
|  | 7.268 | 252 |
| Definition of | 3.22 | 23 |
| Discipline among | 5.165 | 121 |
| Duties of | 5.163–.165 | 120–21 |
|  | 6.054 | 159–60 |
|  | 6.186 | 188 |
| Election of | 5.150 | 117 |
| Equality of | 5.160 | 120 |
| Family of | 5.168 | 122 |
| Freedom of | 6.129 | 175 |
| As hyperetas: Greek, Rowers | 5.155 | 118 |
| And keys of the Kingdom | 5.096 | 102 |
| Maintenance of | 7.218 | 242 |
| Nature of | 5.145–.149 | 115–17 |
| Of New Testament | 5.147 | 116 |
| Office of | 5.159 | 119 |
| Ordering of | 5.161–.162 | 120 |
| Ordination of | 5.151 | 117 |
| Origin of | 5.142 | 115 |
| Power of | 5.157 | 119 |
| Prayer for | 7.293 | 257 |
| And preaching | 5.004 | 77 |
|  | 6.081 | 165 |
|  | 7.268–.269 | 252 |
| Purpose of | 5.142 | 115 |
| Qualifications of | 5.150–.152 | 117 |
| And salvation | 5.142 | 115 |
| Simplicity of | 5.152 | 117 |
| As stewards of the mysteries of God | 5.156 | 118 |
| Stipend for | 5.168 | 122 |
| And visible church | 6.142 | 179 |
| MINISTRIES OF MEN | 9.24 | 290 |

|  | Reference Numbers | Page Numbers |
|---|---|---|
| MINISTRY | 6.067 | 162 |
|  | 6.142 | 179 |
|     Gift of, to church members | 9.38 | 292–93 |
|     Of the gospel | 4.103 | 64 |
|     Maintenance of | 7.218 | 242 |
|     Nature of | 5.155 | 118 |
|     Necessity of | 5.143–.144 | 115 |
|     Offices of | 8.20 | 284 |
|     Ordination to | 9.39 | 293 |
|     Of reconciliation | 5.098 | 102 |
|  | 9.31–.51 | 257–61 |
|     Of the word | 7.268 | 252 |
|  | 8.26 | 284 |
| MISERY OF MAN | 4.003–.011 | 32–34 |
|  | 6.036 | 156 |
|  | 7.019 | 206 |
|  | 7.137 | 228 |
| MISSION: |  |  |
|     Call of church to | 9.31 | 257 |
|     Of Christ | 9.06–.07 | 287–88 |
|     Of the church | 9.31–.46 | 257–60 |
|     Dispersed church and | 9.37 | 292 |
|     Duty of | 9.42 | 293 |
|     Instruments of | 9.40 | 293 |
|     Pattern of | 9.32 | 292 |
|     Unity in | 9.05 | 287 |
| MISSIONS | 6.055–.058 | 160–61 |
|  | 6.187–.190 | 188–89 |
| MODESTY IN APPAREL | 7.248 | 248 |
| MOHAMMEDANS, ERRORS OF | 5.019 | 81 |
| MONARCHIANS, ERRORS OF | 5.019 | 81 |
| MONASTIC VOWS | 6.126 | 174 |
| MONEY, COUNTERFEIT | 4.110 | 66–67 |
| MONKS, STATUS OF | 5.149 | 117 |
| MONOPHYSITES, ERRORS OF | 5.068 | 94 |
| MONOTHEISM | 11.1 | 311 |
| MONOTHELITES, ERRORS OF | 5.068 | 94 |
| MOOD OF PRAYER | 7.295 | 257 |
| MORAL LAW | 6.102 | 169 |
|  | 7.040–.041 | 208 |
|  | 7.202–.208 | 238–39 |
| MOSES | 3.05 | 12 |
|  | 5.081 | 97 |
|  | 5.128 | 110 |

# INDEX

|  | Reference Numbers | Page Numbers |
|---|---|---|
| MURDER | 4.105–.106 | 65 |
|  | 7.067 | 211 |
|  | 7.244 | 247 |
| MURDERERS | 5.255 | 142 |
| MUSIC | 5.221 | 134 |
|  | 9.50 | 295–96 |
| MYSTERY: |  |  |
|   Of God | 5.156 | 118 |
|   Reconciliation as | 9.09 | 288 |
|   Of salvation | 6.050 | 158 |

## N

|  | Reference Numbers | Page Numbers |
|---|---|---|
| NAMES OF CHRIST | 4.029 | 39 |
|  | 4.031 | 40 |
|  | 4.033 | 40–41 |
|  | 4.034 | 41 |
| NATIONAL RESOURCES | 9.46 | 294 |
| NATIONAL SECURITY, RISK TO | 9.45 | 294 |
| NATIONAL SOVEREIGNTY | 9.45 | 294 |
| NATIVITY OF CHRIST, CELEBRATION OF | 5.226 | 135 |
| NATURAL DIVERSITY | 10.4 | 302 |
| NATURE: |  |  |
|   Exploitation of | 11.3 | 311 |
|   Law of | 5.081 | 97 |
|  | 6.118 | 172 |
|   Light of | 6.112 | 171 |
|   Of the ministry | 5.145–.149 | 115–17 |
|  | 5.155 | 118 |
|   Resources of | 9.17 | 289 |
| NATURES, TWO, OF CHRIST | 4.048 | 44 |
|  | 6.044 | 157 |
|  | 7.021 | 206 |
| NAZARETH, JESUS OF | 9.08 | 288 |
| NAZARITES, ERRORS OF | 5.091 | 100 |
| NECESSITY, WORKS OF | 6.119 | 173 |
|  | 7.227 | 244 |
| NEEDY, SERVICE TO | 4.103 | 64 |
|  | 4.111 | 67 |
| NEIGHBOR: |  |  |
|   Alienation from | 9.47 | 294–95 |
|   Conduct toward | 7.074–.081 | 212 |
|  | 7.251–.258 | 248–50 |
|   Duties to | 3.23 | 24 |
|   Exploitation of | 11.3 | 311 |

|  | Reference Numbers | Page Numbers |
|---|---|---|
| **NEIGHBOR** (*Continued*) | | |
|     Good name of | 4.112 | 67 |
|     Love of | 4.107 | 65–66 |
|     Reconciliation with | 5.095 | 101–02 |
|     Service to | 5.114 | 106 |
|     Treatment of | 4.105–.107 | 65–66 |
| | 4.111–.112 | 67 |
|     Winning of | 4.086 | 58 |
| **NESTORIANS, ERRORS OF** | 5.068 | 94 |
| **NESTORIUS** | 3.06 | 13 |
| **NEW AGE, COMING OF** | 9.18 | 289–90 |
| **NEW HUMANITY, THE** | 9.19 | 290 |
| **NEW LIFE IN CHRIST** | 9.21–.26 | 290–91 |
| **NEW POSSIBILITIES OF LIFE** | 10.5 | 303 |
| **NEW TESTAMENT:** | | |
|     Authority of | 9.27–.28 | 291 |
|     Books of | 6.002 | 149–50 |
|     Ceremonial law in | 6.103 | 169 |
|     Covenant under | 6.042 | 157 |
| | 7.145 | 229 |
|     Description of | 9.28 | 291 |
|     Language of | 6.008 | 151 |
|     Ministers in | 5.147 | 116 |
| | 5.155 | 118 |
|     Oath under | 6.121 | 173 |
|     Prophesy concerning | 5.092 | 100 |
|     Rule of faith and practice | 6.002 | 149–50 |
| | 7.002 | 205 |
| | 7.113 | 225 |
|     Sabbath and | 6.118 | 172 |
| | 7.226 | 244 |
|     Sacraments of | 4.068 | 51 |
| | 5.171 | 122–23 |
| | 6.152 | 181 |
| | 6.154–.160 | 181–82 |
| | 7.093 | 214 |
| | 7.274–.275 | 253 |
| | 7.278 | 254 |
|     War and | 6.128 | 174 |
| **NICENE CREED** | 5.078 | 97 |
| | 9.04 | 287 |
|     Prologue | | 2 |
|     Text | 1.1–.3 | 3 |
| **NOAH** | 3.04 | 12 |

INDEX

|  | Reference Numbers | Page Numbers |
|---|---|---|
| NOAH'S ARK | 5.136 | 113 |
| NOTES OF THE TRUE CHURCH | 5.134–.135 | 112 |
| NOVATIANS, ERRORS OF | 5.019 | 81 |
| NUCLEAR WEAPONS | 9.45 | 294 |
| NUMBER OF THE ELECT | 5.056 | 91 |
| NURTURE, BY CHRISTIAN COMMUNITY | 9.24 | 290 |

# O

| | Reference Numbers | Page Numbers |
|---|---|---|
| OATHS (See also Swearing): | | |
| Devout swearing to | 4.101 | 63 |
| | 7.218 | 242 |
| | 7.223 | 243 |
| Lawful | 4.102 | 64 |
| | 6.115 | 172 |
| | 6.120–.123 | 173 |
| Magistrates and | 5.257 | 142 |
| Unlawful | 6.122 | 173 |
| | 7.223 | 243 |
| OBEDIENCE | 10.3 | 302 |
| | 10.5 | 303 |
| | 10.9 | 305 |
| Of Christ | 6.046–.047 | 157–58 |
| | 6.068 | 163 |
| | 6.070 | 163 |
| | 6.106 | 169–70 |
| | 9.08 | 288 |
| To Christ | 6.157 | 182 |
| | 9.03 | 287 |
| And covenant of works | 6.038 | 156 |
| | 6.101 | 169 |
| | 7.012 | 205 |
| | 7.130 | 227 |
| Duty of | 6.130 | 175 |
| Justification and | 6.068 | 163 |
| To the law | 3.15 | 17–18 |
| Of moral law | 6.105 | 169 |
| New | 7.087 | 213 |
| | 7.097 | 214 |
| | 7.186 | 235 |
| | 7.281 | 254–55 |
| Perfect, to God's commandments | 4.114 | 68 |

|  | Reference Numbers | Page Numbers |
|---|---|---|
| OBEDIENCE (*Continued*) | | |
|   Rule of | 6.002 | 149–50 |
| | 6.004 | 150 |
| | 7.040 | 208 |
| | 7.202 | 238 |
|     To superiors | 7.237 | 246 |
|     To will of God | 7.039 | 208 |
| | 7.103 | 215 |
| | 7.201 | 238 |
| | 7.214 | 240 |
| | 7.302 | 258 |
| OBJECTS OF PRAYER | 7.294 | 257 |
| OBLIGATIONS OF BELIEVERS | 6.058 | 161 |
| | 6.190 | 189 |
| OBSERVANCE, OF LORD'S SUPPER | 5.208 | 131–32 |
| OBSTINACY | 7.261 | 251 |
| OFFENSES, AGGRAVATED | 7.261 | 251 |
| OFFERINGS FOR THE POOR | 4.103 | 43 |
| OFFICE: | | |
|   Of the keys | 4.082–.085 | 57–58 |
|   Of the minister | 5.159 | 119 |
| OFFICERS, CHURCH | 9.40 | 293 |
|     Appointment | 6.142 | 179 |
|     And assemblies | 6.173 | 185 |
|     Government of church by | 6.169–.170 | 184 |
|     Of particular churches | 7.155 | 230 |
|     Powers of | 6.170 | 184 |
|     Of presbytery and other judicatories | 6.054 | 159–60 |
| | 6.186 | 188 |
|     And sin | 7.261 | 251 |
| OFFICES, PURPOSE OF | 8.20 | 284 |
| OLD AND NEW TESTAMENTS: | | |
|   Relationship of | 9.27–.28 | 291 |
|   Sacraments of | 5.176 | 123–24 |
| OLD TESTAMENT: | | |
|   Authority of | 9.27–.28 | 291 |
|   Books of | 6.002 | 149–50 |
|   Covenant under | 6.041 | 156 |
|   Description of | 9.28 | 291 |
|   Justification under | 6.073 | 163 |
| | 7.144 | 229 |
|   Language of | 6.008 | 151 |

## INDEX

| | Reference Numbers | Page Numbers |
|---|---|---|
| **OLD TESTAMENT** (*Continued*) | | |
| Rule of faith and life | 6.002 | 149–50 |
| | 7.002 | 205 |
| | 7.113 | 225 |
| Sacraments of | 5.170 | 122 |
| | 5.177 | 124 |
| | 6.153 | 181 |
| Spirits of the dead in | 5.239 | 138 |
| **OMNIPOTENCE OF GOD** | 6.011 | 151–52 |
| | 7.004 | 205 |
| | 7.117 | 225 |
| **OMNIPRESENCE OF GOD** | 6.011 | 151–52 |
| | 7.004 | 205 |
| | 7.117 | 225 |
| **OMNISCIENCE OF GOD** | 6.001–.002 | 149–50 |
| | 7.004 | 205 |
| | 7.117 | 225 |
| **OPPRESSION** | 7.246 | 247 |
| | 7.252 | 248–49 |
| | 10.7 | 304 |
| **OPPRESSORS** | 5.155 | 118 |
| **ORACLES** | 6.142 | 179 |
| **ORDER OF THE TRINITY** | 5.107 | 104 |
| **ORDERS:** | | |
| Of the ministry | 5.162 | 120 |
| Papal | 5.148 | 116–17 |
| **ORDINANCES:** | | |
| Of Christ | 7.088 | 213 |
| | 7.263–.264 | 251 |
| Gospel | 6.042 | 157 |
| | 6.103 | 169 |
| | 7.145 | 229 |
| New Testament | 6.042 | 157 |
| | 6.113–.119 | 172–73 |
| | 7.088 | 213 |
| Old Testament | 6.041 | 156 |
| | 6.103 | 169 |
| | 7.144 | 229 |
| Profitable | 5.171 | 122–23 |
| Sacraments as | 7.092 | 213 |
| | 7.272 | 253 |
| **ORDINATION:** | | |
| Of ministers | 5.151 | 117 |
| Nature of | 9.39 | 293 |
| As an ordinance | 5.171 | 122–23 |

|  | Reference Numbers | Page Numbers |
|---|---|---|
| ORIGINAL SIN | 3.03 | 11 |
|  | 5.039 | 87 |
| ORIGINAL STATE OF MAN (See also Man: Original State of) | 4.006 | 32 |
|  | 4.008 | 33 |
|  | 7.012 | 205 |
|  | 7.130 | 227 |
| ORNAMENTATION OF SANCTUARIES | 5.216 | 133 |
| ORPHANS | 5.235 | 137–38 |
|  | 5.254 | 142 |
|  | 10.7 | 304 |
| ORTHODOX INTERPRETATION OF SCRIPTURE | 5.010 | 79 |
| OUTCASTS, EATING WITH | 11.2 | 311 |
| OVERPOPULATION | 9.47 | 294–95 |

## P

|  | Reference Numbers | Page Numbers |
|---|---|---|
| PAINTERS, AND IMAGES | 5.020–.022 | 81–82 |
| PALESTINIAN JEW, JESUS AS | 9.08 | 288 |
| PAPAL INDULGENCES | 5.104 | 103 |
| PAPAL MASS, AND LORD'S SUPPER | 4.080 | 55–56 |
| PAPAL ORDERS | 5.148 | 116–17 |
| PAPISTS | 5.222 | 134 |
| And the gospel | 5.092 | 100 |
| And Sacraments | 5.171 | 122–23 |
| PARADISE | 4.007 | 33 |
|  | 4.019 | 35–36 |
|  | 5.034 | 86 |
| PARDON OF SINS | 6.068–.069 | 163 |
|  | 6.083 | 165 |
|  | 7.033 | 208 |
|  | 7.105 | 215 |
|  | 7.180 | 234 |
|  | 7.182 | 234 |
|  | 7.304 | 259 |
| PARENTS: |  |  |
| Authority of | 4.104 | 64–65 |
| And baptism | 6.157 | 182 |
| And children | 9.47 | 294–95 |
| First | 5.037 | 87 |
| Honor to | 4.104 | 64–65 |
| PARITY OF THE MINISTRY | 5.160 | 120 |
| PARTICULAR CHURCH: |  |  |
| And Catholic church | 6.143 | 180 |
| Degeneration of | 6.144 | 180 |
| Nature of | 5.128 | 110 |

# INDEX

| | Reference Numbers | Page Numbers |
|---|---|---|
| PASCHAL LAMB | 5.170 | 122 |
| | 5.177 | 124 |
| PASSION OF CHRIST, CELEBRATION OF | 5.226 | 135 |
| PASSIONS, EXCESSIVE | 7.246 | 247 |
| PASTOR: | | |
|     Appointment of | 5.146 | 116 |
|     Christ as | 5.131 | 110–11 |
|     Definition of | 5.147 | 116 |
|     And visitation of the sick | 5.234 | 137 |
| PATRIARCHS | 5.148 | 116–17 |
| PATRIPASSIANS, ERRORS OF | 5.019 | 81 |
| PAUL | 3.18 | 19 |
| | 3.22 | 23 |
| | 4.077 | 54 |
| | 4.079 | 55 |
| | 5.006 | 78 |
| | 5.014 | 80 |
| | 5.024 | 83 |
| | 5.029 | 84 |
| | 5.031 | 85 |
| | 5.111 | 105 |
| | 5.133 | 111–12 |
| | 5.191 | 127 |
| PAUL OF SAMOSATA, ERRORS OF | 5.019 | 81 |
| PAYMENT TO GOD | 4.012–.014 | 34 |
| PEACE | 5.256 | 142 |
| | 10.7 | 304 |
|     Bond of | 10.4 | 302 |
|     Of the church | 6.111 | 171 |
|     Of conscience | 7.036 | 208 |
| | 7.193 | 236–37 |
| | 7.304 | 259 |
|     Maintenance of | 6.128 | 174 |
|     Among nations | 9.45 | 294 |
|     In society | 9.17 | 289 |
| | 11.4 | 312 |
|     And the spirit | 6.099 | 168 |
| PEACEABLENESS | 7.245 | 247 |
| PEACEMAKER, CHURCH AS A | 10.5 | 303 |
| PELAGIANS, ERRORS OF | 5.040 | 87 |
| | 5.051 | 90–91 |
| PELAGIUS, ERRORS OF | 5.040 | 87 |
| PENANCE, DOCTRINE OF | 5.104 | 103 |
| PENITENCE | 6.132 | 176–77 |
| | 6.137 | 178–79 |
| | 7.295 | 257 |

|  | Reference Numbers | Page Numbers |
|---|---|---|
| PERFECTION: | | |
|   After death | 6.076 | 164 |
| | 6.090 | 166 |
| | 6.177 | 186 |
| | 7.082 | 212 |
| | 7.196 | 237 |
|     Attainment of full | 4.115 | 68 |
| PERJURERS | 5.255 | 142 |
| PERJURY | 7.223 | 243 |
| PERSEVERANCE: | | |
|   And election | 6.018 | 153 |
|   Ground of | 6.098 | 168 |
|   Of the justified | 6.072 | 163 |
| | 6.074 | 164 |
| | 6.077 | 164 |
| | 7.036 | 208 |
| | 7.185 | 235 |
|     Necessity of | 6.114 | 172 |
| | 7.295 | 257 |
|     Of the saints | 6.094–.096 | 167–68 |
| | 7.189 | 236 |
| PERSON OF CHRIST | 5.066 | 94 |
| | 9.05 | 287 |
| PERSONAL CRISIS | 9.21 | 290 |
| PERSONS: | | |
|   Of the Godhead | 5.017–.018 | 81 |
| | 6.013 | 152 |
| | 7.006 | 205 |
| | 7.119–.121 | 225–26 |
|     Three | 5.017 | 81 |
| PETER | 5.005 | 78 |
| | 5.010 | 79 |
| | 5.025 | 83 |
| | 5.137 | 113 |
| PETITIONS: | | |
|   To civil magistrates | 6.176 | 186 |
|   And intercession | 9.50 | 295–96 |
| PHARISEES, TEACHING OF | 5.092 | 100 |
| PHAROAH | 3.05 | 12 |
| PHILIPPI, CHURCH IN | 5.006 | 78 |
| | 5.055 | 91 |
| PICTURES, AND INSTRUCTION | 5.021 | 82 |
| PICTURES, LASCIVIOUS | 7.249 | 248 |

# INDEX

|  | Reference Numbers | Page Numbers |
|---|---|---|
| PIETY: | | |
|     Instruction in | 5.003 | 77 |
|     Maintenance of | 6.128 | 174 |
| PITY OF GOD | 6.066 | 162 |
| PLEDGE AND SIGN, BAPTISM AS | 4.073 | 52 |
| POLITICAL LIFE | 9.53 | 296 |
| POLITICAL RIGHTS | 9.44 | 294 |
| POLITICS: | | |
|     Church | 8.28 | 284 |
|     And peace | 9.45 | 294 |
| POLITY: | | |
|     Church | 9.39 | 293 |
|     Presbyterian | 9.40 | 293 |
| POLYGAMY | 5.246 | 140–41 |
| | 7.249 | 248 |
| POLYTHEISM | 7.213–.216 | 240–41 |
| PONTIUS PILATE | 4.038 | 42 |
| POOR (See Poverty) | | |
| POPE, THE (See also Papal: Roman Church) | 5.104 | 103 |
| | 5.131 | 110–11 |
| | 6.130 | 175 |
| | 6.145 | 180 |
|     Decree of, concerning Lord's Supper | 5.197 | 129 |
| POPULATION, EXPANSION OF | 9.46–.47 | 294–95 |
| PORTERS | 5.148 | 116–17 |
| POSSESSIONS OF THE CHURCH | 5.243–.244 | 140 |
| POURING OR SPRINKLING, IN BAPTISM | 6.156 | 182 |
| POVERTY | 9.46 | 294 |
| | 10.7 | 304 |
| | 11.2 | 311 |
| POWER | 6.129 | 175 |
| | 7.107 | 215 |
| | 7.306 | 260 |
|     Of Christ | 5.158 | 119 |
|     Ecclesiastical | 5.159 | 119 |
| | 9.40 | 293 |
|     Of general councils | 3.20 | 20 |
|     Of ministers | 5.157 | 119 |
|     Secular | 9.40 | 293 |
| POWERS: | | |
|     Of civil magistrates | 3.24 | 24 |
|     Civil, rebellion against | 3.24 | 24 |
|     Of the intellect | 5.046 | 89 |
|     Ruling | 8.21 | 284 |

BOOK OF CONFESSIONS

| | Reference Numbers | Page Numbers |
|---|---|---|
| PRAISE TO GOD | 6.112 | 171 |
| | 7.107 | 215 |
| | 7.214 | 240 |
| | 7.306 | 260 |
| PRAISE, AND PRAYER | 9.50 | 295–96 |
| PRAXEAS, ERRORS OF | 5.019 | 81 |
| PRAYER (See also Lord's Prayer) | 4.116–.129 | 68–73 |
| | 7.098–.107 | 214–15 |
| | 7.288–.306 | 256–60 |
|     Acceptable | 7.293–.295 | 257 |
| | 7.297 | 257 |
|     And Bible | 7.099 | 214 |
| | 7.296 | 257 |
|     And canonical hours | 5.222 | 134 |
|     For civil magistrates | 6.130 | 175 |
|     Common language in | 5.218 | 133 |
|     Contents of | 4.117 | 69 |
| | 5.218 | 133 |
|     For the dead | 5.236 | 138 |
|     Definition and discussion of | 6.114–.115 | 172 |
| | 6.117 | 172 |
| | 7.098–.107 | 214–15 |
| | 7.288 | 256 |
|     Dispersed church and | 9.37 | 292 |
|     Free and voluntary | 5.219 | 133–34 |
|     To God only | 7.098 | 214 |
| | 7.288–.289 | 256 |
|     And Holy Spirit | 7.292 | 257 |
| | 11.4 | 312 |
|     For Inferiors | 7.239 | 246 |
|     Lord's | 4.120–.129 | 70–73 |
| | 7.100–.107 | 214–15 |
| | 7.109 | 216 |
| | 7.296–.306 | 257–60 |
|     Method of public | 5.220 | 134 |
| | 7.295 | 257 |
|     Mood of | 7.295 | 257 |
|     Motivation of | 4.120 | 70 |
|     In name of Christ | 7.098 | 214 |
| | 7.288 | 256 |
| | 7.290 | 256 |
| | 7.291 | 256–57 |
|     Necessity of | 4.116 | 68–69 |
|     With and for others | 7.100 | 214 |
| | 7.299 | 257–58 |
| | 10.3 | 302 |

# INDEX

| | Reference Numbers | Page Numbers |
|---|---|---|
| **PRAYER** (See also Lord's Prayer) (*Continued*) | | |
| Petition in | 4.118 | 69 |
| And praise | 9.50 | 295–96 |
| Public | 5.218–.220 | 133–34 |
| Required of all | 7.214 | 240 |
| | 7.218 | 242 |
| Rule for | 7.099 | 214 |
| | 7.296 | 257 |
| For the sick | 5.234 | 137 |
| And sins | 5.101 | 102–3 |
| | 7.261 | 251 |
| For superiors | 7.237 | 246 |
| Thanksgiving | 7.098 | 214 |
| | 7.288 | 256 |
| Time for | 5.223 | 134 |
| Unceasing | 11.4 | 312 |
| And worship | 7.289 | 256 |
| **PREACHING:** | | |
| Duty of | 7.218 | 212 |
| Effective | 9.49 | 295 |
| External | 5.006 | 78 |
| For instruction | 5.021 | 82 |
| And the Kingdom of Heaven | 4.084 | 57 |
| Manner of | 7.269 | 252 |
| Ministers only | 7.268 | 252 |
| And the sacraments | 5.169 | 122 |
| And the true church | 3.18 | 19 |
| Of the Word of God | 5.004 | 77 |
| | 5.211 | 132 |
| | 6.116 | 172 |
| | 7.089–.090 | 213 |
| | 7.268–.270 | 252 |
| **PREDESTINATION** (See also election) | 5.052–.061 | 91–93 |
| And baptism | 6.159 | 182 |
| Of Christ | 5.062 | 93 |
| Doctrine of | 6.016–.021 | 153 |
| | 6.191–.193 | 190–91 |
| Temptation regarding | 5.061 | 92–93 |
| **PREJUDICE** | 10.5 | 303 |
| **PREPARATION FOR THE LORD'S SUPPER** | 5.207 | 131 |
| | 7.097 | 214 |
| | 7.281 | 254–55 |
| **PRESBYTERIAN POLITY** | 9.40 | 293 |
| **PRESBYTERS, OR ELDERS** | 5.147 | 116 |
| | 5.160 | 120 |

BOOK OF CONFESSIONS

| | Reference Numbers | Page Numbers |
|---|---|---|
| PRESENCE OF CHRIST | 4.047 | 44 |
| In Lord's Supper | 5.205 | 131 |
| In the church | 9.07 | 287–88 |
| PRESENT HOPE | 9.21 | 290 |
| PRESENT WITNESS TO CHRIST | 9.01 | 287 |
| PRESUMPTION | 7.215 | 241 |
| | 7.261 | 251 |
| PRETERITION, DOCTRINE OF | 6.020 | 153 |
| | 6.029 | 155 |
| | 6.062 | 161–62 |
| | 6.191–.193 | 190–91 |
| | 7.123 | 226 |
| PRIDE | 7.215 | 241 |
| PRIEST: | | |
| Christ as | 6.043 | 157 |
| | 7.025 | 207 |
| | 7.154 | 230 |
| And confession | 5.095 | 101–02 |
| PRIESTHOOD OF ALL BELIEVERS | 5.154 | 118 |
| PRIMACY IN THE CHURCH | 5.131 | 110–11 |
| PRIORS | 5.148 | 116–17 |
| PRIVATE INTERPRETATION OF SCRIPTURE | 5.010 | 79 |
| PRIVILEGE | 10.7 | 304 |
| PROCLAMATION OF THE GOSPEL | 8.12 | 283 |
| | 9.21 | 290 |
| PRODIGALITY | 7.251 | 248 |
| PROFANITY | 7.055 | 210 |
| | 7.215 | 241 |
| | 7.223 | 243 |
| | 7.300 | 258 |
| PROFESSION OF FAITH IN CHRIST | 6.147 | 180 |
| | 6.157 | 182 |
| | 7.223 | 243 |
| PROGRESS, LIMITED, AND THE KINGDOM | 9.55 | 297 |
| PROLOGUES: | | |
| The Apostles' Creed | | 6 |
| A Brief Statement of Faith—Presbyterian Church (U.S.A.) | | 308 |
| The Confession of 1967 | | 286 |
| The Confession of Belhar | | 300 |
| The Heidelberg Catechism | | 28–29 |
| The Larger Catechism | | 146–48 |
| The Nicene Creed | | 2 |
| The Scots Confession | | 10 |
| The Second Helvetic Confession | | 76 |
| The Shorter Catechism | | 146–48 |

# INDEX

|  | Reference Numbers | Page Numbers |
|---|---|---|
| **PROLOGUES** (*Continued*) | | |
|     The Theological Declaration of Barmen | | 280 |
|     The Westminster Confession of Faith | | 146–48 |
| **PROMISE OF GOD TO ADAM** | 3.04 | 12 |
| **PROMISES:** | | |
|     Carnal and spiritual | 5.087–.088 | 99 |
|     Evangelical | 5.086 | 98–99 |
|     Sins against | 7.261 | 251 |
| **PROPERTIES, IMPARTATION OF** | 5.072 | 95 |
| **PROPERTY:** | | |
|     Church as, of Christ | 8.17 | 283 |
|     Right or title to | 6.148 | 181 |
| **PROPHECY** | 6.001 | 149 |
| **PROPHET, CHRIST AS** | 7.024 | 207 |
| | 7.153 | 230 |
| **PROPHETS:** | | |
|     Definition of | 5.147 | 116 |
|     Teaching of | 9.24 | 290 |
| **PROPITIATION FOR SINS** | 6.191 | 190 |
| **PROSPERITY** | 7.066 | 211 |
| | 7.243 | 247 |
| **PROTECTION** | 7.239 | 246 |
| | 10.1 | 301 |
| | 10.7 | 304 |
| **PROVIDENCE:** | | |
|     Definition and discussion of | 6.024–.030 | 154–55 |
| | 7.011 | 205 |
| | 7.128 | 227 |
|     Of God | 4.027 | 38–39 |
| | 5.029–.031 | 84–85 |
| | 7.011–.012 | 205 |
| | 7.128–.130 | 227 |
| | 9.03 | 287 |
|     Murmuring at | 7.223 | 243 |
|     Scripture and | 6.008 | 151 |
|     Works of | 6.001 | 149 |
| **PROVOSTS** | 5.148 | 116–17 |
| **PRUDENCE** | 6.006 | 150–51 |
| **PUBLIC CONFESSION OF SINS** | 5.095 | 101–02 |
| **PUBLIC MEETINGS FOR WORSHIP** | 5.213 | 132 |
| **PUBLIC WORSHIP:** | | |
|     Discussion of | 6.112–.117 | 171–72 |
|     Form of | 6.104 | 169 |
| | 7.049–.051 | 209 |

|  | Reference Numbers | Page Numbers |
|---|---|---|
| **PUBLIC WORSHIP** (*Continued*) | | |
| Nature of | 9.49 | 295 |
| Oaths and | 6.120 | 173 |
| Purity of | 7.050 | 209 |
| Sacraments in | 6.116 | 172 |
|  | 6.163 | 183 |
| Vows in | 6.108 | 170 |
|  | 6.124–.126 | 174 |
| **PUNISHMENT:** | | |
| Acquittal from | 7.304 | 259 |
| Of body and soul | 4.011 | 34 |
| Capital | 7.246 | 247 |
| Escape from | 4.012 | 34 |
| Eternal | 5.038 | 87 |
| Of evildoers | 7.239 | 246 |
| Of God | 4.010 | 33 |
|  | 4.014 | 34 |
| Of sin | 7.138–.139 | 228 |
| Of the wicked | 7.199 | 237–38 |
| **PURGATORY** | 5.238 | 138 |
| **PURITY OF PARTICULAR CHURCHES** | 6.143 | 180 |

## Q

|  | | |
|---|---|---|
| **QUALIFICATIONS OF MINISTERS** | 5.150–.152 | 117 |
| **QUARRELING** | 7.246 | 247 |
| **QUICUNQUE CREED** (See Athanasius, creed of) | | |

## R

|  | | |
|---|---|---|
| **RACIAL OR ETHNIC DISCRIMINATION** | 9.44 | 294 |
| **READING OF SCRIPTURE** | 5.211 | 132 |
|  | 6.116 | 172 |
|  | 7.089 | 213 |
|  | 7.218 | 212 |
|  | 7.265–.267 | 252 |
| **REBELLION AGAINST SUPERIORS** | 7.238 | 246 |
| **REBELLION AND OVERTHROW OF CIVIL POWERS** | 3.24 | 24 |
| **REBELS** | 5.259 | 143 |
| **REBIRTH:** | | |
| Baptism as water of | 4.071 | 51–52 |
| In faith | 3.03 | 11 |
| Of man | 4.008 | 33 |
| **RECEPTION OF CHRIST** | 5.110 | 105 |

# INDEX

|  | Reference Numbers | Page Numbers |
|---|---|---|
| RECONCILIATION: | | |
| In Christ | 10.3 | 301–2 |
|  | 10.5 | 303 |
| Of Christ | 5.076 | 96 |
| Christ's work of | 10.3 | 301–2 |
| The church as a manifestation of | 10.3 | 301 |
| Descriptions of | 9.09 | 288 |
| Fulfillment of | 9.53–.56 | 296–97 |
| To God | 4.012 | 34 |
|  | 10.3 | 301 |
| God's work of | 9.08–.30 | 288–91 |
| And the Holy Spirit | 9.20–.30 | 290–91 |
| And the Lord's Supper | 9.52 | 296 |
| Ministry of | 5.098 | 102 |
|  | 9.31–.51 | 257–61 |
| As a mystery | 9.09 | 288 |
| Among nations | 9.45 | 294 |
| Need for | 9.06 | 287 |
| With neighbor | 5.095 | 101–02 |
|  | 10.3 | 301 |
| Response to | 9.50 | 295–96 |
| In society | 9.43–.47 | 293–95 |
| Work of | 9.06 | 287 |
| RECREATIONS, LAWFUL | 7.060–.061 | 210–11 |
|  | 7.227 | 244 |
|  | 7.229 | 244 |
|  | 7.245–.246 | 247 |
| REDEEMER, CHRIST AS | 4.015–.017 | 35 |
|  | 9.11 | 288 |
| REDEMPTION | 6.043 | 157 |
|  | 6.047–.050 | 158 |
|  | 7.027 | 207 |
|  | 7.029–.030 | 207 |
|  | 7.159 | 231 |
|  | 7.169 | 233 |
| REFORMATION, THE | 8.05 | 282 |
| Of churches | 5.003 | 77 |
| Of church order | 9.40 | 293 |
| Duty of | 9.03 | 287 |
| In life and doctrine | 9.03 | 287 |
| REFORMED CHURCH, GERMAN | 8.01 | 281 |
|  | 8.06 | 282 |
|  | 8.08 | 282 |
| REGENERATE, THE | 5.047–.049 | 89–90 |
|  | 7.207 | 239 |

BOOK OF CONFESSIONS

|  | Reference Numbers | Page Numbers |
|---|---|---|
| REGENERATION | 3.12–.13 | 15–16 |
| Agent of | 6.065 | 162 |
| And baptism | 6.154 | 181 |
|  | 6.158 | 182 |
| Effectual call and | 6.065–.066 | 162 |
| Elect and | 6.066 | 162 |
| Of infants | 6.066 | 162 |
|  | 6.191–.193 | 190–91 |
| Ministry of the word and | 6.064 | 162 |
| And sin | 6.035 | 155 |
|  | 6.075 | 164 |
| RELATIONS, SEXUAL | 9.47 | 294–95 |
| RELICS, OF SAINTS | 5.027 | 84 |
| RELIGION: |  |  |
| Controversies about | 5.013 | 79 |
| Differences of | 6.130 | 175 |
| Encounter with | 9.41–.42 | 293 |
| God's judgment on | 9.42 | 293 |
| Natural | 6.067 | 162 |
| Non-Christian | 9.42 | 293 |
| True, and civil magistrate | 3.24 | 24 |
| REMARRIAGE | 6.132 | 176–77 |
|  | 6.138–.139 | 179 |
| REMISSION OF SINS | 3.25 | 25 |
|  | 5.099–.100 | 102 |
|  | 5.106 | 104 |
|  | 6.154 | 181 |
| RENEWAL OF LIFE | 5.101 | 102–3 |
| RENUNCIATION OF HUMAN WILL | 4.124 | 71 |
| REPARATION | 7.261 | 251 |
| REPENTANCE | 6.081–.086 | 165–66 |
|  | 7.085 | 213 |
|  | 7.087 | 213 |
|  | 7.186 | 235 |
|  | 7.263 | 251 |
|  | 9.14 | 289 |
|  | 11.4 | 312 |
| And conversion | 5.094 | 100 |
| Definition of | 5.093 | 100 |
| Genuine, parts of | 4.088 | 59 |
| And the gospel | 5.093 | 100 |
| Of man | 5.093–.105 | 100–03 |
| As an ordinance | 5.171 | 122–23 |
| Relapse after | 7.261 | 251 |

# INDEX

| | Reference Numbers | Page Numbers |
|---|---|---|
| REPROBATE, END OF | 3.17 | 19 |
| REPROBATION | 6.020 | 153 |
| | 6.191–.193 | 190–91 |
| RESPONSE, DAILY (See Daily Response) | | |
| RESTITUTION, TIME OF | 3.11 | 15 |
| RESTORATION | 10.7 | 304 |
| RESURRECTION: | | |
|     And believers | 7.038 | 208 |
| | 7.198 | 237 |
|     Of the body | 2.3 | 7 |
| | 3.11 | 15 |
| | 4.057 | 47 |
| | 7.038 | 208 |
| | 7.197 | 237 |
|     Of Christ | 3.10 | 14 |
| | 4.045 | 43 |
| | 5.073 | 95 |
| | 5.226 | 135 |
| | 6.046 | 157–58 |
| | 7.028 | 207 |
| | 7.161–.162 | 231 |
| | 9.08 | 288 |
| | 9.52 | 296 |
| | 11.2 | 311 |
|     Of the dead | 1.3 | 3 |
| | 2.3 | 7 |
|     Doctrine of | 6.177–.179 | 186 |
| | 7.197 | 237 |
|     Of the flesh | 3.25 | 25 |
| | 5.075 | 95–96 |
|     And newness of life | 11.2 | 311 |
|     As a sign | 9.26 | 291 |
|     Testimony to | 3.10 | 14 |
| REVELATION: | | |
|     Of God | 6.001 | 149 |
| | 7.002 | 205 |
| | 7.039–.040 | 208 |
| | 7.112 | 225 |
| | 7.201–.202 | 238 |
|     And religion | 9.41–.42 | 293 |
|     Scripture as | 9.27 | 291 |
|     Source of | 8.12 | 283 |
|     Sufficient | 9.27 | 291 |

| | Reference Numbers | Page Numbers |
|---|---|---|
| REVENGE, DESIRE FOR | 4.105 | 65 |
| | 7.246 | 247 |
| REVERENCE | 6.114 | 172 |
| | 6.116 | 172 |
| | 7.222 | 243 |
| | 7.267 | 252 |
| | 7.295 | 257 |
| REWARD FOR GOOD WORKS | 5.122 | 108 |
| | 6.092 | 167 |
| RIGHTEOUS, THE | 6.177 | 186 |
| | 6.181 | 186–87 |
| | 7.038 | 208 |
| | 7.195 | 237 |
| | 7.200 | 238 |
| RIGHTEOUSNESS | 10.3 | 302 |
| | 10.5 | 303 |
| | 10.7 | 304 |
|     Of Christ | 6.068 | 163 |
| | 6.070 | 163 |
| | 7.033 | 208 |
| | 7.181–.182 | 234 |
| | 7.187 | 235 |
|     Imputed | 5.108 | 104 |
|     Of man | 4.060–.062 | 48–49 |
| RIGHTS, EQUAL | 9.44 | 294 |
| RISK TO NATIONAL SECURITY | 9.45 | 294 |
| RITES: | | |
|     And ceremonies | 5.240–.242 | 138–39 |
|     Diversity of | 5.241 | 139 |
|     External | 5.141 | 114 |
| ROBBERY | 7.252 | 248–49 |
| ROMAN CHURCH | 5.126 | 109 |
|     Head of | 5.132 | 111 |
|     And interpretation of Scripture | 5.010 | 79 |
|     Mass of | 5.210 | 132 |
|     And pope | 5.131 | 110–11 |
|     And the Sacraments | 3.22 | 23 |
|     Sects in | 5.133 | 111–12 |
| ROMANISTS | 3.21 | 22 |
| ROME, POPE AT | 5.131 | 110–11 |
| RULE: | | |
|     Of Christ | 9.54 | 296–97 |
|     Of faith and love | 5.010 | 79 |
|     Law of God as | 6.106 | 169–70 |

# INDEX

|  | Reference Numbers | Page Numbers |
|---|---|---|
| **RULE** (*Continued*) | | |
| Lord's Prayer as | 7.099 | 214 |
|  | 7.296 | 257 |
| Scripture as | 6.002 | 149–50 |
| Synods and councils as | 6.175 | 185 |
| **RULES FOR UNDERSTANDING THE TEN COMMANDMENTS** | 7.209 | 239–40 |

## S

|  | Reference Numbers | Page Numbers |
|---|---|---|
| SABBATH (See Also Lord's Day) | 6.118–.119 | 172–73 |
|  | 7.057–.062 | 210–11 |
|  | 7.225–.231 | 243–45 |
|  | 7.261 | 251 |
| SACERDOTAL CONFESSION AND ABSOLUTION | 5.095 | 101–02 |
| SACRAMENTAL EATING | 5.203 | 130 |
| SACRAMENTAL UNION | 5.180 | 125 |
|  | 6.150 | 181 |
|  | 6.165 | 183 |
| **SACRAMENTS, THE:** | | |
| Abrogation of Old Testament | 5.177 | 124 |
| Administration of | 3.22 | 23 |
|  | 5.166 | 121 |
|  | 5.173–.174 | 123 |
|  | 6.129 | 175 |
|  | 6.152 | 181 |
|  | 6.155 | 182 |
|  | 6.163 | 183 |
|  | 7.218 | 212 |
| Adoration or veneration of | 3.22 | 22 |
| Author of | 5.172 | 123 |
|  | 5.174 | 123 |
| Baptism | 6.154 | 181 |
|  | 7.091 | 213 |
|  | 7.275 | 253 |
| Composition of | 5.178 | 124–25 |
| Consecration of | 5.178 | 124–25 |
| Definition and discussion of | 3.21 | 21–22 |
|  | 4.066 | 50 |
|  | 5.169 | 122 |
|  | 6.149–.153 | 181 |
|  | 7.091–.093 | 213–14 |
|  | 7.271–.274 | 253 |
| Efficacy of | 5.183 | 126 |
| Elements in | 5.178 | 124–25 |
| Holy | 4.065–.068 | 50–51 |

|  | Reference Numbers | Page Numbers |
|---|---|---|
| **SACRAMENTS, THE** (*Continued*) | | |
| Institution of | 3.21 | 21 |
|  | 5.178 | 124–25 |
| Integrity of | 5.173 | 123 |
| Lord's Supper | 6.161 | 182 |
| Means of grace and salvation | 7.091 | 213 |
|  | 7.271 | 253 |
| Ministry through | 8.26 | 284 |
| As mysteries | 5.156 | 118 |
| New Testament | 4.068 | 51 |
|  | 5.171 | 122–23 |
| Number of | 3.21 | 21 |
|  | 4.068 | 51 |
|  | 5.171 | 122–23 |
|  | 7.274 | 253 |
| Of Old and New Testaments | 5.176 | 123–24 |
| Old Testament | 5.170 | 122 |
| Participation in | 4.103 | 64 |
| Parts of | 7.092 | 213 |
|  | 7.273 | 253 |
| And preaching | 5.169 | 122 |
| Purposes of | 3.21 | 21 |
|  | 5.184 | 126 |
| Right administration of | 3.18 | 19 |
| Sanctification of | 5.181 | 125 |
| Signs in | 5.179 | 125 |
| Substance of | 5.175 | 123 |
| As symbols | 3.21 | 21 |
| Under the law | 3.21 | 21 |
| Use of | 4.065 | 50 |
|  | 7.222 | 243 |
| **SACRIFICE:** | | |
| Atoning | 4.037 | 42 |
| Of Christ | 4.066–.067 | 50 |
|  | 4.075 | 53 |
|  | 6.047 | 158 |
|  | 6.162 | 182–83 |
|  | 7.025 | 207 |
|  | 7.162 | 231 |
| Gratitude | 4.043 | 43 |
| Nature of, in communion | 4.080 | 55–56 |
| Voluntary | 3.09 | 14 |
| **SACRIFICES IN OLD TESTAMENT** | 6.041–.042 | 156–57 |
| **SACRILEGE** | 7.219 | 242 |

INDEX

|  | Reference Numbers | Page Numbers |
|---|---|---|
| SAINTS: | | |
| Adoration, invocation, and worship of | 5.025 | 83 |
| Communion of (See also Communion of Saints) | 2.3 | 7 |
| | 3.16 | 18 |
| | 5.125 | 109 |
| | 6.146–.148 | 180–81 |
| Election and predestination of | 5.052 | 91 |
| Festivals of | 5.226 | 135 |
| Images of | 5.020 | 81–82 |
| Mention of | 5.235 | 137–38 |
| Oaths sworn by | 4.102 | 64 |
| Perseverance of | 6.094–.096 | 167–68 |
| | 7.189 | 236 |
| Relics of | 5.027 | 84 |
| Status of | 5.026 | 83–84 |
| Worship of | 6.113 | 172 |
| | 7.215 | 241 |
| SALT OF THE EARTH, CHURCH CALLED TO BE | 10.5 | 303 |
| SALVATION: | | |
| Assurance of | 6.100 | 168–69 |
| And baptism | 6.158 | 182 |
| In Christ | 4.020 | 36 |
| | 4.030 | 39 |
| | 6.064 | 162 |
| | 6.169 | 184 |
| | 7.021 | 206 |
| | 7.170 | 233 |
| Effectual calling to | 6.019 | 153 |
| | 6.047 | 158 |
| | 6.050 | 158 |
| | 6.064–.066 | 162 |
| | 6.191–.193 | 190–91 |
| | 7.020 | 206 |
| | 7.169 | 233 |
| | 7.173 | 233 |
| And election | 5.058 | 92 |
| And good works | 5.119 | 107–8 |
| | 6.091 | 166 |
| Of the impenitent | 4.087 | 59 |
| Limits of | 7.169 | 233 |
| Means of | 7.088 | 213 |
| | 7.091 | 213 |
| | 7.263–.264 | 251 |
| | 7.271 | 253 |

415

|  | Reference Numbers | Page Numbers |
|---|---|---|
| SALVATION (*Continued*) | | |
| And ministers | 5.142 | 115 |
| Mysteries of | 6.050 | 158 |
| Necessity of Lord's Supper to | 5.202 | 130 |
| Offering of | 6.055–.056 | 160 |
| | 6.187–.188 | 188–89 |
| | 6.191 | 190 |
| Outside the church | 5.136–.137 | 113 |
| | 7.173 | 233 |
| Possibility of | 6.141 | 179 |
| Revelation of | 6.056 | 160 |
| | 6.058 | 161 |
| | 6.188 | 189 |
| | 6.190 | 189 |
| Scripture and | 6.005–.007 | 150–51 |
| SAMOSATA, PAUL OF | 5.019 | 81 |
| SAMUEL | 5.031 | 85 |
| SANCTIFICATION | 3.12 | 15–16 |
| Discussion of | 6.075–.077 | 164 |
| | 7.035–.037 | 208 |
| | 7.185 | 235 |
| | 7.187–.188 | 235–36 |
| | 7.193 | 236–37 |
| | 7.196 | 237 |
| Of Lord's Day | 7.060 | 210 |
| | 7.227 | 244 |
| Need of | 8.15 | 283 |
| Of the sacraments | 5.181 | 125 |
| Subjects of | 6.043 | 157 |
| | 6.075 | 164 |
| | 6.077 | 164 |
| | 6.146 | 180 |
| | 7.037 | 208 |
| | 7.185–.189 | 235–36 |
| SANCTUARIES, ORNAMENTATION OF | 5.216 | 133 |
| SARAH | 11.3 | 312 |
| SATAN: | | |
| Christ and | 7.158 | 231 |
| | 7.162 | 231 |
| Compacts with | 7.215 | 241 |
| Kingdom of | 7.301 | 258 |
| Liberty from | 6.108 | 170 |
| Man and | 3.03 | 11 |
| | 7.102 | 215 |
| | 7.301 | 258 |

# INDEX

| | Reference Numbers | Page Numbers |
|---|---|---|
| SATAN (*Continued*) | | |
| Suggestions of | 6.112 | 171 |
| Temptations of | 6.031 | 155 |
| | 6.096 | 168 |
| | 7.131 | 227 |
| | 7.305 | 259 |
| The wicked and | 6.029 | 155 |
| SATISFACTION OF JUSTICE | 6.047 | 158 |
| | 6.068 | 163 |
| | 6.083 | 165 |
| | 7.025 | 207 |
| | 7.148 | 229 |
| | 7.180–.181 | 234 |
| | 7.304 | 259 |
| SAUL | 5.031 | 85 |
| SAVING FAITH | 6.078–.080 | 164 |
| SAVING GRACE: | | |
| Faith as | 7.033 | 208 |
| | 7.085–.086 | 213 |
| | 7.182 | 234 |
| | 7.263 | 251 |
| Repentance as | 7.085 | 213 |
| | 7.087 | 213 |
| | 7.186 | 235 |
| | 7.263 | 251 |
| SAVIOR, CHRIST AS | 4.029 | 39 |
| | 5.077 | 96 |
| SCANDAL | 7.261 | 251 |
| SCHISMS | 5.141 | 114 |
| SCHWENKFELDT, ERRORS OF | 5.070 | 94 |
| SCIENTIFIC LIFE | 9.53 | 296 |
| SCOFFING | 7.255 | 249–50 |
| SCORNFUL CONTEMPT | 7.255 | 249–50 |
| SCOTLAND | 3.18 | 19 |
| SCOTS CONFESSION | 9.04 | 287 |
| Prologue | | 10 |
| Text | 3.01–.25 | 11–26 |
| SCRIPTURE: | | |
| Addition to | 5.002 | 77 |
| Agreement with | 8.04 | 281 |
| Authority of | 3.19 | 20 |
| | 5.001 | 77 |
| Canonical | 3.18 | 19 |
| | 5.011 | 79 |

417

BOOK OF CONFESSIONS

|  | Reference Numbers | Page Numbers |
|---|---|---|
| SCRIPTURE (*Continued*) | | |
| Divorce in | 6.132 | 176–77 |
| And faith | 5.112 | 106 |
| And the fathers | 5.011 | 79 |
| Fidelity to | 9.49 | 295 |
| Guide in prayer | 7.099 | 214 |
|  | 7.296 | 257 |
| Holy Spirit and | 6.005 | 150 |
|  | 6.052 | 159 |
|  | 6.184 | 187 |
|  | 7.089 | 213 |
|  | 7.114 | 225 |
|  | 7.265 | 252 |
| Inspiration of | 6.001–.002 | 149–50 |
|  | 6.008 | 151 |
|  | 6.052 | 159 |
|  | 6.184 | 187 |
| Interpretation of | 3.18 | 19 |
|  | 5.010–.014 | 79–80 |
|  | 9.29 | 291 |
| Languages and circumstances of | 5.010 | 79 |
|  | 7.266 | 252 |
| As literature | 9.29 | 291 |
| Nature of | 9.29 | 291 |
| Oaths in | 6.121 | 173 |
| Obligations concerning | 9.29 | 291 |
| Preaching of | 9.30 | 291 |
| Principal references to | 6.001–.010 | 149–51 |
|  | 7.002–.003 | 205 |
|  | 7.089–.090 | 213 |
|  | 7.112–.116 | 225 |
|  | 7.265–.270 | 252 |
| Principal teaching of | 7.003 | 205 |
|  | 7.115 | 225 |
| And public worship | 6.116 | 172 |
| Reading of | 5.211 | 132 |
|  | 7.266–.267 | 252 |
|  | 9.30 | 291 |
| Relation to synods and councils | 6.174 | 185 |
| As revelation | 9.27 | 291 |
| Rule of faith and practice | 6.002 | 149–50 |
|  | 6.006 | 150–51 |
|  | 6.112 | 171 |
|  | 7.003 | 205 |
|  | 7.113 | 225 |
|  | 7.115 | 225 |

# INDEX

|  | Reference Numbers | Page Numbers |
|---|---|---|
| SCRIPTURE (*Continued*) | | |
| And salvation | 3.18 | 19 |
| Sufficiency of | 7.112 | 225 |
| | 7.114 | 225 |
| Teaching of | 5.003 | 77 |
| And tradition | 5.014 | 80 |
| Vows in | 6.126 | 174 |
| As Word of God | 5.001–.009 | 77–78 |
| | 7.002 | 205 |
| | 7.113–.114 | 225 |
| SECOND CAUSES | 6.025–.026 | 154 |
| SECOND COMING OF CHRIST | 7.028 | 207 |
| | 7.166 | 232 |
| | 8.17 | 283 |
| | 9.32 | 292 |
| | 9.52 | 296 |
| SECOND HELVETIC CONFESSION | 9.04 | 287 |
| Prologue | | 76 |
| Text | 5.001–.260 | 77–143 |
| SECTARIAN DIVISIONS | 9.34 | 292 |
| SECTS, IN ROMAN CHURCH | 5.133 | 111–12 |
| SECULAR POWER | 9.40 | 293 |
| SECURITY, NATIONAL | 9.45 | 294 |
| SEDITION | 11.2 | 311 |
| SEDITIOUS PERSONS | 5.255 | 142 |
| | 5.259 | 143 |
| SELF: | | |
| Alienation from | 9.47 | 294–95 |
| Old and new | 4.088–.090 | 59 |
| SELF-LOVE | 7.215 | 241 |
| SELF-SEEKING | 7.215 | 241 |
| | 10.7 | 304 |
| SEMETIC CULTURE | 9.41 | 293 |
| SEPARATION: | | |
| Based on color | 10.6 | 303 |
| Based on race | 10.5 | 303 |
| | 10.6 | 303 |
| SERMON | 8.26 | 284 |
| SERVETUS, MICHAEL, ERRORS OF | 5.063 | 93 |
| SERVICE: | | |
| Of Christ | 9.32 | 292 |
| Commission to | 9.10 | 288 |
| Courage and hope for | 9.52 | 296 |
| Forms of | 9.48 | 295 |
| Free and grateful | 8.14 | 283 |

|                                          | Reference Numbers | Page Numbers |
|---|---|---|
| SERVICE (*Continued*) | | |
|     To God | 5.114 | 106 |
| | 10.3 | 302 |
|     To the needy | 4.103 | 64 |
|     To neighbor | 5.114 | 106 |
| SETH | 3.18 | 19 |
| SEXUAL RELATIONS | 9.47 | 294–95 |
| SHORTER CATECHISM, THE WESTMINSTER | 9.04 | 287 |
|     Prologue | | 146–48 |
|     Text | 7.001–.110 | 205–16 |
| SICK, VISITATION OF | 5.234 | 137 |
| SIGN, OUTWARD, IN LORD'S SUPPER | 5.196–.197 | 128–29 |
| SIGNS: | | |
|     In Sacraments | 5.179 | 125 |
|     And seals of | 4.066 | 50 |
| | 6.149 | 181 |
| | 6.154 | 181 |
| | 7.092 | 213 |
| | 7.272 | 253 |
|     Of the true church | 5.134–.135 | 112 |
| SIMONY | 5.104 | 103 |
| SIMPLICITY OF MINISTERS | 5.152 | 117 |
| SIN: | | |
|     Against the Holy Spirit | 5.102 | 103 |
|     Aggravations of | 7.261 | 251 |
|     Author of | 5.041 | 87–88 |
|     Confession of | 5.094–.095 | 100–01 |
| | 6.086 | 165–66 |
| | 9.50 | 295–96 |
|     Unto death | 7.293 | 257 |
|     Definition of | 5.037 | 87 |
| | 7.014 | 206 |
| | 7.134 | 227 |
|     Degrees of | 7.083 | 212 |
| | 7.260 | 250 |
|     As disobedience | 6.031–.033 | 155 |
| | 7.015–.017 | 206 |
| | 7.019 | 206 |
| | 7.131 | 227 |
|     First | 7.016–.017 | 206 |
| | 7.019 | 206 |
| | 7.132 | 227 |
| | 7.135 | 227–28 |
| | 7.137 | 228 |

# INDEX

|  | Reference Numbers | Page Numbers |
|---|---|---|
| **SIN** (*Continued*) | | |
| Forgiveness of | 2.3 | 7 |
| | 6.064 | 162 |
| | 6.068 | 163 |
| | 6.072 | 163 |
| | 6.083 | 165 |
| | 7.033 | 208 |
| | 7.105 | 215 |
| | 7.180 | 234 |
| | 7.304 | 259 |
| Freedom from | 4.002 | 31 |
| God and | 5.041 | 87–88 |
| | 6.014 | 152 |
| | 6.027 | 154 |
| | 7.084–.085 | 213 |
| | 7.262–.263 | 251 |
| Greatness of | 4.002 | 31 |
| Guilt of | 6.036 | 156 |
| | 6.084 | 165 |
| | 6.106 | 169–70 |
| | 7.019 | 206 |
| | 7.084 | 213 |
| | 7.137 | 228 |
| | 7.262 | 251 |
| | 7.304 | 259 |
| Justification and | 6.028 | 154–55 |
| | 6.072 | 163 |
| Knowledge of | 4.003 | 32 |
| Of man | 6.053 | 159 |
| | 9.12–.14 | 288–89 |
| Nature of | 5.039 | 87 |
| Original | 3.03 | 11 |
| | 6.032–.036 | 155 |
| | 7.018 | 206 |
| | 7.135–.136 | 227–28 |
| | 7.304 | 259 |
| And prayer | 5.101 | 102–3 |
| | 7.106 | 215 |
| | 7.305 | 259 |
| Pretense of | 6.012 | 152 |
| Propitiation for | 6.191 | 190 |
| Providence and | 6.027 | 154 |
| Punishment of | 6.032–.036 | 155–56 |
| | 6.096 | 168 |
| | 6.177 | 186 |
| | 6.181 | 186–87 |

|   |   | Reference Numbers | Page Numbers |
|---|---|---|---|
| SIN (*Continued*) | | | |
| Punishment of (*Continued*) | | 7.019 | 206 |
| | | 7.137–.139 | 228 |
| | | 7.194 | 237 |
| | | 7.199 | 237–38 |
| Redemption from | | 6.047–.050 | 158 |
| Regeneration and | | 6.035 | 155 |
| | | 6.062 | 161–62 |
| | | 6.108 | 170 |
| Remission of | | 1.3 | 3 |
| | | 2.3 | 7 |
| | | 3.25 | 25 |
| | | 5.099–.100 | 102 |
| | | 6.154 | 181 |
| | | 6.170 | 184 |
| | | 7.275 | 253 |
| Repentance for | | 6.082–.086 | 165–66 |
| Satisfaction | | 4.060 | 48–49 |
| | | 5.076 | 96 |
| | | 5.105 | 103–4 |
| | | 6.047 | 158 |
| | | 6.070 | 163 |
| | | 7.025 | 207 |
| | | 7.154 | 230 |
| | | 7.262 | 251 |
| Transgressions as | | 6.034 | 155 |
| | | 6.036 | 156 |
| | | 7.018 | 206 |
| | | 7.135 | 227–28 |
| Victory over | | 9.08 | 288 |
| | | 10.5 | 303 |
| SINCERITY IN PRAYER | | 7.295 | 257 |
| | | 7.302 | 258 |
| SINGING IN WORSHIP | | 5.221 | 134 |
| SINGING PRAISES | | 6.116 | 172 |
| SINFULNESS, AWARENESS OF | | 4.115 | 68 |
| SINNERS: | | | |
| Forgiveness of | | 11.2 | 311 |
| Justification of | | 7.033 | 208 |
| | | 7.183 | 235 |
| | | 11.4 | 312 |
| SLANDER | | 7.254–.255 | 249–50 |
| SLANDERERS, AND SALVATION | | 4.087 | 59 |
| SLEEP | | 7.245 | 247 |
| SOCIAL CLASSES | | 9.46 | 294 |

# INDEX

|  | Reference Numbers | Page Numbers |
|---|---|---|
| SOCIAL FACTORS | 10.4 | 303 |
| SOCIAL LIFE | 9.53 | 296 |
| SOCIETY: | | |
|     Church scattered in | 9.35 | 292 |
|     Justice and peace in | 9.17 | 289 |
|     Reconciliation in | 9.43–.47 | 293–95 |
|     Renewal of | 9.32 | 292 |
| SOCRATES, HISTORIAN, CITED | 5.219 | 133–34 |
| | 5.230 | 136 |
| | 5.241 | 139 |
| SODOMY | 7.249 | 248 |
| SON, THE, AND BAPTISM | 6.155 | 182 |
| SON OF GOD (See Christ) | | |
| SON OF MAN (See Christ) | | |
| SONGS, LASCIVIOUS | 7.249 | 248 |
| SOUL | 6.023 | 154 |
| | 6.177 | 186 |
|     Of Christ | 5.065 | 94 |
|     Immortality of | 3.17 | 19 |
| | 5.034–.035 | 86 |
| | 7.127 | 226–27 |
|     Of man | 4.057 | 47 |
| | 5.034 | 86 |
|     Of righteous | 7.037 | 208 |
| | 7.196 | 237 |
|     State of, after death | 5.237–.239 | 138 |
|     Of wicked | 7.199 | 237–38 |
| SOVEREIGNTY: | | |
|     Of God | 6.012 | 152 |
| | 6.014 | 152 |
| | 6.020 | 153 |
| | 6.112 | 171 |
| | 6.127 | 174 |
| | 7.052 | 210 |
| | 7.123 | 226 |
| | 7.220 | 242 |
|     National | 9.45 | 294 |
| SPIRIT: | | |
|     Of Christ | 3.12 | 15–16 |
|     And flesh | 3.13 | 16 |
| | 6.076 | 164 |
|     God's | 10.3 | 301 |

|  | Reference Numbers | Page Numbers |
|---|---|---|
| SPIRIT (*Continued*) | | |
| Holy (See Holy Spirit) | | |
| Inward illumination of | 5.005–.007 | 78 |
| And letter | 5.090 | 99 |
| Ministry of | 5.090 | 99 |
| SPIRITS, APPARITION OF | 5.239 | 138 |
| SPIRITUAL: | | |
| Eating | 5.198 | 129 |
| Food | 5.199 | 129 |
| | 5.201 | 130 |
| Gifts | 10.3 | 302 |
| Promises | 5.087–.088 | 99 |
| SPRINKLING OR POURING IN BAPTISM | 5.188 | 127 |
| | 6.156 | 182 |
| STANDARDS, SUBORDINATE | 9.03 | 287 |
| Renewal of | 9.32 | 292 |
| STATE: | | |
| Church and | 6.127–.130 | 174–75 |
| | 8.22–.24 | 284 |
| Commission of | 8.22–.24 | 284 |
| Enemies of | 5.259 | 143 |
| Of man, after death | 6.177–.179 | 186 |
| STEADFASTNESS OF GOD | 10.1 | 301 |
| STEWARDS, MINISTERS AS | 5.156 | 118 |
| STIPEND FOR MINISTERS | 5.168 | 122 |
| STOICS, ERRORS OF | 5.040 | 87 |
| STRIFE IN THE CHURCH | 5.133 | 111–12 |
| STRIKING ANOTHER | 7.246 | 247 |
| SUBDEACONS | 5.148 | 116–17 |
| SUBJECTS, DUTIES OF, TO MAGISTRATES | 5.258 | 143 |
| SUBJECTS OF PRAYER | 7.293 | 257 |
| SUBMISSION TO GOD | 7.103 | 215 |
| | 7.214 | 240 |
| | 7.245 | 247 |
| | 7.295 | 257 |
| | 7.302 | 258 |
| SUBORDINATE STANDARDS, OF THE CHURCH | 9.03 | 287 |
| SUBSTANCE: | | |
| Of Christ | 5.066 | 94 |
| Faith as, hypostasis | 5.113 | 106 |
| Of the Sacraments | 5.175 | 123 |
| SUCCESSION OF BISHOPS | 5.135 | 112 |
| SUFFERING | 10.3 | 302 |
| | 10.7 | 304 |
| | 10.9 | 305 |

# INDEX

|  | Reference Numbers | Page Numbers |
|---|---|---|
| SUFFERING OF CHRIST | 4.037–.040 | 42 |
|  | 5.071 | 94 |
|  | 6.149 | 181 |
|  | 9.32 | 292 |
| SUFFICIENCY OF BAPTISM | 5.186 | 126 |
| SUFFRAGANS | 5.148 | 116–17 |
| SUNDAY (See Lord's Day) |  |  |
| SUPEREROGATION, WORKS OF | 3.15 | 18 |
|  | 6.090 | 166 |
| SUPERIORS | 7.228 | 244 |
|  | 7.235–.240 | 245–46 |
|  | 7.261 | 251 |
| SUPERSTITION | 5.225 | 135 |
| SUPPER, HOLY (See also Lord's Supper) | 3.21 | 21 |
|  | 4.075–.085 | 53–58 |
| SUPREME JUDGE, IN RELIGIOUS CONTROVERSIES | 6.010 | 151 |
| SURETY, CHRIST AS | 6.045 | 157 |
| SURETYSHIPS | 7.251 | 248 |
| SUSPENSION FROM LORD'S TABLE | 6.172 | 185 |
| SWEARING: |  |  |
|     Failure to prevent | 4.100 | 63 |
|     By name of God | 5.028 | 84 |
|     Profane | 6.121 | 173 |
|  | 7.055 | 210 |
|  | 7.223 | 243 |
| SWORD, POWER OF | 6.127 | 174 |
| SYNAGOGUE, OF SATAN | 3.18 | 19 |
| SYNODS: |  |  |
|     And councils | 6.173–.176 | 185–86 |
|     And discipline | 5.167 | 122 |
|     Free | 8.06 | 282 |
|     Gangrian | 5.232 | 136 |

## T

|  |  |  |
|---|---|---|
| TABLE OF THE LAW | 5.226 | 135 |
| TALEBEARING | 7.254–.255 | 249–50 |
| TATIANS, ERRORS OF | 5.232 | 136 |
| TAXES, PAYMENT OF | 5.258 | 143 |
|  | 6.130 | 175 |
| TEACHER: |  |  |
|     Appointment of | 5.146 | 116 |
|     Christ as | 5.146 | 116 |
|     Definition of | 5.147 | 116 |

|  | Reference Numbers | Page Numbers |
|---|---|---|
| TEACHING (See also Education; Instruction) | 9.49 | 295 |
|     Of Apostles and prophets | 9.24 | 290 |
|     The church | 10.7 | 304 |
|     And images | 5.020–.022 | 81–82 |
|     Of the Pharisees | 5.092 | 100 |
|     In Scripture | 5.003 | 77 |
|     In Worship | 5.220 | 134 |
| TECHNOLOGICAL LIFE | 9.53 | 296 |
| TECHNOLOGICAL UNDERSTANDING | 9.46 | 294 |
| TECHNOLOGY, FRUITS OF | 9.46 | 294 |
| TEMPERENCE | 7.245 | 247 |
|  | 7.248 | 248 |
| TEMPLE OF GOD | 5.130 | 110 |
| TEMPTATION: |  |  |
|     Believers and | 6.097–.100 | 168–69 |
|     Freedom from | 7.106 | 215 |
|  | 7.305 | 259 |
|     Providence and | 6.028 | 154–55 |
|     Reasons for | 6.028 | 154–55 |
|  | 7.305 | 259 |
|     Regarding predestination | 5.061 | 92–93 |
|     Rescue from | 4.127 | 72–73 |
|     The wicked and | 6.029 | 155 |
| TEN COMMANDMENTS | 5.081 | 97 |
|  | 5.233 | 137 |
|     Discussion of | 7.041–.083 | 208–12 |
|  | 7.208–.261 | 239–51 |
|     Divisions of | 4.093 | 61 |
|     Keeping of | 7.082 | 212 |
|  | 7.259 | 250 |
|     And moral law | 7.041 | 208 |
|  | 7.208 | 239 |
|     Obedience to | 4.114 | 68 |
|     Preface to | 7.043–.044 | 209 |
|  | 7.210–.211 | 240 |
|     Reasons for | 7.052 | 210 |
|  | 7.056 | 210 |
|  | 7.062 | 211 |
|  | 7.066 | 211 |
|  | 7.210 | 240 |
|  | 7.220 | 242 |
|  | 7.224 | 243 |
|  | 7.230 | 244–45 |
|  | 7.243 | 247 |

# INDEX

|  | Reference Numbers | Page Numbers |
|---|---|---|
| **TEN COMMANDMENTS** (*Continued*) | | |
|   Rules for understanding | 7.209 | 239–40 |
|   Sum of | 7.042 | 208 |
| | 7.212 | 240 |
| | 7.232 | 245 |
|   Text of | 4.092 | 60–61 |
| | 7.108 | 215–16 |
|     First | 7.213–.216 | 240–41 |
|     Second | 7.217–.220 | 241–42 |
|     Third | 7.221–.224 | 243 |
|     Fourth | 7.225–.231 | 243–45 |
|     Fifth | 7.233–.243 | 245–47 |
|     Sixth | 7.244–.246 | 247 |
|     Seventh | 7.247–.249 | 247–48 |
|     Eighth | 7.250–.252 | 248–49 |
|     Ninth | 7.253–.255 | 249–50 |
|     Tenth | 7.256–.258 | 250 |
|   Transgressions of | 7.083 | 212 |
| | 7.260–.261 | 250–51 |
| **TESTAMENTS, TWO, AND THE CHURCH** | 5.129 | 110 |
| **THANKSGIVING** | 4.043 | 43 |
| | 6.114 | 172 |
| | 6.116 | 172 |
| | 7.214 | 240 |
| | 7.237 | 246 |
| | 7.288 | 256 |
| | 9.50 | 295–96 |
| **THEFT** | 4.110 | 66–67 |
| | 7.252 | 248–49 |
| **THEOLOGICAL DECLARATION OF BARMEN** | 9.04 | 287 |
|   Prologue | | 280 |
|   Text | 8.01–.28 | 281–84 |
| **THEOLOGICAL SYSTEMS, AS CONFESSIONS** | 9.02 | 287 |
| **THIEVES, AND SALVATION** | 4.087 | 59 |
| | 5.255 | 142 |
| **TRADITION** | 5.014 | 80 |
| **TRANSLATION OF THE SCRIPTURES** | 6.008 | 151 |
| | 7.266 | 252 |
| **TRANSUBSTANTIATION** | 3.21 | 22 |
| | 4.078 | 55 |
| | 5.210 | 132 |
| | 6.166 | 183 |
| **TRIBUTE TO THE STATE** | 6.130 | 175 |

|  | Reference Numbers | Page Numbers |
|---|---|---|
| TRINITY, THE | 9.05 | 287 |
|   Of the Godhead | 5.016–.018 | 80–81 |
|     Heresies against | 5.019 | 81 |
|     Order of | 5.017 | 81 |
|     Reason for | 4.025 | 37 |
| TRIUMPH OF GOD | 9.55 | 297 |
| TRIUMPHANT, CHURCH | 5.127 | 109–10 |
| TRUE CHURCH, NOTES AND SIGNS OF | 5.134–.135 | 112 |
| TRUE FAITH | 4.020–.021 | 36 |
| TRUTH: |  |  |
|   Aspects of | 6.191–.193 | 190–91 |
|   Evangelical | 8.09–.27 | 283–84 |
|   Maintaining and promoting of | 7.077 | 212 |
|  | 7.251 | 248 |
|  | 7.254 | 249 |
|   Of Scripture | 6.001 | 149 |
|  | 6.005 | 150 |
|  | 6.009 | 151 |
| TURKS, ERRORS OF | 5.071 | 94 |
| TWO NATURES OF CHRIST | 4.048 | 44 |
|  | 5.066 | 94 |
| TWO TABLES OF MOSES | 5.081 | 97 |

## U

|  | Reference Numbers | Page Numbers |
|---|---|---|
| UNBELIEF | 7.215 | 241 |
| UNBELIEVERS: |  |  |
|   Judgment of | 5.204 | 130–31 |
|   And the Lord's Supper | 4.082 | 57 |
|  | 5.204 | 130–31 |
| UNCHASTE PERSONS | 4.087 | 59 |
| UNCHASTITY | 4.108–.109 | 66 |
|  | 7.248 | 248 |
| UNCTION, EXTREME | 5.234 | 137 |
| UNDERSTANDING: |  |  |
|   Of the Lord's Supper | 6.168 | 184 |
|  | 7.097 | 214 |
|  | 7.280–.281 | 254–55 |
|   In worship | 6.114 | 172 |
|  | 6.116 | 172 |
|  | 7.267 | 252 |
|  | 7.295 | 257 |
|  | 7.297 | 257 |

# INDEX

|  | Reference Numbers | Page Numbers |
|---|---|---|
| UNION: | | |
|     With Christ | 6.146 | 180 |
| | 7.176 | 233 |
| | 7.189 | 236 |
|     Sacramental | 5.180 | 125 |
| UNIQUE WITNESS, SCRIPTURE AS | 9.27 | 291 |
| UNITED CHURCH, GERMANY | 8.01 | 281 |
| | 8.06 | 282 |
| | 8.08 | 282 |
| UNITED PRESBYTERIAN CHURCH IN THE UNITED STATES OF AMERICA, THE | 9.04 | 287 |
| UNITY | 10.3 | 301–2 |
| | 10.4 | 302 |
|     Of the church | 5.126 | 109 |
| | 5.129 | 110 |
| | 5.141 | 114 |
| | 9.34 | 292 |
|     Of God | 5.015 | 80 |
| | 6.011 | 151–52 |
| | 6.013 | 152 |
| | 7.006 | 205 |
| | 7.118 | 225 |
|     Of society | 6.112 | 171 |
| UNIVERSAL CHURCH | 10.2 | 301 |
|     Of Christ | 5.002 | 77 |
|     Identity of | 9.03 | 287 |
|     As reconciling community | 9.31 | 291–92 |
| UNJUST DIVORCE | 7.249 | 248 |
| UNREGENERATE: | | |
|     Moral law and | 7.206 | 239 |
|     Works of | 6.093 | 167 |
| UNSAVED, PROVIDENCE AND THE | 6.029 | 155 |
| URBANIZATION, PRESSURES OF | 9.47 | 294–95 |
| USURY | 7.252 | 248–49 |

## V

|  | Reference Numbers | Page Numbers |
|---|---|---|
| VALENTINIANS, ERRORS OF | 5.008 | 78 |
| VALENTINIUS, ERRORS OF | 5.064 | 93–94 |
| VICTORY, OVER SIN AND DEATH | 9.08 | 288 |
| VIRGIN, CHURCH AS | 5.130 | 110 |
| VIRGIN BIRTH OF CHRIST | 4.035–.036 | 41 |
| | 5.062 | 93 |
| | 6.044 | 157 |

|  | Reference Numbers | Page Numbers |
|---|---|---|
| **VIRGIN BIRTH OF CHRIST** (*Continued*) | 7.022 | 206 |
|  | 7.110 | 216 |
|  | 7.147 | 229 |
| **VIRTUE:** | | |
| Human | 9.13 | 289 |
| True | 5.121 | 108 |
| **VISIONS, BIBLICAL** | 9.54 | 296–97 |
| **VISITATION OF THE SICK** | 5.234 | 137 |
| **VOWS:** | | |
| In baptism of adults | 7.277 | 253–54 |
| Definition and discussion of | 6.124–.126 | 174 |
| Of ministers, ruling elders, and deacons | 6.191–.193 | 190–91 |
| Of monks | 5.149 | 117 |
| Sins against | 7.261 | 251 |
| In worship | 6.116 | 172 |
|  | 6.124–.126 | 174 |
|  | 7.218 | 242 |

## W

|  | Reference Numbers | Page Numbers |
|---|---|---|
| **WAGES OF SIN** | 7.194–.195 | 237 |
| **WAR** | 5.256–.258 | 142–43 |
|  | 6.128 | 174 |
| **WASHING, IN BAPTISM** | 4.069–.073 | 51–53 |
|  | 5.188 | 127 |
| **WATCHFULNESS** | 7.305 | 259 |
| **WATER:** | | |
| In baptism | 4.078 | 55 |
|  | 5.188 | 127 |
|  | 6.155–.156 | 182 |
|  | 7.094 | 214 |
|  | 7.275 | 253 |
|  | 9.51 | 296 |
| Of rebirth | 4.071 | 51–52 |
| In Sacraments | 5.178–.180 | 124–25 |
| **WEALTH** | 7.066 | 211 |
|  | 7.074–.075 | 212 |
|  | 7.251 | 248 |
| **WEAPONS, DEVELOPMENT OF** | 9.45 | 294 |
| **WELFARE, COMMON** | 9.17 | 289 |
|  | 9.46 | 294 |
| **WELL-DOERS, REWARDING** | 7.239 | 246 |

# INDEX

|  | Reference Numbers | Page Numbers |
|---|---|---|
| WESTMINSTER, CONFESSION OF FAITH | 9.04 | 287 |
|    Prologue |  | 148 |
|    Text | 6.001–.193 | 149–91 |
| WESTMINSTER—LARGER CATECHISM: |  |  |
|    Prologue |  | 146–48 |
|    Text | 7.111–.306 | 225–60 |
| WESTMINSTER—SHORTER CATECHISM | 9.04 | 287 |
|    Prologue |  | 146–48 |
|    Text | 7.001–.110 | 205–16 |
| WICKED, THE: |  |  |
|    Condition of | 7.139 | 228 |
|    Hardening of | 6.029 | 155 |
|    And Lord's Supper | 6.168 | 184 |
|    Punishment of | 6.181 | 186–87 |
|     | 7.199 | 237–38 |
|    Souls of | 6.177 | 186 |
|     | 7.196 | 237 |
| WIDOWS | 5.235 | 137–38 |
|  | 5.254 | 142 |
|  | 10.7 | 304 |
| WILL, HUMAN: |  |  |
|    Conversion and | 6.062 | 161–62 |
|  | 6.064 | 162 |
|  | 7.031 | 207 |
|  | 7.177 | 234 |
|    Decrees and | 6.014 | 152 |
|  | 6.023 | 154 |
|    Fall and | 6.034 | 155 |
|  | 6.061 | 161 |
|  | 7.135 | 227–28 |
|    Forcing of | 6.014 | 152 |
|  | 6.059 | 161 |
|    Freedom of | 6.023 | 154 |
|  | 6.060 | 161 |
|  | 6.063 | 162 |
|  | 7.103 | 215 |
|  | 7.127 | 226–27 |
|  | 7.131 | 227 |
|    Rejection | 4.124 | 71 |
| WILL OF GOD | 5.042 | 88 |
|  | 5.047 | 89–90 |
|  | 7.103 | 215 |
|  | 7.302 | 258 |
|  | 9.53 | 296 |

| | Reference Numbers | Page Numbers |
|---|---|---|
| **WILL OF GOD** (*Continued*) | | |
| Completeness of | 5.082 | 97 |
| Discernment of | 9.43 | 293 |
| And law of God | 5.080 | 97 |
| **WILLFUL DESERTION** | 7.249 | 248 |
| **WINE, IN THE LORD'S SUPPER** | 5.178–.180 | 124–25 |
| | 6.166 | 183 |
| **WISDOM OF GOD** | 6.001 | 149 |
| | 6.011 | 151–52 |
| | 6.024 | 154 |
| | 7.004 | 205 |
| | 7.117 | 225 |
| **WITNESS:** | | |
| In every age | 8.02 | 281 |
| Church as a | 10.5 | 303 |
| | 10.7 | 304 |
| False | 7.255 | 249–50 |
| Present | 9.01 | 287 |
| | 11.4 | 312 |
| Of the spirit | 6.005 | 150 |
| | 6.098 | 168 |
| | 7.114 | 225 |
| | 7.190 | 236 |
| | 7.261 | 251 |
| Unique and authoritative | 9.27 | 291 |
| **WOMEN:** | | |
| And baptism | 5.191 | 127 |
| Called to all ministries of the church | 11.4 | 312 |
| And ecclesiastical duties | 5.191 | 127 |
| And marriage | 5.246 | 140–41 |
| And men | 9.47 | 294–95 |
| **WORD OF GOD, THE:** | | |
| Christ as | 8.11 | 283 |
| And civil magistrates | 5.254 | 142 |
| Duties of hearers of | 7.090 | 213 |
| | 7.270 | 252 |
| As guide | 7.099 | 214 |
| | 7.296 | 257 |
| Holy Scriptures as | 7.002 | 205 |
| | 7.113 | 225 |
| | 7.114 | 225 |
| Incarnate | 9.27 | 291 |
| Instructions in | 7.090 | 213 |

## INDEX

|  | Reference Numbers | Page Numbers |
|---|---|---|
| **WORD OF GOD, THE** (*Continued*) | | |
| As means of grace | 7.089 | 213 |
| | 7.265 | 252 |
| Nature of | 5.172 | 123 |
| Ordinances concerning | 6.116 | 172 |
| Preaching as | 5.004 | 77 |
| Preaching of | 5.211 | 132 |
| | 6.116 | 172 |
| | 7.268–.269 | 252 |
| Presence of | 9.30 | 291 |
| Reading of | 7.090 | 213 |
| | 7.218 | 242 |
| | 7.266–.267 | 252 |
| Revelation by | 3.03 | 11 |
| And Sacraments | 4.067 | 50 |
| Scripture as | 5.003 | 77 |
| Spoken | 9.30 | 291 |
| Translation of | 6.008 | 151 |
| | 7.266 | 252 |
| True | 5.001–.009 | 77–78 |
| Unity and | 8.01 | 281 |
| Written | 9.27 | 291 |
| **WORKINGS OF THE SPIRIT** | 6.088 | 166 |
| | 6.090 | 166 |
| | 6.093 | 167 |
| | 7.261 | 251 |
| **WORKS:** | | |
| Covenant of | 6.038 | 156 |
| | 6.101 | 169 |
| | 7.012 | 205 |
| | 7.130 | 227 |
| Definition of | 3.14 | 17 |
| Good (See good works) | | |
| Human | 5.116 | 107 |
| Kinds of | 3.14 | 17 |
| Of the regenerate | 5.048 | 90 |
| Trust in | 3.15 | 17–18 |
| **WORLD, THE:** | | |
| Affairs of, church action in | 9.36 | 292 |
| Creation of | 6.022 | 153–54 |
| | 7.009 | 205 |
| | 7.125 | 226 |
| | 11.3 | 311 |

|  | Reference Numbers | Page Numbers |
|---|---|---|
| WORLD, THE (*Continued*) | | |
|     Judgment of | 6.180 | 186 |
| | 7.028 | 207 |
| | 7.161 | 231 |
| | 7.166 | 232 |
|     Nature and purpose of | 9.16 | 289 |
| | 11.4 | 312 |
|     Population of | 9.47 | 294–95 |
|     Study of | 9.49 | 295 |
|     Temptations of | 6.096 | 168 |
| | 7.305 | 259 |
| WORSHIP | 6.012 | 152 |
| | 6.112–.113 | 171–72 |
| | 7.045–.048 | 209 |
| | 7.213–.216 | 240–41 |
| | 7.289 | 256 |
|     Common language in | 5.217–.218 | 133 |
|     Conduct during | 5.215 | 133 |
|     And the gathered church | 9.36 | 292 |
|     Of God | 5.023 | 82–83 |
| | 5.135 | 112 |
|     And idolatry | 4.096–.098 | 62 |
|     In Israel | 5.023 | 82–83 |
|     Meetings for | 5.211–.217 | 132–33 |
|     Neglect of | 5.212 | 132 |
|     Places for | 5.214 | 132–33 |
| | 5.216 | 133 |
|     Prayer in | 5.220 | 134 |
|     Public nature of | 5.231 | 136 |
| | 7.218–.219 | 242 |
| | 9.49 | 295 |
|     Of saints | 5.025 | 83 |
|     Self-devised: Greek, Ethelothraskeia | 5.116 | 107 |
|     Singing in | 5.221 | 134 |
|     Teaching in | 5.220 | 134 |
|     Time of | 5.223 | 134 |
|     And traditions | 5.014 | 80 |
|     Of the trinity | 5.016 | 80 |
| WORTHY BELIEVERS, AND LORD'S SUPPER | 6.167 | 183–84 |
| WOUNDING | 7.246 | 247 |
| WRATH OF GOD | 4.037 | 42 |
| | 9.14 | 289 |
| WRITINGS OF THE FATHERS | 5.011 | 79 |
| WRITTEN WORD OF GOD | 5.011 | 79 |

INDEX

|  | Reference Numbers | Page Numbers |
|---|---|---|
| **Y** | | |
| YAHWEH | 5.028 | 84 |
| YOUTH, INSTRUCTION OF | 5.233 | 137 |
| **Z** | | |
| ZACCHAEUS | 5.101 | 102–3 |
| ZACHARIAS | 5.050 | 90 |
| ZEAL | 7.214–.215 | 240–41 |